THE
OVERSTREET
COMIC BOOK COMPANION

IDENTIFICATION AND PRICE GUIDE

Other **CONFIDENT COLLECTOR** *Titles*
of Interest

THE OVERSTREET COMIC BOOK PRICE GUIDE
by Robert M. Overstreet

THE OVERSTREET COMIC BOOK GRADING GUIDE
by Robert M. Overstreet and Gary M. Carter

ORIGINAL COMIC ART
IDENTIFICATION AND PRICE GUIDE
by Jerry Weist

THE OVERSTREET COMIC BOOK COMPANION

IDENTIFICATION AND PRICE GUIDE

6TH EDITION

ROBERT M. OVERSTREET

The CONFIDENT COLLECTOR™

AVON BOOKS ◭ NEW YORK

Important Notice: All of the information, including valuations, in this book has been compiled from the most reliable sources, and every effort has been made to eliminate errors and questionable data. Nevertheless, the possibility of error always exists in a work of such immense scope. The publisher and the author will not be held responsible for losses which may occur in the purchase, sale, or other transaction of property because of information contained herein. Readers who feel they have discovered errors are invited to *write* and inform us so they may be corrected in subsequent editions.

Cover artwork: Ghost Rider, by Adam Kubert; ™ and © 1992 by Marvel Entertainment Group, Inc. All rights reserved.

THE CONFIDENT COLLECTOR: THE OVERSTREET COMIC BOOK COMPANION IDENTIFICATION AND PRICE GUIDE (6th edition) is an original publication of Avon Books. This work has never before appeared in book form.

AVON BOOKS
A division of
The Hearst Corporation
1350 Avenue of the Americas
New York, New York 10019

Copyright © 1992 by Robert M. Overstreet
The Confident Collector and its logo are trademarked properties of Avon Books.
Published by arrangement with the author
Library of Congress Catalog Card Number: 92-97097
ISBN: 0-380-76911-5

First Avon Books Printing: November 1992

AVON TRADEMARK REG. U.S. PAT. OFF. AND IN OTHER COUNTRIES, MARCA REGISTRADA, HECHO EN U.S.A.

Printed in the U.S.A.

OPM   10 9 8 7 6 5 4 3 2 1

Acknowledgments

COMIC BOOKS

Larry Bigman (Frazetta-Williamson data); Glenn Bray (Kurtzman data); Gary Carter (DC data); J. B. Clifford Jr. (E. C. data); Gary Coddington (Superman data); Wilt Conine (Fawcett data); Al Dellinges (Kubert data); R. C. Holland and Ron Pussell (Seduction and Parade of Pleasure data); Grant Irwin (Quality data); Richard Kravitz (Kelly data); Phil Levine (giveaway data); Fred Nardelli (Frazetta data); Michelle Nolan (love comics); Mike Nolan (MLJ, Timely, Nedor data); George Olshevsky (Timely data); Richard Olson (LOA data); Scott Pell ('50s data); Greg Robertson (National data); Frank Scigliano (Little Lulu data); Gene Seger (Buck Rogers data); Rick Sloane (Archie data); David R. Smith, Archivist, Walt Disney Productions (Disney data); Mike Tiefenbacher, Jerry Sinkovec, and Richard Yudkin (Atlas and National data); Jim Vadeboncoeur Jr. (Williamson and Atlas data); Kim Weston (Disney and Barks data); Andrew Zerbe and Gary Behymer (M. E. data).

My appreciation must also be extended to Ron Pussell, Bruce Hamilton, Steve Geppi, Jon Warren, James Payette, Joe Vereneault, Jay Maybruck, John Verzyl, Terry Stroud, Hugh O'Kennon, John Snyder, Walter Wang, Gary Carter and Gary Colabuono for pricing research; to Tom Inge for his "Chronology of the Development of the American Comic Book;" to Adam Kubert for his outstanding cover art and to Bill Spicer for his kind permission to reprint portions of his and Jerry Bails' America's Four Color Pastime.

BIG LITTLE BOOKS

Special thanks is due Harry B. Thomas for his advice and guidance both in pricing and data presentation; to Bruce Hamilton for his decades of support and knowledge in this field, and to the following people who contributed much needed data for this edition: Mike Tickal, Alan J. Soprych Jr. and Jon Warren.

Table of Contents

THE OVERSTREET COMIC BOOK COMPANION

IDENTIFICATION AND PRICE GUIDE

An Overview to Comic Book Collecting

Introduction

Comic book values listed in this reference work were recorded from convention sales, dealers' lists, adzines, and by special contact with dealers and collectors from coast to coast. Prices paid for rare comics vary considerably from one locale to another. We have attempted to list a realistic average between the lowest and highest range observed. The reader should keep in mind that the prices listed only reflect the market just prior to publication. Any new trends that have developed since the preparation of this book would not be shown.

The values listed are reports, not estimates. Each new edition of the guide is actually an average report of sales that occurred during the year; not an estimate of what we feel the books will be bringing next year. Even though many prices listed will remain current throughout the year, the wise user of this book would keep abreast of current market trends to get the fullest potential out of his invested dollar.

All titles are listed as if they were one word, ignoring spaces, hyphens and apostrophes. Page counts listed will always include covers.

IMPORTANT. Prices listed in this book are in U. S. currency and are for your reference only. This book is not a dealer's price list, although some dealers may base their prices on the values listed. The true value of any comic book is what you are willing to pay. Prices listed herein are an indication of what collectors (not dealers) would probably pay. For one reason or another, these collectors might want certain books badly, or else need specific issues to complete their runs and so are willing to pay more. Dealers are not in a position to pay the full prices listed, but work on a percentage depending largely on the amount of investment required and the quality of material offered. Usually they will pay from 20 to 70 percent of the list price depending on how long it will take them to sell the collection after making the investment; the higher the demand and better the condition, the more the percentage. Most dealers are faced with expenses such as advertising, travel, telephone and mailing, plus convention costs. These costs all go in before the books are sold. The high demand books usually sell right away but there are many other titles that are difficult to sell due to low demand. Sometimes a dealer will have cost tied up in this type of material for several years before finally moving it. Remember, his position is that of handling, demand and overhead. Most dealers are victims of these economics.

Everyone connected with the publication of this book advocates the collecting of comic books for fun and pleasure, as well as for nostalgia, art, and cultural values. Second to this is investment, which, if wisely placed in the best quality books (condition and contents considered), will yield dividends over the long term.

Grading Comic Books

Before a comic book's true value can be assessed, its condition or state of preservation must be determined. In most comic books, the better the condition, the more desirable the book. The scarcer first and/or origin issues in MINT condition will bring several times the price of the same book in POOR condition. The grading of a comic book is done by simply looking at the book and describing its condition, which may range from absolutely perfect newsstand condition (MINT) to extremely worn, dirty, and torn (POOR). Numerous variables influence the evaluation of a comic's condition and **all** must be considered in the final evaluation. More important characteristics include tears, missing pieces, wrinkles, stains, yellowing, brittleness, tape repairs, water marks, spine roll, writing, and cover lustre. The significance of each of these are described more fully in the grading scale definitions. Whenever in doubt, consult with a reputable dealer or experienced collector in your area. The following grading guide is given to aid the panelologist. Consult **The Overstreet Comic Book Grading Guide** for more detailed information on grading comics.

MINT (MT): Near perfect in every way. Only the most subtle bindery or printing defects are allowed. Cover is flat with no surface wear. Cover inks are bright with high reflectivity and minimal fading. Corners are cut square and sharp. Staples are generally centered, clean with no rust. Cover is generally well centered and firmly secured to interior pages. Paper is supple and fresh. Spine is tight and flat.

NEAR MINT (NM): Nearly perfect with only minor imperfections such as tiny corner creases or staple stress lines, a few color flecks, bindery tears, tiny impact creases or a combination of the above where the overall eye appeal is less than Mint. Only the most subtle binding and/or printing defects allowed. Cover is flat with no surface wear. Cover inks are bright with high reflectivity and minimum of fading. Corners are cut square and sharp with ever so slight blunting permitted.

Staples are generally centered, clean with no rust. Cover is well centered and firmly secured to interior pages. Paper is supple and like new. Spine is tight and flat.

VERY FINE (VF): An excellent copy with outstanding eye-appeal. Sharp, bright and clean with supple pages. Cover is relatively flat with minimal surface wear beginning to show. Cover inks are generally bright with moderate to high reflectivity. Slight wear beginning to show including some minute wear at corners. Staples may show some discoloration. Spine may have a few stress lines but is relatively flat. A light ½ inch crease is acceptable. Pages and covers can be yellowish/tannish (at the least) but not brown and will usually be off-white to white.

FINE(FN): An exceptional, above-average copy that shows minor wear, but is still relatively flat and clean with not major creasing or other serious defects. Eye appeal is somewhat reduced because of noticeable surface wear and the accumulation of smaller defects, especially on the spine and edges. A fine condition comic book appears to have been read many times and has been handled with moderate care. Compared to a VF, cover inks are beginning to show a significant reduction in reflectivity but is still highly collectible and desirable.

VERY GOOD (VG): The average used comic book. A comic in this grade shows moderate wear, can have a reading or center crease or a rolled spine, but has not accumulated enough total defects to reduce eye appeal to the point where it is not a desirable copy. Some discoloration, fading and even minor soiling is allowed. No chunks can be missing but a small piece can be out at the corner or edge. Store stamps, name stamps, arrival dates, initials, etc. have no effect on this grade. Cover and interior pages can have minor tears and folds and the centerfold may be loose or detached. One or both staples might be loose, but cover is not completely detached. Common bindery and printing defects do not affect grade. Pages and inside covers may be brown but not brittle. Tape should never be used for comic book repair, however many VG condition comics have minor tape repair.

GOOD (GD): A copy in this grade has all pages and covers, although there may be small pieces missing. Books in this grade are commonly creased, scuffed, abraded and soiled, but completely readable. Often paper quality is low but not brittle. Cover reflectivity is low and in some cases completely absent. Most collectors consider this the lowest collectible grade because comic books in lesser condition are usually incomplete and/or brittle. This grade can have a large accumulation of defects but *still maintains its structural integrity*.

FAIR (FR): A copy in this grade has all pages and most of the covers, although there may be up to ⅓ of the front cover missing or all of the back cover, but not both. A comic in this grade is soiled, ragged and unattractive. Creases and folds are prevalent and paper quality may be very low. The centerfold may be missing if it does not affect a story. Spine may be completely split its entire length. Staples may be gone, and/or cover completely detached. Corners are commonly severely rounded or absent. Coupons may be cut from front cover and/or back cover and/or interior pages. These books are mostly readable although soiling, staining, tears, markings or chunks missing may interfere with reading the complete story. Very often paper quality is low and may even be brittle around the edges but not in the central portion of the pages.

POOR (PR): Most comic books in this grade have been sufficiently degraded to where there is no longer any collector value. Copies in this grade typically have: Pages and/or more than approximately ⅓ of the front cover missing. They may have extremely severe stains, mildew or heavy cover abrasion to the point where cover inks are indistinct/absent. They may have been defaced with paints, varnishes, glues, oil, indelible markers or dyes. Other defects often include severe rips, tears, folding and creasing. Another common defect in this grade is moderate to severe brittleness, often to the point where the comic book literally "falls apart" when examined.

COVERLESS(c): Coverless comics are usually hard to sell and in many cases are worthless.

IMPORTANT: Comics in all grades with fresh extra white pages usually bring more. Books with defects such as pages or panels missing, coupons cut, torn or taped covers and pages, brown or brittle pages, restapled, taped spines, pages or covers, water-marked, printing defects, rusted staples, stained, holed, or other imperfections that distract from the original beauty, are worth less than if free of these defects.

Many of the early strip reprint comics were printed in hardback with dust jackets. Books with dust jackets are worth more. The value can increase from 20 to 50 percent depending on the rarity of this book. Usually, the earlier the book, the greater the percentage. Unless noted, prices listed are without dust jackets. The condition of the dust jacket should be graded independently of the book itself.

Storage of Comic Books

Acids left in comic book paper during manufacture are the primary cause of aging and yellowing. Improper storage can accelerate the aging process.

The importance of storage is proven when looking at the condition of books from larger collections that have surfaced over the last few years. In some cases, an entire collection has brown or yellowed pages approaching brittleness. Collections of this type were probably stored in too much heat or moisture, or exposed to atmospheric pollution (sulfur dioxide) or light. On the other hand, other collections of considerable age (30 to 50 years) have emerged with snow white pages and little signs of aging. Thus we learn that proper storage is imperative to insure the long life of our comic book collections.

Store books in a dark, cool place with an ideal relative humidity of 50 percent and a temperature of 40 to 50 degrees or less. Air conditioning is recommended. Do not use regular cardboard boxes, since most contain harmful acids. Use acid-free boxes instead. Seal books in Mylar (Mylar is a registered trademark of the DuPont company) or other suitable wrappings or bags and store them in the proper containers or cabinets, to protect them form heat, excessive dampness, ultraviolet light (use tungsten filament lights), polluted air, and dust.

Many collectors seal their books in plastic bags and store them in a cool dark room in cabinets or on shelving. Plastic bags should be changed every two to three years, since most contain harmful acids. Cedar chest storage is recommended, but the ideal method of storage is to stack your comics (preferably in Mylar bags) vertically in acid-free boxes. The boxes can be arranged on shelving for easy access. Storage boxes, plastic bags, backing boards, Mylar bags, archival supplies, etc., are available from dealers.

How to Start Collecting

Most collectors of comic books begin by buying new issues in mint condition directly off the newsstand or from their local comic store. (Subscription copies are available from several mail-order services.) Each week new comics appear on the stands that are destined to become true collectors items. The trick is to locate a store that carries a complete line of comics. In several localities this may be difficult. Most panelologists frequent several magazine stands in order not to miss something they want. Even then, it pays to keep in close contact with collectors in other areas. Sooner or later, nearly every collector has to rely upon a friend in Fandom to obtain for him an item that is unavailable locally.

Before you buy any comic to add to your collection, you should carefully inspect its condition. Unlike stamps and coins, defective comics are generally not highly prized. The cover should be properly cut and printed. Remember that every blemish or sign of wear depreciates the beauty and value of your comics.

The serious panelologist usually purchases extra copies of popular titles. He may trade these multiples for items unavailable locally (for example, foreign comics), or he may store the multiples for resale at some future date. Such speculation is, of course, a gamble, but unless collecting trends change radically in the future, the value of certain comics in mint condition should appreciate greatly, as new generations of readers become interested in collecting.

Collecting Back Issues

In addition to current issues, most panelologists want to locate back issues. Some energetic collectors have had great success in running down large hoards of rare comics in their home towns. Occasionally, rare items can be located through agencies that collect old papers and magazines, such as the Salvation Army. The lucky collector can often buy these items for much less than their current market value. Placing advertisements in trade journals, newspapers, etc., can also produce good results. However, don't be discouraged if you are neither energetic nor lucky. Most panelologists build their collections slowly but systematically by placing mail orders with dealers and other collectors.

Comics of early vintage are extremely expensive if they are purchased through a regular dealer or collector, and unless you have unlimited funds to invest in your hobby, you will find it necessary to restrict your collecting in certain ways. However you define your collection, you should be careful to set your goals well within your means.

Proper Handling of Books

Before picking up an old, rare comic book, caution should be exercised to handle it properly. Old comic books are very fragile and can be easily damaged. Because of this, many dealers hesitate to let customers personally handle their rare comics. They would prefer to remove the comic from its bag and show it to the customer themselves. In this way, if the book is damaged, it would be the dealer's responsibility—not the customer's. Remember, the slightest crease or chip could render an otherwise Mint book to Near Mint or even Very Fine. The following steps are provided to aid the novice in the proper handling of comic books: 1. Remove the comic from its protective sleeve or bag very carefully. 2. Gently lay the comic (unopened) in the palm of your hand so that it will stay relatively flat and secure. 3. You can now leaf through the book by carefully rolling or flipping the pages with the thumb and forefinger of your other hand. Caution: Be sure the book always remains relatively flat or slightly rolled. Avoid creating stress points on the covers with your fingers and be particularly cautious in bending covers back too far on Mint books. 4. After examining the book, carefully insert it back into the bag or protective sleeve. Watch corners and edges for folds or tears as you replace the book.

Terminology

Many of the following terms and abbreviations are used in the comic book market and are explained here. For a more complete list of terms, consult **The Overstreet Comic Book Grading Guide:**

a—Story art; **a(i)**—Story art inks; **a(p)**—Story art pencils; **a(r)**— Story art reprint.

B&W—Black and white art.

Bondage cover—Usually denotes a female in bondage.

c—Cover art; **c(i)**—Cover inks; **c(p)**—Cover pencils; **c(r)**—Cover reprint.

Cameo—When a character appears briefly in one or two panels.

Colorist—Artist that applies color to the pen and ink art.

Con—A Convention or public gathering of fans.

Cosmic Aeroplane—Refers to a large collection discovered by Cosmic Aeroplane Books.

Debut—The first time that a character appears anywhere.

Drug propaganda story—Where comic makes an editorial stand about drug abuse.

Drug use story—Shows the actual use of drugs: shooting, taking a trip, harmful effects, etc.

Fanzine—An amateur fan publication.

File Copy—A high grade comic originating from the publisher's file.

First app.—Same as debut.

Flashback—When a previous story is being recalled.

G. A.—Golden Age (1930s–1950s).

Headlight—Protruding breasts.

i—Art inks.

Infinity cover—Shows a scene that repeats itself to infinity.

Inker—Artist that does the inking.

Intro—Same as debut.

JLA—Justice League of America.

JSA—Justice Society of America.

Lamont Larson—Refers to a large high grade collection of comics. Many of the books have Lamont or Larson written on the cover.

Logo—The title of a strip or comic book as it appears on the cover or title page.

Mile High—Refers to a large NM-Mint collection of comics originating from Denver, Colorado (Edgar Church collection).

nd—No date.

nn—No number.

N. Y. Legis. Comm.—New York Legislative Committee to Study the Publication of Comics (1951).

Origin—When the story of the character's creation is given.

p—Art pencils.

Penciler—Artist that does the pencils.

POP—**Parade of Pleasure**, book about the censorship of comics.

Poughkeepsie—Refers to a large collection of Dell Comics' "file copies" believed to have originated from Poughkeepsie, NY.

R or r—Reprint.

Rare—10 to 20 copies estimated to exist.

Reprint comics—Comic books that contain newspaper strip reprints.

S. A.—Silver Age (1956–Present).

Scarce—20 to 100 copies estimated to exist.

Silver proof—A black & white actual size print on thick glossy paper given to the colorist to indicate colors to the engraver.

S&K—Simon and Kirby (artists).

SOTI—**Seduction of the Innocent**, book about the censorship of comics.

Splash panel—A large panel that usually appears at the front of a comic story.

Very rare—1 to 10 copies estimated to exist.

X-over—When one character crosses over into another's strip.

Zine—See Fanzine.

How to Sell Your Comics

If you have a collection of comics for sale, large or small, the following steps should be taken. (1) Make a detailed list of the books for sale, being careful to grade them accurately, showing any noticeable defects; i.e., torn or missing pages, centerfolds, etc. (2) Decide whether to sell or trade wholesale to a dealer all in one lump sum or to go through the long laborious process of advertising and selling piece by piece to collectors. Both have their advantages and disadvantages.

In selling to dealers, you will get the best price by letting everything go at once–the good with the bad–all for one price. Simply select names either from ads in this book or from some of the adzines mentioned below. Send them your list and ask for bids. The bids received will vary depending on the demand, rarity and condition of the books you have. The more in demand, and the better the condition, the higher the bids will be.

On the other hand, you could become a "dealer" and sell the books yourself. Order a copy of one or more of the adzines. Take note how most dealers lay out their ads. Type up your ad copy, carefully pricing each book (using **The Overstreet Comic Book Price Guide** as a reference). Send finished ad copy with payment to adzine editor to be run. You will find that certain books will sell at once while others will not sell at all. The ad will probably have to be retyped, remaining books repriced, and run again. Price books according to how fast you want them to move. If you try to get top dollar, expect a much longer period of time. Otherwise, the better deal you give the collector, the faster they will move. Remember, in being your own dealer, you will have overhead expenses in postage, mailing supplies and advertising cost. Some books might even be returned for refund due to misgrading, etc.

In selling all at once to a dealer, you will get instant cash, immediate profit, and eliminate the long process of running several ads to dispose of the books; but if you have patience, and a small amount of business sense, you could realize more profit selling them directly to collectors yourself.

Where to Buy and Sell

Most of the larger cities have comic book specialty shops that buy and sell old comic books. *The Comics Buyers Guide,* a weekly Tabloid, published by Krause Publications, 700 E. State Street, Iola, WI 54997 and *The Comic Book Marketplace,* P.O. Box 180534, Coronado, CA 92178-0534 are the best sources for buying and selling. These publications are full of ads buying and selling comic books. Comic book conventions are now held the year round in most of the larger cities. These conventions are an excellent source for buying and selling comic books. If you are an inexperienced collector, be sure to compare prices before you buy. Never send large sums of cash through the mail. Send money orders or checks for your personal protection. Beware of bargains, as the items advertised sometimes do not exist, but are only a fraud to get your money.

Learn how to grade properly. You will find that dealers vary considerably in how they grade their comics. For your own protection, your first order to a dealer should consist of an inexpensive book as a test of his grading. This initial order will give you a clue as to how the dealer grades as well as the care he takes in packaging his orders and the promptness in which he gets the order to you.

Directory of Comic and Nostalgia Shops

This is a current up-to-date list, but is not all-inclusive. We cannot assume any responsibility in your dealings with these shops. This list is provided for your information only. When planning your trips, it would be advisable to make appointments in advance.

ALABAMA

Camelot Books
2201 Quintard Avenue
Anniston, AL 36201
PH:205-236-3474

Discount Comic Book Shop
1301 Noble Street
Anniston, AL 36201
PH:205-238-8373

Wizard's Comics & Cards
324 N. Court Street
Florence, AL 35630
PH:205-766-6821

Sincere Comics
3738 Airport Blvd.
Mobile, AL 36608
PH:205-342-2603

Hellen's Comics
113 Mill Street
Oxford, AL 36203
PH:205-835-3040

ARIZONA

Atomic Comics
1318 W. Southern #9
Mesa, AZ 85202
PH:602-649-0807

Ed Kalb – Comics Wanted
(Mail Order Only)
1353 S. Los Alamos
Mesa, AZ 85204

AAA Best Comics Etc.
8336 N. 7th St. #B-C
Phoenix, AZ 85020
PH:602-997-4012

All About Books & Comics
517 E. Camelback
Phoenix, AZ 85012
PH: 602-277-0757

All About Books & Comics West
4208 W. Dunlap
Phoenix, AZ 85051
PH:602-435-0410

All About Books & Comics III
13835 North Tatum, Suite 1
Phoenix, AZ 85032
PH:602-494-1976

Planet Comics
10261 N. Scottsdale Road
Scottsdale, AZ 85254
PH:602-991-1972

The ONE Book Shop
120A E. University Drive
Tempe, AZ 85281
PH:602-967-3551

Fantasy Comics
6009 E. 22nd Street
Tucson, AZ 85711
PH: 602-748-7483

Fantasy Comics
805 E. Ft. Lowell
Tucson, AZ 85719
PH:602-293-3080

ARKANSAS

The Comic Book Store
9307 Treasure Hill
Little Rock, AR 72207
PH:501-227-9777

Pie-Eyes
5215 W. 65th Street
Little Rock, AR 72209
PH:501-568-1414

Collector's Edition Comics
5310 MacArthur Drive
North Little Rock, AR 72118
PH:501-753-2586

Collector's Edition Comics
3217 John F. Kennedy
(Hwy. 107)
North Little Rock, AR 72114
PH:501-753-2586

TNT Collectors Hut
503 W. Hale
Osceola, AR 72370
PH:501-563-5760

CALIFORNIA

Heroes & Legends
5290 Kanan Rd.
Agoura Hills, CA 91301
PH: 818-991-5979

Comic Heaven
24 W. Main Street
Alhambra, CA 91801
PH:818-289-3945

Comic Relief
2138 University Avenue
Berkeley, CA 94704
PH:415-843-5002

Comics & Comix, Inc.
2461 Telegraph Ave.
Berkeley, CA 94704
PH:415-845-4091

Fantasy Kingdom
1802 West Olive Avenue
Burbank, CA 91506
PH:818-954-8432

Crush Comics & Cards
2785 Castro Valley Blvd.
Castro Valley, CA 94546
PH:510-581-4779

Collectors Ink
932-A W. 8th Avenue
Chico, CA 95926
PH:916-345-0958

Comics & Comix, Inc.
6135 Sunrise Blvd.
Citrus Heights, CA 95610
PH:916-969-0717

Flying Colors Comics & Other Cool Stuff
2980 Treat Blvd/Oak Grove Plaza
Concord, CA 94518
PH:510-825-5410

Superior Comics
1630 Superior Avenue
Costa Mesa, CA 92627
PH:714-631-3933

Comics Ink
4267 Overland Avenue
Culver City, CA 90230
PH:310-204-3240

Comic Quest
24344 Muirlands
El Toro, CA 92630
PH:714-951-9668

High Quality Comics
(Mail Order Only)
1106 2nd St. Ste. #110
Encinitas, CA 92024
PH:619-723-7269

Comic Gallery
675-B N. Broadway
Escondido, CA 92025
PH:619-745-5660

Comic Castle
435 5th
Eureka, CA 95501
PH:707-444-2665

Comics & Comix, Inc.
1350 Travis Blvd.
Fairfield, CA 94533
PH:707-427-1202

The Comic Depot
41200 #L Blacow Rd.
Fremont, CA 94538
PH:510-657-5376

Adventureland Comics
106 N. Harbor Blvd.
Fullerton, CA 92632
PH:714-738-3698

Geoffrey's Comics
15530 Crenshaw
Gardena, CA 90249
PH:213-538-3198

Fantasy Illustrated
12553 Harbor Blvd.
Garden Grove, CA 92640
PH:714-537-0087

Shooting Star Comics & Games
618 E. Colorado Blvd. Unit #C
Glendale, CA 91205
PH:818-502-1535

Bud Plant Comic Art
(Free Catalog)
P.O. Box 1689-P
Grass Valley, CA 95945
PH:916-273-2166

The American Comic Book Co.
3972 Atlantic Avenue
Long Beach, CA 90807
PH:310-426-0393

Pacific Comics
5622 E. Second St.
Long Beach, CA 90803
PH:213-434-5136

Golden Apple Comics
7711 Melrose Avenue
Los Angeles, CA 90046
PH:213-658-6047

Golden Apple Comics
8934 West Pico Blvd.
Los Angeles, CA 90034
PH:310-274-2008

Graphitti - Westwood - UCLA
960 Gayley Avenue
Los Angeles, CA 90024
PH:310-824-3656

Pacific Comic Exchange, Inc.
(By Appointment Only)
P. O. Box 34849
Los Angeles, CA 90034
PH:310-836-PCEI

Bonanza Books & Comics
Roseburg Square Center
813 W. Roseburg Avenue
Modesto, CA 95350-5058
PH:209-529-0415

Ninth Nebula: The Comic Book Store
11517 Burbank Blvd.
North Hollywood, CA 91601
PH:818-509-2901

Golden Apple Comics
8962 Reseda Blvd.
Northridge, CA 91324
PH:818-993-7804

Comics & Comix, Inc.
405 California Ave.
Palo Alto, CA 94306
PH:415-328-8100

Lee's Comics
3783 El Camino Real
Palo Alto, CA 94306
PH:415-493-3957

Bud Plant Illustrated Books
c/o Jim Vadeboncoeur, Jr.
3809-C Laguna Avenue
Palo Alto, CA 94306
PH:415-493-1191 (evenings, weekends)

Comics & Comix, Inc.
5050 Rocklin Rd. #9
Rocklin, CA 95677
PH:916-632-2389

Comics & Comix, Inc.
921 K Street
Sacramento, CA 95814
PH:916-442-5142

Comic Gallery
9460-G Mira Mesa Blvd.
San Diego, CA 92126
PH:619-578-9444

Comic Gallery
4224 Balboa Avenue
San Diego, CA 92117
PH:619-483-4853

Comics & Comix, Inc.
650 Irving
San Francisco, CA 94122
PH:415-665-5888

Comics & Comix, Inc.
700 Lombard Street
San Francisco, CA 94133
PH:415-982-3511

Comics And Da-Kind
1643 Noriega Street
San Francisco, CA 94122
PH:415-753-9678

Comics And Da-Kind
1653 Noriega Street
San Francisco, CA 94122
PH:415-753-9678

The Funny Papers
7253 Geary Blvd.
San Francisco, CA 94121
PH:415-752-1914

Gary's Corner Bookstore
1051 San Gabriel Blvd.
San Gabriel, CA 91776
PH:818-285-7575

Comic Collector Shop
73 E. San Fernando
San Jose, CA 95113
PH:408-287-2254

Comics Pendragon
1189 Branham Lane
San Jose, CA 95118
PH:408-265-3233

The Comic Shop
2164 E. 14th Street
San Leandro, CA 94577
PH:510-483-0205

Lee's Comics
2222 S. El Camino Real
San Mateo, CA 94403
PH:415-571-1489 or 571-1595
HOT

**San Mateo Comic Books,
Baseball Cards, & Original Art**
106 South B Street
San Mateo, CA 94401
PH:415-344-1536

R & K Comics
3153 El Camino Real
Santa Clara, CA 95051
PH:408-554-6512

Atlantis Fantasyworld
610 F Cedar Street
Santa Cruz, CA 95060
PH:408-426-0158

Hi De Ho Comics & Fantasy
525 Santa Monica Blvd.
Santa Monica, CA 90401
PH:310-394-2820

Superior Comics
220 Pier Avenue
Santa Monica, CA 90405
PH:213-396-7005

Superhero Universe VIII
Sycamore Plaza
2955-A5 Cochran Street
Simi Valley, CA 93065
PH:805-583-3027 &
800-252-9997

Mark's Comics & Cards
131 E. Fremont Avenue
Sunnyvale, CA 94087
PH:408-739-8165

Superhero Universe IV
18722 Ventura Blvd.
Tarzana, CA 93156
PH:818-774-0969

Heroes & Legends
1165 E. Thousand Oaks Blvd.
Thousand Oaks, CA 91360
PH:805-495-0299

Silver City Comics
4671 Torrence Blvd. at Anza
Torrance, CA 90503
PH:310-542-8034

Ralph's Comic Corner
2377 E. Main Street
Ventura, CA 93003
PH:805-653-2732

**The Second Time Around
Bookshop**
391E Main Street
Ventura, CA 93001
PH:805-643-3154

Graphitti – South Bay!
Airport/Marina Hotel (Rear)
8639 Lincoln Blvd. No. 102
Westchester, L.A., CA 90045
PH:310-641-8661

COLORADO

**Colorado Comic Book
Company, Inc.**
220 N. Tejon Street
Colorado Springs, CO 80903
PH:719-635-2516

Heroes & Dragons
Citadel Mall #2158
Colorado Springs, CO 80909
PH:719-550-9570

CONNECTICUT

The Dragon's Den
43 Greenwich Avenue
Greenwich, CT 06830
PH:203-622-1171

A Timeless Journey
2538 Summer St.
Stamford, CT 06901
PH:203-353-1720

DISTRICT OF COLUMBIA

Another World
1504 Wisconsin Avenue N.W.
Washington, DC 20007
PH:202-333-8651

FLORIDA

Galactic Heroes
1752 Drew Street
Clearwater, FL 34615
PH:813-447-2833

Acevedo's Collectables
4761 S. University Dr.
Davie, FL 33328
PH:305-434-0540

Cliff's Books
209 N. Woodland Blvd. (17-92)
Deland, FL 32720
PH:904-738-9464

Charlie's Comics & Games
1255 W. 46 St. #26
Hialeah, FL 33012
PH:305-557-5994

Coliseum Of Comics
1180 E. Vine Street
Kissimmee, FL 34744
PH:407-870-5322

Comic Warehouse, Inc.
1029 Airport Road North #B6
(Airport Rd. U-Store It)
Naples, FL 33942
PH:813-643-1020

Tropic Comics South, Inc.
743 N.E. 167th St.
N. Miami Beach, FL 33162
PH:305-940-8700

Adventure Into Comics
841 Bennett Road
Orlando, FL 32803
PH:407-896-4047

Cartoon Museum
4300 S. Semoran Blvd.
Suite 109
Orlando, FL 32822
PH:305-273-0141

Coliseum Of Comics
4103 S. Orange Blossom Trail
Orlando, FL 32809
PH:407-422-5757

Enterprise 1701
2814 Corrine Drive
Orlando, FL 32803
PH:407-896-1701

Sincere Comics
3300 N. Pace Blvd.
Pensacola, FL 32505
PH:904-432-1352

Tropic Comics
313 S. State Rd. 7
Plantation, FL 33317
PH:305-587-8878

Comics Inc.
3231 N. Federal Highway
Pompano Beach, FL 33064
PH:305-942-1455

Adventure Into Comics
Flea World Gold Building
Sanford, FL 32716
PH:407-896-4047

Comic & Gaming Exchange
8432 W. Oakland Park Blvd.
Sunrise, FL 33351
PH:305-742-0777

New England Comics
Northdale Court
15836 N. Dale Mabry Highway
Tampa, FL 33618
PH:813-264-1848

Tropic Comics North, Inc.
1018 – 21st St. (U.S. 1)
Vero Beach, FL 32960
PH:407-562-8501

Comics Inc.
6850 Forest Hill Blvd.
West Palm Beach, FL 33413
PH:407-433-9111

GEORGIA

Showcase Collectibles
2880 Holcomb Bridge Road #19
Alpharetta, GA 30202
PH:404-594-0778

Titan Games & Comics Inc.
5436 Riverdale Rd.
College Park, GA 30349
PH:404-996-9129

Comic Company Ltd.
1058 Mistletoe Rd.
Decatur, GA 30033
PH:404-325-2334

Titan Games & Comics IV
2131 Pleasant Hill Rd.
Duluth, GA 30136
PH:404-497-0202

Titan Games & Comics V
937 N. Glynn St. #13
Fayetteville, GA 30214

Titan Games & Comics III
2585 Spring Rd.
Smyrna, GA 30080
PH:404-433-8226

Titan Games & Comics II
3853 C Lawrenceville Hwy.
Tucker, GA 30084
PH:404-491-8067

HAWAII

Compleat Comics Company
1728 Kaahumanu Avenue
Wailuku, Maui, HI 96793
PH:808-242-5875 (b,c,n,q-s)

IDAHO

King's Komix Kastle
1706 N.18th St. (By Appointment)
Boise, ID 83702
PH:208-343-7142

King's Komix Kastle II
2560 Leadville (Drop-In)
Mail: 1706 N. 18th
Boise, ID 83702
PH:208-343-7055

**New Mythology Comics &
Science Fiction**
1725 Broadway
Boise, ID 83706
PH:208-344-6744

ILLINOIS

Friendly Frank's Distribution
(Wholesale Only)
727 Factory Road
Addison, IL 60101

Friendly Frank's Comics
11941 S. Cicero
Alsip, IL 60658
PH:312-371-6760

All-American Comic Shops 3
9118 Ogden Avenue
Brookfield, IL 60513
PH:708-387-9588

AF Books
1856 Sibley Blvd.
Calumet City, IL 60409
PH:708-891-2260

All-American Comic Shops 7
15 River Oaks Drive
Calumet City, IL 60409
PH:708-891-0845

Comic Cavalcade
502 E. John
Champaign, IL 61820
PH: 217-384-2211

All-American Comic Shops 6
6457 W. Archer Avenue
Chicago, IL 60638
PH:312-586-5090

Comics For Heroes
1702 W. Foster
Chicago, IL 60640
PH:312-769-4745

Crash Comics
3804 N. Western
Chicago, IL 60618
PH:312-478-1799

Joe Sarno's Comic Kingdom
5941 West Irving Park Rd.
Chicago, IL 60634
PH:312-545-2231

Larry's Comic Book Store
1219 W. Devon Avenue
Chicago, IL 60660
PH:312-274-1832

Larry Laws
(by appointment only – call first)
831 Cornelia
Chicago, IL 60657
PH:312-477-9247

Mikes on Mars
(An All-American Affiliate 8)
1753 W. 69th Street
Chicago, IL 60637
PH:312-778-6990

Moondog's Comicland
Ford City Shopping Center
7601 S. Cicero
Chicago, IL 60652
PH:312-581-6060

Moondog's Comicland
2301 N. Clark
Chicago, IL 60614
PH:312-248-6060

Toontown Comic Company
3954 N. Southport
Chicago, IL 60613
PH:312-549-6430

Yesterday
1143 W. Addison St.
Chicago, IL 60613
PH:312-248-8087

All-American Comic Shops 5
1701 N. Larkin Avenue
Hillcrest Shopping Center
Crest Hill, IL 60435
PH:815-744-2094

Moondog's Comicland Outlet
114 S. Waukegan
Deerfield, IL 60015
PH:708-272-6080

The Paper Escape
205 W. First St.
Dixon, IL 61021
PH:815-284-7567

Graham Crackers Comics Ltd.
5230 S. Main Street
Downers Grove, IL 60515
PH:708-852-1810

GEM Comics
156 N. York Rd.
Elmhurst, IL 60126
PH:708-833-8787

All-American Comic Shops, Ltd.
3514 W. 95th Street
Evergreen Park, IL 60642
PH:708-425-7555

AF Books
47 E. Lincoln Hwy.
Frankfort, IL 60423
PH:815-469-5092

Galaxy Of Books
Rt. 137 & Sheridan
CNW Great Lakes Train Station
Great Lakes, IL 60064
PH:708-473-1099

Comics Galore
725 W. Hillgrove
LaGrange, IL 60525
PH:708-354-9570

Moondog's Comicland
139 W. Prospect Avenue
Mt. Prospect, IL 60056
PH:708-398-6060

Moondog's Comicland
Randhurst Shopping Center
999 Elmhurst Road
Mt. Prospect, IL 60056
PH:708-577-8668

Graham Crackers Comics Ltd.
5 E. Chicago Avenue
Naperville, IL 60540
PH:708-355-4310

All-American Comic Shops 2
14620 S. LaGrange Rd.
Orland Park, IL 60462
PH:708-460-5556

All-American Comic Shops 4
22305 S. Central Park Ave.
Park Forest, IL 60466
PH:708-748-2509

Tomorrow is Yesterday
5600 N. 2nd St.
Rockford, IL 61111
PH:815-633-0330

Graham Crackers Comics Ltd.
108 E. Main
St. Charles, IL 60174
PH:708-584-0610

Moondog's Comicland
1455 W. Schaumburg Road
Schaumburg, IL 60194
PH:708-529-6060

Comic Quest
805 W. Jefferson
Park Place Plaza
Shorewood, IL 60436
PH:815-741-2327

Unicorn Comics & Cards
216 S. Villa Avenue
Villa Park, IL 60181
PH:708-279-5777

Heroland Comics
6963 W. 111th Street
Worth, IL 60482

Galaxy Of Books
1908 Sheridan Road
Zion, IL 60099
PH:708-872-3313

INDIANA

Pen Comics & Entertainment Store
501 Main Street
Beech Grove, IN 46107
PH:317-782-3450

Books, Comics, & Things
2212 Maplecrest Rd.
Fort Wayne, IN 46815
PH:219-749-4043

Books, Comics, & Things
5950 W. Jefferson Ave.
Ft. Wayne, IN 46802
PH:219-436-0159

Friendly Frank's Distr., Inc.
(Wholesale Only)
3990 Broadway
Gary, IN 46408
PH:219-884-5052

Friendly Frank's Comics
220 Main Street
Hobart, IN 46342
PH:219-942-6020

Blue Moon Comics & Games
8336 West 10th St. Suite E
Indianapolis, IN 46234
PH:317-271-1479

Comic Carnival & Nostalgia Emporium
7311 U.S. 31 South
Indianapolis, IN 46227
PH:317-889-8899

Comic Carnival & Nostalgia Emporium
6265 N. Carrollton Avenue
Indianapolis, IN 46220
PH:317-253-8882

Comic Carnival & Nostalgia Emporium
5002 S. Madison Avenue
Indianapolis, IN 46227
PH:317-787-3773

Comic Carnival & Nostalgia Emporium
982 N. Mitthoeffer Rd.
Indianapolis, IN 46229
PH:317-898-5010

Comic Carnival & Nostalgia Emporium
3837 N. High School Rd.
Indianapolis, IN 46254
PH:317-293-4386

Galactic Greg's
1407 E. Lincolnway
Valparaiso, IN 46383
PH:219-464-0119

IOWA

Oak Leaf Comics
5219 University Avenue
Cedar Falls, IA 50428
PH:319-277-1835

Comic World & Baseball Cards
1626 Central Avenue
Dubuque, IA 52001
PH:319-557-1897

Oak Leaf Comics
23 – 5th S.W.
Mason City, IA 50401
PH:515-424-0333

The Comiclogue
520 Elm
P. O. Box 65304
W. Des Moines, IA 50265
PH:319-279-9006

KENTUCKY

Pac-Rat's, Inc.
1051 Bryant Way
Bowling Green, KY 42103
PH:502-782-8092

Comic Book World
7130 Turfway Rd.
Florence, KY 41042
PH:606-371-9562

Comic Book World
6905 Shepherdsville Road
Louisville, KY 40219
PH:502-964-5500

The Great Escape
2433 Bardstown Road
Louisville, KY 40205
PH:502-456-2216

LOUISIANA

B.T. & W.D. Giles
P. O. Box 271
Keithville, LA 71047
PH:318-925-6654

Excalibur Comics, Cards, & Games
9068 Mansfield Road
Shreveport, LA 71118
PH:318-686-7076

Comix Plus
248 West Hall Avenue
Slidell, LA 70461
PH:504-649-4376

MAINE

Lippincott Books
624 Hammond Street
Bangor, ME 04401
PH:207-942-4398

Moonshadow Comics
359 Maine Mall Rd.
South Portland, ME 04106
PH:207-772-4605

Book Barn
U.S. Rte 1
Wells, ME 04090
PH:207-646-4926

MARYLAND

Universal Comics
5300 East Drive
Arbutus, MD 21227
PH:410-242-4578

Comic Book Kingdom
P. O. Box 3679
4307 Harford Rd.
Baltimore, MD 21214
PH:410-426-4529

Geppi's Comic World
7019 Security Blvd.
Hechinger's Square at
Security Mall
Baltimore, MD 21214
PH:410-298-1758

Geppi's Comic World
Upper Level, Light St. Pavilion
301 Light Street
Baltimore, MD. 21202
PH:410-547-0910

Big Planet Comics
4908 Fairmont Ave.
Bethesda, MD 20814
PH:301-654-6856

The Closet of Comics
7319 Baltimore Avenue
College Park, MD 20740
PH:301-699-0498

Cosmic Comix & Cards
8332 Main Street
Ellicott City, MD 21043
PH:410-461-4161

Zenith Comics & Collectibles Inc.
18200-P Georgia Avenue
Olney, MD 20832
PH:301-774-1345

The Closet of Comics
182 W. Dares Beach Rd.
Prince Frederick, MD 20678
PH:410-535-4731

Geppi's Comic World
8317 Fenton St.
Silver Spring, MD 20910
PH:301-588-2546

MASSACHUSETTS

Comically Speaking
1322 Mass. Avenue
Arlington, MA 02174
PH:617-643-XMEN

Bargain Books & Collectibles
247 South Main Street
Attleboro, MA 02703
PH:508-226-1668

Ayer Comics/Jim
28 Main Street
Ayer, MA 01432
PH:508-772-4994

New England Comics
168 Harvard Avenue
Boston, MA 02134
PH:617-783-1848

Superhero Universe III
41 West Street
Boston, MA 02111
PH:617-423-6676

New England Comics
748 Crescent Street
East Crossing Plaza
Brockton, MA 02402
PH:508-559-5068

New England Comics
316 Harvard Street
Brookline, MA 02146
PH:617-566-0115

New England Comics
12B Eliot Street
Cambridge, MA 02138
PH:617-354-6352

Superhero Universe I
1105 Massachusetts Avenue
Cambridge, MA 02138
PH:617-354-5344

That's Entertainment II
387 Main St.
Fitchburg, MA 01420
PH:508-342-8607

Bop City Comics
Route 9 – Marshall's Mall
Framingham, MA 01701
PH:508-872-2317

New England Comics
12A Pleasant Street
Malden, MA 02148
PH:617-322-2404

Comically Speaking
15 Nason Street
Maynard, MA 01754
PH:508-461-0114

Avalon Comics
P. O. Box 821
Medford, MA 02155
PH:617-391-5614 (mail-order specialist)

New England Comics
732 Washington Street
Norwood, MA 02062
PH:617-769-4552

Imagine That Bookstore
58 Dalton Avenue
Pittsfield, MA 01201
PH:413-445-5934

New England Comics
11 Court Street
Plymouth, MA 02360
PH:508-746-8797

New England Comics
1350 Hancock Street
Quincy, MA 02169
PH:617-770-1848

The Outer Limits
457 Moody Street
Waltham, MA 02154
PH:617-891-0444

Bookstore Restaurant, Inc.
Kendrick Ave.
Wellfleet, MA 02667
PH:508-349-3154

Stan's Toy Chest
8 West Main Street
Westboro, MA 01581
PH:508-366-5091

Best Comic Shop of Worcester
151 Chandler Street
Worcester, MA 01609
PH:508-755-4207

Fabulous Fiction Book Store
984 Main Street
Worcester, MA 01603
PH:508-754-8826

That's Entertainment
151 Chandler St.
Worcester, MA 01609
PH:508-755-4207 (a-v)

MICHIGAN

Tom & Terry Comics
508 Lafayette Avenue
Bay City, MI 48708
PH:517-895-5525

Harley Yee
(By Appointment)
P. O. Box 19578
Detroit, MI 48219-0578
PH: 313-533-2731

Campus Comics
541 E. Grand River
E. Lansing, MI 48823
PH:517-351-4513

Curious Book Shop
307 E. Grand River Ave.
East Lansing, MI 48823
PH:517-332-0112

Amazing Book Store, Inc.
3718 Richfield Rd.
Flint, MI 48506
PH:313-736-3025

Argos Book Shop
1405 Robinson Rd. S.E.
Grand Rapids, MI 49506
PH:616-454-0111

Friendly Frank's Distribution
(Wholesale Only)
976 E. 10 Mile Road
Hazel Park, MI 48030
PH:313-542-2525

Discount Hobby
3307 S. Westnedge Avenue
Kalamazoo, MI 49008-2902
PH:616-344-1818

MINNESOTA

Collector's Connection
21 East Superior Street
Duluth, MN 55802
PH:218-722-9551

Collector's Connection II
1600 Miller Trunk Highway
Miller Hill Mall
Duluth, MN 55811
PH:218-726-1360

College Of Comic Book Knowledge
3151 Hennepin Avenue S.
Minneapolis, MN 55408
PH:612-822-2309

Midway Book & Comic
1579 University Avenue
St. Paul, MN 55104
PH:612-644-7605

MISSISSIPPI

Star Store
4212 N. State
Jackson, MS 39206
PH:601-362-8001

MISSOURI

B & R Comix Center
4747 Morganford
St. Louis, MO 63116
PH:314-353-4013

Mo's Comics & Stories
4530 Gravois
St. Louis, MO 63116
PH:314-353-9500

MONTANA

Paladin Comics
600 15th Street S.
Great Falls, MT 59405
PH:406-771-1535

The Book Exchange
2335 Brooks
Trempers Shopping Center
Missoula, MT 59801
PH:406-728-6342

NEVADA

Fandom's Comicworld of Reno
2001 East Second Street
Reno, NV 89502
PH:702-786-6663

NEW HAMPSHIRE

James F. Payette
P. O. Box 750
Bethlehem, NH 03574
PH:603-869-2097

Granite State Collectables
369 Gage Hill Rd. (Rt. 38)
Pellham, NH 03076
PH:603-898-5086

NEW JERSEY

The Hobby Shop
Strathmore Shopping Center
Route 34
Aberdeen, NJ 07747
PH:908-583-0505

Comic Zone
71 Rt. 73 & Day Avenue
Berlin, NJ 08009
PH:609-768-8186

Fantasy Factory Comics, Inc.
1604 Tilton Road
Cardiff, NJ 08232
PH:609-641-0025

Cliffside Book Center
720 Anderson Avenue
Cliffside, NJ 07010
PH:201-943-1983

Steve's Comic Relief
1555 St. George Avenue
Colonia, NJ 07067
PH:908-382-3736

Steve's Comic Relief
24 Mill Run Plaza
Delran, NJ 08075
PH:609-461-1770

**Shore Video Comics
& BB Cards**
615 Lacey Road
Forked River, NJ 08734
PH:609-693-3831

**Avery Stamps, Cards,
& Comics**
2301 Rt. 9 North
Howell, NJ 07731
PH:908-409-2927

Steve's Comic Relief
165 Mercer Mall
Lawrenceville, NJ 08648
PH:609-482-7548

Comics Plus
1300 Highway 35
Middletown, NJ 07748
PH:908-706-0102

Comic Museum
434 Pine Street
Mount Holly, NJ 08060
PH:609-261-0996

Comicrypt II
521 White Horse Pike
Oaklyn, NJ 08107
PH:609-858-3877

Passaic Book Center
594 Main Avenue
Passaic, NJ 07055
PH:201-778-6646

Sparkle City
(Appointment Only)
P. O. Box 67
Sewell, NJ 08080
PH:609-881-1174

**Philip M. Levine and Sons,
Rare & Esoteric Books**
P.O. Box 246 (Appointment Only)
Three Bridges, NJ 08887
PH:908-788-0532

Steve's Comic Relief
635 Bay Avenue
Toms River, NJ 08753
PH:908-244-5003

Mr. Collector
327 Union Blvd.
Totowa, NJ 07512
PH:201-595-0900

Comics Plus
Ocean Plaza
Hwy. 35 & Sunset Avenue
Wanamassa, NJ 07712
PH:908-922-3308

NEW MEXICO

Captain Comic's Specialty Shop
109 W. 4th Street
Clovis, NM 88101
PH:505-769-1543

NEW YORK

Earthworld Comics
327 Central Avenue
Albany, NY 12206
PH:518-465-5495

Fantaco Enterprises, Inc.
21 Central Avenue
Albany, NY 12210
PH:518-463-1400

Long Island Comics
1670-D Sunrise Hwy.
Bay Shore, NY 11706
PH:516-665-4342

Wow Comics
642 Pelham Parkway South
Bronx, NY 10462
PH:718-829-0461

Wow Comics
652 East 233rd Street
Bronx, NY 10467
PH:718-231-0913

Brain Damage Comics
1301 Prospect Avenue
Brooklyn, NY 11218
PH:718-438-1335

Memory Lane
1301 Prospect Avenue
Brooklyn, NY 11218
PH:718-438-1335

Pinocchio Discounts
1814 McDonald Avenue
Brooklyn, NY 11223
PH:718-645-2573

The Book Stop
384 East Meadow Avenue
East Meadow, NY 11554
PH:516-794-9129

Comics For Collectors
211 West Water Street
Elmira, NY 14901
PH:607-732-2299

Just Kids Nostalgia
326 Main Street
Huntington, NY 11743
PH:516-423-8449

Comics For Collectors
148 The Commons
Ithaca, NY 14810
PH:607-272-3007

Long Beach Books, Inc.
17 East Park Avenue
Long Beach, NY 11561
PH:516-432-2265 or 432-0063

Comics And Hobbies
156 Mamaroneck Avenue
Mamaroneck, NY 10543
PH:914-698-9473

Port Comics & Collectibles
3120 Rt. 112
Medford, NY 11763
PH:516-732-9143

Action Comics
318 E. 84th St.
(Between 1st & 2nd Ave.)
New York, NY 10028
PH:212-249-7344

Big Apple Comics
2489 Broadway (92 - 93 St.)
New York, NY 10025
PH:212-724-0085

Jim Hanley's Universe
126 West 32nd St.
(Between 6th & 7th Ave.)
New York, NY 10001
PH: 212-268-7088

Jim Hanley's Universe
166 Chambers Street at
Greenwich St.
New York, NY 10007
PH:212-349-2930

**Supersnipe Comic Book
Emporium**
Box 1102, Gracie Station
New York, NY 10028

West Side Comics
107 West 86 Street
New York, NY 10024
PH:212-724-0432

Millers Mint Ltd.
313 E. Main Street
Patchogue, NY 11772
PH:516-475-5353

Fantastic Planet
24 Oak Street
Plattsburgh, NY 12901
PH:518-563-2946

**Flash Point Comics,
Cards & Toys**
320 Main Street
Port Jefferson, NY 11777
PH:516-331-9401

**Mint Condition Comic Books
and Baseball Cards, Inc.**
664 Port Washington Blvd.
Port Washington, NY 11050
PH:516-883-0631

Iron Vic Comics
1 Raymond Avenue
Poughkeepsie, NY 12603
PH:914-473-8365

Queensboro Comics
99-17 Queens Blvd., Forest Hills
Queens, NY 11374
PH:718-268-0146

Amazing Comics
12 Gillette Avenue
Sayville, NY 11782
PH:516-567-8069

Electric City Comics
1704 Van Vranken Avenue
Schenectady, NY 12308
PH:518-377-1500

**Electric City Comics –
Rotterdam**
2801 Guilderland Avenue
Schenectady, NY 12306
PH:518-356-1361

Jim Hanley's Universe
350 New Dorp Lane
Staten Island, NY 10306
PH:718-351-6299

Comic Book Heaven
48-14 Skillman Avenue
Sunnyside (Queens), NY 11104
PH:718-899-4175

M. Sagert
P. O. Box 456 – Downtown
Syracuse, NY 13201
PH:315-437-5825

**Twilight Book & Game
Emporium**
1401 N. Salina Street
Syracuse, NY 13208
PH:315-471-3139

Ravenswood, Inc.
263 Genesee St.
Utica, NY 13501
PH:315-735-3699

Iron Vic Comics II
420 Windsor Hwy.
Vail's Gate, NY 12584
PH:914-565-6525

Collector's Comics
3247 Sunrise Hwy.
Wantagh, NY 11793
PH:516-783-8700

The Dragon's Den
2614 Central Avenue
Yonkers, NY 10710
PH:914-793-4630

NORTH CAROLINA

Record Survival
525 Merrimon Avenue
Asheville, NC 28804
PH:704-253-0506

Super Giant Books & Comics
344 Merrimon Avenue
Asheville, NC 28801
PH:704-576-4990

Heroes Aren't Hard To Find
Corner Central Ave. & The Plaza
P. O. Box 9181
Charlotte, NC 28299
PH:704-375-7462

Heroes Aren't Hard To Find
(Mail Order & Wholesale)
P. O. Box 9181
Charlotte, NC 28299
PH:704-376-5766, 800-321-4370

Heroes Are Here
208 South Berkeley Blvd.
Goldsboro, NC 27530
PH:919-751-3131

Acme Comics
348 S. Elm Street
Greensboro, NC 27401
PH:919-272-5994

Acme Comics
2150 Lawndale Dr.
Greensboro, NC 27408
PH:919-574-2263

Parts Unknown: The Comic Book Store
The Cottonmill Square
801 Merritt Drive
Greensboro, NC 27407
PH:919-294-0091

Heroes Are Here, Too
116 E. Fifth Street
Greenville, NC 27584
PH:919-757-0948

The Nostalgia Newsstand
919 Dickinson Ave.
Greenville, NC 27834
PH:919-758-6909

Tales Resold
3936 Atlantic Avenue
Raleigh, NC 27604
PH:919-878-8551

The Booktrader
121 Country Club Rd.
Rocky Mount, NC 27801
PH:919-443-3993

Heroes Aren't Hard To Find
Silas Creek Shopping Center
3234 Silas Creek Parkway
Winston-Salem, NC 27103
PH:919-765-4370

NORTH DAKOTA

Collector's Corner
City Center Mall
Grand Forks, ND 58201
PH:701-772-2518

OHIO

Trade Those Tunes
1320 Whipple Ave., N.W.
Meyer's Lake Plaza
Canton, OH 44708
PH:216-477-5535

Comic Book World
4103 North Bend Road
Cincinnati, OH 45211
PH:513-661-6300

Collectors Warehouse Inc.
5437 Pearl Rd.
Cleveland, OH 44129
PH: 216-842-2896

Dark Star II
1410 W. Dorothy Lane
Dayton, OH 45409
PH:513-293-7307

Bookery Fantasy And Comics
35 North Broad Street
Fairborn, OH 45324
PH:513-879-1408

**Bigg Fredd's Coins &
Collectables**
162 West Main St.
(1 Block E. of US 33 on US 22)
Lancaster, OH, 43130
PH:614-653-5555

Parker's Records & Comics
1222 Suite C, Rt. 28
Milford, OH 45150
PH:513-575-3665

Monarch Cards & Comics
2620 Airport Highway
Toledo, OH 43609
PH:419-382-1451

Funnie Farm Bookstore
328 N. Dixie Drive
Vandalia, OH 45377
PH:513-898-2794

Dark Star Books & Comics
231 Xenia Avenue
Yellow Springs, OH 45387
PH:513-767-9400

OKLAHOMA

New World Comics & Games
6219 N. Meridian
Oklahoma City, OK 73112
PH:405-721-7634

New World Comics & Games
4420 S.E. 44th Street
Oklahoma City, OK 73135
PH:405-677-2559

New World Comics & Games
2203 W. Main
Norman, OK 73069
PH:405-321-7445

Comic Empire Of Tulsa
3122 S. Mingo
Tulsa, OK 74146
PH:918-664-5808

Comics, Cards & Collectibles
4618 East 31st Street
Tulsa, OK 74135
PH:918-749-8500

Starbase 21
2130 S. Sheridan Rd.
Tulsa, OK 74129
PH:918-838-3388

Want List Comics
(Appointment Only)
P.O. Box 701932
Tulsa, OK 74170-1932
PH:918-299-0440

OREGON

Pegasus Books
4390 S.W. Lloyd Street
Beaverton, OR 97005
PH:503-643-4222

Emerald City Comics
770 E. 13th
Eugene, OR 97401
PH:503-345-2568

Nostalgia Collectibles
527 Willamette
Eugene, OR 97401
PH:503-484-9202

It Came From Outer Space
Milwaukie Marketplace
10812 S.E. Oak
Milwaukie, OR 97222
PH:503-786-0865

Pegasus Books
10902 S.E. Main Street
Milwaukie, OR 97222
PH:503-652-2752

Future Dreams Burnside
1800 East Burnside
Portland, OR 97214-1599
PH:503-231-8311

Future Dreams Gateway
10508 N.E. Halsey
Portland, OR 97220
PH:503-255-5245

Future Dreams Comic Art Library
10506 N.E. Halsey
Portland, OR 97220
PH:503-256-1885

It Came From Outer Space II
Plaza 205 Ste. P
9738 S.E. Washington
Portland, OR 97216
PH:503-257-2701

Pegasus Books
4161 N.E. Sandy
Portland, OR 97232
PH:503-284-4693

Pegasus Books
1401 S.E. Division Street
Portland, OR 97214
PH:503-233-0768

PENNSYLVANIA

Cap's Comic Cavalcade
1980 Catasauqua Rd.
Allentown, PA 18103
PH:215-264-5540

Cap's Comic Cavalcade
4672 Broadway
Allentown, PA 18104
PH:215-395-0979

Dreamscape Comics
404 W. Broad Street
Bethlehem, PA 18018
PH: 215-867-1178

Showcase Comics
839 W. Lancaster Ave.
Bryn Mawr, PA 19010
PH:215-527-6236

Time Tunnel Collectibles
1001 Castle Shannon Blvd.
Castle Shannon, PA 15234
PH:412-531-8833

Adventures in Comics
1368 Illinois Avenue
Dormont, PA 15216
PH:412-531-5644

Captain Quality Comics
P. O. Box 812
Drexel Hill, PA 19026
PH:215-359-1622

Dreamscape Comics
25th Street Shopping Center
Easton, PA 18042
PH:215-250-9818

New Dimension Comics
20550 Route 19
Piazza Plaza (Cranberry)
Evans City, PA 16033
PH:412-776-0433

Charlie's Collectors Corner
100 D. West Second Street
Hummelstown, PA 17036
PH:717-566-7216

The Comic Store
2481 Lincoln Hwy. E.
Quality Centers
Lancaster, PA 17602
PH:717-397-8636

The Comic Store
Station Square
28 McGovern Avenue
Lancaster, PA 17602
PH:717-397-8737

Steve's Comic Relief
4153 Woerner Avenue
Levittown, PA 19057
PH:215-945-7954

Showcase Comics II
Granite Run Mall, Rte. 1
Media, PA 19063
PH:215-891-9229

Steve's Comic Relief
2114 South Eagle Road
Newtown, PA 18940
PH:215-579-9225

Fat Jacks Comicrypt
2006 Sansom Street
Philadelphia, PA 19103
PH:215-963-0788

Fat Jacks Comicrypt III
7598 Haverford Avenue
Philadelphia, PA 19151
PH:215-473-6333

Fat Jacks Comicrypt IV
5736 North 5th Street
Philadelphia, PA 19120
PH:215-924-8210

Japanimation and Comics Too
1623 South St.
Philadelphia, PA 19146
PH:215-732-1393

Steve's Comic Relief
1244 Franklin Mills Circle
Philadelphia, PA 19154
PH:215-281-3730

BEM: The Store
622 South Avenue
Pittsburgh, PA 15221
PH:412-243-2736

Comics & Collectibles, Inc.
983 W. County Line Rd.
Rosemore Shopping Center
Warminster, PA 19040
PH:215-675-8708

The Comic Store - West
Northwest Plaza
915 Loucks Road
York, PA 17404

RHODE ISLAND

Starship Excalibur
Lincoln Mall
Lincoln, RI 02865
PH:401-334-3883

Starship Excalibur
60 Washington Street
Providence, RI 02903
PH:401-273-8390

Starship Excalibur
834 Hope Street
Providence, RI 02906
PH:401-861-1177

Starship Excalibur
830-832 Post Road
Warwick Plaza
Warwick, RI 02888
PH:401-941-8890

SOUTH CAROLINA

Super Giant Comics & Records
3464 Cinema Center
Anderson, SC 29621
PH:803-225-9024

Book Exchange
1219 Savannah Hwy.
Charleston, SC 29407
PH:803-556-5051

Heroes Aren't Hard To Find
1415-A Laurens Road
Greenville, SC 29607
PH:803-235-3488

Book Busters
Northwoods Mall
North Charleston, SC 29418
PH:803-569-0836

Heroes Aren't Hard To Find
West Oak Square S/C
2811 Reidville Road
Spartanburg, SC 29301
PH:803-574-1713

Super Giant Comics
Wal-Mart Plaza
7500 Greenville Highway
Spartanburg, SC 29301
PH:803-576-4990

TENNESSEE

Collector's Choice
3405 Keith St., Shoney's Plaza
Cleveland, TN 37311
PH:615-472-6649

Gotham City Comics
2075 Exeter #10
Germantown, TN 38138
PH:901-757-9665

Mountain Empire Collectibles III
1210 North Roan Street
Johnson City, TN 37601
PH:615-929-8245

Mountain Empire Collectibles II
1451 East Center Street
Kingsport, TN 37664
PH:615-245-0364

Collector's Choice
2104 Cumberland Ave.
Knoxville, TN 37916
PH:615-546-2665

Collector's World
Commons S/C-165 N. Peters Rd.
Knoxville, TN 37923
PH:615-531-2943

The Great Escape
Gallatin Road-Old Hickory Blvd.
Madison, TN 37115
PH:615-865-8052

Memphis Comics & Records
665 S. Highland
Memphis, TN 38111
PH:901-452-1304

Collector's World
1511 East Main Street
Murfreesboro, TN 37130
PH:615-895-1120

Collector's World
5751 Nolensville Rd.
Nashville, TN 37211
PH:615-333-9458

The Great Escape
1925 Broadway
Nashville, TN 37203
PH:615-327-0646

Walt's
2604 Franklin Rd.
Nashville, TN 37204
PH:615-298-2506

TEXAS

**Lone Star Comics, Books,
& Games**
511 East Abram Street
Arlington, TX 76010
PH:817-(Metro)-265-0491

**Lone Star Comics, Books,
& Games**
5721 W. I-20 at Green Oaks Blvd.
Arlington, TX 76016
PH:817-478-5405

**Lone Star Comics, Books,
& Games**
11661 Preston Forest Village
Dallas, TX 75230
PH:214-373-0934

Remember When
2431 Valwood Parkway
Dallas, TX 75234
PH:214-243-3439

**Lone Star Comics, Books,
& Games**
6312 Hulen Bend Blvd.
Ft. Worth, TX 76132
PH:817-346-7773

Sonny Johnson
1452 Northwest Highway
Eastgate Center
Garland, TX 75041
PH:214-681-5355

B & D Trophy Shop
4404 N. Shepherd
Houston, TX 77018
PH:713-694-8436

Bedrock City Comic Co.
6521 Westheimer
Houston, TX 77057
PH:713-780-0675

Third Planet
2439 Bissonnnet
Houston, TX 77005
PH:713-528-1067

**Lone Star Comics, Books,
& Games**
931 Melbourne
Hurst, TX 76053
PH:817-595-4375

**Lone Star Comics, Books,
& Games**
2550 N. Beltline Rd.
Irving, TX 75062
PH:817-659-0317

**Lone Star Comics, Books,
& Games**
3600 Gus Thomasson, Suite 107
Mesquite, TX 75150
PH:214-681-2040

**Lone Star Comics, Books,
& Games**
1900 Preston Rd. # 345
Plano, TX 75093
PH:214-985-1953

The Book Cellar
2 South Main Street
Temple, TX 76501
PH:817-773-7545

**Excalibur Comics, Cards,
& Games**
2811 State Line Avenue
Texarkana, TX 75503
PH:903-792-5767

UTAH

The Bookshelf
2456 Washington Blvd.
Ogden, UT 84401
PH:801-621-4752

VERMONT

Comics Outpost
27 Granite Street
Barre, VT 05641
PH:802-476-4553

Comics City, Inc.
6 North Winooski Avenue
Burlington, VT 05401
PH:802-865-3828

**Country Dreamer: Comics,
Sports Cards, And Rare Music**
118 Woodstock Avenue
Rutland, VT 05701
PH:802-773-2298

Comics City, Inc.
67 Eastern Avenue
St. Johnsbury, VT 05814
PH:802-748-3060

VIRGINIA

Capital Comics Center
(Greater D.C. Area)
2008 Mt. Vernon Avenue
Alexandria, VA 22301
PH:703-548-3466

Geppi's Crystal City Comics
1675 Crystal Square Arcade
Arlington, VA 22202
PH:703-521-4618

Mountain Empire Collectibles I
509 State Street
Bristol, VA 24201
PH:703-466-6337

Burke Centre Books
5741 Burke Centre Parkway
Burke, VA 22015
PH:703-250-5114

Fantasia Comics And Records
1419-1/2 University Avenue
Charlottesville, VA 22903
PH:804-971-1029

Fantasia Comics And Records
1861 Seminole Trail
Charlottesville, VA 22901
PH:804-974-7512

Trilogy Shop #3
3916-A6 Portsmouth Blvd.
Chesapeake, VA 23321
PH:804-488-6578

Zeno's Books & Comics
1112 Sparrow Road
Chesapeake, VA 25325
PH:804-420-2344

Hole In The Wall Books
905 West Broad Street
Falls Church, VA 22046
PH:703-536-2511

Marie's Books and Things
1701 Princess Anne Street
Fredericksburg, VA 22401
PH:703-373-5196

Benders
22 South Mallory Street
Hampton, VA 23663
PH:804-723-3741

Franklin Farm Books
13340-B Franklin Farm Road
Herndon, VA 22071
PH:703-437-9530

**World's Best Comics
& Collectibles**
9825 Jefferson Avenue
Newport News, VA 23605
PH:804-595-9005

Trilogy Shop #2
700 E. Little Creek Road
Norfolk, VA 23518
PH:804-587-2540

Trilogy Shop #5
Airline Flea Fair
3535 Airline Blvd.
Portsmouth, VA 23701
PH:804-490-2205

Dave's Comics
7019 Three Chopt Rd.
Richmond, VA 23226
PH:804-282-1211

B & D Comic Shop
3514 Williamson Road, N.W.
Roanoke, VA 24012
PH:703-563-4161

Trilogy Shop #1
5773 Princess Anne Rd.
Virginia Beach, VA 23462
PH:804-490-2205

Trilogy Shop #4
857 S. Lynnhaven Road
Virginia Beach, VA 23452
PH:804-468-0412

WASHINGTON

Psycho 5 Comics & Cards
221 Bellevue Wayne
Bellevue, WA 98004
PH:206-462-2869

Paperback Exchange
2100 N. National Avenue
Chehalis, WA 98532
PH:206-748-4792

Geepy's Comics
618 Bridge Street
Clarkston, WA 99403

Everett Comics And Cards
2936 Colby Avenue
Everett, WA 98201
PH:206-252-8181

Olympic Cards & Comics
311 S. Sound Center
Lacey, WA 98503
PH:206-459-7721

Corner Comics 1
6565 N.E. 181st
Seattle, WA 98155
PH:206-486-XMEN

The Comic Character Shop
Old Firehouse Antique Mall
110 Alaskan Way South
Seattle, WA 98104
PH:206-283-0532

Corner Comics 2
5226 U-Way
Seattle, WA 98105
PH:206-525-9294

**Gemini Book Exchange
& Comic Ctr.**
9614 16th Avenue S.W.
Seattle, WA 98106
PH:206-762-5543

Golden Age Collectables, Ltd.
1501 Pike Place Market
401 Lower Level
Seattle, WA 98101
PH:206-622-9799

Psycho 5 Comics & Cards
12513 Lake City Wayne
Seattle, WA 98125
PH:206-367-1620

Rocket Comics
8544 Greenwood Avenue N.
Seattle, WA 98103
PH:206-784-7300

The Book Exhcange
K-Mart Center
N. 6504 Division
Spokane, WA 99208
PH:509-489-2053

The Book Exchange
University City East
E. 10812 Sprague
Spokane, WA 99206
PH:509-928-4073

Pegasus Books
813 Grand
Vancouver, WA 98661
PH:206-693-1240

Galaxy Comics
1720 5th St., Suite D
Wenatchee, WA 98801
PH:509-663-4330 (b,c,g,q-t)

WEST VIRGINIA

Comic Castle
319 Neville Street
Beckley, WV 25801
PH:304-763-3334

Cheryl's Comics & Toys
5216-1/2 MacCorkle Avenue S.E.
Charleston, WV 25304
PH:304-925-7269

Triple Play Cards, Comics & Collectibles
414 Stratton Street
Logan, WV 25601
PH:304-752-9315

Triple Play Cards, Comics & Collectibles
335 4th Ave.
S. Charleston, WV 25303
PH:304-744-2602

WISCONSIN

Cover to Cover
511 S. Barstow St.
Eau Claire, WI 54701
PH:715-832-4252

River City Hobbies
512 Cass Street
LaCrosse, WI 54601
PH:608-782-5540

Capital City Comics
1910 Monroe Street
Madison, WI 53711
PH:608-251-8445

The Westfield Company of Wisconsin, Inc.
(Comic Subscription Service)
8608 University Green
P. O. Box 470
Middleton, WI 53210
PH:414-332-8199

Capital City Comics
2565 North Downer Street
Milwaukee, WI 53210
PH:414-332-8199

CANADA
ALBERTA

Another Dimension
324-10 Street N.W.
Calgary, Alberta, Can. T2N 1V8
PH:403-283-7078

Another Dimension
7610 Elbow Drive S.W.
Calgary, Alberta, Can. T2V 1K2
PH:403-255-2588

Another Dimension
Unit 110A, 2640-52 Street N.E.
Calgary, Alberta, Can. T1Y 3R5
PH:403-293-1272

Another Dimension
204, 4625 Varsity Drive N.W.
Calgary, Alberta, Can. T3A 0Z9
PH:403-288-1802

Comic Legends Ltd.
Head Office
#205-908-17 Ave. S.W.
Calgary, Alberta, Can. T2T 0A3
PH:403-245-5884

Comic Legends Ltd.
Bay #8-10015 Oakfield Dr. S.W.
Calgary, Alberta, Can. T2T 0A3
PH:403-251-5964

Scorpio Comics, Books, And Sports Cards
7640 Fairmount Dr. S.E.
Calgary, Alberta, Can. T2M 0X8
PH:403-258-0035

Comic Legends Ltd.
1275 3rd Ave. South
Lethbridge, Alberta, Can.
PH:403-327-8558

BRITISH COLUMBIA

L.A. Comics & Books
371 Victoria Street
Kamloops, B.C., Can. V2C 2A3
PH: 604-828-1995

Page After Page
1771 Harvey Avenue
Kelowna, B.C., Can. V1Y 6G4
PH:604-860-6554

Ted's Paperback & Comics
269 Leon Avenue
Kelowna, B.C., Can. V14 6J1
PH:604-763-1258

MANITOBA

International Comic Book Co.
Calvin Slobodian
859 – 4th Avenue
Rivers, Man., Can. R0K 1X0
PH:204-328-7846

Collector's Slave
156 Imperial Ave.
Winnipeg, Man., Can.
PH:204-237-4428

Comic Factory II
380 Donald Street
Winnipeg, Man., Can. R3B 2J2
PH:204-957-1978

Doug Sulipa's Comic World
374 Donald Street
Winnipeg, Man., Can. R3B 2J2
PH:204-943-3642

NOVA SCOTIA

Members Only Comic Service
Mail Order Only
6257 Yale Street
Halifax, N.S., Can. B3L 1C9
PH:902-423-MOCS

ONTARIO

Queen's Comics & Memorabilia
1009 Kingston Rd.
Toronto, Ont., Can. M4E 1T3
PH:416-698-8757

QUEBEC

Capitaine Quebec – Dollard
4305 Blvd. St. Jean
D.D.O., Que., Can. H9H 2A4
PH:514-620-1866

Capitaine Quebec – Centre-Ville
1837 St. Catherine O.
Montreal, Que., Can. H3H 1M2
PH:514-939-9970

Capitaine Quebec – Snowdon
5108 Decarie Blvd.
Montreal, Que., Can. H3X 2H9
PH:514-487-0970

Komico
4210 Decarie Blvd.
Montreal, Que., Can. H4A 3K3
PH:514-489-4009

Premiere Issue
27 – A D'Auteuil
Quebec City (Vieux-Quebec)
Can. G1R 4B9
PH:418-692-3985

Capitaine Quebec – Verdun
4422 Wellington
Verdun, Que., Can. H4G 1W5
PH:514-768-1351

ENGLAND

Adventure Into Comics
No. 9 Half Moon Lane
Herne Hill, London,
England SE249JT
PH:071-738-5002

Stateside Comics PLC
125 East Barnet Road
Barnet, London, EN4 8RF
England
PH:081-449-5535

Stateside Comics PLC at Virgin
First Floor, Virgin Megastore
527 Oxford Street (Opp. Marble
Arch Station)
London W1 England
PH:081-499-8839

FRANCE

Dangeruses Visions
81 Rue De La Monnaie
59800 Lille France
PH:20-06-51-51

Comic Book Conventions

As is the case with most other aspects of comic collecting, comic book conventions, or cons as they are referred to, were originally conceived as the comic-book counterpart to science-fiction fandom conventions. There were many attempts to form successful national cons prior to the time of the first one that materialized, but they were all stillborn. It is interesting that after only three relatively organized years of existence, the first comic con was held. Of course, its magnitude was nowhere near as large as most established cons held today.

What is a comic con? As might be expected, there are comic books to be found at these gatherings. Dealers, collectors, fans, whatever they call themselves can be found trading, selling, and buying the adventures of their favorite characters for hours on end. Additionally if at all possible, cons have guests of honor, usually professionals in the field of comic art, either writers, artists, or editors. The committees put together panels for the con attendees where the assembled pros talk about certain areas of comics, most of the time fielding questions from the assembled audience. At cons one can usually find displays of various and sundry things, usually original art. There might be radio listening rooms; there is most certainly a daily showing of different movies, usually science-fiction or horror type. Of course there is always the chance to get together with friends at cons and just talk about comics; one also has a good opportunity to make new friends who have similar interests and with whom one can correspond after the con.

It is difficult to describe accurately what goes on at a con. The best way to find out is to go to one or more if you can.

The following addresses are those currently available for conventions to be held in the upcoming year. Unfortunately, addresses for certain major conventions are unavailable as this list is being compiled. Once again, the best way to keep abreast of conventions is through the various adzines. Please remember when writing for convention information to include a self-addressed, stamped envelope for reply. Most conventions are non-profit, so they appreciate the help. Here is the list:

Comic Book Convention Calendar for 1993

ATLANTA FANTASY FAIR XVIII, June, 1993, Atlanta Hilton & Towers, Atlanta, GA. Info: Atlanta Fantasy Fair, 4175 Eliza Ct., Lithonia, GA 30058. PH: (404) 985-1230.

BIG-D SUPER COMIC & COLLECTIBLES SHOW (Formally CHILDHOOD TREASURES) July, 1993-Dallas Sheraton Park Central Hotel, Hwy 635 & Coit Rd. Write Don Maris, Box 111266 Arlington, TX 76007. (817) 261-8745

CAROLINA COMIC BOOK FAIR—For info contact New Dimension Comics, 2609 Central Ave., Charlotte, NC 28205. PH: (704) 372-4376.

CAROLINA CON XI—Sept, 1993, Sponsored by The Carolina Pictorial Fiction Assn. Send SASE to Steve Harris, 100 E. Augusta Place, Greenville, SC 29605.

CENTRAL NEW JERSEY COMIC BOOK SHOW—Held monthly on Sundays at the Washington Twp. Volunteer Fire Dept., Rt. 130, Robbinsville. Contact Michael Chaudhuri of EMCEE Conventions, P.O. Box 151, Hightstown, NJ 08520. PH: (609)448-7585.

CHATTANOOGA, TN. SPRING COMICS & COLLECTIBLES SHOW—Feb, 1993, contact Mark Derrick, 3244 Castle Ave, East Ridge, TN 37412. PH: 615/624-3702, before 10:00 p.m.

CHICAGO — BASEBALL CARD & COMIC BOOK SHOW. Held monthly at University of Illinois at Chicago. For more info call Rich at (312) 733-2266.

CHICAGO COMICON—July, 1993, Larry Charet, 1219-A West Devon Ave., Chicago, IL 60660. Phone (312) 274-1832.

COMIC BOOK AND ART EXPO—Nov, 1993, Rosemont Ohare Exposition Center, River Rd. & Kennedy Exp, Rosemont, IL, Midwest Shows, 7516 W. Douglas, Summit, IL 60501, PH: 708/496-8881.

CROWN POINT'S PREMIERE MONTHLY CARD AND COMIC SHOW—Crown Point, IN, Knight's of Columbus, 700 Merrillville Rd. Contact Marilyn Hall, P.O. Box 507, Crown Point, IN 46307. PH: 219-663-8561.

DALLAS FANTASY FAIR, A Bulldog Prod. Convention. For info: Lary Lankford, P.O. Box 820488, Dallas, TX 75382, PH: (214) 349-3367.

DETROIT AREA COMIC BOOK/BASEBALL CARD SHOWS. Held every 2-3 weeks in Royal Oak and Livonia Mich., write: Michael Goldman, Suite 231, 19785 W. 12 Mile Rd., Southfield, MI 48076. PH: (313) 350-2633.

DEF-CON CONVENTIONS—2681 Monroeville Blvd., Monroeville, PA 15146, PH: 412/372-4774. Holds cons in the following cities: Pittsburgh, Erie, State College, Charleston, Morgantown, Elmira, Scranton.

EL PASO FANTASY FESTIVAL—c/o Rita's Fantasy Shop, No. 34 Sunrise Center, El Paso, TX 79904. PH: (915) 757-1143. Late July-Early August.

GREAT EASTERN CONVENTIONS, 225 Everitts Road, Ringoes, NJ 08551, PH: (201) 788-6845. Holds cons in the following cities: Atlanta, Boston, Chicago, Los Angeles, New York and San Francisco.

HEROES CONVENTION '93—June, 1993, Charlotte Apparel Center, 200 N. College St, Charlotte, NC. Contact H. Shelton Drum, P.O. Box 9181, Charlotte, NC 28299, PH: (704) 376-5766 or 1-800-321-4370.

HIGHLAND INDIANA MONTHLY CARD AND COMIC SHOW—Wicker Park Social Center, Ridge Rd. at Indianapolis Blvd., Marilyn Hall, P.O. Box 507, Crown Point, Indiana 46307, PH: 219/663-8561

ILLINOIS/INDIANA—Pinsky Baseball Card & Comic Book Super show, c/o Louis Pinsky, P.O. Box 1072, Lombard, IL 60148-8072, PH: (708) 620-0865. Holds conventions in these cities: Illinois: Alsip, Carol Stream, Countryside/LaGrange, Crystal Lake, Downers Grove, Elgin, Glen Ellyn/Lombard, Itasca, Oakbrook Terrace, Willowbrook/Hinsdale. Indiana: Merrillville.

ISLAND NOSTALGIA COMIC BOOK/BASEBALL CARD SHOWS, Hauppauge, N.Y.-Holiday Inn off L.I.E. exit 55, 10 a.m.-4 p.m. 1740 Express Drive South, Hauppauge, N.Y., For more info call Dennis (516) 724-7422 or Day of Shows only (516) 234-3030, ext 450.

KANSAS CITY COMIC CONVENTION (Formally MO-KAN COMICS FESTIVAL) c/o Kansas City Comic Book Club, 734 North 78th St., Kansas City, KS 66112.

LONG ISLAND COMIC BOOK & COLLECTOR'S CONVENTION (Held monthly). Rockville Centre, Holiday Inn, 173 Sunrise Hwy, Long Island, NY. For info: Cosmic Comics & Books of Rockville Centre, 139 N. Park Ave., Rockville Centre, NY 11570.(516) 763-1133.

LOS ANGELES COMIC BOOK & SCIENCE FICTION CONVENTION, held monthly. For information contact: Bruce Schwartz, 1802 West Olive Ave., Burbank, CA 91506. PH: (818) 954-8432.

MICHIANA COMICON: April, Oct., 1993, South Bend, IN. Contact Jim Rossow, 53100 Poppy Rd., South Bend, IN 46628. PH: (219) 232-8129.

MOBI-CON 93, June, 1993, The Days Inn 3650 Airport Blvd., Mobile, AL. For more info: Mobi-Con, P.O. Box 161257, Mobile, AL 36616.

MOTOR CITY COMIC CON, Dearborn, MI. Held March & Oct. 1993 at the Dearborn Civic Center, 15801 Michigan Ave. Contact Michael Goldman, Suite 231, 19785 W. 12 Mile Rd., Southfield, MI 48076. PH: (313) 350-2633.

NORTHERN ILLINOIS SEASONAL COMIC SHOW—Rockford, IL, contact Mick at Hotstuff Comics, 3833 E. State St., Rockford, IL 61108, PH: 815/227-XMEN (9636).

NOSTALIGA CON—Held in Elizabeth, NJ, Lyndhurst, NJ, Hempstead, NY. Contact George Downes, G.A. Corp., Box 572, Nutley, NJ 07110. PH: (201) 661-3358.

THE ORIGINAL LONG ISLAND MONTHLY COMIC BOOK & BASEBALL CARD SHOW, Held 1st Sunday each month at the Coliseum Motor Inn, 1650 Hempstead Turnpike, East Meadow, Long Island, NY. Contact: Perry Albert, P.O. Box 66, Fredonia, NY 14063. PH: (716) 672-2913.

ORLANDO CON, Sept., 1993, International Inn, Orlando, FL. Info: Jim Ivey, 4300 S. Semoran, Suite 109, Orlando, FL 32822-2453, PH: (407) 273-0141.

SAN DIEGO COMIC-CON—Box 17066, San Diego, CA 92117. Aug, 1993, San Diego Convention Center.

SEATTLE CENTER CON, Apr, July, Oct, 1993, Box 2043, Kirkland, Wash, 98033. Phone (206) 822-5709 or 827-5129.

SEATTLE QUEST NORTHWEST, Seattle, Wash. Write: Ron Church or Steve Sibra, P.O. Box 82676, Kenmore, WA 98028.

WESTERN NEW YORK COMIC BOOK BASEBALL CARD & COLLECTIBLES SHOW—(held monthly), Masonic Lodge, 321 E. Main St., Fredonia, NY. Contact: Perry Albert, P.O. Box 66, Fredonia, NY 14063. PH: (716) 672-2913.

A Chronology of the Development of the American Comic Book

By M. Thomas Inge

Precursors: The facsimile newspaper strip reprint collections constitute the earliest "comic books." The first of these was a collection of Richard Outcault's **Yellow Kid** from the Hearst **New York American** in March 1897. Commercial and promotional reprint collections, usually in cardboard covers, appeared through the 1920s and featured such newspaper strips as **Mutt and Jeff, Foxy Grandpa, Buster Brown,** and **Barney Google.** During 1922 a reprint magazine, **Comic Monthly,** appeared with each issue devoted to a separate strip, and from 1929 to 1930 George Delacorte published 36 issues of **The Funnies** in tabloid format with original comic pages in color, becoming the first four-color comic newsstand publication.

1933: The Ledger syndicate published a small broadside of their Sunday comics on 7" by 9" plates. Employees of Eastern Color Printing Company in New York, sales manager Harry I. Wildenberg and salesman Max C. Gaines, saw it and figured that two such plates would fit a tabloid page, which would produce a book about 7½"×10" when folded. Thus 10,000 copies of **Funnies on Parade,** containing 32 pages of Sunday newspaper reprints, was published for Proctor and Gamble to be given away as premiums. Some of the strips included were: **Joe Palooka, Mutt and Jeff, Hairbreadth Harry,** and **Reg'lar Fellas.** M. C. Gaines was very impressed with this book and convinced Eastern Color that he could sell a lot of them to such big advertisers as Milk-O-Malt, Wheatena, Kinney Shoe Stores, and others to be used as premiums and radio giveaways. So, Eastern Color printed **Famous Funnies: A Carnival of Comics,** and then **Century of Comics,** both as before, containing Sunday newspaper reprints. Mr. Gaines sold these books in quantities of 100,000 to 250,000.

1934: The giveaway comics were so successful that Mr. Gaines believed that youngsters would buy comic books for ten cents like the

"Big Little Books" coming out at that time. So, early in 1934, Eastern Color ran off 35,000 copies of **Famous Funnies, Series 1,** 64 pages of reprints for Dell Publishing Company to be sold for ten cents in chain stores. Since it sold out promptly on the stands, Eastern Color, in May 1934, issued **Famous Funnies** No. 1 (dated July 1934) which became, with issue No. 2 in July, the first monthly comic magazine. The title continued for over 20 years through 218 issues, reaching a circulation peak of over 400,000 copies a month. At the same time, Mr. Gaines went to the sponsors of Percy Crosby's **Skippy,** who was on the radio, and convinced them to put out a Skippy book, advertise it on the air, and give away a free copy to anyone who bought a tube of Phillip's toothpaste. Thus 500,000 copies of **Skippy's Own Book of Comics** was run off and distributed through drug stores everywhere. This was the first four-color comic book of reprints devoted to a single character.

1935: Major Malcolm Wheeler-Nicholson's National Periodical Publications issued in February a tabloid-sized comic publication called **New Fun,** which became **More Fun** after the sixth issue and converted to the normal comic book size after issue eight. **More Fun** was the first comic book of a standard size to publish original material and continued publication until 1949. **Mickey Mouse Magazine** began in the summer, to become **Walt Disney's Comics and Stories** in 1940, and combined original material with reprinted newspaper strips in most issues.

1936: In the wake of the success of **Famous Funnies,** other publishers, in conjunction with the major newspaper strip syndicates, inaugurated more reprint comic books: **Popular Comics** (News-Tribune, February), **Tip Top Comics** (United Features, April), **King Comics** (King Features, April), and **The Funnies** (new series, NEA, October). Four issues of **Wow Comics,** from David McKay and Henle Publications, appeared, edited by S. M. Iger and including early art by Will Eisner, Bob Kane, and Alex Raymond. The first non-reprint comic book devoted to a single theme was **Detective Picture Stories** issued in December by The Comics Magazine Company.

1937: The second single-theme title, **Western Picture Stories,** came in February from The Comics Magazine Company, and the third was **Detective Comics,** an offshoot of **More Fun,** which began in March to be published to the present. The book's initials, "D.C.," have long served to refer to National Periodical Publications, which was purchased from Major Nicholson by Harry Donenfeld late this year.

1938: "DC" copped a lion's share of the comic book market with the publication of **Action Comics** No. 1 in June which contained the first appearance of Superman by writer Jerry Siegel and artist Joe Shuster, a discovery of Max C. Gaines. "The man of steel" inaugurated the "Golden Era" in comic book history. Fiction House, a pulp publisher, entered the comic book field in September with **Jumbo Comics,** featuring Sheena, Queen of the Jungle, and appearing in over-sized format for the first eight issues.

1939: The continued success of "DC" was assured in May with the publication of **Detective Comics** No. 27 containing the first episode of Batman by artist Bob Kane and writer Bill Finger. **Superman Comics** appeared in the summer. Also, during the summer, a black and white premium comic titled **Motion Picture Funnies Weekly** was published to be given away at motion picture theatres. The plan was to issue it weekly and to have continued stories so that the kids would come back week after week not to miss an episode. Four issues were planned but only one came out. This book contains the first appearance and origin of the Sub-Mariner by Bill Everett (8 pages) which was later reprinted in **Marvel Comics.** In November, the first issue of **Marvel Comics** came out, featuring the Human Torch by Carl Burgos and the Sub-Mariner reprint with color added.

1940: The April issue of **Detective Comics** No. 38 introduced Robin the Boy Wonder as a sidekick to Batman, thus establishing the "Dynamic Duo" and a major precedent for later costume heroes who would also have boy companions. **Batman Comics** began in the spring. Over 60 different comic book titles were being issued, including **Whiz Comics** begun in February by Fawcett Publications. A creation of writer Bill Parker and artist C. C. Beck, **Whiz's** Captain Marvel was the only superhero ever to surpass Superman in comic book sales. Drawing on their own popular pulp magazine heroes, Street and Smith Publications introduced **Shadow Comics** in March and **Doc Savage Comics** in May. A second trend was established with the summer appearance of the first issue of **All-Star Comics,** which brought several superheroes together in one story and in its third issue that winter would announce the establishment of the Justice Society of America.

1941: Wonder Woman was introduced in the spring issue of **All-Star Comics** No. 8, the creation of psychologist William Moulton Marston and artist Harry Peter. **Captain Marvel Adventures** began this year. By the end of 1941, over 160 titles were being published, including **Captain America** by Jack Kirby and Joe Simon, **Police Comics** with Jack Cole's Plastic Man and later Will Eisner's Spirit, **Military Comics** with Blackhawk by Eisner and Charles Cuidera, **Daredevil Comics** with the original character by Charles Biro, **Air Fighters** with Airboy also by Biro, and **Looney Tunes & Merrie Melodies** with Porky Pig, Bugs Bunny, and Elmer Fudd, reportedly created by Bob Clampett for the Leon Schlesinger Productions animated films and drawn for the comics by Chase Craig. Also, Albert Kanter's Gilberton

Company initiated the **Classics Illustrated** series with **The Three Musketeers.**

1942: Crime Does Not Pay by editor Charles Biro and publisher Lev Gleason, devoted to factual accounts of criminals' lives, began a different trend in realistic crime stories. **Wonder Woman** appeared in the summer. John Goldwater's character Archie, drawn by Bob Montana, first published in **Pep Comics,** was given his own magazine, **Archie Comics,** which has remained popular over 40 years. The first issue of **Animal Comics** contained Walt Kelly's "Albert Takes the Cake," featuring the new character of Pogo. In mid-1942, the undated Dell Four Color title, No. 9, **Donald Duck Finds Pirate Gold,** appeared with art by Carl Barks and Jack Hannah. Barks, also featured in **Walt Disney's Comics and Stories,** remained the most popular delineator of Donald Duck and later introduced his greatest creation, Uncle Scrooge, in **Christmas on Bear Mountain** (Dell Four Color No. 178). The fantasy work of George Carlson appeared in the first issue of **Jingle Jangle Comics,** one of the most imaginative titles for children ever to be published.

1945: The first issue of **Real Screen Comics** introduced the Fox and the Crow by James F. Davis, and John Stanley began drawing the **Little Lulu** comic book based on a popular feature in the **Saturday Evening Post** by Marjorie Henderson Buell from 1935 to 1944. Bill Woggon's Katy Keene appears in issue No. 5 of **Wilbur Comic**s to be followed by appearances in **Laugh, Pep, Suzie** and her own comic book in 1950. The popularity of Dick Briefer's satiric version of the Frankenstein monster, originally drawn for **Prize Comics** in 1941, led to the publication of **Frankenstein** by Prize publications.

1950: The son of Max C. Gaines, William M. Gaines, who earlier had inherited his father's firm Educational Comics (later Entertaining Comics), began publication of a series of well-written and masterfully drawn titles which would establish a "New Trend" in comics magazines: **Crypt of Terror** (later **Tales from the Crypt**, April), **The Vault of Horror** (April), **The Haunt of Fear** (May), **Weird Science** (May), **Weird Fantasy** (May), **Crime SuspenStories** (October), and **Two-Fisted Tales** (November), the latter stunningly edited by Harvey Kurtzman.

1952: In October "E.C." published the first number of **Mad** under Kurtzman's creative editorship, thus establishing a style of humor which would inspire other publications and powerfully influence the underground comic book movement of the 1960s.

1953: All Fawcett titles featuring Captain Marvel were ceased after many years of litigation in the courts during which National Periodical

Publications claimed that the super-hero was an infringement on the copyrighted Superman.

1954: The appearance of Fredric Wertham's book **Seduction of the Innocent** in the spring was the culmination of a continuing war against comic books fought by those who believed they corrupted youth and debased culture. The U. S. Senate Subcommittee on Juvenile Delinquency investigated comic books and in response the major publishers banded together in October to create the Comics Code Authority and adopted, in their own words, "the most stringent code in existence for any communications media." Before the Code took effect, more than 1,000,000,000 issues of comic books were being sold annually.

1955: In an effort to avoid the Code, "E.C." launched a "New Direction" series of titles, such as **Impact, Valor, Aces High, Extra, M.D.,** and **Psychoanalysis,** none of which lasted beyond the year. **Mad** was changed into a larger magazine format with issue No. 24 in July to escape the Comics Code entirely, and "E.C." closed down its line of comic books altogether.

1956: Beginning with the Flash in **Showcase** No. 4, Julius Schwartz began a popular revival of "DC" superheroes which would lead to the "Silver Age" in comic book history.

1957: Atlas reduced the number of titles published by two-thirds, with **Journey into Mystery** and **Strange Tales** surviving, while other publishers did the same or went out of business. Atlas would survive as a part of the Marvel Comics Group.

1960: After several efforts at new satire magazines (**Trump** and **Humbug**), Harvey Kurtzman, no longer with Gaines, issued in August the first number of another abortive effort, **Help!,** where the early work of underground cartoonists Jay Lynch, Skip Williamson, Gilbert Shelton, and Robert Crumb appeared.

1961: Stan Lee edited in November the first **Fantastic Four,** featuring Mr. Fantastic, the Human Torch, the Thing, and the Invisible Girl, and inaugurated an enormously popular line of titles from Marvel Comics featuring a more contemporary style of superhero.

1962: Lee introduced **The Amazing Spider-Man** in August, with art by Steve Ditko, **The Hulk** in May and **Thor** in August, the last two produced by Dick Ayers and Jack Kirby.

1963: Marvel's **The X-Men,** with art by Jack Kirby, began a successful run in November, but the title would experience a revival and have an even more popular reception in the 1980s.

1965: James Warren issued **Creepy,** a larger black and white comic book, outside Comics Code's control, which emulated the "E.C." horror comic line. Warren's **Eerie** began in September and **Vampirella** in September 1969.

1967: Robert Crumb's **Zap** No. 1 appeared, the first underground comic book to achieve wide popularity, although the undergrounds had began in 1962 with **Adventures of Jesus** by Foolbert Sturgeon (Frank Stack) and 1964 with **God Nose** by Jack Jackson.

1970: Editor Roy Thomas at Marvel begins **Conan the Barbarian** based on fiction by Robert E. Howard with art by Barry Smith, and Neal Adams began to draw for "DC" a series of **Green Lantern/ Green Arrow** stories which would deal with relevant social issues such as racism, urban poverty, and drugs.

1972: The Swamp Thing by Berni Wrightson begins in November from "DC."

1973: In February, "DC" revived the original Captain Marvel with new art by C. C. Beck and reprints in the first issue of **Shazam** and in October **The Shadow** with scripts by Denny O'Neil and art by Mike Kaluta.

1974: "DC" began publication in the spring of a series of oversized facsimile reprints of the most valued comic books of the past under the general title of "Famous First Editions," beginning with a reprint of **Action** No. 1 and including afterwards **Detective Comics** No. 27, **Sensation Comics** No. 1, **Whiz Comics** No. 2, **Batman** No. 1, **Wonder Woman** No. 1, **All-Star Comics** No. 3, **Flash Comics** No. 1, and **Superman** No. 1. Mike Friedrich, an independent publisher, released **Star★Reach** with work by Jim Starlin, Neal Adams, and Dick Giordano, with ownership of the characters and stories invested in the creators themselves.

1975: In the first collaborative effort between the two major comic book publishers of the previous decade, Marvel and "DC" produced together an oversized comic book version of **MGM's Marvelous Wizard of Oz** in the fall, and then the following year in an unprecedented crossover produced **Superman vs. the Amazing Spider-Man,** written by Gerry Conway, drawn by Ross Andru, and inked by Dick Giordano.

1976: Frank Brunner's **Howard the Duck,** who had appeared earlier in Marvel's **Fear** and **Man-Thing,** was given his own book in January, which because of distribution problems became an overnight collector's item. After decades of litigation, Jerry Siegel and Joe Shuster were given financial recompense and recognition by National Periodical Publications for their creation of Superman, after several friends of the team made a public issue of the case.

1977: Stan Lee's **Spider-Man** was given a second birth, fifteen years after his first, through a highly successful newspaper comic strip, which began syndication on January 3 with art by John Romita. This invasion of the comic strip by comic book characters continued with the appearance on June 6 of Marvel's **Howard the Duck,** with story by Steve Gerber and visuals by Gene Colan. In an unusually successful collaborative effort, Marvel began publication of the comic book adaptation of the George Lucas film **Star Wars,** with script by Roy Thomas and art by Howard Chaykin, at least three months before the film was released nationally on May 25. The demand was so great that all six issues of **Star Wars** were reprinted at least seven times, and the installments were reprinted in two volumes of an oversized Marvel Special Edition and a single paperback volume for the book trade. Dave Sim, with an issue dated December, began self-publication of his **Cerebus the Aardvark,** the success of which would help establish the independent market for non-traditional black-and-white comics.

1978: In an effort to halt declining sales, Warner Communications drastically cut back on the number of "DC" titles and overhauled its distribution process in June. The interest of the visual media in comic book characters reached a new high with the Hulk, Spider-Man, and Doctor Strange, the subjects of television shows; with various projects begun to produce film versions of Flash Gordon, Dick Tracy, Popeye, Conan, The Phantom, and Buck Rogers; and with the movement reaching an outlandish peak of publicity with the release of **Superman** in December. Two significant applications of the comic book format to traditional fiction appeared this year: **A Contract with God and Other Tenement Stories** by Will Eisner and **The Silver Surfer** by Stan Lee and Jack Kirby. Eclipse Enterprises published Don McGregor and Paul Gulacy's **Sabre,** the first graphic album produced for the direct sales market, and initiated a policy of paying royalties and granting copyrights to comic book creators. Wendy and Richard Pini's **Elfquest,** a self-publishing project begun this year, eventually became so popular that it achieved bookstore distribution. The magazine **Heavy Metal** brought to American attention the avant-garde comic book work of European artists.

1980: Publication of the November premier issue of **The New Teen Titans,** with art by George Perez and story by Marv Wolfman, brought back to widespread popularity a title originally published by "DC" in 1966.

1981: The distributor Pacific Comics began publishing titles for direct sales through comic shops with the inaugural issue of Jack Kirby's **Captain Victory and the Galactic Rangers** and offered royalties to artists and writers on the basis of sales. "DC" would do the same for regular newsstand comics in November (with payments retroactive to July 1981), and Marvel followed suit by the end of the year. The first issue of **Raw,** irregularly published by Art Spiegelman and Francoise Mouly, carried comic book art into new extremes of experimentation and innovation with work by European and American artists. With issue No. 158, Frank Miller began to write and draw Marvel's **Daredevil** and brought a vigorous style of violent action to comic book pages.

1982: The first slick format comic book in regular size appeared, **Marvel Fanfare** No. 1, with a March date. Fantagraphics Books began publication in July of **Love and Rockets** by Mario, Gilbert, and Jaime Hernandez and brought a new ethnic sensibility and sophistication in style and content to comic book narratives for adults.

1983: This year saw more comic book publishers, aside from Marvel and DC, issuing more titles than had existed in the past 40 years, most small independent publishers relying on direct sales, such as Americomics, Capital, Eagle, Eclipse, First, Pacific, and Red Circle, and with Archie, Charlton, and Whitman publishing on a limited scale. Frank Miller's mini-series **Ronin** demonstrated a striking use of swordplay and martial arts typical of Japanese comic book art, and Howard Chaykin's stylish but controversial **American Flagg** appeared with an October date on its first issue.

1984: A publishing, media, film, and merchandising phenomenon began with the first issue of **Teenage Mutant Ninja Turtles** from Mirage Studios by Kevin Eastman and Peter Laird.

1985: Ohio State University's Library of Communication and Graphic Arts hosted the first major exhibition devoted to the comic book May 19 through August 2. In what was billed as an irreversible decision, the silver age superheroine Supergirl was killed in the seventh (October) issue of **Crisis on Infinite Earths,** a limited series intended to reorganize and simplify the DC universe on the occasion of the publisher's 50th anniversary.

1986: In recognition of its twenty-fifth anniversary, Marvel began publication of several new ongoing titles comprising Marvel's "New Universe," a self-contained fictional world. DC attracted extensive publicity and media coverage with its revisions of the character of **Superman** by John Byrne and of **Batman** in the **Dark Knight** series by Frank Miller. **Watchmen**, a limited-series graphic novel by Alan Moore and artist Dave Gibbons, began publication with a September issue from DC and Marvel's **The 'Nam,** written by Vietnam veteran Doug Murray and penciled by Michael Golden, began with its December issue. DC issued guidelines in December for labelling their titles as either for mature readers or for readers of all ages; in response, many artists and writers publicly objected or threatened to resign.

1987: Art Spiegelman's **Maus: A Survivor's Tale** was nominated for the National Book Critics Circle Award in biography, the first comic book to be so honored. A celebration of Superman's fiftieth birthday began with the opening of an exhibition on his history at the

Smithsonian's Museum of American History in Washington, D.C., in June and a symposium on "The Superhero in America" in October.

1988: Superman's birthday celebration continued with a public party in New York and a CBS television special in February, a cover story in **Time** magazine in March (the first comic book character to appear on the cover), and an international exposition in Cleveland in June. With issue number 601 for May 24, **Action Comics** became the first modern weekly comic book, which ceased publication after 42 issues with the December 13 number. In August, DC initiated a new policy of allowing creators of new characters to retain ownership of them rather than rely solely on work-for-hire.

1989: The fiftieth anniversary of Batman was marked by the release of the film **Batman,** starring Michael Keaton as Bruce Wayne and Jack Nicholson as the Joker; it grossed more money in the weekend it opened than any other motion picture in film history to that time.

1990: The publication of a new **Classics Illustrated** series began in January from Berkley/First with adaptations of Poe's **The Raven and Other Poems** by Gahan Wilson, Dickens' **Great Expectations** by Rick Geary, Carroll's **Through the Looking Glass** by Kyle Baker, and Melville's **Moby Dick** by Bill Sienkiewicz, with extensive media attention. The adaptation of characters to film continued with the most successful in terms of popularity and box-office receipts being **Teenage Mutant Ninja Turtles** and Warren Beatty's **Dick Tracy.** In November, the engagement of Clark Kent and Lois Lane was announced in **Superman** No. 50 which brought public fanfare about the planned marriage.

1991: One of the first modern comic books to appear in the Soviet Union was a Russian version of **Mickey Mouse** published in Moscow on May 16 in a printing of 200,000 copies which were sold out within hours. Issue number one of a new series of Marvel's **X-Men,** with story and art by Chris Claremont and Jim Lee, was published in October in five different editions with a print run of eight million copies, the highest circulation title in the history of the comic book (the closest to it being the August 1990 **Spider-Man** number one, written and drawn by Todd McFarlane, issued in six different editions with over 2.7 million copies in circulation). On December 18, Sotheby's of New York held its first auction of comic book material.

How to Use This Book

The author of this book has included a selection of key titles covering a variety of subjects that are mostly collected. The comic book titles are listed alphabetically for easy reference. All key issues and important contents are pointed out and priced in three grades—good, fine and mint.

Most comic books listed are priced in groups: 11–20, 21–30, 31–50, etc. The prices listed in the right hand column are for each single comic book in that grouping.

The prices shown represent the current range, but since prices do change constantly, the values in this book should be used as a guide only.

A general selection of titles is represented here, so for more detailed information please consult **The Overstreet Comic Book Price Guide**, master guide.

Comic
Book
Listings

ACTION COMICS (...Weekly #601-642)
6/38-No. 583, 9/86; No. 584, 1/87-Present
National Periodical Publ./Detective Comics/DC Comics

	Good	Fine	VF-NM
1-Origin & 1st app. Superman by Siegel & Shuster, Marco Polo, Tex Thompson, Pep Morgan, Chuck Dawson & Scoop Scanlon; 1st app. Zatara & Lois Lane; Superman story missing 4 pgs. which were included when reprinted in Superman #1			
	8,000.00	24,000.00	50,000.00

(Issues 1 through 10 are all scarce to rare)

	Good	Fine	N-Mint
1(1976,1983)-Giveaway; paper cover, 16 pgs. in color; reprints complete Superman story from #1 ('38)			
	1.70	5.00	10.00
1(1987 Nestle Quik giveaway; 1988, 50 cent-c)			
		.25	.50
2	870.00	2175.00	5200.00
3 (Scarce)	700.00	1750.00	4200.00
4-6: 6-1st Jimmy Olsen (called office boy)			
	470.00	1175.00	2800.00
7,10-Superman covers	635.00	1590.00	3800.00
8,9	400.00	1000.00	2400.00
11,12,14: 14-Clip Carson begins, ends #41			
	215.00	535.00	1300.00
13-Superman cover; last Scoop Scanlon			
	335.00	840.00	2000.00
15-Superman cover	315.00	785.00	1900.00
16	170.00	425.00	1000.00
17-Superman cover; last Marco Polo	240.00	600.00	1450.00
18-Origin 3 Aces; 1st X-Ray Vision?	170.00	425.00	1000.00
19-Superman covers begin	215.00	535.00	1300.00
20-"S" left off Superman's chest; Clark Kent works at "Daily Star"			
	200.00	500.00	1200.00
21,22,24,25: 24-Kent at Daily Planet. 25-Last app. Gargantua T. Potts, Tex Thompson's sidekick	125.00	315.00	750.00
23-1st app. Luthor (w/red hair) & Black Pirate; Black Pirate by Moldoff; 1st mention of The Daily Planet (4/40)			
	185.00	465.00	1100.00
26-30	100.00	250.00	600.00

	Good	Fine	N-Mint
31,32: 32-Intro/1st app. Krypto Ray Gun in Superman story by Burnley	75.00	190.00	450.00
33-Origin Mr. America	90.00	225.00	550.00
34-40: 37-Origin Congo Bill. 40-Intro/1st app. Star Spangled Kid & Stripesy	75.00	190.00	450.00
41	66.00	165.00	400.00
42-1st app./origin Vigilante; Bob Daley becomes Fat Man; origin Mr. America's magic flying carpet; The Queen Bee & Luthor app; Black Pirate ends; not in #41	105.00	265.00	625.00
43-46,48-50: 44-Fat Man's i.d. revealed to Mr. America. 45-1st app. Stuff	66.00	165.00	400.00
47-1st Luthor cover in Action Comics	85.00	215.00	500.00
51-1st app. The Prankster	66.00	165.00	400.00
52-Fat Man & Mr. America become the Ameri-commandos; origin Vigilante retold	70.00	175.00	425.00
53-60: 56-Last Fat Man. 59-Kubert Vigilante begins?, ends #70. 60-1st app. Lois Lane as Superwoman	50.00	125.00	300.00
61-63,65-70: 63-Last 3 Aces	45.00	115.00	265.00
64-Intro Toyman	55.00	140.00	325.00
71-79: 74-Last Mr. America	40.00	100.00	240.00
80-2nd app. & 1st Mr. Mxyztplk-c (1/45)	65.00	165.00	380.00
81-90: 83-Intro Hocus & Pocus	40.00	100.00	240.00
91-99: 93-X-Mas-c. 99-1st small logo (7/46)	36.00	90.00	220.00
100	85.00	215.00	500.00
101-Nuclear explosion-c	46.00	115.00	280.00
102-120: 105,117-X-Mas-c	38.00	85.00	225.00
121-126,128-140: 135,136,138-Zatara by Kubert	35.00	85.00	210.00
127-Vigilante by Kubert; Tommy Tomorrow begins	43.00	110.00	260.00
141-157,159-161: 156-Lois Lane as Super Woman. 160-Last 52 pgs.	35.00	85.00	210.00
158-Origin Superman retold	55.00	140.00	325.00
162-180: 168,176-Used in **POP**, pg. 90	25.00	65.00	150.00
181-201: 191-Intro. Janu in Congo Bill. 198-Last Vigilante. 201-Last pre-code issue	25.00	65.00	150.00
202-220	18.00	54.00	125.00
221-240: 224-1st Golden Gorilla story	14.00	43.00	100.00
241,243-251: 248-Congo Bill becomes Congorilla. 251-Last Tommy			

	Good	Fine	N-Mint
Tomorrow	11.00	32.00	75.00

242-Origin & 1st app. Brainiac (7/58); 1st mention of Shrunken City of
Kandor | 70.00 | 210.00 | 500.00

252-Origin & 1st app. Supergirl (5/59); Re-intro Metallo (his 2nd app.
since Superboy #49) | 80.00 | 240.00 | 550.00

| 253-2nd app. Supergirl | 14.00 | 43.00 | 100.00 |

254-1st meeting of Bizarro & Superman-c/story

| | 16.50 | 50.00 | 115.00 |

255-1st Bizarro Lois-c/story & both Bizarros leave Earth to make
Bizarro World | 11.50 | 34.00 | 80.00

256-261: 259-Red Kryptonite used. 261-1st X-Kryptonite which gave
Streaky his powers; last Congorilla in Action; origin & 1st app.
Streaky The Super Cat | 7.00 | 21.00 | 50.00

| 262,264-266,268-270 | 5.30 | 16.00 | 38.00 |
| 263-Origin Bizarro World | 7.00 | 21.00 | 50.00 |

267(8/60)-3rd Legion app; 1st app. Chameleon Boy, Colossal Boy, &
Invisible Kid | 36.00 | 108.00 | 250.00

| 271-275,277-282: Last 10 cent issue | 4.85 | 14.50 | 34.00 |

276(5/61)-6th Legion app; 1st app. Brainiac 5, Phantom Girl,
Triplicate Girl, Bouncing Boy, Sun Boy, & Shrinking Violet;
Supergirl joins Legion | 13.70 | 41.00 | 96.00

| 283(12/61)-Legion of Super-Villains app. | 6.30 | 19.00 | 44.00 |
| 284(1/62)-Mon-el app. | 6.30 | 19.00 | 44.00 |

285(2/62)-12th Legion app; Brainiac 5 cameo; Supergirl's existence
revealed to world | 6.30 | 19.00 | 44.00

286(3/62)-Legion of Super Villains app.	3.15	9.50	22.00
287(4/62)-14th Legion app.(cameo)	3.15	9.50	22.00
288-Mon-el app.; r-origin Supergirl	3.15	9.50	22.00

289(6/62)-16th Legion app.(Adult); Lightning Man & Saturn
Woman's marriage 1st revealed | 3.15 | 9.50 | 22.00

290(7/62)-17th Legion app; Phantom Girl app.

| | 3.15 | 9.50 | 22.00 |

291,292,294-299: 290-1st Supergirl emergency squad. 291-1st
meeting Supergirl & Mr. Mxyzptlk. 292-2nd app. Superhorse (see
Adv. #293). 297-Mon-el app; 298-Legion app.

	2.15	6.50	15.00
293-Origin Comet (Superhorse)	4.70	14.00	33.00
300-(5/63)	2.40	7.25	17.00

301-303,305-308,310-320: 306-Brainiac 5, Mon-el app. 307-Saturn
Girl app. 314-r-origin Supergirl; J.L.A. x-over. 317-Death of Nor-
Kan of Kandor. 319-Shrinking Violet app.

| | 1.50 | 4.50 | 10.00 |

Action Comics #293, © DC Comics

	Good	**Fine**	**N-Mint**
304-Origin & 1st app. Black Flame	1.50	4.50	10.00
309-Legion app.; Batman & Robin-c & cameo	1.60	4.80	11.00
321-333,335-340: 336-Origin Akvar(Flamebird). 340-Origin, 1st app. Parasite	1.00	3.00	7.00
334-Giant G-20; origin Supergirl, Streaky, Superhorse & Legion (all-r)	2.00	6.00	14.00
341-346,348-359: 344-Batman x-over	.85	2.50	5.00
347,360-Giant Supergirl G-33,G-45; 347-Origin Comet-r plus 3 Bizarro stories. 360-Legion-r; r/origin Supergirl	1.30	4.00	9.00
361-372,374-380: 365-Legion app. 370-New facts about Superman's origin. 376-Last Supergirl in Action. 377-Legion begins	.70	2.00	4.00
373-Giant Supergirl G-57; Legion-r	1.05	3.15	7.50
381-402: 392-Last Legion in Action. Saturn Girl gets new costume. 393-402 All Superman issues	.35	1.00	2.00
403-413: All 52pg. issues; 411-Origin Eclipso-(r). 413-Metamorpho begins, ends #418	.35	1.00	2.00
414-424: 419-Intro. Human Target. 421-Intro Capt. Strong; Green Arrow begins. 422,423-Origin Human Target	.35	1.00	2.00
425-Neal Adams-a(p); The Atom begins	.35	1.00	2.00
426-436,438,439: 432-1st S.A. app. The Toyman	.25	.75	1.50

	Good	Fine	N-Mint
437,443-100 pg. giants	.35	1.00	2.00
440-1st Grell-a on Green Arrow	.70	2.00	4.00
441-Grell-a on Green Arrow continues	.40	1.25	2.50

442,444-499: 454-Last Atom. 458-Last Green Arrow. 484-Earth II Superman & Lois Lane wed. 487,488-(44 pgs.). 487-1st app. Microwave Man; origin Atom retold   .25   .75   1.50

500-($1.00, 68 pgs.)-Infinity-c; Superman life story; shows Legion statues in museum   .60   1.20

501-551,554-582: 511-514-New Airwave. 513-The Atom begins. 517-Aquaman begins; ends #541. 521-1st app. The Vixen. 532,536-New Teen Titans cameo. 535,536-Omega Men app. 544-(Mando paper, 68 pgs.)-Origins new Luthor & Brainiac; Omega Men cameo. 546-J.L.A. & New Teen Titans app. 551-Starfire becomes Red-Star   .50   1.00

552,553-Animal Man-c & app. (2/84 & 3/84)

	Good	Fine	N-Mint
	1.00	3.00	6.00
583-Alan Moore scripts	1.15	3.50	7.00
584-Byrne-a begins; New Teen Titans app.	.25	.75	1.50

585-599: 586-Legends x-over. 596-Millennium x-over. 598-1st app. Checkmate   .50   1.00

600-($2.50, 84 pgs., 5/88)	.70	2.00	4.00

601-642-Weekly issues ($1.50, 52 pgs.); 601-Reintro Secret Six. 611-614: Cat woman (new costume in #611). 613-618: Nightwing   .25   .75   1.50

643-Superman & monthly issues begin again; Perez-c/a/scripts begin; cover swipe Superman #1   .25   .75   1.50

644-649,651-661,663-666,668-679: 654-Part 3 of Batman storyline. 655-Free extra 8 pgs. 660-Death of Lex Luthor. 661-Begin $1.00-c. 674-Supergirl logo & cover/story (re-intro). 675-Deathstroke cameo   .50   1.00

650-($1.50, 52 pgs.)-Lobo cameo (last panel)
     .25   .75   1.50

662-Clark Kent reveals i.d. to Lois Lane; story continued in Superman #53   .40   1.25   2.50

667-($1.75, 52 pgs.)	.30	.90	1.80
680-684: 680-Begin $1.25-c		.65	1.30
Annual 1(1987)-Art Adams-c/a(p)	1.00	3.00	6.00
Annual 2(1989, $1.75, 68 pgs.)-Perez-c/a(i)	.35	1.00	2.00

Annual 3('91, $2.00, 68 pgs.)-Armageddon 2001
     .35   1.00   2.00

Annual 4('92, $2.50, 68 pgs.)-Eclipso app.	.40	1.25	2.50

ADDAMS FAMILY (TV cartoon)
Oct, 1974-No. 3, Apr, 1975 (Hanna-Barbera)
Gold Key

	Good	Fine	N-Mint
1	2.85	8.50	20.00
2,3	1.70	5.00	12.00

ADVANCED DUNGEONS & DRAGONS
12/88-#36, 12/91 ($1.25, color) (Newsstand #1 is Holiday, 1988-89)
DC Comics

	Good	Fine	N-Mint
1-Based on TSR role playing game	1.35	4.00	8.00
2	.85	2.50	5.00
3	.70	2.00	4.00
4-10: Later issues $1.50 cover	.40	1.25	2.50
11-15	.30	.85	1.70
16-23	.25	.75	1.50
24-36: 24-Begin $1.75-c. 31-Mandrake-c/a			
	.30	.90	1.80
Annual 1 (1990, $3.95, 68 pgs.)	.70	2.00	4.00

ADVENTURE COMICS (...Presents Dial H For Hero #479-490)
No. 32, 11/38-No. 490, 2/82; No. 491, 9/82-No. 503, 9/83
National Periodical Publications/DC Comics

32-Anchors Aweigh (ends #52), Barry O'Neil (ends #60, not in #33),
  Captain Desmo (ends #47), Dale Daring (ends #47), Federal Men
  (ends #70), The Golden Dragon (ends #36), Rusty & His Pals
  (ends #52) by Bob Kane, Todd Hunter (ends #38) and Tom Brent
  (ends #39) begin   125.00   315.00   750.00
33-38: 37-Cover used on Double Action #2
                                         61.00   75.00   425.00
39(1/39)-Jack Wood begins, ends #42: 1st mention of Marijuana in
  comics   80.00   200.00   475.00

	Good	Fine	VF-NM

40-(Rare, 7/39, on stands 6/10/39)-The Sandman begins; believed to
  be 1st conceived story; Socko Strong begins, ends #54
                                       1040.00   2600.00   6250.00

	Good	Fine	N-Mint

41   183.00   460.00   1100.00
42,44,46,47: All Sandman covers. 44-Opium story. 47-Steve Conrad
  Adventurer begins, ends #76   200.00   500.00   1200.00
43,45   135.00   335.00   800.00

Adventure Comics #86, © DC Comics

	Good	Fine	VF-NM
48-Intro. & 1st app. The Hourman by Bernard Baily			
	800.00	2000.00	4800.00

	Good	Fine	N-Mint
49,50: 50-Cotton Carver by Jack Lehti begins, ends #59?			
	120.00	300.00	725.00
51,60-Sandman-c	150.00	375.00	900.00

52-59: 53-1st app. Jimmy "Minuteman" Martin & the Minutemen of America in Hourman; ends #78. 58-Paul Kirk Manhunter begins (1st app.), ends 72   110.00   275.00   650.00

	Good	Fine	VF-NM
61-1st app. Starman by Jack Burnley	485.00	1210.00	2900.00

	Good	Fine	N-Mint
62-65,67,68,70: 67-Origin The Mist. 70-Last Federal Men			
	100.00	250.00	600.00
66-Origin/1st app. Shining Knight	125.00	310.00	750.00

69-1st app. Sandy the Golden Boy (Sandman's sidekick) by Bob Kane; Sandman dons new costume   115.00   290.00   700.00

71-Jimmy Martin becomes costume aide to the Hourman; 1st app. Hourman's Miracle Ray machine   92.00   230.00   550.00

	Good	Fine	VF-NM
72-1st Simon & Kirby Sandman	460.00	1150.00	2500.00

73-(Scarce)-Origin Manhunter by Simon & Kirby; begin new series   500.00   1250.00   2800.00

	Good	Fine	N-Mint
74-80: 74-Thorndyke replaces Jimmy, Hourman's assistant. 77-			

	Good	Fine	N-Mint

Origin Genius Jones; Mist story. 80-Last Simon & Kirby Manhunter & Burnley Starman 115.00 290.00 700.00

81-90: 83-Last Hourman. 84-Mike Gibbs begins, ends #102
   75.00   190.00   450.00

91-Last Simon & Kirby Sandman 66.00 165.00 400.00

92-99,101,102: 92-Last Manhunter. 102-Last Starman, Sandman, & Genius Jones. Most-S&K-c 50.00 125.00 300.00

100 84.00 210.00 500.00

103-Aquaman, Green Arrow, Johnny Quick, Superboy begin; 1st small logo (4/46) 200.00 500.00 1200.00

104 63.00 150.00 375.00

105-110 50.00 125.00 300.00

111-120: 113-X-Mas-c 45.00 115.00 275.00

121-126,128-130: 128-1st meeting Superboy & Lois Lane
   38.00   95.00   225.00

127-Brief origin Shining Knight retold 40.00 100.00 240.00

131-141,143-149: 132-Shining Knight 1st return to King Arthur time; origin aide Sir Butch 32.00 80.00 190.00

142-Origin Shining Knight & Johnny Quick retold
   36.00   90.00   220.00

150,151,153,155,157,159,161,163-All have 6 pg. Shining Knight stories by Frank Frazetta. 159-Origin Johnny Quick
   43.00   110.00   260.00

152,154,156,158,160,162,164-169: 166-Last Shining Knight. 168-Last 52 pg. issue 25.00 75.00 175.00

170-180 23.00 70.00 160.00

181-199: 189-B&W and color illo in **POP**
   21.00   63.00   145.00

200 35.00 105.00 245.00

201-209: 207-Last Johnny Quick (not in 205). 209-Last Pre-code issue; origin Speedy 25.00 75.00 175.00

210-1st app. Krypto (Superdog) 193.00 580.00 1350.00

211-213,215-220: 220-Krypto app. 20.00 60.00 140.00

214-2nd app. Krypto 22.00 65.00 150.00

221-246: 237-1st Intergalactic Vigilante Squadron (Legion tryout)
   18.00   54.00   125.00

247(4/58)-1st Legion of Super Heroes app.; 1st app. Cosmic Boy, Lightning Boy (later Lightning Lad in #267), & Saturn Girl (origin) 293.00 880.00 2050.00

248-252,254,255: All Kirby Green Arrow. 255-Intro. Red Kryptonite in Superboy (used in #252 but w/no effect)
   12.00   36.00   85.00

	Good	Fine	N-Mint

253-1st meeting of Superboy & Robin; Green Arrow by Kirby
| | 16.00 | 48.00 | 110.00 |

256-Origin Green Arrow by Kirby | 43.00 | 130.00 | 300.00 |

257-259 | 11.00 | 32.00 | 75.00 |

260-1st Silver-Age origin Aquaman (5/59)
| | 43.00 | 130.00 | 300.00 |

261-266,268,270: 262-Origin Speedy in Green Arrow. 270-Congorilla
    begins, ends #281,283 | 8.00 | 24.00 | 56.00 |

267(12/59)-2nd Legion of Super Heroes; Lightning Boy now called
    Lightning Lad; new costumes for Legion
| | 70.00 | 210.00 | 500.00 |

269-Intro. Aqualad; last Green Arrow (not in #206)
| | 14.00 | 43.00 | 100.00 |

271-Origin Luthor | 17.00 | 50.00 | 118.00 |

272-274,277-280: 279-Intro White Kryptonite in Superboy. 280-1st
    meeting Superboy-Lori Lemaris | 5.70 | 17.00 | 40.00 |

275-Origin Superman-Batman team retold (see World's Finest #94)
| | 10.00 | 30.00 | 70.00 |

276-(9/60) Re-intro Metallo (3rd app?); story similar to Superboy #49
| | 5.70 | 17.00 | 40.00 |

281,284,287-289: 281-Last Congorilla. 284-Aquaman ends. 287,288-
    Intro.Dev-Em, the Knave from Krypton. 287-1st Bizarro Perry
    White & Jimmy Olsen. 288-Bizarro-c. 289-Legion cameo
    (statues) | 5.00 | 15.00 | 35.00 |

282(3/61)-5th Legion app; intro/origin Star Boy
| | 12.70 | 38.00 | 88.00 |

283-Intro. The Phantom Zone | 7.50 | 23.00 | 52.00 |

285-1st Tales of the Bizarro World-c/story (ends #299) in Adv.
    (see Action #255) | 9.00 | 27.00 | 62.00 |

286-1st Bizarro Mxyzptlk; Bizarro-c | 7.00 | 21.00 | 50.00 |

290(11/61)-8th Legion app; origin Sunboy in Legion (last 10 cent
    issue) | 11.50 | 34.00 | 80.00 |

291,292,295-298: 292-1st Bizarro Lana Lang & Lucy Lane. 295-1st
    Bizarro Titano | 4.00 | 12.00 | 28.00 |

293(2/62)-13th Legion app; Mon-el & Legion Super Pets (1st app. &
    origin) app. (1st Superhorse). 1st Bizarro Luthor & Kandor
| | 8.00 | 24.00 | 55.00 |

294-1st Bizarro M. Monroe, Pres. Kennedy | 7.50 | 23.00 | 52.00 |

299-1st Gold Kryptonite (8/62) | 4.30 | 13.00 | 30.00 |

300-Tales of the Legion of Super-Heroes series begins (9/62); Mon-el
    leaves Phantom Zone (temporarily), joins Legion
| | 36.00 | 108.00 | 250.00 |

	Good	Fine	N-Mint
301-Origin Bouncing Boy	11.00	32.00	75.00
302-305: 303-1st app. Matter Eater Lad. 304-Death of Lightning Lad in Legion	6.50	19.00	45.00
306-310: 306-Intro. Legion of Substitute Heroes. 307-1st app. Element Lad in Legion. 308-1st app. Lightning Lass in Legion	5.00	15.00	35.00
311-320: 312-Lightning Lad back in Legion. 315-Last new Superboy story; Colossal Boy app. 316-Origins & powers of Legion given. 317-Intro. Dream Girl in Legion; Lightning Lass becomes Light Lass; Hall of Fame series begins. 320-Dev-Em 2nd app.	3.60	11.00	25.00
321-Intro Time Trapper	2.85	8.50	20.00
322-330: 327-Intro Timber Wolf in Legion. 329-Intro The Bizarro Legionnaires	2.65	8.00	18.00
331-340: 337-Chlorophyll Kid & Night Girl app. 340-Intro Computo in Legion	2.15	6.50	15.00
341-Triplicate Girl becomes Duo Damsel	1.50	4.50	10.00
342-345,347,350,351: 345-Last Hall of Fame; returns in 356,371. 351-1st app. White Witch	1.15	3.50	8.00
346,348,349: 346-1st app. Karate Kid, Princess Projectra, Ferro Lad, & Nemesis Kid. 348-Origin Sunboy; intro Dr. Regulus in Legion. 349- Intro Universo & Rond Vidar	1.30	4.00	9.00
352,354-360: 355-Insect Queen joins Legion (4/67)	1.15	3.50	7.00
353-Death of Ferro Lad in Legion	1.60	4.80	11.00
361-364,366,368-370: 369-Intro Mordru in Legion	.85	2.50	5.00
365,367,371,372: 365-Intro Shadow Lass; lists origins & powers of L.S.H. 367-New Legion headquarters. 371-Intro. Chemical King. 372-Timber Wolf & Chemical King join	1.00	3.00	6.00
373,374,376-380: Last Legion in Adventure	.85	2.50	5.00
375-Intro Quantum Queen & The Wanderers	1.00	3.00	6.00
381-389,391-400: 381-Supergirl begins; 1st full length Supergirl story & her 1st solo book (6/69). 399-Unpubbed G.A. Black Canary story. 400-New costume for Supergirl	.25	.75	1.50
390-Giant Supergirl G-69	.85	2.50	5.00
401,402,404-410: 409-420-(52 pg. issues)	.25	.75	1.50
403-68pg. Giant G-81; Legion-r/#304,305,308,312	.85	2.50	5.00

	Good	**Fine**	**N-Mint**

411,413: 413-Hawkman by Kubert; G.A. Robotman-r/Det. #178;
   Zatanna begins, ends #421 .50 1.00

412-Reprints origin/1st app. Animal Man from Strange Adventures
   #180 1.00 3.00 6.00

414-Reprints 2nd Animal Man/Str. Advs. #184
    .70 2.00 4.00

415,420-Animal Man reprints from Strange Adventures #190 (origin
   recap) & #195 .35 1.00 2.00

416-Giant DC-100 Pg. Super Spect. #10; GA-r .60 1.20

417-Morrow Vigilante; Frazetta Shining Knight r-/Adv. #161; origin
   The Enchantress .60 1.20

418,419,421-424: Last Supergirl in Adv. .50 1.00

425-New look, content change to adventure; Toth-a, origin Capt. Fear
    .25 .75 1.50

426-458: 427-Last Vigilante. 435-Mike Grell's 1st comic work
   (9-10/74). 440-New Spectre origin. 441-452-Aquaman app.
   445-447-The Creeper app. 453-458-Superboy app. 453-Intro
   Mighty Girl .50 1.00

459,460,463-466($1.00 size, 68 pgs.): 459-Flash, Deadman, Wonder
   Woman, Gr. Lantern, New Gods begin. 460-Aquaman begins
    .50 1.00

461,462: 461-Justice Society begins; ends 466. 461,462-Death Earth II
   Batman (both $1.00, 68 pgs.) .70 2.00 4.00

467-490: 467-Starman by Ditko, Plastic Man begin, end 478. 469,470-
   Origin Starman. 479-Dial "H" For Hero begins, ends #490
    .50 1.00

491-499: 491-100pg. Digest size begins; r-Legion of Super Heroes/
   Adv. #247 & 267; 493-Challengers of the Unknown begins by
   Tuska w/brief origin .60 1.20

500-All Legion-r (Digest size, 148 pgs.) .25 .80 1.60

501-503-G.A.-r .60 1.20

ADVENTURES INTO THE UNKNOWN

Fall, 1948-No. 174, Aug, 1967 (No. 1-33: 52 pgs.)
American Comics Group

(1st continuous series horror comic)

1-Guardineer-a; adapt. of "Castle of Otranto" by Horace Walpole

	Good	Fine	N-Mint
	65.00	195.00	450.00
2	30.00	90.00	215.00
3-Feldstein-a (9 pgs)	33.00	100.00	235.00
4,5	18.00	54.00	125.00
6-10	13.50	41.00	95.00

	Good	Fine	N-Mint
11-16,18-20: 13-Starr-a	10.00	30.00	70.00
17-Story similar to movie "The Thing"	13.00	40.00	90.00
21-26,28-30	8.50	25.50	60.00
27-Williamson/Krenkel-a (8 pgs.)	14.00	42.00	100.00
31-50: 38-Atom bomb panels	5.70	17.00	40.00
51(1/54)-58 (3-D effect-c/stories). 52-E.C. swipe/Haunt Of Fear #14			
	13.00	40.00	90.00
59-3-D effect story only	8.50	25.50	60.00
60-Woodesque-a by Landau	5.00	15.00	35.00
61-Last pre-code issue (1-2/55)	4.00	12.00	28.00
62-70	3.00	9.00	21.00
71-90	2.00	6.00	14.00
91,96(#95 on inside),107,116-All contain Williamson-a			
	2.85	8.50	20.00
92-95,97-99,101-106,108-115,117-127: 109-113,118-Whitney			
painted-c	1.70	5.00	12.00
100	2.30	7.00	16.00
128-Williamson/Krenkel/Torres-a(r)/Forbidden Worlds #63; last			
10 cent issue	2.00	6.00	14.00
129-150	1.50	4.50	10.00
151-153: 153-Magic Agent app.	1.00	3.00	7.00
154-Nemesis series begins (origin), ends #170			
	1.50	4.50	10.00
155-167,169-174: 157-Magic Agent app.	1.00	3.00	7.00
168-Ditko-a(p)	1.50	4.50	10.00

ADVENTURES OF BOB HOPE, THE
Feb-Mar, 1950-No. 109, Feb-Mar, 1968 (#1-10: 52 pgs.)
National Periodical Publications

	Good	Fine	N-Mint
1-Photo-c	70.00	210.00	500.00
2-Photo-c	36.00	108.00	250.00
3,4-Photo-c	23.00	70.00	160.00
5-10	18.00	54.00	125.00
11-20	11.50	34.00	80.00
21-31 (2-3/55; last precode)	7.00	21.00	50.00
32-40	5.70	17.00	40.00
41-50	4.30	13.00	30.00
51-70	2.85	8.50	20.00
71-93,95-105	1.50	4.50	10.00
94-Aquaman cameo	1.70	5.00	12.00
106-109-All monster-c/stories by N. Adams-c/a			
	2.85	8.50	20.00

ADVENTURES OF CAPTAIN AMERICA
Sept, 1991-No. 4, Dec, 1991 ($4.95, color, squarebound, mini-series)
Marvel Comics

	Good	Fine	N-Mint
1-Embossed-c	.90	2.75	5.50
2-4	.85	2.50	5.00

ADVENTURES OF DEAN MARTIN AND JERRY LEWIS, THE
(The Adventures of Jerry Lewis No. 41 on)
July-Aug, 1952-No. 40, Oct, 1957
National Periodical Publications

1	50.00	150.00	350.00
2	4.50	73.00	170.00
3-10	11.50	34.00	80.00
11-19: Last precode (2/55)	6.50	19.00	45.00
20-30	5.00	15.00	35.00
31-40	3.60	11.00	25.00

ADVENTURES OF JERRY LEWIS, THE (Formerly Adventures of
Dean Martin & Jerry Lewis No. 1-40)
No. 41, Nov, 1957-No. 124, May-June, 1971
National Periodical Publications

41-60	2.85	8.50	20.00
61-80: 68,74-Photo-c	2.30	7.00	16.00
81-91,93-96,98-100: 89-Bob Hope app.	1.30	4.00	9.00
92-Superman cameo	1.70	5.00	12.00
97-Batman/Robin x-over; Joker-c/story	2.85	8.50	20.00
101-104-Neal Adams-c/a; 102-Beatles app.	2.65	8.00	18.00
105-Superman x-over	1.70	5.00	12.00
106-111,113-116	.85	2.50	5.00
112-Flash x-over	1.70	5.00	12.00
117-Wonder Woman x-over	1.00	3.00	6.00
118-124	.70	2.00	4.00

ADVENTURES OF REX THE WONDER DOG, THE
(Rex...No. 1)
Jan-Feb, 1952-No. 45, May-June, 1959; No. 46, Nov-Dec, 1959
National Periodical Publications

1-(Scarce)-Toth-a	67.00	200.00	460.00
2-(Scarce)-Toth-a	31.00	93.00	215.00
3-(Scarce)-Toth-a	24.50	73.00	170.00
4,5	16.50	50.00	115.00

	Good	Fine	N-Mint
6-10	11.50	34.00	80.00
11-Atom bomb-c/story	13.00	40.00	90.00
12-19: Last precode (1-2/55)	6.50	19.00	45.00
20-46	4.50	13.00	32.00

ADVENTURES OF SUPERMAN (Formerly Superman)
No. 424, Jan, 1987-Present
DC Comics

424	.25	.75	1.50
425-449: 426-Legends x-over. 432-1st app. Jose Delgado who becomes Gangbuster in #434. 436-Byrne scripts begin. 436,437-Millennium x-over. 438-New Brainiac app. 440-Batman app.		.50	1.00
450-463,465-479,481-491: 457-Perez plots. 463-Superman/Flash race. 467-Part 2 of Batman story. 473-Hal Jordan, Guy Gardner x-over. 474-Begin $1.00-c. 477-Legion app.		.50	1.00
464-Lobo-c & app. (pre-dates Lobo #1)	.70	2.00	4.00
480-($1.75, 52 pgs.)-Mooney part pencils	.30	.90	1.80
292-296: 292-Begin $1.25-c		.65	1.30
Annual 1 (1987, $1.25, 52 pgs.)-Starlin-c	.25	.70	1.40
Annual 2,3 (1990, 1991, $2.00, 68 pgs.): 2-Byrne-c/a(i); Legion '90 (Lobo) app. 3-Armageddon 2001 x-over			
	.35	1.00	2.00
Annual 4 (1992, $2.50, 68 pgs.)-Eclipso app.	.40	1.25	2.50

ADVENTURES OF THE FLY (The Fly #1-6; becomes Fly Man No. 32-39) Aug, 1959-No. 30, Oct, 1964; No. 31, May, 1965
Archie Publications/Radio Comics

1-Shield app.; origin The Fly; S&K-c/a			
	43.00	130.00	300.00
2-Williamson, S&K-a	24.00	72.00	165.00
3-Origin retold; Davis, Powell-a	16.00	48.00	110.00
4-Neal Adams-a(p)(1 panel); S&K-c; Powell-a; 2 pg. Shield story			
	11.00	32.00	75.00
5-10: 7-Black Hood app. 8,9-Shield x-over. 9-1st app. Cat Girl. 10-Black Hood app.	6.70	20.00	48.00
11-13,15-20: 16-Last 10 cent issue. 20-Origin Fly Girl retold			
	4.00	12.00	28.00
14-Intro. & origin Fly Girl	5.70	17.00	40.00
21-30: 23-Jaguar cameo. 27-29-Black Hood 1 pg. strips. 30-Comet x-over in Fly Girl	2.85	8.50	20.00

	Good	Fine	N-Mint
31-Black Hood, Shield, Comet app.	3.15	9.50	22.00

ADVENTURES OF THE JAGUAR, THE (See Mighty Crusaders)
Sept, 1961-No. 15, Nov, 1963
Archie Publications (Radio Comics)

	Good	Fine	N-Mint
1-Origin Jaguar(1st app?); by J. Rosenberger			
	13.00	40.00	90.00
2,3: 3-Last 10 cent issue	7.00	21.00	50.00
4-6-Catgirl app. (#4's-c is same as splash pg.)			
	5.00	15.00	35.00
7-10	3.60	11.00	25.00
11-15: 13,14-Catgirl, Black Hood app. in both			
	2.85	8.50	20.00

AIRBOY COMICS (Air Fighters Comics No. 1-22)
V2#11, Dec, 1945-V10#4, May, 1953 (No V3#3)
Hillman Periodicals

	Good	Fine	N-Mint
V2#11	32.00	95.00	225.00
12-Valkyrie app.	22.00	65.00	150.00
V3#1,2(no #3)	19.00	57.00	130.00
4-The Heap app. in Skywolf	16.00	48.00	110.00
5-8,10,11: 6-Valkyrie app.	13.00	40.00	90.00
9-Origin The Heap	16.00	48.00	110.00
12-Skywolf & Airboy x-over; Valkyrie app.			
	17.00	51.00	120.00
V4#1-Iron Lady app.	16.00	48.00	110.00
2,3,12: 2-Rackman begins	9.30	28.00	65.00
4-Simon & Kirby-c	11.00	32.00	75.00
5-11-All S&K-a	13.00	40.00	90.00
V5#1-11: 4-Infantino Heap. 5-Skull-c. 10-Origin The Heap			
	6.50	19.00	45.00
12-Krigstein-a(p)	8.50	25.50	60.00
V6#1-3,5-12: 6,8-Origin The Heap	6.50	19.00	45.00
4-Origin retold	8.00	24.00	55.00
V7#1-12: 7,8,10-Origin The Heap	6.50	19.00	45.00
V8#1-3,6-12	5.30	16.00	38.00
4-Krigstein-a	8.00	24.00	55.00
5(#100)	6.50	19.00	45.00
V9#1-12: 2-Valkyrie app. 7-One pg. Frazetta ad			
	5.30	16.00	38.00
V10#1-4	5.30	16.00	38.00

AIR FIGHTERS COMICS (Airboy Comics #23 (V2#11) on)
Nov, 1941; No. 2, Nov, 1942-V2#10, Fall, 1945
Hillman Periodicals

	Good	Fine	N-Mint
V1#1-(Produced by Funnies, Inc.); Black Commander only app.			
	105.00	315.00	725.00
2(11/42)-(Produced by Quality artists & Biro for Hillman); Origin Airboy & Iron Ace; Black Angel, Flying Dutchman & Skywolf begin; Fuje-a;Biro-c/a	170.00	510.00	1200.00
3-Origin The Heap & Skywolf	87.00	260.00	600.00
4	57.00	170.00	400.00
5,6	43.00	130.00	300.00
7-12	35.00	105.00	240.00
V2#1,3-9: 5-Flag-c; Fuje-a. 7-Valkyrie app.			
	31.00	93.00	215.00
2-Skywolf by Giunta; Flying Dutchman by Fuje; 1st meeting Valkyrie & Airboy (she worked for the Nazis in beginning)	42.00	125.00	285.00
10-Origin The Heap & Skywolf	39.00	117.00	275.00

AKIRA
Sept, 1988-Present ($3.50-$3.75, color, deluxe, 68 pgs.)
Epic Comics (Marvel)

	Good	Fine	N-Mint
1	3.35	10.00	20.00
1,2-2nd printings ('89, $3.95)	.70	2.00	4.00
2	2.00	6.00	12.00
3-5	1.50	4.50	9.00
6-15	.90	2.75	5.50
16-35: 17-Begin $3.95-c	.70	2.00	4.00
36 ($4.50)	.75	2.25	4.50

ALF (TV)
Mar, 1988-No. 50, Feb, 1992 ($1.00, color)
Marvel Comics

	Good	Fine	N-Mint
1-Post-a; photo-c	.40	1.25	2.50
2-Post-a	.25	.75	1.50
3-49: 6-Photo-c. 26-Infinity-c. 44-X-Men parody	.50		1.00
50-($1.75, 52 pgs.)-Final issue; photo-c	.30	.90	1.80
Annual 1 (1988, $1.75, 68 pgs.)-Evolutionary War			
	.35	1.00	2.00

	Good	Fine	N-Mint
Annual 2 (1989, $2.00, 68 pgs.)-Sienkiewicz-c			
	.35	1.00	2.00
Annual 3 (1990, $2.00, 68 pgs.)-TMNT parody			
	.35	1.00	2.00
...Comics Digest 1 (1988)-Reprints Alf #1,2	.25	.75	1.50
Holiday Special 1 ($1.75, 1988, 68 pgs.)	.30	.90	1.80
Holiday Special 2 ($2.00, Winter, 1989, 68 pgs.)			
	.35	1.00	2.00
Spring Special 1 (Spr/89, $1.75, 68 pgs.)	.30	.90	1.80

ALIEN LEGION
April, 1984-No. 20, Sept, 1987
Epic Comics (Marvel)

	Good	Fine	N-Mint
1-$2.00 cover, high quality paper	.40	1.25	2.50
2-5	.30	.85	1.70
6-20	.25	.75	1.50

ALIEN LEGION (2nd series)
Aug, 1987 (indicia) (10/87 on-c)-No. 18, Aug, 1990 ($1.25, color)
Epic Comics (Marvel)

	Good	Fine	N-Mint
V2#1	.25	.75	1.50
V2#2-18: 7-Begin $1.50 cover		.60	1.20

ALIENS
1988-No. 6, 1989 ($1.95, B&W, mini-series)
V2#1, Aug, 1989-No. 4, 1990 ($2.25, color, mini-series)
Dark Horse Comics

	Good	Fine	N-Mint
1-Based on movie sequel	5.50	16.50	33.00
1-2nd printing	1.50	4.50	9.00
1-3rd-6th printings; 4th w/new inside front-c			
	.35	1.00	2.00
2	4.00	12.00	24.00
2-2nd printing	.70	2.00	4.00
2-3rd printing w/new inside f/c	.35	1.00	2.00
3	2.00	6.00	12.00
4	1.30	4.00	8.00
5,6	1.00	3.00	6.00
3-6-2nd printings	.35	1.00	2.00
V2#1 ($2.25, color)-Adapts sequel	2.00	6.00	12.00
1-2nd printing ($2.25)	.40	1.15	2.25
2-4	1.00	3.00	6.00

ALIENS: EARTH WAR
June, 1990-No. 4, Oct, 1990 ($2.50, color, mini-series)
Dark Horse Comics

	Good	Fine	N-Mint
1-All have Sam Kieth-a & Bolton painted-c			
	1.70	5.00	10.00
1-2nd printing	.40	1.25	2.50
2	1.30	4.00	8.00
3,4	1.10	3.25	6.50

ALIENS: GENOCIDE
Nov, 1991-No. 4, Feb, 1992 ($2.50, color, mini-series)
Dark Horse Comics

	Good	Fine	N-Mint
1-4: All have Arthur Suydam painted-c	.40	1.25	2.50

Aliens Vs. Predator #1, © Twentieth Century Fox

ALIENS VS. PREDATOR
June, 1990-No. 4, Dec, 1990, ($2.50, color, mini-series)
Dark Horse Comics

1-Painted-c	1.70	5.00	10.00
1-2nd printing	.40	1.25	2.50
0-(7/90, $1.95, B&W)-r/Dark Horse Pres. #34-36			
	2.00	6.00	12.00
2,3	1.00	3.00	6.00
2-4: 2nd printings	.40	1.25	2.50
4-Dave Dorman painted-c	.70	2.00	4.00

ALL-AMERICAN COMICS (...Western #103-126, ...Men of War #127 on)
April, 1939-No. 102, Oct, 1948
National Periodical Publications/All-American

	Good	Fine	N-Mint
1-Hop Harrigan, Scribbly, Toonerville Folks, Ben Webster, Spot Savage, Mutt & Jeff, Red White & Blue, Adv. in the Unknown, Tippie, Reg'lar Fellers, Skippy, Bobby Thatcher, Mystery Men of Mars, Daiseybelle, & Wiley of West Point begin	300.00	750.00	1800.00
2-Ripley's Believe It or Not begins, ends #24	100.00	250.00	600.00
3-5: 5-The American Way begins, ends #10	70.00	175.00	425.00
6,7: 6-Last Spot Savage; Popsicle Pete begins, ends #26, 28. 7-Last Bobby Thatcher	56.00	140.00	335.00
8-The Ultra Man begins	92.00	230.00	550.00
9,10: 10-X-Mas-c	64.00	160.00	380.00
11-15: 12-Last Toonerville Folks. 15-Last Tippie & Reg'lar Fellars	52.00	130.00	315.00

	Good	Fine	VF-NM
16-(Rare)-Origin/1st app. Green Lantern (7/40) & begin series; created by Martin Nodell. Inspired by Aladdin's Lamp; the suggested alter ego name Alan Ladd, was never capitalized on. It was changed to Alan Scott before Alan Ladd became a major film star (he was in two films before this issue)	2,700.00	6,700.00	16,000.00

	Good	Fine	N-Mint
17-(Scarce)-2nd Green Lantern	665.00	1665.00	4000.00
18-N.Y. World's Fair-c/story	465.00	1165.00	2800.00

	Good	Fine	VF-NM
19-Origin/1st app. The Atom (10/40); last Ultra Man	500.00	1250.00	2800.00

	Good	Fine	N-Mint
20-Atom dons costume; Hunkle becomes Red Tornado (1st app.); Rescue on Mars begins, ends #25; 1 pg. origin Green Lantern	210.00	525.00	1250.00
21-23: 21-Last Wiley of West Point & Skippy. 23-Last Daiseybelle; 3 Idiots begin, end #82	136.00	340.00	800.00
24-Sisty & Dinky become the Cyclone Kids; Ben Webster ends. Origin Dr. Mid-Nite & Sargon, The Sorcerer in text with app.	166.00	415.00	1000.00

	Good	Fine	VF-NM

25-Origin/1st story app. Dr. Mid-Nite by Stan Asch; Hop Harrigan
becomes Guardian Angel; last Adventure in the Unknown

	Good	Fine	VF-NM
	355.00	885.00	2000.00
	Good	**Fine**	**N-Mint**

26-Origin/1st story app. Sargon, the Sorcerer

	Good	Fine	N-Mint
	166.00	415.00	1000.00

27: #27-32 are misnumbered in indicia with correct No. appearing on
cover. Intro. Doiby Dickles, Green Lantern's sidekick

	215.00	540.00	1300.00

28-Hop Harrigan gives up costumed i.d.

	92.00	230.00	550.00
29,30	92.00	230.00	550.00

31-40: 35-Doiby learns Green Lantern's i.d.

	65.00	165.00	400.00
41-50: 50-Sargon ends	60.00	150.00	355.00

51-60: 59-Scribbly & the Red Tornado ends

	50.00	125.00	300.00
61-Origin/1st app. Solomon Grundy	185.00	460.00	1100.00

62-70: 70-Kubert Sargon; intro Sargon's helper, Maximillian
O'Leary

	43.00	110.00	255.00

71-88,90-99: 71-Last Red White & Blue. 72-Black Pirate begins (not
in #74-82); last Atom. 73-Winky, Blinky & Noddy begins, ends
#82. 90-Origin Icicle. 99-Last Hop Harrigan

	38.00	95.00	225.00
89-Origin Harlequin	46.00	115.00	275.00

100-1st app. Johnny Thunder by Alex Toth

	75.00	190.00	450.00
101-Last Mutt & Jeff	60.00	150.00	355.00

102-Last Green Lantern, Black Pirate & Dr. Mid-Nite

	75.00	190.00	450.00

ALL-AMERICAN MEN OF WAR (Previously All-American
Western)
No. 127, Aug-Sept, 1952-No. 117, Sept-Oct, 1966
National Periodical Publications

127 (1952)	47.00	140.00	330.00
128 (1952)	30.00	90.00	205.00
2(12-1/'52-53)-5	27.00	80.00	190.00
6-10	16.00	48.00	110.00
11-18: Last precode (2/55)	14.00	43.00	100.00
19-28	10.00	30.00	70.00
29,30,32-Wood-a	11.00	32.00	75.00

	Good	Fine	N-Mint
31,33-40	7.00	21.00	50.00
41-50	5.70	17.00	40.00
51-56,58-70	4.30	13.00	30.00
57-1st Gunner & Sarge by Andru	7.00	21.00	50.00
58-70	4.70	14.00	33.00
71-80	2.85	8.50	20.00
81-100: 82-Johnny Cloud begins, ends #111,114,115. 86-Last 10 cent issue?	1.85	5.50	13.00
101-117: 112-Balloon Buster series begins, ends #114,116; 115-Johnny Cloud app.	1.15	3.50	8.00

ALL-AMERICAN WESTERN (Formerly All-American Comics; Becomes All-American Men of War)
No. 103, Nov, 1948-No. 126, June-July, 1952 (103-121: 52 pgs.)
National Periodical Publications

	Good	Fine	N-Mint
103-Johnny Thunder & his horse Black Lightning continues by Toth, ends #126; Foley of The Fighting 5th, Minstrel Maverick, & Overland Coach begin; Captain Tootsie by Beck; mentioned in Love and Death	29.00	85.00	200.00
104-Kubert-a	20.00	60.00	140.00
105,107-Kubert-a	16.50	50.00	115.00
106,108-110,112: 112-Kurtzman "Pot-Shot Pete," (1 pg.)	13.00	40.00	90.00
111,114-116-Kubert-a	14.00	43.00	100.00
113-Intro. Swift Deer, J. Thunder's new sidekick; classic Toth-c; Kubert-a	16.00	48.00	110.00
117-126: 121-Kubert-a	11.00	32.00	75.00

ALL-FLASH (...Quarterly No. 1-5)
Summer, 1941-No. 32, Dec-Jan, 1947-48
National Periodical Publications/All-American

	Good	Fine	N-Mint
1-Origin The Flash retold by E. Hibbard	500.00	1250.00	2800.00
2-Origin recap	140.00	350.00	850.00
3,4	96.00	240.00	575.00
5-Winky, Blinky & Noddy begins, ends #32	70.00	175.00	425.00
6-10	60.00	150.00	350.00
11-13: 12-Origin The Thinker. 13-The King app.	50.00	125.00	300.00
14-Green Lantern cameo	60.00	150.00	350.00

	Good	Fine	N-Mint
15-31: 18-Mutt & Jeff begins, ends #22	46.00	115.00	275.00
32-Origin The Fiddler; 1st Star Sapphire	56.00	140.00	325.00

ALL-SELECT COMICS (Blonde Phantom No. 12 on)
Fall, 1943-No. 11, Fall, 1946
Timely Comics (Daring Comics)

1-Capt. America, Human Torch, Sub-Mariner begin; Black Widow

	Good	Fine	N-Mint
app.	250.00	625.00	1500.00
2-Red Skull app.	115.00	290.00	700.00
3-The Whizzer begins	75.00	190.00	450.00
4,5-Last Sub-Mariner	60.00	150.00	350.00

6-9: 6-The Destroyer app. 8-No Whizzer

	Good	Fine	N-Mint
	50.00	125.00	300.00

10-The Destroyer & Sub-Mariner app.; last Capt. America & Human Torch issue 50.00 125.00 300.00

11-1st app. Blonde Phantom; Miss America app.; all Blonde Phantom-c by Shores 85.00 215.00 500.00

ALL STAR COMICS (All Star Western No. 58 on)
Summer, 1940-No. 57, Feb-Mar, 1951; No. 58, Jan-Feb, 1976-No. 74, Sept-Oct, 1978
National Periodical Publ./All-American/DC Comics

	Good	Fine	VF-NM
1-The Flash(#1 by Harry Lampert), Hawkman(by Shelly), Hourman, The Sandman, The Spectre, Biff Bronson, Red White & Blue begin; Ultra Man's only app. (#1-3 are quarterly; #4 begins bi-monthly issues)	850.00	2150.00	5100.00
	Good	Fine	N-Mint
2-Green Lantern, Johnny Thunder begin	385.00	965.00	2300.00
	Good	Fine	VF-NM

3-Origin & 1st app. The Justice Society of America; Dr. Fate & The Atom begin, Red Tornado cameo; last Red White & Blue

	Good	Fine	VF-NM
	1600.00	4000.00	9000.00
	Good	Fine	N-Mint
4-1st adventure for J.S.A.	383.00	960.00	2300.00

5-1st app. Shiera Sanders as Hawkgirl

	Good	Fine	N-Mint
	400.00	1000.00	2400.00
6-Johnny Thunder joins JSA	267.00	670.00	1600.00

7-Batman, Superman, Flash cameo; last Hourman; Doiby Dickles app. 285.00 715.00 1700.00

	Good	Fine	VF-NM

8-Origin & 1st app. Wonder Woman (added as 8 pgs. making book 76 pgs.; origin cont'd in Sensation #1); Dr. Fate dons new helmet; Dr.Mid-Nite, Hop Harrigan text stories & Starman begin; Shiera app.; Hop Harrigan JSA guest

	600.00	1500.00	3600.00
	Good	**Fine**	**N-Mint**

9,10: 9-Shiera app. 10-Flash, Green Lantern cameo, Sandman new
costume 235.00 590.00 1400.00

11,12: 11-Wonder Woman begins; Spectre cameo; Shiera app.
12-Wonder Woman becomes JSA Secretary
200.00 500.00 1200.00

13-15: Sandman w/Sandy in #14 & 15; 15-Origin Brain Wave; Shiera
app. 185.00 465.00 1100.00

16-20: 19-Sandman w/Sandy. 20-Dr. Fate & Sandman cameo
135.00 340.00 800.00

21-23: 21-Spectre & Atom cameo; Dr. Fate by Kubert; Dr. Fate,
Sandman end. 22-Last Hop Harrigan; Flag-c. 23-Origin Psycho
Pirate; last Spectre & Starman 115.00 290.00 700.00

24-Flash & Green Lantern cameo; Mr. Terrific only app.; Wildcat,
JSA guest; Kubert Hawkman begins
115.00 290.00 700.00

25-27: 25-The Flash & Green Lantern start again. 27-Wildcat, JSA
guest 110.00 275.00 650.00

28-32 96.00 240.00 575.00

33-Solomon Grundy, Hawkman, Doiby Dickles app.
200.00 500.00 1200.00

34,35-Johnny Thunder cameo in both 88.00 220.00 525.00

36-Batman & Superman JSA guests 185.00 465.00 1100.00

37-Johnny Thunder cameo; origin Injustice Society; last Kubert
Hawkman 120.00 300.00 600.00

38-Black Canary begins; JSA Death issue
140.00 350.00 700.00

39,40: 39-Last Johnny Thunder 90.00 225.00 445.00

41-Black Canary joins JSA; Injustice Society app.
86.00 225.00 435.00

42-Atom & the Hawkman don new costumes
90.00 225.00 450.00

43-49,51-56: 55-Sci/Fi story 90.00 225.00 450.00

50-Frazetta art, 3 pgs. 100.00 250.00 500.00

57-Kubert-a, 6 pgs. (Scarce) 110.00 275.00 550.00

V12#58-74(1976-78)-Flash, Hawkman, Dr. Mid-Nite, Wildcat, Dr.
Fate, Green, Lantern, Star Spangled Kid, & Robin app.; intro

	Good	**Fine**	**N-Mint**
Power Girl. 58-JSA app. 69-1st app. Huntress	.60		1.25

ALL-STAR SQUADRON (See Justice League of America #193)
Sept, 1981-No. 67, March, 1987
DC Comics

	Good	Fine	N-Mint
1-Original Atom, Hawkman, Dr. Mid-Nite, Robotman (origin), Plastic Man, Johnny Quick, Liberty Belle, Shining Knight begin	.50		1.00
2-24: 5-Danette Reilly becomes new Firebrand. 8-Re-intro Steel, the Indestructable Man. 12-Origin G.A. Hawkman retold. 23-Origin/ 1st app. The Amazing Man. 24-Batman app.	.50		1.00
25-1st Infinity, Inc. (9/83)	.50	.50	1.00
26-Origin Infinity, Inc. (2nd app.); Robin app.	.50	.50	1.00
27-46,48,49: 33-Origin Freedom Fighters of Earth-X. 41-Origin Starman	.50		1.00
47-Origin Dr. Fate; McFarlane-a (1st full story)/part-c (7/85)	.50	1.50	3.00
50-Double size; Crisis x-over	.50		1.00
51-67: 51-56-Crisis x-over. 61-Origin Liberty Belle. 62-Origin The Shining Knight. 63-Origin Robotman. 65-Origin Johnny Quick. 66-Origin Tarantula	.50		1.00
Annual 1-3: 1(11/82)-Retells origin of G.A. Atom, Guardian & Wild-cat.2(11/83)-Infinity, Inc. app. 3(9/84)	.50		1.00

ALL STAR WESTERN (Formerly All Star Comics No. 1-57)
No. 58, Apr-May, 1951-No. 119, June-July, 1961
National Periodical Publications

	Good	Fine	N-Mint
58-Trigger Twins (ends #116), Strong Bow, The Roving Ranger & Don Caballero begin	26.30	79.00	185.00
59,60: Last 52 pgs.	12.00	36.00	85.00
61-66: 61-64-Toth-a	10.00	30.00	70.00
67-Johnny Thunder begins; Gil Kane-a	12.00	36.00	85.00
68-81: Last precode (2-3/55)	5.70	17.00	40.00
82-98	4.50	14.00	32.00
99-Frazetta-a r-/Jimmy Wakely #4	6.00	18.00	42.00
100	5.30	16.00	38.00
101-107,109-116,118,119	3.50	10.50	24.00
108-Origin Johnny Thunder	8.50	25.50	60.00
117-Origin Super Chief	6.00	18.00	42.00

ALL-STAR WESTERN (Weird Western Tales No. 12 on)
Aug-Sept, 1970-No. 11, Apr-May, 1972
National Periodical Publications

	Good	Fine	N-Mint
1-Pow-Wow Smith-r; Infantino-a	1.00	3.00	6.00

2-8: 2-Outlaw begins; El Diablo by Morrow begins; has cameos by
Williamson, Torres, Gil Kane, Giordano & Phil Seuling. 3-Origin
El Diablo. 5-Last Outlaw issue. 6-Billy the Kid begins, ends #8

	Good	Fine	N-Mint
	.60	1.75	3.50
9-Frazetta-a, 3 pgs.(r)	.85	2.50	5.00
10-Jonah Hex begins (1st app.)	5.00	15.00	35.00
11-2nd app. Jonah Hex	1.50	4.50	10.00

ALL WINNERS COMICS
Summer, 1941-No. 19, Fall, 1946; No. 21, Winter, 1946-47
    (no No. 20) (No. 21 continued from Young Allies No. 20)
USA No. 1-7/WFP No. 10-19/YAI No. 21

	Good	Fine	VF-NM
1-The Angel & Black Marvel only app.; Capt. America by Simon & Kirby, Human Torch & Sub-Mariner begin			
	425.00	1050.00	2300.00

	Good	Fine	N-Mint
2-The Destroyer & The Whizzer begin; Simon & Kirby Captain			
	185.00	465.00	1100.00
3	140.00	350.00	825.00
4-Classic War-c	160.00	400.00	950.00
5	90.00	225.00	550.00
6-The Black Avenger only app.; no Whizzer story; Hitler, Tojo & Mussolini-c	105.00	260.00	625.00
7-10	75.00	190.00	450.00
11,13-18: 14-16-No Human Torch	50.00	125.00	300.00
12-Red Skull story; last Destroyer; no Whizzer story			
	55.00	140.00	325.00
19-(Scarce)-1st app. & origin All Winners Squad (Capt. America & Bucky, Human Torch & Toro, Sub-Mariner, Whizzer, & Miss America; r-in Fantasy Masterpieces #10			
	115.00	290.00	700.00
21-(Scarce)-All Winners Squad; bondage-c			
	110.00	275.00	650.00
(2nd Series-August, 1948, Marvel Comics (CDS)) 1-The Blonde Phantom, Capt. America, Human Torch, & Sub-Mariner app.			
	95.00	240.00	575.00

ALPHA FLIGHT (See X-Men #120,121 & X-Men/Alpha Flight)
Aug, 1983-Present (#52-on are direct sale only)
Marvel Comics Group

	Good	Fine	N-Mint
1-Byrne-a begins (52 pgs.)-Wolverine & Nightcrawler cameo	.85	2.50	5.00
2-Vindicator becomes Guardian; origin Marrina & Alpha Flight	.40	1.25	2.50
3-11: 3-Concludes origin Alpha Flight. 6-Origin Shaman. 7-Origin Snowbird. 10,11-Origin Sasquatch	.35	1.00	2.00
12-Double size; death of Guardian	.40	1.25	2.50
13-Wolverine app.	2.00	6.00	12.00
14-16: 16-Wolverine cameo	.25	.75	1.50
17-X-Men x-over; Wolverine cameo	1.00	3.00	6.00
18-28: 20-New headquarters. 25-Return of Guardian. 28-Last Byrne issue	.25	.75	1.50
29-32,35-49		.65	1.30
33,34: 33-X-Men (Wolverine) app. 34-Origin Wolverine	1.15	3.50	7.00
50-Double size	.25	.75	1.50
51-Jim Lee's 1st work at Marvel (10/87)	2.00	6.00	12.00
52,53-Wolverine app. 53-1st Lee-a on Wolverine	1.15	3.50	7.00
54,63,64-No Jim Lee-a		.65	1.30
55-62-Jim Lee-a(p)	.70	2.00	4.00
65-74,76-86: 65-Begin $1.50-c. 71-Intro The Sorcerer (villain). 74-Wolverine, Spider-Man & The Avengers app. 89-Original Guardian returns	.25	.75	1.50
75-Double size ($1.95, 52 pgs.)	.35	1.00	2.00
87-90-Wolverine 4 part story w/Jim Lee covers	1.00	3.00	6.00
91-99,101-105,107-114: 91-Dr. Doom app. 94-F.F. x-over. 99-Galactus & Avengers app. 102-Intro Weapon Omega. 105-Begin $1.75-c. 110-112-Infinity War x-overs	.30	.90	1.80
100-($2.00, 52 pgs.)-Avengers & Galactus app.	.35	1.00	2.00
106-Northstar reveals that he is gay	1.70	5.00	10.00
106-2nd printing (1.75)	.30	.90	1.80
Annual 1 (9/86, $1.25)	.30	.90	1.80
Annual 2(12/87, $1.25)		.65	1.30

AMAZING ADULT FANTASY (Formerly Amazing Adventures #1-6; becomes Amazing Fantasy #15)
No. 7, Dec, 1961-No. 14, July, 1962
Marvel Comics Group (AMI)

	Good	Fine	N-Mint
7-Ditko-c/a begins, ends #14	25.00	75.00	175.00
8-Last 10 cent issue	22.00	65.00	150.00
9-14: 12-1st app. Mailbag. 13-Anti-communist story. 14-Professor X prototype	18.00	54.00	125.00

AMAZING ADVENTURES (Becomes Amazing Adult Fantasy #7 on)
June, 1961-No. 6, Nov, 1961
Atlas Comics (AMI)/Marvel Comics No. 3 on

	Good	Fine	N-Mint
1-Origin Dr. Droom (1st Marvel-Age Superhero) by Kirby; Ditko & Kirby-a in all; Kirby c-1-6	61.00	183.00	425.00
2	32.00	96.00	225.00
3-6: 6-Last Dr. Droom	29.00	85.00	200.00

AMAZING ADVENTURES
Aug, 1970-No. 39, Nov, 1976
Marvel Comics Group

	Good	Fine	N-Mint
1-Inhumans by Kirby(p) & Black Widow (1st app. in Tales of Suspense #52) double feature begins	1.15	3.50	8.00
2-4: 2-F.F. brief app. 4-Last Kirby Inhumans	.75	2.25	4.50
5-8-Neal Adams-a(p); 8-Last Black Widow	1.00	3.00	6.00
9,10: Magneto app. 10-Last Inhumans (origin-r by Kirby)	.70	2.00	4.00
11-New Beast begins(origin in flashback); X-Men cameo in flashback (11-17 are all X-Men tie-ins)	1.15	3.50	7.00
12-17: 13-Brotherhood of Evil Mutants x-over from X-Men. 15-X-Men app. 17-Last Beast (origin); X-Men app.	1.00	3.00	6.00
18-War of the Worlds begins; 1st app. Killraven; Neal Adams-a(p)	1.50	4.50	9.00
19-39: 35-Giffen's first story-art, along with Deadly Hands of Kung-Fu #22 (3/76)	.60	1.75	3.50

AMAZING FANTASY (Formerly Amazing Adult Fantasy #7-14)
No. 15, Aug, 1962 (Sept, 1962 shown in indicia)
Marvel Comics Group (AMI)

	Good	Fine	VF-NM
15-Origin/1st app. of Spider-Man by Ditko (11 pgs.); 1st app. Aunt May & Uncle Ben; Kirby/Ditko-c	420.00	1680.00	5000.00

AMAZING-MAN COMICS
No. 5, Sept, 1939-No. 27, Feb, 1942
Centaur Publications

	Good	Fine	N-Mint
5(#1)(Rare)-Origin/1st app. A-Man the Amazing Man by Bill Everett; The Cat-Man by Tarpe Mills (also #8), Mighty Man by Filchock, Minimidget & sidekick Ritty, & The Iron Skull by Burgos begins	1000.00	2500.00	5500.00
6-Origin The Amazing Man retold; The Shark begins; Ivy Menace by Tarpe Mills app.	215.00	645.00	1500.00
7-Magician From Mars begins; ends #11	130.00	390.00	900.00
8-Cat-Man dresses as woman	93.00	280.00	650.00
9-Magician From Mars battles the "Elemental Monster," swiped into The Spectre in More Fun #54 & 55	93.00	280.00	650.00
10,11: 11-Zardi, the Eternal Man begins; ends #16; Amazing Man dons costume; last Everett issue	78.00	235.00	550.00
12,13	77.00	230.00	535.00
14-Reef Kinkaid, Rocke Wayburn (ends #20), & Dr. Hypno (ends #21) begin; no Zardi or Chuck Hardy	60.00	180.00	415.00
15,17-20: 15-Zardi returns; no Rocke Wayburn. 17-Dr. Hypno returns; no Zardi	47.00	140.00	325.00
16-Mighty Man's powers of super strength & ability to shrink & grow explained; Rocke Wayburn returns; no Dr. Hypno; Al Avison (a character) begins, ends #18 (a tribute to the famed artist)	50.00	150.00	350.00
21-Origin Dash Dartwell (drug-use story); origin & only app. T.N.T.	47.00	140.00	325.00
22-Dash Dartwell, the Human Meteor & The Voice app; last Iron Skull & The Shark; Silver Streak app.	47.00	140.00	325.00
23-Two Amazing Man stories; intro/origin Tommy the Amazing Kid; The Marksman only app.	50.00	150.00	350.00
24,27: 24-King of Darkness, Nightshade, & Blue Lady begin; end			

	Good	Fine	N-Mint
#26; 1st app. Super-Ann	47.00	140.00	325.00

25,26 (Scarce)-Meteor Martin by Wolverton in both; 26-Electric Ray

	Good	Fine	N-Mint
app.	78.00	235.00	550.00

AMAZING MYSTERIES (Formerly Sub-Mariner No. 31)
No. 32, May, 1949-No. 35, Jan, 1950
Marvel Comics (CCC)

32-The Witness app; 1st Marvel horror comic

	Good	Fine	N-Mint
	32.00	96.00	225.00
33-Horror format	10.00	30.00	70.00
34,35-Change to Crime. 35-Photo-c	6.50	19.00	45.00

AMAZING SPIDER-MAN, THE (See Amazing Fantasy, Deadly
Foes of Spider-Man, Marvel Tales, Marvel Team-Up,
Spectacular..., Spider-Man, Spider-Man Vs. Wolverine, Spidey
Super Stories, Strange Tales Annual #2, & Web of Spider-Man)
March, 1963-Present
Marvel Comics Group

1-Retells origin by Steve Ditko; 1st Fantastic Four x-over; intro. John Jameson & The Chameleon; Spider-Man's 2nd app.;Kirby-c

	Good	Fine	N-Mint
	390.00	1560.00	4700.00
1-Reprint from the Golden Record Comic set			
	11.00	32.00	75.00
with record (mid-'60s) (still sealed)	20.00	60.00	140.00
2-1st app. the Vulture & the Terrible Tinkerer			
	185.00	555.00	1400.00

3-1st full-length story; Human Torch cameo; intro. & 1st app. Doc Octopus; Dr. Doom & Ant-Man app.

	Good	Fine	N-Mint
	115.00	345.00	850.00
4-Origin & 1st app. The Sandman; Intro. Betty Brant & Liz Allen			
	80.00	240.00	600.00
5-Dr. Doom app.	70.00	210.00	525.00
6-1st app. Lizard	80.00	240.00	600.00

7,8,10: 7-Vs. The Vulture; 1st monthly issue. 8-Fantastic Four app. in back-up story by Ditko/Kirby. 10-1st app. Big Man & The

	Good	Fine	N-Mint
Enforcers	53.00	160.00	400.00
9-Origin & 1st app. Electro (2/64)	56.00	170.00	420.00
11,12: 11-1st app. Bennett Brant	32.00	96.00	240.00
13-1st app. Mysterio	40.00	120.00	300.00

14-(7/64)-1st app. The Green Goblin (c/story)(Norman Osborn); Hulk x-over

	Good	Fine	N-Mint
	100.00	300.00	760.00

	Good	Fine	N-Mint
15-1st app. Kraven the Hunter; 1st mention of Mary Jane Watson (not shown)	35.00	105.00	265.00
16-Spider-Man battles Daredevil (1st x-over 9/64); still in old yellow costume	25.00	75.00	190.00

The Amazing Spider-Man #17, © Marvel Comics

17-2nd app. Green Goblin (c/story); Human Torch x-over (also in #18 & #21)	45.00	135.00	340.00
18-1st app. Ned Leeds who later becomes Hobgoblin; Fantastic Four back-up story; Sandman app.	27.00	80.00	200.00
19-Sandman app.	23.00	70.00	170.00
20-Origin & 1st app. The Scorpion	27.00	80.00	200.00
21,22: 22-1st app. Princess Python	17.00	50.00	125.00
23-3rd app. The Green Goblin (c/story)	25.00	75.00	190.00
24	15.00	45.00	115.00
25-(6/65)-1st app. Mary Jane Watson (cameo; face not shown); 1st app. Spencer Smythe	19.00	57.00	140.00
26-4th app. The Green Goblin (c/story); 1st app. Crime Master; dies in #27	21.00	63.00	160.00
27-5th app. The Green Goblin (c/story)	19.30	58.00	145.00
28-Origin & 1st app. Molten Man	21.00	63.00	160.00
29,30	15.00	45.00	105.00
31-38: 31-1st app. Harry Osborn who later becomes 2nd Green Goblin, Gwen Stacy & Prof. Warren. 34-2nd app. Kraven the Hunter. 36-1st app. Looter. 37-Intro. Norman Osborn. 38-(7/66)-2nd app. Mary Jane Watson cameo; face not shown); last Ditko issue	11.50	34.00	80.00

	Good	Fine	N-Mint

39-The Green Goblin-c/story; Green Goblin's i.d. revealed as
Norman Osborn   13.00   40.00   90.00

40-1st told origin The Green Goblin (c/story)
     21.00   63.00   145.00

41-1st app. Rhino   9.30   28.00   65.00

42-(11/66)-3rd app. Mary Jane Watson (cameo in last 2 panels);
1st time face is shown   9.30   28.00   65.00

43-49: 44,45-2nd & 3rd app. The Lizard. 46-Intro. Shocker.
47,49-3rd & 4th app. Kraven the Hunter
     6.50   19.00   45.00

50-1st app. Kingpin (7/67)   25.00   75.00   175.00

51-2nd app. Kingpin   9.30   28.00   65.00

52-60: 52-1st app. Joe Robertson & 3rd app. Kingpin. 56-1st app.
Capt. George Stacy. 57,58-Ka-Zar app. 59-1st app. Brainwasher
(alias Kingpin)   5.00   15.00   35.00

61-74: 67-1st app. Randy Robertson. 69-Kingpin app. 73-1st app.
Silvermane. 74-Last 12 cent issue   4.30   13.00   30.00

75-89,91-93,95,99: 78,79-1st app. The Prowler. 83-1st app. Schemer
& Vanessa (Kingpin's wife). 84,85-Kingpin-c/story. 93-1st app.
Arthur Stacy   3.60   11.00   25.00

90-Death of Capt. Stacey   3.70   11.00   26.00

94-Origin retold   5.70   17.00   40.00

96-98-Green Goblin app. (97,98-Green Goblin-c); drug books not
approved by CCA   7.00   21.00   50.00

100-Anniversary issue (9/71); Green Goblin cameo (2 pgs.)
     13.50   41.00   95.00

101-1st app. Morbius the Living Vampire; last 15 cent issue
     11.00   32.00   75.00

101-2nd printing (1992, $1.75)   .30   .90   1.80

102-Origin Morbius (25 cents, 52 pgs.)   9.30   28.00   65.00

103-118: 104,111-Kraven the Hunter-c/stories. 108-1st app. Sha-Shan.
109-Dr. Strange-c/story (6/72). 110-1st app. Gibbon. 113-1st app.
Hammerhead   2.30   7.00   16.00

119,120-Spider-Man vs. Hulk   3.15   9.50   22.00

121-Death of Gwen Stacy (killed by Green Goblin) (reprinted in
Marvel Tales #98 & 192)   9.30   28.00   65.00

122-Death of The Green Goblin (c/story) (reprinted in Marvel Tales
#99, 192)   13.50   41.00   95.00

123-128: 124-1st app. Man-Wolf, origin in #125
     2.15   6.50   15.00

129-1st app. Jackal & The Punisher (2/74)
     40.00   120.00   275.00

	Good	Fine	N-Mint

130-133,138-160: 131-Last 20 cent issue. 139-1st app. Grizzly. 140-1st app. Glory Grant. 143-1st app. Cyclone

| | 1.60 | 4.80 | 11.00 |

134-Punisher cameo (7/74); 1st app. Tarantula

| | 2.85 | 8.50 | 20.00 |

135-Punisher app. (8/74)   8.50   25.50   60.00

136-Reappearance of The Green Goblin (Harry Osborn; Norman Osborn's son)   3.15   9.50   22.00

137-Green Goblin-c/story (2nd Harry Osborn)

| | 2.00 | 6.00 | 14.00 |

161-Nightcrawler app. from X-Men; Punisher cameo

| | 1.60 | 4.80 | 11.00 |

162-Punisher, Nightcrawler app.   3.15   9.50   22.00

163-173,181-190: 167-1st app. Will O' The Wisp. 171-Nova app. 181-Origin retold; gives life history of Spidey; Punisher cameo in flashback (1 panel)   1.00   3.00   6.00

174,175-Punisher app.   2.30   7.00   16.00

176-180-Green Goblin app.   1.60   4.80   11.00

191-193,195-199,203-208,210-219: 196-Faked death of Aunt May. 203-2nd app. Dazzler. 210-1st app. Madame Web. 212-1st app. Hydro Man; origin Sandman   1.00   3.00   6.00

194-1st app. Black Cat   1.70   5.00   10.00

200-Giant origin issue (1/80)   3.35   10.00   20.00

201,202-Punisher app.   3.60   11.00   22.00

209-1st app. Calypso   1.35   4.00   8.00

220-237: 225-Foolkiller app. 226,227-Black Cat returns. 236-Tarantula dies. 234-Free 16 pg. insert "Marvel Guide to Collecting Comics." 235-Origin Will-'O-The-Wisp

| | 1.00 | 3.00 | 6.00 |

238-(3/83)-1st app. Hobgoblin (Ned Leeds); came with skin "Tattooz" decal; (price includes decal intact)

| | 8.00 | 24.00 | 55.00 |

239-2nd app. Hobgoblin & 1st battle w/Spidey

| | 4.30 | 13.00 | 30.00 |

240-243,246-248: 241-Origin The Vulture   1.00   3.00   6.00

244-3rd app. Hobgoblin (cameo only)   1.50   4.50   9.00

245-4th app. Hobgoblin (cameo only); Lefty Donovan gains powers of Hobgoblin & battles Spider-Man   2.30   7.00   14.00

249-251: 3 part Hobgoblin/Spider-Man battle. 249-Retells origin & death of 1st Green Goblin. 251-Last old costume

| | 2.00 | 6.00 | 12.00 |

252-Spider-Man dons new black costume (5/84); ties with Marvel

	Good	Fine	N-Mint
Team-Up #141 & Spectacular Spider-Man #90 for 1st new costume (See Marvel S-H Secret Wars #8)	2.30	7.00	14.00
253-1st app. The Rose	1.15	3.50	7.00
254	.85	2.50	5.00
255,263,264,266-273,277-280,282,283: 279-Jack O'Lantern-c/story. 282-X-Factor x-over	.60	1.75	3.50
256-1st app. Puma	.70	2.00	4.00
257-Hobgoblin cameo; 2nd app. Puma	1.50	4.50	9.00
258-Hobgoblin app. (minor)	1.50	4.50	9.00
259-Full Hobgoblin app.; Spidey back to old costume; origin Mary Jane Watson	2.30	7.00	14.00
260-Hobgoblin app.	1.50	4.50	9.00
261-Hobgoblin-c/story; painted-c by Vess	1.70	5.00	10.00
262-Spider-Man unmasked; photo-c	1.00	3.00	6.00
265-1st app. Silver Sable	1.70	5.00	10.00
265-Silver ink 2nd printing (1992, $1.25)	.50	1.50	3.00
274-Zarathos (The Spirit of Vengeance) app. (3/86)	.70	2.00	4.00
275-($1.25, 52 pgs.)-Hobgoblin-c/story; origin-r by Ditko	2.00	6.00	12.00
276-Hobgoblin app.	1.50	4.50	9.00
281-Hobgoblin battles Jack O'Lantern	1.70	5.00	10.00
284-Punisher cameo; Gang War story begins; Hobgoblin-c/story	1.50	4.50	9.00
285-Punisher app.; minor Hobgoblin app.	3.00	9.00	18.00
286,287: 286-Hobgoblin-c & app. (minor). 287-Hobgoblin app. (minor)	1.00	3.00	6.00
288-Full Hobgoblin app.; last Gang War	1.35	4.00	8.00
289-($1.25, 52 pgs.)-Hobgoblin's i.d. revealed as Ned Leeds; death of Ned Leeds; Macendale (Jack O'Lantern) becomes new Hobgoblin	3.70	11.00	22.00
290-292	.75	2.25	4.50
293,294-Part 2 & 5 of Kraven story from Web of Spider-Man. 294-Death of Kraven	1.35	4.00	8.00
295-297	.90	2.75	5.50
298-Todd McFarlane-c/a begins; 1st app. Venom w/o costume (cameo on last pg.)	5.00	15.00	30.00
299-1st Venom with costume (cameo)	2.65	8.00	16.00
300 ($1.50, 52 pgs.; 25th Anniversary)-1st full Venom app.; last black costume	5.30	16.00	32.00
301-305: 301 ($1.00 issues begin). 304-1st bi-weekly issue	2.50	7.50	15.00

	Good	Fine	N-Mint
306-311,313-315: 306-Swipes-c from Action #1			
	1.70	5.00	10.00
312-Hobgoblin battles Green Goblin	3.00	9.00	18.00
316-323,325: 319-Bi-weekly begins again	1.15	3.50	7.00
324-Sabretooth app.; McFarlane cover only	2.00	6.00	12.00
326,327,329: 327-Cosmic Spidey continues from Spect. Spider-Man			
(no McFarlane-c/a)	.60	1.75	3.50
328-Hulk x-over; last McFarlane issue	1.25	3.75	7.50
330,331-Punisher app.	.70	2.00	4.00
332-336,338-343: 341-Tarantula app.	.40	1.25	2.50
337-Hobgoblin app.	.60	1.75	3.50
344-1st app. Cletus Kasady who becomes Carnage			
	1.15	3.50	7.00
345-1st full app. Cletus Kasady; Venom cameo			
	1.70	5.00	10.00
346,347-Venom app.	.75	2.25	4.50
348,349,351-360: 348-Avengers x-over. 351,352-Nova of New Warriors app. 353-Darkhawk app.; brief Punisher app. 354-Punisher cameo & Nova, Night Thrasher (New Warriors), Darkhawk & Moon Knight app. 357, 358-Punisher, Dark Hawk, Moon Knight, Night Thrasher, Nova x-over. 358-3 part gatefold-c. 359-Begin $1.25-c. 360-Carnage cameo	.35	1.00	2.00
350-($1.50, 52pgs.)-Spidey vs. Dr. Doom; pin-ups			
	.50	1.50	3.00
361-Intro Carnage (the spawn of Venom)	1.50	4.50	9.00
361-2nd printing ($1.25-c)		.65	1.30
362,363-Carnage & Venom-c/story	.85	2.50	5.00
364,366-368		.65	1.30
365-($3.95, 84 pgs.)-30th anniversary issue featuring a hologram on-c plus pull-out poster; origin retold	.75	2.25	4.50
Annual 1 (1964, 72 pgs.)-Origin Spider-Man; 1st app. Sinister Six (Dr. Octopus, Electro, Kraven the Hunter, Mysterio, Sandman, Vulture) (41 pg. story); plus gallery of Spidey foes			
	26.30	79.00	185.00
Annual 2 (1965, 25 cents, 72 pgs.)-Reprints from #1,2,5 plus new Doctor Strange story	11.50	34.00	80.00
Special 3 (11/66, 25 cents, 72 pgs.)-Avengers & Hulk x-over; Doctor Octopus reprint from #11,12; Romita/Heath-a			
	5.00	15.00	35.00
Special 4 (11/67, 25 cents, 68 pgs.)-Spidey battles Human Torch (new 41 pg. story)	5.70	17.00	40.00
Special 5 (11/68, 25 cents, 68 pgs.)-New 40 pg. Red Skull story; 1st			

	Good	Fine	N-Mint
app. Peter Parker's parents	2.65	8.00	18.00
Special 6 (11/69, 25 cents, 68 pgs.)-New 41 pg. Sinister Six story plus			
two Kirby/Ditko stories	2.65	8.00	18.00
Special 7 (12/70, 25 cents, 68 pgs.)-All-r (#1,2)			
	2.65	8.00	18.00
Special 8 (12/71)	2.65	8.00	18.00
King Size 9 ('73)-Reprints Spectacular Spider-Man (mag.) #2; 40 pg.			
Green Goblin-c/story	2.65	8.00	18.00
Annual 10 (1976)-Origin Human Fly (vs. Spidey)			
	1.15	3.50	7.00
Annual 11,12: 11 (1977). 12 (1978)-Spider-Man vs. Hulk-r/#119,120			
	1.15	3.50	7.00
Annual 13 (1979)-Byrne/Austin-a (new)	1.35	4.00	8.00
Annual 14 (1980)-Miller-c/a(p), 40 pgs.	1.50	4.50	9.00
Annual 15 (1981)-Miller-c/a(p); Punisher app.			
	3.70	11.00	22.00
Annual 16-20: 16 (1982)-Origin/1st app. new Capt. Marvel (female			
heroine). 17 (1983). 18 (1984). 19 (1985). 20 (1986)-Origin Iron			
Man of 2020	1.00	3.00	6.00
Annual 21 (1987)-Special wedding issue	1.35	4.00	8.00
Annual 22 (1988, $1.75, 68 pgs.)-1st app. Speedball; Evolutionary			
War x-over	1.35	4.00	8.00
Annual 23 (1989, $2.00, 68 pgs.)-Atlantis Attacks; origin Spider-Man			
retold; She-Hulk app.; Byrne-c	1.00	3.00	6.00
Annual 24 (1990, $2.00, 68 pgs.)-Ant-Man app.			
	.60	1.75	3.50
Annual 25 (1991, $2.00, 68 pgs.)-3 pg. origin recap; Iron Man app.;			
Venom story (1st solo story); Ditko-a (6 pgs.)			
	.85	2.50	5.00
Annual 26 (1992, $2.25, 68 pgs.)-Part 1 of solo Venom story			
	.40	1.15	2.30

AMERICA'S BEST COMICS
Feb, 1942-No. 31, July, 1949
Nedor/Better/Standard Publications

	Good	Fine	N-Mint
1-The Woman in Red, Black Terror, Captain Future, Doc Strange, The Liberator, & Don Davis, Secret Ace begin			
	70.00	210.00	500.00
2-Origin The American Eagle; The Woman in Red ends			
	36.00	108.00	250.00
3-Pyroman begins	27.00	80.00	190.00
4	23.00	70.00	160.00

	Good	Fine	N-Mint

5-Last Captain Future (not in #4); Lone Eagle app.

	20.00	60.00	140.00

6,7: 6-American Crusader app. 7-Hitler, Mussolini & Hirohito-c

	18.00	54.00	125.00
8-Last Liberator	17.00	50.00	100.00

9-The Fighting Yank begins; The Ghost app.

	17.00	50.00	100.00

10-14: 10-Flag-c. 14-American Eagle ends

	14.00	43.00	85.00
15-20	13.00	40.00	80.00

21,22: 21-Infinity-c. 22-Capt. Future app.

	12.00	35.00	70.00

23-Miss Masque begins; last Doc Strange

	15.00	45.00	90.00
24-Miss Masque bondage-c	13.00	40.00	80.00
25-Last Fighting Yank; Sea Eagle app.	12.00	35.00	70.00

26-The Phantom Detective & The Silver Knight app.; Frazetta text
illo & some panels in Miss Masque

	15.00	45.00	90.00

27-31: 27,28-Commando Cubs. 27-Doc Strange. 28-Tuska Black
Terror. 29-Last Pyroman

	12.00	35.00	90.00

AMERICA'S GREATEST COMICS
May?, 1941-No. 8, Summer, 1943 (100 pgs.) (Soft cardboard covers)
Fawcett Publications (15 cents)

1-Bulletman, Spy Smasher, Capt. Marvel, Minute Man & Mr.
Scarlet begin; Mac Raboy-c

	150.00	450.00	1050.00
2	70.00	210.00	500.00
3	54.00	160.00	375.00

4,5: 4-Commando Yank begins; Golden Arrow, Ibis the Invincible
& Spy Smasher cameo in Captain Marvel

	50.00	150.00	300.00

6,7: 7-Balbo the Boy Magician app.; Captain Marvel, Bulletman
cameo in Mr. Scarlet

	39.00	118.00	235.00

8-Capt. Marvel Jr. & Golden Arrow app.; Spy Smasher x-over in
Capt. Midnight; no Minute Man or Commando Yank

	39.00	118.00	235.00

ANIMAL COMICS
Dec-Jan, 1941-42-No. 30, Dec-Jan, 1947-48
Dell Publishing Co.

1-1st Pogo app. by Walt Kelly (Dan Noonan art in most issues)

	89.00	270.00	625.00

	Good	Fine	N-Mint
2-Uncle Wiggily begins	38.00	115.00	265.00
3,5	26.00	78.00	180.00
4,6,7-No Pogo	15.00	45.00	105.00
8-10	18.00	54.00	125.00
11-15	11.50	34.00	80.00
16-20	7.50	22.00	52.00
21-30: 25-30-"Jigger" by John Stanley	5.30	16.00	38.00

ANIMAL MAN (Also see Action Comics #552, 553, DC Comics
  Presents #77, 78, Secret Origins #39, Strange Adventures #180 &
  Wonder Woman)
Sept, 1988-Present ($1.25-$1.75, color)
DC Comics

	Good	Fine	N-Mint
1-Bolland c-1-50; Grant Morrison scripts begin			
	3.35	10.00	20.00
2	2.50	7.50	15.00
3,4	1.50	4.50	9.00
5-10: 6-Invasion tie-in	.85	2.50	5.00
11-15: 11-Begin $1.50-c	.75	2.25	4.50
16-20	.70	2.00	4.00
21-26: 24-Arkham Asylum story. 25-Inferior Five app. 26-Last Grant Morrison scripts; part photo-c	.50	1.50	3.00
27-49,51-54: 41-Begin $1.75-c	.30	.90	1.80
50-($2.95, 52 pgs.)	.50	1.50	3.00

AQUAMAN (See Adventure #260, Brave & the Bold, Detective,
  Justice League of America, Showcase #30-33 & World's Finest
  Comics)
Jan-Feb, 1962-No. 56, Mar-Apr, 1971; No. 57, Aug-Sept,
1977-No. 63, Aug-Sept, 1978
National Periodical Publications/DC Comics

	Good	Fine	N-Mint
Showcase #30 (1-2/61)-Origin S.A. Aquaman			
	50.00	150.00	350.00
Showcase #31-33 (3-4/61-7-8/61)-Aquaman			
	24.00	72.00	165.00
1-(1-2/62)-Intro. Quisp	37.00	110.00	260.00
2	16.00	48.00	110.00
3-5	11.00	33.00	77.00
6-10	8.00	24.00	55.00
11-20: 11-1st app. Mera. 18-Aquaman weds Mera; JLA cameo			
	5.70	17.00	40.00
21-32,34-40: 23-Birth of Aquababy. 26-Huntress app.(3-4/66).			

	Good	Fine	N-Mint
29-1st app. Ocean Master, Aquaman's step-brother. 30-Batman & Superman-c & cameo	3.50	10.50	24.00
33-1st app. Aqua-Girl	4.70	14.00	33.00
41-47,49	1.60	4.80	11.00
48-Origin reprinted	1.85	5.50	13.00
50-52-Deadman by Neal Adams	2.85	8.50	20.00
53-56('71): 56-1st app. Crusader	1.10	3.30	6.60
57('77)-63: 58-Origin retold	.70	2.00	4.00

AQUAMAN
Feb, 1986-No. 4, May, 1986 (Mini-series)
DC Comics

1-New costume	.75	2.25	4.50
2-4	.40	1.25	2.50
Special 1 ('88, $1.50, 52 pgs.)	.35	1.00	2.00

AQUAMAN
June, 1989-No. 5, Oct, 1989 ($1.00, mini-series)
DC Comics

1-5: Giffen plots/breakdowns; Swan-p		.50	1.00
Special 1 (Legend of..., $2.00, 1989, 52 pgs.)-Giffen plots/breakdowns; Swan-p	.35	1.00	2.00

AQUAMAN
Dec, 1991-Present ($1.00-$1.25, color)
DC Comics

1	.35	1.00	2.00
2-10,12: 6-Begin $1.25-c. 8-Batman app. 9,10-Sea Devils app.		.65	1.30
11-($2.50)	.40	1.25	2.50

ARMAGEDDON 2001
May, 1991-No. 2, Oct, 1991 ($2.00, squarebound, 68 pgs.)
DC Comics

1-Features many DC heroes; intro Waverider	1.00	3.00	6.00
1-2nd & 3rd printings; 3rd has silver ink-c	.35	1.00	2.00
2	.70	2.00	4.00

ASTONISHING (Formerly Marvel Boy No. 1, 2)
No. 3, April, 1951-No. 63, Aug, 1957
Marvel/Atlas Comics(20CC)

	Good	Fine	N-Mint
3-Marvel Boy continues; 3-5-Marvel Boy-c			
	38.00	115.00	265.00
4-6-Last Marvel Boy; 4-Stan Lee app.	27.00	80.00	190.00
7-10	8.50	25.50	60.00
11,12,15,17,20	6.50	19.00	45.00
13,14,16,19-Krigstein-a	7.00	21.00	50.00
18-Jack The Ripper story	8.00	24.00	55.00
21,22,24	5.00	15.00	35.00
23-E.C. swipe-"The Hole In The Wall" from Vault Of Horror #16			
	6.50	19.00	45.00
25-Crandall-a	6.50	19.00	45.00
26-29: 29-Decapitation-c	4.50	14.00	32.00
30-Tentacled eyeball story	7.00	21.00	50.00
31-37-Last pre-code issue	4.00	12.00	28.00
38-43,46,48-52,56,58,59,61	3.00	9.00	21.00
44-Crandall swipe/Weird Fantasy #22	4.50	14.00	32.00
45,47-Krigstein-a	4.50	14.00	32.00
53,54: 53-Crandall, Ditko-a. 54-Torres-a	3.70	11.00	26.00
55-Crandall, Torres-a	4.50	14.00	32.00
57-Williamson/Krenkel-a (4 pgs.)	5.30	16.00	38.00
60-Williamson/Mayo-a (4 pgs.)	5.30	16.00	38.00
62-Torres, Powell-a	3.15	9.50	22.00
63-Last issue; Woodbridge-a	3.15	9.50	22.00

ASTONISHING TALES (See Ka-Zar)
Aug, 1970-No. 36, July, 1976 (#1-7: 15 cents; #8: 25 cents)
Marvel Comics Group

	Good	Fine	N-Mint
1-Ka-Zar by Kirby(p) & Dr. Doom by Wood double feature begins; Kraven the Hunter-c/story; Nixon cameo			
	2.15	6.50	15.00
2-Kraven the Hunter-c/story; Kirby, Wood-a	1.30	4.00	9.00
3-6: B. Smith-p; Wood-a-#3,4. 5-Red Skull app.			
	2.15	6.50	15.00
7,8: 8-(52 pgs.)-Last Dr. Doom & Kirby-a			
	1.30	4.00	9.00
9-Lorna-r/Lorna #14	.60	1.75	3.50
10-B. Smith-a(p)	1.00	3.00	7.00
11-Origin Ka-Zar & Zabu	.85	2.50	5.00

	Good	Fine	N-Mint
12-Man-Thing by Neal Adams (apps. #13 also)			
	1.00	3.00	6.00
13-24: 20-Last Ka-Zar. 21-It! the Living Colossus begins, ends #24			
	.40	1.25	2.50
25-1st app. Deathlok the Demolisher; full length stories begin, end			
#36; Perez 1st work, 2 pgs. (8/74)	14.00	43.00	100.00
26-28,30	5.00	15.00	35.00
29-r/origin/1st app. Guardians of the Galaxy from Marvel Super-			
Heroes #18 plus-c w/4 pgs. omitted; no Deathlok			
	4.00	12.00	28.00
31-36: 31-Watcher-r/Silver Surfer #3	3.15	9.50	22.00

ATOM, THE (...& Hawkman No. 39 on; see Brave & the Bold, Detective, Showcase #34, & World's Finest)
June-July, 1962-No. 38, Aug-Sept, 1968
National Periodical Publications

	Good	Fine	N-Mint
Showcase #34 (9-10/61)-Origin & 1st app. Silver Age Atom by Kane & Anderson	105.00	315.00	740.00
Showcase #35 (11-12/61)-2nd app. Atom by Gil Kane; last 10 cent issue	57.00	170.00	400.00
Showcase #36 (1-2/62)-3rd app. Atom by Kane			
	43.00	130.00	300.00
1-(6-7/62)-Intro Plant-Master; 1st app. Maya			
	70.00	210.00	500.00
2	25.00	75.00	175.00
3-1st Time Pool story; 1st app. Chronos (origin)			
	16.00	48.00	110.00
4,5: 4-Snapper Carr x-over	11.50	34.00	80.00
6,8-10: 8-Justice League, Dr. Light app.	9.30	28.00	65.00
7-Hawkman x-over (6-7/63; 1st Atom & Hawkman team-up); 1st app. Hawkman since Brave & the Bold tryouts			
	14.00	43.00	100.00
11-15: 13-Chronos-c/story	6.50	19.00	45.00
16-20: 19-Zatanna x-over	4.30	13.00	30.00
21-28,30: 28-Chronos-c/story	2.85	8.50	20.00
29-1st solo Golden Age Atom x-over in S.A.			
	9.30	28.00	65.00
31-35,37,38: 31-Hawkman x-over. 37-Intro. Major Mynah; Hawkman cameo	2.85	8.50	20.00
36-G.A. Atom x-over	3.60	11.00	25.00

ATOM & HAWKMAN, THE (Formerly The Atom)
No. 39, Oct-Nov, 1968-No. 45, Oct-Nov, 1969
National Periodical Publications

	Good	Fine	N-Mint
39-45: 43-Last 12 cent issue; 1st app. Gentlemen Ghost, origin in #44			
	2.15	6.50	15.00

The Avengers #28, © Marvel Comics

AVENGERS, THE (See Marvel Super Action, Marvel Super
    Heroes('66), Solo Avengers, Tales Of Suspense, West Coast
    Avengers & X-Men Vs....)
Sept, 1963-Present
Marvel Comics Group

	Good	Fine	N-Mint
1-Origin & 1st app. The Avengers (Thor, Iron Man, Hulk, Ant-Man, Wasp); Loki app.	147.00	440.00	1025.00
2	46.00	138.00	350.00
3-1st Sub-Mariner x-over (outside the F.F.)	28.50	86.00	225.00
4-Revival of Captain America who joins the Avengers; 1st Silver Age app. of Captain America & Bucky (3/64)	75.00	225.00	525.00
4-Reprint from the Golden Record Comic set	8.00	24.00	55.00
With Record (still sealed)	14.00	43.00	100.00
5-Hulk leaves	18.00	54.00	140.00
6-8: 6-Intro The Masters of Evil. 8-Intro Kang	16.50	50.00	115.00

	Good	Fine	N-Mint
9-Intro Wonder Man who dies in same story			
	18.00	54.00	125.00
10	16.00	48.00	110.00
11-Spider-Man-c & x-over	13.50	41.00	115.00
12-16: 15-Death of Zemo. 16-New Avengers line-up (Hawkeye, Quicksilver, Scarlet Witch join; Thor, Iron Man, Giant-Man, Wasp leave)	11.00	32.00	75.00
17-19: 19-Intro. Swordsman; origin Hawkeye			
	8.00	24.00	55.00
20-22: Wood inks	5.00	15.00	35.00
23-30: 28-Giant-Man becomes Goliath	3.60	11.00	25.00
31-40	2.65	8.00	18.00
41-52,54-56: 43,44-1st app. Red Guardian. 46-Ant-Man returns. 47-Magneto-c/story. 48-Origin/1st app. new Black Knight. 52-Black Panther joins; 1st app. The Grim Reaper. 54-1st app. new Masters of Evil	2.00	6.00	14.00
53-X-Men app.	2.65	8.00	18.00
57-1st app. S.A. Vision	5.00	15.00	35.00
58-Origin The Vision	4.30	13.00	30.00
59-65-Intro. Yellowjacket. 60-Wasp & Yellowjacket wed. 63-Goliath becomes Yellowjacket; Hawkeye becomes the new Goliath. 65-Last 12 cent issue.	2.30	7.00	16.00
66,67: B. Smith-a	2.15	6.50	15.00
68-70	1.50	4.50	10.00
71-1st app. The Invaders; 1st app. Nighthawk; Black Knight joins	1.70	5.00	12.00
72-82,84-86,88-91: 80-Intro. Red Wolf. 82-Daredevil app. 88-Written by Harlan Ellison	1.30	4.00	9.00
83-Intro. The Liberators (Wasp, Valkyrie, Scarlet Witch, Medusa & the Black Widow)	1.50	4.50	10.00
87-Origin The Black Panther	2.00	6.00	14.00
92-Last 15 cent issue; Neal Adams-c	1.60	4.80	11.00
93-(52 pgs.)-Neal Adams-c/a	5.70	17.00	40.00
94-96-Neal Adams-c/a	3.70	11.00	26.00
97-G.A. Capt. America, Sub-Mariner, Human Torch, Patriot, Vision, Blazing Skull, Fin, Angel, & new Capt. Marvel x-over	1.60	4.80	11.00
98-Goliath becomes Hawkeye; Smith c/a(i)			
	3.15	9.50	22.00
99-Smith/Sutton-a	3.15	9.50	22.00
100-(6/72)-Smith-c/a; featuring everyone who was an Avenger			
	5.30	16.00	38.00

	Good	Fine	N-Mint
101-106,108,109: 101-Harlan Ellison scripts			
	1.15	3.50	7.00
107-Starlin-a(p)	1.50	4.50	10.00
110,111-X-Men app.	2.00	6.00	14.00
112-1st app. Mantis	1.50	4.50	10.00
113-120: 116-118-Defenders/Silver Surfer app.			
	1.00	3.00	6.00
121-124,126-130: 123-Origin Mantis	1.00	3.00	6.00
125-Thanos-c & brief app. (7/74)	1.70	5.00	12.00
131-140: 136-Ploog-r/Amazing Advs. #12	.85	2.50	5.00
141-149: 144-Origin & 1st app. Hellcat. 146-25 & 30 cent variants			
exist	.70	2.00	4.00
150-Kirby-a(r); new line-up: Capt. America, Scarlet Witch, Iron Man, Wasp, Yellowjacket, Vision & The Beast			
	.70	2.00	4.00
151-163: 151-Wonderman returns w/new costume			
	.70	2.00	4.00
164-166: Byrne-a	.85	2.50	5.00
167-180	.50	1.50	3.00
181-191: Byrne-a. 181-New line-up: Capt. America, Scarlet Witch, Iron Man, Wasp, Vision, Beast & The Falcon. 183-Ms. Marvel joins. 185-Origin Quicksilver & Scarlet Witch			
	.50	1.50	3.00
192-202: Perez-a. 195-1st Taskmaster. 200-Double size; Ms. Marvel leaves	.35	1.00	2.00
203-213,215-262: 211-New line-up: Capt. America, Iron Man, Tigra, Thor, Wasp & Yellowjacket. 213-Yellowjacket leaves. 215,216-Silver Surfer app. 216-Tigra leaves. 217-Yellowjacket & Wasp return. 221-Hawkeye & She-Hulk join. 227-Capt. Marvel (female) joins; origins of Ant-Man, Wasp, Giant-Man, Goliath, Yellowjacket, & Avengers. 230-Yellowjacket quits. 231-Iron Man leaves. 232-Starfox (Eros) joins. 234-Origin Quicksilver, Scarlet Witch. 236-New logo. 238-Origin Blackout. 240-Spider-Woman revived. 250-($1.00, 52 pgs.)	.35	1.00	2.00
214-Ghost Rider-c/story	.85	2.50	5.00
263-1st app. X-Factor (1/86)(story continues in Fantastic Four #286)			
	.85	2.50	5.00
264-299: 272-Alpha Flight guest star. 291-$1.00 issues begin. 297-Black Knight, She-Hulk & Thor resign. 298-Inferno tie-in			
	.25	.75	1.50
300 ($1.75, 68 pgs.)-Thor joins; Simonson-a			
	.40	1.25	2.50

	Good	**Fine**	**N-Mint**
301-304,306-325,327,329-343: 302-Re-intro Quasar. 314-318-Spider-Man x-over. 320-324-Alpha Flight app. (320-cameo). 341,342-New Warriors app.		.50	1.00
305-Byrne scripts begin	.35	1.00	2.00
326-1st app. Rage	.85	2.50	5.00
328-Origin Rage	.50	1.50	3.00
344-346,348,349,351-356: 344-Begin $1.25-c	.65	1.30	
347-($1.75, 56 pgs.)	.30	.90	1.80
350-($2.50, 68 pgs.)-Gatefold-c	.40	1.25	2.50
Special 1(9/67, 25 cents, 68 pgs.)-New-a; original & new Avengers team-up	5.00	15.00	35.00
Special 2(9/68, 25 cents, 68 pgs.)-New-a; original vs. new Avengers	1.70	5.00	12.00
Special 3(9/69, 25 cents, 68 pgs.)-r/Avengers #4 plus 3 Capt. America stories by Kirby-a; origin Red Skull	2.15	6.50	15.00
Special 4,5: 4(1/71, 25 cents, 68 pgs.)-New Kirby-a (23 pgs.) plus Kirby reprints (23 pgs.). 5(1/72)-Spider-Man x-over	1.00	3.00	6.00
Annual 6(11/76)	.85	2.50	5.00
Annual 7(11/77)-Starlin-c/a; Warlock dies; Thanos app.	4.00	12.00	28.00
Annual 8(1978)-Dr. Strange, Ms. Marvel app.	.75	2.25	4.50
Annual 9(1979)-Newton-a(p)	.60	1.75	3.50
Annual 10(1981)-Golden-p; X-Men cameo; 1st app. Rogue & Madelyne Pryor	1.45	4.00	8.00
Annual 11-16: 11(1982)-Vs. The Defenders. 12(1983). 13(1984). 14(1985). 15(1986). 16(1987)	.60	1.75	3.50
Annual 17(1988)-Evolutionary War x-over	.70	2.00	4.00
Annual 18(1989, $2.00, 68 pgs.)-Atlantis Attacks	.50	1.50	3.00
Annual 19,20(1990, 1991)(both $2.00, 68 pgs.)	.40	1.25	2.50
Annual 21(1992, $2.25, 68 pgs.)-Fantastic Four app.	.40	1.15	2.30

AVENGERS SPOTLIGHT (Formerly Solo Avengers #1-20)
No. 21, Aug, 1989-No. 40, Jan, 1991 (.75-$1.00, color)
Marvel Comics

21 (75 cents)-Byrne-c/a		.50	1.00
22-40 ($1.00): 26-Acts of Vengeance story. 31-34-U.S. Agent series.			

	Good	Fine	N-Mint
36-Heck-i. 37-Mortimer-i. 40-The Black Knight app.			
		.50	1.00

AVENGERS WEST COAST (Formerly West Coast Avengers)
No. 48, Sept, 1989-Present ($1.00-$1.25, color)
Marvel Comics

	Good	Fine	N-Mint
48-49: Byrne-c/a & scripts continue thru #57		.55	1.10
50-Re-intro original Human Torch	.25	.75	1.50
51-74,76-78: 54-Swipes-c/F.F. #1. 70-Spider-Woman app.			
		.65	1.30
75-($1.50, 52 pgs.)-Fantastic Four x-over	.25	.75	1.50
79-88: 79-Dr. Strange x-over; begin $1.25-c		.65	1.30
Annual 7 (1992, $2.25, 68 pgs.)	.40	1.15	2.30

B

BARBIE
Jan, 1991-Present ($1.00, color)
Marvel Comics

	Good	Fine	N-Mint
1-Sealed in plastic bag w/BarbiePink Card; Romita-c			
	.70	2.00	4.00
2-24: 14-begin $1.25-c		.65	1.30

BARBIE & KEN
May-July, 1962-No. 5, Nov-Jan, 1963-64
Dell Publishing Co.

01-053-207(#1)-Based on toy dolls	18.00	54.00	125.00
2-4	14.00	43.00	100.00
5 (Rare)	18.00	54.00	125.00

BARBIE FASHION
Jan, 1991-Present ($1.00, color)
Marvel Comics

1-Sealed in plastic bag w/doorknob hanger			
	.50	1.50	3.00
2-24: 14-Begin $1.25-c		.65	1.30

BATGIRL SPECIAL (See Teen Titans #50)
1988 ($1.50, color, one-shot, 52 pgs)
DC Comics

1	1.35	4.00	8.00

BAT LASH (See Showcase #76 & Weird Western Tales)
Oct-Nov, 1968-No. 7, Oct-Nov, 1969
National Periodical Publications

Showcase #76 (9-10/67)-1st app. Bat Lash	2.85	8.50	20.00
1-(10-11/68)	1.15	3.50	8.00
2-7	.75	2.25	4.50

BATMAN (See The Brave & the Bold, DC Special, Detective, 80-Page
Giants, The Joker, Justice League of America #250, Justice League
Int., Legends of the Dark Knight, Man-Bat, Shadow of the.., 3-D
Batman, Untold Legend of..., Wanted... & World's Finest)
Spring, 1940-Present
National Periodical Publ./Detective Comics/DC Comics

	Good	Fine	VF-NM
1-Origin The Batman retold by Bob Kane; see Detective #33 for 1st origin; 1st app. Joker (2 stories which count as 1st & 2nd app.); 1st app. The Cat (Catwoman); has Batman story without Robin originally planned for Detective #38. This book was created entirely from the inventory of Det. Comics	3,350.00	8,350.00	20,000.00

(Prices vary widely on this book)

	Good	Fine	N-Mint
2-3rd app. The Joker	800.00	2000.00	4800.00
3-1st Catwoman in costume; 1st Puppetmaster app.	585.00	1460.00	3500.00
4-5th app. The Joker	450.00	1125.00	2700.00
5-1st app. of the Batmobile with its bat-head front	335.00	840.00	2000.00
6-10: 8-Infinity-c	240.00	600.00	1450.00
11-Classic Joker-c (2nd Joker-c, 6-7/42)	265.00	660.00	1600.00
12,13,15: 13-Jerry Siegel, creator of Superman appears in a Batman story	200.00	500.00	1200.00
14-2nd Penguin-c (12-1/42-43)	217.00	540.00	1300.00

	Good	Fine	VF-NM
16-Intro Alfred (4-5/43)	275.00	690.00	1650.00

	Good	Fine	N-Mint
17-20: 18-Hitler, Hirohito, Mussolini-c	125.00	315.00	750.00
21,22,24,26,28-30: 22-1st Alfred solo	100.00	250.00	600.00
23-Joker-c/story	150.00	375.00	900.00
25-Only Joker/Penguin team-up	142.00	355.00	850.00
27-Jerry Robinson Christmas-c	125.00	315.00	750.00
31,32,34-36,39: 31-Infinity logo-c. 32-Origin Robin retold	72.00	180.00	425.00
33-Christmas-c	88.00	220.00	525.00
37,40,44-Joker-c/stories	100.00	250.00	600.00
38-Penguin-c	84.00	210.00	500.00
41,45,46: 45-Christmas-c	58.00	146.00	350.00
42-2nd Catwoman-c (8-9/47)	72.00	180.00	425.00
43-Penguin-c	72.00	180.00	425.00
47-1st detailed origin The Batman (6-7/48)	200.00	500.00	1200.00
48-1000 Secrets of Batcave; r-in #203	66.00	165.00	400.00
49-Joker-c/story; 1st Vicki Vale & Mad Hatter	100.00	250.00	600.00

	Good	Fine	N-Mint
50-Two-Face impostor app.	62.00	155.00	375.00

51,53,54,56,57,59,60: 57-Centerfold is a 1950 calendar. 59-1st app.

Deadshot	58.00	145.00	350.00
52,55-Joker-c/stories	75.00	190.00	450.00
58-Penguin-c	62.00	155.00	375.00
61-Origin Batman Plane II	56.00	140.00	340.00
62-Origin Catwoman; Catwoman-c	75.00	190.00	450.00

63,64,67,70-72,74-77,79,80: 72-Last 52 pg. issue. 74-Used in **POP**,

Pg. 90	44.00	110.00	265.00

65,69,84-Catwoman covers. 84-Two-Face app.

	50.00	125.00	300.00
66,73-Joker-c/stories	58.00	145.00	350.00
68,81-Two-Face-c/stories	48.00	120.00	285.00

78-(8-9/53)-Roh Kar, The Man Hunter from Mars story-the 1st
lawman of Mars to come to Earth (green skinned)

	58.00	145.00	350.00

82,83,85-89: 86-Intro Batmarine (Batman's submarine). 89-Last pre-
code issue

	44.00	110.00	265.00

90,91,93-99: 97-2nd app. Bat-Hound-c/story; Joker app.

	30.00	75.00	180.00
92-1st app. Bat-Hound-c/story	40.00	100.00	240.00

Batman #103, © DC Comics

100 (6/56)	150.00	375.00	900.00

101-104,106-109: 103-3rd Bat-Hound-c/story

	29.00	85.00	200.00

	Good	Fine	N-Mint
105-1st Batwoman in Batman (2nd anywhere)			
	36.00	108.00	250.00
110-Joker story	30.00	90.00	210.00
111-120: 113-1st app. Fatman	21.00	63.00	145.00
121,122,124-126,128,130	14.00	43.00	100.00
123-Joker story; Bat-Hound app.	17.00	51.00	120.00
127-Joker story; Superman cameo	17.00	51.00	120.00
129-Origin Robin retold; bondage-c	17.00	51.00	120.00

131-135,137-139,141-143: Last 10 cent issue. 131-Intro 2nd Batman & Robin series. 133-1st Bat-Mite in Batman (3rd app. anywhere).134-Origin The Dummy. 139-Intro old Bat-Girl. 140-Superman guest stars. 141-2nd app. old Bat-Girl

	10.00	30.00	70.00
136-Joker-c/story	16.00	48.00	110.00
140,144-Joker stories	11.00	32.00	75.00
145,148-Joker-c/stories	13.00	40.00	90.00
146,147,149,150	8.00	24.00	55.00

151,153,154,156-158,160-162,164-168,170: 164-New Batmobile (6/64); new look & Mystery Analysts series begins

	5.70	17.00	40.00
152-Joker story	6.50	19.00	45.00
155-1st S.A. app. The Penguin (4/63)	20.00	60.00	140.00
159,163-Joker-c/stories	8.00	24.00	55.00
169-Early S.A. Penguin app.	7.00	21.00	50.00

171-1st S.A. Riddler app.(5/65), 1st since 12/48

	37.00	110.00	260.00

172-175,177,178,180,181,183,184: 181-Batman & Robin poster insert; intro. Poison Ivy

	4.00	12.00	28.00
176-80-Pg. Giant G-17; Joker-c/story	5.70	17.00	40.00
179-2nd app. Silver Age Riddler	9.30	28.00	65.00

182,187-80 Pg. Giants G-24, G-30; Joker-c/stories

	4.50	14.00	32.00
185-80 Pg. Giant G-27	4.00	12.00	28.00
186-Joker-c/story	2.85	8.50	20.00

188-189,191,192,194-196,199: 189-1st S.A. app. Scarecrow

	2.15	6.50	15.00
190-Penguin app.	2.85	8.50	20.00
193-80-Pg. Giant G-37	2.65	8.00	18.00

197-Early S.A. Catwoman app.; new Bat-Girl app.

	5.00	15.00	35.00

198-80-Pg. Giant G-43; Joker-c/story-r/World's Finest #61; Catwoman-r/Det. #211; Penguin-r; origin-r/#47

	6.50	19.00	45.00

	Good	Fine	N-Mint
200-Joker-story; retells origin of Batman & Robin			
	15.00	45.00	105.00
201-Joker story	2.65	8.00	18.00
202,204-207,209,210	1.50	4.50	10.00
203-80 Pg. Giant G-49; r/#48, 61, & Det. 185; Batcave Blueprints			
	2.00	6.00	14.00
208-80 Pg. Giant G-55; New origin Batman by Gil Kane			
	2.65	8.00	18.00
211,212,214-217: 214-Alfred given a new last name-"Pennyworth" (see Detective #96)	1.50	4.50	10.00
213-80-Pg. Giant G-61; 30th anniversary issue (7-8/69); origin Alfred, Joker (r/Det. #168), Clayface; new origin Robin with new facts			
	4.50	14.00	32.00
218-80-Pg. Giant G-67	2.00	6.00	14.00
219-Neal Adams-a	2.85	8.50	20.00
220,221,224-227,229-231	1.50	4.50	9.00
222-Beatles take-off	2.65	8.00	18.00
223,228,233-80-Pg. Giants G-73,G-79,G-85			
	1.85	5.50	11.00
232,237-N. Adams-a. 232-Intro/1st app. Ras Al Ghul. 237-G.A. Batman-r/Det. #37; 1st app. The Reaper; Wrightson/Ellison plots			
	3.15	9.50	22.00
234-1st S.A. app. Two-Face; N. Adams-a; 52 pg. issues begin, end #242	5.70	17.00	40.00
235,236,239-242: 239-XMas-c. 241-Reprint/#5			
	1.35	4.00	8.00
238-DC-8 100 pg. Super Spec.; unpubbed G.A. Atom, Sargon, Plastic Man stories; Doom Patrol origin-r; Batman, Legion, Aquaman-r; N. Adams-c	1.50	4.50	9.00
243-245-Neal Adams-a	2.30	7.00	16.00
246-250,252,253: 253-Shadow app.	1.35	4.00	8.00
251-N. Adams-c/a; Joker-c/story	4.50	14.00	32.00
254,256-259,261-All 100 pg. editions; part-r			
	1.50	4.50	9.00
255-N. Adams-c/a; tells of Bruce Wayne's father who wore bat costume & fought crime (100 pgs.)	2.00	6.00	14.00
260-Joker-c/story (100 pgs.)	3.15	9.50	22.00
262-285,287-290,292,293,295-299: 262-68pgs. 266-Catwoman back to old costume	.85	2.50	5.00
286,291,294-Joker-c/stories	1.15	3.50	7.00
300-Double-size	1.15	3.50	7.00
301-320,322-352,354-356,358,360-365,367,369,370: 304-(44 pgs.).			

	Good	Fine	N-Mint

310-1st app. The Gentleman Ghost. 311-Batgirl reteams w/Batman. 313,314-Two-Face-c/stories. 316-Robin returns. 323,324-Catman & Catwoman app. 332-Catwoman's 1st solo. 325-Death of Comm. Gordon. 345-1st app. new Dr. Death. 357,358-1st app. Killer Croc. 361-1st app. Harvey Bullock .85   2.50   5.00

321,353,359-Joker-c/stories   1.15   3.50   7.00

357-1st app. Jason Todd (3/83); see Det. #524
....1.35   4.00   8.00

366-Jason Todd 1st in Robin costume; Joker-c/story
....4.15   12.50   25.00

368-1st new Robin in costume (Jason Todd)
....3.35   10.00   20.00

371-399,401-403: 386,387-Intro Black Mask (villain). 401-2nd app. Magpie. 403-Joker cameo .40   1.25   2.50

NOTE: *Most issues between 397 & 432 were reprinted in 1989 and sold in multi-packs. Some are not identified as reprints but have newer ads copyrighted after cover dates. 2nd and 3rd printings exist.*

400 ($1.50, 64pgs.)-Dark Knight special; intro by Stephen King; Art Adams/Austin-a   2.50   7.50   15.00

404-Miller scripts begin (end 407); Year 1   2.00   6.00   12.00

405-407: 407-Year 1 ends (See Det. for Year 2)
....85   2.50   5.00

408-410: New Origin Jason Todd (Robin) .85   2.50   5.00

411-416,421-425: 412-Origin/1st app. Mime. 415,416-Millennium tie-ins. 416-Nightwing-c/story .40   1.15   2.35

417-420: "Ten Nights of the Beast" storyline
....1.70   5.00   10.00

426-($1.50, 52 pgs.)-"A Death In The Family" storyline begins, ends #429   1.70   5.00   10.00

427-"A Death In The Family" part 2   1.35   4.00   8.00

428-Death of Robin (Jason Todd)   1.50   4.50   9.00

429-Joker-c/story; Superman app.   .85   2.50   5.00

430-432 .25   .75   1.50

433-435-"Many Deaths of the Batman" story by John Byrne-c/scripts
....40   1.25   2.50

436-Year 3 begins (ends #439); origin original Robin retold by Nightwing (Dick Grayson); 1st app. Timothy Drake
....75   2.25   4.50

436-2nd print .50   1.00

437-439: 437-Origin Robin continued .40   1.25   2.50

440,441: "A Lonely Place of Dying" Parts 1 & 3 .50   1.00

	Good	Fine	N-Mint
442-1st app. Timothy Drake in Robin costume			
	.75	2.25	4.50

443-456,458,459,462-464: 445-447-Batman goes to Russia. 448,449-"The Penguin Affair" parts 1 & 3. 450,451-Joker-c/stories. 452-454-"Dark Knight Dark City" storyline; Riddler app. 455-Alan Grant scripts begin, ends 466,470. 464-Last solo Batman story; free 16 pg. preview of Impact Comics line .25   .75   1.50

457-Timothy Drake officially becomes Robin & dons new costume

	Good	Fine	N-Mint
	1.35	4.00	8.00
457-Direct sale version (has #000 in indicia)	.85	2.50	5.00
460,461-2 part Catwoman story	.35	1.00	2.00
465-Robin returns to action with Batman	.25	.75	1.50
466-476: 470-War of the Gods x-over		.65	1.30
477-488: 477-Begin $1.25-c. 477,478-Photo-c		.65	1.30
Annual 1(8-10/61)-Swan-c	32.00	96.00	225.00
Annual 2	14.00	43.00	100.00
Annual 3(Summer, '62)-Joker-c/story	16.00	48.00	110.00
Annual 4,5	6.50	19.00	45.00
Annual 6,7(7/64, 25 cents, 80 pgs.)	5.00	15.00	35.00
Annual V5#8(1982)-Painted-c	.85	2.50	5.00
Annual 9,10,12: 9(7/85). 10(1986). 12(1988, $1.50)			
	.55	1.65	3.30
Annual 11(1987, $1.25)-Alan Moore scripts			
	1.00	3.00	6.00

Annual 13(1989, $1.75, 68 pgs.)-Gives history of Bruce Wayne, Dick Grayson, Jason Todd, Alfred, Comm. Gordon, Barbara Gordon (Batgirl) & Vicki Vale; Morrow-i .35   1.10   2.20

Annual 14('90, $2.00, 68 pgs.)-Origin Two-Face

	Good	Fine	N-Mint
	.35	1.00	2.00

Annual 15('91, $2.00, 68 pgs.)-Armageddon 2001 x-over; Joker app.; 2nd printing exists .35   1.00   2.00

Special 1 (4/84)-Golden-c/a	.85	2.50	5.00

Full Circle nn (1991, $5.95, stiff-c, 68 pgs.)-Sequel to Batman: Year Two 1.00   3.00   6.00

Holy Terror nn (1991, $4.95, 52 pgs.)-Elseworlds

	Good	Fine	N-Mint
	1.00	3.00	6.00

Lonely Place of Dying (1990, $3.95, 132 pgs.)-r/Batman #440-442 & New Titans #60,61; Perez-c .70   2.00   4.00

BATMAN FAMILY, THE
Sept-Oct, 1975-No. 20, Oct-Nov, 1978 (No.1-4, 17-on: 68 pages)
(Combined with Detective Comics with No. 481)
National Periodical Publications/DC Comics

	Good	Fine	N-Mint
1-Origin Batgirl-Robin team-up (The Dynamite Duo); reprints plus one new story begins; N. Adams-a(r)	.85	2.50	5.00
2-5: 3-Batgirl & Robin learn each's i.d.	.50	1.50	3.00
6,9-Joker's daughter on cover (1st app?)	.70	2.00	4.00
7,8,10,14-16: 10-1st revival Batwoman	.50	1.50	3.00
11-13: Rogers-p. 11-New stories begin; Man-Bat begins	.85	2.50	5.00
17-($1.00 size)-Batman, Huntress begin	.50	1.50	3.00
18-20: Huntress in all. 20-Origin Ragman retold	.30	.90	1.75

BATMAN: SHADOW OF THE BAT
June, 1992-Present ($1.50, color)
DC Comics

	Good	Fine	N-Mint
1	.35	1.00	2.00
2-6	.25	.75	1.50

BATMAN: THE CULT
1988-No. 4, Nov, 1988 ($3.50, color, deluxe mini-series)
DC Comics

	Good	Fine	N-Mint
1-Wrightson-a/painted-c in all	2.00	6.00	12.00
2	1.70	5.00	10.00
3,4	1.50	4.50	9.00

BATMAN: THE DARK KNIGHT
March, 1986-No. 4, 1986
DC Comics

	Good	Fine	N-Mint
1-Miller story & c/a(p); set in the future	7.50	22.50	45.00
1-2nd printing	1.35	4.00	8.00
1-3rd printing	.60	1.75	3.50
2-Carrie Kelly becomes Robin (female)	4.20	12.50	25.00
2-2nd printing	.85	2.50	5.00
2-3rd printing	.50	1.50	3.00
3-Death of Joker; Superman app.	1.70	5.00	10.00
3-2nd printing	.60	1.75	3.50
4-Death of Alfred; Superman app.	1.15	3.50	7.00

BATMAN: THE KILLING JOKE
1988 ($3.50, 52 pgs. color, deluxe, adults)
DC Comics

	Good	Fine	N-Mint
1-Bolland-c/a; Alan Moore scripts	4.15	12.50	25.00
1-2nd thru 8th printings	.85	2.50	5.00

BATMAN: THE OFFICIAL COMIC ADAPTATION OF THE WARNER BROS. MOTION PICTURE
1989 ($2.50, $4.95, 68 pgs.) (Movie adaptation)
DC Comics

	Good	Fine	N-Mint
1-Regular format ($2.50)-Ordway-c/a	.70	2.00	4.00
1-Prestige format ($4.95)-Diff.-c, same insides			
	1.00	3.00	6.00

BATMAN VERSUS PREDATOR
1991-No. 3, 1992 (Mini-series, color)
DC Comics/Dark Horse Comics

1-(Prestige format, $4.95)-1,2-Contain 8 Batman/Predator trading cards; Andy & Adam Kubert-a in all; Suydam-c all Prest.			
	1.15	3.50	7.00
1-(Regular format, $1.95)-No trading cards; diff.-c			
	.70	2.00	4.00
2,3-(Prestige format, $4.95): 2-Extra pin-ups			
	1.00	3.00	6.00
2-(Regular format, $1.95)-No trading cards; diff.-c			
	.60	1.75	3.50
3-(Regular format, $1.95)-No trading cards; diff.-c			
	.50	1.50	3.00

BEVERLY HILLBILLIES (TV)
4-6/63-No. 18, 8/67; No. 19, 10/69; No. 20, 10/70; No. 21, Oct, 1971
Dell Publishing Co.

1-Photo-c	11.00	32.00	75.00
2-Photo-c	5.00	15.00	35.00
3-9: All have photo covers	3.60	11.00	25.00
10-No photo-c	2.00	6.00	14.00
11-21: All have photo covers. 19-r/#1	2.85	8.50	20.00

BEWARE THE CREEPER (See Brave & the Bold, Flash & Showcase)
May-June, 1968-No. 6, March-April, 1969
National Periodical Publications

Showcase #73 (3-4/67)-Origin & 1st app. The Creeper; Ditko-c/a			
	6.50	19.00	45.00
1-(5-6/68)-Ditko-a in all; c-1-5	5.00	15.00	35.00
2-6: 6-G. Kane-c	2.85	8.50	20.00

BEWITCHED (TV)
4-6/65-No. 11, 10/67; No. 12, 10/68-No. 13, 1/69; No. 14, 10/69
Dell Publishing Co.

	Good	Fine	N-Mint
1-Photo-c	10.00	30.00	70.00
2-No photo-c	5.00	15.00	35.00
3-13-All have photo-c	3.60	11.00	25.00
14-No photo-c	2.40	7.20	17.00

BIG SHOT COMICS
May, 1940-No. 104, Aug, 1949
Columbia Comics Group

1-Intro. Skyman; The Face (Tony Trent), The Cloak (Spy Master), Marvelo, Monarch of Magicians, Joe Palooka, Charlie Chan, Tom Kerry, Dixie Dugan, Rocky Ryan begin

	Good	Fine	N-Mint
	87.00	260.00	600.00
2	36.00	108.00	250.00
3-The Cloak called Spy Chief; Skyman-c	30.00	90.00	215.00
4,5	26.30	79.00	185.00
6-10	23.00	70.00	160.00
11-14: 14-Origin Sparky Watts	19.30	58.00	135.00
15-Origin The Cloak	23.00	70.00	160.00
16-20	14.00	43.00	100.00
21-30: 24-Tojo-c. 28-Hitler, Tojo & Mussolini-c. 29-Intro. Capt. Yank; Bo (a dog) newspaper strip reprints by Frank Beck begin, ends #104	11.00	32.00	75.00
31-40: 32-Vic Jordan newspaper strip reprints begin, ends #52; Hitler, Tojo & Mussolini-c	8.50	25.50	60.00
41-50: 42-No Skyman. 43-Hitler-c. 50-Origin The Face retold	7.00	21.00	50.00
51-60	5.30	16.00	38.00
61-70: 63 on-Tony Trent, the Face	4.50	14.00	32.00
71-80: 73-The Face cameo. 74-(2/47)-Mickey Finn begins. 74,80-The Face app. in Tony Trent. 78-Last Charlie Chan strip-r	4.00	12.00	28.00
81-90: 85-Tony Trent marries Babs Walsh. 86-Valentines-c	3.50	10.50	24.00
91-99,101-104: 69-94-Skyman in Outer Space. 96-Xmas-c	2.85	8.50	20.00
100	4.00	12.00	28.00

BIG-3
Fall, 1940-No. 7, Jan, 1942
Fox Features Syndicate

	Good	Fine	N-Mint
1-Blue Beetle, The Flame, & Samson begin			
	88.00	265.00	615.00
2	40.00	120.00	275.00
3-5	30.00	90.00	215.00
6-Last Samson; bondage-c	26.00	78.00	180.00
7-V-Man app.	26.00	78.00	180.00

BIG TOWN (Radio/TV)
Jan, 1951-No. 50, Mar-Apr, 1958 (No. 1-9: 52 pgs.)
National Periodical Publications

1-Dan Barry-a begins	30.00	90.00	215.00
2	14.00	43.00	100.00
3-10	8.50	25.50	60.00
11-20	5.70	17.00	40.00
21-31: Last pre-code (1-2/55)	4.00	12.00	28.00
32-50	2.85	8.50	20.00

BIG VALLEY, THE (TV)
June, 1966-No. 5, Oct, 1967; No. 6, Oct, 1969
Dell Publishing Co.

1: Photo-c #1-5	3.50	10.50	24.00
2-6: 6-Reprints #1	1.70	5.00	12.00

BILL BOYD WESTERN (Movie star; see Hopalong Cassidy)
Feb, 1950-No. 23, June, 1952 (1-3,7,11,14-on: 36 pgs.)
Fawcett Publications

1-Bill Boyd & his horse Midnite begin; photo front/back-c			
	30.00	90.00	210.00
2-Painted-c	16.00	48.00	110.00
3-Photo-c begin, end #23; last photo back-c			
	14.00	43.00	100.00
4-6(52 pgs.)	11.50	34.00	80.00
7,11(36 pgs.)	9.30	28.00	65.00
8-10,12,13(52 pgs.)	10.00	30.00	70.00
14-22	8.50	25.50	60.00
23-Last issue	10.00	30.00	70.00

BILLY THE KID ADVENTURE MAGAZINE
Oct, 1950-No. 30, 1955
Toby Press

	Good	Fine	N-Mint
1-Williamson/Frazetta-a (2 pgs); photo-c			
	16.50	50.00	115.00
2-Photo-c	4.50	14.00	32.00
3-Williamson/Frazetta "The Claws of Death," 4 pgs. plus William-			
son art	18.00	54.00	125.00
4,5,7,8,10: 4,7-Photo-c	3.15	9.50	22.00
6-Frazetta story assist on "Nightmare;" photo-c			
	7.50	23.00	52.00
9-Kurtzman Pot-Shot Pete; photo-c	6.50	19.00	45.00
11,12,15-20: 11-Photo-c	2.65	8.00	18.00
13-Kurtzman-r/John Wayne #12 (Genius)			
	3.00	9.00	21.00
14-Williamson/Frazetta; r-of #1 (2 pgs.)	5.00	15.00	35.00
21,23-30	2.00	6.00	14.00
22-Williamson/Frazetta-r(1pg.)/#1; photo-c			
	3.00	9.00	21.00

BLACK CAT COMICS (...Western #16-19; ...Mystery #30 on)
June-July, 1946-No. 29, June, 1951
Harvey Publications (Home Comics)

	Good	Fine	N-Mint
1-Kubert-a	30.00	90.00	215.00
2-Kubert-a	17.00	51.00	120.00
3,4: 4-The Red Demons begin (The Demon #4, 5)			
	12.00	36.00	85.00
5,6-The Scarlet Arrow app. in ea. by Powell; S&K-a in both. 6-			
Origin Red Demon	16.00	48.00	110.00
7-Vagabond Prince by S&K plus 1 more story			
	16.00	48.00	110.00
8-S&K-a; Kerry Drake begins, ends #13	13.50	41.00	95.00
9-Origin Stuntman (r/Stuntman #1)	16.50	50.00	115.00
10-20: 14,15,17-Mary Worth app. plus Invisible Scarlet O'Neil-			
#15,20,24	11.00	32.00	75.00
21-26	9.30	28.00	65.00
27-Used in **SOTI**, pg. 193; X-Mas-c; 2 pg. John Wayne story			
	11.00	32.00	75.00
28-Intro. Kit, Black Cat's new sidekick	11.00	32.00	75.00
29-Black Cat bondage-c; Black Cat stories			
	10.00	30.00	70.00

BLACK CAT MYSTERY (Formerly Black Cat; ...Western Mystery
#54;...Western #55,56; ...Mystery #57; ...Mystic #58-62; Black Cat
#63-65)No. 30, Aug, 1951-No. 65, April, 1963
Harvey Publications

	Good	Fine	N-Mint
30-Black Cat on cover only	8.50	25.50	60.00
31,32,34,37,38,40	5.30	16.00	38.00
33-Used in **POP**, pg. 89; electrocution-c	6.00	18.00	42.00
35-Atomic disaster cover/story	7.00	21.00	50.00
36,39-Used in **SOTI**: #36-Pgs. 270,271; #39-Pgs. 386-388			
	9.30	28.00	65.00
41-43	5.00	15.00	35.00
44-Eyes, ears, tongue cut out; Nostrand-a	6.00	18.00	42.00
45-Classic "Colorama" by Powell; Nostrand-a			
	10.00	30.00	70.00
46-49,51-Nostrand-a in all	6.00	18.00	42.00
50-Check-a; Warren Kremer?-c showing a man's face burning away			
	10.00	30.00	70.00
52,53 (r-#34 & 35)	4.00	12.00	28.00
54-Two Black Cat stories (2/55, last pre-code)			
	6.50	19.00	45.00
55,56-Black Cat app.	4.30	13.00	30.00
57(7/56)-Simon?-c	3.15	9.50	22.00
58-60-Kirby-a(4)	6.00	18.00	42.00
61-Nostrand-a; "Colorama" r-/45	4.50	14.00	32.00
62(3/58)-E.C. story swipe	3.50	10.50	24.00
63-Giant(10/62); Reprints; Black Cat app.; origin Black Kitten			
	5.00	15.00	35.00
64-Giant(1/63); Reprints; Black Cat app.	5.00	15.00	35.00
65-Giant(4/63); Reprints; Black Cat app.	5.00	15.00	35.00

BLACK GOLIATH
Feb, 1976-No. 5, Nov, 1976
Marvel Comics Group

1: 1-3-Tuska-a(p)	.85	2.50	5.00
2-5	.50	1.50	3.00

BLACKHAWK (Formerly Uncle Sam #1-8; see Military &
Modern Comics)
No. 9, Winter, 1944-No. 243, 10-11/68; No. 244, 1-2/76- No. 250,
1-2/77; No. 251, 10/82-No. 273, 11/84
Comic Magazines(Quality)No. 9-107(12/56); National Periodical Publ.
No. 108(1/57)-250; DC Comics No. 251 on

	Good	Fine	N-Mint
9 (1944)	130.00	390.00	900.00
10 (1946)	57.00	170.00	400.00
11-15: 14-Ward-a; 13,14-Fear app.	43.00	130.00	300.00
16-20: 20-Ward Blackhawk	36.00	108.00	250.00
21-30	26.00	78.00	180.00
31-40: 31-Chop Chop by Jack Cole	19.00	57.00	130.00
41-49,51-60	13.00	40.00	90.00
50-1st Killer Shark; origin in text	16.00	48.00	110.00
61-Used in **POP**, pg. 91	11.50	34.00	80.00
62-Used in **POP**, pg. 92 & color illo	11.50	34.00	80.00
63-70,72-80: 65-H-Bomb explosion panel. 66-B&W and color illos **POP**. 70-Return of Killer Shark. 75-Intro. Blackie the Hawk			
	11.00	32.00	75.00
71-Origin retold; flying saucer-c; A-Bomb panels			
	14.00	43.00	100.00
81-86: Last precode (3/55)	10.00	30.00	70.00
87-92,94-99,101-107	7.00	21.00	50.00
93-Origin in text	8.50	25.50	60.00
100	10.00	30.00	70.00
108-Re-intro. Blackie, the Hawk, their mascot; not in #115			
	32.00	96.00	220.00
109-117	8.00	24.00	55.00
118-Frazetta-r/Jimmy Wakely #4 (3 pgs.)	9.30	28.00	65.00
119-130	5.70	17.00	41.00
131-140: 133-Intro. Lady Blackhawk	4.30	13.00	30.00

Blackhawk #203, © DC Comics

	Good	**Fine**	**N-Mint**
141-163,165,166: 143-Kurtzman-r/Jimmy Wakely #4. 166-Last 10			
cent issue	2.85	8.50	20.00
164-Origin retold	3.60	11.00	25.00
167-180	1.50	4.50	10.00
181-190	1.15	3.50	7.00
191-197,199-202,204-210: Combat Diary series begins. 197-New look			
for Blackhawks	.85	2.50	5.00
198-Origin retold	1.15	3.50	7.00
203-Origin Chop Chop (12/64)	1.00	3.00	6.00
211-243(1968): 228-Batman, Green Lantern, Superman, The Flash			
cameos. 230-Blackhawks become superheroes. 242-Return to old			
costumes	.85	2.50	5.00
244 ('76) -250: 250-Chuck dies	.35	1.00	2.00
251-264: 251-Origin retold; Black Knights return. 252-Intro Domino.			
253-Part origin Hendrickson. 258-Blackhawk's Island destroyed.			
259-Part origin Chop-Chop		.50	1.00
265-273 (75 cent cover price)		.50	1.00

BLACK PANTHER, THE (Also see Fantastic Four #52 &
    Jungle Action)
Jan, 1977-No. 15, May, 1979
Marvel Comics Group

	Good	**Fine**	**N-Mint**
1	1.10	3.25	6.50
2	.75	2.25	4.50
3-10	.60	1.75	3.50
11-15: 14,15-Avengers x-over	.50	1.50	3.00

BLACK PANTHER
July, 1988-No. 4, Oct, 1988 ($1.25, color)
Marvel Comics Group

	Good	**Fine**	**N-Mint**
1-4	.25	.75	1.50

BLACK PANTHER: PANTHER'S PREY
1991-No. 4, 1991 ($4.95, squarebound, mini-series, 52 pgs.)
Marvel Comics

	Good	**Fine**	**N-Mint**
1-4	.85	2.50	5.00

BLACK TERROR (See America's Best & Exciting Comics)
Wint, 1942-43-No. 27, June, 1949
Better Publications/Standard

	Good	**Fine**	**N-Mint**
1-Black Terror, Crime Crusader begin	78.00	234.00	550.00
2	36.00	108.00	250.00

	Good	Fine	N-Mint
3	27.00	80.00	190.00
4,5	21.00	65.00	150.00
6-10: 7-The Ghost app.	16.50	50.00	115.00
11-20: 20-The Scarab app.	13.50	41.00	95.00
21-Miss Masque app.	14.00	43.00	100.00
22-Part Frazetta-a on one Black Terror story			
	16.00	48.00	110.00
23,25-27	13.00	40.00	90.00
24-¼ pg. Frazetta-a	13.50	41.00	95.00

BLONDE PHANTOM (Formerly All-Select #1-11)(Also see
    Marvel Mystery)
No. 12, Winter, 1946-47-No. 22, March, 1949
Marvel Comics (MPC)

12-Miss America begins, ends #14	60.00	180.00	415.00
13-Sub-Mariner begins	40.00	120.00	275.00
14,15; 14-Male bondage-c; Namora app. 15-Kurtzman's "Hey Look"			
	32.00	96.00	225.00
16-Captain America with Bucky app.; Kurtzman's "Hey Look"			
	43.00	130.00	300.00
17-22: 22-Anti Wertham editorial	31.00	93.00	215.00

BLUE BEETLE, THE (Also see Big-3, & Mystery Men)
Winter, 1939-40-No. 60, Aug, 1950
Fox Publ. No. 1-11, 31-60; Holyoke No. 12-30

1-Reprints from Mystery Men 1-5; Blue Beetle origin; Yarko the Great-r/from Wonder/Wonderworld 2-5 all by Eisner; Master Magician app.; (Blue Beetle in 4 different costumes)			
	175.00	440.00	1050.00
2-K-51-r by Powell/Wonderworld 8,9	65.00	195.00	450.00
3-Simon-c	47.00	140.00	325.00
4-Marijuana drug mention story	33.00	100.00	235.00
5-Zanzibar The Magician by Tuska	27.00	80.00	190.00
6-Dynamite Thor begins; origin Blue Beetle			
	26.00	78.00	180.00
7,8-Dynamo app. in both. 8-Last Thor	24.50	73.00	170.00
9,10-The Blackbird & The Gorilla app. in both. 10-Bondage/ hypo-c	23.00	70.00	160.00
11(2/42)-The Gladiator app.	23.00	70.00	160.00
12(6/42)-The Black Fury app.	23.00	70.00	160.00
13-V-Man begins, ends #18; Kubert-a	26.00	78.00	180.00
14,15-Kubert-a in both. 14-Intro. side-kick (c/text only), Sparky			

	Good	Fine	N-Mint
(called Spunky #17-19)	25.00	75.00	175.00
16-18	19.00	58.00	135.00
19-Kubert-a	22.00	65.00	150.00
20-Origin/1st app. Tiger Squadron; Arabian Nights begin			
	23.00	70.00	160.00
21-26: 24-Intro. & only app. The Halo. 26-General Patton story &			
photo	14.00	43.00	100.00
27-Tamaa, Jungle Prince app.	13.00	40.00	90.00
28-30(2/44)	11.00	32.00	75.00
31(6/44), 33-40: "The Threat from Saturn" serial in #34-38			
	8.50	25.50	60.00
32-Hitler-c	11.00	32.00	75.00
41-45	7.00	21.00	50.00
46-The Puppeteer app.	8.00	24.00	55.00
47-Kamen & Baker-a begin	43.00	130.00	300.00
48-50	33.00	100.00	235.00
51,53	30.00	90.00	210.00
52-Kamen bondage-c	43.00	130.00	300.00
54-Used in **SOTI**. Illo-"Children call these 'headlights' comics"			
	60.00	180.00	420.00
55,57(7/48)-Last Kamen issue	30.00	90.00	210.00
56-Used in **SOTI**, pg. 145	30.00	90.00	210.00
58(4/50)-60-No Kamen-a	5.70	17.00	40.00

BLUE BEETLE (Formerly Unusual Tales #1-49)
V2#1, June, 1964-V2#5, Mar-Apr, 1965; V3#50, July, 1965-V3#54,
Feb-Mar, 1966; #1, June, 1967-#5, Nov, 1968
Charlton Comics

V2#1-Origin Dan Garrett-Blue Beetle	5.00	15.00	35.00
2-5,V3#50-54: 5-Weiss illo; 1st published-a?			
	3.60	11.00	25.00
1(1967)-Question series begins by Ditko	8.00	24.00	55.00
2-Origin Ted Kord-Blue Beetle; Dan Garrett x-over			
	3.15	9.50	22.00
3-5 (All Ditko-c/a in #1-5)	2.30	7.00	16.00

BLUE BEETLE (Also Capt. Atom #83-86 & Crisis on Infinite Earths)
June, 1986-No. 24, May, 1988
DC Comics

1-Origin retold; intro. Firefist	.25	.75	1.50
2-24: 2-Origin Firefist. 5-7-The Question app. 11-14-New Teen			

	Good	Fine	N-Mint

Titans x-over. 18-Begin $1.00-c. 20-Justice League app.

	.50	1.00

BLUE RIBBON COMICS (...Mystery Comics No. 9-18)
Nov, 1939-No. 22, March, 1942 (1st MLJ series)
MLJ Magazines

1-Dan Hastings, Richy the Amazing Boy, Rang-A-Tang the Wonder Dog begin; Little Nemo app. (not by W. McCay); Jack Cole-a(3)

	137.00	410.00	950.00

2-Bob Phantom, Silver Fox (both in #3), Rang-A-Tang Club & Cpl. Collins begin; Jack Cole-a 57.00 170.00 400.00

3-J. Cole-a 40.00 120.00 275.00

4-Doc Strong, The Green Falcon, & Hercules begin; origin & 1st app. The Fox & Ty-Gor, Son of the Tiger

	43.00	130.00	300.00

5-8: 8-Last Hercules; 6,7-Biro, Meskin-a. 7-Fox app. on-c 29.00 85.00 200.00

9-(Scarce)-Origin & 1st app. Mr. Justice 107.00 320.00 750.00

10-13: 12-Last Doc Strong. 13-Inferno, the Flame Breather begins, ends #19; Devil-c 50.00 150.00 350.00

14,15,17,18: 15-Last Green Falcon 43.00 130.00 300.00

16-Origin & 1st app. Captain Flag 79.00 235.00 550.00

19-22: 20-Last Ty-Gor. 22-Origin Mr. Justice retold 40.00 120.00 275.00

BOB COLT (Movie star)
Nov, 1950-No. 10, May, 1952
Fawcett Publications

1-Bob Colt, his horse Buckskin & sidekick Pablo begin; photo front/back-c begin 27.00 80.00 190.00

2 18.00 54.00 125.00

3-5 16.00 48.00 110.00

6-Flying Saucer story 13.00 40.00 90.00

7-10: 9-Last photo back-c 11.50 34.00 80.00

BOB STEELE WESTERN (Movie star)
Dec, 1950-No. 10, June, 1952; 1990
Fawcett Publications/AC Comics

1-Bob Steele & his horse Bullet begin; photo front/back-c begin 29.00 85.00 200.00

2 18.00 54.00 125.00

	Good	Fine	N-Mint
3-5: 4-Last photo back-c	14.00	43.00	100.00
6-10: 10-Last photo-c	11.50	34.00	80.00

BOMBA THE JUNGLE BOY (TV)
Sept-Oct, 1967-No. 7, Sept-Oct, 1968 (12 cents)
National Periodical Publications

1-Intro. Bomba; Infantino/Anderson-c	1.70	5.00	12.00
2-7	1.00	3.00	7.00

BOY COMICS (Captain Battle No. 1 & 2; Boy Illustories No. 43-108)
    (Stories by Charles Biro)
No. 3, April, 1942-No. 119, March, 1956
Lev Gleason Publications (Comic House)

3(No.1)-Origin Crimebuster, Bombshell & Young Robin Hood; Yankee Longago, Case 1001-1008, Swoop Storm, & Boy Movies begin; 1st app. Iron Jaw	130.00	390.00	900.00
4-Hitler, Tojo, Mussolini-c	55.00	165.00	385.00
5	43.00	130.00	300.00
6-Origin Iron Jaw; origin & death of Iron Jaw's son; Little Dynamite begins, ends #39	93.00	280.00	650.00
7,9: 7-Flag & Hitler, Tojo, Mussolini-c	36.00	108.00	250.00
8-Death of Iron Jaw	40.00	120.00	275.00
10-Return of Iron Jaw; classic Biro-c	50.00	150.00	350.00
11-14: 11-Classic Iron Jaw-c. 14-Iron Jaw-c	25.00	75.00	175.00
15-Death of Iron Jaw	29.00	85.00	200.00
16,18-20	16.00	48.00	110.00
17-Flag-c	18.00	54.00	125.00
21-26	10.00	30.00	70.00
27-29,31,32-(All 68 pages). 28-Yankee Longago ends. 32-Swoop Storm & Young Robin Hood end	11.00	32.00	75.00
30-(68 pgs.)-Origin Crimebuster retold	14.00	43.00	100.00
33-40: 34-Crimebuster story(2); suicide-c/story	6.50	19.00	45.00
41-50	4.30	13.00	30.00
51-59: 57-Dilly Duncan begins, ends #71	3.50	10.50	24.00
60-Iron Jaw returns	4.30	13.00	30.00
61-Origin Crimebuster & Iron Jaw retold	5.00	15.00	35.00
62-Death of Iron Jaw explained	5.00	15.00	35.00
63-73: 73-Frazetta 1-pg. ad	3.00	9.00	21.00
74-88: 80-1st app. Rocky X of the Rocketeers; becomes "Rocky X"			

	Good	Fine	N-Mint
#101; Iron Jaw, Sniffer & the Deadly Dozen begins, ends #118			
	2.65	8.00	18.00
89-92-The Claw serial app. in all	3.50	10.50	24.00
93-Claw cameo; Rocky X by Sid Check	3.50	10.50	24.00
94-97,99	2.65	8.00	18.00
98-Rocky X by Sid Check	3.50	10.50	24.00
100	2.85	8.50	20.00
101-107,109,111,119: 111-Crimebuster becomes Chuck Chandler.			
119-Last Crimebuster	2.65	8.00	18.00
108,110,112-118-Kubert-a	3.00	9.00	21.00

BOY COMMANDOS (See Detective #64 & World's Finest
Comics #8)
Winter, 1942-43-No. 36, Nov-Dec, 1949
National Periodical Publications

1-Origin Liberty Belle; The Sandman & The Newsboy Legion x-over in Boy Commandos; S&K-a, 48 pgs.			
	200.00	500.00	1200.00
2-Last Liberty Belle; S&K-a, 46 pgs.	88.00	220.00	525.00
3-S&K-a, 45 pgs.	63.00	158.00	375.00
4,5	35.00	88.00	215.00
6-8,10: 6-S&K-a	27.00	68.00	160.00
9-No S&K-a	18.00	46.00	110.00
11-Infinity-c	18.00	46.00	110.00
12-16,18-20	14.00	35.00	85.00
17-Sci/fi-c/story	15.00	38.00	90.00
21,22,24,25: 22-Judy Canova x-over	11.00	27.00	65.00
23-S&K-c/a(all)	12.00	31.00	75.00
26-Flying Saucer story (3-4/48)-4th of this theme			
	11.50	29.00	70.00
27,28,30: 30-Cleveland Indians story	11.00	27.00	65.00
29-S&K story (1)	11.50	29.00	70.00
31-35: 32-Dale Evans app. on-c & story. 34-Intro. Wolf, their mascot			
	11.00	27.00	65.00
36-Intro The Atomobile c/sci-fi story	13.00	33.00	80.00

BRAVE AND THE BOLD, THE
Aug-Sept, 1955-No. 200, July, 1983
National Periodical Publications/DC Comics

1-Viking Prince by Kubert, Silent Knight, Golden Gladiator begin			
	125.00	375.00	865.00
2	55.00	165.00	385.00

	Good	Fine	N-Mint
3,4	30.00	90.00	220.00
5-Robin Hood begins	35.00	110.00	250.00
6-10: 6-Robin Hood by Kubert; Golden Gladiator last app.; Silent Knight; no Viking Prince	25.00	75.00	175.00
11-22,24: 22-Last Silent Knight. 24-Last Viking Prince by Kubert	19.00	57.00	130.00
23-Viking Prince origin by Kubert	24.00	72.00	165.00
25-1st app. Suicide Squad (8-9/59)	20.00	60.00	140.00
26,27-Suicide Squad	13.50	41.00	95.00
28-(2-3/60)-Justice League intro./1st app.; origin Snapper Carr	295.00	890.00	2050.00

The Brave and the Bold #30, © *DC Comics*

29,30-Justice League	107.00	320.00	750.00
31-33-Cave Carson. 31-1st app. Cave Carson (8-9/60)	12.00	36.00	85.00
34-Origin/1st app. Silver-Age Hawkman & Byth by Kubert (2-3/61); 1st S.A. Hawkman tryout series	93.00	275.00	650.00
35,36-Hawkman by Kubert; origin Shadow Thief #36 (6-7/61)	25.00	75.00	175.00
37-Suicide Squad (2nd tryout series)	10.00	30.00	70.00
38,39-Suicide Squad. 38-Last 10 cent issue	10.00	30.00	70.00

	Good	Fine	N-Mint
40,41-Cave Carson Inside Earth; #40 has Kubert art			
	9.30	28.00	65.00
42,44-Hawkman by Kubert (2nd tryout series)			
	13.00	40.00	90.00
43-Origin Hawkman by Kubert retold	16.50	50.00	115.00
45-49-Strange Sports Stories by Infantino	2.85	8.50	20.00
50-The Green Arrow & Manhunter From Mars (10-11/63); team-ups			
begin	11.00	32.00	75.00
51-Aquaman & Hawkman (12-1/63-64); pre-dates Hawkman #1			
	3.15	9.50	22.00
52-Sgt. Rock, Haunted Tank, Johnny Cloud, & Mlle. Marie team-up			
for 1st time by Kubert (c/a)	3.15	9.50	22.00
53-Atom & The Flash by Toth	3.60	11.00	25.00
54-Kid Flash, Robin & Aqualad; 1st app./origin Teen Titans (6-7/64)			
	22.00	65.00	150.00
55-Metal Men & The Atom	2.15	6.50	15.00
56-The Flash & Manhunter From Mars	2.15	6.50	15.00
57-Origin & 1st app. Metamorpho (12-1/64-65)			
	11.50	34.00	80.00
58-Metamorpho by Fradon	5.00	15.00	35.00
59-Batman & Green Lantern; 1st Batman team-up in Brave and the			
Bold	7.00	21.00	50.00
60-Teen Titans (2nd app.)-1st app. new Wonder Girl (Donna Troy),			
who joins Titans (6-7/65)	8.00	24.00	55.00
61,62-Origin Starman & Black Canary by Anderson. 62-1st S.A. app.			
Wildcat (10-11/65); Huntress app.	4.30	13.00	30.00
63-Supergirl & Wonder Woman	1.30	4.00	9.00
64-Batman Versus Eclipso (see H.O.S. #61)			
	5.00	15.00	35.00
65-Flash & Doom Patrol	1.30	4.00	9.00
66-Metamorpho & Metal Men	1.30	4.00	9.00
67-Batman & The Flash by Infantino; Batman team-ups begin, end			
#200	3.15	9.50	22.00
68-Batman/Joker/Riddler/Penguin-c/story	5.70	17.00	40.00
69-78: Batman team-ups. 78-Batgirl app.	2.40	7.25	17.00
79-Batman-Deadman by Neal Adams	3.50	10.50	24.00
80-Batman-Creeper; N. Adams-a	3.15	9.50	22.00
81-Batman-Flash; N. Adams-a	3.15	9.50	22.00
82-Batman-Aquaman; N. Adams-a; origin Ocean Master retold			
	3.15	9.50	22.00
83-Batman-Teen Titans; N. Adams-a	4.70	14.00	33.00
84-Batman(GA)-Sgt. Rock; N. Adams-a	3.15	9.50	22.00

	Good	Fine	N-Mint
85-Batman-Green Arrow; 1st new costume for Green Arrow by Neal Adams	3.15	9.50	22.00
86-Batman-Deadman; N. Adams-a	3.15	9.50	22.00
87-92: Batman team-ups	1.50	4.50	9.00
93-Batman-House of Mystery; N. Adams-a	2.85	8.50	20.00
94-Batman-Teen Titans	1.50	4.50	9.00
95-99: 97-Origin Deadman-r	1.15	3.50	7.00
100-(25 cents, 52 pgs.)-Batman-Green Lantern-Green Arrow-Black Canary-Robin; Deadman-r by N. Adams	2.85	8.50	20.00
101-Batman-Metamorpho; Kubert Viking Prince	.70	2.00	4.00
102-Batman-Teen Titans; N. Adams-a(p)	1.15	3.50	7.00
103-110: Batman team-ups	.70	2.00	4.00
111-Batman/Joker-c/story	1.70	5.00	10.00
112-117: All 100 pgs.; Batman team-ups. 113-Reprints Brave and the Bold #34	1.00	3.00	6.00
118-Batman/Wildcat/Joker-c/story	1.50	4.50	9.00
119-128,131-140: Batman team-ups	.50	1.50	3.00
129,130-Batman/Joker-c/stories	1.70	5.00	10.00
141-Batman vs. Joker-c/story	1.50	4.50	9.00
142-190,192-199: 143,144-(44 pgs.). 148-XMas-c. 149-Batman-Teen Titans. 150-Anniversary issue; Superman. 179-LSH. 182-Batman/Robin. 181-Hawk & Dove. 183-Riddler. 187-Metal Men. 196-Origin Ragman retold. 197-Earth II Batman & Catwoman marry	.50	1.50	3.00
191-Batman/Joker-c/story	1.15	3.50	7.00
200-Double-sized (64 pgs.); printed on Mando paper; Earth One & Earth Two Batman team-up; Intro/1st app. Batman & The Outsiders	1.35	4.00	8.00

BROTHER POWER, THE GEEK (See Saga of Swamp Thing
    Annual)
Sept-Oct, 1968-No. 2, Nov-Dec, 1968
National Periodical Publications

| 1-Origin; Simon-c(i?) | 3.60 | 11.00 | 25.00 |
| 2 | 2.65 | 8.00 | 18.00 |

BROTHERS OF THE SPEAR
June, 1972-No. 17, Feb, 1976; No. 18, May, 1982
Gold Key/Whitman No. 18 on

	Good	Fine	N-Mint
1	1.50	4.50	10.00
2-Painted-c begin, end #17	.85	2.60	6.00
3-10	.70	2.00	4.00
11-17: 13-17-Spiegle-a	.35	1.00	2.00
18-Manning-r/#2; Leopard Girl-r		.50	1.00

BUCK ROGERS (Also see Famous Funnies)
Winter, 1940-41-No. 6, Sept, 1943
Famous Funnies

1-Sunday strip reprints by Rick Yager; begins with strip #190;			
Calkins-c	133.00	400.00	925.00
2 (7/41)-Calkins-c	80.00	240.00	550.00
3 (12/41), 4 (7/42)	65.00	195.00	450.00
5-Story continues with Famous Funnies No. 80; ½ Buck Rogers, ½			
Sky Roads	57.00	170.00	400.00
6-Reprints of 1939 dailies; contains B.R. story "Crater of Doom"			
(2 pgs.) by Calkins not reprinted from Famous Funnies			
	57.00	170.00	400.00

BUCK ROGERS
No. 100, Jan, 1951-No. 9, May-June, 1951
Toby Press

100(#7)	18.00	54.00	125.00
101(#8), 9-All Anderson-a('47-'49-r/dailies)			
	13.50	41.00	95.00

BUCK ROGERS (...in the 25th Century No. 5 on) (TV)
Oct, 1964; No. 2, July, 1979-No. 16, May, 1982 (No #10)
Gold Key/Whitman No. 7 on

1(10128-410)-Painted-c; 12 cents	3.15	9.50	22.00
2(8/79)-Movie adaptation	.35	1.00	2.00
3-9,11-16: 3,4-Movie adaptation; 5-new stories			
	.25	.75	1.50

BULLETMAN (See Master Comics & Nickel Comics)
Sum, 1941-#12, 2/12/43; #14, Spr, 1946-#16, Fall, 1946 (nn 13)
Fawcett Publications

1	186.00	465.00	1100.00
2	82.00	245.00	575.00
3	57.00	170.00	400.00
4,5	50.00	150.00	350.00

	Good	**Fine**	**N-Mint**
6-10: 7-Ghost Stories as told by the night watchman of the cemetery			
begins; Eisnerish-a	43.00	130.00	300.00
11,12,14-16 (nn 13)	35.00	105.00	250.00

BULLWINKLE (TV) (...and Rocky No. 20 on) (Jay Ward)
3-5/62-#11, 4/74; #12, 6/76-#19, 3/78; #20, 4/79-#25, 2/80
Dell/Gold Key

4-Color 1270 (3-5/62)	11.00	32.00	75.00
01-090-209 (Dell, 7-9/62)	11.00	32.00	75.00
1(11/62, Gold Key)	8.50	25.50	60.00
2(2/63)	6.50	19.00	45.00
3(4/72)-11(4/74-Gold Key)	2.15	6.50	15.00
12(6/76)-Reprints	1.15	3.50	7.00
13(9/76), 14-New stories	1.30	4.00	9.00
15-25	1.00	3.00	6.00
Mother Moose Nursery Poems 01-530-207 (5-7/62-Dell)			
	8.00	24.00	55.00

BULLWINKLE (...& Rocky No. 2 on)(TV)
July, 1970-No. 7, July, 1971
Charlton Comics

1	2.65	8.00	18.00
2-7	1.70	5.00	12.00

CAGE (Also see Hero For Hire, Power Man & The Punisher)
Apr, 1992-Present ($1.25, color)
Marvel Comics

	Good	Fine	N-Mint
1-($1.50)-Extra color on-c	.25	.75	1.50
2-10: 3-Punisher-c/cameo. 4-Punisher app.		.65	1.30

CAPTAIN ACTION
Oct-Nov, 1968-No. 5, June-July, 1969 (Based on Ideal toy)
National Periodical Publications

1-Origin; Wood-a; Superman-c app.	4.70	14.00	33.00
2,3,5-Kane/Wood-a	2.85	8.50	20.00
4	2.15	6.50	15.00
...& Action Boy('67)-Ideal Toy Co. giveaway			
	5.15	15.50	36.00

CAPTAIN AERO COMICS (Samson No. 1-6)
V1#7(#1), Dec, 1941-V2#4(#10), Jan, 1943; V3#9(#11), Sept,
    1943-V4#3 (#17), Oct, 1944; #21, Dec, 1944-#26, Aug, 1946 (No
    #18-20)
Holyoke Publishing Co.

V1#7(#1)-Flag-Man & Solar, Master of Magic, Captain Aero, Cap Stone, Adventurer begin	57.00	170.00	400.00
8(#2)-Pals of Freedom app.	33.00	100.00	235.00
9(#3)-Alias X begins; Pals of Freedom app.	33.00	100.00	235.00
10(#4)-Origin The Gargoyle; Kubert-a	33.00	100.00	235.00
11,12(#5,6)-Kubert-a; Miss Victory in #6	27.00	80.00	190.00
V2#1,2(#7,8): 8-Origin The Red Cross; Miss Victory app.	16.00	48.00	110.00
3(#9)-Miss Victory app.	11.50	34.00	80.00
4(#10)-Miss Victory app.	9.30	28.00	65.00
V3#9-V3#13(#11-15): 11,15-Miss Victory app.	7.00	21.00	50.00
V4#2, V4#3(#16,17)	6.00	18.00	42.00
21-24,26-L. B. Cole covers. 22-Intro/origin Mighty Mite	8.50	25.50	60.00
25-L. B. Cole S/F-c	11.00	32.00	75.00

CAPTAIN AMERICA (Formerly Tales of Suspense #1-99; Captain America and the Falcon #134-223 on-c only; see Advs. of..., Avengers #4, The Invaders, Marvel Double Feature, Marvel Super-Action, Marvel Super Heroes)
No. 100, April, 1968-Present
Marvel Comics Group

	Good	Fine	N-Mint
100-Story continued from Tales of Suspense #99; flashback on Cap's revival with Avengers & Sub-Mariner	38.00	115.00	265.00
101	8.50	25.50	60.00
102-108	5.00	15.00	35.00
109-Origin Capt. America	6.50	19.00	45.00
110,111,113-Steranko-c/a. 110-Rick becomes Cap's partner; Hulk x-over; 1st app. Viper. 111-Death of Steve Rogers. 113-Cap's funeral	7.00	21.00	50.00
112-Origin retold	2.85	8.50	20.00
114-116,118-120: 115-Last 12 cent issue	2.15	6.50	15.00
117-1st app. The Falcon (9/69)	3.60	11.00	25.00
121-140: 121-Retells origin. 133-The Falcon becomes Cap's partner; origin Modok. 137,138-Spider-Man x-over. 140-Origin Grey Gargoyle retold	1.30	4.00	9.00
141-153,155-171,176-179: 142-Last 15 cent issue. 143-(52 pgs.). 155-Origin; redrawn with Falcon added. 160-1st app. Solarr. 164-1st app. Nightshade. 176- End of Capt. America	1.00	3.00	6.00
154-1st full app. Jack Monroe who becomes Nomad	1.35	4.00	8.00
172-175-X-Men x-over	1.60	4.80	11.00
180,181,183: 180-Intro/origin of Nomad; Steve Rogers becomes Nomad. 181-Intro & origin of new Capt. America. 183-Death of New Cap; Nomad becomes Cap	.85	2.50	5.00
182,184-200(8/76): 186-True origin The Falcon	.70	2.00	4.00
201-240,242-246: 217-1st app. Marvel Man (later Quasar). 229-Marvel Man app. 233-Death of Sharon Carter. 234,235-Daredevil x-over; 235(7/79)-Miller involved? 244,245-Miller-c	.50	1.50	3.00
241-Punisher app.; Miller-c	7.85	23.50	55.00
247-255-Byrne-a. 255-Origin; Miller-c	.60	1.75	3.50

256-281,284,285,289-322,324-326,329-331: 264-X-Men cameo in flashback. 265,266-Nick Fury & Spider-Man app. 267-1st app. Everyman. 269-1st Team America. 281-'50s Bucky returns. 284-

Captain America #332, © Marvel Comics

	Good	Fine	N-Mint
Patriot (Jack Mace) app. 285-Death of Patriot. 298-Origin Red Skull	.35	1.00	2.00
282-Bucky becomes new Nomad (Jack Monroe) (6/83)	1.35	4.00	8.00
282-Silver ink 2nd printing (1992, $1.75)-Has orig. date	.30	.90	1.80
283-2nd app. Nomad	.70	2.00	4.00
286-288-Deathlok app.	.50	1.50	3.00
323-1st app. new Super Patriot (see Nick Fury)	.70	2.00	4.00
327-Captain America battles Super Patriot	.50	1.50	3.00
328-Origin & 1st app. D-Man	.50	1.50	3.00
332-Old Cap resigns	1.70	5.00	10.00
333-Intro new Captain (Super Patriot)	1.15	3.50	7.00
334	.90	2.75	5.50
335-340: 339-Fall of the Mutants tie-in	.85	2.50	5.00
341-343,345-349	.30	.85	1.70
344-Double size, $1.50	.35	1.10	2.20
350-($1.75, 68 pgs.)-Return of Steve Rogers (original Cap) to original costume	.75	2.25	4.50
351-354: 351-Nick Fury app. 354-1st app. U.S. Agent (see Avengers West Coast)	.30	.85	1.70

355-382,384-396: 373-Bullseye app. 375-Daredevil app. 386-U.S. Agent app. 387-389-Red Skull back-up stories. 396,397-1st app.

	Good	Fine	N-Mint
all new Jack O'Lantern. 398-Galactic Storm x-overs begin	.25	.75	1.50
383-($2.00, 68 pgs.)-50th anniversary issue; Red Skull story; Jim Lee-c(i)	.85	2.50	5.00
397-399,401-410: 398-Galactic Storm x-overs begin	.65	1.30	
400-(2.25, 84 pgs.)-Flip book format w/double gatefold-c & cover pin-ups; reprints Avengers #4 w/cover	.60	1.75	3.50
Special 1(1/71)-Origin retold	2.15	6.50	15.00
Special 2(1/72)-Colan-r/Not Brand Echh; all-r	1.70	5.00	12.00
Annual 3-7: 3(1976). 4(1977, 52 pgs.)-Kirby-c/a(new); Magneto app. 5('81, 52 pgs.). 6('82, 52 pgs.). 7('83, 52 pgs.)	.40	1.25	2.50
Annual 8(9/86)-Wolverine featured	6.50	19.00	45.00
Annual 9(1990, $2.00, 68 pgs.)-Nomad back-up	.85	2.50	5.00
Annual 10('91, $2.00, 68 pgs.)-Origin retold(2 pg.)	.35	1.00	2.00
Annual 11('92, $2.25, 68 pgs.)	.40	1.15	2.30

CAPTAIN AMERICA COMICS
Mar, 1941-No. 75, Jan, 1950; No. 76, 5/54-No. 78, 9/54
　　(No. 74 & 75 titled Capt. America's Weird Tales)
Timely/Marvel Comics (TCI 1-20/CmPS 21-68/MjMC 69-75/Atlas
Comics (PrPl 76-78)

	Good	Fine	VF-NM
1-Origin & 1st app. Captain America & Bucky by S&K; Hurricane, Tuk the Caveboy begin by S&K; Red Skull app. Hitler-c	2,500.00	6,250.00	15,000.00

	Good	Fine	N-Mint
2-S&K Hurricane; Tuk by Avison (Kirby splash); classic Hitler-c	670.00	1675.00	4000.00
3-Red Skull app; Stan Lee's 1st text	465.00	1165.00	2800.00
4-1st full page panel in comics	315.00	790.00	1900.00
5	290.00	725.00	1750.00
6-Origin Father Time; Tuk the Caveboy ends	240.00	600.00	1450.00
7-Red Skull app.; classic-c	240.00	600.00	1450.00
8-10-Last S&K issue, (S&K centerfold #6-10)	200.00	500.00	1200.00

	Good	Fine	N-Mint
11-Last Hurricane, Headline Hunter; Al Avison Captain America begins, ends #20	158.00	395.00	950.00
12-The Imp begins, ends #16; Last Father Time	152.00	380.00	915.00
13-Origin The Secret Stamp; classic-c	165.00	410.00	1000.00
14,15	152.00	380.00	915.00
16-Red Skull unmasks Cap	175.00	438.00	1050.00
17-The Fighting Fool only app.	138.00	345.00	825.00
18,19-Human Torch begins #19	120.00	300.00	725.00
20-Sub-Mariner app.; no H. Torch	120.00	300.00	725.00
21-25: 25-Cap drinks liquid opium	110.00	275.00	650.00
26-30,36: 27-Last Secret Stamp; last 68 pg. issue? 28-60 pg. issues begin? 36-Hitler-c	100.00	250.00	600.00
31-35,38-40	88.00	220.00	525.00
37-Red Skull app.	95.00	240.00	575.00
41-47: 41-Last Jap War-c. 46-German Holocaust-c. 47-Last German War-c	75.00	188.00	450.00
48-58,60	70.00	175.00	425.00
59-Origin retold	135.00	335.00	800.00
61-Red Skull-c/story	100.00	250.00	600.00
62,64,65: 65-"Hey Look" by Kurtzman	70.00	175.00	425.00
63-Intro/origin Asbestos Lady	75.00	188.00	450.00
66-Bucky is shot; Golden Girl teams up with Captain America & learns his i.d; origin Golden Girl	88.00	220.00	525.00
67-Captain America/Golden Girl team-up; Mxyztplk swipe; last Toro in Human Torch	70.00	175.00	425.00
68,70-Sub-Mariner/Namora, and Captain America/Golden Girl team-up in each. 70-Science fiction-c/story	70.00	175.00	425.00
69,71-73: 69-Human Torch/Sun Girl team-up. 71-Anti Wertham editorial; The Witness, Bucky app.	70.00	175.00	425.00
74-(Scarce)(1949)-Titled "C.A.'s Weird Tales;" Red Skull app.	117.00	290.00	700.00
75(2/50)-Titled "C.A.'s Weird Tales;" no C.A. app.; horror cover/ stories	70.00	175.00	425.00
76-78(1954): Human Torch/Toro stories	48.00	120.00	285.00

CAPTAIN AMERICA SPECIAL EDITION
Feb, 1984-No. 2, Mar, 1984 ($2.00, Baxter paper)
Marvel Comics Group

1,2-Steranko-c/a(r)	.40	1.25	2.50

CAPTAIN ATOM
V2#78, Dec, 1965-V2#89, Dec, 1967
Charlton Comics

	Good	Fine	N-Mint
78-Origin retold; Bache-a (3 pgs.)	6.30	19.00	44.00
79-82: 82-Intro. Nightshade (9/66)	4.00	12.00	28.00
83-89: Ted Kord Blue Beetle in all. 84-1st app. new Captain Atom;			
87-89-Nightshade by Aparo in all	3.15	9.50	22.00

CAPTAIN ATOM (Also see Crisis On Infinite Earths)
March, 1987-No. 57, Sept, 1991 (Direct sale only #35 on)
DC Comics

	Good	Fine	N-Mint
1-(44 pgs.)-Origin/1st app. with new costume			
	.35	1.00	2.00
2-49: 5-Firestorm x-over. 6-Intro. new Dr. Spectro. 11-Millennium			
tie-in. 14-Nightshade app. 16-Justice League app. 17-$1.00-c			
begins; Swamp Thing app. 20-Blue Beetle x-over	.60	1.20	
50-($2.00, 52 pgs.)	.35	1.00	2.00
51-57: 57-War of the Gods x-over		.50	1.00
Annual 1 (1988, $1.25)-Intro Major Force	.25	.75	1.50
Annual 2 (1988, $1.50)	.25	.75	1.50

CAPTAIN BATTLE (Boy Comics #3 on) (See Silver Streak Comics)
Summer, 1941-No. 2, Fall, 1941
New Friday Publ./Comic House

	Good	Fine	N-Mint
1-Origin Blackout by Rico; Captain Battle begins			
	60.00	180.00	415.00
2	40.00	120.00	275.00

CAPTAIN BATTLE (2nd Series)
No. 3, Wint, 1942-43-No. 5, Sum, 1943 (#3: 52 pgs., nd)(#5: 68 pgs.)
Magazine Press/Picture Scoop No. 5

	Good	Fine	N-Mint
3-Origin Silver Streak-r/SS#3; Origin Lance Hale-r/Silver Streak;			
Simon-a(r)	35.00	105.00	250.00
4,5: 5-Origin Blackout retold	25.00	75.00	175.00

CAPTAIN BATTLE, JR.
Fall, 1943-No. 2, Winter, 1943-44
Comic House (Lev Gleason)

	Good	Fine	N-Mint
1-The Claw vs. The Ghost	48.00	145.00	335.00
2-Wolverton's Scoop Scuttle; Don Rico-c/a; The Green Claw story			
	40.00	120.00	275.00

CAPTAIN MARVEL (See Life Of..., Marvel Spotlight V2#1 &
   Marvel Super-Heroes #12)
May, 1968-No. 19, Dec, 1969; No. 20, June, 1970-No. 21, Aug, 1970;
   No. 22, Sept, 1972-No. 62, May, 1979
Marvel Comics Group

	Good	Fine	N-Mint
1	12.00	36.00	85.00
2	3.60	11.00	25.00
3-5: 4-Captain Marvel battles Sub-Mariner	2.15	6.50	15.00
6-11: 11-Smith/Trimpe-c; Death of Una	1.50	4.50	10.00
12-24: 14-Capt. Marvel vs. Iron Man; last 12 cent issue. 17-New costume. 21-Capt. Marvel battles Hulk; last 15 cent issue	1.35	4.00	8.00
25-Starlin-c/a begins; Starlin's 1st Thanos saga begins (3/73), ends #34; Thanos cameo (5 panels)	3.60	11.00	25.00
26-2nd full app. Thanos (see Iron Man #55); 1st Thanos-c	4.30	13.00	30.00
27,28-3rd & 4th app. Thanos	2.85	8.50	20.00
29,30-Thanos cameos. 29-C.M. gains more powers	1.30	4.00	9.00
31,32: Thanos app. 31-Last 20 cent. 32-Thanos-c	1.70	5.00	12.00
33-Thanos-c & app.; Capt. Marvel battles Thanos; 1st origin Thanos	3.60	11.00	25.00
34-1st app. Nitro; C.M. contracts cancer which eventually kills him; last Starlin-c/a & last 20 cent issue	1.15	3.50	7.00
35,37-56,58-62: 39-Origin Watcher. 41,43-Wrightson part inks; #43-c(i). 49-Starlin & Weiss-p assists	.25	.75	1.50
36-Reprints origin/1st app. Capt. Marvel from Marvel Super-Heroes #12; Starlin-a (3 pgs.)	.85	2.50	5.00
57-Thanos appears in flashback	1.00	3.00	6.00

CAPTAIN MARVEL ADVENTURES (See America's Greatest,
   Marvel Family, Master Comics #21, Special Edition Comics &
   Whiz Comics) 1941 (March)-No. 150, Nov, 1953 (#1 on stands
   1/16/41)
Fawcett Publications

	Good	Fine	VF-NM
nn(#1)-Captain Marvel & Sivana by Jack Kirby. The cover was printed on unstable paper stock and is rarely found in Fine or Mint condition; blank inside-c	1380.00	3450.00	8300.00

	Good	Fine	N-Mint
2-(Advertised as #3, which was counting Special Edition Comics as the real #1); Tuska-a	215.00	645.00	1500.00
3-Metallic silver-c	130.00	390.00	900.00
4-Three Lt. Marvels app.	93.00	280.00	650.00
5	70.00	210.00	500.00
6-10	55.00	165.00	375.00
11-15: 13-Two-pg. Capt. Marvel pin-up. 15-Comic cards on back-c begin, end #26	43.00	130.00	300.00
16,17: 17-Painted-c	40.00	120.00	275.00
18-Origin & 1st app. Mary Marvel & Marvel Family (12/11/42); painted-c; Mary Marvel by Marcus Swayze	57.00	170.00	400.00
19-Mary Marvel x-over; Christmas-c	35.00	105.00	250.00
20,21-With miniature comic attached to cover	120.00	480.00	1200.00
20,21-Without miniature comic	33.00	100.00	225.00
22-Mr. Mind serial begins	50.00	150.00	350.00
23-25	33.00	100.00	225.00
26-30: 26-Flag-c	25.00	75.00	175.00
31-35: 35-Origin Radar	22.00	65.00	150.00
36-40: 37-Mary Marvel x-over	20.00	60.00	140.00
41-46: 42-Christmas-c. 43-Capt. Marvel 1st meets Uncle Marvel; Mary Batson cameo. 46-Mr. Mind serial ends	17.00	51.00	120.00
47-50	14.00	43.00	100.00
51-53,55-60: 52-Origin & 1st app. Sivana Jr.; Capt. Marvel Jr. x-over	14.00	35.00	85.00
54-Special oversize 68 pg. issue	15.00	38.00	90.00
61-The Cult of the Curse serial begins	14.00	43.00	100.00
62-66-Serial ends; Mary Marvel x-over in #65. 66-Atomic War-c	13.50	34.00	80.00
67-77,79: 69-Billy Batson's Christmas; Uncle Marvel, Mary Marvel, Capt. Marvel Jr. x-over. 71-Three Lt. Marvels app. 79-Origin Mr. Tawny	13.00	32.00	75.00
78-Origin Mr. Atom	14.00	35.00	85.00
80-Origin Capt. Marvel retold	18.00	54.00	125.00
81-84,86-90: 81,90-Mr. Atom app. 82-Infinity-c. 86-Mr. Tawny app.	12.00	30.00	70.00
85-Freedom Train issue	14.00	35.00	85.00
91-99: 96-Mr. Tawny app.	11.00	27.00	65.00
100-Origin retold	18.00	54.00	125.00
101-120: 116-Flying Saucer issue (1/51)	9.00	23.00	55.00

	Good	Fine	N-Mint
121-Origin retold	13.00	32.00	75.00

122-149: 138-Flying Saucer issue (11/52). 141-Pre-code horror story
  "The Hideous Head-Hunter." 142-Used in **POP**, pgs. 92,96

	Good	Fine	N-Mint
	9.00	23.00	55.00
150-(Low distribution)	15.00	38.00	90.00

CAPTAIN MARVEL, JR. (See Marvel Family, Master Comics &
  Whiz)
Nov, 1942-No. 119, June, 1953 (nn 34)
Fawcett Publications

1-Origin Capt. Marvel Jr. retold (Whiz No. 25); Capt. Nazi app.

	Good	Fine	N-Mint
	157.00	470.00	1100.00
2-Vs. Capt. Nazi; origin Capt. Nippon	70.00	210.00	500.00
3,4	50.00	150.00	350.00
5-Vs. Capt. Nazi	43.00	130.00	300.00
6-10: 8-Vs. Capt. Nazi. 9-Flag-c. 10-Hitler-c			
	35.00	105.00	250.00
11,12,15-Capt. Nazi app.	29.00	85.00	200.00

13,14,16-20: 13-Hitler-c. 14-X-Mas-c. 16-Capt. Marvel & Sivana
  x-over. 19-Capt. Nazi & Capt. Nippon app.

	Good	Fine	N-Mint
	24.00	72.00	165.00
21-30: 25-Flag-c	17.00	42.00	100.00
31-33,36-40: 37-Infinity-c	12.00	30.00	70.00

35-#34 on inside; cover shows origin of Sivana Jr. which is not on
  inside. Evidently the cover to #35 was printed out of sequence and
  bound with contents to #34

	12.00	30.00	70.00
41-50	7.50	19.00	45.00
51-70: 53-Atomic Bomb-c/story	6.00	15.00	45.00
71-99,101-104: 104-Used in **POP**, pg. 89	5.00	13.00	30.00
100	6.00	15.00	35.00
105-114,116-119: 119-Electric chair-c	5.00	13.00	30.00

115-Injury to eye-c; Eyeball story w/injury-to-eye panels

	7.50	19.00	45.00

CAPTAIN MIDNIGHT (Radio, films, TV) (See The Funnies, Popular
  Comics) Sept, 1942-No. 67, Fall, 1948 (#1-14: 68 pgs.)
Fawcett Publications

1-Origin Captain Midnight; Captain Marvel cameo on cover

	Good	Fine	N-Mint
	134.00	335.00	800.00
2	63.00	158.00	375.00
3-5	46.00	115.00	275.00
6-10: 9-Raboy-c. 10-Raboy Flag-c	34.00	85.00	200.00

	Good	Fine	N-Mint
11-20: 11,17-Raboy-c	22.00	55.00	135.00
21-30	16.00	40.00	100.00
31-40	13.00	32.00	75.00
41-59,61-67: 54-Sci/fi theme begins?	8.00	24.00	55.00
60-Flying Saucer issue (2/48)-3rd of this theme; see Shadow Comics			
V7#10 & Boy Commandos #26	12.00	36.00	85.00

CAPT. SAVAGE AND HIS LEATHERNECK RAIDERS
(See Sgt. Fury #10)
Jan, 1968-No. 19, Mar, 1970
Marvel Comics Group (Animated Timely Features)

	Good	Fine	N-Mint
1-Sgt. Fury & Howlers cameo	1.15	3.50	8.00
2-10: 2-Origin Hydra. 1-5,7-Ayers/Shores-a			
	.70	2.00	4.00
11-19	.50	1.50	3.00

CAPT. STORM (Also see G. I. Combat #138)
May-June, 1964-No. 18, Mar-Apr, 1967
National Periodical Publications

	Good	Fine	N-Mint
1-Origin	1.70	5.00	12.00
2-18: 3,6,13-Kubert-a. 12-Kubert-c	1.00	3.00	7.00

CAT, THE
Nov, 1972-No. 4, June, 1973
Marvel Comics Group

	Good	Fine	N-Mint
1-Origin & 1st app. The Cat (who later becomes Tigra); Mooney-a(i); Wood-c(i)/a(i)	1.50	4.50	10.00
2,3: 2-Mooney-a(i). 3-Everett inks	1.00	3.00	7.00
4-Starlin/Weiss-a(p)	1.00	3.00	7.00

CATMAN COMICS (Crash No. 1-5)
5/41-No. 17, 1/43; No. 18, 7/43-No. 22, 12/43; No. 23, 3/44-No. 26,
11/44; No. 27, 4/45-No. 30, 12/45; No. 31, 6/46-No. 32, 8/46
Holyoke Publishing Co./Continental Magazines V2#12, 7/44 on

	Good	Fine	N-Mint
1(V1#6)-Origin The Deacon & Sidekick Mickey, Dr. Diamond & Rag-Man; The Black Widow app.; The Catman by Chas. Quinlan & Blaze Baylor begin	80.00	240.00	550.00
2(V1#7)	40.00	120.00	275.00
3(V1#8), 4(V1#9): 3-The Pied Piper begins			
	29.00	85.00	200.00
5(V2#10)-Origin Kitten; The Hood begins (c-redated), 6,7			

	Good	Fine	N-Mint
(V2#11,12)	24.00	72.00	165.00
8(V2#13,3/42)-Origin Little Leaders; Volton by Kubert begins (his 1st comic book work)	33.00	100.00	225.00
9,10(V2#14,15): 10-Origin Blackout; Phantom Falcon begins	22.00	65.00	150.00
11(V3#1)-Kubert-a	22.00	65.00	150.00
12(V3#2)-15, 17, 18(V3#8, 7/43)	18.00	45.00	110.00
16 (V3#5)-Hitler, Tojo, Mussolini, Stalin-c	23.00	56.00	135.00
19 (V2#6)-Hitler, Tojo, Mussolini-c	23.00	56.00	135.00
20(V2#7)-23(V2#10, 3/44)	18.00	45.00	110.00
nn(V3#13, 5/44)-Rico-a; Schomburg bondage-c	17.00	42.00	100.00
nn(V2#12, 7/44)	17.00	42.00	100.00
nn(V3#1, 9/44)-Origin The Golden Archer; Leatherface app.	17.00	42.00	100.00
nn(V3#2, 11/44)-L. B. Cole-c	20.00	60.00	140.00
27-Origin Kitten retold; L. B. Cole Flag-c	22.00	65.00	150.00
28-Catman learns Kitten's I.D.; Dr. Macabre, Deacon app.; L. B. Cole-c/a	24.00	72.00	165.00
29-32-L. B. Cole-c; bondage-#30	20.00	60.00	140.00

CATWOMAN (Also see Action Comics Weekly #611-614 & Batman)
Feb, 1989-No. 4, May, 1989 ($1.50, mini-series, mature readers)
DC Comics

Catwoman #3, © DC Comics

	Good	Fine	N-Mint
1	2.50	7.50	15.00
2	1.50	4.50	9.00
3,4: 3-Batman cameo. 4-Batman app.	1.00	3.00	6.00

CEREBUS THE AARDVARK
Dec, 1977-Present ($1.70-$2.00, B&W)
Aardvark-Vanaheim

1-2000 print run; most copies poorly printed			
	30.00	90.00	180.00

NOTE: *There is a counterfeit version known to exist. It can be distinguished from the original in the following ways: inside cover is glossy instead of flat, black background on the front cover is blotted or spotty.*

	Good	Fine	N-Mint
2-Dave Sim art in all	13.00	40.00	80.00
3-Origin Red Sophia	12.00	35.00	70.00
4-Origin Elrod the Albino	7.50	22.50	45.00
5,6	6.00	18.00	36.00
7-10	3.85	11.50	23.00
11,12: 11-Origin Capt. Coachroach	4.20	12.50	25.00
13-15: 14-Origin Lord Julius	2.30	7.00	14.00
16-20	1.50	4.50	9.00
21-Scarcer	7.50	22.50	45.00
22-Low distribution; no cover price	2.30	7.00	14.00
23-30: 26-High Society storyline begins	1.15	3.50	7.00
31-Origin Moonroach	1.50	4.50	9.00
32-40	.75	2.25	4.50
41-50,52: 52-Cutey Bunny app.	.60	1.80	3.60
51-Not reprinted; Cutey Bunny app.	2.30	7.00	14.00
53-Intro. Wolveroach (cameo)	.90	2.70	5.40
54-Wolveroach 1st full story	1.20	3.60	7.20
55,56-Wolveroach app.	.90	2.70	5.40
57-60	.55	1.60	3.20
61,62: Flaming Carrot app.	.75	2.25	4.50
63-68	.60	1.80	3.60
69-75	.50	1.45	2.90
76-79	.45	1.35	2.70
80-160: 104-Flaming Carrot app. 112/113-Double issue. 137-Begin $2.25-c; 151,152-2nd printings exist	.40	1.15	2.30

CHALLENGERS OF THE UNKNOWN (See Showcase #6, 7, 11, 12)
    4-5/58-No. 77, 12-1/70-71; No. 78, 2/73-No. 80, 6-7/73; No. 81, 6-7/77-No. 87, 6-7/78
National Periodical Publications/DC Comics

	Good	Fine	N-Mint
Showcase #6 (1-2/57)-Origin & 1st app. Challengers of the Unknown by Kirby (1st DC S.A. super-hero team)			
	150.00	450.00	1050.00
Showcase #7 (3-4/57)-2nd app. by Kirby	82.00	246.00	575.00
Showcase #11,12 (11-12/57, 1-2/58)-3rd & 4th app. Challengers by Kirby (2nd tryout series)	72.00	216.00	500.00
1-(4-5/58)-Kirby/Stein-a(2)	115.00	345.00	800.00
2-Kirby/Stein-a(2)	57.00	170.00	400.00
3-Kirby/Stein-a(2)	47.00	140.00	330.00
4-8-Kirby/Wood-a plus c-#8	40.00	120.00	275.00
9,10	20.00	60.00	140.00
11-15: 14-Origin Multi-Man	13.00	40.00	88.00
16-22: 18-Intro. Cosmo, the Challengers Spacepet. 22-Last 10 cent issue	9.30	28.00	66.00
23-30	5.00	15.00	35.00
31-Retells origin of the Challengers	5.70	17.00	40.00
32-40	2.65	8.00	18.00
41-60: 43-New look begins. 48-Doom Patrol app. 49-Intro. Challenger Corps. 51-Sea Devils app. 55-Death of Red Ryan. 60-Red Ryan returns	1.60	4.80	11.00
61-73,75-77: 64,65-Kirby origin-r, parts 1 & 2. 66-New logo. 68-Last 12 cent issue. 69-1st app. Corinna	.70	2.00	4.00
74-Deadman by Tuska/N. Adams	1.60	4.80	11.00
78-87: 82-Swamp Thing begins	.50	1.50	3.00

CHALLENGERS OF THE UNKNOWN (2nd series)
Mar, 1991-No. 8, Oct, 1991 ($1.75, color, mini-series)
DC Comics

1-Bolland-c	.40	1.25	2.50
2-8: 6-Kane-c(p). 7-Steranko-c swipe by Arthur Adams			
	.30	.90	1.80

CHAMBER OF DARKNESS (Monsters on the Prowl #9 on)
Oct, 1969-No. 8, Dec, 1970
Marvel Comics Group

1-Buscema-a(p)	4.30	13.00	30.00
2-Neal Adams scripts	1.50	4.50	10.00

	Good	Fine	N-Mint
3-Smith, Buscema-a	1.60	4.80	11.00
4-A Conanesque tryout by Smith (4/70); reprinted in Conan #16;			
Marie Severin/Everett-c	5.00	15.00	35.00
5,6,8: 5-H.P. Lovecraft adaptation	.85	2.50	5.00
7-Wrightson-c/a, 7pgs. (his 1st work at Marvel); Wrightson draws			
himself in 1st & last panels; Kirby/Ditko-r			
	2.15	6.50	15.00
1-(1/72; 25 cent Special)	1.15	3.50	7.00

CHAMPIONS, THE
October, 1975-No. 17, Jan, 1978
Marvel Comics Group

1-Origin & 1st app. The Champions (The Angel, Black Widow,			
Ghost Rider, Hercules, Ice Man); Venus x-over			
	1.70	5.00	12.00
2-10,16: 2,3-Venus x-over	1.15	3.50	8.00
11-15,17-Byrne-a	1.30	4.00	9.00

CHECKMATE (See Action Comics #598)
April, 1988-No. 33, Jan, 1991 ($1.25)
DC Comics

1-12		.65	1.30
13-30: $1.50, new format	.25	.75	1.50
31-33 ($2.00-c)	.35	1.00	2.00

CLASSIC X-MEN (Becomes X-Men Classic #46 on)
Sept, 1986-No. 45, Mar, 1990 (#27 on: $1.25)
Marvel Comics Group

1-Begins-r of New X-Men	1.70	5.00	10.00
2-4	1.00	3.00	6.00
5-9	.85	2.50	5.00
10-Sabretooth app.	1.35	4.00	8.00
11-15	.60	1.75	3.50
16,18-20	.50	1.50	3.00
17-Wolverine-c	1.15	3.50	7.00
21-25,27-30: 27-r/X-Men #121	.35	1.00	2.00
26-r/X-Men #120; Wolverine-c/app.	1.15	3.50	7.00
31-38,40-42,44,45: 35-r/X-Men #129	.30	.90	1.80
39-New Jim Lee back-up story (2nd-a on X-Men)			
	1.35	4.00	8.00
43-Byrne-c/a(r); $1.75, double-size	.40	1.25	2.50

CLAW THE UNCONQUERED
5-6/75-No. 9, 9-10/76; No. 10, 4-5/78-No. 12, 8-9/78
National Periodical Publications/DC Comics

	Good	Fine	N-Mint
1	.35	1.00	2.00
2,3: 3-Nudity panel	.25	.75	1.50
4-12: 9-Origin		.60	1.20

CLUE COMICS
Jan, 1943-No. 15(V2#3), May, 1947
Hillman Periodicals

1-Origin The Boy King, Nightmare, Micro-Face, Twilight, & Zippo	60.00	180.00	350.00
2	24.00	73.00	170.00
3-5	20.00	50.00	120.00
6,8,9: 8-Palais-c/a(2)	13.00	32.00	75.00
7-Classic torture-c	18.00	45.00	110.00
10-Origin The Gun Master	14.00	35.00	85.00
11	9.00	23.00	55.00
12-Origin Rackman; McWilliams-a, Guardineer-a(2)	13.00	32.00	75.00
V2#1-Nightmare new origin; Iron Lady app.; Simon & Kirby-a	18.00	45.00	110.00
V2#2-S&K-a(2)-Bondage/torture-c; man attacks & kills people with electric iron. Infantino-a	18.00	45.00	110.00
V2#3-S&K-a(3)	18.00	45.00	110.00

COMEDY COMICS (1st Series) (Formerly Daring Mystery No. 1-8)
No. 9, April, 1942-No. 34, Fall, 1946
Timely Comics (TCI 9,10)

9-(Scarce)-The Fin by Everett, Capt. Dash, Citizen V, & The Silver Scorpion app.; Wolverton-a; 1st app. Comedy Kid; satire on Hitler & Stalin	125.00	315.00	750.00
10-(Scarce)-Origin The Fourth Musketeer, Victory Boys; Monstro, the Mighty app.	75.00	225.00	525.00
11-Vagabond, Stuporman app.	25.00	75.00	175.00
12,13	7.00	21.00	50.00
14-Origin & 1st app. Super Rabbit	27.00	80.00	190.00
15-20	5.70	17.00	40.00
21-32	4.30	13.00	30.00
33-Kurtzman-a (5 pgs.)	5.70	17.00	40.00
34-Intro Margie; Wolverton-a (5 pgs.)	8.50	25.50	60.00

COMEDY COMICS (2nd Series)
May, 1948-No. 10, Jan, 1950
Marvel Comics (ACI)

	Good	Fine	N-Mint
1-Hedy, Tessie, Millie begin; Kurtzman's "Hey Look"(he draws himself)	17.00	51.00	120.00
2	5.70	17.00	40.00
3,4-Kurtzman's "Hey Look"(?&3)	8.00	24.00	55.00
5-10	3.00	9.00	21.00

COMIC CAVALCADE
Winter, 1942-43-No. 63, June-July, 1954
(Contents change with No. 30, Dec-Jan, 1948-49 on)
All-American/National Periodical Publications

	Good	Fine	VF-NM
1-The Flash, Green Lantern, Wonder Woman, Wildcat, The Black Pirate by Moldoff (also #2), Ghost Patrol, and Red White & Blue begin; Scribbly app., Minute Movies	300.00	750.00	1800.00

	Good	Fine	N-Mint
2-Mutt & Jeff begin; last Ghost Patrol & Black Pirate; Minute Movies	134.00	335.00	800.00
3-Hop Harrigan & Sargon, the Sorcerer begin; The King app.	100.00	250.00	600.00
4,5: 4-The Gay Ghost, The King, Scribbly, & Red Tornado app. 5-Christmas cover	88.00	220.00	525.00
6-10: 7-Red Tornado & Black Pirate app.; last Scribbly. 9-X-mas-c	66.00	165.00	400.00
11,12,14-20: 12-Last Red White & Blue. 15-Johnny Peril begins, ends #29. 19-Christmas-c	58.00	145.00	350.00
13-Solomon Grundy app.; X-mas-c	100.00	250.00	600.00
21-23: 23-Harry Lampert-c (Toth swipes)	58.00	145.00	350.00
24-Solomon Grundy x-over in Green Lantern	66.00	165.00	400.00
25-28: 25-Black Canary app.; X-mas-c. 26-28-Johnny Peril app. 28-Last Mutt & Jeff	44.00	110.00	265.00
29-(10-11/48)-Last Flash, Wonder Woman, Green Lantern & Johnny Peril; Wonder Woman invents "Thinking Machine;" 1st computer in comics?	50.00	125.00	300.00
30-(12-1/48-49)-The Fox & the Crow, Dodo & the Frog & Nutsy Squirrel begin	26.00	78.00	180.00
31-35	11.50	34.00	80.00

	Good	Fine	N-Mint
36-49	8.50	25.50	60.00
50-62(Scarce)	11.00	32.00	75.00
63(Rare)	18.00	54.00	125.00

Conan the Barbarian #4, © Marvel Comics

CONAN THE BARBARIAN (See Chamber of Darkness #4 & King
    Conan)
Oct, 1970-Present
Marvel Comics Group

	Good	Fine	N-Mint
1-Origin/1st app. Conan (in comics) by Barry Smith; Kull app.; #1-9 are 15 cent issues	23.00	70.00	160.00
2	8.50	25.50	60.00
3-(Low distribution in some areas)	14.00	43.00	100.00
4,5	7.00	21.00	50.00
6-9: 8-Hidden panel message, pg. 14	4.50	14.00	32.00
10,11 (25 cent giants): 10-Black Knight-r; Kull story by Severin	5.70	17.00	40.00
12,13: 12-Wrightson-c(i)	3.50	10.50	24.00
14,15-Elric app.	5.00	15.00	35.00
16,19,20: 16-Conan-r/Savage Tales #1	2.85	8.50	20.00
17,18-No Barry Smith-a	1.50	4.50	9.00
21,22: 22-Has reprint from #1	2.65	8.00	18.00
23-1st app. Red Sonja (2/73)	3.15	9.50	22.00
24-1st full story Red Sonja; last Smith-a	3.15	9.50	22.00
25-John Buscema-c/a begins	1.50	4.50	9.00
26-30	.85	2.50	5.00

	Good	Fine	N-Mint
31-36,38-40	.50	1.50	3.00
37-Neal Adams-c/a; last 20 cent issue	1.00	3.00	6.00
41-57,59,60: 44,45-N. Adams-i(Crusty Bunkers). 45-Adams-c. 48-Origin retold. 59-Origin Belit.	.35	1.00	2.00
58-2nd Belit app.	.50	1.50	3.00
61-99: 68-Red Sonja story cont'd from Marvel Feature #7. 84-Intro. Zula. 85-Origin Zula. 87-r/Savage Sword of Conan #3 in color		.50	1.00
100-(52 pg. Giant)-Death of Belit	.40	1.25	2.50
101-114,116-199		.50	1.00
115-Double size		.60	1.20
200,250: 200-($1.50, 52 pgs.). 250-($1.50, 60 pgs.)	.25	.75	1.50
201-249,251,252: 232-Young Conan storyline begins; Conan is born. 244-Return of Zula		.50	1.00
253-262: 253-Begin $1.25-c		.65	1.30
King Size 1(1973, 35 cents)-Smith-r/#2,4; Smith-c	1.35	4.00	8.00
Annual 2(1976, 50 cents)-New full length story	.60	1.75	3.50
Annual 3(1978)-Chaykin/N. Adams-r	.35	1.00	2.00
Annual 4,5: 4(1978)-New full length story. 5(1979)-New full length Buscema story & part-c	.25	.75	1.50
Annual 6(1981)-Kane-c/a	.25	.75	1.50
Annual 7-9: 7(1982)-Based on novel "Conan of the Isles" (new-a). 8(1984).9(1984)		.60	1.25
Annual 10-12: 10(1985). 11(1986). 12(1987)		.60	1.25
Special Edition 1 (Red Nails)	.60	1.75	3.50

CONAN THE KING (Formerly King Conan)
No. 20, Jan, 1984-No. 55, Nov, 1989
Marvel Comics Group

	Good	Fine	N-Mint
20-55: 48-55 ($1.50)	.25	.75	1.50

COSMIC BOY (See The Legion of Super-Heroes)
Dec, 1986-No. 4, Mar, 1987 (Mini-series)
DC Comics

		Fine	N-Mint
1-4-Legends tie-in, all issues		.50	1.00

COSMIC ODYSSEY
1988-No. 4, 1988 ($3.50, color, squarebound)
DC Comics

	Good	Fine	N-Mint
1-4: Superman, Batman, Green Lantern app.			
	.60	1.75	3.50

CRACKAJACK FUNNIES
June, 1938-No. 43, Jan, 1942
Dell Publishing Co.

	Good	Fine	N-Mint
1-Dan Dunn, Freckles, Myra North, Wash Tubbs, Apple Mary, The Nebbs, Don Winslow, Tom Mix, Buck Jones, Major Hoople, Clyde Beatty, Boots begin	100.00	300.00	700.00
2	47.00	140.00	325.00
3	33.00	100.00	225.00
4,5: 5-Nude woman on cover	26.00	78.00	180.00
6-8,10	22.00	65.00	150.00
9-(3/39)-Red Ryder strip-r begin by Harman; 1st app. in comics & 1st cover app.	29.00	85.00	200.00
11-14	19.00	58.00	135.00
15-Tarzan text feature begins by Burroughs (9/39); not in #26,35	22.00	65.00	150.00
16-24	14.00	43.00	100.00
25-The Owl begins; in new costume #26 by Frank Thomas	35.00	105.00	235.00
26-30: 28-Part Owl-c. 29-Ellery Queen begins	26.00	78.00	180.00
31-Owl covers begin, end #42	23.00	70.00	160.00
32-Origin Owl Girl	29.00	85.00	200.00
33-38: 36-Last Tarzan issue	17.00	51.00	120.00
39-Andy Panda begins (intro/1st app.)	20.00	60.00	140.00
40-43: 42-Last Owl cover	16.00	48.00	110.00

CRACK COMICS (...Western No. 63 on)
May, 1940-No. 62, Sept, 1949
Quality Comics Group

	Good	Fine	N-Mint
1-Origin The Black Condor by Lou Fine, Madame Fatal, Red Torpedo, Rock Bradden & The Space Legion; The Clock, Alias the Spider, Wizard Wells, & Ned Brant begin; Powell-a; Note: Madame Fatal is a man dressed up as a woman	200.00	600.00	1400.00
2	93.00	280.00	650.00
3	70.00	210.00	485.00
4	60.00	180.00	420.00
5-10: 5-Molly The Model begins. 10-Tor, the Magic Master begins	47.00	140.00	325.00

	Good	Fine	N-Mint
11-20: 13-1 pg. J. Cole-a. 18-1st app. Spitfire?	42.00	125.00	285.00
21-24-Last Fine Black Condor	32.00	95.00	220.00
25,26	22.00	65.00	150.00
27-(1/43)-Intro & origin Captain Triumph by Alfred Andriola (Kerry Drake artist) & begin series	45.00	135.00	315.00
28-30	19.00	57.00	130.00
31-39: 31-Last Black Condor	11.00	32.00	75.00
40-46	8.00	24.00	55.00
47-57,59,60-Capt. Triumph by Crandall	8.50	25.50	60.00
58,61,62-Last Captain Triumph	6.50	19.00	45.00

CRACK WESTERN (Formerly Crack Comics)
No. 63, Nov, 1949-No. 84, May, 1953 (36pgs., 63-68,74-on)
Quality Comics Group

	Good	Fine	N-Mint
63(#1)-Two-Gun Lil (origin & 1st app.)(ends #84), Arizona Ames, his horse Thunder (with sidekick Spurs & his horse Calico), Frontier Marshal (ends #70), & Dead Canyon Days (ends #69) begin; Crandall-a	12.00	36.00	85.00
64,65-Crandall-a	10.00	30.00	70.00
66,68-Photo-c. 66-Arizona Ames becomes A. Raines (ends #84)	8.50	25.50	60.00
67-Randolph Scott photo-c; Crandall-a	10.00	30.00	70.00
69(52pgs.)-Crandall-a	8.50	25.50	60.00
70(52pgs.)-The Whip (origin & 1st app.) & his horse Diablo begin (ends #84); Crandall-a	8.50	25.50	60.00
71(52pgs.)-Frontier Marshal becomes Bob Allen F. Marshal (ends #84); Crandall-c/a	10.00	30.00	70.00
72(52pgs.)-Tim Holt photo-c	8.00	24.00	55.00
73(52pgs.)-Photo-c	5.30	16.00	38.00
74-76,78,79,81,83-Crandall-c	6.50	19.00	45.00
77,80,82	4.00	12.00	28.00
84-Crandall-c/a	8.50	25.50	60.00

CRASH COMICS (Catman Comics No. 6 on)
May, 1940-No. 5, Nov, 1940
Tem Publishing Co.

	Good	Fine	N-Mint
1-The Blue Streak, Strongman (origin), The Perfect Human, Shangra begin; Kirby-a	115.00	345.00	800.00
2-Simon & Kirby-a	57.00	170.00	400.00
3,5-Simon & Kirby-a	43.00	130.00	300.00

	Good	Fine	N-Mint
4-Origin & 1st app. The Catman; S&K-a			
	75.00	225.00	525.00

CREATURES ON THE LOOSE (Formerly Tower of Shadows
No. 1-9)
No. 10, March, 1971-No. 37, Sept, 1975 (New-a & reprints)
Marvel Comics Group

	Good	Fine	N-Mint
10-First King Kull story; Wrightson-a; 15 cents			
	3.15	9.50	22.00
11-37: 16-Origin Warrior of Mars (begins? ends #21). 21,22-Steranko-c. 22-29-Thongor-c/stories. 30-Manwolf begins			
	.35	1.00	2.00

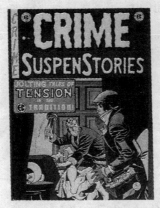

Crime SuspenStories #14, © William M. Gaines

CRIME SUSPENSTORIES (Formerly Vault of Horror No. 12-14)
No. 15, Oct-Nov, 1950-No. 27, Feb-Mar, 1955
E. C. Comics

	Good	Fine	N-Mint
15-Identical to #1 in content; #1 printed on outside front cover. #15 (formerly "The Vault of Horror") printed and blackened out on inside front cover with Vol. 1, No. 1 printed over it			
	90.00	270.00	625.00
1	68.00	205.00	475.00
2	40.00	120.00	285.00
3-5	27.00	80.00	190.00
6-10	22.00	65.00	150.00
11,12,14,15	15.00	45.00	105.00

	Good	Fine	N-Mint
13,16-Williamson-a	18.00	54.00	125.00
17-Williamson/Frazetta-a (6 pgs.)	20.00	60.00	140.00
18,19: 19-Used in **SOTI**, pg. 235	13.00	40.00	90.00
20-Cover used in **SOTI**, illo-"Cover of a children's comic book"			
	16.50	50.00	115.00
21,24-27	9.30	28.00	65.00
22,23-Used in Senate investigation on juvenile delinquency. 22-Ax decapitation-c	13.50	41.00	95.00

CRISIS ON INFINITE EARTHS
Apr, 1985-No. 12, Mar, 1986 (12 issue maxi-series)
DC Comics

	Good	Fine	N-Mint
1-1st DC app. Blue Beetle & Detective Karp from Charlton; Perez-c on all	.85	2.50	5.00
2-6: 6-Intro Charlton's Capt. Atom, Nightshade, Question, Judomaster, Peacemaker & Thunderbolt	.50	1.50	3.00
7-Double size; death of Supergirl	.85	2.50	5.00
8-Death of Flash	1.00	3.00	6.00
9-11: 9-Intro. Charlton's Ghost. 10-Intro. Charlton's Banshee, Dr. Spectro, Image, Punch & Jewellee	.40	1.25	2.50
12-(52 pgs.)-Deaths of Dove, Kole, Lori Lemaris, Sunburst, G.A. Robin & Huntress; Kid Flash becomes new Flash			
	.85	2.50	5.00

CRYPT OF SHADOWS
Jan, 1973-No. 21, Nov, 1975 (#1 & 2 are 20 cents)
Marvel Comics Group

	Good	Fine	N-Mint
1-Wolverton-r/Advs. Into Terror #7	.35	1.00	2.00
2-21: 2-Starlin/Everett-c		.60	1.20

D

DALE EVANS COMICS (Also see Queen of the West...)
Sept-Oct, 1948-No. 24, July-Aug, 1952 (No. 1-19: 52 pgs.)
National Periodical Publications

	Good	Fine	N-Mint
1-Dale Evans & her horse Buttermilk begin; Sierra Smith begins by			
Alex Toth	40.00	120.00	280.00
2-Alex Toth-a	20.00	60.00	140.00
3-11-Alex Toth-a	17.00	51.00	120.00
12-24	8.50	25.50	60.00

DAMAGE CONTROL (See Marvel Comics Presents #19)
5/89-No. 4, 8/89; V2#1, 12/89-No. 4, 2/90 ($1.00, color) V3#1,
6/91-No. 4, 9/91 ($1.25, all are mini-series)
Marvel Comics

V1#1-3		.50	1.00
4-Wolverine app.	.25	.75	1.50
V2#1,3		.60	1.20
2,4-Punisher app.	.30	.90	1.80
V3#1-4 ($1.25): 1-Spider-Man app. 2-New Warriors app. 3,4-Silver			
Surfer app. 4-Infinity Gauntlet parody		.65	1.30

DAREDEVIL (...& the Black Widow #92-107 on-c only; see Marvel
Super Heroes, '66 & Spider-Man and...) April, 1964-Present
Marvel Comics Group

1-Origin & 1st app. Daredevil; reprinted in Marvel Super Heroes #1			
(1966); death of Battling Murdock; intro Foggy Nelson & Karen			
Page	130.00	390.00	900.00
2-Fantastic Four cameo; 2nd app. Electro (Spidey villain)			
	43.00	130.00	300.00
3-Origin & 1st app. The Owl	29.00	85.00	200.00
4,5: 5-New Costume; Wood-a begins	17.00	51.00	120.00
6,8-10: 8-Origin/1st app. Stilt-Man	12.00	36.00	85.00
7-Daredevil battles Sub-Mariner & dons new red costume			
	13.50	41.00	95.00
11-15: 12-Romita's 1st work at Marvel; 1st app. Plunderer. 13-Facts			
about Ka-Zar's origin; Kirby-a	7.00	21.00	50.00
16,17-Spider-Man x-over	9.30	28.00	65.00
18-20: 18-Origin & 1st app. Gladiator	5.30	16.00	38.00

	Good	Fine	N-Mint
21-30: 24-Ka-Zar app. 27-Spider-Man x-over			
	3.60	11.00	25.00
31-40: 39-1st Exterminator (later Death-Stalker)			
	2.85	8.50	20.00
41-49: 41-Death Mike Murdock. 42-1st app. Jester. 43-Vs. Captain America. 45-Statue of Liberty photo-c			
	2.00	6.00	14.00
50-53: 50-52-B. Smith-a. 53-Origin retold			
	2.30	7.00	16.00
54,55,58-60: 54-Spider-Man x-over	1.30	4.00	9.00
56-1st app. Death's Head (9/69)	1.50	4.50	10.00
57-Reveals i.d. to Karen Page	1.50	4.50	10.00
61-99: 62-1st app. Nighthawk. 81-Oversize issue; Black Widow begins	1.15	3.50	8.00
100-Origin retold	2.65	8.00	18.00
101-104,106,108-113,115-120	1.00	3.00	6.00
105-Origin Moondragon by Starlin	1.70	5.00	12.00
107-Starlin-c	1.15	3.50	7.00
114-1st app. Deathstalker	1.35	4.00	8.00
121-130,133-137: 124-1st app. Copperhead; Black Widow leaves. 126-1st new Torpedo	.60	1.75	3.50
131-Origin Bullseye (1st app. in Nick Fury #15)			
	2.85	8.50	20.00
132-Bullseye app.	.85	2.50	5.00
138-Ghost Rider-c/story; Byrne-a	1.60	4.80	11.00
139-157: 142-Nova cameo. 146-Bullseye app. 148-30 & 35 cent issues exist. 150-1st app. Paladin. 151-Reveals i.d. to Heather Glenn. 155-Black Widow returns. 156-1960s Daredevil app.	.60	1.75	3.50
158-Frank Miller art begins (5/79); origin/death of Deathstalker (see Spect. Spider-Man for Miller's 1st D.D.)			
	6.85	21.50	48.00
159	3.15	9.50	22.00
160,161	1.60	4.80	11.00
162-Ditko-a, no Miller-a	.50	1.50	3.00
163,164: 163-Hulk cameo. 164-Origin	1.50	4.50	9.00
165-167,170	1.15	3.50	7.00
168-Origin/1st app. Elektra	3.50	10.50	24.00
169-Elektra app.	1.50	4.50	9.00
171-175: 174,175-Elektra app.	.85	2.50	5.00
176-180-Elektra app. 179-Anti-smoking issue mentioned in the Congressional Record	.60	1.75	3.50

Daredevil #249, © Marvel Comics

	Good	Fine	N-Mint
181-Double size; death of Elektra; Punisher cameo out of costume			
	1.50	4.50	10.00
182-184-Punisher app. by Miller (drug issues)			
	2.00	6.00	14.00
185-191: 187-New Black Widow. 189-Death of Stick. 190-Double size; Elektra returns, part origin. 191-Last Miller Daredevil			
	.35	1.00	2.00
192-195,197-210: 208-Harlan Ellison scripts			
	.25	.75	1.50
196-Wolverine app.	1.70	5.00	12.00
211-225: 219-Miller scripts		.50	1.00
226-Frank Miller plots begin	.25	.75	1.50
227-Miller scripts begin	.85	2.50	5.00
228-233-Last Miller scripts	.40	1.25	2.50
234-237,239,240,242-247		.50	1.00
238-Mutant Massacre; Sabretooth app.	1.00	3.00	6.00
241-Todd McFarlane-a(p)	.60	1.75	3.50
248,249-Wolverine app.	1.00	3.00	6.00
250,251,253,258: 250-1st app. Bullet. 258-Intro The Bengal (a villain)			
		.50	1.00
252-(52 pgs.); Fall of the Mutants	.50	1.50	3.00
254-Origin & 1st app. Typhoid Mary	3.00	9.00	18.00
255-2nd app. Typhoid Mary	1.35	4.00	8.00
256-3rd app. Typhoid Mary	1.15	3.50	7.00
257-Punisher app. (x-over w/Punisher #10)	4.30	13.00	30.00
259,260-Typhoid Mary app. 260-Double size			
	.70	2.00	4.00

	Good	Fine	N-Mint
261-291,294,296-299: 272-Intro Shotgun (villain). 282-Silver Surfer app. (cameo in #281). 283-Capt. America app. 297-Typhoid Mary app.; Kingpin storyline begins		.50	1.00
292,293-Punisher app.	.50	1.50	3.00
295-Ghost Rider app.	.40	1.25	2.50
300-($2.00, double size)-Kingpin story ends	.60	1.75	3.50
301-310: 301-Begin $1.25-c. 305,306-Spider-Man app.		.65	1.30
Special 1(9/67, 25 cents, 68 pgs.)-new art	2.85	8.50	20.00
Special 2,3: 2(2/71, 25 cents, 52 pgs.)-Entire book has Powell/Wood-r; Wood-c. 3(1/72)-reprints	1.50	4.50	10.00
Annual 4(10/76)	.85	2.50	5.00
Annual 4(#5)('89, $2.00, 68 pgs.)-Atlantis Attacks	.40	1.25	2.50
Annual 6(1990, $2.00, 68 pgs.)-Sutton-a	.35	1.00	2.00
Annual 7(1991, $2.00, 68 pgs.)-Guice-a (7 pgs.)	.35	1.00	2.00
Annual 8(1992, $2.25, 68 pgs.)-Deathlok app.	.40	1.15	2.30

DAREDEVIL AND THE PUNISHER (Child's Play trade paperback)
1988 ($4.95, color, squarebound, one-shot; 2nd & 3rd printings exist)
Marvel Comics

	Good	Fine	N-Mint
1-r/Daredevil #182-184 by Miller	1.35	4.00	8.00

DAREDEVIL COMICS (See Silver Streak Comics)
July, 1941-No. 134, Sept, 1956 (Charles Biro stories)
Lev Gleason Publications (Funnies, Inc. No. 1)

	Good	Fine	VF-NM
1-No. 1 titled "Daredevil Battles Hitler;" The Silver Streak, Lance Hale, Cloud Curtis, Dickey Dean, Pirate Prince team up w/Daredevil and battle Hitler; Daredevil battles the Claw; Origin of Hitler feature story. Hitler photo app. on-c	368.00	920.00	2200.00

	Good	Fine	N-Mint
2-London, Pat Patriot, Nightro, Real American No. 1, Dickie Dean, Pirate Prince, & Times Square begin; intro. & only app. The Pioneer, Champion of America	157.00	470.00	1100.00
3-Origin of 13	93.00	280.00	650.00
4	80.00	240.00	550.00
5-Intro. Sniffer & Jinx; Ghost vs. Claw begins by Bob Wood, ends #20	70.00	210.00	500.00

	Good	Fine	N-Mint
6-(#7 on indicia)	60.00	180.00	415.00
7-10: 8-Nightro ends	50.00	150.00	350.00
11-London, Pat Patriot end; bondage/torture-c			
	45.00	135.00	315.00
12-Origin of The Claw; Scoop Scuttle by Wolverton begins			
(2-4 pgs.), ends #22, not in #21	70.00	210.00	500.00
13-Intro. of Little Wise Guys	70.00	210.00	500.00
14	35.00	105.00	250.00
15-Death of Meatball	53.00	160.00	370.00
16,17	32.00	95.00	225.00
18-New origin of Daredevil-Not same as Silver Streak #6			
	67.00	200.00	465.00
19,20	27.00	80.00	190.00
21-Reprints cover of Silver Streak #6(on inside) plus intro. of The			
Claw from Silver Streak #1	38.00	115.00	265.00
22-30	18.00	54.00	125.00
31-Death of The Claw	35.00	105.00	250.00
32-37,39,40: 35-Two Daredevil stories begin, end #68 (35-40 are			
64 pgs.)	12.00	36.00	85.00
38-Origin Daredevil retold from #18	23.00	70.00	160.00
41-50: 42-Intro. Kilroy in Daredevil	8.00	24.00	55.00
51-69-Last Daredevil issue (12/50)	5.70	17.00	40.00
70-Little Wise Guys take over book; McWilliams-a; Hot Rock			
Flanagan begins, ends #80	3.60	11.00	25.00
71-79,81: 79-Daredevil returns	2.65	8.00	18.00
80-Daredevil x-over	3.00	9.00	21.00
82,90-One page Frazetta ad in both	3.00	9.00	21.00
83-89,91-99,101-134	2.15	6.50	15.00
100	4.30	13.00	30.00

DARING COMICS (Formerly Daring Mystery)
No. 9, Fall, 1944-No. 12, Fall, 1945
Timely Comics (HPC)

9-Human Torch & Sub-Mariner begin	45.00	135.00	310.00
10-The Angel only app.	40.00	120.00	275.00
11,12-The Destroyer app.	40.00	120.00	275.00

DARING MYSTERY COMICS (Comedy Comics No. 9 on; title
changed to Daring Comics with No. 9) 1/40-No. 5, 6/40; No. 6,
9/40; No. 7, 4/41-No. 8, 1/42
Timely Comics (TPI 1-6/TCI 7,8)

	Good	Fine	VF-NM

1-Origin The Fiery Mask by Joe Simon; Monako, Prince of Magic, John Steele, Soldier of Fortune, Doc Doyle begin; Flash Foster & Barney Mullen, Sea Rover only app; bondage-c

	Good	Fine	VF-NM
	735.00	1840.00	4400.00

	Good	Fine	N-Mint

2-(Rare)-Origin The Phantom Bullet & only app.; The Laughing Mask & Mr. E only app.; Trojak the Tiger Man begins, ends #6; Zephyr Jones & K-4 & His Sky Devils app., also #4

	370.00	925.00	2200.00

3-The Phantom Reporter, Dale of FBI, Breeze Barton, Captain Strong & Marvex the Super-Robot only app.; The Purple Mask begins   250.00   625.00   1500.00

4-Last Purple Mask; Whirlwind Carter begins; Dan Gorman, G-Man app.   160.00   400.00   950.00

5-The Falcon begins; The Fiery Mask, Little Hercules app. by Sagendorf in the Segar style; bondage-c

	160.00	400.00	950.00

6-Origin & only app. Marvel Boy by S&K; Flying Flame, Dynaman, & Stuporman only app.; The Fiery Mask by S&K; S&K-c

	200.00	500.00	1200.00

7-Origin The Blue Diamond, Captain Daring by S&K, The Fin by Everett, The Challenger, The Silver Scorpion & The Thunderer by Burgos; Mr. Millions app.   185.00   465.00   1100.00

8-Origin Citizen V; Last Fin, Silver Scorpion, Capt. Daring by Borth, Blue Diamond & The Thunderer; S&K-c; Rudy the Robot only app.   150.00   375.00   900.00

DARKHAWK
Mar, 1991-Present ($1.00, color)
Marvel Comics

	Good	Fine	N-Mint
1-Origin/1st app. Darkhawk; Hobgoblin cameo	1.85	5.50	11.00
2,3-Spider-Man & Hobgoblin app.	1.35	4.00	8.00
4	1.00	3.00	6.00
5	.85	2.50	5.00
6-Captain America & Daredevil x-over	.75	2.25	4.50
7,8	.70	2.00	4.00
9-Punisher app.	1.00	3.00	6.00
10-12: 11,12-Tombstone app. 12-Begin $1.25-c	.40	1.25	2.50
13,14-Venom-c/story	.70	2.00	4.00
15-20; 19-Spider-Man app.		.65	1.30

	Good	Fine	N-Mint
Annual 1 (1992, $2.25, 68 pgs.)	.40	1.15	2.30

DARK SHADOWS (TV)
March, 1969-No. 35, Feb, 1976 (Photo-c: 2-7)
Gold Key

	Good	Fine	N-Mint
1(30039-903)-With pull-out poster (25 cents)	18.00	54.00	125.00
1-Without poster	8.00	24.00	55.00
2	7.00	21.00	50.00
3-With pull-out poster	11.00	32.00	75.00
3-Without poster	6.50	19.00	45.00
4-7: Last photo-c	7.00	21.00	50.00
8-10	5.00	15.00	35.00
11-20	3.60	11.00	25.00
21-35: 30-last painted-c	2.65	8.00	18.00
Story Digest 1 (6/70)-Photo-c	4.30	13.00	30.00

DARK SHADOWS
June, 1992-No. 4, Sept, 1992 ($2.50, color, mini-series)
Innovation Publishing

	Good	Fine	N-Mint
1-Based on NBC TV mini-series; painted-c/a	.50	1.50	3.00
2-4	.40	1.25	2.50

DATE WITH DEBBI (Also see Debbi's Dates)
Jan-Feb, 1969-No. 17, Sept-Oct, 1971; No. 18, Oct-Nov, 1972
National Periodical Publications

	Good	Fine	N-Mint
1	1.50	4.50	10.00
2-5	1.00	3.00	6.00
6-18	.70	2.00	4.00

DAZZLER, THE (Also see X-Men #130)
March, 1981-No. 42, Mar, 1986
Marvel Comics Group

	Good	Fine	N-Mint
1,2-X-Men app.	.35	1.00	2.00
3-37,39-42: 10,11-Galactus app. 21-Double size; photo-c. 42-The Beast app.		.50	1.00
38-Wolverine-c/app.; X-Men app.	.85	2.50	5.00

DC COMICS PRESENTS
July-Aug, 1978-No. 97, Sept, 1986 (Superman team-ups in all)
DC Comics

	Good	Fine	N-Mint
1-12,14-25: 19-Batgirl	.25	.75	1.50
13-Legion of Super Heroes (also in #43 & 80)			
	.40	1.25	2.50

26-(10/80)-Green Lantern; intro Cyborg, Starfire, Raven, New Teen Titans; Starlin-c/a; Sargon the Sorcerer back-up; 16 pgs. preview of the New Teen Titans   1.15   3.50   7.00

27-40,42-71,73-76,79-84,86-97: 31,58-Robin. 35-Man-Bat. 52-Doom Patrol. 82-Adam Strange. 83-Batman & Outsiders. 86-88-Crisis x-over. 88-Creeper   .25   .75   1.50

41-Superman/Joker-c/story   .50   1.50   3.00

72-Joker/Phantom Stranger-c/story   .50   1.50   3.00

77,78-Animal Man app. (77-cover app. also)
| | 1.00 | 3.00 | 6.00 |

85-Swamp Thing; Alan Moore scripts   .70   2.00   4.00

Annual 1-4: 1(9/82)-G.A. Superman. 2(7/83)-Intro/origin Superwoman. 3(9/84)-Shazam. 4(10/85)-Superwoman
| | | .60 | 1.20 |

DC SPECIAL
10-12/68-No. 15, 11-12/71; No. 16, Spr/75-No. 29, 8-9/77
National Periodical Publications

1-All Infantino issue; Flash, Batman, Adam Strange-r (begin 68 pg., 25 cent issues, ends #15)   1.00   3.00   7.00

2-15: 5-All Kubert issue; Viking Prince, Sgt. Rock-r. 12-Viking Prince; Kubert-c/a. 15-G.A. Plastic Man origin-r/Police #1; origin Woozy by Cole; last 68 pg. issue   .75   2.25   4.50

16-29: 16-Super Heroes Battle Super Gorillas. 22-Origin Robin Hood. 28-Earth Shattering Disaster Stories; Legion of Super-Heroes story. 29-Secret Origin of the Justice Society
| | .50 | 1.50 | 3.00 |

DC SUPER-STARS
March, 1976-No. 18, Winter, 1978 (No. 3-18: 52 pgs.)
National Periodical Publications/DC Comics

1-(68 pgs.)-Re-intro Teen Titans plus Teen Titans-r
| | .60 | 1.75 | 3.50 |

2-7,9,11-14,16,18: 2-6,8-Adam Strange; 2-(68 pgs.)-r/1st Adam Strange/Hawkman team-up from Mystery in Space #90 plus Atomic Knights origin-r. 13-Sergio Aragones Special
| | | .50 | 1.00 |

8-r/1st Space Ranger from Showcase #15, Adam Stranger/Mystery

	Good	Fine	N-Mint
in Space #89 & Star Rovers-r/M.I.S. #80	.60	1.75	3.50
10-Strange Sports Stories; Batman/Joker-c/story	.70	2.00	4.00
15-Batman Spectacular; Golden & Rogers-a	.40	1.25	2.50

17-Secret Origins of Super-Heroes(origin of The Huntress); origin
   Green Arrow by Grell; Legion app.; Earth II Batman & Catwoman
   marry (1st revealed; also see B&B #197)

	.35	1.00	2.00

DEADLY FOES OF SPIDER-MAN
May, 1991-No. 4, Aug, 1991 ($1.00, color, mini-series)
Marvel Comics

1-Punisher, Kingpin, Rhino, others app.	.60	1.75	3.50
2-4: 2,4-Rhino, Kingpin app.	.35	1.00	2.00

DEATHLOK (Also see Astonishing Tales #25)
July, 1990-No. 4, Oct, 1990 ($3.95, limited series, 52 pgs.)
Marvel Comics

1-Guice-a(p)	1.85	5.50	11.00
2-4: 2-Guice-a(p). 3,4-Denys Cowan-a, c-4	1.35	4.00	8.00

DEATHLOK
July, 1991-Present ($1.75, color)
Marvel Comics

1-Silver ink cover; Denys Cowan-c/a(p) begins	.70	2.00	4.00
2-5: 2-Forge (X-Men) app. 3-Vs. Dr. Doom. 5-X-Men & F.F. x-over	.50	1.50	3.00
6-10: 6,7-Punisher x-over. 9,10-Ghost Rider-c/story	.35	1.00	2.00
11-18	.30	.90	1.80
Annual 1 (1992, $2.50, 68 pgs.)-Guice-a(p)	.40	1.25	2.50

DEATHLOK SPECIAL
May, 1991-No. 4, Late-June, 1991 ($2.00, bi-weekly mini-series)
Marvel Comics

1-4: r/1-4('90) w/new Guice-c #1,2; Cowan c-3,4	.45	1.40	2.80
1-2nd printing (white cover)	.40	1.15	2.30

DEATH'S HEAD
Dec, 1988-No. 10, Dec, 1989 ($1.75, color)
Marvel Comics

	Good	Fine	N-Mint
1-Dragon's Claws spin-off	1.85	5.50	11.00
2	.90	2.75	5.50
3,4	.75	2.25	4.50
5-10: 9-Simonson-c	.50	1.50	3.00

DEATH'S HEAD II
Mar, 1992-No. 4, June, 1992 ($1.75, color, mini-series)
Marvel Comics UK, Ltd.

1	1.25	3.75	7.50
2	.75	2.25	4.50
3,4	.50	1.50	3.50

DEATHSTROKE: THE TERMINATOR (Also see Marvel & DC Present, New Teen Titans #2, New Titans & Tales of the Teen Titans #42-44)
Aug, 1991-Present ($1.75, color)
DC Comics

1-New Titans spin-off	1.35	4.00	8.00
1-Gold 2nd printing (1992, $1.75)	.35	1.00	2.00
2	.85	2.50	5.00
3-5	.50	1.50	3.00

6-18: 6,8-Batman cameo. 7,9-Batman-c/story. 9-Intro new Vigilante (female). 10-1st full app. new Vigilante; Perez-a(i)

	.30	.90	1.80

Annual 1 (1992, $3.50, 68 pgs.)-Eclipso, Vigilante app.

	.60	1.75	3.50

DEBBI'S DATES (Also see Date With Debbi)
Apr-May, 1969-No. 11, Dec-Jan, 1970-71
National Periodical Publications

1	1.50	4.50	10.00
2-11: 4-Neal Adams text illo.	.85	2.50	5.00

DEFENDERS, THE (Also see Marvel Feature; The New...#140-on)
Aug, 1972-No. 152, Feb, 1986
Marvel Comics Group

	Good	Fine	N-Mint
1-The Hulk, Doctor Strange, & Sub-Mariner begin			
	6.30	19.00	44.00
2	2.85	8.50	20.00
3-5: 4-Valkyrie joins	2.15	6.50	15.00
6-9: 9-Avengers app.	1.85	5.50	13.00
10-Hulk vs. Thor; Avengers app.	2.40	7.25	17.00
11-14: 12-Last 20 cent issue	1.45	4.40	8.80
15,16-Magneto & Brotherhood of Evil Mutants app. from X-Men			
	1.50	4.50	10.00
17-20: 17-Power Man x-over (11/74)	1.10	3.30	6.60
21-25: 24,25-Son of Satan app.	.90	2.75	5.50
26-29-Guardians of the Galaxy app. (#26 is 8/75; pre-dates Marvel Presents #3). 27-1st app. Starhawk	1.85	5.50	11.00
30-50: 31,32-Origin Nighthawk. 35-Intro New Red Guardian. 44-Hellcat joins. 45-Dr. Strange leaves	.75	2.20	4.40
51-60: 53-1st app. Lunatik in cameo (Lobo lookalike). 55-Origin Red Guardian; Lunatik cameo. 56-1st full Lunatik story			
	.70	2.00	4.00
61-72: 61-Lunatik & Spider-Man app. 70-73-Lunatik (origin #71)			
	.55	1.65	3.30
73-75-Foolkiller II app. (Greg Salinger). 74-Nighthawk resigns			
	.60	1.75	3.50
76-95,97-124,126-151: 77-Origin Omega. 78-Original Defenders return thru #101. 94-1st Gargoyle. 100-(52 pgs.). 104-The Beast joins. 105-Son of Satan joins. 106-Death of Nighthawk. 120,121-Son of Satan-c/stories. 122-Final app. Son of Satan (2 pgs.). 129-New Mutants cameo (3/84, early x-over). 150-Dbl. size; origin Cloud	.35	1.10	2.20
96-Ghost Rider app.	.75	2.20	4.40
125-Double size; 1st app. Mad Dog; intro new Defenders			
	.50	1.50	3.00
152-Double size; ties in with X-Factor & Secret Wars II			
	.45	1.40	2.80
Annual 1 (1976, 52 pgs.)-New book-length story			
	.70	2.00	4.00

DEFENDERS OF DYNATRON CITY
Feb, 1992-No. 6, July, 1992 ($1.25, color, limited series)
Marvel Comics

	Good	Fine	N-Mint
1-Painted-c; Lucasarts characters	.30	.90	1.80
2-Origin	.25	.75	1.50
3-6		.65	1.30

DEMON, THE (See Detective Comics No. 482-485)
Aug-Sept, 1972-V3#16, Jan, 1974
National Periodical Publications

	Good	Fine	N-Mint
1-Origin; Kirby-c/a in 1-16	2.15	6.50	13.00
2-5	1.15	3.50	7.00
6-16	1.00	3.00	6.00

DETECTIVE COMICS
March, 1937-Present
National Periodical Publications/DC Comics

	Good	Fine	V-Fine
1-(Scarce)-Slam Bradley & Spy by Siegel & Shuster, Speed Saunders by Guardineer, Flat Foot Flannigan by Gustavson, Cosmo, the Phantom of Disguise, Buck Marshall, Bruce Nelson begin; Chin Lung-c from "Claws of the Red Dragon" serial; Flessel-c (1st?)	3200.00	8000.00	14,000.00

	Good	Fine	VF-NM
2 (Rare)	750.00	1875.00	4500.00
3 (Rare)	600.00	1500.00	3600.00

	Good	Fine	N-Mint
4,5: 5-Larry Steele begins	315.00	780.00	1900.00
6,7,9,10	210.00	525.00	1250.00
8-Mister Chang-c	265.00	660.00	1600.00
11-17,19: 17-1st app. Fu Manchu in Det.	185.00	465.00	1100.00
18-Fu Manchu-c	240.00	600.00	1450.00
20-The Crimson Avenger begins (1st app.)	280.00	700.00	1700.00
21,23-25	130.00	325.00	800.00
22-1st Crimson Avenger-c (12/38)	190.00	475.00	1150.00
26	155.00	390.00	925.00

	Good	Fine	VF-NM
27-The Batman & Commissioner Gordon begin (1st app.) by Bob Kane (5/39); Batman-c (1st)	10,000.00	30,000.00	60,000.00

(Prices vary widely on this book)

	Good	Fine	N-Mint
27(1984)-Oreo Cookies giveaway (32 pgs., paper-c, r-/Det. 27, 38 & Batman No. 1 (1st Joker)	3.00	9.00	21.00
28-2nd app. The Batman	900.00	2250.00	5400.00

	Good	Fine	VF-NM
29-Batman-c; Doctor Death app.	965.00	2400.00	5800.00

	Good	Fine	N-Mint
30,32: 30-Dr. Death app. 32-Batman uses gun			
	415.00	1040.00	2500.00

	Good	Fine	VF-NM
31-Classic Batman-c; 1st Julie Madison, Bat Plane (Bat-Gyro) & Batarang	965.00	2400.00	5800.00
33-Origin The Batman (1st told origin); Batman gunholster-c	1300.00	3250.00	7800.00

	Good	Fine	N-Mint
34-Steve Malone begins; 2nd Crimson Avenger-c			
	350.00	875.00	2100.00
35-Batman-c begin; hypo-c	535.00	1335.00	3200.00
36,37: 36-Origin Hugo Strange. 37-Cliff Crosby begins; last Batman solo story	385.00	960.00	2300.00

	Good	Fine	VF-NM
38-Origin/1st app. Robin the Boy Wonder (4/40)			
	1415.00	3550.00	8500.00

	Good	Fine	N-Mint
39	330.00	825.00	2000.00
40-Origin & 1st app. Clay Face (Basil Karlo); 1st Joker cover app. (6/40); Joker story intended for this issue was used in Batman #1 instead	400.00	1000.00	2400.00
41-Robin's 1st solo	215.00	535.00	1300.00
42-44: 44-Crimson Avenger-new costume			
	150.00	375.00	900.00
45-1st Joker story in Det. (4th story in all)			
	225.00	560.00	1350.00
46-50: 48-1st time car called Batmobile; Gotham City 1st mention. 49-Last Clay Face	135.00	340.00	810.00
51-57	108.00	270.00	650.00
58-1st Penguin app.; last Speed Saunders			
	235.00	585.00	1400.00
59-Last Steve Malone; 2nd Penguin; Wing becomes Crimson Avenger's aide	117.00	291.00	700.00
60-Intro. Air Wave	117.00	290.00	700.00
61,63: 63-Last Cliff Crosby; 1st app. Mr. Baffle			
	100.00	250.00	600.00
62-Joker-c/story (2nd Joker-c, 4/42)	150.00	375.00	900.00
64-Origin & 1st app. Boy Commandos by Simon & Kirby (6/42); Joker app.	267.00	665.00	1600.00
65-Boy Commandos-c	132.00	335.00	800.00
66-Origin & 1st app. Two-Face	183.00	460.00	1100.00
67-1st Penguin-c (9/42)	117.00	291.00	700.00

	Good	Fine	N-Mint
68-Two-Face-c/story	92.00	230.00	550.00
69-Joker-c/story	117.00	290.00	700.00
70	87.00	215.00	520.00
71-Joker-c/story	105.00	260.00	625.00
72-75: 73-Scarecrow-c/story. 74-1st Tweedledum & Tweedledee; S&K-a	80.00	200.00	480.00
76-Newsboy Legion & The Sandman x-over in Boy Commandos; S&K-a; Joker-c/story	121.00	302.00	725.00
77-79: All S&K-a	80.00	200.00	480.00
80-Two-Face app.; S&K-a	92.00	230.00	550.00
81,82,84,86-90: 81-1st Cavalier app. 89-Last Crimson Avenger	71.00	178.00	425.00
83-1st "Skinny" Alfred; last S&K Boy Commandos? Most issues #84 on signed S&K are not by them	80.00	200.00	480.00
85-Joker-c/story; Last Spy	93.00	235.00	560.00
91,102-Joker-c/story	87.00	215.00	520.00
92-98: 96-Alfred's last name "Beagle" revealed, later changed to "Pennyworth"-214	64.00	160.00	385.00
99-Penguin-c	88.00	220.00	525.00
100 (6/45)	96.00	240.00	575.00
101,103-108,110-113,115-117,119: 114-1st small logo (8/46)	58.00	145.00	350.00
109,114,118-Joker-c/stories	80.00	200.00	480.00
120-Penquin-c	83.00	210.00	500.00
121,123,125,127,129,130	56.00	140.00	335.00
122,126: 122-1st Catwoman-c(4/47). 126-Penguin-c	75.00	190.00	450.00
124,128-Joker-c/stories	73.00	185.00	440.00
131-136,139	48.00	120.00	285.00
137-Joker-c/story; last Air Wave	64.00	160.00	385.00
138-Origin Robotman; series ends #202	83.00	210.00	500.00
140-The Riddler-c/story (1st app., 10/48)	167.00	415.00	1000.00
141,143-148,150: 150-Last Boy Commandos	50.00	125.00	300.00
142-2nd Riddler-c/story	80.00	200.00	475.00
149-Joker-c/story	65.00	165.00	400.00
151-Origin & 1st app. Pow Wow Smith	55.00	135.00	325.00
152,154,155,157-160: 152-Last Slam Bradley	50.00	125.00	300.00
153-1st Roy Raymond app.; origin The Human Fly	55.00	135.00	325.00

	Good	Fine	N-Mint
156(2/50)-The new classic Batmobile	62.00	155.00	375.00
161-167,169,170,172-176: Last 52 pgs.	55.00	135.00	325.00
168-Origin the Joker	200.00	500.00	1200.00
171-Penguin-c	67.00	167.00	400.00

177-179,181-186,188,189,191,192,194-199,201,202,204,206-210,
212,214-216: 185-Secret of Batman's utility belt. 187-Two-Face
app. 202-Last Robotman & Pow Wow Smith. 216-Last precode

(2/55)	37.00	92.00	220.00
180,193-Joker-c/story	41.00	102.00	245.00
187-Two-Face-c	41.00	102.00	245.00
190-Origin Batman retold	55.00	135.00	325.00
200	50.00	125.00	300.00
203,211-Catwoman-c	41.00	102.00	245.00
205-Origin Batcave	55.00	135.00	325.00
213-Origin Mirror Man	48.00	120.00	290.00
217-224	33.00	85.00	200.00

225-(11/55)-1st app. Martian Manhunter-John Jones, later changed to
J'onn J'onzz; origin begins; also see Batman #78

	286.00	715.00	2000.00
226-Origin Martian Manhunter continued	65.00	195.00	450.00
227-229	37.00	110.00	260.00

230-1st app. Mad Hatter; brief origin recap of Martian Manhunter

	43.00	130.00	300.00
231-Brief origin recap Martian Manhunter	24.00	73.00	170.00
232,234,237-240: 239-Painted-c	24.00	73.00	170.00

Detective Comics #271, © DC Comics

	Good	Fine	N-Mint
233-Origin & 1st app. Batwoman	86.00	260.00	600.00
235-Origin Batman & his costume	38.00	114.00	265.00
236-J'onn J'onzz talks to parents and Mars-1st since being stranded on earth	29.00	85.00	200.00
241-260: 246-Intro. Diane Meade, J. Jones' girl. 257-Intro. & 1st app. Whirly Bats	19.00	56.00	130.00
261-J. Jones tie-in to sci/fi movie "Incredible Shrinking Man"	14.00	43.00	100.00
262-264,266-270: 261-1st app. Dr. Double X. 262-Origin Jackal	14.00	43.00	100.00
265-Batman's origin retold with new facts	24.00	72.00	165.00
267-Origin & 1st app. Bat-Mite	16.00	48.00	110.00
271-Manhunter origin recap	12.00	36.00	85.00
272,274-280: 276-2nd Bat-Mite	11.00	32.00	75.00
273-J'onn J'onzz i.d. revealed for 1st time	12.00	36.00	85.00
281-297: 287-Origin J'onn J'onzz retold. 292-Last Roy Raymond. 293-Aquaman begins, ends #300. 297-Last 10 cent issue (11/61)	8.00	24.00	55.00
298-1st modern Clayface (Matt Hagen)	13.00	40.00	90.00
299,300(2/62)	5.00	15.00	35.00
301(3/62)-J'onn J'onzz returns to Mars (1st since stranded on Earth 6½ years before)	5.70	17.00	40.00
302-326,329,330: 311-Intro. Zook in John Jones; 1st app. Cat-Man. 318,325-Cat-Man-c/story. 322-Bat-Girl's 1st/only app. in Det. 326-Last J'onn J'onzz, story cont'd in H.O.M. #143; intro. Idol-Head of Diabolu	4.30	13.00	30.00
327(5/64)-Elongated Man begins, ends #383; 1st new look Batman with new costume	5.00	15.00	35.00
328-Death of Alfred; Bob Kane biog, 2 pg.	8.00	24.00	55.00
331,333-340,342-358,360-364,366-368,370: 344-1st app. The Outsider. 345- Intro Block Buster. 351-Elongated Man new costume. 355-Zatanna x-over in Elongated Man. 356-Alfred brought back in Batman	2.85	8.50	20.00
332,341,365-Joker-c/stories	3.60	11.00	26.00
359-Intro/origin new Batgirl	3.60	11.00	26.00
369(1/67)-Neal Adams-a; early S.A. Catwoman cameo; story continued in Batman #197	3.50	10.50	24.00
371-1st new Batmobile from tv show (1/68)	2.15	6.50	15.00
372-386,389,390: 375-New Batmobile-c. 385-Last 12 cent-c?	1.70	5.00	12.00
387-r/1st Batman story from #27; Joker-c	4.00	12.00	28.00
388-Joker-c/story	2.65	8.00	18.00

	Good	Fine	N-Mint

391-394,396,398,399,401,403,405,406,409: 392-1st app. Jason Bard.
    401-2nd Batgirl/Robin team-up   1.35   4.00   9.00

395,397,402,404,407,408,410-Neal Adams-a
                     2.15   6.50   15.00

400-(6/70)-Origin & 1st app. Man-Bat; 1st Batgirl/Robin team-up;
    Neal Adams-a   3.15   9.50   22.00

411-420: 413-Last 15 cent issue. 414-25 cent, 52 pgs. begin, end #424.
    418-Creeper x-over   1.35   4.00   9.00

421-436: 424-Last Batgirl; 1st She-Bat. 426,430,436-Elongated Man
    app. 428, 434-Hawkman begins, ends #467
                     1.15   3.50   8.00

437-New Manhunter begins by Simonson, ends #443
                     1.70   5.00   12.00

438-445 (All 100 pgs.): 439-Origin Manhunter. 440-G.A. Manhunter,
    Hawkman, Dollman, Gr. Lantern; Toth-a. 441-G.A. Plastic Man,
    Batman, Ibis-r. 442-G.A. Newsboy Legion, Bl. Canary, Elongated
    Man, Dr. Fate-r. 443-Origin The Creeper-r; death of Manhunter;
    G.A. Gr. Lantern, Spectre-r. 444-G.A. Kid Eternity-r. 445-G.A.
    Dr. Midnite-r   1.50   4.50   10.00

446-460: 457-Origin retold & updated   1.15   3.50   7.00

461-465,469,470,480: 463,464-1st app. Black Spider; 480 (44 pgs.)
                     .85   2.50   5.00

466-468,471-474,478,479-Rogers-a in all. 466-1st app. Signalman
    since Batman #139. 469-Intro/origin Dr. Phosphorous. 470,471-
    1st modern app. Hugo Strange. 474-1st app. new Deadshot. 478-
    1st app. 3rd Clayface (Preston Payne). 479-(44 pgs.)
                     2.00   6.00   12.00

475,476-Joker-c/stories; Rogers-a   2.85   8.50   20.00

477-Neal Adams-a(r); Rogers-a, 3 pgs.   2.15   6.50   15.00

481-(Combined with Batman Family, 12/78-1/79)(Begin $1.00, 68 pg.
    issues, ends #495); 481-495-Batgirl, Robin solo stories
                     1.50   4.50   10.00

482-Starlin/Russell, Golden-a; The Demon begins (origin-r), ends
    #485 (by Ditko #483-485)   1.15   3.50   7.00

483-40th Anniversary issue; origin retold; Newton Batman begins
                     1.35   4.00   8.00

484-499: 484-Origin Robin. 485-Death of Batwoman. 487-The Odd
    Man by Ditko. 489-Robin/Batgirl team-up. 490-Black Lightning
    begins. 491-(#492 on inside)   .70   2.00   4.00

501-503,505-523: 512-2nd app. new Dr. Death. 519-Last Batgirl. 521-
    Green Arrow series begins. 523-Solomon Grundy app.
                     .60   1.75   3.50

	Good	Fine	N-Mint
500-($1.50)-Batman/Deadman team-up	1.15	3.50	7.00
504-Joker-c/story	1.10	3.25	6.50
524-2nd app. Jason Todd (cameo)(3/83)	.75	2.25	4.50
525-3rd app. Jason Todd (See Batman #357)	.60	1.75	3.50

526-Batman's 500th app. in Detective Comics ($1.50, 68 pgs.); contains
    55 pg. Joker story; Bob Kane pin-up   1.60   4.80   11.00

527-531,533,534,536-568,571: 542-Jason Todd quits as Robin
    (becomes Robin again #547). 549,550-Alan Moore scripts(Gr.
    Arrow). 554-1st new Black Canary. 566-Batman villains profiled.
    567-Harlan Ellison scripts   .40   1.25   2.50

| 532,569,570-Joker-c/stories | .85 | 2.50 | 5.00 |

535-Intro new Robin (Jason Todd)-1st appeared in Batman
                                         .90   2.75   5.50

572 (60 pgs., $1.25)-50th Anniversary of Det.	.60	1.75	3.50
573	.40	1.25	2.50
574-Origin Batman & Jason Todd retold	.85	2.50	5.00
575-Year 2 begins, ends #578	2.00	6.00	14.00
576-578: McFarlane-c/a	1.70	5.00	12.00

579-597,601-610: 579-New bat wing logo. 589-595-(52 pgs.)-Each
    contain free 16 pg. Batman stories. 604-607-Mudpack storyline;
    604,607-Contain Batman mini-posters. 610-Faked death of
    Penguin   .25   .75   1.50

598-($2.95, 84 pgs.)-"Blind Justice" storyline begins by Batman
    movie writer Sam Hamm, ends #600   1.50   4.50   9.00

| 599 | 1.35 | 2.00 | 4.00 |

600-($2.95, 84 pgs.)-50th Anniversary of Batman in Det.; 1 pg. Neal
    Adams pin-up, among other artists   1.00   3.00   6.00

611-626,628-654: 615-"The Penquin Affair" part 2 (See Batman
    #448,449). 617-Joker-c/story. 624-1st new Catwoman(w/death)
    & 1st new Batwoman. 645-Begin $1.25-c   .65   1.30

627-($2.95, 84 pgs.)-Batman's 600th app. in Det.; reprints 1st story/#27
    plus 3 versions (2 new) of same story   .55   1.60   3.20

Annual 1 (1988, $1.50)	.85	2.50	5.00
Annual 2 (1989, $2.00, 68 pgs.)	.70	2.00	4.00
Annual 3 (1990, $2.00, 68 pgs.)	.35	1.00	2.00
Annual 4 (1991, $2.00, 68 pgs.)-Painted-c	.35	1.00	2.00
Annual 5 (1992, $2.50, 68 pgs.)-Eclipso app.	.40	1.25	2.50

DICK TRACY (...Monthly #1-24; see Popular Comics &
    Super Comics)
Jan, 1948-No. 24, Dec, 1949
Dell Publishing Co.

	Good	Fine	N-Mint
1-1934 reprints	40.00	120.00	280.00
2,3	22.00	65.00	150.00
4-10	19.00	56.00	130.00
11-18: 13-Bondage-c	14.00	43.00	100.00

19-1st app. Sparkle Plenty, B.O. Plenty & Gravel Gertie in a 3-pg.

	Good	Fine	N-Mint
strip not by Gould	16.00	48.00	110.00

20-1st app. Sam Catchem; c/a not by Gould

	Good	Fine	N-Mint
	12.00	36.00	85.00
21-24-Only 2 pg. Gould-a in each	12.00	36.00	85.00

DICK TRACY (Continued from Dell series)(...Comics Monthly
#25-140)
No. 25, Mar, 1950-No. 145, April, 1961
Harvey Publications

25	16.00	48.00	110.00
26-28,30: 28-Bondage-c	12.00	36.00	85.00
29-1st app. Gravel Gertie in a Gould-r	16.00	48.00	110.00

31,32,34,35,37-40: 40-Intro/origin 2-way wrist radio

	11.00	32.00	75.00

33-"Measles the Teen-Age Dope Pusher"

	12.00	36.00	85.00
36-1st app. B.O. Plenty in a Gould-r	12.00	36.00	85.00
41-50	9.30	28.00	65.00
51-56,58-80: 51-2 pgs. Powell-a	8.50	25.50	60.00
57-1st app. Sam Catchem, Gould-r	11.00	32.00	75.00
81-99,101-140	6.50	19.00	45.00
100	7.00	21.00	50.00
141-145 (25 cents)(titled "Dick Tracy")	6.00	18.00	42.00

DISNEY'S DUCKTALES (TV)
Oct, 1988-No. 13, May, 1990 (1,2,9-11: $1.50; 3-8: 95 cents, color)
Gladstone Publishing

1-Barks-r	.60	1.75	3.50

2-11: 2,4-6,9-11-Barks-r. 7-Barks-r(1 pg.)

	.35	1.00	2.00

12,13 ($1.95, 68 pgs.)-Barks-r; 12-r/F.C. #495

	.35	1.10	2.20

DOC SAVAGE
Oct, 1972-No. 8, Jan, 1974
Marvel Comics Group

	Good	Fine	N-Mint
1	1.15	3.50	7.00
2-8: 2,3-Steranko-c	.70	2.00	4.00

DOC SAVAGE COMICS (Also see Shadow Comics)
May, 1940-No. 20, Oct, 1943 (1st app. in Doc Savage pulp, 3/33)
Street & Smith Publications

1-Doc Savage, Cap Fury, Danny Garrett, Mark Mallory, The Whisperer, Captain Death, Billy the Kid, Sheriff Pete & Treasure Island begin; Norgil, the Magician app.

	170.00	425.00	1000.00

2-Origin & 1st app. Ajax, the Sun Man; Danny Garrett, The Whisperer end

	70.00	210.00	510.00
3	57.00	170.00	400.00
4-Treasure Island ends; Tuska-a	45.00	135.00	315.00

5-Origin & 1st app. Astron, the Crocodile Queen, not in #9 & 11; Norgil the Magician app.

	35.00	105.00	250.00

6-9: 6-Cap Fury ends; origin & only app. Red Falcon in Astron story. 8-Mark Mallory ends; Charlie McCarthy app. on cover. 9-Supersnipe app.

	29.00	85.00	200.00
10-Origin & only app. The Thunderbolt	29.00	85.00	200.00
11,12	23.00	70.00	160.00

V2#1-8(#13-20): 16-The Pulp Hero, The Avenger app. 17-Sun Man ends; Nick Carter begins

	23.00	70.00	160.00

DOCTOR SOLAR, MAN OF THE ATOM (Also see Solar...)
10/62-No. 27, 4/69; No. 28, 4/81-No. 31, 3/82
Gold Key/Whitman No. 28 on (Painted-c No. 1-27)

1-Origin/1st app. Dr. Solar (1st Gold Key comic-No. 10000-210)

	12.70	38.00	88.00
2-Prof. Harbinger begins	5.70	17.00	40.00

3-5: 5-Intro. Man of the Atom in costume

	4.30	13.00	30.00
6-10,15: 15-Origin retold	2.85	8.50	20.00
11-14,16-20	2.40	7.20	17.00
21-27	1.85	5.50	13.00

28-31: 29-Magnus Robot Fighter begins. 31-The Sentinel app.

	.35	1.00	2.00

DOCTOR STRANGE (Formerly Strange Tales #1-168) (Also see The Defenders & Marvel Premiere)
No. 169, 6/68-No. 183, 11/69; 6/74-No. 81, 2/87
Marvel Comics Group

	Good	Fine	N-Mint
169(#1)-Origin retold; panel swipe/M.D. #1-c			
	11.50	34.00	80.00
170-176	4.50	14.00	32.00
177-New costume	4.30	13.00	30.00
178-183: 178-Black Knight app. 180-Photo montage-c. 181-Brunner-			
c(part-i)	4.00	12.00	28.00
1(6/74)-Brunner-c/a	4.00	12.00	28.00
2	2.15	6.50	15.00
3-5	1.35	4.00	8.00
6-10	1.00	3.00	6.00
11-20	.75	2.25	4.50
21-26: 21-Origin-r/Doctor Strange #169	.60	1.75	3.50
27-77,79-81: 56-Origin retold	.25	.75	1.50
78-New costume	.40	1.25	2.50
Annual 1 (1976, 52 pgs.)-New Russell-a (35 pgs.)			
	.70	2.00	4.00

DOCTOR STRANGE CLASSICS
Mar, 1984-No. 4, June, 1984 ($1.50 cover price; Baxter paper)
Marvel Comics Group

1-4: Ditko-r; Byrne-c. 4-New Golden pin-up			
	.35	1.00	2.00

DOCTOR STRANGE/GHOST RIDER SPECIAL
April, 1991 ($1.50, color)
Marvel Comics

1-Same-c & contents as Dr. Strange S.S. #28			
	.85	2.50	5.00

DOCTOR STRANGE/SILVER DAGGER (Special Edition)
Mar, 1983 ($2.50, Baxter paper)
Marvel Comics

1-r/Dr. Strange #1,2,4,5; Wrightson-c	.50	1.50	3.00

DOCTOR STRANGE, SORCERER SUPREME
Nov, 1988-Present (Mando paper, $1.25-1.50, direct sales only)
Marvel Comics

1 ($1.25)	.85	2.50	5.00
2-10,12-14,16-27,29,30 ($1.50): 3-New Defenders app. 5-Guice-c/a			
begins. 26-Werewolf by Night app.	.25	.75	1.50
11-Hobgoblin app.	.85	2.50	5.00
15-Unauthorized Amy Grant photo-c	.85	2.50	5.00

	Good	Fine	N-Mint
28-Ghost Rider story cont'd from G.R. #12; same cover & contents as Doctor Strange/Ghost Rider Special #1	.85	2.50	5.00
31-Infinity Gauntlet x-over (Silver Surfer app.)	.50	1.50	3.00
32-36-Infinity Gauntlet x-overs. 33-Thanos-c & cameo. 36-Warlock app.	.50	1.50	3.00
37-48: 37-Silver Surfer app. 38-Begin $1.75-c. 41-Wolverine-c/story	.30	.90	1.80
Annual 2 (1992, $2.25, 68 pgs.)-New Defenders app.	.40	1.15	2.30

DOCTOR WHO (Also see Marvel Premiere #57-60)
Oct, 1984-No. 23, Aug, 1986 ($1.50, Direct sales, Baxter paper)
Marvel Comics Group

	Good	Fine	N-Mint
1-($1.50 cover)-British-r		.50	1.00
2-23		.50	1.00

Dollman #10, © Quality Comics

DOLL MAN (Also see Feature Comics #27)
Fall, 1941-No. 7, Fall, '43; No. 8, Spring, '46-No. 47, Oct, 1953
Quality Comics Group

1-Dollman (by Cassone) & Justin Wright begin			
	115.00	345.00	800.00
2-The Dragon begins; Crandall-a(5)	57.00	170.00	400.00

	Good	Fine	N-Mint
3,4	43.00	130.00	300.00
5-Crandall-a	32.00	95.00	225.00
6,7(1943)	24.00	72.00	165.00
8(1946)-1st app. Torchy by Bill Ward	26.00	78.00	180.00
9	20.00	60.00	140.00
10-20	16.00	48.00	110.00
21-30	13.00	40.00	90.00
31-36,38,40: Jeb Rivers app. #32-34	11.50	34.00	80.00
37-Origin Dollgirl; Dollgirl bondage-c	14.00	43.00	100.00
39-"Narcotics...the Death Drug"-c-/story	11.00	32.00	75.00
41-47	8.00	24.00	55.00

DONALD DUCK ADVENTURES (Walt Disney's...#4 on)
Nov, 1987-No. 20, Apr, 1990
Gladstone Publishing

	Good	Fine	N-Mint
1	.55	1.65	3.30
2-r/F.C. #308	.35	1.10	2.20
3,4,6,7,9-11,13,15-18: 3-r/F.C. #223. 4-r/F.C. #62. 9-r/F.C. #159. 16-r/F.C. #291; Rosa-c. 18-r/F.C. #318; Rosa-c	.30	.85	1.70
5,8-Don Rosa-a	.35	1.10	2.20
12($1.50, 52 pgs.)-Rosa-c/a w/Barks poster	.35	1.10	2.20
14-r/F.C. #29, "Mummy's Ring"	.40	1.25	2.50
19 ($1.95, 68 pgs.)-Barks-r/F.C. #199	.35	1.00	2.00
20 ($1.95, 68 pgs.)-Barks-r/F.C. #189 & cover-r	.35	1.00	2.00

DOOM PATROL, THE (Formerly My Greatest Adventure No. 1-85; see Brave and the Bold & Showcase No. 94-96) No. 86, 3/64-No. 121, 9-10/68; No. 122, 2/73-No. 124, 6-7/73
National Periodical Publications

	Good	Fine	N-Mint
86-1 pg. origin (#86-121 are 12 cent issues)	9.30	28.00	65.00
87-99: 88-Origin The Chief. 91-Intro. Mento. 99-Intro. Beast Boy (later became the Changeling in New Teen Titans)	6.00	18.00	42.00
100-Origin Beast Boy; Robot-Maniac series begins (12/65)	7.00	21.00	50.00
101-110: 102-Challengers/Unknown app. 105-Robot-Maniac series ends. 106-Negative Man begins (origin)	3.50	10.50	24.00
111-120	2.85	8.50	20.00

	Good	Fine	N-Mint
121-Death of Doom Patrol; Orlando-c	8.50	25.50	60.00
122-124: All reprints	.40	1.25	2.50

DOOM PATROL
Oct, 1987-Present (New format, direct sale, $1.50 #19 on)
DC Comics

	Good	Fine	N-Mint
1	.35	1.00	2.00
2-18: 3-1st app. Lodestone. 4-1st app. Karma. 8,15,16-Art Adams-c(i). 18-Invasion		.50	1.00
19-New format & Grant Morrison scripts begin			
	2.50	7.50	15.00
20-25	1.50	4.50	9.00
26-30: 29-Superman app.	.85	2.50	5.00
31-40: 39-Preview of World Without End	.35	1.00	2.00
41-49,51-56,58-62	.25	.75	1.50
50,57-($2.50, 52 pgs.)	.40	1.25	2.50
...And Suicide Squad Special 1(3/88, $1.50)	.25	.75	1.50
Annual 1 ('88, $1.50, 52 pgs.)-No Morrison scripts			
	.25	.75	1.50

DRAGONLANCE
Dec, 1988-No. 34, Sept, 1991 ($1.25-$1.50, color, Mando paper)
DC Comics

	Good	Fine	N-Mint
1-Based on TSR game	.90	2.75	5.50
2	.70	2.00	4.00
3-5	.60	1.75	3.50
6-10: 6-Begin $1.50-c	.50	1.50	3.00
11-15	.35	1.00	2.00
16-34: 25-Begin $1.75-c. 30-32-Kaluta-c	.30	.90	1.80
Annual 1 (1990, $2.95, 68 pgs.)	.50	1.50	3.00

DURANGO KID, THE (Charles Starrett starred in Columbia's Durango Kid movies)
Oct-Nov, 1949-No. 41, Oct-Nov, 1955 (All 36 pgs.)
Magazine Enterprises

	Good	Fine	N-Mint
1-Charles Starrett photo-c; Durango Kid & his horse Raider begin; Dan Brand & Tipi (origin) begin by Frazetta & continue through #16	43.00	130.00	300.00
2(Starrett photo-c)	25.00	75.00	175.00
3-5(All-Starrett photo-c)	21.50	64.00	150.00
6-10: 7-Atomic weapon-c/story	11.00	32.00	75.00
11-16-Last Frazetta issue	8.00	24.00	55.00

	Good	Fine	N-Mint
17-Origin Durango Kid	10.00	30.00	70.00
18-Fred Meagher-a on Dan Brand begins	5.70	17.00	40.00
19-30: 19-Guardineer-c/a(3) begin, end #41. 23-Intro. The Red			
Scorpion	5.70	17.00	40.00
31-Red Scorpion returns	5.00	15.00	35.00
32-41-Bolle/Frazetta-a (Dan Brand)	6.50	19.00	45.00

DYNAMO (Also see T.H.U.N.D.E.R. Agents)
Aug, 1966-No. 4, June, 1967 (25 cents)
Tower Comics

1-Crandall/Wood, Ditko/Wood-a; Weed series begins; NoMan &			
Lightning cameos; Wood-c/a	3.60	11.00	25.00
2-4: Wood-c/a in all	2.65	8.00	18.00

80 PAGE GIANT (...Magazine No. 2-15) (25 cents)
8/64-No. 15, 10/65; No. 16, 11/65-No. 89, 7/71 (All reprints)
National Periodical Publications (#1-56: 84 pgs.; #57-89: 68 pages)

	Good	Fine	N-Mint
1-Superman Annual	12.50	50.00	100.00
2-Jimmy Olsen	6.70	20.00	48.00
3,4: 3-Lois Lane. 4-Flash-G.A.-r; Infantino-a			
	4.30	13.00	30.00
5-Batman; has Sunday newspaper strip; Catwoman-r; Batman's Life Story-r (25th anniversary special)	5.70	17.00	40.00
6-Superman	4.30	13.00	30.00
7-Sgt. Rock's Prize Battle Tales; Kubert-c/a			
	4.30	13.00	30.00
8-More Secret Origins-origins of JLA, Aquaman, Robin, Atom, & Superman; Infantino-a	13.50	41.00	95.00
9-11: 9-Flash (r/Flash #106,117,123 & Showcase #14); Infantino-a. 10-Superboy. 11-Superman; all Luthor issue			
	4.30	13.00	30.00
12-Batman; has Sunday newspaper strip	5.00	15.00	35.00
13,14: 13-Jimmy Olsen. 14-Lois Lane	4.30	13.00	30.00
15-Superman and Batman; Joker-c/story	5.70	17.00	40.00

NOTE: *No. 16 through 89 can be found under their own titles.*

ELEKTRA: ASSASSIN
Aug, 1986-No. 8, Mar, 1987 (Limited series)(Adults)
Epic Comics (Marvel)

1-Miller scripts in all	.85	2.50	5.00
2	.70	2.00	4.00
3-7	.50	1.50	3.00
8	.75	2.25	4.50

ELEKTRA SAGA, THE
Feb, 1984-No. 4, June, 1984 ($2.00, Baxter paper)
Marvel Comics Group

1-4-r/Daredevil 168-190; Miller-c/a	1.00	3.00	6.00

ELVIRA'S HOUSE OF MYSTERY
Jan, 1986-No. 11, Jan, 1987
DC Comics

	Good	Fine	N-Mint
1 ($1.50, 68 pgs.)-Photo back-c	.40	1.25	2.50
2-10: 6-Reads sideways. 7-Sci/fic issue. 9-Photo-c			
	.25	.70	1.40
11-Double-size Halloween issue; Dave Stevens-c			
	.35	1.00	2.00
Special #1 (3/87, $1.25)-Haunted Holidays	.25	.75	1.50

E-MAN
Oct, 1973-No. 10, Sept, 1975 (Painted-c No. 7-10)
Charlton Comics

1-Origin E-Man; Staton c/a in all	2.15	6.50	15.00
2-4: 2,4-Ditko-a. 3-Howard-a	1.25	3.75	7.50
5-Miss Liberty Belle app. by Ditko	1.00	3.00	6.00
6,7,9,10-Early Byrne-a in all (#6 is 1/75)	1.25	3.75	7.50
8-Full-length story; Nova begins as E-Man's partner			
	1.30	4.00	9.00

EMERALD DAWN (See Green Lantern: Emerald Dawn)

ETERNALS, THE
July, 1976-No. 19, Jan, 1978
Marvel Comics Group

1-Origin	.50	1.50	3.00
2-19: 2-1st app. Ajak & The Celestials. 14,15-Cosmic powered			
Hulk-c/story	.35	1.00	2.00
Annual 1(10/77)	.40	1.25	2.50

EXCALIBUR (Also see Marvel Comics Presents #31)
1987; Oct, 1988-Present ($1.50, Baxter)($1.75 #24 on)
Marvel Comics

Special Edition nn (The Sword is Drawn)(1987, $3.25)-This is the 1st			
Excalibur comic	2.50	7.50	15.00
Special Edition nn (2nd print, 10/88, $3.50)	1.00	3.00	6.00
Special Edition nn (3rd print, 12/89, 4.50)	.75	2.25	4.50
1($1.50, 10/88)-X-Men spin-of; Nightcrawler, Shadowcat (Kitty			
Pryde), Capt. Britain, Phoenix & Meggan begin			
	2.00	6.00	12.00
2	1.00	3.00	6.00
3,4	.70	2.00	4.00
5-10	.50	1.50	3.00
11-15: 10,11-Rogers/Austin-a	.35	1.00	2.00

	Good	Fine	N-Mint

16-23: 19-Austin-i. 21-Intro Crusader X. 22-Iron Man x-over.

	.25	.75	1.50

24-40,42-49,51-58: 32-($1.50). 24-John Byrne app. in story; begin
  $1.75-c. 27-B. Smith-a(p). 37-Dr. Doom & Iron Man app.

	.30	.90	1.80

41-X-Men (Wolverine) app.; Cable cameo	.35	1.00	2.00
50-($2.75, 56 pgs.)	.45	1.40	2.80

...Air Apparent nn (12/91, $4.95)-Simonson-c

	.85	2.50	5.00

...Mojo Mayhem nn ($4.50, 12/89)-Art Adams/Austin-c/a

	.85	2.50	5.00

...The Possession nn (7/91, $2.95, 52 pgs.)-Excalibur Special on-c

	.50	1.50	3.00

FAMOUS FUNNIES
1933-No. 218, July, 1955
Eastern Color

	Good	Fine	VF-NM

A Carnival of Comics (probably the second comic book), 36 pgs., no date given, no publisher, no number; contains strip reprints of The Bungle Family, Dixie Dugan, Hairbreadth Harry, Joe Palooka, Keeping Up With the Jones, Mutt & Jeff, Reg'lar Fellers, S'Matter Pop, Strange As It Seems, and others. This book was sold by M. C. Gaines to Wheatena, Milk-O-Malt, John Wanamaker, Kinney Shoe Stores, & others to be given away as premiums and radio giveaways (1933).   435.00   1080.00   2600.00

Series 1-(Very rare)(nd-early 1934)(68 pgs.) No publisher given (Eastern Color Printing Co.); sold in chain stores for 10 cents. 35,000 print run. Contains Sunday strip reprints of Mutt & Jeff, Reg'lar Fellers, Nipper, Hairbreadth Harry, Strange As It Seems, Joe Palooka, Dixie Dugan, The Nebbs, Keeping Up With the Jones, and others. Inside front and back covers and pages 1-16 of Famous Funnies Series 1, #s 49-64 reprinted from **Famous Funnies**, **A Carnival of Comics**, and most of pages 17-48 reprinted from **Funnies on Parade**. This was the first comic book sold.
                    1200.00   3000.00   7200.00

No. 1-(Rare)(7/34-on stands 5/34)-Eastern Color Printing Co. First monthly newsstand comic book. Contains Sunday strip reprints of Toonerville Folks, Mutt & Jeff, Hairbreadth Harry, S'Matter Pop, Nipper, Dixie Dugan, The Bungle Family, Connie, Ben Webster, Tailspin Tommy, The Nebbs, Joe Palooka, & others.

	Good	Fine	VF-NM
	1000.00	2500.00	6000.00
2 (Rare)	250.00	625.00	1500.00
3-Buck Rogers Sunday strip reprints by Rick Yager begins, ends #218; not in #191-208; the number of the 1st strip reprinted is pg. 190, Series No. 1	285.00	710.00	1700.00
4	86.00	257.00	600.00
5	72.00	215.00	500.00
6-10	57.00	170.00	400.00

	Good	Fine	N-Mint
11,12,18-Four pgs. of Buck Rogers in each issue, completes stories in Buck Rogers #1 which lacks these pages; #18-Two pgs. of Buck Rogers reprinted in Daisy Comics #1	50.00	150.00	350.00

	Good	Fine	N-Mint
13-17,19,20: 14-Has two Buck Rogers panels missing. 17-1st Christmas-c on a newsstand comic	36.00	107.00	250.00
21,23-30: 27-War on Crime begins; part photo-c. 29-X-Mas-c	26.00	78.00	180.00
22-Four pgs. of Buck Rogers needed to complete stories in Buck Rogers #1	28.00	85.00	200.00
31-34,36,37,39,40: 33-Careers of Baby Face Nelson & John Dillinger traced	19.00	58.00	135.00
35-Two pgs. Buck Rogers omitted in B. Rogers #2	21.00	62.00	145.00
38-Full color portrait of Buck Rogers	19.00	58.00	135.00
41-60: 41,53-X-Mas-c. 55-Last bottom panel, pg. 4 in Buck Rogers redrawn in Buck Rogers #3	13.00	40.00	90.00
61-64,66,67,69,70	11.00	32.00	75.00
65,68-Two pgs. Kirby-a-"Lightnin & the Lone Rider"	11.50	34.00	80.00
71,73,77-80: 80-Buck Rogers story continues from Buck Rogers #5	9.30	28.00	65.00
72-Speed Spaulding begins by Marvin Bradley (artist), ends #88. This series was written by Edwin Balmer & Philip Wylie (later appeared as film & book "When Worlds Collide")	10.00	30.00	70.00
74-76-Two pgs. Kirby-a in all	8.50	25.00	60.00
81-Origin Invisible Scarlet O'Neil; strip begins #82, ends #167	7.00	21.00	50.00
82-Buck Rogers-c	8.50	25.50	60.00
83-87,90: 87 has last Buck Rogers full page-r. 90-Bondage-c	7.00	21.00	50.00
88-Buck Rogers in "Moon's End" by Calkins, 2 pgs.(not reprints). Beginning with #88, all Buck Rogers pages have rearranged panels	8.00	24.00	55.00
89-Origin Fearless Flint, the Flint Man	8.00	24.00	55.00
91-93,95,96,98-99,101-110: 105-Series 2 begins (Strip Page #1)	5.30	16.00	38.00
94-Buck Rogers in "Solar Holocaust" by Calkins, 3 pgs.(not reprints)	6.50	19.00	45.00
97-War Bond promotion, Buck Rogers by Calkins, 2 pgs.(not reprints)	6.50	19.00	45.00
100	6.50	19.00	45.00
111-130	5.00	15.00	30.00
131-150: 137-Strip page No. 110 omitted	3.70	11.00	22.00
151-162,164-168	3.00	9.00	18.00

	Good	Fine	N-Mint
163-St. Valentine's Day-c	3.70	11.00	22.00
169,170-Two text illos. by Williamson, his 1st comic book work			
	6.70	20.00	40.00
171-180: 171-Strip pgs. 227,229,230, Series 2 omitted. 172-Strip Pg. 232 omitted	3.00	9.00	18.00
181-190: Buck Rogers ends with start of strip pg. 302, Series 2			
	2.30	7.00	14.00
191-197,199,201,203,206-208: No Buck Rogers			
	2.00	6.00	12.00
198,202,205-One pg. Frazetta ads; no Buck Rogers			
	2.50	7.50	15.00
200-Frazetta 1 pg. ad	2.65	8.00	16.00
204-Used in **POP**, pgs. 79,99	2.65	8.00	16.00
209-Buck Rogers begins with strip pg. 480, Series 2; Frazetta-c			
	30.00	90.00	210.00
210-216: Frazetta-c. 211-Buck Rogers ads by Anderson begins, ends #217. 215-Contains B. Rogers strip pg. 515-518, series 2 followed by pgs. 179-181, Series 3	30.00	90.00	210.00
217,218-B. Rogers ends with pg. 199, Series 3			
	2.65	8.00	18.00

FANTASTIC COMICS
Dec, 1939-No. 23, Nov, 1941
Fox Features Syndicate

	Good	Fine	N-Mint
1-Intro/origin Samson; Stardust, The Super Wizard, Sub Saunders (by Kiefer), Space Smith, Capt. Kidd begin	140.00	420.00	1000.00
2-Powell text illos	72.00	215.00	500.00
3-5: 3-Powell text illos	57.00	170.00	400.00
6-9: 6,7-Simon-c	48.00	145.00	335.00
10-Intro/origin David, Samson's aide	36.00	107.00	250.00
11-17,19,20,22: 16-Stardust ends	29.00	85.00	200.00
18-1st app. Black Fury & sidekick Chuck; ends #23			
	32.00	96.00	225.00
21,23: 21-The Banshee begins(origin); ends #23; Hitler-c. 23-Origin The Gladiator	32.00	96.00	225.00

FANTASTIC FOUR (See Marvel Triple Action)
Nov, 1961-Present
Marvel Comics Group

1-Origin/1st app. The Fantastic Four (Reed Richards: Mr. Fantastic,

	Good	Fine	N-Mint

Johnny Storm: The Human Torch, Sue Storm: The Invisible Girl, & Ben Grimm: The Thing); origin/1st app. The Mole Man (Marvel's 1st super-hero group since the G.A.)   390.00   1560.00   4700.00

1-Golden Record Comic Set Reprint (mid-'60s)-cover not identical
   to original   12.00   36.00   85.00
   with record (still sealed)   24.00   72.00   165.00

2-Vs. The Skrulls (last 10 cent issue)   186.00   560.00   1300.00

3-Fantastic Four don costumes & establish Headquarters; brief 1 pg. origin; intro The Fantasti-Car; Human Torch drawn w/two left hands on-c   122.00   366.00   850.00

4-1st Silver Age Sub-Mariner app. (5/62)
          122.00   366.00   850.00

5-Origin & 1st app. Doctor Doom   130.00   390.00   900.00

6-Sub-Mariner, Dr. Doom team up; 1st Marvel villain team-up
          82.00   246.00   575.00

7-10: 7-1st app. Kurrgo. 8-1st app. Puppet-Master & Alicia Masters. 9-Sub-Mariner app. 10-Stan Lee & Jack Kirby app. in story
          60.00   180.00   420.00

11-Origin/1st app. The Impossible Man   43.00   130.00   300.00

12-Fantastic Four Vs. The Hulk (1st x-over)
          47.00   140.00   325.00

13-Intro. The Watcher; 1st app. The Red Ghost
          35.00   105.00   240.00

14-19: 14-Sub-Mariner x-over. 15-1st app. Mad Thinker. 16-1st Ant-Man x-over (7/63). 18-Origin/1st app. The Super Skrull. 19-Intro. Rama-Tut   25.00   75.00   175.00

The Fantastic Four #14, © Marvel Comics

	Good	Fine	N-Mint
20-Origin/1st app. The Molecule Man	26.30	79.00	185.00
21-Intro. The Hate Monger; 1st Sgt. Fury x-over (11/63)			
	14.00	43.00	100.00
22-24	11.50	34.00	80.00

25,26-The Hulk vs. The Thing (their 1st battle). 26-1st Avengers
x-over (5/64)   26.00   78.00   180.00

27-1st Doctor Strange x-over (6/64)	13.00	40.00	90.00
28-Early X-Men x-over (7/64)	14.00	43.00	100.00
29,30: 30-Intro. Diablo	9.30	28.00	65.00

31-40: 31-Early Avengers x-over. 33-1st app. Attuma; part photo-c.
35-Intro/1st app. Dragon Man. 36-Intro/1st app. Madam Medusa
& the Frightful Four (Sandman, Wizard, Paste Pot Pete). 39-Wood
inks on Daredevil (early x-over)   7.00   21.00   50.00

41-47: 41-43-Frightful Four app. 44-Intro. Gorgan. 45-Intro. The
Inhumans (12/65). 46-1st app. Black Bolt

         5.00   15.00   35.00

48-Partial origin/1st app. The Silver Surfer & Galactus (3/66);
Galactus cameo in last panel; 1st of 3 part story

         52.00   156.00   360.00

49-2nd app. Silver Surfer & Galactus	11.00	32.00	75.00
50-Silver Surfer battles Galactus	14.00	43.00	100.00
51,54: 54-Inhumans cameo	4.00	12.00	28.00
52-1st app. The Black Panther (7/66)	6.50	19.00	45.00
53-Origin & 2nd app. The Black Panther	5.70	17.00	40.00
55-Thing battles Silver Surfer	5.70	17.00	40.00

56-60: Silver Surfer x-over. 59,60-Inhumans cameo

         5.00   15.00   35.00

61-65,68-70: 61-Silver Surfer cameo   3.60   11.00   25.00

66-(9/67)-Begin 2 part origin Him (Warlock); does not app. in #66

         11.00   32.00   75.00

67-(10/67)-1st app. Him (cameo on last page); see Thor #165,166 for
next app.   12.00   36.00   85.00

71,73,78-80: 73-Spider-Man, D.D., Thor x-over

         2.85   8.50   20.00

72,74-77: Silver Surfer app. in all   3.15   9.50   22.00

81-88: 81-Crystal joins & dons costume. 82,83-Inhumans app. 84-87-
Dr. Doom app. 88-Last 12 cent issue   2.15   6.50   15.00

89-99,101,102: 94-Intro. Agatha Harkness. 102,103-Fantastic Four
vs. Sub-Mariner   1.70   5.00   12.00

100 (7/70)	7.00	21.00	50.00

103-111: 108-Last Kirby issue (not in #103-107)

         1.50   4.50   10.00

	Good	Fine	N-Mint
112-Hulk Vs. Thing (7/71)	3.60	11.00	25.00
113-115: 115-Last 15 cent issue	1.30	4.00	9.00
116-120: 116-(52 pgs.)	1.15	3.50	8.00
121-123-Silver Surfer x-over. 122,123-Galactus			
	1.50	4.50	10.00
124,125,127,129-149: 129-Intro. Thundra. 130-Sue leaves F.F. 131- Quicksilver app. 132-Medusa joins. 133-Thundra Vs. Thing. 142- Kirbyish-a by Buckler begins. 143-Dr. Doom app.			
	1.00	3.00	6.00
126-Origin F.F. retold; cover swipe of F.F. #1			
	1.15	3.50	7.00
128-Four pg. insert of F.F. Friends & Foes	1.15	3.50	7.00
150-Crystal & Quicksilver's wedding	1.15	3.50	7.00
151-154,158-160: Origin Thundra. 159-Medusa leaves; Sue rejoins			
	.85	2.50	5.00
155-157: Silver Surfer in all	1.00	3.00	6.00
161-180: 164-The Crusader (old Marvel Boy) revived (origin #165). 176-Re-intro Impossible Man; Marvel artists app.			
	.50	1.50	3.00
181-199: 190,191-Fantastic Four break up	.35	1.00	2.00
200-(11/78, 52 pgs.)-F.F. re-united vs. Dr. Doom			
	.70	2.00	4.00
201-208,219,222-231	.25	.75	1.50
209-216,218,220,221-Byrne-a. 209-1st Herbie the Robot. 220-Brief origin	.35	1.00	2.00
217-Dazzler app. by Byrne	.50	1.50	3.00
232-Byrne-a begins	.60	1.75	3.50
233-235,237-249,251-260: All Byrne-a. 238-Origin Frankie Ray. 252- Reads sideways; Annihilus app.; contains skin "Tattooz" decals. 260-Alpha Flight app.	.40	1.25	2.50
236-20th Anniversary issue(11/81, 64 pgs., $1.00)-Brief origin F.F. Byrne-c/a(p); new Kirby-a(p)	.60	1.75	3.50
250-(52 pgs.)-Spider-Man x-over; Byrne-a; Skrulls impersonate New X-Men	.60	1.75	3.50
261-285: 261-Silver Surfer. 262-Origin Galactus; Byrne writes & draws himself into story. 264-Swipes-c of F.F. #1	.40	1.25	2.50
286-2nd app. X-Factor continued from Avengers #263; story continues in X-Factor #1	.70	2.00	4.00
287-295: 292-Nick Fury app.		.50	1.00
296-($1.50)-Barry Smith-c/a; Thing rejoins	.35	1.05	2.10
297-305,307-318,320-330: 300-Johnny Storm & Alicia Masters wed.			

	Good	Fine	N-Mint
312-X-Factor x-over. 327-Mr. Fantastic & Invisible Girl return			
		.50	1.00
306-New team begins	.25	.75	1.50
319-Double size	.35	1.00	2.00
331-346,351-357,359,360: 334-Simonson-c/scripts begin. 337-Simonson-a begins. 342-Spider-Man cameo. 356-F.F. vs. The New Warriors; Paul Ryan-c/a begins		.50	1.00
347-Ghost Rider, Wolverine, Spider-Man, Hulk-c/stories thru #349; Arthur Adams-c/a(p) in each	.85	2.50	5.00
347-Gold 2nd printing	.35	1.00	2.00
348,349	.50	1.50	3.00
348-Gold 2nd printing		.50	1.00
350-($1.50, 52 pgs.)-Dr. Doom app.	.40	1.25	2.50
358-(11/91, $2.25, 88 pgs.)-30th anniversary issue; gives history of F.F.; die cut-c; Art Adams back-up story-a			
	.40	1.25	2.50
361-370: 361-Begin $1.25-c. 362-Spider-Man app.		.65	1.30
Annual 1('63)-Origin F.F.; Ditko-i	36.00	108.00	250.00
Annual 2('64)-Dr. Doom origin & c/story	26.30	79.00	185.00
Annual 3('65)-Reed & Sue wed; r/#6,11	11.50	34.00	80.00
Special 4(11/66)-G.A. Torch x-over & origin retold; r/#25,26 (Hulk vs. Thing)	6.00	18.00	42.00
Special 5(11/67)-New art; Intro. Psycho-Man; early Black Panther, Inhumans & Silver Surfer (1st solo story) app.			
	6.00	18.00	42.00
Special 6(11/68)-Intro. Annihilus; birth of Franklin Richards; new 48 pg. movie length epic; no reprints	4.30	13.00	30.00
Special 7(11/69)-All reprints	2.65	8.00	18.00
Special 8(12/70). 9(12/71). 10('73)-All reprints			
	1.50	4.50	9.00
Annual 11-14: 11(1976). 12(1978). 13(1978)-New-a. 14(1979)-New-a			
	.85	2.50	5.00
Annual 15-20: 15(1980). 16(1981). 17(1983)-New Byrne-c/a. 18(1984). 19(1985). 20(1987)	.50	1.50	3.00
Annual 21(1988)-Evolutionary War x-over	.55	1.70	3.40
Annual 22(1989, $2.00, 64 pgs.)-Atlantis Attacks x-over; Sub-Mariner & The Avengers app.; Buckler-a	.35	1.00	2.00
Annual 23('90, $2.00, 68 pgs.)-Byrne-c; Guice-p			
	.35	1.00	2.00
Annual 24('91, $2.00, 68 pgs.)-2 pg. origin recap of F.F.; Guardians of the Galaxy x-over	.35	1.00	2.00
Annual 25('92, $2.25, 68 pgs.)	.40	1.15	2.30

	Good	Fine	N-Mint
Special Edition 1 (5/84)-r/Annual #1; Byrne-c/a			
	.35	1.05	2.10

FANTASTIC FOUR ROAST
May, 1982 (75 cents, one shot, direct sale only)
Marvel Comics Group

1-Celebrates 20th anniversary of F.F.#1; X-Men, Ghost Rider & many others cameo; Golden, Miller, Buscema, Rogers, Byrne, Anderson art; Hembeck/Austin-c	.60	1.80	3.60

FANTASTIC FOUR VS. X-MEN
Feb, 1987-No. 4, June, 1987 (Mini-series)
Marvel Comics

1	.60	1.75	3.50
2-4: 4-Austin-a(i)	.40	1.25	2.50

FANTASY MASTERPIECES (Marvel Super Heroes No. 12 on)
Feb, 1966-No. 11, Oct, 1967; Dec, 1979-No. 14, Jan, 1981
Marvel Comics Group

1-Photo of Stan Lee (12 cent-c #1,2)	3.60	11.00	25.00
2-r/1st Fin Fang Foom from Strange Tales #89			
	1.30	4.00	9.00
3-8: 3-G.A. Capt. America-r begin, end #6; 1st 25 cent Giant; Colan reprint. 7-Begin G.A. Sub-Mariner, Torch-r/M. Mystery. 8-Torch battles the Sub-Mariner-r/Marvel Mystery #9			
	1.60	4.80	11.00
9-Origin Human Torch-r/Marvel Comics #1			
	2.00	6.00	14.00
10,11: 10-r/origin & 1st app. All Winners Squad from All Winners #19. 11-r/origin of Toro(H.T. #1) & Black Knight			
	1.30	4.00	9.00
V2#1(12/79)-52 pgs.; 75 cents; r/origin Silver Surfer from S. Surfer #1 with editing; J. Buscema-a	.75	2.25	4.50
2-14-Reprints Silver Surfer #2-14	.50	1.50	3.00

FEAR (Adventure into...)
Nov, 1970-No. 31, Dec, 1975 (No.1-6: Giant Size)
Marvel Comics Group

1-Fantasy & Sci-Fi reprints in early issues			
	1.15	3.50	8.00
2-6	.75	2.25	4.50
7-9	.50	1.50	3.00

	Good	Fine	N-Mint
10-Man-Thing begins, ends #19; Morrow/Chaykin-c/a			
	1.15	3.50	8.00
11,12: 11-N. Adams-c. 12-Starlin/Buckler-a			
	.70	2.00	4.00
13,14,16-18: 17-Origin/1st app. Wundarr	.40	1.25	2.50
15-1st full-length Man-Thing story	.70	2.00	4.00
19-Intro. Howard the Duck; Val Mayerik-a			
	2.15	6.50	15.00
20-Morbius, the Living Vampire begins; Gulacy-a(p)			
	1.25	3.75	7.50
21-25	.70	2.00	4.00
26-31: 31-Morbius ends	.50	1.50	3.00

FEATURE COMICS (Formerly Feature Funnies)
No. 21, June, 1939-No. 144, May, 1950
Quality Comics Group

	Good	Fine	N-Mint
21-Strips continue from Feature Funnies	28.00	86.00	200.00
22-26: 23-Charlie Chan begins	22.00	65.00	150.00
26-(nn, nd)-c-in one color, (10 cents, 36 pgs.; issue No. blanked out. 2 variations exist, each contain half of the regular #26)			
	6.00	18.00	42.00
27-(Rare)-Origin/1st app. Dollman by Eisner			
	170.00	510.00	1200.00
28-1st Lou Fine Dollman	75.00	225.00	525.00
29,30	46.00	138.00	325.00
31-Last Clock & Charlie Chan issue	40.00	120.00	275.00
32-37: 32-Rusty Ryan & Samar begin. 34-Captain Fortune app. 37-Last Fine Dollman	28.00	86.00	200.00
38-41: 38-Origin the Ace of Space. 39-Origin The Destroying Demon, ends #40. 40-Bruce Blackburn in costume			
	22.00	65.00	150.00
42,43,45-50: 42-USA, the Spirit of Old Glory begins. 46-Intro. Boyville Brigadiers in Rusty Ryan. 48-USA ends			
	14.00	43.00	100.00
44-Dollman by Crandall begins, ends #63; Crandall-a(2)			
	21.00	63.00	145.00
51-60: 56-Marijuana story in "Swing Session." 57-Spider Widow begins. 60-Raven begins, ends #71	11.50	34.00	80.00
61-68 (5/43)	11.00	32.00	75.00
69,70-Phantom Lady x-over in Spider Widow			
	11.50	34.00	80.00

	Good	**Fine**	**N-Mint**
71-80,100: 71-Phantom Lady x-over. 72-Spider Widow ends			
	8.00	24.00	55.00
81-99	6.50	19.00	45.00
101-144: 139-Last Dollman. 140-Intro. Stuntman Stetson			
	5.00	15.00	35.00

FEATURE FUNNIES (Feature Comics No. 21 on)
Oct, 1937-No. 20, May, 1939
Harry "A" Chesler

	Good	Fine	N-Mint
1(V9#1-indicia)-Joe Palooka, Mickey Finn, The Bungles, Jane Arden, Dixie Dugan, Big Top, Ned Brant, Strange As It Seems, & Off the Record strip reprints begin	167.00	500.00	1000.00
2-The Hawk app. (11/37); Goldberg-c	69.00	205.00	480.00
3-Hawks of Seas begins by Eisner, ends #12; The Clock begins; Christmas-c	50.00	150.00	350.00
4,5	36.00	107.00	250.00
6-12: 11-Archie O'Toole by Bud Thomas begins, ends #22	28.00	86.00	200.00
13-Espionage, Starring Black X begins by Eisner, ends #20	32.00	95.00	225.00
14-20	25.00	75.00	175.00

FIGHT COMICS
Jan, 1940-No. 83, 11/52; No. 84, Wint, 1952-53; No. 85, Spring, 1953; No. 86, Summer, 1954
Fiction House Magazines

	Good	Fine	N-Mint
1-Origin Spy Fighter, Starring Saber; Fine/Eisner-c; Eisner-a	107.00	320.00	750.00
2-Joe Louis life story	47.00	140.00	325.00
3-Rip Regan, the Power Man begins	43.00	130.00	300.00
4,5: 4-Fine-c	32.00	95.00	225.00
6-10: 6,7-Powell-c	27.00	81.00	190.00
11-14: Rip Regan ends	24.00	72.00	165.00
15-1st Super American	32.00	95.00	225.00
16-Captain Fight begins; Spy Fighter ends	32.00	95.00	225.00
17,18: Super American ends	27.00	81.00	190.00
19-Captain Fight ends; Senorita Rio begins (origin & 1st app.); Rip Carson, Chute Trooper begins	27.00	81.00	190.00
20	21.00	63.00	145.00
21-30	13.00	40.00	90.00

	Good	Fine	N-Mint
31,33-50: 31-Decapitation-c. 44-Capt. Flight returns. 48-Used in Love and Death by Legman	11.50	34.00	80.00
32-Tiger Girl begins	12.00	36.00	85.00
51-Origin Tiger Girl; Patsy Pin-Up app.	19.00	57.00	130.00
52-60,62-65-Last Baker issue	9.30	28.00	65.00
61-Origin Tiger Girl retold	11.50	34.00	80.00
66-78: 78-Used in **POP**, pg. 99	8.50	25.50	60.00
79-The Space Rangers app.	8.50	25.50	60.00
80-85	7.00	21.00	50.00
86-Two Tigerman stories by Evans; Moreira-a			
	8.50	25.50	60.00

FIGHTING YANK (See America's Best & Startling Comics)
Sept, 1942-No. 29, Aug, 1949
Nedor/Better Publ./Standard

	Good	Fine	N-Mint
1-The Fighting Yank begins; Mystico, the Wonder Man app; bondage-c	72.00	215.00	500.00
2	36.00	107.00	250.00
3	24.00	72.00	165.00
4	19.00	57.00	130.00
5-10: 7-The Grim Reaper app.	14.00	43.00	100.00
11-20: 11-The Oracle app. 12-Hirohito bondage-c. 18-The American Eagle app.	13.00	40.00	90.00
21,23,24: 21-Kara, Jungle Princess app. 24-Miss Masque app.			
	14.00	43.00	100.00
22-Miss Masque-c/story	17.00	51.00	120.00
25-Robinson/Meskin-a; strangulation, lingerie panel; The Cavalier app.	17.00	51.00	120.00
26-29: All-Robinson/Meskin-a. 28-One pg. Williamson-a			
	14.00	43.00	100.00

FIRESTAR
March, 1986-No. 4, June, 1986 (From Spider-Man TV series)
Marvel Comics Group

	Good	Fine	N-Mint
1-X-Men & New Mutants app.	.50	1.50	3.00
2-Wolverine-c by Art Adams (p)	1.00	3.00	6.00
3,4	.35	1.00	2.00

FIRESTORM (See DC Comics Presents, Flash #289, & Justice League of America #179)
March, 1978-No. 5, Oct-Nov, 1978
DC Comics

	Good	Fine	N-Mint
1-Origin & 1st app.	.50	1.50	3.00
2-5: 2-Origin Multiplex. 3-Origin Killer Frost. 4-1st app. Hyena			
	.35	1.00	2.00

FLASH, THE (See Adventure, The Brave and the Bold, Crisis On
Infinite Earths, DC Comics Presents, DC Special, DC Super-Stars,
Green Lantern, Justice League of America, Showcase, & World's
Finest)

No. 105, Feb-Mar, 1959-No. 350, Oct, 1985
National Periodical Publ./DC Comics

	Good	Fine	VF-NM
Showcase #4 (9-10/56)-Origin & 1st app. The Flash (1st DC S.A. super hero) & The Turtle; Kubert-a			
	750.00	3000.00	7500.00
Showcase #8 (5-6/57)-2nd app. The Flash; origin & 1st app. Capt. Cold			
	300.00	900.00	2100.00

	Good	Fine	N-Mint
Showcase #13 (3-4/58)-Origin Mr. Element			
	200.00	600.00	1400.00
Showcase #14 (5-6/58)-Origin Dr. Alchemy, formerly Mr. Element			
	200.00	600.00	1400.00
105-(2-3/59)-Origin Flash(retold), & Mirror Master			
	215.00	640.00	1500.00
106-Origin Grodd & Pied Piper; Flash's 1st visit to Gorilla City; begin Grodd the Super Gorilla trilogy, ends #108 (Scarce)			
	75.00	225.00	525.00
107,108-Grodd trilogy ends	40.00	120.00	275.00
109	35.00	110.00	250.00
110-Intro/origin The Weather Wizard & Kid Flash who later becomes Flash in Crisis On Infinite Earths #12; begin Kid Flash trilogy, ends #112 (also in #114,116,118)	65.00	195.00	450.00
111	22.00	65.00	150.00
112-Origin & 1st app. Elongated Man (4-5/60); also apps. in #115,119,130	25.00	75.00	175.00
113-Origin & 1st app. Trickster	23.00	70.00	160.00
114-Captain Cold app. (see Showcase #8)	19.00	58.00	135.00
115,116,118-120: 119-Elongated Man marries Sue Dearborn. 120-Flash & Kid Flash team-up for 1st time			
	14.00	43.00	100.00
117-Origin & 1st app. Capt. Boomerang	18.00	54.00	125.00
121,122: 122-Origin & 1st app. The Top	10.00	30.00	70.00
123-Re-intro. Golden Age Flash; origins of both Flashes; 1st mention			

	Good	Fine	N-Mint
of an Earth II where DC G. A. heroes live			
	57.00	170.00	400.00
124-Last 10 cent issue	9.30	28.00	65.00
125-128,130: 128-Origin Abra Kadabra	7.50	22.50	52.00
129-2nd G.A. Flash x-over; JSA cameo in flashback			
	19.00	57.00	132.00
131-136,138,140: 131-Early Green Lantern x-over (9/62). 136-1st Dexter Miles. 140-Origin & 1st app. Heat Wave			
	7.50	22.50	52.00
137-G.A. Flash x-over; J.S.A. cameo (1st S.A. app.)(1st real app. since 2-3/51); 1st S.A. app. Vandall Savage			
	31.00	93.00	215.00
139-Origin & 1st app. Prof. Zoom	10.00	30.00	70.00
141-150: 142-Trickster app.	5.00	15.00	35.00

The Flash #151, © DC Comics

	Good	Fine	N-Mint
151-G.A. Flash vs. The Shade	6.50	19.00	45.00
152-159	3.60	11.00	25.00
160-80-Pg. Giant G-21-G.A.-r Flash & Johnny Quick			
	5.00	15.00	35.00
161-168,170: 165-Silver Age Flash weds Iris West. 167-New facts about Flash's origin. 168-Green Lantern-c/story. 170-Dr. Mid-Nite, Dr. Fate, G.A. Flash x-over	3.15	9.50	22.00
169-80-Pg. Giant G-34	5.00	15.00	35.00
171-174,176,177,179,180: 171-JLA, Green Lantern, Atom flashbacks. 173-G.A. Flash x-over. 174-Barry Allen reveals I.D. to wife			
	2.40	7.25	17.00

	Good	Fine	N-Mint
175-2nd Superman/Flash race (12/67); JLA cameo			
	8.00	24.00	55.00
178-80-Pg. Giant G-46	3.50	10.50	24.00
181-186,188-195,197-200: 186-Re-intro. Sargon			
	1.50	4.50	9.00
187,196: 68-Pg. Giants G-58, G-70	2.30	7.00	16.00
201-204,206-210: 201-New G.A. Flash story. 208-52 pg. issues begin, end #213,215,216. 206-Elongated Man begins			
	.85	2.50	5.00
205-68-Pg. Giant G-82	1.30	4.00	9.00
211-213,216,220: 211-G.A. Flash origin-r/#104. 213-Reprints #137			
	.85	2.50	5.00
214-DC 100 Page Super Spectacluar DC-11; origin Metal Men-r/ Showcase #37; never before pubbed G.A. Flash story			
	1.00	3.00	7.00
215 (52 pgs.)-Flash-r/Showcase #4; G.A. Flash x-over, r-in #216			
	1.50	4.50	10.00
217-219: Neal Adams-a in all. 217-Green Lantern/Green Arrow series begins. 219-Last Green Arrow	1.30	4.00	9.00
221-225,227,228,230,231	.85	2.50	5.00
226-Neal Adams-a	1.00	3.00	7.00
229,232,233-(All 100pgs.)-G.A. Flash-r & new-a			
	1.00	3.00	6.00
234-274,277-288,290: 243-Death of The Top. 246-Last Gr. Lantern. 256-Death of The Top retold. 265-267-(44 pgs.). 267-Origin Flash's uniform. 270-Intro The Clown. 286-Intro/origin Rainbow Raider	.50	1.50	3.00
275,276-Iris West Allen dies	.50	1.50	3.00
289-Perez 1st DC art; new Firestorm series begins, ends #304			
	.85	2.50	5.00
291-299,301-305: 291-Intro/origin Colonel Computron. 298-Intro/ origin new Shade. 301-Atomic Bomb-c. 303-The Top returns. 305-G.A. Flash x-over	.40	1.25	2.50
300-(52pgs.)-Origin Flash retold; 25th ann. ish			
	.70	2.00	4.00
306-Dr. Fate by Giffen begins, ends #313	.40	1.25	2.50
307-313: Giffen-a. 309-Origin Flash retold	.35	1.00	2.00
314-349: 318-323-Creeper back-ups. 323,324-Two part Flash vs. Flash story. 324-Death of Reverse Flash (Prof. Zoom). 328-Iris West Allen's death retold. 344-Origin Kid Flash	.35	1.00	2.00
350-Double size ($1.25)	.85	2.50	5.00

	Good	Fine	N-Mint
Annual 1(10-12/63, 84pgs.)-Origin Elongated Man & Kid Flash-r; origin Grodd, G.A. Flash-r	32.00	96.00	220.00

FLASH
June, 1987-Present (75 cents, $1.00 #17 on)
DC Comics

	Good	Fine	N-Mint
1-Guice-c/a begins; New Teen Titans app.	1.50	4.50	9.00
2	1.00	3.00	6.00
3-Intro. Kilgore	.70	2.00	4.00
4-6: 5-Intro. Speed McGee	.50	1.50	3.00
7-10: 7-1st app. Blue Trinity. 8,9-Millennium tie-ins. 9-1st app. The Chunk	.40	1.25	2.50
11-20: 12-Free extra 16 pg. Dr. Light story. 19-Free extra 16 pg. Flash story	.35	1.00	2.00
21-30: 28-Capt. Cold app. 29-New Phantom Lady app.	.25	.75	1.50
31-49,51-65: 40-Dr. Alchemy app.		.50	1.00
50-($1.75, 52 pgs.)	.30	.90	1.80
66-72: 66-Begin $1.25-c		.65	1.30
Annual 1 (1987, $1.25)	.60	1.75	3.50
Annual 2 (1988, $1.50)	.50	1.50	3.00
Annual 3 (1989, $1.75, 68 pgs.)-Gives history of G.A., Silver Age, & new Flash in text	.40	1.25	2.50
Annual 4 (1991, $2.00, 68 pgs.)-Armaggedon 2001	.35	1.00	2.00
Annual 5 (1992, $2.50, 68 pgs.)-Eclipso app.	.40	1.25	2.50
Special 1 (1990, $2.95, 84 pgs.)-50th anniversary issue; Kubert-c	.60	1.75	3.50
...TV Special 1 (1991, $3.95, 76 pgs.)-Photo-c plus behind the scenes photos of TV show; Saltares-a, Byrne scripts	.70	2.00	4.00

FLASH COMICS (The Flash No. 105 on) (Also see All-Flash)
Jan, 1940-No. 104, Feb, 1949
National Periodical Publications/All-American

	Good	Fine	VF-NM
1-The Flash (origin/1st app.) by Harry Lampert, Hawkman (origin/1st app.) by Gardner Fox, The Whip, & Johnny Thunder (origin/1st app.) by Stan Asch; Cliff Cornwall by Moldoff, Minute			

	Good	Fine	VF-NM

Movies begin; Moldoff (Shelly) cover; 1st app. Shiera Sanders who later becomes Hawkgirl, #24 (on sale 11/10/39)

	Good	Fine	N-Mint
	1800.00	4500.00	10,800.00
2-Rod Rian begins, ends #11	370.00	915.00	2200.00
3-The King begins, ends #41	290.00	730.00	1750.00
4-Moldoff (Shelly) Hawkman begins	250.00	625.00	1500.00
5	217.00	540.00	1300.00
6,7	175.00	440.00	1050.00
8-10	133.00	335.00	800.00
11-20: 12-Les Watts begins; "Sparks" #16 on. 17-Last Cliff Cornwall			
	100.00	250.00	600.00
21-23	88.00	220.00	525.00
24-Shiera becomes Hawkgirl (12/41)	117.00	290.00	700.00
25-30: 28-Last Les Sparks. 29-Ghost Patrol begins(origin, 1st app.),			
ends #104	72.00	180.00	435.00
31-40: 33-Origin Shade	62.00	155.00	375.00
41-50	58.00	145.00	350.00
51-61: 59-Last Minute Movies. 61-Last Moldoff Hawkman			
	48.00	120.00	285.00
62-Hawkman by Kubert begins	61.00	152.00	365.00
63-70: 66-68-Hop Harrigan in all	48.00	120.00	285.00
71-85: 80-Atom begins, ends #104	48.00	120.00	285.00
86-Intro. The Black Canary in Johnny Thunder; rare in Mint due to			
black ink smearing on white cover	133.00	335.00	800.00
87-90: 88-Origin Ghost. 89-Intro villain Thorn			
	62.00	155.00	375.00
91,93-99: 98-Atom dons new costume	75.00	190.00	450.00
92-1st solo Black Canary	117.00	290.00	700.00
100 (10/48),103(Scarce)-52 pgs. each	133.00	335.00	800.00
101,102(Scarce)	108.00	270.00	650.00
104-Origin The Flash retold (Scarce)	233.00	585.00	1400.00

FLINTSTONES, THE (TV)
No. 2, Nov-Dec, 1961-No. 60, Sept, 1970 (Hanna-Barbera)
Dell Publ. Co./Gold Key No. 7 (10/62) on

2	7.00	21.00	50.00
3-6(7-8/62)	5.00	15.00	35.00
7 (10/62; 1st GK)	5.00	15.00	35.00
8-10: Mr. & Mrs. J. Evil Scientist begin?	4.30	13.00	30.00
11-1st app. Pebbles (6/63)	5.70	17.00	40.00
12-15,17-20	3.60	11.00	25.00

	Good	Fine	N-Mint
16-1st app. Bamm-Bamm (1/64)	4.30	13.00	30.00
21-30: 24-1st app. The Grusomes app.	2.85	8.50	20.00
31-33,35-40: 31-Xmas-c. 33-Meet Frankenstein & Dracula. 39-Reprints	2.65	8.00	18.00
34-1st app. The Great Gazoo	3.60	11.00	25.00
41-60: 45-Last 12 cent issue	2.15	6.50	15.00
At N.Y. World's Fair('64)-J.W. Books(25 cents)-1st printing; no date on-c (29 cent version exists, 2nd print?)	3.60	11.00	25.00
At N.Y. World's Fair (1965 on-c; re-issue). NOTE: Warehouse find in 1984	.85	2.50	5.00
Bigger & Boulder 1(#30013-211) (Gold Key Giant, 11/62, 25 cents, 84 pgs.)	7.00	21.00	50.00
Bigger & Boulder 2-(25 cents)(1966)-reprints B&B #1	5.70	17.00	40.00
...With Pebbles & Bamm Bamm(100 pgs., G.K.)-30028-511 (paper-c, 25 cents)(11/65)	5.70	17.00	40.00

FLINTSTONES, THE (TV)(...& Pebbles)
Nov, 1970-No. 50, Feb, 1977 (Hanna-Barbera)
Charlton Comics

1	4.00	12.00	28.00
2	2.00	6.00	14.00
3-7,9,10	1.50	4.50	10.00
8-"Flintstones Summer Vacation," 52 pgs. (Summer, 1971)	1.70	5.00	12.00
11-20	1.15	3.50	8.00
21-50: 37-Byrne text illos (early work). 36-Mike Zeck illos (early work). 42-Byrne-a (2 pgs.)	1.00	3.00	6.00

FLY, THE (See Adventures of... & Flyman)

FLY MAN (Formerly Adventures of The Fly; Mighty Comics #40 on)
   No. 32, July, 1965-No. 39, Sept, 1966 (Also see Mighty Crusaders)
Mighty Comics Group (Radio Comics) (Archie)

32,33-Comet, Shield, Black Hood, The Fly & Flygirl x-over. 33-Re-intro Wizard, Hangman	3.15	9.50	22.00
34-36: 34-Shield begins. 35-Origin Black Hood. 36-Hangman x-over in Shield; re-intro. & origin of Web	2.00	6.00	14.00
37-39: 37-Hangman, Wizard x-over in Flyman; last Shield issue. 38-Web story. 39-Steel Sterling story	2.00	6.00	14.00

FOOLKILLER (Also see The Amazing Spider-Man #225, The
Defenders #73, Man-Thing #3 & Omega the Unknown #8)
Oct, 1990-No. 10, Oct, 1991 ($1.75, color, limited series)
Marvel Comics

	Good	Fine	N-Mint
1-Origin 3rd Foolkiller; Greg Salinger app.			
	.50	1.50	3.00
2-5: DeZuniga-a(i) in 1-4	.35	1.00	2.00
6,7,9,10	.30	.90	1.80
8-Spider-Man x-over	.40	1.25	2.50

FORBIDDEN WORLDS
7-8/51-No. 34, 10-11/54; No. 35, 8/55-No. 145, 8/67 (No. 1-5:
52 pgs.; No. 6-8: 44 pgs.)
American Comics Group

	Good	Fine	N-Mint
1-Williamson/Frazetta-a (10 pgs.)	68.00	205.00	475.00
2	34.00	100.00	240.00
3-Williamson/Wood/Orlando-a (7 pgs.)	36.00	108.00	250.00
4	17.00	51.00	120.00
5-Krenkel/Williamson-a (8 pgs.)	28.00	85.00	200.00
6-Harrison/Williamson-a (8 pgs.)	25.00	75.00	175.00
7,8,10	12.00	36.00	85.00
9-A-Bomb explosion story	14.00	43.00	100.00
11-20	8.50	25.50	60.00
21-33: 24-E.C. swipe by Landau	5.70	17.00	40.00
34(10-11/54)(Scarce)-Last pre-code issue; A-Bomb explosion story			
	5.70	17.00	40.00
35(8/55)-Scarce	5.00	15.00	35.00
36-62	3.60	11.00	25.00
63,69,76,78-Williamson-a in all; w/Krenkel #69			
	4.30	13.00	30.00
64-68,70-72,74,75,77,79-90: 65-"There's a New Moon Tonight" listed in #114 as holding 1st record fan mail response. 86-Flying saucer-c	2.65	8.00	18.00
73-1st app. Herbie by Ogden Whitney	19.00	57.00	130.00
91-93,95-100	1.70	5.00	12.00
94-Herbie app.	4.50	14.00	32.00
101-109,111-113,115,117-120	1.30	4.00	9.00
110,114,116-Herbie app. 114-1st Herbie-c; contains list of editor's top 20 ACG stories. 116-Herbie goes to Hell			
	2.85	8.50	20.00
121-124: 124-Magic Agent app.	1.30	4.00	9.00

	Good	Fine	N-Mint

125-Magic Agent app.; intro. & origin Magicman series, ends #141

	1.50	4.50	10.00
126-130	1.15	3.50	8.00

131-141: 133-Origin/1st app. Dragonia in Magicman (1-2/66); returns
   in #138. 136-Nemesis x-over in Magicman. 140-Mark Midnight
   app. by Ditko

	1.10	3.25	7.00
142-145	1.00	3.00	6.00

FOREVER PEOPLE, THE
Feb-Mar, 1971-No. 11, Oct-Nov, 1972
National Periodical Publications

1-Superman x-over; Kirby-c/a begins; 1st full app. Darkseid (3rd
   anywhere; ties with New Gods #1)

	3.15	9.50	22.00

2-5: 3,4,6,8-Darkseid apps. 4-G.A. reprints begin, end #9. 5,11-
   Darkseid cameos

	1.70	5.00	12.00
6-11: 9,10-Deadman app.	1.15	3.50	8.00

FOUR FAVORITES
Sept, 1941-No. 32, Dec, 1947
Ace Magazines

1-Vulcan, Lash Lightning, Magno the Magnetic Man & The Raven
   begin; flag-c

	54.00	160.00	375.00
2-The Black Ace only app.	27.00	81.00	190.00
3-Last Vulcan	22.00	65.00	150.00

4,5: 4-The Raven & Vulcan end; Unknown Soldier begins, ends
   #28. 5-Captain Courageous begins, ends #28; not in #6

	21.00	62.00	145.00
6-8: 6-The Flag app.; Mr. Risk begins	17.00	51.00	120.00

9,11-Kurtzman-a; 11-Hitler, Mussolini, Hirohito-c; L.B. Cole-a

	23.00	70.00	160.00
10-Classic Kurtzman-c/a	26.00	78.00	180.00
12-L.B. Cole-a	12.00	36.00	85.00
13-20: 18,20-Palais-c/a	11.00	32.00	75.00

21-No Unknown Soldier; The Unknown app.

	8.00	24.00	55.00

22-26: 22-Captain Courageous drops costume. 23-Unknown Soldier
   drops costume. 26-Last Magno

	8.00	24.00	55.00
27-32: 29-Hap Hazard app.	6.50	19.00	45.00

FOX AND THE CROW
Dec-Jan, 1951-52-No. 108, Feb-Mar, 1968
National Periodical Publications

	Good	Fine	N-Mint
1	60.00	180.00	425.00
2(Scarce)	30.00	90.00	210.00
3-5	19.00	58.00	135.00
6-10	12.00	36.00	85.00
11-20	8.50	25.50	60.00
21-40: 22-Last precode (2/55)	5.30	16.00	38.00
41-60	3.70	11.00	26.00
61-80	2.65	8.00	18.00
81-94	1.70	5.00	12.00
95-Stanley & His Monster begins (origin)(1st app?)			
	2.30	7.00	15.00
96-99,101-108	1.00	3.00	7.00
100	1.30	4.00	9.00

FRANKENSTEIN
Jan, 1973-No. 18, Sept, 1975
Marvel Comics Group

	Good	Fine	N-Mint
1-Ploog-c/a begins, ends #6	2.15	6.50	15.00
2-5,8,9: 8,9-Dracula app.	1.00	3.00	6.00
6,7,10	.70	2.00	4.00
11-18	.50	1.50	3.00

FROM BEYOND THE UNKNOWN
10-11/69-No. 25, 11-12/73 (No. 7-11: 64 pgs.; No. 12-17: 52 pgs.)
National Periodical Publications

	Good	Fine	N-Mint
1	.85	2.50	5.00
2-10: 7-Intro. Col. Glenn Merrit	.50	1.50	3.00
11-25: Star Rovers-r begin #18,19. Space Museum in #23-25			
	.35	1.00	2.00

FUNNIES, THE (New Funnies No. 65 on)
Oct, 1936-No. 64, May, 1942
Dell Publishing Co.

	Good	Fine	N-Mint
1-Tailspin Tommy, Mutt & Jeff, Alley Oop (1st app?), Capt. Easy, Don Dixon begin	125.00	312.00	750.00
2-Scribbly by Mayer begins	50.00	150.00	350.00
3	43.00	130.00	300.00
4,5: 4-Christmas-c	36.00	108.00	250.00
6-10	28.00	85.00	200.00
11-20: 16-Christmas-c	25.00	75.00	175.00
21-29: 25-Crime Busters by McWilliams(4 pgs.)			
	20.00	60.00	140.00

	Good	Fine	N-Mint

30-John Carter of Mars (origin) begins by Edgar Rice Burroughs
| | 57.00 | 170.00 | 400.00 |

31-44: 33-John Coleman Burroughs art begins on John Carter. 35-(9/39)-Mr. District Attorney begins-based on radio show
| | 36.00 | 108.00 | 250.00 |

45-Origin/1st app. Phantasmo, the Master of the World (Dell's 1st super-hero) & his sidekick Whizzer McGee
| | 26.00 | 78.00 | 180.00 |

46-50: 46-The Black Knight begins, ends #62
| | 23.00 | 70.00 | 160.00 |

51-56-Last ERB John Carter of Mars	23.00	70.00	160.00
57-Intro. & origin Captain Midnight	60.00	180.00	425.00
58-60	24.00	72.00	165.00
61-Andy Panda begins by Walter Lantz	25.00	75.00	175.00

62,63: 63-Last Captain Midnight-c; bondage-c
| | 24.00 | 72.00 | 165.00 |

64-Format change; Oswald the Rabbit, Felix the Cat, Li'l Eight Ball app.; origin & 1st app. Woody Woodpecker in Oswald; last Capt. Midnight
| | 50.00 | 150.00 | 350.00 |

GABBY HAYES ADVENTURE COMICS
Dec, 1953
Toby Press

	Good	Fine	N-Mint
1-Photo-c	8.50	25.50	60.00

GABBY HAYES WESTERN (Movie star)
Nov, 1948-No. 50, Jan, 1953; No. 51, Dec, 1954-No. 59, Jan, 1957
Fawcett Publications/Charlton Comics No. 51 on

1-Gabby & his horse Corker begin; Photo front/back-c begin			
	28.00	86.00	200.00
2	14.00	43.00	100.00
3-5	10.00	30.00	70.00
6-10: 9-Young Falcon begins	8.50	25.50	60.00
11-20: 19-Last photo back-c	6.50	19.00	45.00
21-49: 20,22,24,26,28,29-(52 pgs.)	4.30	13.00	30.00
50-(1/53)-Last Fawcett issue; last photo-c?			
	5.00	15.00	35.00
51-(12/54)-1st Charlton issue; photo-c	5.00	15.00	35.00
52-59(1955-57): 53,55-Photo-c. 58-Swayze-a			
	2.65	8.00	18.00

GENE AUTRY COMICS (Movie, Radio star; singing cowboy)
(Dell takes over with No. 11)
1941 (On sale 12/31/41)-No. 10, 1943 (68 pgs.)
Fawcett Publications

1 (Rare)-Gene Autry & his horse Champion begin			
	200.00	500.00	1200.00
2	64.00	192.00	450.00
3-5	43.00	130.00	300.00
6-10	39.00	118.00	275.00

GENE AUTRY COMICS (...& Champion No. 102 on)
No. 11, 1943-No. 121, Jan-Mar, 1959 (TV-later issues)
Dell Publishing Co.

11 (1943, 60 pgs.)-Continuation of Fawcett series; photo back-c			
	43.00	130.00	300.00
12 (2/44, 60 pgs.)	42.00	126.00	290.00
4-Color 47(1944, 60 pgs.)	39.00	118.00	275.00

	Good	Fine	N-Mint
4-Color 57(11/44),66('45)(52 pgs. each)			
	34.00	103.00	240.00
4-Color 75,83('45, 36 pgs. each)	29.00	85.00	200.00
4-Color 93,100('45-46, 36 pgs. each)	23.00	70.00	160.00
1(5-6/46, 52 pgs.)	39.00	118.00	275.00
2(7-8/46)-Photo-c begin, end #111	20.00	60.00	140.00
3-5: 4-Intro Flapjack Hobbs	16.00	48.00	110.00
6-10	11.50	34.00	80.00
11-20: 20-Panhandle Pete begins	8.50	25.50	60.00
21-29(36 pgs.)	6.50	19.00	45.00
30-40(52 pgs.)	6.50	19.00	45.00
41-56(52 pgs.)	5.00	15.00	35.00
57-66(36 pgs.): 58-X-mas-c	3.15	9.50	22.00
67-80(52 pgs.)	3.70	11.00	26.00
81-90(52 pgs.): 82-X-mas-c. 87-Blank inside-c			
	2.85	8.50	20.00
91-99(36 pgs. No. 91-on). 94-X-mas-c	2.00	6.00	14.00
100	2.85	8.50	20.00
101-111-Last Gene Autry photo-c	2.00	6.00	14.00
112-121-All Champion painted-c	1.50	4.50	10.00

GET SMART (TV)
June, 1966-No. 8, Sept, 1967 (All have Don Adams photo-c)
Dell Publishing Co.

1	6.50	19.00	45.00
2-Ditko-a	5.00	15.00	35.00
3-8: 3-Ditko-a(p)	4.00	12.00	28.00

GHOST RIDER, THE
Feb, 1967-No. 7, Nov, 1967 (Western hero)(All 12 cent-c)
Marvel Comics Group

1-Origin Ghost Rider; Kid Colt-r begin	4.00	12.00	28.00
2-7: 6-Last Kid Colt-r; All Ayers-c/a(p)	1.70	5.00	12.00

GHOST RIDER (See The Champions, Marvel Spotlight #5, Marvel
Team-Up #15, 58, Marvel Two-In-One #8 & The Original Ghost
Rider Rides Again)
Sept, 1973-No. 81, June, 1983 (Super-hero)
Marvel Comics Group

1-Johnny Blaze, the Ghost Rider begins; 1st app. (cameo) Daimon
Hellstrom (Son of Satan)   11.00   32.00   75.00
2-1st full app. Daimon Hellstrom; shows partial view of costume;

	Good	Fine	N-Mint
story continued in Marvel Spotlight #12			
	4.70	14.00	33.00
3-5: 3-Ghost Rider gets new cycle; Son of Satan app. continued from Marvel Spotlight #12	4.00	12.00	28.00
6-10: 10-Reprints origin/1st app. from Marvel Spotlight #5; Ploog-a			
	2.40	7.25	17.00
11-19	2.15	6.50	15.00
20-Daredevil x-over; Byrne-a	2.40	7.25	17.00
21-30: 22-1st app. Enforcer. 29,30-Vs. Dr. Strange			
	1.25	3.75	8.80
31-49	1.10	3.30	6.60
50-Double size	1.10	3.30	7.70
51-67,69-76,78-80: 80-Brief origin recap	.75	2.20	4.40
68,77-Origin retold	1.10	3.30	6.60
81-Death of Ghost Rider (Demon leaves Blaze)			
	1.70	5.00	10.00

Ghost Rider V2#16, © Marvel Comics

GHOST RIDER (Also see Doctor Strange/Ghost Rider Special & Marvel Comics Presents)
V2#1, May, 1990-Present ($1.50/$1.75, color)
Marvel Comics

V2#1-($1.95, 52 pgs.)-Origin/1st app. new Ghost Rider; Kingpin app.

| | 3.60 | 11.00 | 25.00 |

	Good	Fine	N-Mint
1-Gold 2nd printing	1.15	3.50	7.00
2	2.65	8.00	18.00
3-Kingpin app.	1.70	5.00	12.00
4-Scarcer	2.85	8.50	20.00
5-Punisher app.; Jim Lee-c	2.85	8.50	20.00
5-Gold 2nd printing	1.50	4.50	10.00
6-Punisher app.	1.50	4.50	10.00
7-10: 9-X-Factor app.	.85	2.50	5.00
11-14: 12,13-Dr. Strange/cont'd in D.S. #28. 13-Painted-c. 14-			
Johnny Blaze vs. Ghost Rider	.50	1.50	3.00
15-Glow in the dark-c; begin $1.75-c	1.30	4.00	9.00
15-2nd printing	.50	1.50	3.00
16,17-Spider-Man/Hobgoblin app.	.60	1.75	3.50
18-24,29-32: 18-Painted-c.	.30	.90	1.80
25-($2.75, 52 pgs.)-Contains pop-up scene as bonus			
	.50	1.50	3.00
26,27-X-Men x-over; Jim Lee-c(p)	.50	1.50	3.00
28-($2.50)-Part 1 of Rise of the Midnight Sons; polybagged with			
foldout poster & gatefold centerfold spread			
	.50	1.50	3.00

GHOST RIDER; WOLVERINE; PUNISHER: HEARTS OF DARKNESS
Dec, 1991 ($4.95, color, one-shot, 52 pgs.)
Marvel Comics

	Good	Fine	N-Mint
1-Double gatefold-c; John Romita, Jr.-c/a(p)			
	.85	2.50	5.00

GHOSTS (Ghost No. 1)
Sept-Oct, 1971-No. 112, May, 1982 (No. 1-5: 52 pgs.)
National Periodical Publications/DC Comics

	Good	Fine	N-Mint
1	.85	2.60	6.00
2-Wood-a(i)	.70	2.00	4.00
3-5	.50	1.50	3.00
6-20	.35	1.00	2.00
21-96	.25	.75	1.50
97-99-The Spectre app.	.35	1.00	2.00
100-112: 100-Infinity-c		.50	1.00

G. I. COMBAT
Oct, 1952-No. 43, Dec, 1956
Quality Comics Group

	Good	Fine	N-Mint
1-Crandall-c	22.00	65.00	150.00
2	8.50	25.50	60.00
3-5,10-Crandall-c/a	8.50	25.50	60.00
6-Crandall-a	7.00	21.00	50.00
7-9	5.00	15.00	35.00
11-20	3.60	11.00	25.00
21-31,33,35-43	2.85	8.50	20.00
32-Nuclear attack-c	5.70	17.00	40.00
34-Crandall-a	4.50	14.00	32.00

G. I. COMBAT
No. 44, Jan, 1957-No. 288, Mar, 1987
National Periodical Publications/DC Comics

	Good	Fine	N-Mint
44	23.00	70.00	160.00
45	11.50	34.00	80.00
46-50	8.00	24.00	55.00
51-60	5.30	16.00	38.00
61-66,68-80	3.85	11.50	25.00
67-1st Tank Killer	6.70	20.00	47.00
81,82,84-86	3.50	9.50	22.00
83-1st Big Al, Little Al, & Charlie Cigar	3.85	11.50	27.00
87-1st Haunted Tank	6.70	20.00	47.00
88-90: Last 10 cent issue	1.70	5.00	12.00
91-113,115-120	1.30	4.00	9.00
114-Origin Haunted Tank	3.15	9.50	22.00
121-137,139,140: 136-Last 12 cent issue	1.00	3.00	7.00
138-Intro. The Losers (Capt. Storm, Gunner/Sarge, Johnny Cloud) in Haunted Tank (10-11/69)	1.15	3.50	8.00
141-200: 146-148-(25 cent, 68 pgs.). 149-154-(52 pgs.). 150-Ice Cream Soldier story (tells how he got his name). 151-Capt. Storm story. 151,153-Medal of Honor series by Maurer	.60	1.75	3.50
201-281: 246-($1.50, 76pgs.)-30th Anniversary issue	.35	1.00	2.00
282-288 (75 cents): 282-New advs. begin	.35	1.00	2.00

G. I. JOE AND THE TRANSFORMERS
Jan, 1987-No. 4, Apr, 1987 (Mini-series)
Marvel Comics Group

	Good	Fine	N-Mint
1	.25	.75	1.50
2-4		.50	1.00

G. I. JOE, A REAL AMERICAN HERO
June, 1982-Present
Marvel Comics Group

	Good	Fine	N-Mint
1-Printed on Baxter paper	1.50	4.50	9.00
2-Printed on reg. paper	1.50	4.50	9.00
2-10 (2nd printings)	.30	.90	1.80
3-5,7,9,10	1.00	3.00	6.00
6,8	1.15	3.50	7.00
11-Intro Airborne	.70	2.00	4.00
12	.85	2.50	5.00
13-15	.60	1.75	3.50
14 (2nd printing)	.30	.90	1.80
16-20	.50	1.50	3.00
17-19 (2nd printings)	.25	.70	1.40
21,22	.85	2.50	5.00
23-25	.50	1.50	3.00
21,23,25 (2nd printings)	.25	.70	1.40
26,27-Origin Snake-Eyes parts 1 & 2	.75	2.25	4.50
26,27 (2nd printings)		.45	.90
28-30	.50	1.50	3.00
29,30 (2nd printings)		.45	.90
31-35: 33-New headquarters	.40	1.25	2.50
34-37 (2nd printings)		.45	.90
36-40	.35	1.00	2.00
41-49	.25	.75	1.50
50-Double size; intro Special Missions	.50	1.50	3.00
51-58		.60	1.20
51 (2nd printing)		.35	.70
59,61-99,101-120: 94-96,103-Snake-Eyes app.		.65	1.30
60-Todd McFarlane-a	.30	.90	1.80
100 ($1.50, 52 pgs.)	.25	.75	1.50
121-124: 121-Begin $1.25-c		.65	1.30
Special Treasury Edition (1982)-r/#1	1.20	3.60	7.20
...Yearbook 1 ('84)-r/#1; Golden-c	1.05	3.15	6.30
...Yearbook 2 ('85)-Golden-c/a	.60	1.80	3.60
...Yearbook 3 ('86, 68 pgs.)	.45	1.35	2.70
...Yearbook 4 (2/88)	.25	.80	1.60

G. I. JOE ORDER OF BATTLE, THE
Dec, 1986-No. 4, Mar, 1987 (Mini-series)
Marvel Comics Group

	Good	Fine	N-Mint
1	.40	1.25	2.50
2-4	.25	.75	1.50

G. I. JOE SPECIAL MISSIONS (Indicia title: Special Missions)
Oct, 1986-No. 28, Dec, 1989 ($1.00, color)
Marvel Comics Group

1	.50	1.50	3.00
2	.30	.90	1.80
3-28		.50	1.00

GODZILLA
August, 1977-No. 24, July, 1979 (Based on movie series)
Marvel Comics Group

1-Mooney-i	.85	2.50	5.00
2-10: 2-Tuska-i. 3-Champions app.(w/o Ghost Rider)			
	.70	2.00	4.00
11-24: 20-F.F. app. 21,22-Devil Dinosaur app.			
	.40	1.25	2.50

GREEN ARROW (See Action #440, Adventure, Brave & the Bold,
    Detective #521, Flash #217, Green Lantern #76 & Justice League
    of America #4)
May, 1983-No. 4, Aug, 1983 (Mini-series)
DC Comics

1-Origin; Speedy cameo	.70	2.00	4.00
2-4	.50	1.50	3.00

GREEN ARROW
Feb, 1988-Present ($1.00, mature readers)(Painted-c #1-3)
DC Comics

1-Mike Grell scripts in all	1.85	5.50	11.00
2	.85	2.50	5.00
3	.50	1.50	3.00
4-12	.35	1.00	2.00
13-20	.30	.90	1.80
21-49,51-70: 27,28-Warlord app. 35-38-Co-stars Black Canary (bi-weekly); Bill Wray-i. 40-Grell-a. 47-Begin $1.50-c			
	.25	.75	1.50
50-($2.50, 52 pgs.)	.40	1.25	2.50
Annual 1 ('88, $2.00)-No Grell scripts	.35	1.00	2.00
Annual 2 ('89, $2.50, 68 pgs.)-No Grell scripts; recaps origin Green Arrow, Speedy, Black Canary & others	.40	1.25	2.50

	Good	Fine	N-Mint
Annual 3 ('90, $2.50, 68 pgs.)-Bill Wray-a	.40	1.25	2.50
Annual 4 ('91, $2.95, 68 pgs.)-50th ann. issue	.50	1.50	3.00
Annual 5 ('92, $3.00, 68 pgs.)-Batman, Black Canary			
	.50	1.50	3.00

GREEN ARROW: THE LONG BOW HUNTERS
Aug, 1987-No. 3, Oct, 1987 ($2.95, color, mature readers)
DC Comics

1-Grell-c/a in all	2.15	6.50	15.00
1,2-2nd printings	.35	1.00	2.00
2	1.35	4.00	8.00
3	.85	2.50	5.00

GREEN HORNET, THE (TV)
Feb, 1967-No. 3, Aug, 1967 (All have photo-c)
Gold Key

1-All have Bruce Lee photo-c	13.00	40.00	90.00
2,3	9.30	28.00	65.00

GREEN HORNET, THE (Also see Tales of the...)
Nov, 1989-No. 14, Feb, 1991 ($1.75, color)
V2#1, Sept, 1991-Present ($1.95, color)
Now Comics

1 ($2.95, double-size)-Steranko painted-c; G.A. Green Hornet			
	3.35	10.00	20.00
1-2nd printing ('90, $3.95)-New Butler-c	.70	2.00	4.00
2	1.70	5.00	10.00
3-5: 5-Death of original (1930s) Green Hornet			
	1.00	3.00	6.00
6-8: 6-Dave Dorman painted-c	.50	1.50	3.00
9-14	.35	1.00	2.00
V2#1-11,13,14: 1-Butler painted-c	.35	1.00	2.00
V2#12-($2.50)-Comes polybagged w/G.H. button			
	.50	1.50	3.00

GREEN HORNET COMICS (...Racket Buster #44) (Radio, movies)
Dec, 1940-No. 47, Sept, 1949 (See All New #13,14)
Helnit Publ. Co.(Holyoke) No. 1-6/Family Comics(Harvey) No. 7-on

1-Green Hornet begins(1st app.); painted-c			
	157.00	470.00	1100.00
2	68.00	205.00	475.00
3	57.00	170.00	400.00

	Good	Fine	N-Mint
4-6 (8/41)	43.00	130.00	300.00
7 (6/42)-Origin The Zebra; Robin Hood & Spirit of 76 begin			
	39.00	118.00	275.00
8-10	34.00	100.00	235.00
11,12-Mr. Q in both	28.00	85.00	200.00
13-20	24.00	72.00	165.00
21-30: 24-Sci-Fi-c	22.00	65.00	150.00
31-The Man in Black Called Fate begins	21.50	64.00	155.00
32-36: 36-Spanking panel	19.00	58.00	135.00
37-Shock Gibson app. by Powell; S&K Kid Adonis reprinted from			
Stuntman #3	21.00	63.00	145.00
38-Shock Gibson, Kid Adonis app.	19.00	58.00	135.00
39-Stuntman story by S&K	23.00	70.00	160.00
40,41	15.00	45.00	90.00
42-47-Kerry Drake in all. 45-Boy Explorers on cover only. 46-"Case			
of the Marijuana Racket" cover/story; Kerry Drake app.			
	15.00	45.00	90.00

GREEN LAMA (Also see Prize Comics #7)
Dec, 1944-No. 8, March, 1946
Spark Publications/Prize No. 7 on

		Good	Fine	N-Mint
1-Intro. The Green Lama, Lt. Hercules & The Boy Champions; Mac				
Raboy-c/a #1-8		68.00	205.00	475.00
2-Lt. Hercules borrows the Human Torch's powers for one panel				
		50.00	150.00	350.00
3,6-8: 7-X-mas-c; Raboy craft tint art		34.00	102.00	235.00
4-Dick Tracy take-off in Lt. Hercules story by H. L. Gold (sci-				
fiction writer)		34.00	102.00	235.00
5-Lt. Hercules story; Little Orphan Annie, Smilin' Jack & Snuffy				
Smith take-off (5/45)		34.00	102.00	235.00

GREEN LANTERN (1st Series) (See All-American, All Flash
    Quarterly, All Star Comics & Comic Cavalcade)
Fall, 1941-No. 38, May-June, 1949
National Periodical Publications/All-American

	Good	Fine	VF-NM
1-Origin retold	835.00	2100.00	5000.00
	Good	**Fine**	**N-Mint**
2-1st book-length story	400.00	1000.00	2400.00
3	270.00	670.00	1600.00
4-Classic war-c	200.00	500.00	1200.00
5	140.00	350.00	850.00

	Good	Fine	N-Mint
6-8: 8-Hop Harrigan begins	120.00	290.00	700.00
9,10: 10-Origin Vandal Savage	105.00	260.00	625.00
11-17,19,20: 12-Origin Gambler	88.00	220.00	525.00
18-Christmas-c	100.00	250.00	600.00

21-30: 27-Origin Sky Pirate. 30-Origin/1st app. Streak the Wonder

	Good	Fine	N-Mint
Dog by Toth	75.00	190.00	450.00
31-35	63.00	155.00	375.00
36-38: 37-Sargon the Sorcerer app.	92.00	230.00	550.00

GREEN LANTERN (Green Lantern Corps. #206 on; see Adventure
Comics, Brave & the Bold, Flash, Justice League of America &
Showcase)
7-8/60-No. 89, 4-5/72; No. 90, 8-9/76-No. 205, 10/86
National Periodical Publications/DC Comics

Showcase #22 (9-10/59)-Origin & 1st app. Silver Age Green Lantern

	Good	Fine	N-Mint
by Gil Kane	265.00	800.00	1850.00
Showcase #23,24 (11-12/59, 1-2/60)	92.00	275.00	640.00

1-(7-8/60)-Origin retold; Gil Kane-a begins

	Good	Fine	N-Mint
	180.00	540.00	1250.00
2-1st Pieface	65.00	195.00	450.00
3	40.00	120.00	275.00

Green Lantern #5 (3-4/61), © DC Comics

4,5: 5-Origin & 1st app. Hector Hammond

	Good	Fine	N-Mint
	30.00	90.00	210.00

6-10: 6-Intro Tomar-re the alien G.L. 7-Origin Sinestro. 8-1st 5700
A.D. story; painted-c. 9-1st Jordan Brothers; last 10 cent issue

	Good	Fine	N-Mint
	20.00	60.00	140.00
11,12,14,15: 14-Origin/1st app. Sonar	14.00	43.00	100.00

	Good	Fine	N-Mint
13-Flash x-over	17.00	51.00	120.00
16-20: 16-Origin Star Sapphire. 20-Flash x-over			
	12.00	36.00	85.00
21-30: 21-Origin Dr. Polaris. 23-1st Tattooed Man. 24-Origin Shark.			
9-JLA cameo; 1st Blackhand	11.00	32.00	75.00
31-39	8.00	24.00	55.00
40-1st app. Crisis (10/65); 2nd solo G.A. Green Lantern in Silver Age			
(see Showcase #55); origin The Guardians; Doiby Dickles app.			
	42.00	126.00	290.00
41-44,46-50: 42-Zatanna x-over. 43-Flash x-over			
	5.30	16.00	38.00
45-G.A. Green Lantern x-over	7.00	21.00	50.00
51,53-58	3.30	10.00	23.00
52-G.A. Green Lantern x-over	4.30	13.00	30.00
59-1st app. Guy Gardner (3/68)	17.50	52.00	122.00
60,62-69: 69-Wood inks; last 12 cent issue			
	2.30	7.00	16.00
61-G.A. Green Lantern x-over	3.15	9.50	22.00
70-75	1.85	5.50	13.00
76-Begin Green Lantern/Green Arrow series (by Neal Adams #76-			
89) ends #122	11.50	34.00	80.00
77	4.50	14.00	32.00
78-80	3.70	11.00	26.00
81-84: 82-Wrightson-i(1 pg.). 83-G.L. reveals i.d. to Carol Ferris. 84-			
N. Adams/Wrightson-a(22 pgs.); last 15 cent-c			
	3.15	9.50	22.00
85,86(52 pgs.)-Drug propaganda books. 86-G.A. Green Lantern-r;			
Toth-a			
87(52 pgs.): 2nd app. Guy Gardner (cameo); 1st app. John Stewart			
(becomes Green Lantern in #182)	2.85	8.50	20.00
88(52 pgs.,'72)-Unpubbed G.A. Green Lantern story; Green Lantern-r/			
Showcase #23. N. Adams-a(1 pg.)	.70	2.00	5.00
89(4-5/72, 52 pgs.)-G.A. Green Lantern-r	1.50	4.50	10.00
90(8-9/76)-99	.50	1.50	3.00
100-(Giant)-1st app. new Air Wave	.85	2.50	5.00
101-111,113-115,117-119: 107-1st Tales of the G.L. Corps story. 108-			
110-(44pgs)-G.A. Green Lantern. 111-Origin retold; G.A. Green			
Lantern app.	.40	1.25	2.50
112-G.A. Green Lantern origin retold	1.00	3.00	6.00
116-1st app. Guy Gardner as a Green Lantern			
	2.85	8.50	20.00
120,121,124-135,138-140,142-149: 130-132-Tales of the G.L. Corps.			

	Good	**Fine**	**N-Mint**

132-Adam Strange series begins, ends 147. 142,143-Omega Men app.; Perez-c. 144-Omega Men cameo. 148-Tales of the G.L. Corps begins, ends #173 — .25 / .75 / 1.50

122-Last Green Lantern/Green Arrow team-up
.35 / 1.00 / 2.00

123-Green Lantern back to solo action; 2nd app. Guy Gardner as Green Lantern — .85 / 2.50 / 5.00

136,137-1st app. Citadel; Space Ranger app. .40 / 1.25 / 2.50

141-1st app. Omega Men — .40 / 1.25 / 2.50

150-Anniversary issue, 52 pgs.; no G.L. Corps
.40 / 1.25 / 2.50

151-170: 159-Origin Evil Star. 160,161-Omega Men app. 181-Hal Jordan resigns as G.L. 182-John Stewart becomes new G.L.; origin recap of Hal Jordan as G.L. .25 / .75 / 1.50

171-193,196-199,201-205: 185-Origin new G.L. (John Stewart). 188-I.D. revealed; Alan Moore back-up scripts. 191-1st app. Star Sapphire. 198-Crisis x-over. 199-Hal Jordan returns as a member of G.L. Corps (3 G.L.s now). 201-Green Lantern Corps begins (is cover title & says premiere issue) .25 / .75 / 1.50

194-Crisis x-over; Hal Jordan/Guy Gardner battle; Guardians choose Guy Gardner to become new G.L. .40 / 1.25 / 2.50

195-Guy Gardner becomes Green Lantern; Crisis x-over
1.85 / 5.50 / 11.00

200-Double-size — .40 / 1.25 / 2.50

Special 1 (1988), 2 (1989)-(Both $1.50, 52 pgs.)
.40 / 1.25 / 2.50

GREEN LANTERN
June, 1990-Present ($1.00, color)
DC Comics

1-Hal Jordan, John Stewart & Guy Gardner return; Batman app.
.60 / 1.75 / 3.50

2,3 — .35 / 1.00 / 2.00

4-8 — .60 / 1.20

9-12-Guy Gardner solo story .40 / 1.25 / 2.50

13-($1.75, 52 pgs.) .35 / 1.00 / 2.00

14-18,20-24,26 — .50 / 1.00

19-($1.75, 52 pgs.)-50th anniversary issue; Mart Nodell (original G.A. artist) part-p on G.A. Gr. Lantern; G. Kane-c
.30 / .90 / 1.80

25-($1.75, 52 pgs.)-Hal Jordan battles Guy Gardner
.35 / 1.00 / 2.00

	Good	Fine	N-Mint
27-32: 27-Begin $1.25-c		.65	1.30
Annual 1 (1992, $2.50, 68 pgs.)-Eclipso app.			
	.40	1.25	2.50

GREEN LANTERN CORPS, THE (Formerly Green Lantern)
No. 206, Nov, 1986-No. 224, May, 1988
DC Comics

	Good	Fine	N-Mint
206-223: 220,221-Millennium tie-ins		.50	1.00
224-Double size last issue	.25	.75	1.50
Corps Annual 2 (12/86)-Alan Moore scripts	.25	.75	1.50
Corps Annual 3 (8/87)-Moore scripts; Byrne-a			
	.25	.75	1.50

GREEN LANTERN: EMERALD DAWN
Dec, 1989-No. 6, May, 1990 ($1.00, color, mini-series)
DC Comics

	Good	Fine	N-Mint
1-Origin retold; Giffen plots in all	2.00	6.00	12.00
2	1.35	4.00	8.00
3,4	.85	2.50	5.00
5,6	.50	1.50	3.00

GREEN LANTERN: EMERALD DAWN II (Emerald Dawn II #1 & 2)
Apr, 1991-No. 6, Sept, 1991 ($1.00, color, mini-series)
DC Comics

	Good	Fine	N-Mint
1	.25	.75	1.50
2-6		.50	1.00

GREEN MASK, THE (Also see Mystery Men)
Summer, 1940-No. 9, 2/42; No. 10, 8/44-No. 11, 11/44; V2#1, Spring, 1945-No. 6, 10-11/46
Fox Features Syndicate

	Good	Fine	N-Mint
V1#1-Origin The Green Mask & Domino; reprints/Mystery Men #1-3,5-7; Lou Fine-c	107.00	320.00	750.00
2-Zanzibar The Magician by Tuska	54.00	162.00	375.00
3-Powell-a; Marijuana story	34.00	100.00	235.00
4-Navy Jones begins, ends #6	26.00	78.00	180.00
5	23.00	70.00	160.00
6-The Nightbird begins, ends #9	19.00	58.00	135.00
7-9	16.00	48.00	110.00
10,11: 10-Origin One Round Hogan & Rocket Kelly			
	13.00	40.00	90.00

	Good	Fine	N-Mint
V2#1	10.00	30.00	70.00
2-6	8.50	25.50	60.00

GUARDIANS OF THE GALAXY (Also see Marvel Presents #3,
    Marvel Super-Heroes #18 & Marvel Two-In-One #5)
    June, 1990-Present ($1.00, color)
    Marvel Comics

	Good	Fine	N-Mint
1-Valentino-c/a(p) begin; painted-c	1.35	4.00	8.00
2,3: 2-Zeck-c(i)	.85	2.50	5.00
4-6: 5-McFarlane-c(i)	.60	1.75	3.50
7-10: 7-Intro Malevolence (Mephisto's daughter); Perez-c(i). 8-Intro Rancor (descendant of Wolverine) in cameo. 9-1st full app. Rancor; Rob Liefeld-c(i). 10-Jim Lee-c(i)			
	.50	1.50	3.00
11,12,15: 15-Starlin-c(i)	.35	1.00	2.00
13,14-1st app. Spirit of Vengeance (futuristic Ghost Rider). 14-Spirit of Vengeance vs. The Guardians	1.00	3.00	6.00
16-($1.50, 52 pgs.)-Starlin-c(i)	.35	1.00	2.00
17-20: 17-20-31st century Punishers storyline		.65	1.30
21-23,26-32: 21-Rancor app.; begin $1.25-c. 22-Reintro Starhawk. 26-Origin revealed		.65	1.30
24-Silver Surfer-c/story; Ron Lim-c(i)	.50	1.50	3.00
25-($2.50, 52 pgs.)-Foil stamped-c; Silver Surfer app.			
	.50	1.50	3.00
25-(without foil-c; printing error)	.25	1.00	2.00
Annual 1 (1991, $2.00, 68 pgs.)-2 pg. origin	.40	1.25	2.50
Annual 2 (1992, $2.25, 68 pgs.)	.40	1.15	2.30

GUNSMOKE (TV)
No. 679, 2/56-No. 27, 6-7/61; 2/69-No. 6, 2/70
Dell Publishing Co./Gold Key (All have James Arness photo-c)

	Good	Fine	N-Mint
4-Color 679(No. 1)	10.00	30.00	70.00
4-Color 720,769,797,844	5.00	15.00	35.00
6(11-1/57-58), 7	5.00	15.00	35.00
8,9,11,12-Williamson-a in all, 4 pgs. each			
	6.00	18.00	42.00
10-Williamson/Crandall-a, 4 pgs.	6.00	18.00	42.00
13-27	4.50	14.00	32.00
Gunsmoke Film Story (11/62-G.K. Giant) #30008-211			
	5.70	17.00	40.00
1 (Gold Key)	2.65	8.00	18.00
2-6('69-70)	1.50	4.50	10.00

HANNA-BARBERA SUPER TV HEROES (TV)
April, 1968-No. 7, Oct, 1969 (Hanna-Barbera)
Gold Key

	Good	Fine	N-Mint
1-The Birdman, The Herculoids(ends #2), Moby Dick, Young Samson & Goliath(ends #2,4), and The Mighty Mightor begin; Spiegle-a in all	11.00	32.00	75.00
2-The Galaxy Trio app.; Shazzan begins	7.00	21.00	50.00
3-7: The Space Ghost app. in #3,5-7	5.70	17.00	40.00

HARBINGER
Jan, 1992-Present ($1.95-$2.50, color)
Valiant

1	2.50	7.50	15.00
2	1.25	3.75	7.50
3	.60	1.75	3.50
4	1.00	3.00	6.00
5-12: 10-1st app. HARD Corps	.40	1.25	2.50

HAUNT OF FEAR
No. 15, May-June, 1950-No. 28, Nov-Dec, 1954
E. C. Comics

15(#1, 1950)(Scarce)	157.00	470.00	1100.00
16	80.00	240.00	550.00
17-Origin of Crypt of Terror, Vault of Horror, & Haunt of Fear; used in **SOTI**, pg. 43; last pg. Ingels-a used by N.Y. Legis. Comm.; story "Monster Maker" based on Frankenstein			
	80.00	240.00	550.00
4	57.00	170.00	400.00
5-Injury-to-eye panel, pg. 4	43.00	130.00	300.00
6-10: 8-Shrunken head cover. 10-Ingels biog.			
	31.00	92.00	215.00
11-13,15-18: 11-Kamen biog. 12-Feldstein biog. 16,18-Ray Bradbury adaptations. 18-Ray Bradbury biog.			
	22.00	65.00	150.00
14-Origin Old Witch by Ingels	31.00	92.00	215.00
19-Used in **SOTI**, ill.-"A comic book baseball game" & Senate investigation on juvenile delinq. bondage/decapitation-c			
	28.00	85.00	200.00

	Good	Fine	N-Mint
20-Feldstein-r/Vault of Horror #12	20.00	60.00	140.00
21,22,25,27: 27-Cannibalism story; Wertham cameo			
	13.00	40.00	90.00
23-Used in **SOTI**, pg. 241	14.00	43.00	100.00
24-Used in Senate Investigative Report, pg.8			
	13.00	40.00	90.00
26-Contains anti-censorship editorial, "Are you a Red Dupe?"			
	13.00	40.00	90.00
28-Low distribution	14.00	43.00	100.00

HAWK AND DOVE
Oct, 1988-No. 5, Holiday, 1988 ($1.00, color, mini-series)
DC Comics

1-Rob Liefeld-c/a(p) in all	.85	2.50	5.00
2-5	.50	1.50	3.00

HAWK AND DOVE
June, 1989-No. 28, Oct, 1991 ($1.00-$1.25, color)
DC Comics

1	.25	.75	1.50
2-24: 12-New Titans app. 18,19-The Creeper app.		.50	1.00
25,28 ($2.00, 52 pgs.): 28-War of the Gods			
	.35	1.00	2.00
26,27 ($1.25-c)		.65	1.30
Annual 1,2: 1-(1990, $2.00, 68 pgs.). 2-(1991, $2.00, 68 pgs.)-			
Armaggedon 2001 x-over	.35	1.00	2.00

The Hawk and the Dove #2 (10-11/68), © DC Comics

HAWK AND THE DOVE, THE (See Showcase #75 & Teen Titans)
Aug-Sept, 1968-No. 6, June-July, 1969
National Periodical Publications

	Good	Fine	N-Mint
Showcase #75 (7-8/67)-Origin & 1st app. Hawk and the Dove; Ditko-c/a	7.00	21.00	50.00
1-Ditko-c/a	5.00	15.00	35.00
2-6: 5-Teen Titans cameo	3.60	11.00	25.00

HAWKMAN (See Atom #7, Atom &..., The Brave & the Bold, Detective, Hawkworld, Justice League of America #31, Mystery in Space & Showcase)
Apr-May, 1964-No. 27, Aug-Sept, 1968
National Periodical Publications

	Good	Fine	N-Mint
Brave and the Bold #34 (2-3/61)-Origin & 1st app. S.A. Hawkman & Byth by Kubert; 1st S.A. Hawkman tryout	93.00	280.00	650.00
Brave and the Bold #35,36 (4-5/61, 6-7/61): Hawkman by Kubert. 36-Origin Shadow Thief	25.00	75.00	175.00
Brave and the Bold #42,44 (6-7/62, 10-11/62)-Hawkman by Kubert; 2nd Hawkman tryout series	12.00	36.00	85.00
Brave and the Bold #43 (8-9/62)-Hawkman origin retold by Kubert (see Mystery in Space for 3rd tryout series)	16.50	50.00	115.00
1-(4-5/64)-Anderson-c/a begins, ends #21	36.00	108.00	250.00
2	13.50	41.00	95.00
3,5	9.50	28.50	66.00
4-Origin & 1st app. Zatanna	11.00	33.00	77.00
6-10: 9-Atom cameo; Hawkman & Atom learn each other's I.D.; 2nd app. Shadow Thief	6.30	19.00	44.00
11-15	4.50	14.00	32.00
16-27: 18-Adam Strange x-over (cameo #19). 25-G.A. Hawkman-r by Moldoff. 27-Kubert-c	3.15	9.50	22.00

HAWKMAN
Aug, 1986-No. 17, Dec, 1987
DC Comics

	Good	Fine	N-Mint
1		.60	1.20
2-17: 10-Byrne-c		.50	1.00
Special #1 ('86, $1.25)	.25	.75	1.50

HAWKWORLD
1989-No. 3, 1989 ($3.95, prestige format, mini-series)
DC Comics

	Good	Fine	N-Mint
Book 1-Hawkman dons new costume	1.70	5.00	10.00
Book 2,3-Truman-c/a/scripts in #1-3	1.15	3.50	7.00

HAWKWORLD
June, 1990-Present ($1.50, on-going series)
DC Comics

1-Hawkman spin-off	.70	2.00	4.00
2-5	.40	1.25	2.50
6-26: 15,16-War of the Gods x-over	.25	.75	1.50
27-30: 27-Begin $1.75-c	.50	1.50	3.00
Annual 1 (1990, $2.95, 68 pgs.)-Flash app.	.50	1.50	3.00
Annual 2,3 ($2.95, 68 pgs.): 2(1991)-2nd print exists with silver ink-c.			
3(1992)-Eclipso app.	.50	1.50	3.00

HELLBLAZER (John Constantine) (See Saga of Swamp Thing #37)
Jan, 1988-Present ($1.25-1.50, adults)
DC Comics

1	2.50	7.50	15.00
2-5	1.50	4.50	9.00
6-10	.70	2.00	4.00
11-20	.50	1.50	3.00
21-30: 25,26-Grant Morrison scripts	.40	1.25	2.50
31-39: 36-Preview of World Without End	.30	.90	1.80
40-($2.25, 52 pgs.)-Preview of Kid Eternity			
	.40	1.25	2.50
41-49: 44-Begin $1.75-c	.40	1.25	2.50
50-($3.00, 52 pgs.)	.50	1.50	3.00
51-60	.30	.90	1.80
Annual 1 ('89, $2.95, 68 pgs.)	.70	2.00	4.00

HERBIE (See Forbidden Worlds & Unknown Worlds)
April-May, 1964-No. 23, Feb, 1967 (All 12 cents)
American Comics Group

1-Whitney-c/a in most issues	11.50	34.00	80.00
2-4	7.00	20.00	40.00
5-Beatles, Dean Martin, F. Sinatra app.	7.00	21.00	50.00
6,7,9,10	5.00	15.00	30.00
8-Origin The Fat Fury	5.70	17.00	40.00
11-23: 14-Nemesis & Magicman app. 17-r/2nd Herbie from For-			

	Good	Fine	N-Mint

bidden Worlds #94. 23-r/1st Herbie from F.W. #73

	3.15	9.50	22.00

HEROES FOR HOPE STARRING THE X-MEN
Dec, 1985 ($1.50, one-shot, 52pgs., proceeds donated to famine relief)
Marvel Comics Group

1-Stephen King scripts; Byrne, Miller, Corben-a; Wrightson/J.
Jones-a (3 pgs.); Art Adams-c   .60   1.75   3.50

HERO FOR HIRE (Power Man No. 17 on)
June, 1972-No. 16, Dec, 1973
Marvel Comics Group

1-Origin & 1st app. Luke Cage; 1-3-Tuska-a(p)

	4.00	12.00	28.00

2-5: 3-1st app. Mace. 4-1st Phil Fox of the Bugle

	1.70	5.00	12.00

6-10   1.00   3.00   6.00

11-16: 14-Origin retold. 15-Everett Subby-r('53). 16-Origin Stilletto;
death of Rackham   .85   2.50   5.00

HEX (Replaces Jonah Hex)
Sept, 1985-No. 18, Feb, 1987 (Story continues from Jonah Hex 92)
DC Comics

1-Hex in post-atomic war world; origin   .25   .75   1.50
2-10,14-18: 6-Origin Stiletta   .50   1.00
11-13: All contain future Batman storyline. 13-Intro The Dogs of War
(origin #15)   .35   1.00   2.00

HISTORY OF THE DC UNIVERSE
Sept, 1986-No. 2, Nov, 1986 ($2.95)
DC Comics

1-Perez-c/a   .60   1.75   3.50
2   .50   1.50   3.00

HIT COMICS
July, 1940-No. 65, July, 1950
Quality Comics Group

1-Origin Neon, the Unknown & Hercules; intro. The Red Bee; Bob
& Swab, Blaze Barton, the Strange Twins, X-5 Super Agent,
Casey Jones & Jack & Jill (ends #7) begin

	215.00	645.00	1500.00

2-The Old Witch begins, ends #14   100.00   300.00   700.00

	Good	Fine	N-Mint
3-Casey Jones ends; transvestism story-"Jack & Jill"			
	80.00	240.00	550.00
4-Super Agent (ends #17), & Betty Bates (ends #65) begin; X-5 ends			
	64.00	192.00	450.00
5-Classic cover	100.00	300.00	700.00
6-10: 10-Old Witch by Crandall (4 pgs.); 1st work in comics			
	54.00	160.00	375.00
11-17: 13-Blaze Barton ends. 17-Last Neon; Crandall Hercules in all			
	50.00	150.00	350.00
18-Origin Stormy Foster, the Great Defender; The Ghost of Flanders			
begins; Crandall-c	57.00	170.00	400.00
19,20	50.00	150.00	350.00
21-24: 21-Last Hercules. 24-Last Red Bee & Strange Twins			
	43.00	130.00	300.00
25-Origin Kid Eternity and begins by Moldoff			
	57.00	170.00	400.00
26-Blackhawk x-over in Kid Eternity	47.00	140.00	325.00
27-29	26.00	78.00	180.00
30,31-"Bill the Magnificent" by Kurtzman, 11 pgs. in each			
	23.00	70.00	160.00
32-40: 32-Plastic Man x-over. 34-Last Stormy Foster			
	11.50	34.00	80.00
41-50	9.00	27.00	55.00
51-60-Last Kid Eternity	8.35	25.00	50.00
61,63-Crandall-c/a; Jeb Rivers begins #61	9.00	27.00	55.00
62	7.50	22.00	45.00
64,65-Crandall-a	8.35	25.00	50.00

HOGAN'S HEROES (TV) (No. 1-7 have photo-c)
June, 1966-No. 8, Sept, 1967; No. 9, Oct, 1969
Dell Publishing Co.

1	4.00	12.00	28.00
2,3-Ditko-a(p)	2.65	8.00	18.00
4-9: 9-Reprints #1	1.70	5.00	12.00

HOPALONG CASSIDY (See Bill Boyd Western & Master Comics;
   Bill Boyd starred as H. Cassidy in the movies; H. Cassidy in
   movies, radio & TV)
Feb, 1943; No. 2, Summer, 1946-No. 85, Jan, 1954
Fawcett Publications

1 (1943, 68 pgs.)-H. Cassidy & his horse Topper begin (on sale			
1/8/43)-Captain Marvel on-c	167.00	415.00	1000.00

	Good	Fine	N-Mint
2-(Sum, '46)	50.00	150.00	350.00
3,4: 3-(Fall, '46, 52 pgs. begin)	24.00	70.00	165.00
5-"Mad Barber" story mentioned in **SOTI**, pgs. 308,309			
	22.00	65.00	150.00
6-10	17.00	51.00	120.00
11-19: 11,13-19-Photo-c	12.00	36.00	85.00
20-29 (52 pgs.)-Painted/photo-c	9.30	28.00	65.00
30,31,33,34,37-39,41 (52 pgs.)-Painted-c	5.70	17.00	40.00
32,40 (36 pgs.)-Painted-c	5.00	15.00	35.00
35,42,43,45 (52 pgs.)-Photo-c	6.00	18.00	42.00
36,44,48 (36 pgs.)-Photo-c	5.00	15.00	35.00
46,47,49-51,53,54,56 (52 pgs.)-Photo-c	5.50	16.00	38.00
52,55,57-70 (36 pgs.)-Photo-c	4.00	12.00	28.00
71-84-Photo-c	3.50	10.50	24.00
85-Last Fawcett issue; photo-c	4.30	13.00	30.00

HOPALONG CASSIDY (TV)
No. 86, Feb, 1954-No. 135, May-June, 1959 (All-36 pgs.)
National Periodical Publications

86-Photo covers continue	19.00	58.00	135.00
87	11.50	34.00	80.00
88-90	8.50	25.50	60.00
91-99 (98 has #93 on-c & is last precode issue, 2/55)			
	6.50	19.00	45.00
100	8.00	24.00	55.00
101-108-Last photo-c	5.00	15.00	35.00
109-135: 124-Painted-c	4.30	13.00	30.00

HOT WHEELS (TV)
Mar-Apr, 1970-No. 6, Jan-Feb, 1971
National Periodical Publications

1	3.60	11.00	25.00
2,4,5	1.70	5.00	12.00
3-Neal Adams-c	2.85	8.50	20.00
6-Neal Adams-c/a	3.50	10.50	24.00

HOUSE OF MYSTERY, THE (Also see Brave & the Bold #93 &
    Elvira's...)
Dec-Jan, 1951-52-No. 321, Oct, 1983 (No. 199-203: 52 pgs.)
National Periodical Publications/DC Comics

1	72.00	215.00	500.00
2	28.00	85.00	200.00

House of Mystery #156, © DC Comics

	Good	Fine	N-Mint
3	25.00	75.00	175.00
4,5	22.00	65.00	150.00
6-10	16.00	48.00	110.00
11-15	13.00	40.00	90.00
16(7/53)-25	8.50	25.50	60.00
26-35(2/55)-Last pre-code issue; 30-Woodish-a			
	7.00	21.00	50.00
36-49	5.00	15.00	35.00
50-Text story of Orson Welles' War of the Worlds broadcast			
	4.30	13.00	30.00
51-60	3.15	9.50	22.00
61,63,65,66,70,72-Kirby-a	3.15	9.50	22.00
62,64,67-69,71,73-75,77-83,86-99	2.15	6.50	15.00
76,84,85-Kirby-a	2.85	8.50	20.00
100 (7/60)	2.65	8.00	18.00
101-116: Last 10 cent issue. 109-Toth, Kubert-a			
	2.15	6.50	15.00
117-119,121-130	1.60	4.80	11.00
120-Toth-a	2.00	6.00	14.00
131-142	1.30	4.00	9.00
143-J'onn J'onzz, Manhunter begins (6/64), ends #173; story continues from Detective #326	11.00	32.00	75.00
144	5.70	17.00	40.00
145-155,157-159: 149-Toth-a. 158-Origin/1st app. Diabolu Idol-Head in J'onn J'onzz	4.30	13.00	30.00
156-Robby Reed begins (origin), ends #173	4.50	14.00	32.00

	Good	Fine	N-Mint
160-(7/66)-Robby Reed becomes Plastic Man in this issue only; 1st S.A. app. Plastic Man; intro Marco Xavier (Martin Manhunter) & Vulture Crime Organization; ends #173			
	5.70	17.00	40.00
161-173: 169-Origin/1st app. Gem Girl	2.85	8.50	20.00
174-177,182: 174-Mystery format begins. 182-Toth-a			
	1.00	3.00	7.00
178-Neal Adams-a; last 12 cent issue	1.50	4.50	10.00
179-N. Adams/Orlando, Wrightson-a (1st pro work, 3 pgs.)			
	2.65	8.00	18.00
180,181,183: Wrightson-a (3, 10, & 3 pgs.). 180-Kane-Wood-a(2).			
183-Wood-a	1.00	3.00	7.00
184-Kane/Wood, Toth-a	.85	2.50	5.00
185-Williamson/Kaluta-a; 3 pgs. Howard-a			
	1.15	3.50	8.00
186-N. Adams-a; Wrightson-a, 10 pgs.	1.15	3.50	8.00
187,190: 187-Toth-a. 190-Toth-a(r)	.50	1.50	3.00
188,191,195-Wrightson-a (8, 3 & 10 pgs.). 195-Swamp creature story by Wrightson similar to Swamp Thing (10/71)			
	1.15	3.50	8.00
189-Wood-a	.50	1.50	3.00
192-194,196-198,200-203,205-223,225-227: 194-Toth, Kirby-a; 48 pgs. begin, end #198. 207-Wrightson-a. 221-Wrightson/Kaluta-a (8 pgs.). 226-Wrightson-r; Phantom Stranger-r			
	.50	1.50	3.00
199-Wood, Kirby-a; 52pgs. begin, end 203	.70	2.00	4.00
204-Wrightson-a, 9 pgs.	.70	2.00	4.00
224-N. Adams/Wrightson-a(r); begin 100 pg. issues; Phantom Stranger-r	.85	2.50	5.00
228-N. Adams inks; Wrightson-r	.70	2.00	4.00
229-321: 229-Wrightson-a(r); Toth-r; last 100 pg. issue. 230-68 pgs. 251-259, 84 pgs. 251-Wood-a	.50	1.50	3.00

HOUSE OF SECRETS (Combined with The Unexpected after #154)
11-12/56-No. 80, 9-10/66; No. 81, 8-9/69-No. 140, 2-3/76; No. 141, 8-9/76-No. 154, 10-11/78
National Periodical Publications/DC Comics

	Good	Fine	N-Mint
1-Drucker-a; Moreira-c	52.00	156.00	360.00
2-Moreira-a	22.50	67.00	155.00
3-Kirby-c/a	19.00	57.00	132.00
4,8-Kirby-a	10.00	30.00	70.00
5-7,9-11: 11-Lou Cameron-a(unsigned)	8.00	24.00	55.00

	Good	Fine	N-Mint
12-Kirby-c/a	9.30	28.00	65.00
13-15	6.00	18.00	42.00
16-20	4.50	14.00	32.00
21,22,24-30	3.70	11.00	26.00
23-Origin/1st app. Mark Merlin & begin series			
	4.50	14.00	32.00
31-47,49,50: Last 10 cent issue	2.40	7.25	17.00
48-Toth-a	2.85	8.50	20.00
51-60: 58-Origin Mark Merlin retold	1.60	4.80	11.00
61-First Eclipso (7-8/63) and begin series	8.50	25.50	60.00
62	4.30	13.00	30.00
63-65,67-Toth-a on Eclipso (see Brave & the Bold #64)			
	2.85	8.50	20.00
66-1st Eclipso-c (also #67,70,78,79); Toth-a on Eclipso			
	5.70	17.00	40.00

68-80: 73-Mark Merlin ends, Prince Ra-Man begins. 76-Prine Ra-Man vs. Eclipso. 80-Eclipso, Prince Ra-Man end

	2.65	8.00	18.00

81-91: 81-Mystery format begins. 82-N. Adams-c(i). 85-N. Adams-a(i). 87-Wrightson & Kaluta-a. 90-Buckler (early work)/N. Adams-a

	.55	1.65	3.30

92-1st app. Swamp Thing (6-7/71) by Berni Wrightson(p) w/Jeff Jones/Kaluta/Weiss ink assists (8 pgs.)

	23.00	70.00	160.00
93-100: 94-Wrightson inks. 96-Wood-a	.55	1.65	3.30
101-154: 140-Origin The Patchworkman		.50	1.00

HOWARD THE DUCK (Also see Fear & Man-Thing)
Jan, 1976-No. 31, May, 1979; No. 32, Jan, 1986; No. 33, Sept, 1986
Marvel Comics Group

1-Brunner-c/a; Spider-Man x-over (low distr.)			
	1.50	4.50	10.00
2-11: 2-Brunner-c/a (low distr.). 3-Buscema-a(p)			
	.35	1.00	2.00
12-1st app. Kiss (cameo, 3/77)	.70	2.00	4.00
13-Kiss app. (1st full story)	.85	2.50	5.00
14-33: 16-Album issue; 3pgs. comics		.50	1.00
Annual 1(1977, 52 pgs.)-Mayerik-a		.50	1.00

HUEY, DEWEY AND LOUIE JUNIOR WOODCHUCKS
     (Disney)
Aug, 1966-No. 81, 1984 (See Walt Disney's C&S #125)
Gold Key No. 1-61/Whitman No. 62 on

	Good	Fine	N-Mint
1	3.00	9.00	21.00
2,3(12/68)	2.00	6.00	14.00
4,5(4/70)-Barks-r	2.00	6.00	14.00
6-17-Written by Barks	1.30	4.00	9.00
18,27-30	.85	2.50	5.00
19-23,25-Written by Barks. 22,23,25-Barks-r			
	1.00	3.00	6.00
24,26-Barks-r	1.00	3.00	6.00
31-57,60-81: 41,70,80-Reprints	.35	1.00	2.00
58,59-Barks-r	.50	1.50	3.00

HUMAN FLY, THE
Sept, 1977-No. 19, Mar, 1979
Marvel Comics Group

	Good	Fine	N-Mint
1-Origin; Spider-Man x-over	.70	2.00	4.00
2-Ghost Rider app.	1.00	3.00	6.00
3-19: 9-Daredevil x-over	.25	.75	1.50

HUMAN TORCH, THE (Red Raven #1)(See All-Select, All Winners, Marvel Mystery, Mystic Comics (2nd series), Sub-Mariner, USA & Young Men)
No. 2, Fall, 1940-No. 15, Spring, 1944; No. 16, Fall, 1944-No. 35, Mar, 1949; No. 36, April, 1954-No. 38, Aug, 1954
Timely/Marvel Comics (TP 2,3/TCI 4-9/SePI 10/SnPC 11-25/CnPC 26-35/Atlas Comics (CPC 36-38))

	Good	Fine	VF-NM
2(#1)-Intro/Origin Toro; The Falcon, The Fiery Mask, Mantor the Magician, & Microman only app.; Human Torch by Burgos, Sub-Mariner by Everett begin (origin of each in text)			
	700.00	1750.00	4200.00

	Good	Fine	N-Mint
3(#2)-40pg. H.T. story; H.T. & S.M. battle over who is best artist in text-Everett or Burgos	267.00	670.00	1600.00
4(#3)-Origin The Patriot in text; last Everett Sub-Mariner; Sid Greene-a	217.00	540.00	1300.00
5(#4)-The Patriot app; Angel x-over in Sub-Mariner (Summer, 1941)	150.00	375.00	900.00
5-Human Torch battles Sub-Mariner (Fall, '41)			
	217.00	540.00	1300.00
6,7,9	100.00	250.00	600.00
8-Human Torch battles Sub-Mariner; Wolverton-a, 1 pg.			
	158.00	395.00	950.00

	Good	Fine	N-Mint
10-Human Torch battles Sub-Mariner; Wolverton-a, 1 pg.			
	117.00	290.00	700.00
11-15	75.00	190.00	450.00
16-20: 20-Last War issue	58.00	145.00	350.00
21-30: 23(Sum/46)-Becomes Junior Miss 24?			
	50.00	125.00	300.00
31-Namora x-over in Sub-Mariner (also #30); last Toro			
	42.00	105.00	250.00
32-Sungirl, Namora app.; Sungirl-c	42.00	105.00	250.00
33-Capt. America x-over	45.00	112.00	270.00
34-Sungirl solo	42.00	105.00	250.00
35-Captain America & Sungirl app. (1949)			
	45.00	112.00	270.00
36-38(1954)-Sub-Mariner in all	38.00	95.00	225.00

HUMAN TORCH, THE (Also see Avengers West Coast, Fantastic
   Four, The Invaders, Saga of the Original... & Strange Tales #101)
Sept, 1974-No. 8, Nov, 1975
Marvel Comics Group

1: 1-8-r/stories from Strange Tales #101-108			
	.85	2.50	5.00
2-8: 1st H.T. title since G.A. 7-vs. Sub-Mariner			
	.50	1.50	3.00

ICEMAN (Also see The Champions & X-Men #94)
Dec, 1984-No. 4, June, 1985 (Limited series)
Marvel Comics Group

	Good	Fine	N-Mint
1	.35	1.00	2.00
2,4	.25	.75	1.50
3-The Defenders, Champions (Ghost Rider) & the original X-Men			
x-over	.40	1.25	2.50

I DREAM OF JEANNIE (TV)
April, 1965-No. 2, Dec, 1966 (Photo-c)
Dell Publishing Co.

1,2-Barbara Eden photo-c	5.00	15.00	35.00

I LOVE LUCY COMICS (TV) (Also see The Lucy Show)
No. 535, Feb, 1954-No. 35, Apr-June, 1962 (All photo-c)
Dell Publishing Co.

4-Color 535(#1)	29.00	85.00	200.00
4-Color 559(#2, 5/54)	17.00	51.00	120.00
3 (8-10/54)-5	11.50	34.00	80.00
6-10	8.50	25.50	60.00
11-20	7.00	21.00	50.00
21-35	6.50	19.00	45.00

INCREDIBLE HULK, THE (See The Avengers #1, The Defenders
#1, Marvel Comics Presents #26 & She-Hulk)
May, 1962-No. 6, Mar, 1963; No. 102, Apr, 1968-Present
Marvel Comics Group

1-Origin & 1st app. (skin is grey colored)			
	245.00	735.00	2200.00
2-1st green skinned Hulk	100.00	300.00	700.00
3-Origin retold; 1st app. Ringmaster	70.00	210.00	500.00
4,5: 4-Brief origin retold	65.00	195.00	450.00
6-Intro. Teen Brigade	65.00	195.00	450.00
102-(Formerly Tales to Astonish)-Origin retold; story continued from			
Tales to Astonish #101	21.00	63.00	145.00
103	8.50	25.50	60.00
104-Rhino app.	8.00	24.00	55.00
105-108: 105-1st Missing Link	5.70	17.00	40.00

	Good	Fine	N-Mint
109,110: 109-Ka-Zar app.	4.00	12.00	28.00
111-117: 117-Last 12 cent issue	2.85	8.50	20.00
118-121,123-125: 118-Sub-Mariner x-over	1.50	4.50	10.00
122-Hulk battles Thing (12/69)	1.85	5.50	13.00

126-140: 126-1st Barbara Norriss (Valkyrie). 131-1st Jim Wilson, Hulk's new sidekick. 136-1st Xeron, The Star-Slayer. 140-Written by Harlan Ellison; 1st Jarella, Hulk's love

	Good	Fine	N-Mint
	1.30	3.85	7.70
141-1st app. Doc Samson	1.10	3.30	6.60

The Incredible Hulk #109, © *Marvel Comics*

142-144,146-161,163-171,173-175: 149-1st The Inheritor. 155-1st app. Shaper. 161-The Mimic dies; Beast app. 163-1st app. The Gremlin. 164-1st Capt. Omen & Colonel John D. Armbruster. 166-1st Zzzax. 168-1st The Harpy. 169-1st Bi-Beast

	Good	Fine	N-Mint
	.90	2.75	5.50
145-(52 pgs.)-Origin retold	1.30	3.85	7.70
162-1st app. The Wendigo; Beast app.	1.10	3.30	6.60
172-X-Men cameo; origin Juggernaut retold			
	1.10	3.30	6.60
176-Warlock cameo (1 panel only, 6/74)	1.00	3.00	7.00
177-Warlock dies (last panel, 7/74)	1.50	4.50	10.00
178-Rebirth of Warlock (8/74)	2.15	6.50	15.00
179-No Warlock	.85	2.50	5.00
180-(10/74)-1st app. Wolverine (cameo last pg.)			
	8.50	25.50	60.00

	Good	Fine	N-Mint
181-1st full Wolverine story	38.00	114.00	265.00
182-Wolverine cameo; 1st Crackajack Jackson			
	6.50	19.50	45.00
183-199: 185-Death of Col. Armbruster	.60	1.75	3.50
200-Silver Surfer app.; anniversary issue	3.15	9.50	22.00
201-240: 212-1st The Constrictor. 227-Original Avengers app. 233-Marvel Man app. 234-(4/79)-1st app. Quasar (formerly Marvel Man & changes name to Quasar)	.50	1.50	3.00
241-249,251-271: 271-Rocket Raccoon app.	.35	1.00	2.00
250-Giant size; Silver Surfer app.	.85	2.50	5.00
272-299: 272-Sasquatch & Wendigo app.; Wolverine & Alpha Flight cameo in flashback. 278,279-Most Marvel characters app. (Wolverine in both). 279-X-Men & Alpha Flight cameos. 282-284-She-Hulk app. 293-Fantastic Four app.	.35	1.00	2.00
300-(10/84, 52 pgs.)-Spider-Man app in new black costume on-c & 2 pg. cameo	.70	2.00	4.00
301-313: 312-Origin Hulk retold	.40	1.25	2.50
314-Byrne-c/a begins, ends #319	.85	2.50	5.00
315-319: 319-Bruce Banner & Betty Talbot wed	.40	1.25	2.50
320-323,325,327-329	.35	1.00	2.00
324-1st app. Grey Hulk since #1 (c-swipe of #1)	1.70	5.00	10.00
326-Grey vs. Green Hulk	.85	2.50	5.00
330-1st McFarlane issue (4/87)	3.60	11.00	25.00
331-Grey Hulk series begins	2.70	8.00	16.00
332-334,336-339: 336,337-X-Factor app.	1.85	5.50	11.00
335-No McFarlane-a	.50	1.50	3.00
340-Hulk battles Wolverine by McFarlane	6.50	19.00	45.00
341-344	1.15	3.50	7.00
345-($1.50, 52 pgs.)	1.35	4.00	8.00
346-Last McFarlane issue	1.00	3.00	6.00
347-349,351-358,360-366	.50	1.50	3.00
350-Double size	.70	2.00	4.00
359-Wolverine app. (illusion only)	.75	2.25	4.50
367-1st Dale Keown-a on Hulk (3/90)	2.50	7.50	15.00
368-Sam Kieth-c/a	1.85	5.50	11.00
369,370-Dale Keown-c/a. 370,371-Original Defenders app.	1.00	3.00	6.00
371,373-376: Keown-c/a. 376-Green vs. Grey Hulk	.70	2.00	4.00

	Good	Fine	N-Mint
372-Green Hulk app.; Keown-c/a	2.00	6.00	12.00
377-1st all new Hulk; fluorescent-c; Keown-c/a			
	2.50	7.50	15.00
377-Gold 2nd printing	.85	2.50	5.00
378,380,389: No Keown-a. 380-Doc Samson app.		.50	1.00
379-Keown-a	.70	2.00	4.00
381-388,390-392: Keown-a. 385-Infinity Gauntlet x-over. 390-Begin			
$1.25-c	.25	.75	1.50
393-($2.50, stiff-c, 72 pgs.)-Green foil stamped-c; 30th anniversary			
issue w/pin-ups of classic battles; swipes cover to #1			
	.70	2.00	4.00
393-($2.50)-2nd printing	.35	1.00	2.00
394-No Keown-c/a		.65	1.30
395,396-Punisher-c/stories; Keown-c/a	.25	.75	1.50
397,398		.65	1.30
Special 1 (10/68, 25 cents, 68 pg.)-New 51 pg. story, Hulk battles The			
Inhumans; Steranko-c	5.70	17.00	40.00
Special 2 (10/69, 25 cents, 68 pg.)-Origin retold			
	3.60	11.00	25.00
Special 3 (1/71, 25 cents, 68 pg.)	1.15	3.50	8.00
Annual 4 (1/72)	1.00	3.00	6.00
Annual 5 (1976)	.70	2.00	4.00
Annual 6 (1977)	.35	1.00	2.00
Annual 7 (1978)-Byrne/Layton-c/a; Iceman & Angel app. in book-			
length story	.50	1.50	3.00
Annual 8-16: 8 ('79)-Book-length Sasquatch-c/story. 9 ('80). 10 ('81).			
11 ('82)-Miller-p(5 pgs.), Buckler-a(p). 12 ('83). 13 ('84). 14			
('85). 15 ('86). 16 ('90, $2.00, 68 pgs.)-She-Hulk app.			
	.35	1.00	2.00
Annual 17 (1991, $2.00, 68 pgs.)-Origin retold			
	.35	1.00	2.00
Annual 18 (1992, $2.25, 68 pgs.)-Part 1 of Return of the Defenders; no			
Keown-c/a	.40	1.15	2.30
...Versus Quasimodo 1 (3/83, one-shot)-Based on Saturday morning			
cartoon		.50	1.00

INCREDIBLE HULK AND WOLVERINE, THE
Oct, 1986 (One shot, $2.50, color)
Marvel Comics Group

	Good	Fine	N-Mint
1-r-/1st app. Wolverine from Incred. Hulk #180,181; Wolverine back-up by Austin(i); Byrne-c	2.00	6.00	12.00

INFERIOR FIVE, THE (Inferior 5 #11, 12) (See Showcase #62, 63, 65)
3-4/67-No. 10, 9-10/68; No. 11, 8-9/72-No. 12, 10-11/72
National Periodical Publications (#1-10: 12 cents)

	Good	Fine	N-Mint
Showcase #62 (5-6/66)-Origin & 1st app.	5.00	15.00	35.00
Showcase #63,65 (7-8/66, 11-12/66)-2nd & 3rd app.			
	2.65	8.00	18.00
1-(3-4/67)-Sekowsky-a(p)	4.30	13.00	30.00
2-Plastic Man app.; Sekowsky-a(p)	2.15	6.50	15.00
3-10: 10-Superman x-over	1.50	4.50	10.00
11,12-Orlando-c/a; both r-/Showcase #62,63			
	1.50	4.50	10.00

INFINITY GAUNTLET (The... #2 on; see Warlock & the Infinity...)
July, 1991-No. 6, Dec, 1991 ($2.50, color, limited series)
Marvel Comics

1-Thanos-c/stories in all; Starlin scripts in all			
	1.15	3.50	7.00
2	.70	2.00	4.00
3,4	.50	1.50	3.00
5,6-Ron Lim-c/a	.85	2.50	5.00

INFINITY, INC. (See All-Star Squadron #25)
Mar, 1984-No. 53, Aug, 1988 ($1.25, Baxter paper, 36 pgs.)
DC Comics

1-Brainwave, Jr., Fury, The Huntress, Jade, Northwind, Nuklon, Obsidian, Power Girl, Silver Scarab, Star Spangled Kid begin
    .50   1.50   3.00
2-5: 2-Dr. Midnite, G.A. Flash, W. Woman, Dr. Fate, Hourman, Green Lantern, Wildcat app. 5-Nudity panels
    .35   1.00   2.00
6-13,38-49,51-53: 46,47-Millennium tie-ins
    .25   .80   1.60
14-Todd McFarlane-a (5/85, 2nd full story) .70 2.00 4.00
15-37-McFarlane-a (20,23,24: 5 pgs. only; 33: 2 pgs.); 18-24-Crisis x-over. 21-Intro new Hourman & Dr. Midnight. 26-New Wildcat app. 31-Star Spangled Kid becomes Skyman. 32-Green Fury becomes Green Flame. 33-Origin Obsidian
    .50   1.50   3.00
50 ($2.50, 52 pgs.)   .40   1.25   2.50
Annual 1,2: 1(12/85)-Crisis x-over. 2('88, $2.00)
    .35   1.00   2.00

	Good	Fine	N-Mint
Special 1 ('87, $1.50)	.25	.75	1.50

INFINITY WAR
June, 1992-No. 6, Nov, 1992 ($2.50, color, mini-series)
Marvel Comics

1-Starlin scripts and Ron Lim-a(p) in all	.70	2.00	4.00
2-6	.40	1.25	2.50

INHUMANS, THE (See Amazing Adventures, Fantastic Four 45, & Thor 146)
Oct, 1975-No. 12, Aug, 1977
Marvel Comics Group

1: #1-4 are 25 cent issues	.50	1.50	3.00
2-12: 9-Reprints Amazing Adventures #1,2('70)	.25	.75	1.50
Special 1(4/90, $1.50, 52 pgs.)-F.F. cameo	.25	.75	1.50

INVADERS, THE (TV)
Oct, 1967-No. 4, Oct, 1968 (All have photo-c)
Gold Key

1-Spiegle-a in all	5.00	15.00	35.00
2-4	3.60	11.00	25.00

INVADERS, THE (Also see The Avengers #71)
August, 1975-No. 40, May, 1979; No. 41, Sept, 1979
Marvel Comics Group

1-Captain America & Bucky, Human Torch & Toro, & Sub-Mariner begin; #1-7 are 25 cent issues	1.35	4.00	8.00
2-10: 2-1st app. Mailbag & Brain-Drain. 3-Battle issue; intro U-Man. 6-Liberty Legion app; intro/1st app. Union Jack; two cover prices, 25 & 30 cents. 7-Intro Baron Blood; Human Torch origin retold. 9-Origin Baron Blood. 10-G.A. Capt. America-r	.90	2.75	5.50
11-19: 11-Origin Spitfire; intro The Blue Bullet. 14-1st app. The Crusaders. 16-Re-intro The Destroyer. 17-Intro Warrior Woman. 18-Reintro The Destroyer w/new origin. 19-Hitler-c/story	.70	2.00	4.00
20-Reprints origin/1st app. Sub-Mariner from Motion Picture Funnies Weekly with color added & brief write-up about MPFW; 1st app. new Union Jack II	.85	2.50	5.00
21-Reprints Marvel Mystery #10 (battle issue)	.60	1.75	3.50

	Good	Fine	N-Mint
22,23,25-40: 22-New origin Toro. 25-All new-a begins. 28-Intro new Human Top & Golden Girl. 29-Intro Teutonic Knight. 31-Frankenstein-c/story. 32, 33-Thor app. 34-Mighty Destroyer joins. 35-The Whizzer app.	.40	1.25	2.50
24-r/Marvel Mystery #17 (team-up issue; all-r)	.50	1.50	3.00
41-Double size last issue	.50	1.50	3.00
Annual 1(9/77)-Schomburg, Rico stories (new); Schomburg-c/a (1st for Marvel in 30 years); Avengers app.; re-intro The Shark & The Hyena	.50	1.50	3.00

INVASION
Holiday, 1988-'89-No. 3, Jan, 1989 ($2.95, mini-series, 84 pgs.)
DC Comics

	Good	Fine	N-Mint
1-McFarlane/Russell-a	.60	1.75	3.50
2,3: 2-McFarlane/Russell-a	.50	1.50	3.00

IRON FIST (Also see Marvel Premiere & Power Man)
Nov, 1975-No. 15, Sept, 1977
Marvel Comics Group

	Good	Fine	N-Mint
1-Iron Fist battles Iron Man (#1-6: 25 cent-c)	3.60	11.00	25.00
2	1.70	5.00	12.00
3-5	1.30	4.00	9.00
6-10: 8-Origin retold	1.15	3.50	7.00
11-13: 12-Capt. America app.	1.00	3.00	6.00
14-1st app. Sabretooth	12.00	36.00	85.00
15-New X-Men app., Byrne-a (30 & 35 cents)	3.15	9.50	22.00

IRON MAN (Also see The Avengers #1, Marvel Double Feature, & Tales of Suspense #39)
May, 1968-Present
Marvel Comics Group

	Good	Fine	N-Mint
1-Origin; Colan-c/a(p); story continued from Iron Man & Sub-Mariner #1	47.00	140.00	325.00
2	14.00	43.00	100.00
3	11.00	32.00	75.00
4,5	8.00	24.00	55.00
6-10: 9-Iron Man battles Hulk	5.70	17.00	40.00
11-15: 15-Last 12 cent issue	4.50	14.00	32.00

	Good	Fine	N-Mint
16-20	2.85	8.50	20.00

21-24,26-42: 22-Death of Janice Cord. 27-Intro Fire Brand. 33-1st
app. Spy-master. 35-Nick Fury & Daredevil x-over. 42-Last 15

cent issue	2.15	6.50	15.00
25-Iron Man battles Sub-Mariner	2.65	8.00	18.00
43-Intro The Guardsman; 25 cent giant	2.15	6.50	15.00

44-46,48-50: 46-The Guardsman dies. 50-Princess Python app.

	1.50	4.50	10.00

Iron Man #7, © Marvel Comics

47-Origin retold; Smith-a(p)	2.30	7.00	16.00
51-53: 53-Starlin part pencils	1.15	3.50	8.00

54-Iron Man battles Sub-Mariner; Everett part-c; 1st app. Moon-

dragon	2.00	6.00	14.00

55-1st app. Drax the Destroyer, Kronos, & Thanos (2/73); Starlin-c/a;

1st app. Mentor & Starfox	14.00	43.00	100.00
56-Starlin-a	2.85	8.50	20.00

57-67,69,70: 59-Firebrand returns. 65-Origin Dr. Spectrum. 67-Last

20 cent issue	1.25	3.75	7.50
68-Starlin-c; origin retold	1.50	4.50	10.00

71-99: 72-Cameo portraits of N. Adams, Brunner. 76-r/#9. 86-1st
app. Blizzard. 87-Origin Blizzard. 89-Last 25 cent issue. 96-1st

app. new Guardsman	.85	2.50	5.00
100-(7/77)-Starlin-c	1.50	4.50	10.00

101-117: 101-Intro DreadKnight. 109-1st app. new Crimson Dynamo
& 1st app. Vanguard. 110-Origin Jack of Hearts retold

	.85	2.50	5.00

	Good	Fine	N-Mint
118-Byrne-a(p)	1.00	3.00	6.00

119,120,123-128-Tony Stark recovers from alcohol problem. 120,
121-Sub-Mariner x-over. 125-Ant-Man app.

	.75	2.20	4.40

121,122,129-149: 122-Origin. 131,132-Hulk x-over

	.40	1.20	2.40
150-Double size	.55	1.65	3.30

151-168: 152-New armor. 161-Moon Knight app. 167-Tony Stark
alcohol problem starts again   .35   1.00   2.00

169-New Iron Man (Jim Rhodes replaces Tony Stark)

	1.45	4.40	8.80
170	.85	2.50	5.00
171	.50	1.50	3.00

172-199: 172-Captain America x-over. 186-Intro Vibro. 190-Scarlet
Witch app. 191-198-Tony Stark returns as original Iron Man. 192-
Both Iron Men battle   .35   1.00   2.00

200-(11/85, $1.25, 52 pgs.)-Tony Stark returns as new Iron Man (red &
white armor) thru #230   .75   2.20   4.40

201-224: 213-Intro new Dominic Fortune. 214-Spider-Woman apps.
in new black costume (1/87)   .25   .75   1.50

225-Double size ($1.25)   .90   2.75   5.50

226-243,245-249: 228-Vs. Capt. America. 231-Intro new Iron Man.
233-Ant-man app. 234-Spider-Man x-over. 243-Tony Stark loses
use of legs. 247-Hulk x-over   .25   .75   1.50

244-($1.50, 52 pgs.)-New Armor makes him walk

	.75	2.20	4.40
250-($1.50, 52 pgs.)-Dr. Doom-c/story	.30	.85	1.70

251-274,276-288: 258-Byrne scripts begin. 271-Fin Fang Foom app.
277-Begin $1.25-c   .65   1.30

275-($1.50, 52 pgs.)   .25   .75   1.50

Special 1(8/70)-Sub-Mariner x-over; Everett-c

	2.65	8.00	18.00
Special 2(11/71)	1.15	3.50	8.00
Annual 3(1976)-Man-Thing app.	.70	2.00	4.00
King Size 4(8/77)-Newton-a(i)	.50	1.50	3.00

Annual 5-9: 5(1982)-New-a. 6(1983)-New Iron Man(J. Rhodes) app.
7(1984). 8(1986)-X-Factor app. 9(1987)

	.35	1.00	2.00

Annual 10(1989, $2.00, 68 pgs.)-Atlantis Attacks x-over; P. Smith-a;
Layton/Guice-a; Sub-Mariner app.   .40   1.25   2.50

Annual 11,12 ($2.00, 68 pgs.): 11-(1990)-Origin Mrs. Arbogast by

	Good	Fine	N-Mint

Ditko. 12-(1991)-1 pg. origin recap; Ant-Man back-up story

	.35	1.00	2.00

Annual 13 (1992, $2.25, 68 pgs.)-Darkhawk app.

	.40	1.25	2.50

IRON MAN & SUB-MARINER
April, 1968 (One Shot) (Pre-dates Iron Man #1 & Sub-Mariner #1)
Marvel Comics Group

1-Iron Man story by Colan/Craig continued from Tales of Suspense #99 & continued in Iron Man #1; Sub-Mariner story by Colan continued from Tales to Astonish #101 & continued in Sub-Mariner #1; Colan/Everett-c 21.00 63.00 145.00

I SPY (TV)
Aug, 1966-No. 6, Sept, 1968 (Photo-c)
Gold Key

1-Bill Cosby, Robert Culp photo covers	14.00	43.00	100.00
2-6: 3,4-McWilliams-a	8.50	25.50	60.00

JACKIE GLEASON (TV)
1948-No. 2, 1948; Sept, 1955-No. 4, Dec, 1955?
St. John Publishing Co.

	Good	Fine	N-Mint
1(1948)	47.00	140.00	325.00
2(1948)	36.00	108.00	250.00
1(1955)(TV)-Photo-c	39.00	120.00	275.00
2-4	25.00	75.00	175.00

JACKIE GLEASON AND THE HONEYMOONERS (TV)
June-July, 1956-No. 12, Apr-May, 1958
National Periodical Publications

1	57.00	170.00	400.00
2	43.00	130.00	300.00
3-11	32.00	95.00	225.00
12 (Scarce)	47.00	140.00	325.00

JESSE JAMES
8/50-No. 9, 11/52; No. 15, 10/53-No. 29, 8-9/56
Avon Periodicals

	Good	Fine	N-Mint
1-Kubert Alabam-r/Cowpuncher #1	11.00	33.00	76.00
2-Kubert-a(3)	8.50	25.50	60.00
3-Kubert Alabam-r/Cowpuncher #2	7.00	21.00	50.00
4,9-No Kubert	2.85	8.50	20.00
5,6-Kubert Jesse James-a(3); 5-Wood-a(1 pg.)			
	7.00	21.00	50.00
7-Kubert Jesse James-a(2)	6.00	18.00	42.00
8-Kinstler-a(3)	4.00	12.00	28.00
15-Kinstler-r/#3	2.15	6.50	15.00
16-Kinstler-r/#3 & Sheriff Bob Dixon's Chuck Wagon #1 with name			
changed to Sheriff Tom Wilson	2.65	8.00	18.00

17-19,21: 17-Jesse James r-/#4; Kinstler-c idea from Kubert splash in
#6. 18-Kubert Jesse James r-/#5. 19-Kubert Jesse James-r. 21-
Two Jesse James r-/#4, Kinstler r-/#4   1.70   5.00   12.00

20-Williamson/Frazetta-a; r-Chief Vic. Apache Massacre; Kubert
Jesse James r-/#6; Kit West story by Larsen

	8.50	25.50	60.00
22,23-No Kubert	1.60	4.80	11.00

	Good	Fine	N-Mint

24-New McCarty strip by Kinstler; Kinstler-r

	1.60	4.80	11.00

25-New McCarty Jesse James strip by Kinstler; Jesse James r-/#7,9

	1.60	4.80	11.00

26,27-New McCarty Jesse James strip plus a Kinstler/McCann Jesse James-r

	1.60	4.80	11.00

28,29: 28-Reprints most of Red Mountain, Featuring Quantrells Raiders

	1.60	4.80	11.00

Annual(nn, 1952, 25 cents, 100 pgs.)-"...Brings Six-Gun Justice to the West;" 3 earlier issues rebound; Kubert, Kinstler-a(3)

	17.00	51.00	120.00

JETSONS, THE (TV)
Jan, 1963-No. 36, Oct, 1970 (Hanna-Barbera)
Gold Key

	Good	Fine	N-Mint
1	19.30	58.00	135.00
2	11.00	32.00	75.00
3-10	8.00	24.00	55.00
11-20	5.70	17.00	40.00
21-36	4.30	13.00	30.00

JETSONS, THE (TV) (Hanna-Barbera)
Nov, 1970-No. 20, Dec, 1973
Charlton Comics

	Good	Fine	N-Mint
1	6.85	20.50	48.00
2	3.60	11.00	25.00
3-10	2.65	8.00	18.00
11-20	1.70	5.00	12.00

JOHN CARTER, WARLORD OF MARS (Also see Weird Worlds)
June, 1977-No. 28, Oct, 1979
Marvel Comics Group

	Good	Fine	N-Mint
1-Origin by Gil Kane	.25	.75	1.50
2-17,19-28: 11-Origin Dejah Thoris		.50	1.00
18-Miller-a(p)	.35	1.00	2.00
Annuals 1-3: 1(1977). 2(1978). 3(1979)-All 52 pgs. with new book-length stories	.25	.75	1.50

JOHN WAYNE ADVENTURE COMICS (Movie star)
Winter, 1949-50-No. 31, May, 1955 (Photo-c: 1-12,17,25-on)
Toby Press

	Good	**Fine**	**N-Mint**
1 (36 pgs.)-Photo-c begin	54.00	160.00	375.00
2 (36 pgs.)-Williamson/Frazetta-a(2) 6 & 2 pgs. (one story-r/Billy the Kid #1); photo back-c	45.00	135.00	310.00
3 (36 pgs.)-Williamson/Frazetta-a(2), 16 pgs. total; photo back-c	45.00	135.00	310.00
4 (52 pgs.)-Williamson/Frazetta-a(2), 16 pgs. total	45.00	135.00	310.00
5 (52 pgs.)-Kurtzman-a-(Alfred "L" Newman in Potshot Pete)	32.00	95.00	220.00
6 (52 pgs.)-Williamson/Frazetta-a, 10 pgs; Kurtzman a-"Pot-Shot Pete," 5 pgs.; & "Genius Jones," 1 pg.	43.00	130.00	300.00
7 (52 pgs.)-Williamson/Frazetta-a, 10 pgs.	34.00	100.00	240.00
8 (36 pgs.)-Williamson/Frazetta-a(2), 12 & 9 pgs.	43.00	130.00	300.00
9-11: Photo western-c	23.00	70.00	160.00
12-Photo war-c; Kurtzman-a, 2 pgs. "Genius"	23.00	70.00	160.00
13-15: 13-Line-drawn-c begin, end #24	20.00	60.00	140.00
16-Williamson/Frazetta-r/Billy the Kid #1	22.00	65.00	150.00
17-Photo-c	23.00	70.00	160.00
18-Williamson/Frazetta-a (r/#4 & 8, 19 pgs.)	25.00	75.00	175.00
19-24: 23-Evans-a?	18.00	54.00	125.00
25-Photo-c return; end #31; Williamson/Frazetta-r/Billy the Kid #3	25.00	75.00	175.00
26-28,30-Photo-c	22.00	65.00	150.00
29,31-Williamson/Frazetta-a in each (r/#4, 2)	23.00	70.00	160.00

JOKER, THE (See Batman, Batman: The Killing Joke, Brave & the Bold, Detective, Justice League Annual #2)
May, 1975-No. 9, Sept-Oct, 1976
National Periodical Publications

1-Two-Face app.	3.25	9.75	22.50
2,3	1.80	5.40	12.60
4-6	1.55	4.65	10.80
7,8	1.15	3.45	8.10
9-Catwoman-c/story	1.50	4.50	10.00

JONAH HEX (See All-Star Western, Hex and Weird Western Tales)
Mar-Apr, 1977-No. 92, Aug, 1985
National Periodical Publications/DC Comics

	Good	Fine	N-Mint
1	1.70	5.00	12.00
2-6,8-10: 9-Wrightson-c	.85	2.50	5.00
7-Explains Hex's face disfigurement	1.00	3.00	6.00
11-20: 12-Starlin-c	.50	1.50	3.00
21-50: 31,32-Origin retold	.35	1.00	2.00
51-92: 92-Story continued in Hex #1		.50	1.00

JONNY QUEST (TV)
December, 1964 (Hanna-Barbera)
Gold Key

	Good	Fine	N-Mint
1 (10139-412)	19.00	57.00	130.00

JONNY QUEST (TV)
June, 1986-No. 31, Dec, 1988 (Hanna-Barbera)
Comico

	Good	Fine	N-Mint
1	.70	2.00	4.00
2	.45	1.30	2.60
3,5-Dave Stevens-c	.50	1.50	3.00
4,6-14	.25	.75	1.50
15-31: 15-Begin $1.75-c. 30-Adapts TV episode			
	.30	.90	1.80
Special 1(9/88, $1.75), 2(10/88, $1.75)	.25	.75	1.50

JOURNEY INTO MYSTERY (1st Series) (Thor No. 126 on)
6/52-No. 48, 8/57; No. 49, 11/58-No. 125, 2/66
Atlas(CPS No. 1-48/AMI No. 49-68/Marvel No. 69 (6/61) on)

	Good	Fine	N-Mint
1	85.00	250.00	600.00
2	43.00	130.00	300.00
3,4	33.00	100.00	225.00
5-11	20.00	60.00	140.00
12-20,22: 22-Davisesque-a; last pre-code issue (2/55)			
	17.00	51.00	120.00
21-Kubert-a; Tothish-a by Andru	19.00	57.00	130.00
23-32,35-38,40: 24-Torres?-a	9.30	28.00	65.00
33-Williamson-a	12.00	36.00	85.00
34,39: 34-Krigstein-a. 39-Wood-a	11.00	32.00	75.00
41-Crandall-a; Frazettaesque-a by Morrow			
	8.00	24.00	55.00

	Good	Fine	N-Mint
42,48-Torres-a	8.00	24.00	55.00
43,44-Williamson/Mayo-a in both	8.50	25.50	60.00
45,47,52,53	7.00	21.00	50.00

Journey Into Mystery #111, © Marvel Comics

	Good	Fine	N-Mint
46-Torres & Krigstein-a	8.50	25.50	60.00
49-Matt Fox, Check-a	8.50	25.50	60.00
50,54: 50-Davis-a. 54-Williamson-a	7.00	21.00	50.00
51-Kirby/Wood-a	7.00	21.00	50.00
55-61,63-75: 66-Return of Xemnu. 74-Contents change to Fantasy.			
75-Last 10 cent issue	6.85	20.50	48.00
62-1st app. Xemnu (Titan) called "The Hulk"			
	10.00	30.00	70.00
76,77,79-82: 80-Anti-communist propaganda story			
	5.70	17.00	40.00
78-The Sorceror (Dr. Strange prototype) app. (3/62)			
	8.00	24.00	55.00
83-Origin & 1st app. The Mighty Thor by Kirby (8/62) and begin			
series; Thor-c also begin	230.00	690.00	1600.00
83-Reprint from the Golden Record Comic Set			
	8.50	25.50	60.00
with the record (1966) (still sealed)	14.00	43.00	100.00
84-2nd app. Thor	70.00	210.00	500.00
85-1st app. Loki & Heimdall; Odin cameo (1 panel)			
	40.00	120.00	275.00

	Good	Fine	N-Mint
86-1st full app. Odin	25.00	75.00	175.00
87-89: 89-Reprints origin Thor from #83	18.00	54.00	125.00
90-No Kirby-a	11.00	32.00	75.00
91,92,94-96-Sinnott-a	9.30	28.00	65.00
93,97-Kirby-a; Tales of Asgard series begins #97 (origin which concludes in #99)	13.00	40.00	90.00
98-100-Kirby/Heck-a. 98-Origin/1st app. The Human Cobra. 99-1st app. Surtur & Mr. Hyde	8.50	25.50	60.00
101-108,110: 102-Intro Sif. 103-1st app. Enchantress. 105-109-Ten extra pgs. Kirby-a in each. 107-1st app. Grey Gargoyle. 108-Early Dr. Strange & Avengers x-over (9/64)	5.70	17.00	40.00
109-Magneto-c & app.	6.50	19.00	45.00
111,113,114,116-125: 118-1st app. Destroyer. 119-Intro Hogun, Fandrall, Volstagg. 124-Hercules-c/story	5.00	15.00	35.00
112-Thor Vs. Hulk (1/65). 112,113-Origin Loki	11.50	34.00	80.00
115-Detailed origin Loki	5.70	17.00	40.00
Annual 1('65, 25 cents, 72 pgs.)-New Thor vs. Hercules story; Kirby-c/a; r/#85,93,95,97	11.50	34.00	80.00

JOURNEY INTO MYSTERY (2nd Series)
Oct, 1972-No. 19, Oct, 1975
Marvel Comics Group

	Good	Fine	N-Mint
1-Robert Howard adaptation; Starlin/Ploog-a	.85	2.50	5.00
2,3,5-Bloch adaptation; 5-Last new story	.50	1.50	3.00
4,6-19: 4-H. P. Lovecraft adaptation	.35	1.00	2.00

JUNGLE ACTION (...& Black Panther #18-21?)
Oct, 1972-No. 24, Nov, 1976
Marvel Comics Group

	Good	Fine	N-Mint
1-Lorna, Jann-r (All reprints in 1-4)	.85	2.50	5.00
2-4	.60	1.75	3.50
5-Black Panther begins; new stories begin	1.00	3.00	6.00
6-18: 8-Origin Black Panther. 9-Contains pull-out centerfold	.60	1.75	3.50
19-24: 19-23-KKK x-over. 23-r-/#22. 24-1st Wind Eagle	.40	1.25	2.50

JUNGLE TALES OF TARZAN
Dec, 1964-No. 4, July, 1965
Charlton Comics

	Good	Fine	N-Mint
1	2.65	8.00	18.00
2-4	2.00	6.00	14.00

JUSTICE LEAGUE (...International #7-25; ...America #26 on)
May, 1987-Present (Also see Legends #6)
DC Comics

1-Batman, Green Lantern(Guy Gardner), Blue Beetle, Mr. Miracle,
  Capt. Marvel & Martian Manhunter begin

	1.70	5.00	10.00
2	1.00	3.00	6.00
3-Regular cover (white background)	.85	2.50	5.00

3-Limited cover (yellow background, Superman logo)

	13.00	40.00	90.00
4-Booster Gold joins	.70	2.00	4.00

5,6: 5-Origin Gray Man; Batman vs. Guy Gardner; Creeper app.

	.40	1.25	2.50

7-Double size ($1.25); Capt. Marvel & Dr. Fate resign; Capt. Atom,
  Rocket Red join

	.50	1.50	3.00
8-10: 9,10-Millennium x-over	.35	1.00	2.00
11-23: 16-Bruce Wayne-c/story. 18-21-Lobo app.	.60		1.20
24-($1.50)-1st app. Justice League Europe	.25	.75	1.50

25-49,51-62: 31,32-Justice League Europe x-over. 58-Lobo app. 61-
  New team begins; swipes-c to JLA #1

		.50	1.00
50-($1.75, 52 pgs.)	.30	.90	1.80
63-70: 63-Begin $1.25-c		.65	1.30
Annual 1 (1987)	.50	1.50	3.00
Annual 2 (1988)-Joker-c/story	.70	2.00	4.00
Annual 3 (1989, $1.75, 68 pgs.)	.30	.90	1.75
Annual 4 (1990, $2.00, 68 pgs.)	.50	1.50	3.00

Annual 5 (1991, $2.00, 68 pgs.)-Armageddon 2001 x-over; 2nd
  printing exists with silver ink-c

	.35	1.00	2.00

Annual 6 (1992, $2.50, 68 pgs.)-Woman Wonder app.

	.40	1.25	2.50
Special 1 ('90, $1.50, 52 pgs.)-Giffen plots	.25	.75	1.50
Special 2('91, $2.95, 52 pgs.)-Staton-a(p)	.50	1.50	3.00

Spectacular 1 (1992, $1.50, 52 pgs.)-Intro new JLA & new JLE teams,
  ties into Justice League #61 & JLE #37   .25   .75   1.50

JUSTICE LEAGUE EUROPE
April, 1989-Present (75 cents; $1.00 #5 on)
DC Comics

	Good	Fine	N-Mint
1-Giffen plots in all; breakdowns in 1-8,13-30			
	.35	1.00	2.00
2-38: 7-9-Batman app. 7,8-JLA x-over. 20,21-Rogers-c/a(p). 33,34-Lobo vs. Despero. 37-New team begins; swipes-c to JLA #9			
		.65	1.30
39-46: 39-Begin $1.25-c		.65	1.30
Annual 1 (1990, $2.00, 68 pgs.)-Return of the Global Guardians; Giffen plots/breakdowns	.35	1.00	2.00
Annual 2 ('91, $2.00, 68pgs.)-Armageddon 2001; Giffen-p; Golden-i; Rogers-p	.35	1.00	2.00
Annual 3 ('92, $2.50, 68 pgs.)	.40	1.25	2.50

JUSTICE LEAGUE OF AMERICA (See Brave & the Bold #28-30 & Mystery In Space #75)
Oct-Nov, 1960-No. 261, Apr, 1987 (91-99,139-157: 52 pgs.)
National Periodical Publications/DC Comics

	Good	Fine	N-Mint
Brave and the Bold #28 (2-3/60)-Intro/1st app. Justice League of America; origin Snapper Carr	293.00	880.00	2050.00
Brave and the Bold #29,30 (4-5/60, 6-7/60)			
	110.00	330.00	750.00
1-(10-11/60)-Origin Despero; Aquaman, Batman, Flash, Green Lantern, J'onn J'onzz, Superman & Wonder Woman continue from Brave and the Bold	107.00	620.00	1450.00
2	60.00	180.00	425.00
3-Origin/1st app. Kanjar Ro	45.00	135.00	315.00
4-Green Arrow joins JLA	35.00	105.00	240.00
5-Origin Dr. Destiny	26.30	79.00	185.00
6-8,10: 6-Origin Prof. Amos Fortune. 7-Last 10 cent issue. 10-Origin Felix Faust; 1st app. Time Lord			
	22.00	65.00	150.00
9-Origin J.L.A. (1st origin)	32.00	96.00	220.00
11-15: 12-Origin & 1st app. Dr. Light. 13-Speedy app. 14-Atom joins JLA	16.00	48.00	110.00
16-20: 17-Adam Strange flashback	12.00	36.00	85.00
21-"Crisis on Earth-One;" re-intro. of JSA (1st S.A. app. Hourman & Dr. Fate)	22.00	65.00	150.00
22-"Crisis on Earth-Two;" JSA x-over (story continued from #21)			
	19.00	58.00	135.00

	Good	Fine	N-Mint
23-28: 24-Adam Strange app. 28-Robin app.			
	6.50	19.00	45.00
29,30-JSA x-over; 1st Silver Age app. Starman. 29-"Crisis on Earth-Three"	7.00	21.00	50.00
31-Hawkman joins JLA, Hawkgirl cameo	4.30	13.00	30.00
32-Intro & Origin Brain Storm	3.60	11.00	25.00
33,35,36,40,41: 41-Intro & origin The Key			
	3.15	9.50	22.00
34-Joker-c/story	4.00	12.00	28.00
37,38-JSA x-over (1st S.A. app. Mr. Terrific #38). 38-"Crisis on Earth-A"	5.70	17.00	40.00
39-Giant G-16; r/B&B #28,30 & JLA #5	3.60	11.00	25.00
42-45: 42-Metamorpho app. 43-Intro. Royal Flush Gang			
	2.00	6.00	14.00
46-JSA x-over; 1st S.A. app. Sandman	5.70	17.00	40.00
47-JSA x-over	2.85	8.50	20.00
48-Giant G-29; r/JLA #2,3 & B&B #29	2.85	8.50	20.00
49-54,57,59,60	1.70	5.00	12.00

Justice League of America #55, © DC Comics

	Good	Fine	N-Mint
55-Intro. Earth 2 Robin (1st G.A. Robin in S.A.)			
	3.60	11.00	25.00
56-JLA vs. JSA	2.15	6.50	15.00
58-Giant G-41; r/JLA #6,8,1	1.70	5.00	12.00
61-63,66,68-72: 69-Wonder Woman quits. 71-Manhunter leaves. 72-Last 12 cent issue	1.15	3.50	8.00
64,65-JSA app. 64-Origin/1st app. S.A. Red Tornado			
	1.30	4.00	9.00

	Good	Fine	N-Mint
67-Giant G-53; r/JLA #4,14,31	1.30	4.00	9.00
73,74,77-80: 74-Black Canary joins. 78-Re-intro Vigilante			
	.85	2.50	5.00
75-2nd app. Green Arrow in new costume	1.00	3.00	6.00
76-Giant G-65	1.00	3.00	6.00
81-84,86-92: 83-Death of Spectre	.70	2.00	4.00
85,93-(Giant G-77,G-89; 68 pgs.)	1.00	3.00	6.00
94-Reprints 1st Sandman story (Adv. #40) & origin/1st app. Starman (Adv. #61); Deadman x-over; N. Adams-a(4 pgs.); begin 25 cent, 52 pg. issues, ends #99	2.65	8.00	18.00
95-Origin Dr. Fate & Dr. Midnight reprint (More Fun #67, All-American #25)	1.00	3.00	7.00
96-Origin Hourman (Adv. #48); Wildcat-r			
	1.00	3.00	7.00
97-Origin JLA retold; Sargon, Starman-r	.85	2.50	5.00
98,99: 98-G.A. Sargon, Starman-r. 99-G.A. Sandman, Starman, Atom-r; last 52 pg. issue	.85	2.50	5.00
100-(8/72)	.85	2.50	5.00
101,102: JSA x-overs. 102-Red Tornado dies			
	1.00	3.00	6.00
103-106,109: 103-Phantom Stranger joins. 105-Elongated Man joins. 106-New Red Tornado joins. 109-Hawkman resigns			
	.50	1.50	3.00
107,108-G.A. Uncle Sam, Black Condor, The Ray, Dollman, Phantom Lady & The Human Bomb (JSA) x-over			
	1.00	3.00	6.00
110-116: All 100 pgs. 111-Shining Knight, Green Arrow-r. 112-Crimson Avenger, Vigilante, origin Starman-r			
	.70	2.00	4.00
117-190: 117-Hawkman rejoins. 120,121,138-Adam Strange app. 128-Wonder Woman rejoins. 129-Death of Red Tornado. 135-137-G.A. Bulletman, Bulletgirl, Spy Smasher, Mr. Scarlet, Pinky & Ibis x-over. 137-Superman battles G.A. Capt. Marvel. 139-157-(52 pgs.). 144-Origin retold; origin J'onn J'onnz. 145-Red Tornado resurrected. 158-160-(44 pgs.). 161-Zatanna joins & new costume. 171-Mr. Terrific murdered. 178-Cover similar to #1; J'onn J'onzz app. 179-Firestorm joins. 181-Green Arrow leaves			
	.35	1.00	2.00
191-199: 192,193-Real origin Red Tornado. 193-1st app. All-Star Squadron as free 16 pg. insert	.25	.75	1.50
200-Anniversary issue (76 pgs., $1.50); origin retold; Green Arrow rejoins	.50	1.50	3.00

	Good	Fine	N-Mint
201-220: 203-Intro/origin new Royal Flush Gang. 207,208-JSA, JLA, & All-Star Squadron team-up. 219,220-True origin Black Canary	.25	.75	1.50
221-250 (75 cents): 228-Re-intro Martian Manhunter. 233-New JLA begins. 243-Aquaman leaves. 244,245-Crisis x-over. 250-Batman rejoins	.25	.75	1.50
251-260: 253-1st told origin Despero. 258-Death of Vibe. 258-261-Legends x-over. 260-Death of Steel		.50	1.00
261-Last issue	.60	1.75	3.50
Annual 1(1983)	.40	1.25	2.50
Annual 2(1984)-Intro new J.L.A.	.25	.75	1.50
Annual 3(1985)-Crisis x-over	.25	.75	1.50

JUSTICE SOCIETY OF AMERICA (See Adventure #461)
April, 1991-No. 8, Nov, 1991 ($1.00, color, limited series)
DC Comics

	Good	Fine	N-Mint
1-Flash	.30	.90	1.80
2-Black Canary		.65	1.30
3-Green Lantern	.25	.75	1.50
4-8: 4-Hawkman. 5-Flash/Hawkman. 6-Green Lantern/Black Canary. 7-JSA		.50	1.00

KAMANDI, THE LAST BOY ON EARTH
Oct-Nov, 1972-No. 59, Sept-Oct, 1978
National Periodical Publications/DC Comics

	Good	Fine	N-Mint
1-Origin	2.65	8.00	18.00
2	1.70	5.00	12.00
3-5: 4-Intro. Prince Tuftan of the Tigers	1.15	3.50	8.00
6-10	1.00	3.00	6.00
11-20	.70	2.00	4.00
21-40: 29-Superman x-over. 31-Intro Pyra. 32-(68 pgs.)-r/origin from #1; 4 pg. biog. of Jack Kirby with B&W photos			
	.50	1.50	3.00
41-59: 59-(44 pgs.)-The return of Omac by Starlin-c/a(p)			
	.40	1.25	2.50

KARATE KID (See Action, Adventure, Legion of Super-Heroes, & Superboy)
Mar-Apr, 1976-No. 15, July-Aug, 1978 (Legion spin-off)
National Periodical Publications/DC Comics

1-Meets Iris Jacobs; Estrada/Staton-a	.35	1.00	2.00
2-15: 2-Major Disaster app. 15-Continued into Kamandi #58			
	.25	.75	1.50

KA-ZAR (Also see X-Men #10)
Aug, 1970-No. 3, Mar, 1971 (Giant-Size, 68 pgs.)
Marvel Comics Group

1-Reprints earlier Ka-Zar stories; Avengers x-over in Hercules; Daredevil, X-Men app; hidden profanity-c			
	1.50	4.50	10.00
2,3-Daredevil-r. 2-Ka-Zar origin, X-Men-r			
	1.15	3.50	8.00

KA-ZAR
Jan, 1974-No. 20, Feb, 1977 (Regular size)
Marvel Comics Group

1	.40	1.25	2.50
2-20	.25	.75	1.50

KID ETERNITY
1991-No. 3, 1991 ($4.95, mini-series, mature readers, 52 pgs.)

DC Comics	Good	Fine	N-Mint
1-3: Grant Morrison scripts	.85	2.50	5.00

KING COMICS (Strip reprints)
Apr, 1936-No. 159, Feb, 1952 (Winter on cover)
David McKay Publications/Standard No. 156-on

	Good	Fine	VF-NM
1-Flash Gordon by Alex Raymond; Brick Bradford, Popeye, Henry & Mandrake the Magician begin	500.00	1250.00	3000.00

	Good	Fine	N-Mint
2	175.00	440.00	1050.00
3	125.00	315.00	750.00
4	80.00	240.00	550.00
5	61.00	183.00	425.00
6-10: 9-X-Mas-c	39.00	120.00	275.00
11-20	32.00	95.00	225.00
21-30	25.00	75.00	175.00
31-40: 33-Last Segar Popeye	22.00	65.00	150.00
41-50: 46-Little Lulu, Alvin & Tubby app. as text illos by Marge Buell. 50-The Lone Ranger begins	19.00	58.00	135.00
51-60: 52-Barney Baxter?	14.00	43.00	100.00
61-The Phantom begins	12.00	36.00	85.00
62-80: 76-Flag-c	10.00	30.00	70.00
81-99: 82-Blondie begins?	8.50	25.50	60.00
100	11.00	32.00	75.00
101-114: 114-Last Raymond issue (1 pg.); Flash Gordon by Austin Briggs begins, ends #155	8.00	24.00	55.00
115-145: 117-Phantom origin retold	5.70	17.00	40.00
146,147-Prince Valiant in both	4.30	13.00	30.00
148-155-Flash Gordon ends	4.30	13.00	30.00
156-159	3.60	11.00	25.00

KING CONAN (Conan The King No. 20 on)
March, 1980-No. 19, Nov, 1983 (52 pgs.)

Marvel Comics Group			
1	.40	1.25	2.50
2-6: 4-Death of Thoth Amon	.30	.90	1.80
7-19: 7-1st Paul Smith-a, 2 pgs. (9/81)	.30	.90	1.80

KITTY PRYDE AND WOLVERINE
Nov, 1984-No. 6, April, 1985 (6 issue mini-series)
Marvel Comics Group

	Good	Fine	N-Mint
1 (From X-Men)	1.15	3.50	7.00
2-6	.70	2.00	4.00

KOBRA
Feb-Mar, 1976-No. 7, Mar-Apr, 1977
National Periodical Publications

1-Art plotted by Kirby; only 25 cent issue	.25	.75	1.50
2-7: (30 cent-c) 3-Giffen-a		.50	1.00

KORAK, SON OF TARZAN (Edgar Rice Burroughs)
Jan, 1964-No. 45, Jan, 1972 (Painted-c No. 1-?)
Gold Key

1-Russ Manning-a	4.50	14.00	32.00
2-11-Russ Manning-a	2.30	7.00	16.00
12-21: 12,13-Warren Tufts-a. 14-Jon of the Kalahari ends. 15-Mabu, Jungle Boy begins. 21-Manning-a	1.70	5.00	12.00
22-30	1.15	3.50	8.00
31-45	1.00	3.00	6.00

KORAK, SON OF TARZAN (Also see Tarzan #230)
V9#46, May-June, 1972-V12#56, Feb-Mar, 1974; No. 57, May-June,
1975-No. 59, Sept-Oct, 1975 (Edgar Rice Burroughs) National
Periodical Publications

46-(52 pgs.)-Carson of Venus begins (origin); Pellucidar feature; Weiss-a	.25	.75	1.50
47-59: 49-Origin Korak retold. 56-Last Carson of Venus		.50	1.00

KRYPTON CHRONICLES
Sept, 1981-No. 3, Nov, 1981
DC Comics

1-Buckler-c(p)	.25	.75	1.50
2,3		.50	1.00

KULL THE CONQUEROR (...the Destroyer #11 on; see Marvel Preview)
June, 1971-No. 2, Sept, 1971; No. 3, July, 1972-No. 15, Aug, 1974;
No. 16, Aug, 1976-No. 29, Oct, 1978
Marvel Comics Group

1-Andru/Wood-a; origin Kull; 15 cent-c	1.15	3.50	8.00
2-5: 2-Last 15 cent issue. 3-13: 20 cent-c	.70	2.00	4.00
6-10	.50	1.50	3.00

	Good	Fine	N-Mint
11-29: 11-15-Ploog-a. 14-16: 25 cent-c	.35	1.00	2.00

KULL THE CONQUEROR
Dec, 1982-No. 2, Mar, 1983 (52 pgs., printed on Baxter paper)
Marvel Comics Group

1,2: 1-Buscema-a(p)	.35	1.00	2.00

KULL THE CONQUEROR (No. 9,10 titled "Kull")
5/83-No. 10, 6/85 (52 pgs.; $1.25-60 cents; Mando paper)
Marvel Comics Group

V3#1-10: Buscema-a in #1-3,5-10		.50	1.00

LAND OF THE GIANTS (TV)
Nov, 1968-No. 5, Sept, 1969 (All have photo-c)
Gold Key

	Good	Fine	N-Mint
1	3.60	11.00	25.00
2-5	2.15	6.50	15.00

Lash LaRue Western #6, © Fawcett Publications

LASH LARUE WESTERN (Movie star; king of the bullwhip)
Sum, 1949-No. 46, Jan, 1954 (36 pgs., 1-7,9,13,16-on)
Fawcett Publications

	Good	Fine	N-Mint
1-Lash & his horse Black Diamond begin; photo front/back-c begin			
	72.00	215.00	500.00
2(11/49)	34.00	100.00	235.00
3-5	29.00	85.00	200.00
6,7,9: 6-Last photo back-c; intro. Frontier Phantom (Lash's twin brother)			
	22.00	65.00	150.00
8,10 (52 pgs.)	23.00	70.00	160.00
11,12,14,15 (52 pgs.)	14.00	43.00	100.00
13,16-20 (36 pgs.)	13.00	40.00	90.00
21-30: 21-The Frontier Phantom app.	11.00	32.00	75.00
31-45	9.30	28.00	65.00
46-Last Fawcett issue & photo-c	10.00	30.00	70.00

LASH LARUE WESTERN (Continues from Fawcett series)
No. 47, Mar-Apr, 1954-No. 84, June, 1961
Charlton Comics

	Good	Fine	N-Mint
47-Photo-c	9.30	28.00	65.00
48	8.00	24.00	55.00
49-60	6.00	18.00	42.00
61-66,69,70: 52-r/#8; 53-r/#22	5.00	15.00	35.00
67,68-(68 pgs.). 68-Check-a	5.70	17.00	40.00
71-83	3.60	11.00	25.00
84-Last issue	4.30	13.00	30.00

LASSIE (TV) (M-G-M's... #1-36)
June, 1950-No. 70, July, 1969
Dell Publishing Co./Gold Key No. 59 (10/62) on

	Good	Fine	N-Mint
1 (52 pgs.)-Photo-c; inside lists One Shot #282 in error			
	9.00	28.00	55.00
2-Painted-c begin	5.00	15.00	30.00
3-10	3.35	10.00	20.00
11-19: 12-Rocky Langford (Lassie's master) marries Gerry Lawrence. 15-1st app. Timbu	2.30	7.00	14.00
20-22-Matt Baker-a	3.35	10.00	20.00
23-40: 33-Robinson-a. 39-1st app. Timmy as Lassie picks up her TV family	1.70	5.00	10.00
41-70: 63-Last Timmy. 64-r/#19. 65-Forest Ranger Corey Stuart begins, ends #69. 70-Forest Rangers Bob Ericson & Scott Turner app. (Lassie's new masters)	1.15	3.50	7.00

LEADING COMICS (...Screen Comics No. 42 on)
Winter, 1941-42-No. 41, Feb-Mar, 1950
National Periodical Publications

	Good	Fine	N-Mint
1-Origin The Seven Soldiers of Victory; Crimson Avenger, Green Arrow & Speedy, Shining Knight, The Vigilante, Star Spangled Kid & Stripesy begin. The Dummy (Vigilante villain) app.			
	215.00	540.00	1300.00
2-Meskin-a	72.00	215.00	500.00
3	57.00	170.00	400.00
4,5	50.00	150.00	350.00
6-10	43.00	130.00	300.00
11-14(Spring, 1945)	32.00	95.00	225.00
15-(Sum,'45)-Content change to funny animal			
	13.00	40.00	90.00
16-22,24-30	6.00	18.00	42.00

	Good	Fine	N-Mint
23-1st app. Peter Porkchops by Otto Feur			
	14.00	43.00	100.00
31,32,34-41	4.50	14.00	32.00
33-(Scarce)	7.00	21.00	50.00

LEADING SCREEN COMICS (Formerly Leading Comics)
No. 42, Apr-May, 1950-No. 77, Aug-Sept, 1955
National Periodical Publications

42	6.00	18.00	42.00
43-77	4.00	12.00	28.00

LEGENDS
Nov, 1986-No. 6, Apr, 1987 (75 cents, mini-series)
DC Comics

1-Byrne-c/a(p) in all; 1st app. new Capt. Marvel			
	.35	1.10	2.20
2-5: 3-1st app. new Suicide Squad; death of Blockbuster			
	.25	.70	1.40
6-1st app. new Justice League	1.00	3.00	6.00

LEGENDS OF NASCAR, THE
1990-Present (Color)(#1 3rd printing (1/91) says 2nd printing inside)
Vortex Comics

1-Bill Elliot biog.; Trimpe-a ($1.50-c)	4.15	12.50	25.00
1-2nd printing (11/90, $2.00-c)	1.35	4.00	8.00
1-3rd print; contains Maxx racecards ($3.00-c)			
	1.15	3.50	7.00
2-Richard Petty	.70	2.00	4.00
3-Ken Schrader (7/91)	.40	1.25	2.50
4-12: 4-Bobby Allison; Spiegle-a(p); Adkins part-i. 5-Sterling Marlin. 6-Bill Elliott	.35	1.00	2.00

LEGENDS OF THE DARK KNIGHT (Batman)
Nov, 1989-Present ($1.50/$1.75, color)
DC Comics

1-"The Shaman of Gotham" begins, ends #5; outer cover has four different color variations, all worth same			
	.90	2.75	5.50
2	.50	1.50	3.00
3-5	.35	1.10	2.20
6-10-"Gothic" by Grant Morrison (scripts)			
	.50	1.50	3.00

	Good	Fine	N-Mint
11-18: 11-15-Gulacy/Austin-a. 14-Catwoman app.			
	.35	1.00	2.00
19-40: 19-Begin $1.75-c	.30	.90	1.80
Annual 1 (1991, $3.95, 68 pgs.)	.70	2.00	4.00

L.E.G.I.O.N. '89 (Becomes L.E.G.I.O.N. '90 #11-22; becomes ...'91 #23-34; becomes ...'92 #35 on; also see Lobo) Feb, 1989-Present ($1.50, color)
DC Comics

1-Giffen plots/breakdowns in #1-12	.35	1.00	2.00
2-22,24-48: 3-Lobo app. #3 on. 4-1st Lobo-c this title. 5-Lobo joins Legion. 28-Giffen-c(p). 31-Capt. Marvel app.			
	.25	.75	1.50
23-($2.50, 52 pgs.)	.40	1.25	2.50
Annual 1 (1990, $2.95, 68 pgs.)-Lobo, Superman			
	.50	1.50	3.00
Annual 2 (1991, $2.95, 68 pgs.)-Alan Grant script			
	.50	1.50	3.00
Annual 3 (1992, $2.95, 68 pgs.)-Justice League app.			
	.50	1.50	3.00

LEGION OF SUPER-HEROES (See Action, Adventure, Secrets of the..., Superboy, & Superman)
Feb, 1973-No. 4, July-Aug, 1973
National Periodical Publications

1-Legion & Tommy Tomorrow reprints begin			
	1.15	3.50	8.00
2-4: 2-Forte-r. 3-r/Adv. #340. Action #240. 4-r/Adv. #341, Action #233; Mooney-r	.85	2.50	5.00

LEGION OF SUPER-HEROES, THE (Formerly Superboy and...; Tales of The Legion No. 314 on)
No. 259, Jan, 1980-No. 313, July, 1984
DC Comics

259(#1)-Superboy leaves Legion	.50	1.50	3.00
260-270: 265-Contains 28pg. insert "Superman & the TR5-80 Computer;" Origin Tyroc; Tyroc leaves Legion			
	.35	1.00	2.00
271-284: 272-Blok joins; origin; 20pg. insert-Dial "H" For Hero. 277-Intro Reflecto. 280-Superboy re-joins legion. 282-Origin Reflecto. 283-Origin Wildfire	.25	.75	1.50
285,286-Giffen back up story	.35	1.00	2.00

	Good	Fine	N-Mint
287-Giffen-a on Legion begins	.45	1.40	2.80
288-290: 290-294-Great Darkness saga	.35	1.00	2.00
291-293	.25	.75	1.50
294-Double size (52 pgs.); Giffen-a(p)	.30	.90	1.80
295-299,301-305: 297-Origin retold		.60	1.20

300-Double size, 64 pgs., Mando paper; c/a by almost everyone at DC

	.35	1.00	2.00
306-313 (75 cent-c): 306-Brief origin Star Boy		.50	1.00

Annual 1(1982, 52 pgs.)-Giffen-c/a; 1st app./origin new Invisible Kid
who joins Legion .35 1.00 2.00

Annual 2,3: 2(1983, 52 pgs.)-Giffen-c; Karate Kid & Princess
Projectra wed & resign. 3(1984, 52 pgs.)

	.25	.75	1.50

LEGION OF SUPER-HEROES
Aug, 1984-No. 63, Aug, 1989 ($1.25-$1.75, deluxe format)
DC Comics

1	.35	1.00	2.00

2-10: 4-Death of Karate Kid. 5-Death of Nemesis Kid

	.25	.80	1.60

11-14: 12-Cosmic Boy, Lightning Lad, & Saturn Girl resign. 14-Intro
new members: Tellus, Sensor Girl, Quislet .60 1.20

15-18: 15-17-Crisis tie-ins. 18-Crisis x-over

	.25	.80	1.60

19-25: 25-Sensor Girl i.d. revealed as Princess Projectra

	.60	1.20

26-36,39-44: 35-Saturn Girl rejoins. 40-$1.75 cover price begins.
42,43-Millennium tie-ins. 44-Origin Quislet 55 1.10

37,38-Death of Superboy	1.70	5.00	10.00
45 ($2.95, 68 pgs.)	.50	1.50	3.00
46-49,51-62		.55	1.10
50-Double size, $2.50	.40	1.25	2.50
63-Final issue	.25	.70	1.40
Annual 1 (10/85, 52 pgs.)-Crisis tie-in	.30	.90	1.80
Annual 2 (1986, 52 pgs.). 3 (1987, 52 pgs.)	.25	.80	1.60
Annual 4 (1988, $2.50, 52 pgs.)	.35	1.00	2.00

LEGION OF SUPER-HEROES
Nov, 1989-Present ($1.75, color)
DC Comics

1-Giffen-c/a(p) & scripts in all (4 pg.-a only #18)

	.40	1.25	2.50

	Good	Fine	N-Mint
2-36: 8-Origin. 13-Free poster by Giffen showing new costumes. 21,22-No Giffen-a. 23-Lobo & Darkseid app.			
	.30	.90	1.80
Annual 1-3 (1990, 1991, 1992, $3.50, 68 pgs.)			
	.60	1.75	3.50

LIFE OF CAPTAIN MARVEL, THE
Aug, 1985-No. 5, Dec, 1985 ($2.00 cover; Baxter paper)
Marvel Comics Group

	Good	Fine	N-Mint
1-Reprints Starlin issues of Capt. Marvel #25-34 plus Marvel Feature #12 (all with Thanos)	1.10	3.25	6.50
2-5: 4-New Thanos back-c by Starlin	.70	2.00	4.00

LOBO (Also see Action #650, Advs. of Superman, Justice League, L.E.G.I.O.N. '89, Mister Miracle, Omega Men #3 & Superman #41)
Nov, 1990-No. 4, Feb, 1991 ($1.50, color, mini-series)

	Good	Fine	N-Mint
1-(99 cents)-Giffen plots/Breakdowns in all			
	.85	2.50	5.00
2-Legion '89 spin-off	.40	1.25	2.50
3,4	.35	1.00	2.00
...Paramilitary Christmas Special 1 (1991, $2.39, 52 pgs.)			
	.40	1.20	2.40

LOBO'S BACK
May, 1992-No. 4, Aug, 1992 ($1.50, color, mini-series, mature readers)
DC Comics

	Good	Fine	N-Mint
1-4: Simon Bisley-c/a in all. 1-Has 3 covers on book			
	.35	1.00	2.00

LOGAN'S RUN
Jan, 1977-No. 7, July, 1977
Marvel Comics Group

	Good	Fine	N-Mint
1: 1-5-Based on novel & movie	.60	1.75	3.50
2-5,7: 6,7-New stories adapted from novel			
	.40	1.25	2.50
6-1st Thanos solo story (back-up story)	2.65	8.00	18.00

LOIS LANE (See Showcase #9, 10 & Superman's Girlfriend...)

The Lone Ranger #5, © The Lone Ranger

LONE RANGER, THE (Movie, radio & TV; Clayton Moore starred
as Lone Ranger in the movies; No. 1-37: strip reprints)(Also see
King Comics)
Jan-Feb, 1948-No. 145, May-July, 1962
Dell Publishing Co.

	Good	Fine	N-Mint
1 (36pgs.)-The L. Ranger, his horse Silver, companion Tonto & his horse Scout begin	57.00	170.00	400.00
2 (52pgs. begin, end #41)	27.00	80.00	190.00
3-5	22.00	65.00	150.00
6,7,9,10	17.00	51.00	120.00
8-Origin retold; Indian back-c begin, end #35	22.00	65.00	155.00
11-20: 11-"Young Hawk" Indian boy serial begins, ends #145	11.50	34.00	80.00
21,22,24-31: 51-Reprint. 31-1st Mask logo	9.30	28.00	65.00
23-Origin retold	13.00	40.00	90.00
32-37: 32-Painted-c begin. 36-Animal photo back-c begin, end #49. 37-Last newspaper-r issue; new outfit	7.00	21.00	50.00
38-41 (All 52 pgs.)	6.00	18.00	42.00
42-50 (36pgs.)	5.00	15.00	35.00
51-74 (52pgs.): 71-Blank inside-c	5.00	15.00	35.00
75-99: 76-Flag-c. 79-X-mas-c	4.00	12.00	28.00
100	5.70	17.00	40.00
101-111: Last painted-c	4.30	13.00	30.00

	Good	Fine	N-Mint
112-Clayton Moore photo-c begin, end #145			
	16.00	48.00	110.00
113-117	8.00	24.00	55.00
118-Origin Lone Ranger, Tonto, & Silver retold; Special anniversary			
issue	14.00	43.00	100.00
119-145: 139-Last issue by Fran Striker	7.00	21.00	50.00

LONE RANGER, THE
9/64-No. 16, 12/69; No. 17, 11/72; No. 18, 9/74-No. 28, 3/77
Gold Key (Reprints in #13-20)

	Good	Fine	N-Mint
1-Retells origin	2.85	8.50	20.00
2	1.50	4.50	10.00
3-10: Small Bear-r in #6-12	1.00	3.00	7.00
11-17	.85	2.50	6.00
18-28	.70	2.40	5.00
Golden West 1(10/66, #30029-610)-Giant; r/most Golden West #3-			
including Clayton Moore photo front/back-c			
	6.50	19.00	45.00

LONGSHOT
Sept, 1985-No. 6, Feb, 1986 (Limited series)
Marvel Comics Group

	Good	Fine	N-Mint
1-Arthur Adams/Whilce Portacio-a in all	2.70	8.00	16.00
2	2.30	7.00	14.00
3-5: 4-Spider-Man app.	2.00	6.00	12.00
6-Double size	2.50	7.50	15.00

LOST IN SPACE (TV) (Space Family Robinson..., on Space Station
One) (Formerly Space Family Robinson)
No. 37, 10/73-No. 54, 11/78; No. 55, 3/81-No. 59, 5/82
Gold Key

	Good	Fine	N-Mint
37-48: All have Spiegle-a & painted-c	.60	1.75	3.50
49-59: Reprints-#49,50,55-59	.35	1.00	2.00

LUCY SHOW, THE (TV)
June, 1963-No. 5, June, 1964 (Photo-c: 1,2)
Gold Key

	Good	Fine	N-Mint
1	8.00	24.00	55.00
2	5.70	17.00	40.00
3-5: Photo back-c,1,2,4,5	5.00	15.00	35.00

M

MACHINE MAN (Also see 2001, A Space Odyssey)
Apr, 1978-No. 9, Dec, 1978; No. 10, Aug, 1979-No. 19, Feb, 1981
Marvel Comics Group

	Good	Fine	N-Mint
1	.50	1.50	3.00
2-17	.25	.75	1.50
18-Wendigo, Alpha Flight-ties into X-Men #140	.85	2.50	5.00
19-1st app. Jack O'Lantern (Macendale, who later becomes Hobgoblin II)	2.00	6.00	12.00

MACHINE MAN
Oct, 1984-No. 4, Jan, 1985 (Limited-series)
Marvel Comics Group

	Good	Fine	N-Mint
1-Barry Smith-c/a(p) in all	.25	.75	1.50
2-4		.60	1.20

MAGIK (Illyana and Storm Limited Series)
Dec, 1983-No. 4, Mar, 1984 (60 cents, mini-series)
Marvel Comics Group

	Good	Fine	N-Mint
1-Characters from X-Men; Inferno begins; X-Men cameo (Buscema pencils in 1,2; c-1p	.40	1.25	2.50
2-4: 2-Nightcrawler app. & X-Men cameo	.35	1.00	2.00

MAGNUS (...Robot Fighter)
May, 1991-Present ($1.75, color, high quality paper)
Valiant Comics

	Good	Fine	N-Mint
1-Nichols/Layton-c/a; 1-8 have trading cards	3.35	10.00	20.00
2	1.70	5.00	10.00
3,4	1.00	3.00	6.00
5-1st app. Rai; 5-8 contain Rai mini-series #1-4 in flip book format	1.15	3.50	7.00
6-8: 8-Begin $1.95-c	.85	2.50	5.00
0-Origin issue; Layton-a; ordered through mail w/coupons from 1st 8 issues plus 50 cents; B. Smith trading card	10.00	30.00	60.00

	Good	**Fine**	**N-Mint**
0-Same as above except sold in shops w/o card			
	3.35	10.00	20.00
9-11	.70	2.00	4.00
12-($3.25, 44 pgs.)	.60	1.75	3.50
13-18: 13-Begin $2.25-c. 16-True origin revealed			
	.40	1.15	2.30

MAGNUS, ROBOT FIGHTER (...4000 A.D.)(See Doctor Solar)
Feb, 1963-No. 46, Jan, 1977 (Painted covers)
Gold Key

1-Origin & 1st app. Magnus; Aliens (1st app.) series begins			
	19.00	57.00	130.00
2,3	10.00	30.00	70.00
4-10: 10-Simonson fan club illo (5/65, 1st-a?)			
	6.50	19.00	45.00
11-20	4.50	14.00	32.00
21,24-28: 22-Origin-r/#1. 28-Aliens ends	2.85	8.50	20.00
22,23-12 cent and 15 cent editions exist	2.85	8.50	20.00
29-46-Reprints	1.60	4.80	11.00

MAN-BAT (See Batman Family, Brave & the Bold, & Detective #400)
Dec-Jan, 1975-76-No. 2, Feb-Mar, 1976; Dec, 1984
National Periodical Publications/DC Comics

1-Ditko-a(p); Aparo-c; Batman, She-Bat app.			
	.75	2.25	4.50
2-Aparo-c	.50	1.50	3.00
1 (12/84)-N. Adams-r(3)/Det.(Vs. Batman on-c)			
	.70	2.00	4.00

MAN FROM U.N.C.L.E., THE (TV)
Feb, 1965-No. 22, April, 1969 (All photo covers)
Gold Key

1	11.50	34.00	80.00
2-Photo back c-2-8	8.00	24.00	55.00
3-10: 7-Jet Dream begins (all new stories)			
	5.00	15.00	35.00
11-22: 21,22-Reprint #10 & 7	4.00	12.00	28.00

MAN-THING (See Fear, Marvel Comics Presents & Marvel Fanfare)
Jan, 1974-No. 22, Oct, 1975; V2#1, Nov, 1979-V2#11, July, 1981
Marvel Comics Group

	Good	Fine	N-Mint
1-Howard the Duck(2nd app.) cont./Fear #19			
	2.00	6.00	14.00
2	1.15	3.50	7.00
3-1st app. original Foolkiller	.85	2.50	5.00
4-Origin Foolkiller; last app. 1st Foolkiller			
	.60	1.75	3.50
5-11-Ploog-a. 11-Foolkiller cameo (flashback)			
	.40	1.25	2.50
12-22: 19-1st app. Scavenger. 20-Spidey cameo. 21-Origin Scavenger, Man-Thing. 22-Howard the Duck cameo			
	.35	1.00	2.00
V2#1(1979)-11: 6-Golden-c		.50	1.00

MARC SPECTOR: MOON KNIGHT (Also see Moon Knight)
June, 1989-Present ($1.50, color, direct sale only)
Marvel Comics

	Good	Fine	N-Mint
1	.85	2.50	5.00
2-7: 4-Intro new Midnight	.40	1.25	2.50
8,9-Punisher app.	1.15	3.50	7.00
10-18	.35	1.00	2.00
19-21-Spider-Man & Punisher app.	1.00	3.00	6.00
22-24,26-31,34-44: 20-Guice-c. 21-23-Cowan-c(p)			
	.25	.75	1.50
25-($2.50, 52 pgs.)-Ghost Rider app.	.50	1.50	3.00
32,33-Hobgoblin II (Macendale) & Spider-Man (in black costume) app.	.50	1.50	3.00
35-38-Punisher story	.35	1.00	2.00
39-44: 39-New costume	.30	.90	1.80

MARRIED ... WITH CHILDREN (TV)
June, 1990-No. 7, Dec?, 1990 ($1.75, color)
V2#1, July, 1991-Present ($1.95, color)
Now Comics

	Good	Fine	N-Mint
1-Based on Fox TV show	1.15	3.50	7.00
1-2nd printing ($1.75)	.50	1.50	3.00
2-Photo-c	.85	2.50	5.00
2-2nd printing ($1.75)	.30	.90	1.80
3	.35	1.10	2.20
4-7	.30	.90	1.80
V2#1-14: 1,4,5,12-Photo-c. 12-14-Kelly Bundy Specials; polybagged with Kelly poster inside each	.35	1.00	2.00

MARVEL AND DC PRESENT (Featuring the Uncanny X-Men and
   the New Teen Titans)
1982 ($2.00, one shot, 68 pgs., printed on Baxter paper)
Marvel Comics Group/DC Comics

	Good	Fine	N-Mint
1-Deathstroke the Terminator app.; Simonson/Austin-c/a			
	2.15	6.50	15.00

MARVEL CHILLERS
Oct, 1975-No. 7, Oct, 1976 (All 25 cent issues)
Marvel Comics Group

	Good	Fine	N-Mint
1-Intro. Modred the Mystic; Kane-c(p)	.50	1.50	3.00

2-7: 3-Tigra, the Were-Woman begins (origin), ends #7. Chaykin/
Wrightson-c. 4-Kraven app. 5-Red Wolf app. 6-Byrne-a(p);
Buckler-c(p); Red Wolf app. 7-Kirby-c; Tuska-p

	.25	.75	1.50

MARVEL COLLECTORS ITEM CLASSICS (Marvel's Greatest
   #23 on)
Feb, 1965-No. 22, Aug, 1969 (68 pgs.)
Marvel Comics Group(ATF)

	Good	Fine	N-Mint
1-Fantastic Four, Spider-Man, Thor, Hulk, Iron Man-r begin; all are 25 cent cover price	5.00	15.00	35.00
2 (4/66)-4	2.85	8.50	20.00
5-22	1.30	4.00	9.00

MARVEL BOY (Astonishing #3 on; see Marvel Super Action #4)
Dec, 1950-No. 2, Feb, 1951
Marvel Comics (MPC)

	Good	Fine	N-Mint
1-Origin Marvel Boy by Russ Heath	39.00	120.00	275.00
2-Everett-a	32.00	95.00	225.00

MARVEL COMICS (Marvel Mystery Comics #2 on)
October, November, 1939
Timely Comics (Funnies, Inc.)

	Good	Fine	VF-NM
1-Origin Sub-Mariner by Bill Everett (1st newsstand app.); intro Human Torch by Carl Burgos, Kazar the Great (1st Tarzan clone), & Jungle Terror (only app.); intro. The Angel by Gustavson, The Masked Raider (ends #12); biography of Burgos & Everett			
	6700.00	16,700.00	40,000.00

(Prices vary widely on this book)

MARVEL COMICS PRESENTS
Early Sept, 1988-Present ($1.25-$1.50, color, bi-weekly)
Marvel Comics

	Good	Fine	N-Mint
1-Wolverine by Buscema in #1-10	1.70	5.00	10.00
2-5	.85	2.50	5.00
6-10: 6-Sub-Mariner app. 10-Colossus begins	.70	2.00	4.00

11-32,34-37: 17-Cyclops begins. 19-1st app. Damage Control. 24-Havok begins. 25-Origin/1st app. Nth Man. 26-Hulk begins by Rogers. 29- Quasar app. 31-Excalibur begins by Austin (i). 33-Capt. America. 37-Devil-Slayer app.   .35   1.00   2.00

| 33-Jim Lee-a | .50 | 1.50 | 3.00 |

38-Wolverine begins by Buscema; Hulk app.
.85   2.50   5.00

39-47,51-53: 39-Spider-Man app. 46-Liefeld Wolverine-c
.50   1.50   3.00

48-50-Wolverine & Spider-Man team-up. 48-Wasp app. 50-Silver Surfer. 50-53-Comet Man; Bill Mumy scripts
.85   2.50   5.00

54-61-Wolverine/Hulk; 54-Werewolf by Night begins; The Shroud by Ditko. 58-Iron Man by Ditko. 59-Punisher
1.00   3.00   6.00

| 62-Deathlok & Wolverine stories | 1.35 | 4.00 | 8.00 |
| 63-Wolverine | .70 | 2.00 | 4.00 |

64-71-Wolverine/Ghost Rider 8 part story. 70-Liefeld Ghost Rider/Wolverine-c   .75   2.25   4.50

72-Begin 13 part Weapon-X story(Wolverine origin) by B. Windsor-Smith (Prologue)   1.35   4.00   8.00

73-Weapon-X part 1; Black Knight, Sub-Mariner
.85   2.50   5.00

74-Weapon-X part 2; Black Knight, Sub-Mariner
.70   2.00   4.00

75-80: 77-Mr. Fantastic story. 78-Iron Man by Steacy. 80,81-Capt. America by Ditko/Austin   .50   1.50   3.00

81-84: 81-Daredevil by Rogers/Williamson. 82-Power Man. 83-Human Torch by Ditko(a&scripts). 84-Last Weapon-X (24 pg. conclusion)   .40   1.25   2.50

85-Begin 8 part Wolverine story (1st Kieth-a on Wolverine); begin 8 part Beast story; Liefeld-a(p)   .85   2.50   5.00

| 86-89 | .50 | 1.50 | 3.00 |

90-Begin 8 part Ghost Rider & Cable story; begin flip book format with two covers   .70   2.00   4.00

	Good	Fine	N-Mint
91-94: 93-Begin 6 part Wolverine story	.40	1.25	2.50
95-98: 95-Begin $1.50-c. 98-Begin 2 part Ghost Rider story			
	.35	1.00	2.00

99,101-107,112-116: 99-Spider-Man story. 101-Begin 6 part Ghost Rider/Dr. Strange story & 8 part Wolverine/Nightcrawler story; Punisher story. 107-Begin 6 part Ghost Rider & Werewolf by Night story   .25   .75   1.50

100-Full length Ghost Rider/Wolverine story by Kieth w/Tim Vigil assists   .40   1.25   2.50

108-111: 4 part Thanos story by Starlin (scripts). 109-Begin 8 part Wolverine & Typhoid Mary story   .35   1.00   2.00

MARVEL DOUBLE FEATURE
Dec, 1973-No. 21, Mar, 1977
Marvel Comics Group

1-Capt. America, Iron Man-r/T.O.S. begin			
	.70	2.00	4.00
2-16,20,21	.35	1.00	2.00
17-Reprints story/Iron Man & Sub-Mariner #1			
	.50	1.50	3.00
18,19-Colan/Craig-r from Iron Man #1 in both			
	.70	2.00	4.00

MARVEL FANFARE
March, 1982-No. 60, Jan, 1992 ($1.25-$2.25, slick paper, direct sale)
Marvel Comics Group

1-Spider-Man/Angel team-up; 1st Paul Smith-a; Daredevil app.			
	1.70	5.00	12.00
2-Spider-Man, Ka-Zar, The Angel. F.F. origin retold			
	1.70	5.00	10.00
3,4-X-Men & Ka-Zar. 4-Deathlok app.	1.50	4.50	9.00
5-Dr. Strange, Capt. America	.70	2.00	4.00

6-15: 6-Spider-Man, Scarlet Witch. 7-Incredible Hulk. 8-Dr. Strange; Wolf Boy begins. 9-Man-Thing. 10-13-Black Widow. 14-The Vision. 15-The Thing by Barry Smith, c/a   .40   1.25   2.50

16-32,34-50: 16,17-Skywolf. 18-Capt. America by Miller. 19-Cloak and Dagger. 20-Thing/Dr. Strange. 21-Thing/Dr. Strange/ Hulk. 22,23-Iron Man vs. Dr. Octopus. 24-26-Weirdworld. 27-Daredevil/Spider-Man. 28-Alpha Flight. 29-Hulk. 30-Moon Knight. 31,32-Captain America. 34-37-Warriors Three. 38-Moon

	Good	Fine	N-Mint

Knight/Dazzler. 39-Moon Knight/Hawkeye. 40-Angel/Rogue & Storm. 41-Dr. Strange. 42-Spider-Man. 43-Sub-Mariner/Human Torch. 44-Iron Man Vs. Dr. Doom by Ken Steacy. 45-All pin-up issue by Steacy, Art Adams & others. 46-Fantastic Four. 47-Hulk. 48-She-Hulk/Vision. 49-Dr. Strange/Nick Fury. 50-X-Factor; begin $2.25-c   .40   1.25   2.50

33-X-Men, Wolverine app.; Punisher pin-up

                                    1.00   3.00   6.00

51-($2.95, 52 pgs.)-Silver Surfer; Fantastic Four & Capt. Marvel app.; 51,52-Colan/Williamson back-up (Dr. Strange)

                                  .60   1.75   3.50

52,53: 52-54-Black Knight; 53-Iron Man back up

                                  .40   1.25   2.50

54,55-Wolverine back-ups. 55-Power Pack .60   1.75   3.50

56-60: 56-59-Shanna the She-Devil. 58-Vision & Scarlet Witch back-up. 60-Black Panther, Rogue & Daredevil stories

                                  .40   1.25   2.50

MARVEL FEATURE (See Marvel Two-In-One)
Dec, 1971-No. 12, Nov, 1973 (No. 1,2: 25 cents)(1-3: Quarterly)
Marvel Comics Group

1-Origin/1st app. The Defenders (Sub-Mariner, Hulk & Dr. Strange); Dr. Strange solo story plus '50s Sub-Mariner-r; Neal Adams-c   7.00   21.00   50.00

2,3: 2-1950s Sub-Mariner-r. 3-Defenders ends

                                3.60   11.00   25.00

4-Re-intro Antman(1st app. since '60s), begin series; brief origin

                                1.30   4.00   9.00

5-10: 6-Wasp app. & begins team-ups. 8-Origin Antman & Wasp-r/ TTA #44. 9-Iron Man app. 10-Last Antman

                                .85   2.50   5.00

11-Thing vs. Hulk; 1st Thing solo book (9/73); origin Fantastic Four retold   1.00   3.00   7.00

12-Thing/Iron Man; early Thanos app. 1.30   4.00   9.00

MARVEL FEATURE (Also see Red Sonja)
Nov, 1975-No. 7, Nov, 1976 (Story continues in Conan #68)
Marvel Comics Group

1-Red Sonja begins (pre-dates Red Sonja #1); adapts Howard short story; Adams-r/Savage Sword of Conan #1

                                .60   1.75 .   3.50

	Good	Fine	N-Mint
2-7: Thorne-c/a in #2-7. 7-Battles Conan	.35	1.00	2.00

MARVEL MYSTERY COMICS (Formerly Marvel Comics)
No. 2, Dec, 1939-No. 92, June, 1949
Timely /Marvel Comics (TP 2-17/TCI 18-54/MCI 55-92)

	Good	Fine	VF-NM
2-American Ace begins, ends #3; Human Torch (blue costume) by Burgos, Sub-Mariner by Everett continue; 2pg. origin recap of Human Torch	900.00	2250.00	5400.00

	Good	Fine	N-Mint
3-New logo from Marvel pulp begins	500.00	1250.00	3000.00
4-Intro. Electro, the Marvel of the Age (ends #19), The Ferret, Mystery Detective (ends #9)	417.00	1040.00	2500.00

	Good	Fine	VF-NM
5 (Scarce)	635.00	1580.00	3800.00

	Good	Fine	N-Mint
6,7	270.00	670.00	1600.00
8-Human Torch & Sub-Mariner battle	335.00	835.00	2000.00

	Good	Fine	VF-NM
9-(Scarce)-Human Torch & Sub-Mariner battle	500.00	1250.00	3000.00

	Good	Fine	N-Mint
10-Human Torch & Sub-Mariner battle, conclusion; Terry Vance, the Schoolboy Sleuth begins, ends #57	225.00	560.00	1350.00
11	183.00	460.00	1100.00
12-Classic Kirby-c	167.00	415.00	1000.00
13-Intro. & 1st app. The Vision by S&K; Sub-Mariner dons new costume, ends #15	208.00	520.00	1250.00
14-16	117.00	290.00	700.00
17-Human Torch/Sub-Mariner team-up by Burgos/Everett; pin-up on back-c	133.00	335.00	800.00
18	108.00	270.00	650.00
19-Origin Toro in text	113.00	285.00	680.00
20-Origin The Angel in text	108.00	270.00	650.00
21-Intro. & 1st app. The Patriot; not in #46-48; pin-up on back-c	100.00	250.00	600.00
22-25: 23-Last Gustavson Angel; origin The Vision in text. 24-Injury-to-eye story	83.00	210.00	500.00
26-30: 27-Ka-Zar ends; last S&K Vision who battles Satan. 28-Jimmy Jupiter in the Land of Nowhere begins, ends #48; Sub-Mariner vs. The Flying Dutchman	78.00	195.00	470.00

Marvel Mystery Comics #23, © Marvel Comics

	Good	Fine	N-Mint
31-Sub-Mariner by Everett ends, begins again #84			
	75.00	190.00	450.00
32-1st app. The Boboes	75.00	190.00	450.00
33,35-40: 40-Zeppelin-c	75.00	190.00	450.00
34-Everett, Burgos, Martin Goodman, Funnies, Inc. office appear in story & battles Hitler; last Burgos Human Torch			
	86.00	215.00	515.00
41-43,45-48: 46-Hitler-c. 48-Last Vision; flag-c			
	67.00	170.00	400.00
44-Classic Super Plane-c	67.00	170.00	400.00
49-Origin Miss America	86.00	215.00	515.00
50-Mary becomes Miss Patriot (origin)	67.00	170.00	400.00
51-60: 53-Bondage-c	63.00	156.00	375.00
61,62,64-Last German War-c	58.00	145.00	350.00
63-Classic Hitler War-c; The Villainess Cat-Woman only app.			
	63.00	156.00	375.00
65,66-Last Japanese War-c	58.00	145.00	350.00
67-75: 74-Last Patriot. 75-Young Allies begin			
	54.00	135.00	325.00
76-78: 76-Ten Chapter Miss America serial begins, ends #85			
	54.00	135.00	325.00
79-New cover format; Super Villains begin on cover; last Angel			
	50.00	125.00	300.00
80-1st app. Capt. America in Marvel Comics			
	67.00	170.00	400.00

	Good	Fine	N-Mint
81-Captain America app.	58.00	145.00	350.00
82-Origin Namora; 1st Sub-Mariner/Namora team-up; Captain America app.	100.00	250.00	600.00
83,85: 83-Last Young Allies. 85-Last Miss America; Blonde Phantom app.	50.00	125.00	300.00
84-Blonde Phantom, Sub-Mariner by Everett begins; Captain America app.	70.00	175.00	420.00
86-Blonde Phantom i.d. revealed; Captain America app.; last Bucky app.	58.00	145.00	350.00
87-1st Capt. America/Golden Girl team-up	63.00	156.00	375.00
88-Golden Girl, Namora, & Sun Girl (1st in Marvel Comics) x-over; Captain America, Blonde Phantom app.; last Toro	58.00	145.00	350.00
89-1st Human Torch/Sun Girl team-up; 1st Captain America solo; Blonde Phantom app.	60.00	150.00	360.00
90-Blonde Phantom un-masked; Captain America app.	62.00	155.00	370.00
91-Capt. America app.; intro Venus; Blonde Phantom & Sub-Mariner end	62.00	155.00	370.00
92-Feature story on the birth of the Human Torch and the death of Professor Horton (his creator); 1st app. The Witness in Marvel Comics; Captain America app.	92.00	230.00	550.00

MARVEL PREMIERE
April, 1972-No. 61, Aug, 1981 (A tryout book for new characters)
Marvel Comics Group

1-Origin Warlock (pre #1) by Gil Kane/Adkins; origin Counter-Earth; Hulk & Thor cameo (#1-14 are 25 cent-c)	5.30	16.00	38.00
2-Warlock ends; Kirby Yellow Claw-r	3.60	11.00	25.00
3-Dr. Strange series begins (pre #1, 7/72), B. Smith-a(p); Smith-c?	3.85	11.50	27.00
4-Smith/Brunner-a	1.70	5.00	12.00
5-9	1.00	3.00	7.00
10-Death of the Ancient One	1.50	4.50	10.00
11-14: 11-Dr. Strange origin-r by Ditko. 14-Last Dr. Strange (3/74), gets own title 3 months later	.85	2.50	5.00
15-Origin/1st app. Iron Fist (5/74), ends #25	5.00	15.00	35.00
16-24: Iron Fist in all. 16-Hama's 1st Marvel-a	1.50	4.50	10.00

	Good	Fine	N-Mint
25-1st Byrne Iron Fist (moves to own title next)			
	1.70	5.00	12.00
26,27: 26-Hercules. 27-Satana	.85	2.50	5.00
28-Legion of Monsters (Ghost Rider, Man-Thing, Morbius, Were-wolf)			
	1.70	5.00	12.00

29-49,51-56,61: 29,30-The Liberty Legion. 29-1st modern app. Patriot. 31-1st app. Woodgod; last 25 cent issue. 32-1st app. Monark Starstalker. 33,34-1st color app. Solomon Kane. 35-Origin/1st app. 3-D Man. 38-1st Weird-world. 41-1st Seeker 3001! 42-Tigra. 44-Jack of Hearts (1st solo book, 10/78). 47-Origin/1st app. new Ant-Man. 48-Ant-Man. 49-The Falcon (1st solo book, 8/79). 51,52-Black Panther. 54-1st Caleb Hammer. 56-1st color app. Dominic Fortune. 61-Star Lord

	Good	Fine	N-Mint
	.25	.75	1.50
50-1st comic book app. Alice Cooper	.85	2.50	5.00
57-Dr. Who (1st U.S. app.)	.50	1.50	3.00
58-60-Dr. Who	.35	1.00	2.00

MARVEL PRESENTS
October, 1975-No. 12, Aug, 1977 (#1-5 are 25 cent-c)
Marvel Comics Group

	Good	Fine	N-Mint
1-Origin & 1st app. Bloodstone	.90	2.75	5.50
2-Origin Bloodstone continued; Kirby-c	.70	2.00	4.00
3-Guardians of the Galaxy (1st solo book, 2/76) begins, ends #12			
	3.15	9.50	22.00
4-7,9-12: 9,10-Origin Starhawk	2.15	6.50	15.00
8-Reprints story from Silver Surfer #2	2.20	6.60	15.50

MARVEL PREVIEW (Magazine)
Feb, 1975-No. 24, Winter, 1980 (B&W) ($1.00)
Marvel Comics Group

	Good	Fine	N-Mint
1-Man Gods From Beyond the Stars; Neal Adams-a(i) & cover; Nino-a	.35	1.00	2.00
2-Origin The Punisher (see Amaz. Spider-Man 129); 1st app. Dominic Fortune; Morrow-c	24.50	73.00	170.00

3-10: 3-Blade the Vampire Slayer. 4-Star-Lord & Sword in the Star (origins & 1st app.). 5,6-Sherlock Holmes. 6-N. Adams frontis-piece. 7-Satana, Sword in the Star app. 8-Legion of Monsters. 9-Man-God; origin Star Hawk, ends #20. 10-Thor the Mighty. 10,11-Starlin frontispiece in each   .35   1.00   2.00

11-20,22-24: 11-Star-Lord; Byrne-a. 12-Haunt of Horror. 15-Star-

	Good	Fine	N-Mint
Lord. 16-Detectives. 17-Black Mark by G. Kane. 18-Star-Lord. 19-Kull. 20-Bizarre Advs. 22-King Arthur. 23-Bizarre Adventures; Miller-a. 24-Debut Paradox	.35	1.00	2.00
21-Moon Knight (pre-dates Moon Knight #1); The Shroud by Ditko-a	.70	2.00	4.00

MARVEL SAGA, THE
Dec, 1985-No. 25, Dec, 1987
Marvel Comics Group

1	.25	.75	1.50
2-25		.50	1.00

MARVEL'S GREATEST COMICS (Marvel Collectors Item Classics #1-22)
No. 23, Oct, 1969-No. 96, Jan, 1981
Marvel Comics Group

23-30: Begin Fantastic Four-r/#30s?-116	.50	1.50	3.00
31-34,38-96: 42-Silver Surfer-r/F.F.(others?)	.35	1.00	2.00
35-37-Silver Surfer-r/Fantastic Four #48-50	.35	1.00	2.00

MARVEL SPECTACULAR
Aug, 1973-No. 19, Nov, 1975
Marvel Comics Group

1-Thor-r from mid-sixties begin by Kirby	.35	1.00	2.00
2-19	.25	.75	1.50

MARVEL SPOTLIGHT (...& Son of Satan #19, 20, 23, 24)
Nov, 1971-No. 33, Apr, 1977; V2#1, July, 1979-V2#11, Mar, 1981
Marvel Comics Group (A try-out book for new characters)

1-Origin Red Wolf (1st solo book, pre #1); Wood inks, Neal Adams-c; only 15 cent issue	2.65	8.00	18.00
2-(25 cents, 52 pgs.)-Venus-r by Everett; origin/1st app. Werewolf By Night (begins) by Ploog; N. Adams-c	3.60	11.00	25.00
3,4: 4-Werewolf By Night ends (2/72)	1.70	5.00	12.00
5-Origin/1st app. Ghost Rider (8/72) & begins	14.00	43.00	100.00
6-8: 6-Origin G.R. retold. 8-Last Ploog issue	7.00	21.00	50.00

	Good	Fine	N-Mint

9-11-Last Ghost Rider(gets own title next mo.)

	5.70	17.00	40.00

12-Origin & 2nd full app. The Son of Satan (10/73); story cont'd from
Ghost Rider #2 & into #3; series begins, ends #24

	1.15	3.50	8.00

13-21,23,24: 14-Last 20 cent issue. 24-Last Son of Satan (10/75); gets
own title 12/75

	.70	2.00	4.00

22-Ghost Rider-c & cameo (5 panels)   1.30   4.00   9.00

25-27,30,31: 25-Sinbad. 26-Scarecrow. 27-Sub-Mariner. 29-Last 25
cent issue. 30-The Warriors Three. 31-Nick Fury

	.50	1.50	3.00

28,29: Moon Knight (28-1st solo app., 6/76)

	1.30	4.00	9.00

32-1st app./partial origin Spider-Woman (2/77); Nick Fury app.

	1.15	3.50	7.00

33-Deathlok; 1st app. Devil-Slayer   1.15   3.50   7.00

V2#1-11: 1-4,8-Capt. Marvel. 5-Dragon Lord. 6,7-StarLord; origin #6.
9-11-Capt. Universe (see Micronauts #8)   .50   1.00

MARVEL SUPER ACTION
May, 1977-No. 37, Nov, 1981
Marvel Comics Group

1-Reprints Capt. America #100 by Kirby   .40   1.25   2.50
2,3,5-13: r/Capt. America #101,102,103-111. 11-Origin-r. 12,13-
Classic Steranko-c/a(r)   .25   .75   1.50
4-Marvel Boy-r(origin)/M. Boy #1   .25   .75   1.50
14-37: r/Avengers #55,56, Annual 2, others   .50   1.00

MARVEL SUPER HERO CONTEST OF CHAMPIONS
June, 1982-No. 3, Aug, 1982 (Mini-Series)
Marvel Comics Group

1-3: Features nearly all Marvel characters currently appearing in
their comics   1.00   3.00   6.00

MARVEL SUPER HEROES
October, 1966 (25 cents, 68 pgs.) (1st Marvel One-shot)
Marvel Comics Group

1-r/origin Daredevil from D.D. #1; r/Avengers #2; G.A. Sub-
Mariner-r/Marvel Mystery #8 (H. Torch app.)

	8.50	25.50	60.00

MARVEL SUPER-HEROES (Formerly Fantasy Masterpieces #1-11)

No. 12, 12/67-No. 31, 11/71; No. 32, 9/72-No. 105, 1/82
Marvel Comics Group

	Good	Fine	N-Mint
12-Origin & 1st app. Capt. Marvel of the Kree; G.A. Human Torch, Destroyer, Capt. America, Black Knight, Sub-Mariner-r (#12-20 all contain new stories and reprints & are 25 cents, 68 pgs.)	13.00	40.00	90.00
13-2nd app. Capt. Marvel; G.A. Black Knight, Torch, Vision, Capt. America, Sub-Mariner-r	6.50	19.00	45.00
14-Amazing Spider-Man (5/68, new-a by Andru/Everett); G.A. Sub-Mariner, Torch, Mercury (1st Kirby-a at Marvel), Black Knight, Capt. America reprints	10.00	30.00	70.00
15-Black Bolt cameo in Medusa (new-a); Black Knight, Sub-Mariner, Black Marvel, Capt. America-r	1.70	5.00	12.00
16-Origin & 1st app. S. A. Phantom Eagle; G.A. Torch, Capt. America, Black Knight, Patriot, Sub-Mariner-r	1.70	5.00	12.00
17-Origin Black Knight (new-a); G.A. Torch, Sub-Mariner-r; reprint from All-Winners Squad #21 (cover & story)	1.70	5.00	12.00
18-Origin/1st app. Guardians of the Galaxy; G.A. Sub-Mariner, All-Winners Squad-r	8.00	24.00	55.00
19-Ka-Zar (new-a); G.A. Torch, Marvel Boy, Black Knight, Sub-Mariner reprint; Smith-c(p); Tuska-a(r)	1.70	5.00	12.00
20-Doctor Doom (5/69); r/Young Men #24 w/-c	1.70	5.00	12.00
21-31: All-r issues. 31-Last Giant issue	1.00	3.00	6.00
32-105: 32-Hulk/Sub-Mariner-r begin from TTA. 56-r/origin Hulk/Inc. Hulk #102; Hulk-r begin		.50	1.00

MARVEL SUPER-HEROES
May, 1990-Present ($2.95-$2.25, 84 pgs.)
Marvel Comics

	Good	Fine	N-Mint
1-Moon Knight, Hercules, Black Panther, Magik, Brother Voodoo, Speedball (by Ditko) & Hellcat; Hembeck-a	.60	1.75	3.50
2,4-5: 2-Rogue, Speedball (by Ditko), Iron Man, Falcon, Tigra & Daredevil. 4-Spider-Man/Nick Fury, Daredevil, Speedball,			

	Good	Fine	N-Mint
Wonder Man, Spitfire & Black Knight; Byrne-c. 5-Thor, Dr. Strange, Thing & She-Hulk; Speedball by Ditko(p)	.50	1.50	3.00
V2#3-Retells origin Capt. America w/new facts; Blue Shield, Capt. Marvel, Speedball, Wasp; Hulk by Ditko/Rogers	.60	1.75	3.50
V2#6-8 ($2.25-c): 6,7-X-Men, Cloak & Dagger, The Shroud & Marvel Boy in each. 8-X-Men, Namor & Iron Man (by Ditko)	.50	1.50	3.00
V2#9 ($2.50-c)-West Coast Avengers; Iron Man back-up	.50	1.50	3.00
V2#10 ($2.50)-Namor, Fantastic Four, Thor, Ms. Marvel	.50	1.50	3.00

MARVEL SUPER HEROES SECRET WARS (See Secret
   Wars II)
May, 1984-No. 12, Apr, 1985 (Limited series)
Marvel Comics Group

	Good	Fine	N-Mint
1	.60	1.75	3.50
1-3-2nd printings		.50	1.00
2-7,9-12: 6-The Wasp dies. 7-Intro. new Spider-Woman. 12-($1.00, 52 pgs.)	.35	1.00	2.00
8-Spider-Man's new costume explained as Alien costume (later becomes Venom)	1.70	5.00	10.00

MARVEL TALES (...Annual #1,2: ...Starring Spider-Man #123 on)
1964-Present (No. 1-32: 72 pgs.)
Marvel Comics Group (NPP earlier issues)

	Good	Fine	N-Mint
1-Reprints origins of Spider-Man/Amazing Fantasy #15, Hulk/Inc. Hulk #1, Ant-Man/T.T.A. #35, Giant Man/T.T.A. #49, Iron Man/T.O.S. #39,48, Thor/J.I.M. #83 & r/Sgt. Fury #1	29.00	85.00	200.00
2 ('65)-r/X-Men #1(origin), Avengers #1(origin), origin Dr. Strange-r/Strange Tales #115 & origin Hulk(Hulk #3)	9.30	28.00	65.00
3 (7/66)-Spider-Man, Strange Tales, Journey into Mystery, Tales to Astonish-r begin (r/Strange Tales #101)	4.30	13.00	30.00
4,5	2.00	6.00	14.00
6-8,10: 10-Reprints 1st Kraven/Amaz. S-M #15	1.30	4.00	9.00
9-r/Amazing Spider-Man #14 w/cover	1.60	4.80	11.00
11-32: 11-Spider-Man battles Daredevil-r/Amaz. Spider-Man #16.			

	Good	Fine	N-Mint

13-Origin Marvel Boy-r/M. Boy #1. 22-Green Goblin-c/story-r/
Amazing Spider-Man #27. 30-New Angel story. 32-Last 72 pg.
issue   1.00   3.00   6.00

33-105: 33-Kraven-r; 52 pgs. 34-Begin reg. size issues. 75-Origin
Spider-Man-r. 77-79-Drug issues-r/A. Spider-Man #96-98. 98-
Death of Gwen Stacy-r/A. Spider-Man #121 (Green Goblin). 99-
Death Green Goblin-r/A. Spider-Man #122. 100-(52 pgs.)-New
Hawkeye/Two Gun Kid story. 101-105-All Spider-Man-r
                                                          .25   .75   1.50

106-1st Punisher-r/Amazing Spider-Man #129
                                                         1.30   4.00   9.00

107-133-All   Spider-Man-r.   111,112-r/Spider-Man   #134,135
(Punisher). 113,114-r/Spider-Man #136,137(Green Goblin)
                                                                    .50   1.00

134-136-Dr. Strange-r begin; SpM stories continue. 134-Dr. Strange-
r/Strange Tales #110   .50   1.00

137-Origin-r Dr. Strange; shows original unprinted-c & origin Spider-
Man/Amazing Fantasy #15   .85   2.50   5.00

137-Nabisco giveaway   .50   1.00

138-Reprints all Amazing Spider-Man #1; begin reprints of Spider-
Man with covers similar to originals   .85   2.50   5.00

139-144: r/Amazing Spider-Man #2-7   .35   1.00   2.00

145-191,193-199: Spider-Man-r continue w/#8 on. 149-Contains skin
"Tattooz." 150-($1.00, 52pgs.)-r/Spider-Man Annual 1(Kraven
app.). 153-r/1st Kraven/Spider-Man #15. 155-r/2nd Gr. Goblin/
Spider-Man #17. 161, 164,165-Gr. Goblin-c/stories-r/Spider-Man
#23,26,27. 178,179-Green Goblin-c/story-r/Spider-Man #39,40.
187,189-Kraven-r. 191-($1.50, 68 pgs.)-r/Spider-Man #96-98.
193-Byrne-r/Marvel Team-up begin w/scripts
                                                                    .60   1.20

192-($1.25, 52 pgs.)-r/Spider-Man #121,122
                                                          .35   1.00   2.00

200-Double size ($1.25)-Miller-c & r/Annual #14
                                                          .25   .75   1.50

201-208,210-221: 208-Last Byrne-r. 210,211-r/Spidey 134,135.
212,213-r/Giant Size Spidey 4. 214,215-r/Spidey 161,162
                                                                    .50   1.00

209-Reprints 1st app. The Punisher/Amazing Spider-Man #129;
Punisher reprints begin, end #222   .40   1.25   2.50

222-Reprints origin Punisher/Spectacular Spider-Man #83; last
Punisher reprint   .50   1.00

223-McFarlane-c begin, end #239   .25   .75   1.50

	Good	Fine	N-Mint

224-249,251,252,254-257: 233-Spider-Man/X-Men team-ups begin; r/X-Men #35. 234-r/Marvel Team-Up #4. 235,236-r/M. Team-Up Annual #1. 237, 238-r/M. Team-Up #150. 239,240-r/M. Team-Up #38,90 (Beast). 242-r/M. Team-Up #89. 243-r/M. Team-Up #117 (Wolverine). 251-253-r/Spider-Man #100-102 (Gr. Goblin-c/ story in #251). 254-r/M. Team-Up #15(Ghost Rider); new painted-c. 255,256-Spider-Man & Ghost Rider-r/Marvel Team-Up #58,91. 257-Hobgoblin-r begin(r/A. Spider-Man #238)

		.50	1.00

250-($1.50, 52pgs.)-r/1st Karma/M. Team-Up #100

	.25	.75	1.50

253-($1.50, 52 pgs.)-r/Amaz. S-M #102 .25 .75 1.50

258-270: 258-r/A. Spider-Man #239; begin $1.25-c. 259-261-r/A. Spider-Man #249-251 (Hobgoblin). 265-r/ A. Spidey Annual #2

		.65	1.30

MARVEL TEAM-UP
March, 1972-No. 150, Feb, 1985
Marvel Comics Group

NOTE: *Spider-Man team-ups in all but Nos. 18, 23, 26, 29, 32, 35, 97, 104, 105, 137.*

	Good	Fine	N-Mint
1-Human Torch	8.00	24.00	55.00
2,3-H-T	3.15	9.50	22.00
4-X-Men	5.30	16.00	38.00

5-10: 5-Vision. 6-Thing. 7-Thor. 8-The Cat. 9-Iron Man. 10-H-T

	1.50	4.50	10.00

11-14,16-20: 11-Inhumans. 12-Werewolf. 13-Capt. America. 14-Sub-Mariner. 16-Capt. Marvel. 17-Mr. Fantastic. 18-H-T/Hulk. 19-Ka-Zar. 20-Black Panther; last 20 cent issue

	1.15	3.50	8.00

15-1st Spider-Man/Ghost Rider team-up (11/73)

	2.15	6.50	15.00

21-30: 21-Dr. Strange. 22-Hawkeye. 23-H-T/Iceman (X-Men cameo). 24-Brother Voodoo. 25-Daredevil. 26-H-T/Thor. 27-Hulk. 28-Hercules. 29-H-T/Iron Man. 30-Falcon

	1.00	3.00	6.00

31-45,47-50: 31-Iron Fist. 32-H-T/Son of Satan. 33-Nighthawk. 34-Valkyrie. 35-H-T/Dr. Strange. 36-Frankenstein. 37-Man-Wolf. 38-Beast. 39-H-T. 40-Sons of the Tiger/H-T. 41-Scarlet Witch. 42-The Vision. 43-Dr. Doom; retells origin. 44-Moondragon. 45-Killraven. 47-Thing. 48-Iron Man; last 25 cent issue. 49-Dr.

	Good	Fine	N-Mint

Strange; Iron Man app. 50-Iron Man; Dr. Strange app.

	.85	2.50	5.00
46-Spider-Man/Deathlok team-up	1.85	5.50	11.00

51,52,56,57: 51-Iron Man; Dr. Strange app. 52-Capt. America. 56-
Daredevil. 57-Black Widow   .60   1.75   3.50

53-Hulk; Woodgod & X-Men app., 1st Byrne-a on X-Men (1/77)

	2.00	6.00	12.00

54,59,60: 54-Hulk; Woodgod app. 59-Yellowjacket/The Wasp. 60-
The Wasp (Byrne-a in all)   1.00   3.00   6.00

55-Warlock-c/story; Byrne-a	1.35	4.00	8.00
58-Ghost Rider	1.00	3.00	6.00

61-70: All Byrne-a; 61-H-T. 62-Ms. Marvel. 63-Iron Fist. 64-
Daughters of the Dragon. 65-Capt. Britain (1st U.S. app.). 66-
Capt. Britain; 1st app. Arcade. 67-Tigra; Kraven the Hunter app.
68-Man-Thing. 69-Havok (from X-Men). 70-Thor

	.55	1.65	3.30

71-74,76-78,80: 71-Falcon. 72-Iron Man. 73-Daredevil. 74-Not
Ready for Prime Time Players (Belushi). 76-Dr. Strange. 77-Ms.
Marvel. 78-Wonder Man. 80-Dr. Strange/Clea

	.50	1.50	3.00

75,79: 75-Power Man. 79-Mary Jane Watson as Red Sonja. Both
have Byrne-a(p)   .55   1.65   3.30

81-85,87,88,90: 81-Satana. 82-Black Widow. 83-Nick Fury. 84-
Shang-Chi. 85-Shang-Chi/Black Widow/Nick Fury. 87-Black
Panther. 88-Invisible Girl. 90-Beast   .35   1.00   2.00

86-Guardians of the Galaxy	.70	2.00	4.00
89-Nightcrawler (from X-Men)	.50	1.50	3.00
91-Ghost Rider	.85	2.50	5.00

92-99: 92-Hawkeye. 93-Werewolf by Night. 94-SpM vs. The Shroud.
95-Mockingbird (intro.); Nick Fury app. 96-Howard the Duck.
97-Spider-Woman/Hulk. 98-Black Widow. 99-Machine Man

	.35	1.00	2.00

100-(Double-size)-Fantastic Four/Storm/Black Panther; origin/1st
app. Karma, one of the New Mutants; origin Storm; X-Men
x-over; Miller-a/c(p); Byrne (on X-Men app. only)

	1.70	5.00	10.00

101-116: 101-Nighthawk(Ditko-a). 102-Doc Samson. 103-Ant-Man.
104-Hulk/Ka-Zar. 105-Hulk/Powerman/Iron Fist. 106-Capt.
America. 107-She-Hulk. 108-Paladin; Dazzler cameo. 109-
Dazzler; Paladin app. 110-Iron Man. 111-Devil-Slayer. 112-King
Kull. 113-Quasar. 114-Falcon. 115-Thor. 116-Valkyrie

	.25	.75	1.50

	Good	Fine	N-Mint
117-Wolverine-c/story	2.00	6.00	12.00

118-140,142-149: 118-Professor X; Wolverine app. (4 pgs.); X-Men cameo. 119-Gargoyle. 120-Dominic Fortune. 121-Human Torch. 122-Man-Thing. 123-Daredevil. 124-The Beast. 125-Tigra. 126-Hulk & Powerman/Son of Satan. 127-The Watcher. 128-Capt. America; Spider-Man/Capt. America photo-c. 129-The Vision. 130-Scarlet Witch. 131-Frogman. 132-Mr. Fantastic. 133-Fantastic-4. 134-Jack of Hearts. 135-Kitty Pryde; X-Men cameo. 136-Wonder Man. 137-Aunt May/Franklin Richards. 138-Sandman. 139-Nick Fury. 140-Black Widow. 142-Capt. Marvel. 143-Starfox. 144-Moon Knight. 145-Iron Man. 146-Nomad. 147-Human Torch; SpMback to old costume. 148-Thor. 149-Cannonball .25 .75 1.50

141-Daredevil; SpM/Black Widow app. (Spidey in new black costume #141-146; #141 ties w/Amaz. S-M #252 for 1st black costume)

	.50	1.50	3.00
150-X-Men ($1.00, double-size); B. Smith-c	.60	1.75	3.50
Annual 1(1976)-SpM/New X-Men (early app.)			
	2.00	6.00	14.00

Annuals 2-7: 2(1979)-SpM/Hulk. 3(1980)-Hulk/Power Man/Machine Man/Iron Fist; Miller-c(p). 4(1981)-SpM/Daredevil/Moon Knight/Power Man/Iron Fist; brief origins of each; Miller-c; Miller scripts on Daredevil. 5(1982)-SpM/The Thing/Scarlet Witch/Dr. Strange/Quasar. 6(1983)-SpM/New Mutants (early app.), Cloak & Dagger. 7(1984)-Alpha Flight; Byrne-c(i) .35 1.00 2.00

MARVEL TRIPLE ACTION
Feb, 1972-No. 24, Mar, 1975; No. 25, Aug, 1975-No. 47, Apr, 1979
Marvel Comics Group

1-(25 cent giant, 52pgs.)-Dr. Doom, Silver Surfer, The Thing begin, end #4 ('66 reprints from Fantastic Four)

	.50	1.50	3.00
2-47: 45-r/X-Men #45. 46-r/Avengers #53(X-Men)	.50		1.00

MARVEL TWO-IN-ONE (...Featuring ... #82? on; see The Thing)
January, 1974-No. 100, June, 1983
Marvel Comics Group

1-Thing team-ups begin; Man-Thing	2.65	8.00	18.00

2-4: 2-Sub-Mariner; last 20 cent issue. 3-Daredevil. 4-Capt.
America	1.15	3.50	8.00
5-Guardians of the Galaxy	2.30	7.00	16.00

Marvel Two-in-One #4, © Marvel Comics

	Good	Fine	N-Mint
6-Dr. Strange (11/74)	2.00	6.00	14.00
7,9,10	1.00	3.00	6.00
8-Early Ghost Rider app. (3/75)	1.50	4.50	10.00
11-20: 17-Spider-Man. 18-Last 25 cent issue			
	.70	2.00	4.00
21-26,28,29,31-40: 29-Spider-Woman cameo. 39-Vision			
	.50	1.50	3.00
27-Deathlok	1.15	3.50	7.00
30-2nd full app. Spider-Woman	.85	2.50	5.00
41,42,44-49: 42-Capt. America. 45-Capt. Marvel. 46-Thing battles			
Hulk-c/story	.25	.75	1.50
43,50,53,55-Byrne-a	.40	1.25	2.50
51-The Beast, Nick Fury, Ms. Marvel; Miller-p			
	.50	1.50	3.00
52-Moon Knight app.	.50	1.50	3.00
54-Death of Deathlok: Byrne-a	2.30	7.00	16.00
56-68,70-79,81,82: 60-Intro. Impossible Woman. 61-63-Warlock			
app. 71-1st app. Maelstrom. 76-Iceman		.50	1.00
69-Guardians of the Galaxy	.70	2.00	4.00
80-Ghost Rider	1.00	3.00	6.00
83,84: 83-Sasquatch. 84-Alpha Flight app.	.35	1.00	2.00
85-99: 90-Spider-Man. 93-Jocasta dies. 96-X-Men-c & cameo			
		.50	1.00
100-Double size, Byrne scripts	.25	.75	1.50

	Good	Fine	N-Mint
Annual 1(1976, 52 pgs.)-Thing/Liberty Legion			
	.35	1.00	2.00
Annual 2(1977, 52 pgs.)-Thing/Spider-Man; 2nd death of Thanos; end of Thanos saga; Starlin-c/a	3.60	11.00	25.00
Annual 3,4: 3(1978, 52 pgs.). 4(1979, 52 pgs.)			
	.25	.75	1.50
Annual 5-7: 5(1980, 52 pgs.)-Hulk. 6(1981, 52 pgs.)-1st app. American Eagle. 7(1982, 52 pgs.)-The Thing/Champion; Sasquatch, Colossus app.		.50	1.00

MARY MARVEL COMICS (Monte Hale #29 on) (Also see Captain Marvel #18, Marvel Family & Wow)
Dec, 1945-No. 28, Sept, 1948
Fawcett Publications

1-Captain Marvel intro. Mary on-c; intro/origin Georgia Sivana	Good	Fine	N-Mint
	67.00	200.00	470.00
2	34.00	100.00	235.00
3	24.00	70.00	165.00
4	19.00	55.00	130.00
5-8: 8-Bulletgirl x-over in Mary Marvel			
	16.00	48.00	110.00
9,10	12.00	36.00	85.00
11-20	10.00	30.00	70.00
21-28	8.50	25.50	60.00

MASTER COMICS
Mar, 1940-No. 133, Apr, 1953 (No. 1-6: oversized issues)
(#1-3: 15 cents, 52 pgs.; #4-6: 10 cents, 36 pgs.)
Fawcett Publications

	Good	Fine	VF-NM
1-Origin Master Man; The Devil's Dagger, El Carim, Master of Magic, Rick O'Say, Morton Murch, White Rajah, Shipwreck Roberts, Frontier Marshal, Streak Sloan, Mr. Clue begin (all features end #6)	250.00	625.00	1500.00

	Good	Fine	N-Mint
2	133.00	335.00	800.00
3-5	92.00	230.00	550.00
6-Last Master Man	100.00	250.00	600.00

NOTE: *#1-6 rarely found in near mint to mint condition due to large-size.*
7-(10/40)-Bulletman, Zoro, the Mystery Man (ends #22), Lee Granger, Jungle King, & Buck Jones begin; only app. The War

	Good	Fine	N-Mint
Bird & Mark Swift & the Time Retarder			
	150.00	375.00	900.00
8-The Red Gaucho (ends #13), Captain Venture (ends #22) & The Planet Princess begin	72.00	215.00	500.00
9,10: 10-Lee Granger ends	57.00	171.00	400.00
11-Origin Minute-Man	150.00	375.00	900.00
12	72.00	215.00	500.00
13-Origin Bulletgirl	117.00	290.00	700.00
14-16: 14-Companions Three begins, ends #31			
	57.00	170.00	400.00
17-20: 17-Raboy-a on Bulletman begins. 20-Captain Marvel cameo app. in Bulletman	57.00	170.00	400.00

	Good	Fine	VF-NM
21-(12/41; Scarce)-Captain Marvel & Bulletman team up against Capt. Nazi; origin Capt. Marvel Jr's most famous nemesis Captain Nazi who will cause creation of Capt. Marvel Jr. in Whiz #25. Part I of trilogy origin of Capt. Marvel Jr.			
	193.00	580.00	1400.00
22-(1/42)-Captain Marvel Jr. moves over from Whiz #25 & teams with Bulletman against Captain Nazi; part III of trilogy origin of Capt. Marvel Jr. & his 1st cover and adventure			
	171.00	515.00	1200.00

	Good	Fine	N-Mint
23-Capt. Marvel Jr. c/stories begins; fights Capt. Nazi by himself			
	135.00	405.00	950.00
24,25,29: 29-Hitler & Tojo-c	53.00	160.00	370.00
26-28,30-Capt. Marvel Jr. vs. Capt. Nazi. 30-Flag-c			
	53.00	160.00	370.00
31,32: 32-Last El Carim & Buck Jones; Balbo, the Boy Magician intro. in El Carim	37.00	110.00	260.00
33-Balbo, the Boy Magician (ends #47), Hopalong Cassidy (ends #49) begins	37.00	110.00	260.00
34-Capt. Marvel Jr. vs. Capt. Nazi	37.00	110.00	260.00
35	37.00	110.00	260.00
36-40: 40-Flag-c	34.00	100.00	235.00
41-Bulletman, Capt. Marvel Jr. & Bulletgirl x-over in Minute-Man; only app. Crime Crusaders Club (Capt. Marvel Jr., Minute-Man, Bulletman & Bullet-girl)-only team in Fawcett Comics	36.00	107.00	250.00
42-47,49: 47-Hitler becomes Corpl. Hitler Jr. 49-Last Minute-Man			
	20.00	60.00	140.00

	Good	Fine	N-Mint
48-Intro. Bulletboy; Capt. Marvel cameo in Minute-Man			
	24.00	73.00	170.00
50-Radar, Nyoka the Jungle Girl begin; Capt. Marvel x-over in Radar; origin Radar	16.00	48.00	110.00
51-58	11.00	32.00	75.00
59-62: Nyoka serial "Terrible Tiara" in all; 61-Capt. Marvel Jr. 1st meets Uncle Marvel	12.00	36.00	85.00
63-80	8.50	25.50	60.00
81,83-87,89-91,95-99: 88-Hopalong Cassidy begins (ends #94). 95-Tom Mix begins (ends #133)	7.00	21.00	50.00
82,88,92-94-Krigstein-a	8.00	24.00	55.00
100	8.00	24.00	55.00
101-106-Last Bulletman	5.70	17.00	40.00
107-132: 132-B&W and color illos in **POP**	5.00	15.00	35.00
133-Bill Battle app.	6.50	19.00	45.00

MASTER OF KUNG FU (Formerly Special Marvel Edition)
No. 17, April, 1974-No. 125, June, 1983
Marvel Comics Group

	Good	Fine	N-Mint
17-Starlin-a; intro Black Jack Tarr	2.15	6.50	15.00
18-20: 19-Man-Thing app.	1.35	4.00	8.00
21-23,25-30	.85	2.50	5.00
24-Starlin, Simonson-a	1.00	3.00	6.00
31-99: 33-1st Leiko Wu. 43-Last 25 cent issue			
	.40	1.25	2.50
100-Double size	.50	1.50	3.00
101-117,119-124	.35	1.00	2.00
118,125-Double size issues	.40	1.25	2.50
Annual 1(4/76)-Iron Fist	.70	2.00	4.00

MEPHISTO VS... (See Silver Surfer #3)
Apr, 1987-No. 4, July, 1987 ($1.50, mini-series)
Marvel Comics Group

	Good	Fine	N-Mint
1-Fantastic Four; Austin-i	.35	1.00	2.00
2-4: 2-X-Factor. 3-X-Men. 4-Avengers	.25	.80	1.60

METAL MEN (See Brave & the Bold, DC Comics Presents, and Showcase)
4-5/63-No. 41, 12-1/69-70; No. 42, 2-3/73-No. 44, 7-8/73; No. 45, 4-5/76-No. 56, 2-3/78
National Periodical Publications/DC Comics

	Good	Fine	N-Mint
Showcase #37 (3-4/62)-1st app. Metal Men			
	43.00	130.00	300.00
Showcase #38-40 (5-6/62-9-10/62)-Metal Men			
	25.00	75.00	175.00
1-(4-5/63)	32.00	96.00	220.00
2	13.00	40.00	90.00
3-5	8.00	24.00	55.00
6-10	5.00	15.00	35.00
11-20	3.70	11.00	26.00
21-26,28-30	2.40	7.25	17.00
27-Origin Metal Men	5.30	16.00	38.00
31-41(1968-70): 38-Last 12 cent issue. 41-Last 15 cent issue			
	1.85	5.50	13.00
42-44(1973)-Reprints	1.00	3.00	6.00
45('76)-49-Simonson-a in all	1.00	3.00	6.00
50-56: 50-Part-r. 54,55-Green Lantern x-over			
	1.00	3.00	6.00

METAMORPHO (See Action Comics, Brave & the Bold &
World's Finest)
July-Aug, 1965-No. 17, Mar-Apr, 1968 (All 12 cent issues)
National Periodical Publications

	Good	Fine	N-Mint
Brave and the Bold #57 (12-1/64-65)-Origin & 1st app. Metamorpho			
by Ramona Fraden	11.50	34.00	80.00
Brave and the Bold #58 (2-3/65)-2nd app.	5.00	15.00	35.00
1-(7-8/65)	9.30	28.00	65.00
2,3	5.15	15.50	36.00
4-6	2.85	8.50	20.00
7-9	2.30	7.00	16.00
10-Origin & 1st app. Element Girl (1-2/67)			
	3.15	9.50	22.00
11-17	1.70	5.00	12.00

MICKEY AND DONALD (Walt Disney's...#3 on)
Mar, 1988-No. 18, May, 1990 (95 cents, color)
Gladstone Publishing

	Good	Fine	N-Mint
1-Don Rosa-a; r/1949 Firestone giveaway			
	1.00	3.00	6.00
2	.40	1.25	2.50
3-Infinity-c	.35	1.00	2.00
4-8: Barks-r		.60	1.20

	Good	Fine	N-Mint
9-15: 9-r/1948 Firestone giveaway; X-Mas-c		.50	1.00
16 ($1.50, 52 pgs.)-r/FC #157	.25	.75	1.50
17,18 ($1.95, 68 pgs.): 17-Barks M.M.-r/FC #79 plus Barks D.D.-r;			
Rosa-a; X-Mas-c. 18-Kelly-c(r); Barks-r			
	.35	1.00	2.00

MICRONAUTS
Jan, 1979-No. 59, Aug, 1984 (Mando paper #53 on)
Marvel Comics Group

1-Intro/1st app. Baron Karza	.35	1.10	2.20
2-5		.60	1.20
6-36,39-59: 7-Man-Thing app. 8-1st app. Capt. Universe (8/79). 9-			
1st app. Cilicia. 13-1st app. Jasmine. 15-Death of Microtron. 15-			
17-Fantastic Four app. 17-Death of Jasmine. 20-Ant-Man app. 21-			
Microverse series begins. 25-Origin Baron Karza. 25-29-Nick			
Fury app. 27-Death of Biotron. 34,35-Dr. Strange app. 35-Double			
size; origin Microverse; intro Death Squad. 40-Fantastic Four app.			
57-Double size. 59-Golden painted-c		.50	1.00
37-Nightcrawler app.; X-Men cameo (2 pgs.)			
	.35	1.00	2.00
38-First direct sale	.25	.80	1.60
nn-Reprints #1-3; blank UPC; diamond on top		.50	1.00
Annual 1(12/79)-Ditko-c/a	.40	1.25	2.50
Annual 2(10/80)-Ditko-c/a	.35	1.00	2.00

MICRONAUTS (The New Voyages)
Oct, 1984-No. 20, May, 1986
Marvel Comics Group

V2#1-20: 1-Golden-a. 2-Guice/Arthur Adams-c		.50	1.00

MIGHTY COMICS (...Presents) (Formerly Flyman)
No. 40, Nov, 1966-No. 50, Oct, 1967 (All 12 cent issues)
Radio Comics (Archie)

40-Web	1.70	5.00	12.00
41-50: 41-Shield, Black Hood. 42-Black Hood. 43-Shield, Web &			
Black Hood. 44-Black Hood, Steel Sterling & The Shield. 45-			
Shield & Hangman; origin Web retold. 46-Steel Sterling, Web &			
Black Hood. 47-Black Hood & Mr. Justice. 48-Shield & Hang-			
man; Wizard x-over in Shield. 49-Steel Sterling & Fox; Black			
Hood x-over in Steel Sterling. 50-Black Hood & Web; Inferno			
x-over in Web	1.50	4.50	10.00

MIGHTY CRUSADERS, THE (Also see Adventures of the Fly & Fly Man)
Nov, 1965-No. 7, Oct, 1966 (All 12 cent issues)
Mighty Comics Group (Radio Comics)

	Good	Fine	N-Mint
1-Origin The Shield	3.60	11.00	25.00
2-Origin Comet	2.00	6.00	14.00
3-Origin Fly-Man	1.70	5.00	12.00
4-Fireball, Inferno (1st S.A. app.), Firefly, Web, Fox, Bob Phantom, Black-jack, Hangman, Zambini, Kardak, Steel Sterling, Mr. Justice, Wizard,Capt. Flag, Jaguar x-over			
	2.15	6.50	15.00
5-Intro. Ultra-Men (Fox, Web, Capt. Flag) & Terrific Three (Jaguar, Mr. Justice, Steel Sterling)	1.70	5.00	12.00
6,7: 7-Steel Sterling feature; origin Fly-Girl			
	1.70	5.00	12.00

MIGHTY MARVEL WESTERN, THE
Oct, 1968-No. 46, Sept, 1976 (#1-14: 68 pgs.; #15,16: 52 pgs.)
Marvel Comics Group (LMC earlier issues)

	Good	Fine	N-Mint
1-Begin Kid Colt, Rawhide Kid, Two-Gun Kid-r			
	1.00	3.00	6.00
2-10	.50	1.50	3.00
11-20	.35	1.00	2.00
21-46: 24-Kid Colt-r end. 25-Matt Slade-r begin. 31-Baker-r. 32-Origin-r/Ringo Kid #23; Williamson-r/Kid Slade #7. 37-Williamson, Kirby-r/Two-Gun Kid #51			
		.60	1.20

MILITARY COMICS (Becomes Modern Comics #44 on)
Aug, 1941-No. 43, Oct, 1945
Quality Comics Group

	Good	Fine	VF-NM
1-Origin/1st app. Blackhawk by C. Cuidera (Eisner scripts); Miss America, The Death Patrol by Jack Cole (also #2-7,27-30), & The Blue Tracer by Guardineer; X of the Underground, The Yankee Eagle, Q-Boat & Shot & Shell, Archie Atkins, Loops & Banks by Bud Ernest (Bob Powell)(ends #13) begin			
	350.00	875.00	2100.00
	Good	Fine	N-Mint
2-Secret War News begins (by McWilliams #2-16); Cole-a			
	143.00	430.00	1000.00
3-Origin/1st app. Chop Chop	115.00	345.00	800.00
4	100.00	300.00	700.00

	Good	Fine	N-Mint
5-The Sniper begins; Miss America in costume #4-7			
	79.00	235.00	550.00
6-9: 8-X of the Underground begins (ends #13). 9-The Phantom Clipper begins (ends #16)	67.00	200.00	465.00
10-Classic Eisner-c	72.00	215.00	500.00
11-Flag-c	54.00	160.00	375.00
12-Blackhawk by Crandall begins, ends #22			
	72.00	215.00	500.00
13-15: 14-Private Dogtag begins (ends #83)			
	50.00	150.00	350.00
16-20: 16-Blue Tracer ends. 17-P.T. Boat begins			
	43.00	130.00	300.00
21-31: 22-Last Crandall Blackhawk. 27-Death Patrol revived			
	39.00	120.00	275.00
32-43	34.00	100.00	240.00

MISSION IMPOSSIBLE (TV)
May, 1967-No. 4, Oct, 1968; No. 5, Oct, 1969 (All have photo-c)
Dell Publishing Co.

1	5.00	15.00	35.00
2-5: 5-reprints #1	3.50	10.50	24.00

Mister Miracle #6 (1-2/72), © DC Comics

MISTER MIRACLE
3-4/71-V4#18, 2-3/74; V5#19, 9/77-V6#25, 8-9/78; 1987
National Periodical Publications/DC Comics

	Good	Fine	N-Mint
1-(#1-3 are 15 cents)	2.00	6.00	14.00
2,3	1.30	4.00	9.00
4-8: 4-Boy Commandos-r begin; all 52 pgs.			
	1.15	3.50	8.00
9,10: 9-Origin Mr. Miracle; Darkseid app.			
	1.00	3.00	6.00
11-18: 15-Intro/1st app. Shilo Norman. 18-Barda & Scott Free wed;			
New Gods and Darkseid app.	.85	2.50	5.00
19-25 (1977-1978)	.50	1.50	3.00
Special 1(1987, $1.25, 52 pgs.)	.35	1.00	2.00

MISTER MIRACLE
Jan, 1989-No. 28, June, 1991 (1.00-$1.25, color)
DC Comics

	Good	Fine	N-Mint
1-Spin-off from Justice League International			
	.25	.75	1.50
2-28: 9-Intro Maxi-Man. 13,14-Lobo app. 22-1st new Mr. Miracle.			
27,28-($1.25). 27-Justice League app.		.50	1.00

MODERN COMICS (Formerly Military Comics #1-43)
No. 44, Nov, 1945-No. 102, Oct, 1950
Quality Comics Group

	Good	Fine	N-Mint
44-Blackhawk continues	34.00	100.00	235.00
45-52: 49-1st app. Fear, Lady Adventuress			
	20.00	60.00	140.00
53-Torchy by Ward begins (9/46)	25.00	75.00	175.00
54-60: 55-J. Cole-a	17.00	51.00	120.00
61-77,79,80: 73-J. Cole-a	16.00	48.00	110.00
78-1st app. Madame Butterfly	17.00	51.00	120.00
81-99,101: 82,83-One pg. J. Cole-a. 83-Last 52 pg. issue?			
	16.00	48.00	110.00
100	16.00	48.00	110.00
102-(Scarce)-J. Cole-a; Spirit by Eisner app.			
	19.00	56.00	130.00

MOD SQUAD (TV)
Jan, 1969-No. 3, Oct, 1969-No. 8, April, 1971
Dell Publishing Co.

	Good	Fine	N-Mint
1-Photo-c	2.30	7.00	16.00
2-8: 2-4-Photo-c. 8-Reprints #2	1.50	4.50	10.00

MONKEES, THE (TV)
March, 1967-No. 17, Oct, 1969 (#1-4,6,7,10 have photo-c)
Dell Publishing Co.

	Good	Fine	N-Mint
1	8.00	24.00	55.00
2-4,6,7,10: All photo-c	4.70	14.00	33.00
5,8,9,11-17: 17 reprints #1	3.15	9.50	22.00

MONSTERS ON THE PROWL (Chamber of Darkness #1-8)
No. 9, 2/71-No. 27, 11/73; No. 28, 6/74-No. 30, 10/74
Marvel Comics Group (No. 13,14: 52 pgs.)

9-Barry Smith inks	.70	2.00	4.00
10-30: 16-King Kull app.; Severin-c	.35	1.00	2.00

MONTE HALE WESTERN (Movie star; Formerly Mary Marvel #1-28)
No. 29, Oct, 1948-No. 88, Jan, 1956
Fawcett Publications/Charlton No. 83 on

29-(#1, 52 pgs.)-Photo-c begin, end #82; Monte Hale & his horse Pardner begin	29.00	85.00	200.00
30-(52 pgs.)-Big Bow and Little Arrow begin, end #34; Captain Tootsie by Beck	16.00	48.00	110.00
31-36,38-40-(52 pgs.): 34-Gabby Hayes begins, ends #80. 39-Captain Tootsie by Beck	13.00	40.00	90.00
37,41,45,49-(36 pgs.)	8.00	24.00	55.00
42-44,46-48,50-(52 pgs.): 47-Big Bow & Little Arrow app.	8.50	25.50	60.00
51,52,54-56,58,59-(52 pgs.)	6.50	19.00	45.00
53,57-(36 pgs.): 53-Slim Pickens app.	5.30	16.00	38.00
60-81: 36 pgs. #60-on. 80-Gabby Hayes ends	5.30	16.00	38.00
82-Last Fawcett issue (6/53)	7.00	21.00	50.00
83-1st Charlton issue (2/55); B&W photo back-c begin. Gabby Hayes returns, ends #86	7.00	21.00	50.00
84 (4/55)	5.30	16.00	38.00
85-86	5.00	15.00	35.00
87,88: 87-Wolverton-r, pg. 88-Last issue	5.30	16.00	38.00

MOON KNIGHT (Also see Marc Spector..., Marvel Preview #21, Marvel Spotlight & Werewolf by Night #32)
November, 1980-No. 38, July, 1984 (Mando paper No. 33 on)
Marvel Comics Group

	Good	Fine	N-Mint
1-Origin resumed in #4; begin Sienkiewicz-c/a	.70	2.00	4.00

2-34,36-38: 4-Intro Midnight Man. 16-The Thing app. 25-Double

size	.25	.75	1.50

35-($1.00, 52 pgs.)-X-men app.; F.F. cameo

	.35	1.00	2.00

MORE FUN COMICS (Formerly New Fun Comics #1-6)
No. 7, Jan, 1936-No. 127, Nov-Dec, 1947 (No. 7,9-11: paper-c)
National Periodical Publications

	Good	Fine	F-VF
7(1/36)-Oversized, paper-c; 1 pg. Kelly-a	500.00	1250.00	2000.00

	Good	Fine	V-Fine
8(2/36)-Oversized (10×12"), slick-c; 1 pg. Kelly-a	333.00	835.00	2000.00

9(3-4/36)(Very rare, 1st comic-sized issue)-Last Henri Duval by

Siegel & Shuster	333.00	835.00	2000.00
10,11(7/36): 11-1st "Calling All Cars" by Siegel & Shuster	208.00	520.00	1250.00
12(8/36)-Slick-c begin	183.00	460.00	1100.00
V2#1(9/36, #13)	175.00	440.00	1050.00

2(10/36, #14)-Dr. Occult in costume (1st in color)(Superman
proto-type-1st DC appearance), ends #17

	900.00	2250.00	4500.00

	Good	Fine	VF-NM

V2#3(11/36, #15), 16(V2#4), 17(V2#5)-Cover numbering begins #16.
16-Xmas-c. Last Superman tryout issue

	330.00	1000.00	2000.00
18-20(V2#8, 5/37)	108.00	270.00	650.00

	Good	Fine	N-Mint
21(V2#9)-24(V2#12, 9/37)	83.00	210.00	500.00

25(V3#1, 10/37)-27(V3#3, 12/37): 27-Xmas-c

	83.00	210.00	500.00
28-30: 30-1st non-funny cover	83.00	210.00	500.00
31-35: 32-Last Dr. Occult	75.00	190.00	450.00

36-40: 36-The Masked Ranger begins, ends #41. 39-Xmas-c

	71.00	175.00	425.00
41-50	58.00	145.00	350.00

51-The Spectre app. (in costume) in one panel ad at end of Buc-
caneer story

	233.00	585.00	1400.00

	Good	Fine	VF-NM
52-(2/40)-Origin/1st app. The Spectre (in costume splash panel only), Part 1 by Bernard Baily; last Wing Brady	2000.00	5000.00	12,000.00
53-Origin The Spectre (in costume at end of story), Part 2; Capt. Desmo begins	1370.00	3400.00	8200.00
54-The Spectre in costume; last King Carter	500.00	1250.00	3000.00
55-(Scarce)-Dr. Fate begins (Intro & 1st app.); last Bulldog Martin	535.00	1335.00	3200.00

	Good	Fine	N-Mint
56-60: 56-Congo Bill begins; classic Dr. Fate-c. 58-Classic Spectre-c	225.00	560.00	1350.00
61-66: 61-Classic Dr. Fate-c. 63-Last St. Bob Neal. 64-Lance Larkin begins. 65-Classic Spectre-c	167.00	415.00	1000.00

	Good	Fine	VF-NM
67-Origin (1st) Dr. Fate; last Congo Bill & Biff Bronson	285.00	710.00	1700.00

	Good	Fine	N-Mint
68-70: 68-Clip Carson begins. 70-Last Lance Larkin	138.00	345.00	825.00

	Good	Fine	VF-NM
71-Origin/1st app. Johnny Quick by Mort Wysinger	250.00	625.00	1500.00

	Good	Fine	N-Mint
72-Dr. Fate's new helmet; last Sgt. Carey, Sgt. O'Malley & Captain Desmo	117.00	291.00	700.00

	Good	Fine	VF-NM
73-Origin & 1st app. Aquaman (11/41); intro. Green Arrow & Speedy	417.00	1050.00	2500.00

	Good	Fine	N-Mint
74-2nd Aquaman	142.00	354.00	850.00
75-80: 76-Last Clip Carson; Johnny Quick by Meskin begins, ends #97. 80-Last large logo	125.00	310.00	750.00
81-88: 81-1st small logo. 87-Last Radio Squad	83.00	210.00	500.00
89-Origin Green Arrow & Speedy Team-up	100.00	250.00	600.00
90-99: 93-Dover & Clover begin. 97-Kubert-a. 98-Last Dr. Fate	55.00	138.00	330.00
100	83.00	210.00	500.00

	Good	Fine	VF-NM
101-Origin & 1st app. Superboy (3/44)(not by Siegel & Shuster); last Spectre issue	333.00	835.00	2000.00

	Good	Fine	N-Mint
102-2nd Superboy	100.00	250.00	600.00
103-3rd Superboy	67.00	170.00	400.00
104-107: 104-1st Superboy-c. 105-Superboy-c. 107-Last J. Quick & Superboy	57.00	140.00	340.00
108-120: 108-Genius Jones begins	9.30	28.00	65.00
121-124,126: 121-123,126-Post-c	8.00	24.00	55.00
125-Superman on cover	43.00	130.00	300.00
127-(Scarce)-Post-c/a	17.00	51.00	120.00

MS. MARVEL (Also see The Avengers #183)
Jan, 1977-No. 23, Apr, 1979
Marvel Comics Group

	Good	Fine	VF-NM
1-1st app. Ms. Marvel; Scorpion app. in #1,2	.60	1.75	3.50
2-Origin	.50	1.50	3.00
3-10: 5-Vision app.	.35	1.00	2.00
11-23: 18-Avengers x-over. 19-Capt. Marvel app. 20-New costume. 23-Vance Astro (leader of the Guardians) app.	.25	.75	1.50

MUNSTERS, THE (TV)
Jan, 1965-No. 16, Jan, 1968 (All photo-c?)
Gold Key

1 (10134-501)-Photo-c	16.00	48.00	110.00
2	8.00	24.00	55.00
3-5: 4,6-Photo-c	6.50	19.00	45.00
6-16: 16-Photo-c	5.70	17.00	40.00

MY FAVORITE MARTIAN (TV)
1/64; No.2, 7/64-No. 9, 10/66 (No. 1,3-9 have photo-c)
Gold Key

1-Russ Manning-a	8.50	25.50	60.00
2	3.60	11.00	25.00
3-9	4.30	13.00	30.00

MY GREATEST ADVENTURE (Doom Patrol #86 on)
Jan-Feb, 1955-No. 85, Feb, 1964
National Periodical Publications

1-Before CCA	70.00	210.00	500.00

	Good	Fine	N-Mint
2	33.00	100.00	225.00
3-5	23.00	70.00	160.00
6-10: 6-Science fiction format begins	17.00	51.00	120.00
11-15,19	12.00	36.00	85.00
16-18,20,21,28-Kirby-a; 18-Kirby-c	13.50	41.00	95.00
22-27,29,30	7.00	21.00	50.00
31-40	5.70	17.00	40.00
41-57,59	3.60	11.00	25.00
58,60,61-Toth-a; Last 10 cent issue	3.15	9.50	22.00
62-79: 77-Toth-a	2.00	6.00	14.00
80-(6/63)-Intro/origin Doom Patrol and begin series; origin Robot-man, Negative Man, & Elasti-Girl	29.00	85.00	200.00
81-85: 81,85-Toth-a	11.50	34.00	80.00

MYSTERIES OF UNEXPLORED WORLDS
Aug, 1956; No. 2, Jan, 1957-No. 48, Sept, 1965
Charlton Comic

	Good	Fine	N-Mint
1	16.00	48.00	110.00
2-No Ditko	6.50	19.00	45.00
3,4,8,9-Ditko-a	10.00	30.00	70.00
5,6-Ditko-c/a (all)	11.50	34.00	80.00
7-(2/58, 68 pgs.); Ditko-a(4)	11.50	34.00	80.00
10-Ditko-c/a(4)	11.50	34.00	80.00
11-Ditko-c/a(3)-signed J. Kotdi	11.50	34.00	80.00
12,19,21-24,26-Ditko-a	8.00	24.00	55.00
13-18,20	2.30	7.00	16.00
25,27-30	1.70	5.00	12.00
31-45	.85	2.60	6.00
46(5/65)-Son of Vulcan begins (origin)	1.70	5.00	12.00
47,48	1.00	3.00	7.00

MYSTERY IN SPACE
4-5/51-No. 110, 9/66; No. 111, 9/80-No. 117, 3/81 (#1-3: 52 pgs.)
National Periodical Publications

1-Frazetta-a, 8 pgs.; Knights of the Galaxy begins			
	185.00	555.00	1300.00
2	70.00	210.00	500.00
3	57.00	170.00	400.00
4,5	43.00	130.00	300.00
6-10: 7-Toth-a. 8-Last Knights of the Galaxy			
	36.00	108.00	250.00
11-15: 13-Toth-a	23.00	70.00	160.00

	Good	Fine	N-Mint
16-18,20-25: Interplanetary Insurance feature by Infantino in all. 24-Last precode issue	20.00	60.00	140.00
19-Virgil Finlay-a	23.00	70.00	160.00
26-40: 26-Space Cabbie begins	14.00	43.00	100.00
41-52: 47-Space Cabbie feature ends	12.00	36.00	85.00
53-Adam Strange begins (8/59, 10 pg. story) (1st app. in Showcase)	86.00	260.00	600.00
54	32.00	96.00	225.00
55	19.00	57.00	130.00
56-60: 59-Kane/Anderson-a	13.50	41.00	95.00

Mystery in Space #89, © DC Comics

	Good	Fine	N-Mint
61-71: 61-1st app. Adam Strange foe Ulthoon. 62-1st app. A.S. foe Mortan. 63-Origin Vandor. 66-Star Rovers begin. 68-Dust Devils app. 71-Last 10 cent issue	8.50	25.50	60.00
72-74,76-80	6.50	19.00	45.00
75-JLA x-over in Adam Strange (5/62)	17.00	51.00	120.00
81-86	3.60	11.00	25.00
87-(11/63)-Adam Strange/Hawkman double feature	11.00	32.00	75.00
88-90: 88-89-Adam Strange & Hawkman stories. 90-A. Strange & Hawkman team-up for 1st time (3/64); Hawkman moves to own title next month (Hawkman's 3rd tryout title)	6.50	19.00	45.00

	Good	Fine	N-Mint
91-103: 91-End Infantino art on Adam Strange. 92-Space Ranger begins (6/64), ends #103. 92-94,96,98-Space Ranger-c. 94,98-Adam Strange/Space Ranger team-up. 102-A. Strange ends (no Space Ranger). 103-Origin Ultra, the Multi-Alien; last Space Ranger	1.70	5.00	12.00
104-110: 110-(9/66)-Last 10 cent issue	.85	2.50	5.00
V17#111(9/80)-117: 117-Newton-a(3 pgs.)	.35	1.00	2.00

MYSTERY MEN COMICS
Aug, 1939-No. 31, Feb, 1942
Fox Features Syndicate

	Good	Fine	N-Mint
1-Intro/1st app. The Blue Beetle, The Green Mask, Rex Dexter of Mars by Briefer, Zanzibar by Tuska, Lt. Drake, D-13-Secret Agent by Powell, Chen Chang, Wing Turner, & Captain Denny Scott	190.00	475.00	1150.00
2	80.00	240.00	550.00
3 (10/39)	67.00	200.00	475.00
4-Capt. Savage begins	57.00	170.00	400.00
5	45.00	135.00	315.00
6-8	42.00	125.00	290.00
9-The Moth begins	35.00	105.00	240.00
10-Wing Turner by Kirby	35.00	105.00	240.00
11-Intro. Domino	26.00	79.00	185.00
12,14-18	24.00	72.00	165.00
13-Intro. Lynx & sidekick Blackie	27.00	80.00	190.00
19-Intro. & 1st app. Miss X (ends #21)	27.00	80.00	190.00
20-31: 26-The Wraith begins	22.50	67.00	155.00

MYSTIC COMICS (1st Series)
March, 1940-No. 10, Aug, 1942
Timely Comics (TPI 1-5/TCI 8-10)

	Good	Fine	VF-NM
1-Origin The Blue Blaze, The Dynamic Man, & Flexo the Rubber Man; Zephyr Jones, 3X's & Deep Sea Demon app.; The Magician begins; c-from Spider pulp V18#1, 6/39	583.00	1460.00	3500.00

	Good	Fine	N-Mint
2-The Invisible Man & Master Mind Excello begin; Space Rangers, Zara of the Jungle, Taxi Taylor app.	216.00	540.00	1300.00
3-Origin Hercules, who last appears in #4	166.00	415.00	1000.00

4-Origin The Thin Man & The Black Widow; Merzak the Mystic

	Good	Fine	N-Mint

app.; last Flexo, Dynamic Man, Invisible Man & Blue Blaze(some issues have date sticker on cover; others have July w/August overprint in silver color); Roosevelt assassination-c

	190.00	475.00	1150.00

5-Origin The Black Marvel, The Blazing Skull, The Sub-Earth Man, Super Slave & The Terror; The Moon Man & Black Widow app.

	188.00	470.00	1125.00

6-Origin The Challenger & The Destroyer

	166.00	415.00	1000.00

7-The Witness begins (origin); origin Davey & the Demon; last Black Widow; Hitler opening Pandora's Box-c by Simon & Kirby

	150.00	375.00	900.00
8	108.00	270.00	650.00

9-Gary Gaunt app.; last Black Marvel, Mystic & Blazing Skull; Hitler-c

	108.00	270.00	650.00

10-Father Time, World of Wonder, & Red Skeleton app.; last Challenger &Terror

	108.00	270.00	650.00

MYSTIC COMICS (2nd Series)
Oct, 1944-No. 4, Winter, 1944-45
Timely Comics (ANC)

1-The Angel, The Destroyer, The Human Torch, Terry Vance the Schoolboy Sleuth, & Tommy Tyme begin

	Good	Fine	N-Mint
	100.00	250.00	600.00
2-Last Human Torch & Terry Vance	58.00	145.00	350.00

3-Last Angel (two stories) & Tommy Tyme

	54.00	135.00	325.00
4-The Young Allies app.	50.00	125.00	300.00

'NAM, THE
Dec, 1986-Present
Marvel Comics Group

	Good	Fine	N-Mint
1-Golden a(p)/c begins, ends #13	1.25	3.80	7.60
1 (2nd printing)	.30	.95	1.90
2	.80	2.40	4.80
3,4	.65	1.90	3.80
5-7: 7-Only 2 pgs. Golden-a	.50	1.45	2.90
8-10	.30	.95	1.90
11-20: 12-Severin-a; Golden-c only	.25	.70	1.40
21-51: 25-begin $1.50-c. 32-Death R. Kennedy		.55	1.10
52-Frank Castle (The Punisher) app.	.95	2.85	5.70
53-Frank Castle (The Punisher) app.	.65	1.90	3.80
52,53-Gold 2nd printings	.25	.70	1.40
54-64: 58-Silver logo	.25	.75	1.50
65-74: 65-Begin $1.75-c. 67-69-Punisher 3 part story			
	.30	.90	1.80

NAMOR, THE SUB-MARINER (See Prince Namor & Sub-Mariner)
Apr, 1990-Present ($1.00, color)
Marvel Comics

1-Byrne-c/a/scripts in all	.60	1.75	3.50
2-5: 5-Iron Man app.	.35	1.00	2.00
6-11: 8,10,16-Re-intro Iron Fist (8-cameo only)			
	.25	.75	1.50
12-($1.50, 52 pgs.)-Re-intro. The Invaders	.35	1.00	2.00
13-22: 18-Punisher cameo (1 panel); 21-Wolverine cameo			
		.50	1.00
23-34: $1.25-c. 24-Namor vs. Wolverine		.65	1.30
Annual 1(1991, $2.00, 68 pgs.)-3 pg. origin recap			
	.35	1.00	2.00
Annual 2(1992, $2.25, 68 pgs.)-New Defenders app.			
	.40	1.15	2.30

NATIONAL COMICS
July, 1940-No. 75, Nov, 1949
Quality Comics Group

1-Uncle Sam begins; Origin sidekick Buddy by Eisner; origin Won-

	Good	**Fine**	**N-Mint**

der Boy & Kid Dixon; Merlin the Magician (ends #45); Cyclone, Kid Patrol, Sally O'Neil Policewoman, Pen Miller (ends #22), Prop Powers (ends #26), & Paul Bunyan (ends #22) begin

	Good	**Fine**	**N-Mint**
	193.00	580.00	1350.00
2	93.00	280.00	650.00
3-Last Eisner Uncle Sam	70.00	210.00	500.00
4-Last Cyclone	53.00	160.00	365.00
5-(11/40)-Quicksilver begins (3rd w/lightning speed?); origin Uncle Sam	65.00	195.00	450.00
6-11: 8-Jack & Jill begins (ends #22). 9-Flag-c	50.00	150.00	350.00
12	36.00	108.00	250.00
13-16-Lou Fine-a	44.00	132.00	310.00
17,19-22	34.00	102.00	235.00
18-(12/41)-Shows orientals attacking Pearl Harbor; on stands one month before actual event	40.00	120.00	275.00
23-The Unknown & Destroyer 171 begin	36.00	108.00	250.00
24-26,28,30: 26-Wonder Boy ends	25.00	75.00	175.00
27-G-2 the Unknown begins (ends #46)	25.00	75.00	175.00
29-Origin The Unknown	25.00	75.00	175.00
31-33: 33-Chic Carter begins (ends #47)	23.00	70.00	160.00
34-40: 35-Last Kid Patrol. 39-Hitler-c	14.00	43.00	100.00
41-50: 42-The Barker begins (1st app?); The Barker covers begin. 48-Origin The Whistler	11.00	32.00	75.00
51-Sally O'Neil by Ward, 8 pgs. (12/45)	14.00	43.00	100.00
52-60	8.00	24.00	55.00
61-67: 67-Format change; Quicksilver app.	5.70	17.00	40.00
68-75: The Barker ends	4.00	12.00	28.00

NEW FUN COMICS (Becomes More Fun #7 on)
Feb, 1935-No. 6, Oct, 1935 (10x15'', No. 1-4,6: slick covers)
(No. 1-5: 36 pgs; 68 pgs. No. 6-on)
National Periodical Publications

	Good	**Fine**	**V-Fine**
V1#1 (1st DC comic); 1st app. Oswald The Rabbit. Jack Woods (cowboy) begins	3000.00	7500.00	15,000.00
2(3/35)-(Very Rare)	1085.00	2700.00	6500.00
3-5(8/35): 5-Soft-c	500.00	1250.00	3000.00

6(10/35)-1st Dr. Occult by Siegel & Shuster (Leger & Reughts); last "New Fun" title; Henri Duval (ends #9) by Siegel & Shuster

	Good	Fine	V-Fine
begins; paper-c	500.00	1250.00	3000.00

NEW FUNNIES (The Funnies #1-64; Walter Lantz...#109 on; New TV... #259, 260, 272, 273; TV Funnies #261-271)
No. 65, July, 1942-No. 288, Mar-Apr, 1962
Dell Publishing Co.

	Good	Fine	N-Mint
65(#1)-Andy Panda in a world of real people, Raggedy Ann & Andy, Oswald the Rabbit (with Woody Woodpecker x-overs), Li'l Eight Ball & Peter Rabbit begin	45.00	135.00	315.00
66-70: 67-Billy & Bonnie Bee by Frank Thomas & Felix The Cat begin. 69-Kelly-a (2 pgs.); The Brownies begin (not by Kelly)	22.00	65.00	150.00
71-75: 72-Kelly illos. 75-Brownies by Kelly?	13.50	41.00	95.00
76-Andy Panda (Carl Barks & Pabian-a); Woody Woodpecker x-over in Oswald ends	57.00	171.00	400.00
77,78: 78-Andy Panda in a world with real people ends	13.50	41.00	95.00
79-81	9.30	28.00	65.00
82-Brownies by Kelly begins; Homer Pigeon begins	11.00	32.00	75.00
83-85-Brownies by Kelly in ea. 83-X-mas-c. 85-Woody Woodpecker, 1 pg. strip begins	11.00	32.00	75.00
86-90: 87-Woody Woodpecker stories begin	5.30	16.00	38.00
91-99	3.60	11.00	25.00
100 (6/45)	4.30	13.00	30.00
101-110	3.00	9.00	18.00
111-120: 119-X-mas-c	2.00	6.00	12.00
121-150: 131,143-X-mas-c	1.70	5.00	10.00
151-200: 155-X-mas-c. 168-X-mas-c. 182-Origin & 1st app. Knothead & Splinter. 191-X-mas-c	1.40	3.50	7.00
201-240	1.20	3.00	6.00
241-288: 270,271-Walter Lantz c-app. 281-1st story swipe/WDC&S #100	1.00	2.50	5.00

NEW GODS, THE (New Gods #12 on)(See Adventure #459)
2-3/71-V2#11, 10-11/72; V3#12, 7/77-V3#19, 7-8/78
National Periodical Publications/DC Comics

	Good	Fine	N-Mint
1-Intro/1st app. Orion; 3rd app. Darkseid (cameo; ties w/Forever People #1) (#1-3 are 15 cent issues)	2.85	8.50	20.00

	Good	Fine	N-Mint
2-Darkseid-c/story (2nd full app., 4-5/71)			
	2.15	6.50	15.00
3-Last 15 cent issue	1.85	5.50	13.00
4-9: (25 cent giants): 4-Darkseid cameo; origin Manhunter-r. 5,7, 8-Young Gods feature. 7-Darkseid app.; origin Orion. 9-1st app.			
Bug	1.50	4.50	10.00
10,11	1.15	3.50	8.00
12-19: 12-New costume Orion	.50	1.50	3.00

NEW GODS, THE
May, 1984-No. 6, Nov,1984 ($2.00, direct sale; Baxter paper)
DC Comics

	Good	Fine	N-Mint
1-New Kirby-c begin; r-/New Gods #1&2			
	.35	1.00	2.00
2-6: 6-Original art by Kirby	.35	1.00	2.00

NEW GODS
Feb, 1989-No. 28, Aug, 1991 ($1.50, color)
DC Comics

	Good	Fine	N-Mint
1-Russell-i	.40	1.25	2.50
2-28: 2-4-Starlin scripts. 17-Darkseid app.	.25	.75	1.50

NEW MUTANTS, THE
March, 1983-No. 100, April, 1991
Marvel Comics Group

	Good	Fine	N-Mint
1	1.70	5.00	10.00
2,3: 3,4-Ties into X-Men #167	1.00	3.00	6.00
4-10: 10-1st app. Magma	.70	2.00	4.00
11-17,19,20: 13-Kitty Pryde app.	.50	1.50	3.00
18-Intro. new Warlock	1.70	5.00	10.00
21-Double size; new Warlock origin	1.70	5.00	10.00
22-30: 23-25-Cloak & Dagger app.	.50	1.50	3.00
31-58: 50-Double size. 58-Contains pull-out mutant registration form			
	.40	1.25	2.50
59-Fall of The Mutants begins, ends #61	.70	2.00	4.00
60-($1.25, 52 pgs.)	.50	1.50	3.00
61-Fall of The Mutants ends	.40	1.25	2.50
62,64-72,74-85: 68-Intro Spyder. 76-X-Factor & X-Terminator app.			
85-Liefeld-c begin	.25	.75	1.50
63-X-Men & Wolverine app.; begin $1.00-c			
	.70	2.00	4.00
73-($1.50, 52 pgs.)	.40	1.25	2.50

	Good	Fine	N-Mint
86-Rob Liefeld-a begins; McFarlane-c(i) swiped from Ditko splash pg.; Cable cameo (last page teaser)	2.65	8.00	18.00
87-1st full app. Cable (3/90)	9.30	28.00	65.00
87-2nd printing; gold metallic ink-c ($1.00)	.25	.75	1.50
88-2nd app. Cable	4.30	13.00	30.00
89-3rd app. Cable	2.40	7.25	17.00
90,91: 90-New costumes. 90,91-Sabretooth app.	1.85	5.50	13.00
92-No Liefeld-a; Liefeld-c	.90	2.75	5.50
93,94-Cable vs. Wolverine	2.40	7.25	17.00
95-97-X-Tinction Agenda x-over. 97-Wolverine & Cable-c, but no app.	1.85	5.50	13.00
95-Gold 2nd printing	.50	1.50	3.00
98-1st app. Deadpool; 1st app. of Gideon & Domino of X-Force; 2nd Shatterstar (cameo)	1.70	5.00	12.00
99-1st app. of Feral of X-Force	1.30	3.85	7.70
100-($1.50, 52 pgs.)-1st app. X-Force (cameo)	1.85	5.50	11.00
100-Gold ink 2nd printing	.75	2.25	4.50
100-Silver ink 3rd printing	.25	.75	1.50
Annual 1 (1984)	1.00	3.00	6.00
Annual 2 (1986, $1.25)	.50	1.50	3.00
Annual 3 (1987, $1.25)	.35	1.00	2.00
Annual 4(1988, $1.75)-Evolutionary War x-over	.70	2.00	4.00
Annual 5(1989, $2.00, 68 pgs.)-Atlantis Attacks; 1st Liefeld-a on New Mutants	3.15	9.50	22.00
Annual 6('90, $2.00, 68 pgs.)-1st new costumes by Liefeld (3 pgs.); 1st app. (cameo) Shatterstar (of X-Force)	.35	1.00	2.00
Annual 7('91, $2.00, 68 pgs.)-Liefeld pin-up only; X-Terminators back-up story	.35	1.00	2.00
Special 1-Special Edition ('85, 68 pgs.)-ties in with X-Men Alpha Flight mini-series; Art Adams/Austin-a	1.15	3.50	7.00
Summer Special 1(Sum/90, $2.95, 84 pgs.)	.50	1.50	3.00

NEW TEEN TITANS, THE (See DC Comics Presents 26, Marvel and DC Present & Teen Titans; Tales of the Teen Titans #41 on)
November, 1980-No. 40, March, 1984
DC Comics

1-Robin, Kid Flash, Wonder Girl, The Changeling, Starfire, The

	Good	Fine	N-Mint
Raven, Cyborg begin; partial origin	1.70	5.00	10.00
2-1st app. Deathstroke the Terminator	2.00	6.00	14.00

3-9: 3,4-Origin Starfire. 3-Intro The Fearsome 5. 4-J.L.A. app. 6-Origin Raven. 7-Cyborg origin. 8-Origin Kid Flash retold. 9-Minor cameo Deathstroke on last pg.   .70   2.00   4.00

The New Teen Titans #10 (8/81), © DC Comics

10-2nd app. Deathstroke the Terminator; origin Changeling retold
1.70   5.00   10.00

11-20: 13-Return of Madame Rouge & Capt. Zahl; Robotman revived. 14-Return of Mento; origin Doom Patrol. 15-Death of Madame Rouge & Capt. Zahl; intro. new Brotherhood of Evil. 16-1st app. Capt. Carrot (free 16 pg. preview). 18-Return of Starfire. 19-Hawkman teams-up   .25   .75   1.50

21-30: 21-Intro Night Force in free 16 pg. insert; intro Brother Blood. 23-1st app. Vigilante (not in costume), & Blackfire. 24-Omega Men app. 25-Omega Men cameo; free 16 pg. preview Masters of the Universe. 26-1st Terra. 27-Free 16 pg. preview Atari Force. 29-The New Brotherhood of Evil & Speedy app. 30-Terra joins the Titans   .60   1.20

31-33,35-38,40: 38-Origin Wonder Girl		.50	1.00
34-3rd app. Deathstroke the Terminator	.85	2.50	5.00
39-Last Dick Grayson as Robin; Kid Flash quits			
	.35	1.00	2.00
Annual 1(11/82)-Omega Men app.	.25	.70	1.40
Annual 2(9/83)-1st app. Vigilante in costume	.30	.90	1.80
Annual 3(1984)-Death of Terra		.50	1.00

NEW TEEN TITANS, THE (The New Titans #50 on)
Aug, 1984-No. 49, Nov, 1988 ($1.25-$1.75; deluxe format)
DC Comics

	Good	Fine	N-Mint
1-New storyline; Perez-c/a begins	.70	2.00	4.00
2,3: 2-Re-intro Lilith	.45	1.40	2.80
4-10: 5-Death of Trigon. 7-9-Origin Lilith. 8-Intro Kole. 10-Kole			
joins	.30	.90	1.80
11-19: 13,14-Crisis x-over		.60	1.20
20-Robin(Jason Todd) joins; original Teen Titans return			
	.35	1.00	2.00
21-49: 37-Begin $1.75-c. 38-Infinity, Inc. x-over. 47-Origin all			
Titans	.25	.70	1.40
Annual 1 (9/85)-Intro. Vanguard	.35	1.00	2.00
Annual 2 (8/86; $2.50): Byrne c/a(p); origin Brother Blood; intro new			
Dr. Light	.40	1.25	2.50
Annual 3 (11/87)-Intro. Danny Chase	.35	1.00	2.00
Annual 4 ('88, $2.50)-Perez-c	.40	1.15	2.30

NEW TITANS, THE (Formerly The New Teen Titans)
No. 50, Dec, 1988-Present ($1.75, color)
DC Comics

	Good	Fine	N-Mint
50-Perez-c/a begins; new origin Wonder Girl			
	.75	2.25	4.50
51-59: 50-55-Painted-c. 55-Nightwing (Dick Grayson) forces Danny			
Chase to resign; Batman app. in flashback			
	.40	1.25	2.50
60-A Lonely Place of Dying Part 2 continues from Batman #440; new			
Robin tie-in; Timothy Drake app.	1.10	3.25	6.50
61-A Lonely Place of Dying Part 4	.70	2.00	4.00
62-65: Deathstroke the Terminator app. 65-Timothy Drake (Robin)			
app.	.85	2.50	5.00
66-69,71: 71-(44 pgs.)-10th anniversary issue; Deathstroke cameo			
	.50	1.50	3.00
70-1st Deathstroke solo cover/story	.60	1.75	3.50
72-79: Deathstroke in all. 74-Intro. Pantha	.50	1.50	3.00
80-94: Deathstroke in all. 83,84-Deathstroke kills his son, Jericho.			
85-The Teen Titans app. (new group). 87-Nightwing dons new			
costume; Superman x-over. 89,90-Team Titans app.			
	.30	.90	1.80
Annual 5,6 (1989, 1990, $3.50, 68 pgs.)	.60	1.75	3.50
Annual 7 (1991, $3.50, 68 pgs.)-Armaggedon 2001 x-over; 1st app.			
Teen Titans (new group)	.60	1.75	3.50

	Good	Fine	N-Mint
Annual 8 (1992, $3.50, 68 pgs.)	.60	1.75	3.50

NEW WARRIORS, THE (See Thor #411,412)
July, 1990-Present ($1.00, color)
Marvel Comics

	Good	Fine	N-Mint
1-Williamson-i; Bagley-c/a(p) in 1-13, Annual 1			
	2.85	8.50	20.00
1-Gold 2nd printing (7/91)	.50	1.50	3.00
2-Williamson-c/a(i)	1.70	5.00	12.00
3: 1,3-Guice-c(i)	1.35	4.00	8.00
4,5	1.10	3.25	6.50
6,7,10: 7-Punisher cameo (last pg.)	.70	2.00	4.00
8,9-Punisher app.	1.00	3.00	6.00
11-14: 14-Darkhawk & Namor x-over	.40	1.25	2.50
15-24: 17-Fantastic Four & Silver Surfer x-over. 19-Gideon (of X-Force) app. 20-Begin $1.25-c	.25	.75	1.50
20-24,26-30: 20-Begin $1.25-c		.65	1.30
25-($2.50, 52 pgs.)-Die-cut cover; Darkhawk app.			
	.40	1.25	2.50
Annual 1 (1991, $2.00, 68 pgs.)-Origins all members; X-Force (formerly New Mutants) x-over before X-Force #1			
	.70	2.00	4.00
Annual 2 (1992, $2.25, 68 pgs.)-Spider-Man app.			
	.40	1.15	2.30

NICKEL COMICS
May, 1940-No. 8, Aug, 1940 (36 pgs.; Bi-Weekly; 5 cents)
Fawcett Publications

	Good	Fine	N-Mint
1-Origin/1st app. Bulletman	118.00	355.00	825.00
2	53.00	160.00	375.00
3	47.00	140.00	325.00
4-The Red Gaucho begins	43.00	130.00	300.00
5-8: 8-World's Fair-c; Bulletman moved to Master Comics #7 in Oct.			
	38.00	115.00	265.00

NICK FURY, AGENT OF SHIELD (See Marvel Spotlight #31 & Shield)
6/68-No. 15, 11/69; No. 16, 11/70-No. 18, 3/71
Marvel Comics Group

	Good	Fine	N-Mint
1	5.00	15.00	35.00
2-4: 4-Origin retold	2.85	8.50	20.00
5-Classic-c	3.50	10.50	24.00

	Good	Fine	N-Mint
6,7	1.60	4.80	11.00

8-11,13: 9-Hate Monger begins (ends #11). 11-Smith-c. 13-1st app.

Super-Patriot; last 12 cent issue	1.00	3.00	6.00
12-Smith-c/a	1.15	3.50	8.00
14	.60	1.75	3.50

15-(15 cents)-1st app. & death of Bullseye(11/69)

| | 2.85 | 8.50 | 20.00 |

16-18-(25 cents, 52 pgs.)-r/Strange Tales #135-143

| | .35 | 1.00 | 2.00 |

NICK FURY, AGENT OF SHIELD (Also see Strange Tales #135)
Dec, 1983-No. 2, Jan, 1984 ($2.00, Baxter paper, 52 pgs.)
Marvel Comics Group

| 1,2-r/Nick Fury #1-4; new Steranko-c | .35 | 1.00 | 2.00 |

NICK FURY, AGENT OF S.H.I.E.L.D.
Sept, 1989-Present ($1.50, color)
Marvel Comics

V2#1-26,30,31: 10-Capt. America app. 13-Return of The Yellow
Claw. 15-Fantastic Four app. 30,31-Deathlok app.

	.25	.75	1.50
27-29-Wolverine-c/stories	.35	1.00	2.00
32-42: 32-Begin $1.75-c. 36-Cage app.	.30	.90	1.80

NICK FURY VS. SHIELD
June, 1988-No. 6, Dec, 1988 ($3.50, 52 pgs, color, deluxe format)
Marvel Comics

1-Steranko-c	1.70	5.00	10.00
2	2.00	6.00	12.00
3	.85	2.50	5.00
4-6	.60	1.75	3.50

NIGHTCRAWLER
Nov, 1985-No. 4, Feb, 1986 (Mini-series from X-Men)
Marvel Comics Group

| 1-Cockrum-c/a | .50 | 1.50 | 3.00 |
| 2-4 | .35 | 1.00 | 2.00 |

NOMAD (See Captain America #180)
Nov, 1990-No. 4, Feb, 1991 ($1.50, color)
Marvel Comics

| 1: 1,4-Captain America app. | .40 | 1.25 | 2.50 |

	Good	Fine	N-Mint
2-4	.35	1.00	2.00

NOMAD
V2#1, May, 1992-Present ($1.75, color)
Marvel Comics

1-($2.00)-Gatefold-c with map/wanted poster			
	.40	1.25	2.50
2-8: 4-Daredevil app.	.30	.90	1.80

NOMAN (See Thunder Agents)
Nov, 1966-No. 2, March, 1967 (25 cents, 68 pgs.)
Tower Comics

1-Wood/Williamson-c; Lightning begins; Dynamo cameo; Kane-a(p) & Whitney-a	4.30	13.00	30.00
2-Wood-c only; Dynamo x-over; Whitney-a			
	2.85	8.50	20.00

NOT BRAND ECHH (Brand Echh #1-4)
Aug, 1967-No. 13, May, 1969 (No. 9-13: 25 cents, 68 pages)
Marvel Comics Group (LMC)

1: 1-8 are 12 cent issues	2.85	8.50	20.00
2-4: 3-Origin Thor, Hulk & Capt. America; Monkees, Alfred E. Neuman cameo. 4-X-Men app.	1.70	5.00	12.00
5-8: 5-Origin/intro. Forbush Man. 7-Origin Fantastical-4 & Stuporman. 8-Beatles cameo; X-Men satire	1.70	5.00	12.00
9-13-All Giants. 9-Beatles cameo. 10-All-r; The Old Witch, Crypt Keeper & Vault Keeper cameos. 12,13-Beatles cameo, Avengers satire #12	2.00	6.00	14.00

NOVA (The Man Called...No. 22-25)
Sept, 1976-No. 25, May, 1979
Marvel Comics Group

1-Origin/1st app. Nova	1.00	3.00	6.00
2-11: 4-Thor x-over	.50	1.50	3.00
12-Spider-Man x-over	.70	2.00	4.00
13-25: 13-Intro Crime-Buster. 14-Last 30 cent issue. 18-Yellow Claw app.	.35	1.00	2.00

NTH MAN THE ULTIMATE NINJA (See Marvel Comics Presents #25)
Aug, 1989-No. 16, Sept, 1990 ($1.00, color)
Marvel Comics

	Good	Fine	N-Mint
1-Ninja mercenary	.25	.80	1.60
2-16: 8-Dale Keown-a(p); 1st at Marvel? (1/90)		.50	1.00

NUKLA
Oct-Dec, 1965-No. 4, Sept, 1966
Dell Publishing Co.

	Good	Fine	N-Mint
1-Origin Nukla (super hero)	2.00	6.00	14.00
2,3	1.15	3.50	8.00
4-Ditko-a, c(p)	1.50	4.50	10.00

OFFICIAL HANDBOOK OF THE MARVEL UNIVERSE, THE
Jan, 1983-No. 15, May, 1984
Marvel Comics Group

	Good	Fine	N-Mint
1-Lists Marvel heroes & villains (letter A)			
	1.00	3.00	6.00
2 (B-C)	.85	2.50	5.00
3-5: 3-(C-D). 4-(D-G). 5-(H-J)	.70	2.00	4.00
6-9: 6-(K-L). 7-(M). 8-(N-P); Punisher-c. 9-(Q-S)			
	.50	1.50	3.00
10-15: 10-(S). 11-(S-U). 12-(V-Z); Wolverine-c. 13,14-Book of the Dead. 15-Weaponry catalogue	.40	1.25	2.50

OFFICIAL HANDBOOK OF THE MARVEL UNIVERSE, THE
Dec, 1985-No. 20, April?, 1987 ($1.50 cover; maxi-series)
Marvel Comics Group

V2#1-Byrne-c	.70	2.00	4.00
2-5: 2,3-Byrne-c	.50	1.50	3.00
6-10	.40	1.25	2.50
11-20	.35	1.00	2.00

OFFICIAL HANDBOOK OF THE MARVEL UNIVERSE, THE
July, 1989-No. 8, Mid-Dec, 1990 ($1.50, color, mini-series, 52 pgs.)
Marvel Comics

V3#1-8: 1-McFarlane-a(2 pgs.)	.25	.75	1.50

OFFICIAL MARVEL INDEX TO THE AMAZING SPIDER-MAN
Apr, 1985-No. 9, Dec, 1985 ($1.25, color)
Marvel Comics Group

1 ($1.00-c)	.40	1.25	2.50
2-9: 5,6,8,9-Punisher-c	.35	1.00	2.00

OMAC (One Man Army, ...Corps. #4 on; also see Warlord)
Sept-Oct, 1974-No. 8, Nov-Dec, 1975
National Periodical Publications

1-Origin	.85	2.50	5.00
2-8: 8-2pg. Neal Adams ad	.50	1.50	3.00

OMAC: ONE MAN ARMY CORPS
1991-No. 4, 1991 ($3.95, B&W, mini-series, mature readers, 52 pgs.)
DC Comics

	Good	Fine	N-Mint
Book One-Four: John Byrne-c/a & scripts	.70	2.00	4.00

OMEGA MEN, THE (See Green Lantern #141)
Dec, 1982-No. 38, May, 1986 ($1.00-$1.50; Baxter paper)
DC Comics

1	.25	.75	1.50
2,4,6-8,11-18,21-36,38: 2-Origin Broot. 7-Origin The Citadel; Lobo app? 26, 27-Alan Moore scripts. 30-Intro new Primus. 31-Crisis x-over. 34,35-Teen Titans x-over		.50	1.00
3-1st app. Lobo (5 pgs.)(6/83); Lobo-c	1.70	5.00	10.00
5,9-2nd & 3rd app. Lobo (cameo, 2 pgs. each)	.70	2.00	4.00
10-1st full Lobo story	1.70	5.00	10.00
19-Lobo cameo	.25	.75	1.50
20-2nd full Lobo story	1.00	3.00	6.00
37-1st solo Lobo story (8 pg. back-up by Giffen)	.50	1.50	3.00
Annual 1(11/84, 52 pgs.), 2(11/85)	.25	.75	1.50

OMEGA THE UNKNOWN
March, 1976-No. 10, Oct, 1977
Marvel Comics Group

1-1st app. Omega	.70	2.00	4.00
2-7,10: 2-Hulk app. 3-Electro app.	.35	1.00	2.00
8-1st app. 2nd Foolkiller (Greg Salinger), 1 panel only (cameo)	1.00	3.00	6.00
9-1st full app. Foolkiller	1.35	4.00	8.00

ORIGINAL GHOST RIDER RIDES AGAIN, THE
July, 1991-No. 7, Jan, 1992, ($1.50, color, mini-series, 52 pgs.)
Marvel Comics

1-Reprints Ghost Rider #68(origin),69 w/covers	.25	.75	1.50
2-7: Reprints G.R. #70-81 w/covers	.25	.75	1.50

OUR ARMY AT WAR (Sgt. Rock #302 on)
Aug, 1952-No. 301, Feb, 1977
National Periodical Publications

	Good	Fine	N-Mint
1	68.00	205.00	475.00
2	34.00	100.00	235.00
3,4: 4-Krigstein-a	29.00	86.00	200.00
5-7	19.00	58.00	135.00
8-11,14-Krigstein-a	19.00	58.00	135.00
12,15-20	14.00	43.00	100.00
13-Krigstein-c/a; flag-c	19.00	58.00	135.00
21-31: Last precode (2/55)	10.00	30.00	70.00
32-40	8.50	25.50	60.00
41-60	7.00	21.00	50.00
61-70	5.30	16.00	38.00
71-80	4.00	12.00	28.00

81-1st Sgt. Rock app. (4/59) by Andru & Esposito in Easy Co. story

	93.00	280.00	650.00

82-Sgt. Rock cameo in Easy Co. story (6 panels)

	19.30	58.00	135.00
83-1st Kubert Sgt. Rock (6/59)	30.00	90.00	210.00
84,86-90	11.00	32.00	75.00
85-Origin & 1st app. Ice Cream Soldier	12.00	36.00	85.00
91-All Sgt. Rock issue	33.00	100.00	230.00

92-100: 92-1st app. Bulldozer. 95-1st app. Zack

	6.50	19.00	45.00

101-120: 101-1st app. Buster. 111-1st app. Wee Willie & Sunny. 113-1st app. Wildman & Jackie Johnson. 118-Sunny dies

	3.15	9.50	22.00

121-127,129-150: 126-1st app. Canary. 139-1st app. Little Sure Shot

	1.85	5.50	13.00
128-Training & origin Sgt. Rock	11.00	32.00	75.00
151-Intro. Enemy Ace by Kubert	8.50	25.50	60.00

152,154,156,157,159-163,165-170: 157-2 pg. pin-up. 162,163-Viking Prince x-over in Sgt. Rock

	1.60	4.80	11.00
153-2nd app. Enemy Ace	5.00	15.00	35.00
155-3rd app. Enemy Ace	2.15	6.50	15.00

158-Origin & 1st app. Iron Major(1965), formerly Iron Captain

	1.85	5.50	13.00
164-Giant G-19	1.85	5.50	13.00
171-176,178-181	1.30	4.00	9.00
177-(80 pg. Giant G-32)	1.50	4.50	10.00

182,183,186-Neal Adams-a. 186-Origin retold

	1.30	4.00	9.00

184,185,187-189,191-199: 184-Wee Willie dies. 189-Intro. The Teen-age Underground Fighters of Unit 3

	1.00	3.00	7.00

	Good	Fine	N-Mint
190-(80 pg. Giant G-44)	1.15	3.50	8.00
200-12 pg. Rock story told in verse; Evans-a			
	1.50	4.50	10.00
201-Krigstein-r/#14	1.00	3.00	6.00
202,204-215: 204,205-All reprints; no Sgt. Rock			
	.70	2.00	4.00
203-(80 pg. Giant G-56)-All-r, no Sgt. Rock	1.00	3.00	6.00
216,229-(80 pg. Giants G-68, G-80)	.85	2.50	5.00
217-228,230-239,241,243-301: 249-Wood-a. 280-200th app. Sgt. Rock;			
reprints Our Army at War #81,83	.70	2.00	4.00
240-Neal Adams-a	.85	2.50	5.00
242-(50 cent issue DC-9)-Kubert-c	.85	2.50	5.00

OUR FIGHTING FORCES
Oct-Nov, 1954-No. 181, Sept-Oct, 1978
National Periodical Publications/DC Comics

	Good	Fine	N-Mint
1-Grandenetti-c/a	47.00	140.00	330.00
2	23.00	70.00	160.00
3-Kubert-c; last precode (3/55)	20.00	60.00	138.00
4,5	15.00	45.00	105.00
6-9	12.00	36.00	85.00
10-Wood-a	13.50	41.00	95.00
11-20	10.00	30.00	70.00
21-30	6.00	18.00	42.00
31-40	5.15	15.50	36.00
41-Unknown Soldier tryout	6.00	18.00	42.00
42-44	4.50	14.00	32.00
45-Gunner & Sarge begin (ends #94)	16.50	50.00	115.00
46	8.00	24.00	55.00
47	5.15	15.50	36.00
48-50	3.70	11.00	26.00
51-64: 64-Last 10 cent issue	2.30	7.00	16.00
65-70	1.50	4.50	10.00
71-90	1.00	3.00	6.00
91-100: 95-Devil-Dog begins, ends 98. 99-Capt. Hunter begins, ends			
#106	.70	2.00	4.00
101-181: 106-Hunters Hellcats begin. 116-Mlle. Marie app. 121-Intro.			
Heller. 123-Losers (Capt. Storm, Gunner/Sarge, Johnny Cloud)			
begin. 134,146-Toth-a	.50	1.50	3.00

OUTLAW KID, THE
Aug, 1970-No. 30, Oct, 1975
Marvel Comics Group

	Good	Fine	N-Mint
1,2-Reprints; 1-Orlando-r, Wildey-r(3)	.70	2.00	4.00
3,9-Williamson-a(r)	.35	1.00	2.00
4-8: 8-Crandall-r		.75	1.50
10-30: 10-Origin; new-a in #10-16. 27-Origin-r/#10	.50		1.00

OUTSIDERS, THE
Nov, 1985-No. 28, Feb, 1988
DC Comics

1-Has tri-fold splash page; Aparo-c/a in most

	.25	.75	1.50

2-28: 2-Gives McFarlane art credits intended for Infinity, Inc. by mistake. 4-Metamorpho back-up by Staton. 7-Includes cut-out Outsiders trading cards. 18-Eclipso app. 18-26-Batman returns. 21-1st app. Clayface IV. 22- E.C. parody; Orlando-a. 25-Atomic Knight joins. 27,28-Millennium tie-ins

		.50	1.00

Annual 1 (12/86; $2.50)-Intro Strike Force Kobra

	.35	1.00	2.00
Special 1 (7/87, $1.50)	.25	.75	1.50

P

PACIFIC PRESENTS (Also see Starslayer #2, 3)
Oct, 1982-No. 2, Apr, 1983; No. 3, Mar, 1984-No. 4, June, 1984
Pacific Comics

	Good	Fine	N-Mint
1-Chapter 3 of The Rocketeer; Stevens-c/a			
	1.70	5.00	10.00
2-Chapter 4 of The Rocketeer (4th app.); nudity; Stevens-c/a			
	1.35	4.00	8.00
3,4: 3-1st app. Vanity	.35	1.00	2.00

PEACEMAKER, THE
V3#1, Mar, 1967-No. 5, Nov, 1967 (All 12 cent cover price)
Charlton Comics

1-Fightin' Five begins	1.50	4.50	10.00
2,3,5	1.00	3.00	6.00
4-Origin The Peacemaker	1.50	4.50	10.00

PEACEMAKER (Also see Crisis On Infinite Earths)
Jan, 1988-No. 4, April, 1988 ($1.25, mini-series)
DC Comics

1-4		.65	1.30

PEBBLES & BAMM BAMM (TV)
Jan, 1972-No. 36, Dec, 1976 (Hanna-Barbera)
Charlton Comics

1	3.00	9.00	21.00
2-10	1.50	4.50	10.00
11-36	1.00	3.00	7.00

PEBBLES FLINTSTONE (TV)
Sept, 1963 (Hanna-Barbera)
Gold Key

1 (10088-309)	5.70	17.00	40.00

PEP COMICS
Jan, 1940-No. 411?, 1987
MLJ Magazines/Archie Publications #56 (3/46) on

	Good	Fine	VF-NM

1-Intro. The Shield by Irving Novick (1st patriotic hero); origin The Comet by Jack Cole, The Queen of Diamonds & Kayo Ward; The Rocket, The Press Guardian (The Falcon #1 only), Sergeant Boyle, Fu Chang, & Bentley of Scotland Yard

	Good	Fine	VF-NM
	275.00	690.00	1650.00

	Good	Fine	N-Mint
2-Origin The Rocket	86.00	260.00	600.00
3	72.00	215.00	500.00
4-Wizard cameo	57.00	170.00	400.00
5-Wizard cameo in Shield story	57.00	170.00	400.00

Pep Comics #10, © *Archie Comics*

6-10: 8-Last Cole Comet; no Cole-a in #6,7			
	43.00	130.00	300.00
11-Dusty, Shield's sidekick begins; last Press Guardian, Fu Chang			
	50.00	150.00	350.00
12-Origin Fireball; last Rocket & Queen of Diamonds			
	61.00	182.00	425.00
13-15	39.00	118.00	275.00
16-Origin Madam Satan; blood drainage-c			
	61.00	182.00	425.00
17-Origin The Hangman; death of The Comet			
	132.00	395.00	925.00
18-20-Last Fireball	39.00	118.00	275.00
21-Last Madam Satan	39.00	118.00	275.00

	Good	Fine	VF-NM
22-Intro. & 1st app. Archie, Betty, & Jughead(12/41); (also see Jackpot)	290.00	730.00	1750.00

	Good	Fine	N-Mint
23	67.00	200.00	465.00
24,25	57.00	170.00	400.00
26-1st app. Veronica Lodge	72.00	215.00	500.00
27-30: 30-Capt. Commando begins	47.00	140.00	325.00
31-35: 34-Bondage/Hypo-c	38.00	115.00	265.00
36-1st Archie-c	61.00	180.00	425.00
37-40	29.00	86.00	200.00
41-50: 41-Archie-c begin. 47-Last Hangman issue; infinity-c. 48-Black Hood begins (5/44); ends #51,59,60	20.00	60.00	140.00
51-60: 52-Suzie begins. 56-Last Capt. Commando. 59-Black Hood not in costume; spanking & lingerie panels; Archie dresses as his aunt; Suzie ends. 60-Katy Keene begins, ends #154	14.00	43.00	100.00
61-65-Last Shield. 62-1st app. Li'l Jinx	11.00	32.00	75.00
66-80: 66-G-Man Club becomes Archie Club (2/48); Nevada Jones by Bill Woggon	7.00	21.00	50.00
81-99	5.00	15.00	35.00
100	6.50	19.00	45.00
101-130	2.30	7.00	16.00
131-149	1.30	4.00	9.00
150-160-Super-heroes app. in each (see note). 150 (10/61?)-2nd or 3rd app. The Jaguar? 157-Li'l Jinx story	1.50	4.50	10.00
161-167,169-200	.70	2.00	4.00
168-Jaguar app.	.85	2.60	6.00
201-260	.35	1.00	2.00
261-411: 383-Marvelous Maureen begins (Sci/fi). 393-Thunderbunny begins	.50		1.00

NOTE: *The Fly app. in 151, 154, 160. Flygirl app. in 153, 155, 156, 158. Jaguar app. in 150, 152, 157, 159, 168.*

PETER PARKER (See The Spectacular Spider-Man)

PETER PORKER, THE SPECTACULAR SPIDER-HAM
May, 1985-No. 17, Sept, 1987
Star Comics (Marvel)

1-Michael Golden-c	.35	1.00	2.00
2-17: 13-Halloween issue		.50	1.00

PHANTOM, THE (nn 29-Published overseas only)
Nov, 1962-No. 17, July, 1966; No. 18, Sept, 1966-No. 28, Dec,
    1967; No. 30, Feb, 1969-No. 74, Jan, 1977
Gold Key (#1-17)/King (#18-28)/Charlton (#30 on)

	Good	Fine	N-Mint
1-Manning-a	7.00	21.00	50.00
2-King, Queen & Jack begins, ends #11	3.60	11.00	25.00
3-10	2.85	8.50	20.00
11-17: 12-Track Hunter begins	2.15	6.50	15.00
18-Flash Gordon begins; Wood-a	2.65	8.00	18.00
19,20-Flash Gordon ends (both by Gil Kane)			
	1.70	5.00	12.00
21-24,26,27: 21-Mandrake begins. 20,24-Girl Phantom app. 26-Brick Bradford app.	1.70	5.00	12.00
25-Jeff Jones-a(4 pgs.); 1 pg. Williamson ad			
	1.70	5.00	12.00
28(nn)-Brick Bradford app.	1.50	4.50	10.00
30-40: 36,39-Ditko-a	1.15	3.50	7.00
41-66: 46-Intro. The Piranha. 62-Bolle-c	.85	2.50	5.00
67-71,73-Newton-c/a; 67-Origin retold	.50	1.50	3.00
72,74: 74-Newton Flag-c; Newton-a	.50	1.50	3.00

PHANTOM, THE
May, 1988-No. 4, Aug, 1988 ($1.25, color, mini-series)
DC Comics

1-Orlando-c/a in all	.35	1.00	2.00
2-4	.25	.75	1.50

PHANTOM, THE
Mar, 1989-No. 13, Mar, 1990 ($1.50, color)
DC Comics

1-Brief origin	.35	1.00	2.00
2-13	.25	.75	1.50

PHANTOM STRANGER, THE (See Showcase #80)
May-June, 1969-No. 41, Feb-Mar, 1976
National Periodical Publications

1-Only 12 cent issue	4.70	14.00	33.00
2,3: 2-? are 15 cents	1.85	5.50	13.00
4-Neal Adams-a	2.15	6.50	15.00
5-7	1.40	4.25	9.50
8-14	1.25	3.75	7.50

	Good	Fine	N-Mint
15-19: All 25 cent, 52 pg. giants	.75	2.25	4.50
20-41: 22-Dark Circle begins. 23-Spawn of Frankenstein begins by Kaluta; series ends #30. 31-The Black Orchid begins. 39-41-Deadman app.	.60	1.75	3.50

PHANTOM STRANGER (See Justice League of America #103)
Oct, 1987-No. 4, Jan, 1988 (75 cents, color, mini-series)
DC Comics

1-Mignola/Russell-c/a in all	.25	.75	1.50
2-4		.50	1.00

PHOENIX (...The Untold Story)
April, 1984 ($2.00, One shot)
Marvel Comics Group

1-Byrne/Austin-r/X-Men 137 with original unpublished ending			
	1.50	4.50	9.00

PINK PANTHER, THE (TV)
April, 1971-No. 87, 1984
Gold Key

1-The Inspector begins	1.70	5.00	12.00
2-10	.85	2.50	5.00
11-30: Warren Tufts-a #16-on	.60	1.75	3.50
31-60	.40	1.25	2.50
61-87	.35	1.00	2.00

PLANET COMICS
1/40-No. 62, 9/49; No. 63, Wint, 1949-50; No. 64, Spring, 1950; No. 65, 1951(nd); No. 66-68, 1952(nd); No. 69, Wint, 1952-53; No. 70-72, 1953(nd); No. 73, Winter, 1953-54
Fiction House Magazines

	Good	Fine	VF-NM
1-Origin Auro, Lord of Jupiter; Flint Baker & The Red Comet begin; Eisner/Fine-c	535.00	1335.00	3200.00
	Good	**Fine**	**N-Mint**
2-(Scarce)	267.00	665.00	1600.00
3-Eisner-c	208.00	520.00	1250.00
4-Gale Allen and the Girl Squadron begins			
	183.00	460.00	1100.00
5,6-(Scarce)	167.00	415.00	1000.00
7-12: 12-The Star Pirate begins	133.00	335.00	800.00
13-14: 13-Reff Ryan begins	108.00	270.00	650.00

	Good	Fine	N-Mint
15-(Scarce)-Mars, God of War begins (11/42)			
	200.00	500.00	1200.00
16-20,22	100.00	250.00	600.00
21-The Lost World & Hunt Bowman begin			
	105.00	260.00	625.00
23-26: 26-The Space Rangers begin	92.00	235.00	550.00
27-30	63.00	190.00	440.00
31-35: 33-Origin Star Pirates Wonder Boots, reprinted in #52. 35-Mysta of the Moon begins	54.00	160.00	375.00
36-45: 41-New origin of "Auro, Lord of Jupiter." 42-Last Gale Allen. 43-Futura begins	48.00	145.00	335.00
46-60: 53-Used in **SOTI**, pg. 32	36.00	107.00	250.00
61-64	26.00	77.00	180.00
65-68,70: 65-70-All partial-r of earlier issues			
	26.00	77.00	180.00
69-Used in **POP,** pgs. 101,102	26.00	77.00	180.00
71-73-No series stories	19.00	57.00	135.00

PLASTIC MAN (Also see Police Comics & Smash Comics #17)
Sum, 1943-No. 64, Nov, 1956
Vital Publ. No. 1,2/Quality Comics No. 3 on

nn(#1)-"In The Game of Death;" Jack Cole-c/a begins; ends-#64?			
	165.00	495.00	1150.00
nn(#2, 2/44)-"The Gay Nineties Nightmare"			
	89.00	268.00	625.00
3 (Spr, '46)	59.00	175.00	410.00
4 (Sum, '46)	50.00	150.00	350.00
5 (Aut, '46)	43.00	130.00	300.00
6-10	34.00	100.00	235.00
11-20	29.00	85.00	200.00
21-30: 26-Last non-r issue?	24.00	70.00	165.00
31-40: 40-Used in **POP**, pg. 91	18.00	54.00	125.00
41-64: 53-Last precode issue	14.00	43.00	100.00

PLASTIC MAN (See DC Special #15 & House of Mystery #160)
11-12/66-No. 10, 5-6/68; V4#11, 2-3/76-No. 20, 10-11/77
National Periodical Publications/DC Comics

1-2nd app. Silver Age Plastic Man (see House of Mystery #160 for 1st app.); Gil Kane-c/a; 12 cent issues begin			
	4.70	14.00	33.00
2-5: 4-Infantino-c; Mortimer-a	2.15	6.50	15.00

	Good	Fine	N-Mint
6-10('68): 10-Sparling-a; last 12 cent issue			
	1.15	3.50	8.00
V4#11('76)-20: 11-20-Fraden-p. 17-Origin retold			
	.35	1.00	2.00

PLASTIC MAN
Nov, 1988-No. 4, Feb, 1989 ($1.00, mini-series)
DC Comics

	Good	Fine	N-Mint
1-4: 1-Origin; Woozy Winks app.		.50	1.00

PLOP!
Sept-Oct, 1973-No. 24, Nov-Dec, 1976
National Periodical Publications

	Good	Fine	N-Mint
1-20: Sergio Aragones-a. 1,5-Wrightson-a	.60	1.75	3.50
21,22,24 (52 pgs.)	.70	2.00	4.00
23-No Aragones-a (52 pgs.)	.25	.75	1.50

POLICE COMICS
Aug, 1941-No. 127, Oct, 1953
Quality Comics Group (Comic Magazines)

	Good	Fine	N-Mint
1-Origin Plastic Man (1st app.) by Jack Cole, The Human Bomb by Gustavson, & No. 711; intro. Chic Carter by Eisner, The Firebrand by Reed Crandall, The Mouthpiece, Phantom Lady, & The Sword; r-in DC Special #15	385.00	960.00	2300.00
2-Plastic Man smuggles opium	157.00	470.00	1100.00
3	115.00	343.00	800.00
4	107.00	320.00	750.00
5-Plastic Man forced to smoke marijuana	107.00	320.00	750.00
6,7	100.00	300.00	700.00
8-Manhunter begins (origin)	115.00	345.00	800.00
9,10	89.00	270.00	625.00
11-The Spirit strip reprints begin by Eisner(Origin-strip #1)	143.00	430.00	1000.00
12-Intro. Ebony	89.00	270.00	625.00
13-Intro. Woozy Winks; last Firebrand	89.00	270.00	625.00
14-19: 15-Last No. 711; Destiny begins	59.00	180.00	415.00
20-The Raven x-over in Phantom Lady; features Jack Cole himself	59.00	180.00	415.00
21,22-Raven & Spider Widow x-over in Phantom Lady #21; cameo in Phantom Lady #22	46.00	140.00	325.00

	Good	Fine	N-Mint
23-30: 23-Last Phantom Lady. 24-26-Flatfoot Burns by Kurtzman in all	40.00	120.00	280.00
31-41-Last Spirit-r by Eisner	28.00	85.00	200.00
42,43-Spirit-r by Eisner/Fine	25.00	75.00	175.00
44-Fine Spirit-r begin, end #88,90,92	22.00	65.00	150.00
45-50-(#50 on-c, #49 on inside)(1/46)	22.00	65.00	150.00
51-60: 58-Last Human Bomb	17.00	51.00	120.00
61-88: 63-(Some issues have #65 printed on cover, but #63 on inside) Kurtzman-a, 6 pgs.	14.00	43.00	100.00
89,91,93-No Spirit	13.00	40.00	90.00
90,92-Spirit by Fine	14.00	43.00	100.00
94-99,101,102: Spirit by Eisner in all; 101-Last Manhunter. 102-Last Spirit & Plastic Man by Jack Cole	19.00	57.00	130.00
100	22.00	65.00	150.00
103-Content change to crime; Ken Shannon begins (1st app.)	11.00	32.00	75.00
104-111,114-127-Crandall-a most issues	7.00	21.00	50.00
112-Crandall-a	7.00	21.00	50.00
113-Crandall-c/a(2), 9 pgs. each	8.00	24.00	55.00

POPULAR COMICS
Feb, 1936-No. 145, July-Sept, 1948
Dell Publishing Co.

	Good	Fine	V-Fine
1-Dick Tracy (1st comic book app.), Little Orphan Annie, Terry & the Pirates, Gasoline Alley, Don Winslow, Harold Teen, Little Joe, Skippy, Moon Mullins, Mutt & Jeff, Tailspin Tommy, Smitty, Smokey Stover, Winnie Winkle & The Gumps begin (all strip-r)	300.00	750.00	1500.00

	Good	Fine	VF-NM
2	85.00	260.00	600.00
3	70.00	215.00	500.00
4,5: 5-Tom Mix begins	54.00	160.00	375.00
6-10: 8,9-Scribbly, Reglar Fellers app.	43.00	130.00	300.00

	Good	Fine	N-Mint
11-20: 12-Xmas-c	36.00	107.00	250.00
21-27: 27-Last Terry & the Pirates, Little Orphan Annie, & Dick Tracy	25.00	75.00	175.00
28-37: 28-Gene Autry app. 31,32-Tim McCoy app. 35-Christmas-c; Tex Ritter app.	22.00	65.00	150.00
38-43-Tarzan in text only. 38-Gang Busters (radio) & Zane Grey's			

	Good	Fine	N-Mint
Tex Thorne begins? 43-1st non-funny-c?			
	24.00	73.00	170.00
44,45: 45-Tarzan-c	17.00	51.00	120.00
46-Origin Martan, the Marvel Man	23.00	70.00	160.00
47-50	16.00	48.00	110.00
51-Origin The Voice (The Invisible Detective) strip begins			
	17.00	51.00	120.00
52-59: 55-End of World story	13.00	40.00	90.00
60-Origin Professor Supermind and Son	13.50	41.00	95.00
61-71: 63-Smilin' Jack begins	11.50	34.00	80.00
72-The Owl & Terry & the Pirates begin; Smokey Stover reprints			
begin	19.00	58.00	135.00
73-75	13.50	41.00	95.00
76-78-Capt. Midnight in all	17.00	51.00	120.00
79-85-Last Owl	12.00	36.00	85.00
86-99: 98-Felix the Cat, Smokey Stover-r begin			
	9.30	28.00	65.00
100	11.00	32.00	75.00
101-130	6.00	18.00	42.00
131-145: 142-Last Terry & the Pirates	5.00	15.00	35.00

POWER MAN (Formerly Hero for Hire; ...& Iron Fist #68
  on; see Cage)
No. 17, Feb, 1974-No. 125, Sept, 1986
Marvel Comics Group

	Good	Fine	N-Mint
17-Luke Cage continues; Iron Man app.	1.50	4.50	10.00
18-20: 18-Last 20 cent issue	1.00	3.00	7.00
21-31: 31-Part Neal Adams-i. 34-Last 25 cents			
	.75	2.25	4.50
32-48: 36-r/Hero For Hire #12. 41-1st app. Thunderbolt. 45-Starlin-c. 48-Byrne-a; Powerman/Iron Fist 1st meet			
	.50	1.50	3.00
49,50-Byrne-a(p); 50-Iron Fist joins Cage	.50	1.50	3.00
51-56,58-60: 58-Intro El Aguila	.25	.75	1.50
57-New X-Men app. (6/79)	.85	2.50	5.00
61-65,67-77,79-83,85-124: 75-Double size. 77-Daredevil app. 87-Moon Knight app. 90-Unus app. 109-The Reaper app. 100-Double size; origin K'un L'un			
		.50	1.00
66-2nd app. Sabretooth (see Iron Fist #14)	4.30	13.00	30.00
78-3rd app. Sabretooth (cameo under cloak)			
	1.70	5.00	12.00

	Good	Fine	N-Mint
84-4th app. Sabretooth	1.70	5.00	12.00
125-Double size; death of Iron Fist	.35	1.00	2.00
Annual 1(1976)-Punisher cameo in flashback	.70	2.00	4.00

POWER PACK
Aug, 1984-No. 62, Feb, 1991
Marvel Comics Group

	Good	Fine	N-Mint
1-($1.00, 52 pgs.)	.60	1.75	3.50
2-5	.40	1.25	2.50
6-8-Cloak & Dagger app. 6-Spider-man app.	.25	.75	1.50
9-18		.60	1.20
19-Dbl. size; Cloak & Dagger, Wolverine app.	1.70	5.00	10.00
20-24		.50	1.00
25-Double size	.30	.90	1.80
26-Begin direct sale; Cloak & Dagger app.		.50	1.00
27-Mutant massacre; Wolverine & Sabretooth app.	2.15	6.50	13.00
28,30-43: 42-1st Inferno tie-in		.50	1.00
29-Spider-Man & Hobgoblin app.	.35	1.00	2.00
44,45,47-49,51-62: 44-Begin $1.50-c		.50	1.00
46-Punisher app.	.85	2.50	5.00
50-Double size ($1.95)	.25	.75	1.50
Holiday Special 1 (2/92, $2.25, 68 pgs.)	.35	1.00	2.00

PREDATOR (Also see Aliens Vs. Predator)
May, 1989-No. 4, 1990 ($2.25, color, mini-series)
Dark Horse Comics

	Good	Fine	N-Mint
1-Based on movie; 1st app. Predator	4.70	14.00	33.00
1-2nd printing	1.15	3.50	7.00
2	2.30	7.00	16.00
3	1.70	5.00	10.00
4	1.15	3.50	7.00

PREDATOR: BIG GAME
Mar, 1991-No. 4, June, 1991 ($2.50, color, mini-series)
Dark Horse Comics

	Good	Fine	N-Mint
1: 1-3-Contain 2 Dark Horse trading cards	.70	2.00	4.00
2-4	.50	1.50	3.00

PREDATOR COLD WAR
Sept, 1991-No. 4, Dec, 1991 ($2.50, color, mini-series)
Dark Horse Comics

	Good	Fine	N-Mint
1-All have painted-c	.70	2.00	4.00
2-4	.50	1.50	3.00

PREDATOR 2
Feb, 1991-No. 2, June, 1991 ($2.50, color, mini-series)
Dark Horse Comics

	Good	Fine	N-Mint
1-Adapts movie; trading cards inside; photo-c	.60	1.75	3.50
2-Trading cards inside; photo-c	.40	1.25	2.50

PRINCE NAMOR, THE SUB-MARINER (Also see Namor ...)
Sept, 1984-No. 4, Dec, 1984 (Mini-series)
Marvel Comics Group

	Good	Fine	N-Mint
1	.35	1.00	2.00
2-4		.60	1.20

PRISONER, THE (TV)
1988-No. 4, Jan, 1989 ($3.50, mini-series, squarebound)
DC Comics

	Good	Fine	N-Mint
1-Book A	.75	2.25	4.50
2-4: Book B-D	.60	1.75	3.50

PRIZE COMICS (...Western #69 on)
March, 1940-No. 68, Feb-Mar, 1948
Prize Publications

	Good	Fine	N-Mint
1-Origin Power Nelson, The Futureman & Jupiter, Master Magician; Ted O'Neil, Secret Agent M-11, Jaxon of the Jungle, Bucky Brady & Storm Curtis begin	100.00	300.00	700.00
2-The Black Owl begins	47.00	140.00	325.00
3,4	38.00	115.00	265.00
5,6: Dr. Dekkar, Master of Monsters app. in each	36.00	107.00	250.00
7-(Scarce)-Black Owl by S&K; origin/1st app. Dr. Frost & Frankenstein; The Green Lama, Capt. Gallant, The Great Voodini & Twist Turner begin	79.00	235.00	550.00
8,9-Black Owl & Ted O'Neil by S&K	43.00	130.00	300.00
10-12,14-20: 11-Origin Bulldog Denny. 16-Spike Mason begins	36.00	107.00	250.00

	Good	Fine	N-Mint
13-Yank & Doodle begin (origin)	40.00	120.00	280.00
21-24	25.00	75.00	175.00
25-30	14.00	43.00	100.00
31-33	11.50	34.00	80.00

34-Origin Airmale, Yank & Doodle; The Black Owl joins army, Yank & Doodle's father assumes Black Owl's role

	13.00	40.00	90.00

35-40: 35-Flying Fist & Bingo begin. 37-Intro. Stampy, Airmale's sidekick; Hitler-c

	10.00	30.00	70.00

41-50: 45-Yank & Doodle learn Black Owl's I.D. (their father). 48-Prince Ra begins

	7.00	21.00	50.00

51-62,64-68: 53-Transvestism story. 55-No Frankenstein. 57-X-Mas-c. 64-Black Owl retires. 65,66-Frankenstein-c by Briefer

	6.50	19.00	45.00
63-Simon & Kirby c/a	8.50	25.50	60.00

PRIZE COMICS WESTERN (Formerly Prize Comics #1-68)
No. 69(V7#2), Apr-May, 1948-No. 119, Nov-Dec, 1956
Prize Publications (Feature) (No. 69-84: 52 pgs.)

69(V7#2)	8.50	25.50	60.00
70-75	6.50	19.00	45.00

76-Randolph Scott photo-c; "Canadian Pacific" movie adaptation

	8.50	25.50	60.00

77-Photo-c; Severin, Mart Bailey-a; "Streets of Laredo" movie adapt.

	7.00	21.00	50.00

78-Photo-c; Kurtzman-a, 10 pgs.; Severin, Mart Bailey-a; "Bullet Code," & "Roughshod" movie adapt.

	10.00	30.00	70.00

79-Photo-c; Kurtzman-a, 8 pgs.; Severin & Elder, Severin, Mart Bailey-a; "Stage To Chino" movie adapt.

	10.00	30.00	70.00
80,81-Photo-c; Severin/Elder-a(2)	7.00	21.00	50.00

82-Photo-c; 1st app. The Preacher by Mart Bailey; Severin/Elder-a(3)

	7.00	21.00	50.00
83,84	5.70	17.00	40.00

85-American Eagle by John Severin begins (1-2/50)

	14.00	43.00	100.00
86,92,101-105	6.50	19.00	45.00

87-91,93-99,110,111-Severin/Elder a(2-3) each

	7.00	21.00	50.00
100	8.50	25.50	60.00
106-108,112	4.50	14.00	32.00
109-Severin/Williamson-a	7.00	21.00	50.00

	Good	Fine	N-Mint
113-Williamson/Severin-a(2)/Frazetta?	8.00	24.00	55.00
114-119: Drifter series in all; by Mort Meskin #114-118			
	3.60	11.00	25.00

PUNISHER (See Amazing Spider-Man #129, Captain America #241, Daredevil #182-184, 257, Daredevil and the..., Ghost Rider V2#5, 6, Marc Spector #8 & 9, Marvel Preview #2, Marvel Tales, Power Pack #46, Spectacular Spider-Man #81-83, 140, 141, 143 & new Strange Tales #13 & 14)
Jan, 1986-No. 5, May, 1986 (Mini-series)
Marvel Comics Group

	Good	Fine	N-Mint
1-Double size	6.70	20.00	47.00
2	3.60	11.00	25.00
3-Has 2 cover prices, 75 & 95(w/UPC) cents			
	2.50	7.50	15.00
4,5	2.00	6.00	12.00

PUNISHER
July, 1987-Present
Marvel Comics Group

	Good	Fine	N-Mint
V2#1	5.00	15.00	30.00
2	2.50	7.50	15.00
3-5	1.50	4.50	9.00
6,7	1.35	4.00	8.00
8-Portacio/Williams-c/a begins, ends #18			
	1.70	5.00	10.00

The Punisher #29, © Marvel Comics

	Good	Fine	N-Mint
9-Scarcer, lower distribution	1.85	5.50	11.00
10-Daredevil app.; ties in w/Daredevil #257			
	4.50	13.50	27.00
11-15: 13-18-Kingpin app.	1.15	3.50	7.00
16-20: 19-Stroman-c/a. 20-Portacio-c(p)			
	.85	2.50	5.00
21-24,26-30: 24-1st app. Shadowmasters			
	.50	1.50	3.00
25-Double size ($1.50)-Shadowmasters app.			
	.70	2.00	4.00
31-40	.35	1.00	2.00
41-49		.65	1.30
50-($1.50, 52 pgs.)	.25	.75	1.50
51-59: 57-Photo-c; came with outer-c. 59-Punisher is severely cut & has skin grafts (has black skin)		.50	1.00
60-74: 60-Begin $1.25-c. 60,61-Luke Cage app. 62-Punisher back to white skin		.65	1.30
Annual 1 (1988)-Evolutionary War x-over	2.00	6.00	12.00
Annual 2 (1989, $2.00, 68 pgs.)-Atlantis Attacks x-over; Jim Lee-a(p) (back-up story, 6 pgs.); Moon Knight app.			
	1.15	3.50	7.00
Annual 3 (1990, $2.00, 68 pgs.)	.35	1.00	2.00
Annual 4 (1991, $2.00, 68 pgs.)-Golden-c(p)	.35	1.00	2.00
Annual 5 (1992, $2.25, 68 pgs.)	.40	1.15	2.30
Summer Special 1 (8/91, $2.95, 52 pgs.)	.50	1.50	3.00
Summer Special 2 (1992, $2.50, 52 pgs.)	.40	1.25	2.50
...and Wolverine in African Saga nn (1989, $5.95, 52 pgs.)-Reprints Punisher War Journal #6 & 7; Jim Lee-c/a(r)			
	1.00	3.00	6.00
...Bloodlines nn (1991, $5.95, 68 pgs.)	1.00	3.00	6.00
...G-Force nn (1992, $4.95, 52 pgs.)-Painted-c			
	.85	2.50	5.00
...Movie Special 1 (6/90, $5.95, 68 pgs.)	1.00	3.00	6.00
...: No Escape nn (1990, $4.95, 52 pgs.)-New-a			
	1.00	3.00	6.00
...The Prize nn (1990, $4.95, 68 pgs.)-New-a	.85	2.50	5.00

PUNISHER ARMORY, THE
July, 1990 ($1.50); No. 2, June, 1991 ($1.75); No. 3, Apr, 1992 ($2.00)
Marvel Comics

1-r/weapons pgs. from War Journal; Jim Lee-c			
	.60	1.75	3.50

	Good	Fine	N-Mint
2-Jim Lee-c	.40	1.15	2.25
3-Jusko painted-c	.35	1.00	2.00

PUNISHER: P.O.V.
1991-No. 4, 1991 ($4.95, color, mini-series, 52 pgs.)
Marvel Comics

1-4: Starlin scripts & Wrightson painted-c/a in all. 2-Nick Fury app.			
	.85	2.50	5.00

PUNISHER WAR JOURNAL, THE
Nov, 1988-Present ($1.50-$1.75, color)
Marvel Comics

1-Origin The Punisher; Jim Lee-c/a begins; Matt Murdock cameo;			
1st Lee-a on Punisher	3.35	10.00	20.00
2-Daredevil x-over	2.30	7.00	14.00
3-5: 3-Daredevil x-over	1.70	5.00	10.00
6-Two part Wolverine story begins	3.35	10.00	20.00
7-Wolverine story ends	1.70	5.00	10.00
8-10	1.15	3.50	7.00
11-13,17-19: 19-Last Jim Lee-c/a	.85	2.50	5.00
14-16,20-22: No Jim Lee-a. 13-15-Heath-i. 14,15-Spider-Man x-over			
	.40	1.25	2.50
23-28,31-48: 23-Begin $1.75-c. 31-Andy & Joe Kubert art. 36-Photo-c. 45-Daredevil & Nomad app. (cont'd in D.D. #308)			
	.30	.90	1.80
29,30-Ghost Rider app.	.40	1.25	2.50

PUNISHER WAR ZONE
Mar, 1992-Present ($1.75, color)
Marvel Comics

1-($2.25)-Special die-cut-c; Romita, Jr.-c/a begins			
	.60	1.75	3.50
2	.40	1.25	2.50
3-10	.30	.90	1.80

Q

QUASAR (See Avengers #302, Captain America #217, Incredible
   Hulk #234 & Marvel Team-Up #113)
Oct, 1989-Present ($1.00-$1.25, color) (Direct sale #17 on)
Marvel Comics

	Good	Fine	N-Mint
1-Origin; formerly Marvel Boy/Marvel Man			
	.35	1.00	2.00
2-5: 3-Human Torch app.	.25	.75	1.50
6-Venom cameo (2 pgs.)	.35	1.00	2.00
7-Cosmic Spidey app.	.40	1.25	2.50
8-15,18-24: 11-Excalibur x-over. 14-McFarlane-c. 20-Fantastic			
Four app. 23-Ghost Rider x-over		.60	1.20
16-($1.50, 52 pgs.)	.25	.75	1.50
17-Flash parody (Buried Alien)	.35	1.00	2.00
25-($1.50, 52 pgs.)-New costume Quasar	.25	.75	1.50
26-Infinity Guantlet x-over; Thanos-c/story	.35	1.00	2.00
27-Infinity Guantlet x-over	.25	.75	1.50
28-30		.50	1.00
31-40: Thanos cameo in flashback. 31-D.P. 7 guest stars; begin $1.25-c			
		.65	1.30

NOTE: *#32-34 have newsstand versions which are renumbered on the
cover starting with #1. Indicias still have original number.*

QUEEN OF THE WEST, DALE EVANS (TV)(Also see
   Dale Evans Comics)
No. 479, 7/53-No. 22, 1-3/59 (All photo-c; photo back c-4-8, 15)
Dell Publishing Co.

4-Color 479(#1, '53)	10.00	30.00	70.00
4-Color 528(#2, '54)	6.50	19.00	45.00
3(4-6/54)-Toth-a	7.00	21.00	50.00
4-Toth, Manning-a	7.00	21.00	50.00
5-10-Manning-a. 5-Marsh-a	5.00	15.00	35.00
11,19,21-No Manning 21-Tufts-a	3.70	11.00	26.00
12-18,20,22-Manning-a	4.30	13.00	30.00

QUESTION, THE (Also see Crisis on Infinite Earths)
Feb, 1987-No. 36, Mar, 1990 ($1.50-$1.75, color, mature readers)
DC Comics

	Good	Fine	N-Mint
1-Sienkiewicz painted-c	.50	1.50	3.00
2-5	.35	1.00	2.00
6-36: 8-Intro. The Mikado. 16-Begin $1.75-c			
	.25	.75	1.50
Annual 1(9/88, $2.50)-Sienkiewicz-c(i)	.40	1.25	2.50
Annual 2('89, $3.50, 68 pgs.)-Green Arrow app.			
	.60	1.75	3.50

RAGMAN (See Batman Family #20 and Brave & The Bold #196)
Aug-Sept, 1976-No. 5, June-July, 1977
National Periodical Publications/DC Comics No. 5

	Good	Fine	N-Mint
1-Origin	.50	1.50	3.00
2-5: 2-Origin ends; Kubert-c. 4-Drug use story			
	.25	.75	1.50

RAGMAN (2nd series)
Oct, 1991-No. 8, May, 1992 ($1.50, color, mini-series)
DC Comics

1-Giffen plots/breakdowns	.50	1.50	3.00
2-8: 3-Origin. 8-Batman app.	.25	.75	1.50

RAI (Also see Magnus #5-8)
Mar, 1992-Present ($1.95-$2.25, color)
Valiant

1	1.50	4.50	9.00
2,3	.85	2.50	5.00
4-8: 5-Begin $2.25-c	.40	1.15	2.30
0 (8/92)	.40	1.15	2.30

RAT PATROL, THE (TV)
March, 1967-No. 5, Nov, 1967; No. 6, Oct, 1969
Dell Publishing Co.

1-Christopher George photo-c	4.00	12.00	28.00
2	3.00	9.00	21.00
3-6: 3-6-Photo-c	2.30	7.00	16.00

RAWHIDE KID
3/55-No. 16, 9/57; No. 17, 8/60-No. 151, 5/79
Atlas/Marvel Comics (CnPC No. 1-16/AMI No. 17-30)

1-Rawhide Kid, his horse Apache & sidekick Randy begin; Wyatt Earp app.; #1 was not code approved	37.00	110.00	260.00
2	17.00	51.00	120.00
3-5	11.00	32.00	75.00
6-10: 7-Williamson-a (4 pgs.)	7.00	21.00	50.00
11-16: 16-Torres-a	5.70	17.00	40.00

	Good	Fine	N-Mint
17-Origin by Jack Kirby	9.30	28.00	65.00
18-22,24-30	4.30	13.00	30.00
23-Origin retold by Jack Kirby	7.00	21.00	50.00
31,32,36-44,46: 40-Two-Gun Kid x-over. 42-1st Larry Lieber issue.			
46-Toth-a	3.60	11.00	25.00
33-35-Davis-a. 35-Intro & death of The Raven			
	4.00	12.00	28.00
45-Origin retold	4.00	12.00	28.00
47-70: 50-Kid Colt x-over. 64-Kid Colt story. 66-Two-Gun Kid story.			
67-Kid Colt story	1.70	5.00	12.00
71-86: 79-Williamson-a(r). 86-Origin-r; Williamson-a r-/Ringo Kid			
#13 (4 pgs.)	1.00	3.00	7.00
87-89	.85	2.50	5.00
100-Origin retold & expanded	1.00	3.00	7.00
101-120	.40	1.25	2.50
121-151	.25	.75	1.50
Special 1(9/71, 25 cents, 68 pgs.)-All Kirby/Ayers-r			
	.85	2.50	5.00

RAY, THE
Feb,1992-No. 6, July, 1992 ($1.00, color, mini-series)
DC Comics

1	.85	2.50	5.00
2	.50	1.50	3.00
3-6	.25	.75	1.50

RED RAVEN COMICS (Human Torch #2 on; also see X-Men #44)
August, 1940 (Also see Sub-Mariner #26, 2nd series)
Timely Comics

	Good	Fine	VF-NM
1-Origin Red Raven; Comet Pierce & Mercury by Kirby, The Human			
Top & The Eternal Brain; intro. Magar, the Mystic & only app.;			
Kirby-c	670.00	1670.00	4000.00

RED RYDER COMICS (Movies, radio)(Also see Crackajack
Funnies)
9/40; No. 3, 8/41-No. 5, 12/41; No. 6, 4/42-No. 151, 4-6/57
Hawley Publ. No. 1-5/Dell Publishing Co.(K.K.) No. 6 on

	Good	Fine	N-Mint
1-Red Ryder, his horse Thunder, Little Beaver & his horse Papoose			
strip reprints begin by Fred Harman; 1st meeting of Red & Little			
Beaver; Harman line-drawn-c #1-85	93.00	280.00	650.00

	Good	Fine	N-Mint
3-(Scarce)-Alley Oop, King of the Royal Mtd., Capt. Easy, Freckles & His Friends, Myra North & Dan Dunn strip-r begin			
	57.00	171.00	400.00
4,5	32.00	95.00	225.00
6-1st Dell issue	32.00	95.00	225.00
7-10	25.00	75.00	175.00
11-20	19.00	57.00	130.00
21-32-Last Alley Oop, Dan Dunn, Capt. Easy, Freckles			
	12.00	36.00	85.00
33-40 (52 pgs.)	8.00	24.00	55.00
41 (52 pgs.)-Rocky Lane photo back-c; photo back-c begin, end #57			
	8.50	25.50	60.00
42-46 (52 pgs.): 46-Last Red Ryder strip-r	6.50	19.00	45.00
47-53 (52 pgs.): 47-New stories on Red Ryder begin			
	5.00	15.00	35.00
54-57 (36 pgs.)	4.00	12.00	28.00
58-73 (36 pgs.): 73-Last King of the Royal Mtd; strip-r by Jim Gary			
	3.70	11.00	26.00
74-85,93 (52 pgs.)-Harman line-drawn-c	4.00	12.00	28.00
86-92 (52 pgs.)-Harman painted-c	4.00	12.00	28.00
94-96 (36 pgs.)-Harman painted-c	3.00	9.00	21.00
97,98,107,108 (36 pgs.)-Harman line-drawn-c			
	3.00	9.00	21.00
99,101-106 (36 pgs.)-Jim Bannon Photo-c	3.00	9.00	21.00
100 (36 pgs.)-Bannon photo-c	3.60	11.00	25.00
109-118 (52 pgs.)-Harman line-drawn-c	2.30	7.00	16.00
119-129 (52 pgs.): 119-Painted-c begin, not by Harman, end #151			
	2.00	6.00	14.00
130-144 (#130 on have 36 pgs.)	1.70	5.00	12.00
145-148: 145-Title change to Red Ryder Ranch Magazine with photos			
	1.50	4.50	10.00
149-151: 149-Title changed to Red Ryder Ranch Comics			
	1.50	4.50	10.00

RED SONJA (Also see Conan #23 & Marvel Feature)
1/77-No. 15, 5/79; V1#1, 2/83-V2#2, 3/83; V3#1, 8/83-V3#4, 2/84;
    V3#5, 1/85-V3#13, 1986
Marvel Comics Group

1-Created by Robert E. Howard	.50	1.50	3.00
2-5	.35	1.00	2.00
6-15, V1#1,V2#2		.50	1.00
V3#1-4 ($1.00, 52 pgs.)		.60	1.20

	Good	Fine	N-Mint
5-13 (65-75 cents)		.50	1.00

RED WOLF (See Avengers #80 & Marvel Spotlight #1)
May, 1972-No. 9, Sept, 1973
Marvel Comics Group

1-Gil Kane/Severin-c; Shores-a; western hero begins			
	.50	1.50	3.00
2-5: 2-Shores-a; Gil Kane-c	.25	.75	1.50
6-Red Wolf as super hero begins	.50	1.50	3.00
7-9: 9-Origin sidekick, Lobo (wolf)	.25	.75	1.50

RIMA, THE JUNGLE GIRL
Apr-May, 1974-No. 7, Apr-May, 1975
National Periodical Publications

1-Origin, part 1 (#1-5: 20 cent-c, 6,7: 25 cents)			
	.50	1.50	3.00
2-4-Origin, part 2,3,&4	.25	.75	1.50
5-7: 7-Origin & only app. Space Marshal		.50	1.00

RIP HUNTER TIME MASTER (See Showcase #20, 21, 25, 26)
Mar-Apr, 1961-No. 29, Nov-Dec, 1965
National Periodical Publications

Showcase #20 (5-6/59)-Origin & 1st app. Rip Hunter; Moriera-a			
	52.00	156.00	360.00
Showcase #21 (7-8/59)-2nd app. Rip Hunter; Sekowsky-c/a			
	24.00	72.00	165.00
Showcase #25,26 (3-4/60, 5-6/60)-3rd & 4th app. Rip Hunter by			
Kubert	17.00	51.00	120.00
1-(3-4/61)	36.00	108.00	250.00
2	18.00	54.00	125.00
3-5: 5-Last 10 cent issue	11.00	32.00	75.00
6,7-Toth-a in each	8.50	25.50	60.00
8-15	6.00	18.00	42.00
16-20	5.15	15.50	36.00
21-29: 29-G. Kane-c	4.00	12.00	28.00

ROBIN (See Batman #457, Detective, New Teen Titans, Robin II &
   Teen Titans)
Jan, 1991-No. 5, May, 1991 ($1.00, color, mini-series)
DC Comics

1-Free poster by N. Adams; Bolland-c on all			
	2.00	6.00	12.00

Robin #2, © DC Comics

	Good	Fine	N-Mint
1-2nd printing (without poster)	.70	2.00	4.00
1-3rd printing	.35	1.00	2.00
2	.85	2.50	5.00
2-2nd printing		.50	1.00
3-5	.40	1.25	2.50

ROBIN II (The Joker's Wild)
Oct, 1991-No. 4, Dec, 1991 ($1.50, color, mini-series)
DC Comics

1-(Direct sale, $1.50)-With 4 different-c; same hologram on each

	.25	.75	1.50

1-(Newsstand, $1.00)-No hologram; 1 version

		.50	1.00

1-Collector's set ($10.00)-Contains all 5 versions bagged with holo-
gram trading card inside

	3.35	5.00	10.00

2-(Direct sale, $1.50)-With 3 different-c

	.25	.75	1.50

2-4-(Newsstand, $1.00)-1 version of each

		.50	1.00

2-Collector's set ($8.00)-Contains all 4 versions bagged with holo-
gram trading card inside

	1.35	4.00	8.00

3-(Direct sale, $1.50)-With 2 different-c

	.25	.75	1.50

3-Collector's set ($6.00)-Contains all 3 versions bagged with holo-
gram trading card inside

	1.00	3.00	6.00

4-(Direct sale, $1.50)-Only one version

	.25	.75	1.50

4-Collector's set ($4.00)-Contains both versions bagged with Bat-
Signal hologram trading card

	.70	2.00	4.00

Annual 1 (1992, $2.50, 68 pgs.)-Eclipso app.; Kieth-c

	.40	1.25	2.50

	Good	Fine	N-Mint

Deluxe Complete Set ($30.00)-Contains all 14 versions of #1-4 plus a new hologram trading card; numbered & limited to 25,000; comes with slip-case & 2 acid free backing boards

	5.00	15.00	30.00

ROBOCOP
March, 1990-No. 23, Jan, 1992 ($1.50, color)
Marvel Comics

	Good	Fine	N-Mint
1-Based on movie	1.70	5.00	10.00
2	1.00	3.00	6.00
3-6	.60	1.75	3.50
7-10	.35	1.10	2.20
11-20	.30	.90	1.80
21-23	.25	.70	1.40
nn (7/90, $4.95, color, 52 pgs.)-Adapts 1st movie			
	.75	2.25	4.50

ROBOCOP 2
Aug, 1990; Late Aug, 1990-#3, Late Sept, 1990 ($1.00, mini-series)
Marvel Comics

	Good	Fine	N-Mint
nn-(8/90, $4.95, color, 68 pgs.)-Adapts sequel			
	.85	2.50	5.00
1: #1-3 reprint no number issue	.50	1.50	3.00
2,3: 2-Guice-c(i)	.35	1.00	2.00

ROCKETEER ADVENTURE MAGAZINE, THE (Also see Pacific Presents & Starslayer)
July, 1988-No. 2, July, 1989 ($2.00-$2.75, color)
Comico

	Good	Fine	N-Mint
1-Dave Stevens-c/a in all; Kaluta back-up-a			
	1.70	5.00	10.00
2 (7/89, $2.75)-Stevens/Dorman painted-c			
	1.00	3.00	6.00

ROCKETEER SPECIAL EDITION, THE
Nov, 1984 ($1.50, color, Baxter paper)(Chapter 5 of Rocketeer serial)
Eclipse Comics

	Good	Fine	N-Mint
1-Stevens-c/a; Kaluta back-c; pin-ups inside			
	2.50	7.50	15.00

ROCKY LANE WESTERN (Allan Rocky Lane starred in Republic movies & TV (for a short time as Allan Lane, Red Ryder & Rocky Lane)
May, 1949-No. 87, Nov, 1959
Fawcett Publications/Charlton No. 56 on

	Good	Fine	N-Mint
1 (36 pgs.)-Rocky, his stallion Black Jack, & Slim Pickens begin; photo-c begin, end #57; photo back-c	54.00	160.00	375.00
2 (36 pgs.)-Last photo back-c	22.00	65.00	150.00
3-5 (52 pgs.): 4-Captain Tootsie by Beck	16.00	48.00	110.00
6,10 (36 pgs.)	12.00	36.00	85.00
7-9 (52 pgs.)	13.00	40.00	90.00
11-13,15-17 (52 pgs.): 15-Black Jack's Hitching Post begins, ends #25	10.00	30.00	70.00
14,18 (36 pgs.)	8.50	25.50	60.00
19-21,23,24 (52 pgs.): 20-Last Slim Pickens. 21-Dee Dickens begins, ends #55,57,65-68	8.50	25.50	60.00
22,25-28,30 (36 pgs. begin)	8.00	24.00	55.00
29-Classic complete novel "The Land of Missing Men,"-hidden land of ancient temple ruins (r-in #65)	10.00	30.00	70.00
31-40	7.00	21.00	50.00
41-54	5.70	17.00	40.00
55-Last Fawcett issue (1/54)	6.50	19.00	45.00
56-1st Charlton issue (2/54)-Photo-c	8.50	25.50	60.00
57,60-Photo-c	5.70	17.00	40.00
58,59,61-64: 59-61-Young Falcon app. 64-Slim Pickens app.	4.00	12.00	28.00
65-R-/#29, "The Land of Missing Men"	4.30	13.00	30.00
66-68: Reprints #30,31,32	3.60	11.00	25.00
69-78,80-86	3.60	11.00	25.00
79-Giant Edition, 68 pgs.	4.50	14.00	32.00
87-Last issue	4.30	13.00	30.00

ROD CAMERON WESTERN (Movie star)
Feb, 1950-No. 20, April, 1953
Fawcett Publications

	Good	Fine	N-Mint
1-Rod Cameron, his horse War Paint, & Sam The Sheriff begin; photo front/back-c begin	38.00	115.00	265.00
2	19.00	57.00	130.00
3-Novel length story "The Mystery of the Seven Cities of Cibola"	16.00	48.00	110.00

	Good	Fine	N-Mint
4-10: 9-Last photo back-c	12.00	36.00	85.00
11-19	11.00	32.00	75.00
20-Last issue & photo-c	11.50	34.00	80.00

ROGER RABBIT
June, 1990-No. 18, Nov, 1991 ($1.50, color)
Disney Comics

1-All new stories	.50	1.50	3.00
2,3	.30	1.00	2.00
4-18	.25	.75	1.50

ROM
December, 1979-No. 75, Feb, 1986
Marvel Comics Group

1-Based on a Parker Bros. toy; origin/1st app.			
	.40	1.25	2.50
2-5		.60	1.20
6-16: 13-Saga of the Space Knights begins		.50	1.00
17,18-X-Men app.	.40	1.25	2.50
19-24,26-30: 19-X-Men cameo. 24-F.F. cameo; Skrulls, Nova & The New Champions app. 26,27-Galactus app.		.50	1.00
25-Double size		.60	1.20
31-75: 31,32-Brother of Evil Mutants app. 32-X-Men cameo. 34,35-Sub-Mariner app. 41,42-Dr. Strange app. 50-Double size; Skrulls app. 56,57-Alpha Flight app. 58,59-Ant-Man app. 65-West Coast Avengers & Beta Ray Bill app. 65,66-X-Men app.		.50	1.00
Annual 1,4: 1(1982, 52 pgs.). 4(1985, 52 pgs.)		.60	1.20
Annual 2,3: 2(1983, 52 pgs.). 3(1984, 52 pgs.)		.50	1.00

RONIN
July, 1983-No. 6, Apr, 1984 ($2.50, mini-series, 52 pgs.)
DC Comics

1-Miller script, c/a in all	1.00	3.00	6.00
2	.85	2.50	5.00
3-5	.70	2.00	4.00
6-Scarcer	1.35	4.00	8.00

ROOM 222 (TV)
Jan, 1970; No. 2, May, 1970-No. 4, Jan, 1971
Dell Publishing Co.

1-4: 2,4-Photo-c. 3-Marijuana story. 4 r-/#1			
	3.15	9.50	22.00

ROOTS OF THE SWAMPTHING
July, 1986-No. 5, Nov, 1986 ($2.00, Baxter paper, 52 pgs.)
DC Comics

	Good	Fine	N-Mint
1-5: r/Swamp Thing #1-10 by Wrightson & House of Myst.-r; 1-new Wrightson-c(2-5-r). 4-Batman-c/story-r/S.T. #7. 5-r/Swamp Thing #9 & 1st app./House of Secrets #92	.40	1.25	2.50

ROY ROGERS COMICS (...& Trigger #92(8/55)-on)(Roy starred in Republic movies, radio & TV) (Singing cowboy) (See Dale Evans & Queen of the...)
Jan, 1948-No. 145, Sept-Oct, 1961 (#1-19: 36 pgs.)
Dell Publishing Co.

	Good	Fine	N-Mint
1-Roy, his horse Trigger, & Chuck Wagon Charley's Tales begin; photo-c begin, end #145	50.00	150.00	350.00
2	23.00	70.00	160.00
3-5	18.00	54.00	125.00
6-10	13.00	40.00	90.00
11-19: 19-...Charley's Tales ends	9.30	28.00	65.00
20 (52 pgs.)-Trigger feature begins, ends #46	9.30	28.00	65.00
21-30 (52 pgs.)	8.00	24.00	55.00
31-46 (52 pgs.): 37-X-mas-c	6.00	18.00	42.00
47-56 (36 pgs.): 47-Chuck Wagon Charley's Tales returns, ends #133. 49-X-mas-c. 55-Last photo back-c	4.50	14.00	32.00
57 (52 pgs.)-Heroin drug propaganda story	5.30	16.00	38.00
58-70 (52 pgs.): 61-X-mas-c	4.30	13.00	30.00
71-80 (52 pgs.): 73-X-mas-c	3.60	11.00	25.00
81-91 (36 pgs. #81-on): 85-X-mas-c	2.85	8.50	20.00
92-99,101-110,112-118: 92-Title changed to Roy Rogers and Trigger (8/55)	2.85	8.50	20.00
100-Trigger feature returns, ends #133?	4.50	14.00	32.00
111,119-124-Toth-a	5.00	15.00	35.00
125-131: 125-Toth-a (1 pg.)	3.60	11.00	25.00
132-144-Manning-a. 144-Dale Evans featured	4.00	12.00	28.00
145-Last issue	5.00	15.00	35.00

S

SAGA OF RA'S AL GHUL, THE (See Batman #232)
Jan, 1988-No. 4, Apr, 1988 ($2.50, color, mini-series)
DC Comics

	Good	Fine	N-Mint
1-Batman reprints; Neal Adams-a(r) in all	.75	2.25	4.50
2-4: 4-New N. Adams/Nebres-c	.65	1.90	3.75

SAGA OF SWAMP THING, THE (Swamp Thing #39-41,46 on)
May, 1982-Present (Later issues for mature readers; #86 on: $1.50)
DC Comics

	Good	Fine	N-Mint
1-Origin retold; Phantom Stranger series begins; ends #13; Yeates-c/a begins	.25	.75	1.50
2-15: 2-Photo-c from movie		.50	1.00
16-19: Bissette-a. 13-Last Yeates-a	.35	1.00	2.00
20-1st Alan Moore issue	3.15	9.50	22.00
21-New origin	2.85	8.50	20.00
22-25: 24-JLA x-over; Last Yeates-c	1.30	4.00	8.00
26-30	.90	2.75	5.50
31-33: 33-r/1st app. from House of Secrets #92			
	.50	1.50	3.00
34	1.50	4.50	9.00
35,36	.35	1.10	2.25
37-1st app. John Constantine, apps. thru #40			
	1.25	3.75	7.50
38-40: John Constantine app.	.70	2.00	4.00
41-45: 44-Batman cameo	.30	.90	1.75
46-51: 46-Crisis x-over; Batman cameo & John Constantine app. 50-($1.25, 52 pgs.)-Deadman, Dr. Fate, Demon			
	.25	.75	1.50
52-Arkham Asylum-c/story; Joker-c/cameo			
	.50	1.50	3.00
53-($1.25, 52 pgs.)-Arkham Asylum; Batman-c/story			
	.70	2.00	4.00
54-64: 58-Spectre preview. 64-Last Moore issue			
		.60	1.25
65-99,101-126: 65-Direct only begins. 70,76-John Constantine x-over. 79-Superman-c/story. 84-Sandman cameo. 85-Jonah Hex app. 110-Begin $1.75-c	.30	.90	1.80

	Good	Fine	N-Mint
100 ($2.50, 52 pgs.)	.40	1.25	2.50
Annual 1(1982, $1.00)-Movie Adaptation; painted-c	.50		1.00
Annual 2(1985)-Alan Moore scripts, Bissette-a(p)			
	.50	1.50	3.00
Annual 3(1987, $2.00)-New format; Bolland-c			
	.35	1.00	2.00
Annual 4(1988, $2.00)-Batman-c/story	.50	1.50	3.00
Annual 5(1989, $2.95, 68 pgs.)-Batman cameo; re-intro Brother			
Power, 1st app. since 1968	.50	1.50	3.00
Annual 6(1991, $2.95, 68 pgs.)	.50	1.50	3.00

SAGA OF THE ORIGINAL HUMAN TORCH (See Avengers West Coast)
Apr, 1990-No. 4, July, 1990 ($1.50, color, limited series)
Marvel Comics

1-Buckler-c/a(p) in all; origin	.40	1.25	2.50
2-4: 3-Hitler-c	.25	.75	1.50

SAMSON (Becomes Captain Aero #7 on; also see Big 3 Comics)
Fall, 1940-No. 6, Sept, 1941 (See Fantastic Comics)
Fox Features Syndicate

1-Powell-a, signed "Rensie;" Wing Turner by Tuska app; Fine-c?			
	68.00	205.00	475.00
2-Dr. Fung by Powell; Fine-c?	34.00	103.00	240.00
3-Navy Jones app.; Simon-c	27.00	81.00	190.00
4-Yarko the Great, Master Magician by Eisner begins; Fine-c?			
	24.00	70.00	165.00
5,6: 6-Origin The Topper	22.00	65.00	150.00

SANDMAN, THE (See Adventure Comics #40 & World's Finest #3)
Winter, 1974; No. 2, Apr-May, 1975-No. 6, Dec-Jan, 1975-76
National Periodical Publications

1-Kirby-a; Joe Simon scripts	1.00	3.00	6.00
2-6: 6-Kirby/Wood-c/a	.70	2.00	4.00

SANDMAN
Jan, 1989-Present ($1.50, color, mature readers)
DC Comics

1 ($2.00, 52 pgs.)-Gaiman scripts begin; Kieth-a(p)			
	5.00	15.00	35.00

Sandman #3 (3/89), © DC Comics

	Good	Fine	N-Mint
2-Sam Kieth-a(p) in #1-5	3.60	11.00	25.00
3-5: 3-John Constantine app.	2.85	8.50	20.00
6-8: 8-Regular ed. has Jeanette Kahn publishorial & American Cancer Society ad w/no indicia on inside front-c	2.00	6.00	12.00
8-Limited ed. (600+ copies?); has Karen Berger editorial and next issue teaser (has indicia)	16.00	48.00	110.00
9-13	1.25	3.75	7.50
14-($2.50, 52 pgs.)	1.60	4.75	9.50
15-20: 16-Photo-c	.70	2.00	4.00
21-27: Seasons of Mist storyline. 24-Russell-i	.70	2.00	4.00
28-30	.40	1.25	2.50
31-35,37-44	.25	.75	1.50
36-($2.50, 52 pgs.)	.40	1.25	2.50
Special 1('91, $3.50, 68 pgs.)-Glow in the dark-c	.85	2.50	5.00

SAVAGE SHE-HULK, THE (See The Avengers, & The Sensational She-Hulk)
Feb, 1980-No. 25, Feb, 1982
Marvel Comics Group

1-Origin & 1st app. She-Hulk	.85	2.50	5.00
2-10	.40	1.25	2.50
11-25: 25-(52 pgs.)	.35	1.00	2.00

SCOOBY DOO (...Where are you? #1-16,26; ...Mystery Comics
  #17-25,27 on) (TV)
March, 1970-No. 30, Feb, 1975 (Hanna-Barbera)
Gold Key

	Good	Fine	N-Mint
1	3.60	11.00	25.00
2-5	2.15	6.50	15.00
6-10	1.50	4.50	10.00
11-20: 11-Tufts-a	1.00	3.00	7.00
21-30	.70	2.00	4.00

SCOOBY DOO (TV)
April, 1975-No. 11, Dec, 1976 (Hanna Barbera)
Charlton Comics

1	1.70	5.00	12.00
2-5	.85	2.50	5.00
6-11	.70	2.00	4.00

SCOOBY-DOO (TV)
Oct, 1977-No. 9, Feb, 1979 (Hanna-Barbera)
Marvel Comics Group

1-Dyno-Mutt begins	.50	1.50	3.00
2-9	.25	.75	1.50

SEA DEVILS (See Showcase #27-29)
Sept-Oct, 1961-No. 35, May-June, 1967
National Periodical Publications

Showcase #27 (7-8/60)-1st app. Sea Devils

	48.00	145.00	335.00

Showcase #28,29 (9-10/60, 11-12/60)-2nd & 3rd app. Sea Devils

	25.00	75.00	175.00
1-(9-10/61)	34.00	102.00	240.00
2-Last 10 cent issue	15.00	45.00	105.00
3-5: 3-Begin 12 cent issues thru #35	9.30	28.00	65.00
6-10	5.30	16.00	38.00
11,12,14-20	3.70	11.00	26.00
13-Kubert, Colan-a	4.30	13.00	30.00
21-35: 22-Intro. International Sea Devils; origin & 1st app. Capt. X & Man Fish	2.85	8.50	20.00

SECRET AGENT (TV)
Nov, 1966-No. 2, Jan, 1968
Gold Key

	Good	Fine	N-Mint
1,2-Photo-c	3.00	9.00	21.00

SECRET ORIGINS (See 80 Page Giant #8)
Aug-Oct, 1961 (Annual) (Reprints)
National Periodical Publications

1('61)-Origin Adam Strange (Showcase #17), Green Lantern (G.L. #1), Challengers (partial/Showcase #6, 6 pgs. Kirby-a). J'onn J'onzz (Det. #225), The Flash (Showcase #4). Green Arrow (1 pg. text). Superman-Batman team (W. Finest #94). Wonder Woman (Wonder Woman #105)   22.50   67.00   155.00

SECRET ORIGINS
Feb-Mar, 1973-No. 6, Jan-Feb, 1974; No. 7, Oct-Nov, 1974
National Periodical Publications (All origin reprints)

1-Superman (Action #1, 1st time since G.A.), Batman (Batman #33), Ghost (Flash #88), The Flash (Showcase #4)
		1.30	4.00	9.00

2-4: 2-Green Lantern (Showcase #22), Atom (Showcase #34), & Supergirl (Action #252). 3-Wonder Woman (W.W. #1), Wildcat (Sensation #1). 4-Vigilante (Action #42) by Meskin, Kid Eternity (Hit #25)   .70   2.00   4.00

5-7: 5-The Spectre by Baily (More Fun?). 6-Blackhawk (Military #1) & Legion of Super-Heroes (Adv?). 7-Robin (Detective #38), Aquaman (More Fun #73?)   .50   1.50   3.00

SECRET ORIGINS
4/86-No. 50, 8/90 (All origins) (52 pgs. #6 on) (#27 on: $1.50)
DC Comics

1-Origin Superman	.60	1.75	3.50
2-Blue Beetle	.50	1.50	3.00
3-5: 3-Shazam. 4-Firestorm. 5-Crimson Avenger/Shadow/Doll Man			
	.40	1.25	2.50
6-G.A. Batman	.70	2.00	4.00

7-10: 7-Green Lantern (Guy Gardner) /G.A. Sandman. 8-Doll Man. 9-G.A. Flash/Skyman. 10-Phantom Stranger w/Alan Moore scripts; Legends spin-off   .40   1.15   2.25

11,12,14-26: 11-G.A. Hawkman/Power Girl. 12-Challs of Unknown/ G.A. Fury. 14-Suicide Squad; Legends spin-off. 15-Spectre/ Deadman. 16-G.A. Hour-man/Warlord. 17-Adam Strange/Dr.

	Good	Fine	N-Mint

Occult. 18-G.A. Gr. Lantern/The Creeper. 19-Uncle Sam/The Guardian. 20-Batgirl/G.A. Dr. Mid-Nite. 21-Jonah Hex/Black Condor. 22-Manhunters. 23-Floronic Man/Guardians of the Universe. 24-Blue Devil/Dr. Fate. 25-LSH/Atom. 26-Black Lightning/Miss America .35 1.00 2.00

13-Origin Nightwing; Johnny Thunder app. .70 2.00 4.00

27-38,40-44: 27-Zatara/Zatanna. 28-Midnight/Nightshade. 29-Power of the Atom/Mr. America. 30-Plastic Man/Elongated Man. 31-JSA. 32-JLA. 33-35-JLI. 36-Green Lantern/Poison Ivy. 37-Legion Of Substitute Heroes/Doctor Light. 38-Green Arrow/Speedy; Grell scripts. 40-All Ape issue. 41-Rogues Gallery of Flash. 42-Phantom Girl/Grim Ghost. 43-Original Hawk & Dove/Cave Carson/Chris KL-99. 44-Batman app.; story based on Det. #40 .30 .90 1.80

39-Animal Man-c/story continued in Animal Man #10; Grant Morrison scripts; Batman app. .70 2.00 4.00

45-49: 45-Blackhawk/El Diablo. 46-JLA/LSH/New Titans. 47-LSH. 48-Ambush Bug/Stanley & His Monster/Rex the Wonder Dog/Trigger Twins. 49-Newsboy Legion/Silent Knight/brief origin Bouncing Boy .25 .75 1.50

50-($3.95, 100 pgs.)-Batman & Robin in text, Flash of Two Worlds, Johnny Thunder, Dolphin, Black Canary & Space Museum .70 2.00 4.00

Annual 1 (8/87)-Capt. Comet/Doom Patrol .35 1.00 2.00

Annual 2 ('88, $2.00)-Origin Flash II & Flash III .35 1.00 2.00

Annual 3 ('89, $2.95, 84 pgs.)-Teen Titans; 1st app. new Flamebird who replaces original Bat-Girl .50 1.50 3.00

Special 1 (10/89, $2.00)-Batman villains: Penguin, Riddler, & Two-Face; Bolland-c .40 1.25 2.50

SECRET SIX (See Action Comics Weekly)
Apr-May, 1968-No. 7, Apr-May, 1969 (12 cents)
National Periodical Publications

	Good	Fine	N-Mint
1-Origin	3.15	9.50	22.00
2-7	2.00	6.00	14.00

SECRET SOCIETY OF SUPER-VILLAINS
May-June, 1976-No. 15, June-July, 1978
National Periodical Publications/DC Comics

1-Origin; JLA cameo & Capt. Cold app. .25 .75 1.50
2-5: 2-Re-intro/origin Capt. Comet; Gr. Lantern x-over. 5-Green

	Good	Fine	N-Mint
Lantern, Hawkman x-over; Darkseid app.		.60	1.20
6-15: 9,10-Creeper x-over. 11-Capt. Comet; Orlando-i. 15-G.A.			
Atom, Dr. Midnite, & JSA app.		.50	1.00

SECRETS OF HAUNTED HOUSE
4-5/75-#5, 12-1/75-76; #6, 6-7/77-#14, 10-11/78; #15, 8/79-#46, 3/82
National Periodical Publications/DC Comics

	Good	Fine	N-Mint
1		.60	1.20
2-46: 31-Mr. E series begins, ends #41		.50	1.00

SECRETS OF SINISTER HOUSE (Sinister House of Secret Love #1-4)
No. 5, June-July, 1972-No. 18, June-July, 1974
National Periodical Publications

	Good	Fine	N-Mint
5-9: 7-Redondo-a	.25	.75	1.50
10-Neal Adams-a(i)	.50	1.50	3.00
11-18: 17-Barry-a; early Chaykin 1 pg. strip		.50	1.00

SECRETS OF THE LEGION OF SUPER-HEROES
Jan, 1981-No. 3, March, 1981 (Mini-series)
DC Comics

	Good	Fine	N-Mint
1-Origin of the Legion		.60	1.20
2,3: 2-Retells origins of Brainiac 5, Shrinking Violet, Sun-Boy, Bouncing Boy, Ultra-Boy, Matter-Eater Lad, Mon-El, Karate Kid, & Dream Girl		.50	1.00

SECRET WARS II (Also see Marvel Super Heroes...)
July, 1985-No. 9, Mar, 1986 (Maxi-series)
Marvel Comics Group

	Good	Fine	N-Mint
1-Byrne/Austin-c	.30	.90	1.80
2-9: 9-Double sized (75 cents)		.65	1.30

SENSATIONAL SHE-HULK, THE (Also see Savage She-Hulk)
V2#1, 5/89-Present ($1.50, color, deluxe format) (She-Hulk #21 on)
Marvel Comics

	Good	Fine	N-Mint
V2#1-Byrne-c/a(p)/scripts begin, end #8	.50	1.50	3.00
2-8: 4-Reintro G.A. Blonde Phantom	.35	1.10	2.20
9-46: 14-17-Howard the Duck app. 21-23-Return of the Blonde Phantom. 22-All Winners Squad app. 25-Thor app. 26-Excalibur app.; Guice-c. 29-Wolverine app. (3 pgs.). 30-Hobgoblin-c &			

	Good	Fine	N-Mint
cameo. 31-36-Byrne-c/a/ scripts. 36-Begin $1.75-c			
	.30	.90	1.80

SENSATION COMICS (Sensation Mystery #110 on)
Jan, 1942-No. 109, May-June, 1952
National Periodical Publ./All-American

	Good	Fine	N-Mint
1-Origin Mr. Terrific(1st app.), Wildcat(1st app.), The Gay Ghost, & Little Boy Blue; Wonder Woman(cont'd from All Star #8), The Black Pirate begin; intro. Justice & Fair Play Club			
	450.00	1125.00	2700.00
2	170.00	515.00	1200.00
3-W. Woman gets secretary's job	100.00	300.00	700.00
4-1st app. Stretch Skinner in Wildcat	86.00	260.00	600.00
5-Intro. Justin, Black Pirate's son	64.00	193.00	450.00
6-Origin/1st app. Wonder Woman's magic lasso			
	64.00	193.00	450.00
7-10	52.00	155.00	365.00
11,12,14-20	44.00	133.00	310.00
13-Hitler, Tojo, Mussolini-c	50.00	150.00	350.00
21-30	34.00	100.00	235.00
31-33	27.00	81.00	190.00
34-Sargon, the Sorcerer begins, ends #36; begins again #52			
	27.00	81.00	190.00
35-40: 38-Xmas-c	22.00	65.00	155.00
41-50: 43-The Whip app.	19.00	55.00	130.00
51-60: 51-Last Black Pirate. 56,57-Sargon by Kubert			
	16.50	50.00	115.00
61-80: 63-Last Mr. Terrific. 65,66-Wildcat by Kubert. 68-Origin Huntress	16.50	50.00	115.00
81-Used in **SOTI**, pg. 33,34; Krigstein-a	18.00	54.00	125.00
82-90: 83-Last Sargon. 86-The Atom app. 90-Last Wildcat			
	13.00	40.00	90.00
91-Streak begins by Alex Toth	13.00	40.00	90.00
92,93: 92-Toth-a, 2 pgs.	12.00	36.00	85.00
94-1st all girl issue	14.00	43.00	100.00
95-99,101-106: Wonder Woman ends. 99-1st app. Astra, Girl of the Future, ends 106. 105-Last 52 pgs.	14.00	43.00	100.00
100	22.00	65.00	150.00
107-(Scarce)-1st mystery issue; Toth-a	26.00	77.00	180.00
108-(Scarce)-Johnny Peril by Toth(p)	23.00	70.00	160.00
109-(Scarce)-Johnny Peril by Toth(p)	26.00	77.00	180.00

SENSATION MYSTERY (Formerly Sensation #1-109)
No. 110, July-Aug, 1952-No. 116, July-Aug, 1953
National Periodical Publications

	Good	Fine	N-Mint
110-Johnny Peril continues	16.00	48.00	110.00
111-116-Johnny Peril in all	16.00	48.00	110.00

SERGEANT BILKO (Phil Silvers) (TV)
May-June, 1957-No. 18, Mar-Apr, 1960
National Periodical Publications

1	32.00	95.00	225.00
2	20.00	60.00	140.00
3-5	15.00	45.00	105.00
6-18: 11,12,15,17-Photo-c	13.00	40.00	90.00

SGT. BILKO'S PVT. DOBERMAN (TV)
June-July, 1958-No. 11, Feb-Mar, 1960
National Periodical Publications

1	20.00	60.00	140.00
2	13.00	40.00	90.00
3-5: 5-Photo-c	10.00	30.00	70.00
6-11: 6,9-Photo-c	7.00	21.00	50.00

SGT. FURY (& His Howling Commandos)(See Special Marvel
  Edition)
May, 1963-No. 167, Dec, 1981
Marvel Comics Group (BPC earlier issues)

1-1st app. Sgt. Nick Fury (becomes agent of Shield in Strange Tales
  #135; Kirby/Ayers-c/a   40.00   120.00   275.00
2-Kirby-a   18.00   54.00   125.00
3-5: 3-Reed Richards x-over. 4-Death of Junior Juniper. 5-1st Baron
  Strucker app.; Kirby-a   11.00   32.00   75.00
6-10: 8-Baron Zemo, 1st Percival Pinkerton app. 10-1st app. Capt.
  Savage (the Skipper)   8.00   24.00   55.00
11,12,14-20: 14-1st Blitz Squad. 18-Death of Pamela Hawley
                                  4.30   13.00   30.00
13-Captain America & Bucky app.(12/64); 1st Capt. America x-over
  outside The Avengers; Kirby-a 12.00   36.00   85.00
21-30: 25-Red Skull app. 27-1st app. Eric Koenig; origin Fury's eye
  patch   2.65   8.00   18.00
31-50: 34-Origin Howling Commandos. 35-Eric Koenig joins
  Howlers. 43-Bob Hope, Glen Miller app. 44-Flashback-Howlers

	Good	Fine	N-Mint
1st mission	1.70	5.00	12.00

51-100: 64-Capt. Savage & Raiders x-over. 76-Fury's Father app. in
WWI story. 98-Deadly Dozen x-over. 100-Captain America, Fantastic Four cameos; Stan Lee, Martin Goodman & others app.

	Good	Fine	N-Mint
	1.00	3.00	7.00
101-167: 101-Origin retold. 167-reprints #1	.70	2.00	4.00

Annual 1('65, 25 cents, 72 pgs.)-r/#4,5 & new-a

	Good	Fine	N-Mint
	6.50	19.00	45.00
Special 2('66)	2.15	6.50	15.00
Special 3('67)	1.50	4.50	10.00
Special 4('68)	1.15	3.50	8.00
Special 5-7('69-11/71)	.85	2.60	6.00

SGT. ROCK (Formerly Our Army at War; see Brave & the Bold #52)
No. 302, March, 1977-No. 422, July, 1988
National Periodical Publications/DC Comics

	Good	Fine	N-Mint
302	1.15	3.50	8.00
303-310	1.00	3.00	6.00
311-320: 318-Reprints	.70	2.00	4.00
321-350	.50	1.50	3.00

351-422: 422-1st Joe, Adam, Andy Kubert-a team

	Good	Fine	N-Mint
	.25	.75	1.50
Annual 2-4: 2(1982), 3(1983), 4(1984)	.40	1.25	2.50

SGT. ROCK SPECIAL (Sgt. Rock #14 on)
Oct, 1988-No. 21, Feb, 1992 ($2.00, color, quarterly, 52 pgs.)
DC Comics

	Good	Fine	N-Mint
1	.40	1.25	2.50

2-8,10-21: All reprints; 5-r/1st Sgt. Rock/Our Army At War #81. 7-
Tomahawk-r by Thorne. 10-All Rock issue. 11-r/1st Haunted
Tank story. 12-All Kubert issue; begins monthly. 13-Dinosaur
story by Heath(r). 14-Enemy Ace-r (22 pgs.) by Adams/Kubert.
15-Enemy Ace (22 pgs.) by Kubert. 16-Iron Major c/story. 16,17-
Enemy Ace-r. 19-Batman-c/story-r   .35   1.00   2.00

	Good	Fine	N-Mint
9-Enemy Ace-r by Kubert	.40	1.25	2.50

SGT. ROCK'S PRIZE BATTLE TALES (See 80 Page Giant #7)
Winter, 1964 (One Shot) (Giant-80 pgs.)
National Periodical Publications

	Good	Fine	N-Mint
1-Kubert, Heath-r; new Kubert-c	7.00	21.00	50.00

SERGIO ARAGONES' GROO THE WANDERER
March, 1985-Present
Epic Comics (Marvel)

	Good	Fine	N-Mint
1-Aragones-c/a in all	2.85	8.50	20.00
2	1.70	5.00	12.00
3-5	1.50	4.50	9.00
6-10	1.15	3.50	7.00
11-20	.85	2.50	5.00
21-26	.60	1.80	3.60
27,28,30-35	.45	1.35	2.70
29	.75	2.25	4.50
36-49	.30	.90	1.80
50-65: 50-($1.50, double size)	.25	.70	1.40
66-86: 86-$1.25-c		.60	1.20
87-96: 87-Begin $2.25, direct sale only, high quality paper issues			
	.40	1.15	2.30

SHADE, THE CHANGING MAN
June-July, 1977-No. 8, Aug-Sept, 1978 (Also see Suicide Squad #16)
National Periodical Publications/DC Comics

1-Ditko-c/a in all	.60	1.75	3.50
2-8	.35	1.00	2.00

SHADE, THE CHANGING MAN (2nd series)
July, 1990-Present ($1.50, color, mature readers)
DC Comics

1-($2.50, 52 pgs.)	.40	1.25	2.50
2-16: 6-Preview of World Without End	.30	.90	1.80
17-30: 17-Begin $1.75-c	.30	.90	1.80

SHADOW, THE
Aug, 1964-No. 8, Sept, 1965 (All 12 cents)
Archie Comics (Radio Comics)

1	3.50	10.50	24.00
2-8: 3,4,6,7-The Fly 1 pg. strips. 7-Shield app.			
	2.15	6.50	15.00

SHADOW, THE
Oct-Nov, 1973-No. 12, Aug-Sept, 1975
National Periodical Publications

1-Kaluta-a begins	3.15	9.50	22.00

	Good	Fine	N-Mint
2	1.85	5.50	13.00
3-Kaluta/Wrightson-a	2.40	7.25	17.00
4,6-Kaluta-a ends. 4-Chaykin, Wrightson part-i			
	1.60	4.80	11.00
5,7-12: 11-The Avenger (pulp character) x-over			
	1.00	3.00	7.00

SHADOW, THE
May, 1986-No. 4, Aug, 1986 (Mini-series, mature readers)
DC Comics

1-Chaykin-a in all	1.15	3.50	7.00
2-4	.75	2.25	4.50

SHADOW, THE
Aug, 1987-No. 19, Jan, 1989 ($1.50, mature readers)
DC Comics

1	.50	1.50	3.00
2-19: 7-Rogers-c/a. 13-Death of Shadow. 18-E.C.-c swipe			
	.35	1.00	2.00
Annual 1,2: 1(12/87, $2.25)-Orlando-a 2(12/88, $2.50)			
	.40	1.25	2.50

SHADOW COMICS (Pulp, radio)
March, 1940-V9#5, Aug, 1949
Street & Smith Publications

V1#1-Shadow, Doc Savage, Bill Barnes, Nick Carter, Frank Merriwell, Iron Munro, the Astonishing Man begin			
	235.00	585.00	1400.00
2-The Avenger begins, ends #6; Capt. Fury only app.			
	79.00	235.00	550.00
3(nn-5/40)-Norgil the Magician app.	64.00	193.00	450.00
4,5: 4-The Three Musketeers begins, ends #8. 5-Doc Savage ends			
	54.00	160.00	375.00
6,8,9: 9-Norgil the Magician app.	43.00	130.00	300.00
7-Origin & 1st app. Hooded Wasp & Wasplet; series ends V3#8			
	49.00	150.00	345.00
10-Origin The Iron Ghost, ends #11; The Dead End Kids begins, ends #14	43.00	130.00	300.00
11-Origin The Hooded Wasp & Wasplet retold			
	43.00	130.00	300.00
12-Dead End Kids app.	37.00	110.00	260.00
V2#1,2(11/41): 2-Dead End Kids story	33.00	100.00	230.00

	Good	Fine	N-Mint
3-Origin & 1st app. Supersnipe; series begins; Little Nemo story			
	43.00	130.00	300.00
4,5: 4-Little Nemo story	32.00	95.00	220.00
6-9: 6-Blackstone the Magician app.	29.00	85.00	200.00
10-12: 10-Supersnipe app.	29.00	85.00	200.00
V3#1-12: 10-Doc Savage begins, not in V5#5, V6#10-12, V8#4			
	26.00	77.00	180.00
V4#1-12	24.00	70.00	165.00
V5#1-12	22.00	65.00	150.00
V6#1-11: 9-Intro. Shadow, Jr.	20.00	60.00	140.00
12-Powell-c/a; atom bomb panels	22.00	65.00	150.00
V7#1,2,5,7-9,12: 2,5-Shadow, Jr. app.; Powell-a			
	22.00	65.00	150.00
3,6,11-Powell-c/a	23.00	70.00	160.00
4-Powell-c/a; Atom bomb panels	27.00	80.00	185.00
10(1/48)-Flying Saucer issue; Powell-c/a (2nd of this theme; see			
The Spirit 9/28/47)	29.00	85.00	200.00
V8#1-12-Powell-a. 8-Powell Spider-c/a	23.00	70.00	160.00
V9#1,5-Powell-a	22.00	65.00	150.00
2-4-Powell-c/a	23.00	70.00	160.00

SHADOWMAN
May, 1992-Present ($2.50, color)
Valiant

1	.85	2.50	5.00
2-8	.40	1.25	2.50

SHADOW OF THE BATMAN
Dec, 1985-No. 5, Apr, 1986 ($1.75 cover; mini-series)
DC Comics

1-Detective-r (all have wraparound-c)	1.70	5.00	10.00
2,3,5: 3-Penguin-c & cameo. 5-Clayface app.			
	1.15	3.50	7.00
4-Joker-c/story	1.50	4.50	9.00

SHANNA, THE SHE-DEVIL
Dec, 1972-No. 5, Aug, 1973 (All are 20 cent issues)
Marvel Comics Group

1-1st app. Shanna; Steranko-c; Tuska-a(p)	.70	2.00	4.00
2-Steranko-c; heroin drug story	.50	1.50	3.00
3-5	.35	1.00	2.00

SHAZAM! (TV)(See World's Finest #253)
Feb, 1973-No. 35, May-June, 1978
National Periodical Publications/DC Comics

	Good	Fine	N-Mint
1-1st revival of original Captain Marvel since G.A. (origin retold), by Beck; Capt. Marvel Jr. & Mary Marvel x-over			
	.50	1.50	3.00
2-35: 2,6-Infinity photo-c; re-intro Mr. Mind & Tawney. 4-Origin retold. 5-Capt. Marvel Jr. origin retold. 8-(100 pgs.)-r/Capt. Marvel Jr. by Raboy; origin/C.M. #80; origin Mary Marvel/C.M. #18. 10-Last C.C. Beck issue. 11-Shaffenberger-a begins. 12-17-(All 100 pgs.). 15-Lex Luthor x-over. 25-1st app. Isis. 30-1st DC app. 3 Lt. Marvels. 31-1st DC app. Minuteman. 34-Origin Capt. Nazi & Capt. Marvel Jr. retold	.25	.75	1.50

SHAZAM: THE NEW BEGINNING
Apr, 1987-No. 4, July, 1987 (Mini-series; Legends spin-off)
DC Comics

	Good	Fine
1-New origin Captain Marvel; Marvel Family cameos		
	.60	1.20
2-4: Sivana & Black Adam app.	.50	1.00

SHIELD (Nick Fury & His Agents of...) (Also see Nick Fury)
Feb, 1973-No. 5, Oct, 1973 (All 20 cents)
Marvel Comics Group

	Good	Fine	N-Mint
1-Steranko-c	.75	2.25	4.50
2-Steranko flag-c	.35	1.00	2.00
3-5: 1-5 all contain reprints from Strange Tales #146-155. 3-5-are cover-r; 3-Kirby/Steranko-c(r). 4-Steranko-c(r)			
	.35	1.00	2.00

SHOCK SUSPENSTORIES
Feb-Mar, 1952-No. 18, Dec-Jan, 1954-55
E. C. Comics

	Good	Fine	N-Mint
1-Classic Feldstein electrocution-c; Ray Bradbury adaptation			
	57.00	170.00	400.00
2	34.00	100.00	235.00
3	23.00	70.00	160.00
4-Used in **SOTI**, pg. 387,388	23.00	70.00	160.00
5-Hanging-c	22.00	65.00	150.00
6,7: 6-Classic bondage-c. 7-Classic face melting-c			
	27.00	81.00	190.00

	Good	**Fine**	**N-Mint**
8-Williamson-a	23.00	70.00	160.00

9-11: 9-Injury to eye panel. 10-Junkie story

	19.00	57.00	130.00

12-"The Monkey"-classic junkie cover/story; drug propaganda issue

	22.00	65.00	155.00

13-Frazetta's only solo story for E.C., 7 pgs.

	27.00	81.00	190.00

14-Used in Senate Investigation hearings	14.00	43.00	100.00

15-Used in 1954 Reader's Digest article, "For the Kiddies to Read"

	14.00	43.00	100.00

| 16-"Red Dupe" editorial; rape story | 13.00 | 40.00 | 90.00 |
| 17,18 | 13.00 | 40.00 | 90.00 |

SHOGUN WARRIORS
Feb, 1979-No. 20, Sept, 1980 (Based on Mattel toys)
Marvel Comics Group

1-Raydeen, Combatra, & Dangard Ace begin			
	.50	1.50	3.00
2-10	.35	1.00	2.00
11-20: 11-Austin-c. 12-Simonson-c	.25	.75	1.50

Showcase #8, © DC Comics

SHOWCASE
3-4/56-No. 93, 9/70; No. 94, 8-9/77-No. 104, 9/78
National Periodical Publications/DC Comics

	Good	Fine	N-Mint
1-Fire Fighters	150.00	450.00	1050.00

2-King of the Wild; Kubert-a (animal stories)

	Good	Fine	N-Mint
	52.00	156.00	360.00
3-The Frogmen	43.00	130.00	300.00

	Good	Fine	VF-NM

4-Origin/1st app. The Flash (1st DC Silver Age hero, Sept-Oct, 1956) & The Turtle; Kubert-a; reprinted in Secret Origins #1 ('61 & '73)

	Good	Fine	VF-NM
	750.00	3000.00	7500.00

	Good	Fine	N-Mint
5-Manhunters	60.00	180.00	420.00

6-Origin/1st app. Challengers of the Unknown by Kirby, partly r-/in Secret Origins #1 & Challengers #64,65 (1st DC Silver Age super-hero team)

	150.00	450.00	1050.00

7-Challengers of the Unknown by Kirby r-in/Challengers of the Unknown #75

	82.00	245.00	575.00

	Good	Fine	VF-NM

8-The Flash; origin & 1st app. Capt. Cold

	300.00	900.00	2100.00

	Good	Fine	N-Mint

9-Lois Lane (Pre-#1, 7-8/57) (1st Showcase character to win own series)

	122.00	365.00	850.00
10-Lois Lane; Jor-el cameo	103.00	310.00	725.00

11,12-Challengers of the Unknown by Kirby

	72.00	215.00	500.00
13-The Flash; origin Mr. Element	200.00	600.00	1400.00

14-The Flash; origin Dr. Alchemy, former Mr. Element

	200.00	600.00	1400.00
15-Space Ranger (1st app., 7-8/58)	72.00	215.00	500.00
16-Space Ranger	47.00	140.00	325.00

17-Adventures on Other Worlds; origin/1st app. Adam Strange (11-12/58)

	103.00	310.00	720.00

18-Adventures on Other Worlds (A. Strange)

	55.00	165.00	380.00

19-Adam Strange; 1st Adam Strange logo

	55.00	165.00	380.00

20-Origin & 1st app. Rip Hunter (5-6/59); Moriera-a

	52.00	155.00	360.00
21-Rip Hunter; Sekowsky-c/a	24.00	72.00	165.00

22-Origin & 1st app. Silver Age Green Lantern by Gil Kane (9-10/59); reprinted in Secret Origins #2

	265.00	795.00	1850.00

	Good	Fine	N-Mint
23,24-Green Lantern. 23-Nuclear explosion-c			
	92.00	275.00	640.00
25,26-Rip Hunter by Kubert	17.00	51.00	120.00
27-1st app. Sea Devils (7-8/60); Heath-c/a			
	48.00	145.00	335.00
28,29-Sea Devils; Heath-c/a	25.00	75.00	175.00
30-Origin Silver Age Aquaman (1-2/61) (see Adventure #260 for 1st S.A. origin)	47.00	140.00	330.00
31-33-Aquaman	24.00	72.00	165.00
34-Origin & 1st app. Silver Age Atom by Kane & Anderson (9-10/61); reprinted in Secret Origins #2			
	106.00	320.00	740.00
35-The Atom by Gil Kane; last 10 cent issue			
	57.00	170.00	400.00
36-The Atom by Gil Kane (1-2/62)	43.00	130.00	300.00
37-1st app. Metal Men (3-4/62)	43.00	130.00	300.00
38-40-Metal Men	25.00	75.00	175.00
41,42-Tommy Tomorrow (parts 1&2). 42-Origin			
	7.00	21.00	50.00
43-Dr. No (James Bond); Nodel-a; (1st DC Silver Age movie adaptation) (based on Ian Fleming novel & movie)			
	36.00	108.00	250.00
44-Tommy Tomorrow	5.00	15.00	35.00
45-Sgt. Rock; origin retold; Heath-c	11.50	34.00	80.00
46,47-Tommy Tomorrow	3.60	11.00	25.00
48,49-Cave Carson	2.65	8.00	18.00
50,51-I Spy (Danger Trail-r by Infantino), King Farady story (#50 is not a reprint)	3.15	9.50	22.00
52-Cave Carson	2.65	8.00	18.00
53,54-G.I. Joe; Heath-a	2.85	8.50	20.00
55-Dr. Fate & Hourman. (3-4/65)-Origin of each in text; 1st solo app. G.A. Green Lantern in Silver Age (pre-dates Gr. Lantern #40); 1st S.A. app. Solomon Grundy	8.00	24.00	55.00
56-Dr. Fate & Hourman	3.60	11.00	25.00
57,58-Enemy Ace by Kubert	5.70	17.00	40.00
59-Teen Titans (3rd app., 11-12/65)	8.00	24.00	55.00
60-1st Silver Age app. The Spectre; Anderson-a (1-2/66); origin in text	11.50	34.00	80.00
61,64-The Spectre by Anderson	5.70	17.00	40.00
62-Origin & 1st app. Inferior Five (5-6/66)			
	5.00	15.00	35.00
63,65-Inferior Five	2.65	8.00	18.00

	Good	Fine	N-Mint
66,67-B'wana Beast	1.15	3.50	8.00
68,69,71-Maniaks	1.15	3.50	8.00
70-Binky (9-10/67)-Tryout issue	1.15	3.50	8.00
72-Top Gun (Johnny Thunder-r)-Toth-a	1.15	3.50	8.00
73-Origin/1st app. Creeper; Ditko-c/a (3-4/67)			
	6.50	19.00	45.00
74-Intro/1st app. Anthro; Post-c/a (5-6/67)	5.00	15.00	35.00
75-Origin/1st app. Hawk & the Dove; Ditko-c/a			
	7.00	21.00	50.00
76-1st app. Bat Lash (9-10/67)	2.85	8.50	20.00
77-1st app. Angel & The Ape	3.60	11.00	25.00
78-Jonny Double	1.50	4.50	10.00
79-Dolphin; Aqualad origin-r	2.15	6.50	15.00
80-Phantom Stranger-r; Neal Adams-c	1.15	3.50	8.00
81-Windy & Willy	.85	2.60	6.00
82-1st app. Nightmaster by Grandenetti & Giordano; Kubert-c			
	4.70	14.00	33.00
83,84-Nightmaster by Wrightson w/Jones/Kaluta ink assist in each; Kubert-c. 84-Origin retold; last 12 cent-c?			
	4.70	14.00	33.00
85-87-Firehair; Kubert-a	1.15	3.50	8.00
88-90-Jason's Quest: 90-Manhunter 2070 app.			
	.70	2.00	4.00
91-93-Manhunter 2070; origin-92	.70	2.00	4.00
94-Intro/origin new Doom Patrol & Robotman			
	.85	2.60	6.00
95,96-The Doom Patrol. 95-Origin Celsius	.50	1.50	3.00
97-99-Power Girl; origin-97,98; JSA cameos			
	.50	1.50	3.00
100-(52 pgs.)-Most Showcase characters featured			
	.50	1.50	3.00
101-103-Hawkman; Adam Strange x-over	.50	1.50	3.00
104-(52 pgs.)-O.S.S. Spies at War	.50	1.50	3.00

SILVER SABLE AND THE WILD PACK (See Amazing Spider-Man #265)
June, 1992-Present ($1.25, color)
Marvel Comics

	Good	Fine	N-Mint
1-($2.00)-Embossed, silver foil stamped-c; Spidey app.			
	.35	1.00	2.00
2-6		.65	1.30

SILVER STREAK COMICS
Dec, 1939-No. 21, May, 1942; No. 22-24, 1946 (Silver logo-#1-5)
Your Guide Publs. No. 1-7/New Friday Publs. No. 8-17/Comic House
   Publ./Newsbook Publ.

	Good	Fine	VF-NM
1-(Scarce)-Intro The Claw by Cole (r-/in Daredevil #21), Red Reeves, Boy Magician, & Captain Fearless; The Wasp, Mister Midnight begin; Spirit Man app. Silver metallic-c begin, end #5	435.00	1085.00	2600.00

	Good	Fine	N-Mint
2-The Claw by Cole; Simon c/a	171.00	515.00	1200.00
3-1st app. & origin Silver Streak (2nd with lightning speed); Dickie Dean the Boy Inventor, Lance Hale, Ace Powers, Bill Wayne, & The Planet Patrol begin	143.00	430.00	1000.00
4-Sky Wolf begins; Silver Streak by Jack Cole (new costume); 1st app. Jackie, Lance Hale's sidekick	79.00	235.00	550.00
5-Jack Cole c/a(2)	93.00	280.00	650.00

	Good	Fine	VF-NM
6-(Scarce)-Origin & 1st app. Daredevil (blue & yellow costume) by Jack Binder; The Claw returns; classic Cole Claw-c	350.00	875.00	2100.00
7-Claw vs. Daredevil (new costume-blue & red) by Jack Cole & 3 other Cole stories (38 pgs.)	240.00	605.00	1450.00

	Good	Fine	N-Mint
8-Claw vs. Daredevil by Cole; last Cole Silver Streak	121.00	365.00	850.00
9-Claw vs. Daredevil by Cole	93.00	280.00	650.00
10-Origin Captain Battle; Claw vs. Daredevil by Cole	82.00	245.00	575.00
11-Intro. Mercury by Bob Wood, Silver Streak's sidekick; conclusion Claw vs. Daredevil by Rico	57.00	171.00	400.00
12-14: 13-Origin Thun-Dohr	47.00	140.00	330.00
15-17-Last Daredevil issue	43.00	130.00	300.00
18-The Saint begins; by Leslie Charteris	36.00	107.00	250.00
19-21(1942): 20,21 have Wolverton's Scoop Scuttle	24.00	70.00	165.00
22,24(1946)-Reprints	14.00	43.00	100.00
23-Reprints?; bondage-c	14.00	43.00	100.00

SILVER SURFER, THE (See Fantastic Four, Fantasy Masterpieces
   V2#1, Marvel Presents #8, Marvel's Greatest Comics & Tales To
   Astonish #92)
Aug, 1968-No. 18, Sept, 1970; June, 1982 (No. 1-7: 68 pgs.)
Marvel Comics Group

	Good	Fine	N-Mint
1-More detailed origin by John Buscema (p); The Watcher back-up			
stories begin (origin), end #7	36.00	108.00	250.00
2	12.00	36.00	85.00
3-1st app. Mephisto	11.00	32.00	75.00
4-Low distribution; Thor & Loki app.	37.00	110.00	260.00
5-7-Last giant size. 5-The Stranger app. 6-Brunner inks. 7-1st app.			
Frankenstein's monster (cameo); Brunner-c			
	37.00	110.00	260.00
8-10: 8-18-(15 cent issues)	5.70	17.00	40.00
11-13,15-18: 15-Silver Surfer vs. Human Torch; Fantastic Four app.			
18-Vs. The Inhumans; Kirby-c/a	4.30	13.00	30.00
14-Spider-Man x-over	5.70	17.00	40.00
V2#1 (6/82, 52 pgs.)-Byrne-c/a	1.70	5.00	10.00

SILVER SURFER, THE
V3#1, July, 1987-Present
Marvel Comics Group

	Good	Fine	N-Mint
V3#1-Double size ($1.25)	1.70	5.00	10.00
2	.70	2.00	4.00
3-10	.40	1.25	2.50
11-14	.35	1.00	2.00
15-Ron Lim-c/a begins (9/88)	1.70	5.00	10.00
16,17	1.00	3.00	6.00
18-20	.70	2.00	4.00
21-24,26-30,33,37,39-43	.35	1.00	2.00
25,31 ($1.50, 52 pgs.): 25-Skrulls app.	.40	1.25	2.50
32,39-No Ron Lim-c/a	.25	.75	1.50
34-Thanos returns (cameo); Starlin scripts begin			
	2.00	6.00	12.00
35-1st full Thanos app. in Silver Surfer	2.00	6.00	12.00
36-Recaps history of Thanos; Capt. Marvel & Warlock app.			
	1.15	3.50	7.00
38-Silver Surfer battles Thanos	1.35	4.00	8.00
44,45,49-Thanos stories (c-44,45)	.50	1.50	3.00
46,47-Return of Adam Warlock	1.35	4.00	8.00
48-Last Starlin scripts	.35	1.00	2.00
50-($1.50, 52 pgs.)-Silver Surfer battles Thanos; embossed silver			
foil stamped-c; thick cover stock	1.50	4.50	9.00
50-2nd printing	.50	1.50	3.00
51-53: Infinity Gauntlet x-over	.50	1.50	3.00
54-57: Infinity Gauntlet x-overs. 54-Rhino app. 55,56-Thanos-c &			
app. 57-Thanos-c & cameo	.40	1.25	2.50

	Good	Fine	N-Mint
58,59: Infinity Gauntlet x-overs; Thanos joins. 58-Ron Lim-c only. 59-Thanos battles Silver Surfer-c/story			
	.70	2.00	4.00
60-66	.25	.75	1.50
67-69: Infinity War x-over	.25	.75	1.50
70-74		.65	1.30
Annual 1 (1988, $1.75)-Evolutionary War x-over; 1st Ron Lim-a on this title	1.15	3.50	7.00
Annual 2 ('89, $2.00, 68 pgs.)-Atlantis Attacks; Lim-c/a			
	.40	1.25	2.50
Annual 3 (1990, $2.00, 68 pgs.)	.40	1.25	2.50
Annual 4 (1991, $2.00, 68 pgs.)-3 pg. origin story; Silver Surfer battles the Guardians of the Galaxy	.40	1.25	2.50
Annual 5 (1992, $2.25, 68 pgs.)-New Defenders app.			
	.40	1.25	2.50

SILVER SURFER, THE
Dec, 1988-No. 2, Jan, 1989 ($1.00, limited series)
Epic Comics (Marvel)

1,2: By Stan Lee (scripts) & Moebius (art)	.35	1.00	2.00

SINISTER HOUSE OF SECRET LOVE, THE (Secrets of Sinister... #5 on)
Oct-Nov, 1971-No. 4, Apr-May, 1972
National Periodical Publications

1	.35	1.00	2.00
2-4: 2-Jeff Jones-c. 3-Toth-a, 36 pgs.		.50	1.00

SKULL, THE SLAYER
August, 1975-No. 8, Nov, 1976
Marvel Comics Group

1-Origin; Gil Kane-c	.25	.75	1.50
2-8: 2-Gil Kane-c. 8-Kirby-c		.50	1.00

SLEEPWALKER
June, 1991-Present ($1.00-$1.25, color)
Marvel Comics

1-1st app?	.50	1.50	3.00
2-5: 4-Williamson-i. 5-Spider-Man-c/story	.35	1.00	2.00
6-10: 7-Infinity Gauntlet x-over. 8-Vs. Deathlok			
	.25	.75	1.50
11-18: 11-Ghost Rider-c/story		.65	1.30

SMASH COMICS
Aug, 1939-No. 85, Oct, 1949
Quality Comics Group

	Good	Fine	N-Mint
1-Origin Hugh Hazard & His Iron Man, Bozo the Robot, Espionage, Starring Black X by Eisner, & Invisible Justice; Chic Carter & Wings Wendall begin	86.00	257.00	600.00
2-The Lone Star Rider app; Invisible Hood gains power of invisibility	39.00	118.00	275.00
3-Captain Cook & John Law begin	27.00	80.00	185.00
4,5: 4-Flash Fulton begins	24.00	73.00	170.00
6-12: 12-One pg. Fine-a	20.00	60.00	140.00
13-Magno begins; last Eisner issue; The Ray app. in full page ad; The Purple Trio begins	20.00	60.00	140.00
14-Intro. The Ray by Lou Fine & others	121.00	365.00	850.00
15,16	57.00	171.00	400.00
17-Wun Cloo becomes plastic super-hero by Jack Cole (9 months before Plastic Man)	57.00	171.00	400.00
18-Midnight by Jack Cole begins (origin)	68.00	205.00	475.00
19-22: Last Fine Ray; The Jester begins-#22	41.00	122.00	285.00
23,24: 24-The Sword app.; last Chic Carter; Wings Wendall dons new costume #24,25	34.00	103.00	240.00
25-Origin Wildfire	41.00	122.00	285.00
26-30: 28-Midnight-c begin	32.00	95.00	220.00
31,32,34: Ray by Rudy Palais; also #33	24.00	70.00	165.00
33-Origin The Marksman	29.00	85.00	200.00
35-37	24.00	70.00	165.00
38-The Yankee Eagle begins; last Midnight by Cole	24.00	70.00	165.00
39,40-Last Ray issue	19.00	57.00	130.00
41,43-50	8.50	25.50	60.00
42-Lady Luck begins by Klaus Nordling	10.00	30.00	70.00
51-60	7.00	21.00	50.00
61-70	6.00	18.00	42.00
71-85	5.30	16.00	38.00

SOLAR (Man of the Atom; also see Doctor Solar)
Sept, 1991-Present ($1.75, color, 44 pgs.)
Valiant

	Good	Fine	N-Mint
1-Layton-i on Solar; Barry Windsor-Smith-c/a	1.25	3.75	7.50

	Good	Fine	N-Mint
2-Layton-i on Solar, Smith-a in all	.70	2.00	4.00
3-7 (#5-7: $1.95-c)	.40	1.25	2.50
8,9,11-16: 8-Begin $2.25-c	.40	1.15	2.30
10-($3.95)-Black embossed-c; 1st app. Eternal Warrior			
	1.70	5.00	10.00
10-2nd printing ($3.95)	.70	2.00	4.00

SOLO AVENGERS (Becomes Avengers Spotlight #21 on)
Dec, 1987-No. 20, July, 1989 (75 cents-$1.00)
Marvel Comics

1-Jim Lee-a on back-up story	.35	1.00	2.00
2-5		.60	1.20
6-20: 11-Intro Bobcat		.50	1.00

SON OF SATAN (Also see Marvel Spotlight #12)
Dec, 1975-No. 8, Feb, 1977
Marvel Comics Group

1-Mooney-a; Kane-c(p), Starlin splash(p)	.70	2.00	4.00
2-8: 2-Origin The Possessor. 8-Heath-a	.40	1.25	2.50

SPACE FAMILY ROBINSON (TV)(...Lost in Space #15-36;
    becomes Lost in Space #37 on)
Dec, 1962-No. 36, Oct, 1969 (All painted covers)
Gold Key

1-(Low distribution); Spiegle-a in all	20.00	60.00	140.00
2(3/63)-Family becomes lost in space	8.00	24.00	55.00
3-10: 6-Captain Venture begins	4.70	14.00	33.00
11-20	2.85	8.50	20.00
21-36	1.85	5.50	13.00

SPACE GHOST (TV) (Also see Hanna-Barbera Super TV Heroes
    #3-7)
March, 1967 (Hanna-Barbera) (TV debut was 9/10/66)
Gold Key

1 (10199-703)-Spiegle-a	19.30	58.00	135.00

SPAWN
July, 1992-Present ($1.95, color)
Image Comics

1-Todd McFarlane-c/a begins	.50	1.50	3.00
1-2nd printing	.35	1.00	2.00
2-4	.35	1.00	2.00

SPECIAL EDITION COMICS
1940 (August) (One Shot, 68 pgs.)
Fawcett Publications

	Good	Fine	VF-NM
1-1st book devoted entirely to Captain Marvel; C.C. Beck-c/a; only app. of Capt. Marvel with belt buckle; Capt. Marvel apps. with button-down flap; 1st story (came out before Captain Marvel #1)	335.00	1000.00	2500.00

SPECIAL EDITION X-MEN
Feb, 1983 (One Shot) (Baxter paper, $2.00)
Marvel Comics Group

	Good	Fine	N-Mint
1-r/Giant-Size X-Men #1 plus one new story	2.00	6.00	12.00

SPECIAL MARVEL EDITION (Master of Kung Fu #17 on)
Jan, 1971-No. 16, Feb, 1974
Marvel Comics Group

1-Thor-r by Kirby; 68 pgs.	.85	2.50	5.00
2-4: Thor-r by Kirby; 68 pg. Giant	.70	2.00	4.00
5-14: Sgt. Fury-r; 11-Reprints Sgt. Fury #13 (Captain America app.)	.60	1.75	3.50
15-Master of Kung Fu (Shang-Chi) begins (1st app., 12/73); Starlin-a; origin/1st app. Nayland Smith & Dr. Petric	4.00	12.00	28.00
16-1st app. Midnight; Starlin-a (2nd Shang-Chi)	2.85	8.50	20.00

SPECIAL MISSIONS (See G.I. Joe...)

SPECTACULAR SPIDER-MAN, THE (Magazine)
July, 1968-No. 2, Nov, 1968 (35 cents)
Marvel Comics Group

1-(Black & White)	6.50	19.00	45.00
2-(Color)-Green Goblin-c & 40 pg. story; Romita painted-c (reprinted in King Size Spider-Man #9)	9.30	28.00	65.00

SPECTACULAR SPIDER-MAN, THE (Peter Parker...#54-132,134)
Dec, 1976-Present
Marvel Comics Group

1-Origin retold; return of Tarantula	5.30	16.00	38.00

The Spectacular Spider-Man #4, © Marvel Comics

	Good	Fine	N-Mint
2-Kraven the Hunter app.	2.15	6.50	15.00
3-5: 4-Vulture app.	1.60	4.80	11.00
6-10: 6-8-Morbius app. 9,10-White Tiger app.			
	1.70	5.00	10.00
11-20: 17,18-Champions cameo (Ghost Rider)			
	1.00	3.00	6.00
21,24-26: 21-Scorpion app. 26-Daredevil app.			
	.85	2.50	5.00
22,23-Moon Knight app.	1.35	4.00	8.00
27-Miller's 1st art on Daredevil (7/79); also see Captain America			
#235	2.30	7.00	16.00
28-Miller Daredevil (p)	1.85	5.50	13.00
29-55,57,59: 33-Origin Iguana. 38-Morbius app.			
	.70	2.00	4.00
56-1st Spider-Man/Jack O'Lantern battle (7/81)			
	1.35	4.00	8.00
58-Byrne-a(p)	.85	2.50	5.00
60-Double size; origin retold with new facts revealed			
	.70	2.00	4.00
61-63,65-68,71-74: 65-Kraven the Hunter app.			
	.50	1.50	3.00
64-1st app. Cloak & Dagger (3/82)	2.65	8.00	16.00
69,70-Cloak & Dagger app.	1.50	4.50	9.00
75-Double size	.70	2.00	4.00
76-80: 79-Punisher cameo	.50	1.50	3.00
81,82-Punisher, Cloak & Dagger app.	2.30	7.00	14.00

	Good	Fine	N-Mint
83-Origin Punisher retold	3.00	9.00	18.00

84,86-99: 90-Spider-man's new black costume, last panel (ties w/Amazing Spider-Man #252 & Marvel Team-Up #141). 94-96-Cloak & Dagger app. 98-Intro The Spot .50   1.50   3.00

85-Hobgoblin(Ned Leeds) app. (12/83); gains powers of original Green Goblin (see Amazing Spider-Man #238)

	3.60	11.00	25.00
100-(3/85)-Double size	.70	2.00	4.00

101-115,117,118,120-129: 107-110-Death of Jean DeWolff. 111-Secret Wars II tie-in. 128-Black Cat new costume

	.40	1.25	2.50
116,119-Sabretooth-c/story	.85	2.50	5.00
130-Hobgoblin app.	.70	2.00	4.00
131-Six part Kraven tie-in	1.00	3.00	6.00
132-Kraven tie-in	.85	2.50	5.00
133-139: 139-Origin Tombstone	.35	1.00	2.00
140-Punisher cameo app.	.50	1.50	3.00
141-Punisher app.	1.35	4.00	8.00
142,143-Punisher app.	.85	2.50	5.00
144-146,148-157: 151-Tombstone returns	.35	1.00	2.00
147-1st app. new Hobgoblin (Macendale)	2.50	7.50	15.00

158-Spider-Man gets new powers (1st Cosmic Spidey, continued in Web of Spider-Man #59) 2.00   6.00   12.00

	1.35	4.00	8.00
159-Cosmic Spider-Man app.	1.35	4.00	8.00

160-170: 161-163-Hobgoblin app. 168-170-Avengers x-over. 169-1st app. The Outlaws .25   .75   1.50

171-184: 180,181,183,184-Green Goblin app.		.50	1.00
185-188,190-196: 185-Begin $1.25-c		.65	1.30

189-($2.95, 52 pgs.)-30th anniversary issue; hologram on-c; gatefold Hobgoblin poster; origin retold; Green Goblin story

	.50	1.50	3.00

Annuals 1-7: 1(1979). 2(1980)-Origin/1st app. Rapier. 3(1981)-Last Man-Wolf. 4(1984). 5(1985). 6(1985). 7(1987)

	.50	1.50	3.00

Annual 8 ('88, $1.75)-Evolutionary War x-over

	.70	2.00	4.00

Annual 9 ('89, $2.00, 68 pgs.)-Atlantis Attacks

	.50	1.50	3.00

Annual 10 ('90, $2.00, 68 pgs.)-McFarlane-a

	.40	1.25	2.50

Annual 11 ('91, $2.00, 68 pgs.)-Iron Man app.

	.35	1.00	2.00

	Good	Fine	N-Mint

Annual 12 ('92, $2.25, 68 pgs.)-Venom back-up story

| | .40 | 1.15 | 2.30 |

SPECTRE, THE (See Adventure Comics #431 & Showcase)
Nov-Dec, 1967-No. 10, May-June, 1969 (All 12 cents)
National Periodical Publications

Showcase #60 (1-2/66)-1st Silver Age app. The Spectre; Anderson-a;			
origin in text	11.50	34.00	80.00
Showcase #61,64 (3-4/66, 9-10/66)-2nd & 3rd app. The Spectre by			
Anderson	5.70	17.00	40.00
1-(11-12/67)-Anderson-c/a	6.50	19.00	45.00
2-5-Neal Adams-c/a; 3-Wildcat x-over	4.70	14.00	33.00
6-8,10: 6-8-Anderson inks. 7-Hourman app.			
	2.15	6.50	15.00
9-Wrightson-a	2.65	8.00	18.00

SPECTRE, THE (See Saga of Swamp Thing #58)
Apr, 1987-No. 31, Oct, 1989 ($1.00, new format)
DC Comics

1-Colan-a(p) begins	.40	1.25	2.50
2-10: 9-Nudity panels	.25	.75	1.50
11-31: 10-Batman cameo. 10,11-Millennium tie-ins	.60		1.25
Annual 1 (1988, $2.00)-Deadman app.	.35	1.00	2.00

SPEED COMICS (New Speed)
10/39-#11, 8/40; #12, 3/41-#44, 1-2/47 (#14-16: pocket size, 100 pgs.)
Brookwood Publ./Speed Publ./Harvey Publications No. 14 on

1-Origin Shock Gibson; Ted Parrish, the Man with 1000 Faces			
begins; Powell-a	93.00	280.00	650.00
2-Powell-a	47.00	140.00	325.00
3	29.00	86.00	200.00
4,5: 4-Powell-a?	24.00	73.00	170.00
6-11: 7-Mars Mason begins, ends #11	20.00	60.00	140.00
12 (3/41; shows #11 in indicia)-The Wasp begins; Major Colt app.			
(Capt. Colt #12)	24.00	73.00	170.00
13-Intro. Captain Freedom & Young Defenders; Girl Commandos,			
Pat Parker, War Nurse begins; Major Colt app.			
	29.00	86.00	200.00
14-16 (100 pg. pocket size, 1941): 15-Pat Parker dons costume, last in			
costume #23; no Girl Commandos	23.00	70.00	160.00
17-Black Cat begins (reprints origin); not in #40,41			
	37.00	110.00	260.00

	Good	Fine	N-Mint
18-20	19.00	58.00	135.00
21,22,25-30: 26-Flag-c	17.00	51.00	120.00
23-Origin Girl Commandos	25.00	75.00	175.00
24-Pat Parker team-up with Girl Commandos			
	17.00	51.00	120.00
31-44: 38-Flag-c	14.00	43.00	100.00

SPIDER-MAN (See Amazing..., Marvel Tales, Marvel Team-Up,
   Spectacular..., Spidey Super Stories, & Web Of...)
Aug, 1990-Present ($1.75, color)
Marvel Comics

1-Silver edition, direct sale only (unbagged)
                                        1.70   4.00   8.00

1-Silver bagged edition; direct sale, no price on comic, but $2.00 on
   plastic bag (still sealed)(125,000 print run)
    4.15   12.50   25.00

1-Regular edition w/Spidey face in UPC area (unbagged); green-c
    .85   2.50   5.00

1-Regular bagged edition w/Spidey face in UPC area (price is for
   still sealed only); green cover (125,000)
    2.50   7.50   15.00

1-Newsstand bagged w/UPC code (sealed)
    1.15   3.50   7.00

1-Gold edition, 2nd printing (unbagged) with Spider-Man in box
   (400,000-450,000)   1.15   3.50   7.00

1-Gold 2nd printing w/UPC code; sold in Wal-Mart; not scarce
    1.00   3.00   6.00

1-Platinum ed. mailed to retailers only (10,000 print run); has new
   McFarlane-a & editorial material instead of ads; stiff-c, no cover
   price   50.00 150.00 350.00

2-McFarlane-c/a/scripts continue   1.00   3.00   6.00

3-5   .70   2.00   4.00

6,7-Ghost Rider & Hobgoblin app.   1.00   3.00   6.00

8-Wolverine cameo; Wolverine storyline begins
    .50   1.50   3.00

9-12: 12-Wolverine storyline ends   .50   1.50   3.00

13-15,18-25,27-30: 13,14-Spidey in black costume. 15-Larsen-c/a;
   Beast-c/story. 18-Ghost Rider-c/story. 19-Hulk & Hobgoblin-c &
   app. 21-Deathlok app. 22-Ghost Rider, Deathlok, Hobgoblin,
   Hulk app.   .30   .90   1.80

16-X-Force-c/story w/Liefeld assists; continues in X-Force #4; reads
   sideways   .40   1.25   2.50

	Good	Fine	N-Mint
17-Thanos-c/story; Williamson-c/a(i)	.40	1.25	2.50
26-(3.50)-Hologram on-c; 3-part gatefold poster; 30th anniversary issue; origin retold	.60	1.75	3.50

SPIDER-MAN AND DAREDEVIL
March, 1984 ($2.00, one-shot, deluxe paper)
Marvel Comics Group

1-r/Spectacular Spider-Man #26-28 by Miller			
	.50	1.50	3.00

SPIDER-MAN AND HIS AMAZING FRIENDS
Dec, 1981 (One shot) (See Marvel Action Universe)
Marvel Comics Group

1-Adapted from NBC TV cartoon show; Green Goblin-c/story; 1st Spidey, Firestar, Iceman team-up; Spiegle-p			
	.35	1.00	2.00

SPIDER-MAN VS. WOLVERINE
Feb, 1987 (One-shot); V2#1, 1990 (Both have 68 pgs.)
Marvel Comics Group

1-Williamson-c/a(i); intro Charlemagne; death of Ned Leeds (old Hobgoblin)	3.35	10.00	20.00
V2#1 (1990, $4.95)-Reprints #1 (2/87)	.85	2.50	5.00

SPIDER-WOMAN (Also see The Avengers #240, Marvel Spotlight #32 & Marvel Two-In-One #29)
April, 1978-No. 50, June, 1983 (New logo #47 on)
Marvel Comics Group

1-New complete origin & mask added	.85	2.50	5.00
2-36,39-49: 6,19-Werewolf by Night app. 20,28,29-Spider-Man app. 46-Kingpin app. 49-Tigra app.	.25	.75	1.50
37,38-New X-Men x-over; 37-1st Siryn; origin retold; photo-c			
	.50	1.50	3.00
50-(52 pgs.)-Death of Spider-Woman; photo-c			
	.50	1.50	3.00

SPIDEY SUPER STORIES (Spider-Man)
Oct, 1974-No. 57, Mar, 1982 (35 cents) (no ads)
Marvel/Children's TV Workshop

1-(Stories simplified)	.50	1.50	3.00
2-12: 2-Kraven. 6-Iceman	.35	1.00	2.00
13-38,40-44,46-57: 33-Hulk. 34-Sub-Mariner. 38-F.F. 44-Vision.			

	Good	Fine	N-Mint
45-Dr. Doom	.25	.75	1.50
39-Thanos-c/story	.70	2.00	4.00
45-Silver Surfer app.	.50	1.50	3.00

SPIRIT, THE (1st Series)(Also see Police Comics #11)
1944-No. 22, Aug, 1950
Quality Comics Group (Vital)

	Good	Fine	N-Mint
nn(#1)-"Wanted Dead or Alive"	47.00	141.00	330.00
nn(#2)-"Crime Doesn't Pay"	30.00	90.00	210.00
nn(#3)-"Murder Runs Wild"	23.00	70.00	160.00
4,5	16.50	50.00	115.00
6-10	15.00	45.00	105.00
11	13.50	41.00	95.00
12-17-Eisner-c	23.00	70.00	160.00
18-21-Strip-r by Eisner; Eisner-c	32.00	95.00	220.00
22-Used by N.Y. Legis. Comm; Classic Eisner-c			
	46.00	137.00	320.00
Super Reprint #11-r-/Quality Spirit #19 by Eisner			
	1.30	4.00	9.00
Super Reprint #12-r-/Quality Spirit #17 by Fine			
	1.00	3.00	7.00

SPIRIT, THE (2nd Series)
Spring, 1952-No. 5, 1954
Fiction House Magazines

	Good	Fine	N-Mint
1-Not Eisner	23.00	70.00	160.00
2-Eisner-c/a(2)	25.00	75.00	175.00
3-Eisner/Grandenetti-c	17.00	50.00	115.00
4-Eisner/Grandenetti-c; Eisner-a	20.00	60.00	140.00
5-Eisner-c/a(4)	26.00	77.00	180.00

SPIRIT, THE
Oct, 1966-No. 2, Mar, 1967 (Giant Size, 25 cents, 68 pgs.)
Harvey Publications

	Good	Fine	N-Mint
1-Eisner-r plus 9 new pgs.(Origin Denny Colt, Take 3, plus 2 filler pages)	4.00	12.00	24.00
2-Eisner-r plus 9 new pgs.(Origin of the Octopus)			
	4.00	12.00	24.00

SPYMAN (Top Secret Adventures on cover)
Sept, 1966-No. 3, Feb, 1967 (12 cents)
Harvey Publications (Illustrated Humor)

	Good	Fine	N-Mint
1-Steranko-a(p)-1st pro work; 1 pg. Neal Adams ad; Tuska-c/a; Crandall-a(i)	2.85	8.50	20.00
2,3: Simon-c. 2-Steranko-a(p)	2.00	6.00	14.00

STALKER
June-July, 1975-No. 4, Dec-Jan, 1975-76
National Periodical Publications

1-Origin & 1st app; Ditko/Wood-c/a	.40	1.25	2.50
2-4-Ditko/Wood-c/a	.25	.75	1.50

STARFIRE (See New Teen Titans & Teen Titans #18)
Aug-Sept, 1976-No. 8, Oct-Nov, 1977
National Periodical Publications/DC Comics

1-Origin (CCA stamp fell off cover art; so it was approved by code)			
	.25	.75	1.50
2-8		.50	1.00

STARRIORS
Aug, 1984-No. 4, Feb, 1985 (Limited-series)
Marvel Comics Group

1-Based on Tomy Toy robots		.60	1.20
2-4		.50	1.00

STARSLAYER
Feb, 1982-No. 6, Apr, 1983; No. 7, Aug, 1983-No. 34, Nov, 1985
Pacific Comics/First Comics No. 7 on

1-Origin; excessive blood & gore; 1 pg. Rocketeer cameo which continues in #2	.50	1.50	3.00
2-Origin/1st full app. the Rocketeer by Dave Stevens (Chapter 1 of Rocketeer saga; see Pacific Presents #1,2)	3.15	9.50	22.00
3-Chapter 2 of Rocketeer saga by Stevens	2.30	7.00	16.00
4	.35	1.00	2.00
5-2nd app. Groo the Wanderer by Aragones	1.00	3.00	6.00
6,7: 7-Grell-a ends	.35	1.00	2.00
8-34: 10-1st app. Grimjack (11/83, ends #17). 18-Starslayer meets Grimjack. 20-The Black Flame begins(1st app.), ends #33. 27-Book length Black Flame story		.50	1.00

STAR SPANGLED COMICS (...War Stories #131 on)
Oct, 1941-No. 130, July, 1952
National Periodical Publications

	Good	Fine	N-Mint
1-Origin Tarantula; Captain X of the R.A.F., Star Spangled Kid (see Action #40) & Armstrong of the Army begin			
	200.00	500.00	1200.00
2	88.00	220.00	525.00
3-5	47.00	141.00	330.00
6-Last Armstrong of the Army	33.00	100.00	230.00

	Good	Fine	VF-NM
7-Origin/1st app. The Guardian by S&K, & Robotman by Paul Cassidy; The Newsboy Legion & TNT begin; last Captain X			
	250.00	625.00	1500.00

	Good	Fine	N-Mint
8-Origin TNT & Dan the Dyna-Mite	107.00	321.00	750.00
9,10	86.00	257.00	600.00
11-17	72.00	215.00	500.00
18-Origin Star Spangled Kid	93.00	280.00	650.00
19-Last Tarantula	72.00	215.00	500.00
20-Liberty Belle begins	72.00	215.00	500.00
21-29-Last S&K issue; 23-Last TNT. 25-Robotman by Jimmy Thompson begins	57.00	171.00	400.00
30-40: 31-S&K-c	25.00	75.00	175.00
41-50	22.00	65.00	155.00
51-64: Last Newsboy Legion & The Guardian; last Liberty Belle? #53 by S&K	22.00	65.00	155.00
65-Robin begins with cover app. (2/47); Batman cameo in 1 panel; Robin-c begin, end #95	75.00	225.00	525.00
66-Batman cameo in Robin story	50.00	150.00	350.00
67,68,70-80: 72-Burnley Robin-c	40.00	120.00	280.00
69-Origin/1st app. Tomahawk by F. Ray	50.00	150.00	350.00
81-Origin Merry, Girl of 1000 Gimmicks in Star Spangled Kid story			
	30.00	90.00	210.00
82,85: 82-Last Robotman?	30.00	90.00	210.00
83-Tomahawk enters the lost valley, a land of dinosaurs; Capt. Compass begins, ends #130	30.00	90.00	210.00
84,87 (Rare): 87-Batman cameo in Robin	45.00	135.00	315.00
86-Batman cameo in Robin story; last Star Spangled Kid			
	35.00	105.00	245.00
88(1/49)-94: Batman-c/stories in all. 91-Federal Men begin, end #93. 94-Manhunters Around the World begin, end #121			
	40.00	120.00	280.00

	Good	Fine	N-Mint
95-Batman story; last Robin-c	35.00	105.00	245.00
96,98-Batman cameo in Robin stories. 96-1st Tomahawk-c			
	25.00	75.00	175.00
97,99	19.00	58.00	135.00
100	25.00	75.00	175.00
101-109,118,119,121: 121-Last Tomahawk-c			
	18.00	54.00	125.00
110,111,120-Batman cameo in Robin stories. 120-Last 52 pgs.			
	19.00	58.00	135.00
112-Batman & Robin story	22.00	65.00	150.00
113-Frazetta-a (10 pgs.)	30.00	90.00	210.00
114-Retells Robin's origin (3/51); Batman & Robin story			
	27.00	80.00	185.00
115,117-Batman app. in Robin stories	19.00	58.00	135.00
116-Flag-c	19.00	56.00	130.00
122-(11/51)-Ghost Breaker-c/stories begin (origin), ends #130			
	19.00	56.00	130.00
123-126,128,129	13.00	40.00	90.00
127-Batman cameo	14.00	43.00	100.00
130-Batman cameo in Robin story	16.00	48.00	110.00

STAR SPANGLED WAR STORIES (Star Spangled Comics #1-130;
   The Unknown Soldier #205 on; also see Showcase) No. 131,
   8/52-No. 133, 10/52; No. 3, 11/52-No. 204, 2-3/77
National Periodical Publications

131(#1)	47.00	140.00	330.00
132	28.00	84.00	195.00
133-Used in **POP**, pg. 94	24.00	72.00	165.00
3-6: 4-Devil Dog Dugan app. 6-Evans-a	20.00	60.00	140.00
7-10	14.00	43.00	100.00
11-20	12.00	36.00	85.00
21-30: Last precode (2/55)	9.30	28.00	65.00
31-33,35-40	6.50	19.00	45.00
34-Krigstein-a	7.00	21.00	50.00
41-50	5.00	15.00	35.00
51-83: 67-Easy Co. story without Sgt. Rock			
	4.30	13.00	30.00
84-Origin Mlle. Marie	8.50	25.50	60.00
85-89-Mlle. Marie in all	5.00	15.00	35.00
90-1st dinosaur issue-c/story (4-5/60)	22.00	65.00	150.00
91,93-No dinosaur stories	3.60	11.00	25.00
92,94-99: All dinosaur-c/stories	9.30	28.00	65.00

	Good	Fine	N-Mint
100-Dinosaur-c/story	11.50	34.00	80.00
101-133,135-137-Last dinosaur story; Heath Birdman-#129,131			
	6.50	19.00	45.00
134-Neal Adams-a; dinosaur story	7.00	21.00	50.00
138-Enemy Ace-c/stories begin by Joe Kubert (4-5/68)			
	4.30	13.00	30.00
139-143,145: 145-Last 12 cent issue (6-7/69)			
	2.15	6.50	15.00
144-Neal Adams/Kubert-a	2.40	7.25	17.00
146-Enemy Ace-c only	1.15	3.50	8.00
147,148-Enemy Ace stories	1.50	4.50	10.00
149,150-Viking Prince by Kubert. 150-Last new Enemy Ace story by Kubert	1.50	4.50	10.00
151-1st Unknown Soldier (6-7/70); Enemy Ace-r begin			
	2.85	8.50	20.00
152,153,155-Enemy Ace reprints	1.15	3.50	8.00
154-Origin Unknown Soldier	2.15	6.50	15.00
156-1st Battle Album	1.00	3.00	6.00
157-161: 161-Last Enemy Ace reprint	.70	2.00	4.00
162-204: 167-Chaykin-a. 181-183-Enemy Ace vs. Balloon Buster serial app.	.25	.75	1.50

STARTLING COMICS
June, 1940-No. 53, May, 1948
Better Publications (Nedor)

	Good	Fine	N-Mint
1-Origin Captain Future-Man Of Tomorrow, Mystico (By Eisner/Fine), The Wonder Man; The Masked Rider begins; drug use story	82.00	245.00	575.00
2	34.00	103.00	240.00
3	27.00	81.00	190.00
4	22.00	65.00	150.00
5-9	16.00	48.00	110.00
10-The Fighting Yank begins (origin/1st app.)			
	68.00	205.00	475.00
11-15: 12-Hitler, Hirohito, Mussolini-c	20.00	60.00	140.00
16-Origin The Four Comrades; not in #32,35			
	23.00	70.00	160.00
17-Last Masked Rider & Mystico	14.00	43.00	100.00
18-Pyroman begins (origin)	39.00	118.00	275.00
19	16.00	48.00	110.00
20-The Oracle begins; not in #26,28,33,34			
	16.00	48.00	110.00

	Good	Fine	N-Mint
21-Origin The Ape, Oracle's enemy	14.00	43.00	100.00
22-33	13.00	40.00	90.00
34-Origin The Scarab & only app.	14.00	43.00	100.00
35-Hypodermic syringe attacks Fighting Yank in drug story			
	14.00	43.00	100.00
36-43: 36-Last Four Comrades. 38-Bondage/torture-c. 40-Last Capt. Future & Oracle. 41-Front Page Peggy begins; A-Bomb-c. 43-Last Pyroman	13.00	40.00	90.00
44-Lance Lewis, Space Detective begins; Ingels-c			
	22.00	65.00	150.00
45-Tygra begins (Intro/origin)	22.00	65.00	150.00
46-Ingels-c/a	22.00	65.00	150.00
47,48,50-53: 50.51-Sea-Eagle app.	16.00	48.00	110.00
49-Robot-c; last Fighting Yank	19.00	56.00	130.00

STAR TREK (TV)
7/67; No. 2, 6/68; No. 3, 12/68; No. 4, 6/69-No. 61, 3/79
Gold Key

1-Photo-c begin, end #9	40.00	120.00	275.00
2	22.00	65.00	150.00
3-5	18.00	54.00	125.00
6-9	14.00	43.00	100.00
10-20	8.00	24.00	55.00
21-30	5.70	17.00	40.00
31-40	3.60	11.00	25.00
41-61: 52-Drug propaganda story	2.15	6.50	15.00

STAR TREK
April, 1980-No. 18, Feb, 1982
Marvel Comics Group

1-r/Marvel Super Special; movie adapt.	.75	2.25	4.50
2-18: 5-Miller-c	.50	1.50	3.00

STAR TREK (Also see Who's Who In Star Trek)
Feb, 1984-No. 56, Nov, 1988 (Mando paper, 75 cents)
DC Comics

1-Sutton-a(p) begin	1.50	4.50	9.00
2-5	.90	2.75	5.50
6-10: 7-Origin Saavik	.75	2.25	4.50
11-20	.50	1.50	3.00
21-32	.35	1.10	2.20
33-($1.25, 52 pgs.)-20th anniversary issue	.60	1.75	3.50

	Good	Fine	N-Mint
34-49: 37-Painted-c. 49-Begin $1.00-c	.25	.75	1.50
50-($1.50, 52 pgs.)	.40	1.25	2.50
51-56		.50	1.00
Annual 1-3: 1(1985). 2(1986). 3(1988, $1.50)			
	.40	1.25	2.50

STAR TREK
Oct, 1989-Present ($1.50-$1.75, color)
DC Comics

1-Capt. Kirk and crew	1.15	3.50	7.00

Star Trek #3 (12/89), © Paramount Pictures

2,3	.50	1.50	3.00
4-23,25-30	.35	1.00	2.00
24-($2.95, 68 pgs.)-40 pg. epic w/pin-ups	.50	1.50	3.00
31-40	.30	.90	1.80
Annual 1,2('90, '91, $2.95, 68 pgs.): 1-Morrow-a			
	.50	1.50	3.00
Annual 3(1992, $3.50, 68 pgs.)-Painted-c	.60	1.75	3.50

STAR TREK – THE MODALA IMPERATIVE
Late July, 1991-No. 4, Late Sept, 1991 ($1.75, color, mini-series)
DC Comics

1	.40	1.25	2.50
2-4	.35	1.00	2.00

STAR TREK: THE NEXT GENERATION (TV)
Feb, 1988-No. 6, July, 1988 (Mini-series, based on TV show)
DC Comics

	Good	Fine	N-Mint
1 (52 pgs.)-Sienkiewicz painted-c	1.35	4.00	8.00
2-6 ($1.00)	.85	2.50	5.00

STAR TREK: THE NEXT GENERATION (TV)
Oct, 1989-Present ($1.50-$1.75, color)
DC Comics

	Good	Fine	N-Mint
1-Capt. Picard and crew from TV show	1.35	4.00	8.00
2,3	.70	2.00	4.00
4-10	.40	1.25	2.50
11-20	.35	1.00	2.00
21-23,25-30: 21-Begin $1.75-c	.35	1.00	2.00
24-($2.50, 52 pgs.)	.40	1.25	2.50
31-40	.30	.90	1.80
Annual 1 (1990, $2.95, 68 pgs.)	.60	1.75	3.50
Annual 2 (1991, $3.50, 68 pgs.)	.70	2.00	4.00

STAR TREK: THE NEXT GENERATION – THE MODALA IMPERATIVE
Early Sept, 1991-No. 4, 1991 ($1.75, color, mini-series)
DC Comics

	Good	Fine	N-Mint
1	.40	1.25	2.50
2-4	.35	1.00	2.00

STAR WARS (Movie)
July, 1977-No. 107, Sept, 1986
Marvel Comics Group

	Good	Fine	N-Mint
1-(Regular 30 cent edition)-Price in square w/UPC code			
	2.50	7.50	15.00
1-(35 cent cover; limited distribution-1500 copies?)-Price in square w/UPC code (see note below)	50.00	150.00	350.00
2-4: 4-Battle with Darth Vader	.85	2.50	5.00
5-10: 6-Dave Stevens inks	.50	1.50	3.00
11-20	.35	1.00	2.00
21-38	.25	.75	1.50
39-44-The Empire Strikes Back-r by Williamson in all			
	.35	1.00	2.00
45-107: 92,100-($1.00, 52 pgs.). 107-Portacio-a(i)	.50	1.00	

	Good	Fine	N-Mint
1-9-Reprints; has "reprint" in upper lefthand corner of cover or on inside or price and number inside a diamond with no date or UPC on cover; 30 cents and 35 cents issues published		.50	1.00
Annual 1 (12/79)	.35	1.00	2.00
Annual 2 (11/82), 3(12/83)		.60	1.20

NOTE: *The rare 35 cent edition has the cover price in a square box, and the UPC box in the lower left hand corner has the UPC code lines running through it.*

STAR WARS: DARK EMPIRE
Dec, 1991-No. 6, Oct, 1992 ($2.95, color, mini-series)
Dark Horse Comics

	Good	Fine	N-Mint
1-Dave Dorman painted-c on all	2.00	6.00	12.00
1-3: 2nd printings	.50	1.50	3.00
2	1.00	3.00	6.00
3-6	.60	1.75	3.50

STRAIGHT ARROW (Radio)
Feb-Mar, 1950-No. 55, Mar, 1956 (All 36 pgs.)
Magazine Enterprises

	Good	Fine	N-Mint
1-Straight Arrow (alias Steve Adams) & his palomino Fury begin; 1st mention of Sundown Valley & the Secret Cave; Whitney-a	23.00	70.00	160.00
2-Red Hawk begins (1st app?) by Powell (Origin), ends #55	11.50	34.00	80.00
3-Frazetta-c	14.00	42.00	100.00
4,5: 4-Secret Cave-c	6.00	18.00	42.00
6-10	4.65	14.00	32.00
11-Classic story "The Valley of Time," with an ancient civilization made of gold	5.00	15.00	35.00
12-19	3.50	10.50	24.00
20-Origin Straight Arrow's Shield	5.30	16.00	38.00
21-Origin Fury	6.00	18.00	42.00
22-Frazetta-c	10.00	30.00	70.00
23,25-30: 25-Secret Cave-c. 28-Red Hawk meets The Vikings	3.50	10.50	24.00
24-Classic story "The Dragons of Doom!" with prehistoric pteradactyls	4.65	14.00	32.00
31-38: 36-Red Hawk drug story by Powell	3.00	9.00	21.00
39-Classic story "The Canyon Beast," with a dinosaur egg hatching a			

	Good	Fine	N-Mint
Tyranosaurus Rex	3.60	11.00	25.00
40-Classic story "Secret of The Spanish Specters," with Conquistadors' lost treasure	3.60	11.00	25.00
41,42,44-54: 45-Secret Cave-c	2.30	7.00	16.00
43-1st app. Blaze, Straight Arrow's Warrior dog	3.00	9.00	21.00
55-Last issue	3.50	10.50	24.00

STRANGE ADVENTURES
Aug-Sept, 1950-No. 244, Oct-Nov, 1973 (No. 1-12: 52 pgs.)
National Periodical Publications

	Good	Fine	N-Mint
1-Adaptation of "Destination Moon;" Kris KL-99 & Darwin Jones begin; photo-c	150.00	450.00	1050.00
2	72.00	215.00	500.00
3,4	47.00	140.00	325.00
5-8,10: 7-Origin Kris KL-99	39.00	115.00	270.00
9-Captain Comet begins (6/51, Intro/origin)	100.00	300.00	700.00
11-20: 12,13,17,18-Toth-a	30.00	90.00	210.00
21-30	22.00	65.00	150.00
31,34-38	19.00	58.00	135.00
32,33-Krigstein-a	20.00	60.00	140.00
39-Ill. in **SOTI**-"Treating police contemptuously" (top right)	26.00	77.00	180.00
40-49-Last Capt. Comet; not in 45,47,48	18.00	54.00	125.00
50-53-Last precode issue (2/55)	12.00	36.00	85.00
54-70	7.00	21.00	50.00
71-99	5.30	16.00	38.00
100	8.00	24.00	55.00
101-110: 104-Space Museum begins by Sekowsky	4.00	12.00	28.00
111-116,118,119: 114-Star Hawkins begins, ends #185; Heath-a in Wood E.C. style	3.60	11.00	25.00
117-Origin/1st app. Atomic Knights (6/60)	32.00	96.00	220.00
120-2nd app. Atomic Knights	14.00	43.00	100.00
121,122,124,125,127,128,130,131,133,134: 124-Origin Faceless Creature. 134-Last 10 cent issue	3.15	9.50	22.00
123,126-3rd & 4th app. Atomic Knights	8.00	24.00	55.00
129,132,135,138,141,144,147-Atomic Knights app.	4.30	13.00	30.00
136,137,139,140,142,143,145,146,148,149,151,152,154,155,157-159	2.65	8.00	18.00

	Good	Fine	N-Mint
150,153,156,160: Atomic Knights in each. 153-2nd app. Faceless Creature; atomic explosion-c (6/63). 159-Star Rovers app.; Gil Kane/Anderson-a. 160-Last Atomic Knights			
	3.60	11.00	25.00
161-179: 161-Last Space Museum. 163-Star Rovers app. 170-Infinity-c. 177-Origin Immortal Man	1.50	4.50	10.00
180-Origin/1st app. Animal Man	26.00	77.00	180.00
181-183,185-189: 187-Origin The Enchantress			
	1.00	3.00	7.00
184-2nd app. Animal Man by Gil Kane	14.00	43.00	100.00
190-1st app. Animal Man in costume	17.00	51.00	120.00
191-194,196-200,202-204	.85	2.50	5.00
195-1st full length Animal Man story	10.00	30.00	70.00
201-Last Animal Man; 2nd full length story	5.00	15.00	35.00
205-Intro/origin Deadman by Infantino (10/67)			
	5.70	17.00	40.00
206-Neal Adams-a begins	4.30	13.00	30.00
207-210	2.85	8.50	20.00
211-216: 211-Space Museum-r. 216-Last Deadman			
	2.15	6.50	15.00
217-221,223-231: 217-Adam Strange & Atomic Knights-r begin. 218-Last 12 cent issue. 226-New Adam Strange text story w/illos by Anderson (8 pgs.). 226-236-(68-52 pgs.). 231-Last Atomic Knights reprint	.70	2.00	4.00
222-New Adam Strange story; Kane/Anderson-a			
	1.15	3.50	8.00
232-244	.35	1.00	2.00

STRANGE SPORTS STORIES (See Brave & the Bold)
Sept-Oct, 1973-No. 6, July-Aug, 1974
National Periodical Publications

Brave and the Bold #45-49 (12-1/62-63-8-9/63)-Strange Sports Stories			
by Infantino	2.85	8.50	20.00
1	1.00	3.00	6.00
2-6: 3-Swan/Anderson-a	.50	1.50	3.00

STRANGE TALES (... Featuring Warlock #178-181; becomes Doctor Strange #169 on)
June, 1951-#168, May, 1968; #169, Sept, 1973-#188, Nov, 1976
Atlas (CCPC #1-67/ZPC #68-79/VPI #80-85)/Marvel #86(7/61) on

| 1 | 113.00 | 340.00 | 790.00 |

	Good	Fine	N-Mint
2	48.00	145.00	340.00
3,5: 3-Atom bomb panels	37.00	110.00	260.00
4-"The Evil Eye," cosmic eyeball story	42.00	125.00	290.00
6-9	26.00	79.00	185.00
10-Krigstein-a	28.00	84.00	195.00
11-14,16-20	15.00	45.00	105.00
15-Krigstein-a	16.00	48.00	110.00
21,23-27,29-32,34-Last precode issue(2/55): 27-Atom bomb panels			
	13.00	40.00	90.00
22-Krigstein, Forte/Fox-a	12.00	36.00	85.00
28-Jack Katz story used in Senate Investigation report, pgs. 7 & 169			
	12.00	36.00	85.00
33-Davis-a	13.00	40.00	90.00
35-41,43,44	8.50	25.50	60.00
42,45,59,61-Krigstein-a; #61 (2/58)	9.30	28.00	65.00
46-57,60: 53,56-Crandall-a. 60-(8/57)	7.00	21.00	50.00
58,64-Williamson-a in each, with Mayo-#58			
	8.00	24.00	55.00
62,63,65,66: 62-Torres-a. 66-Crandall-a	6.50	19.00	45.00
67-78,80: Ditko/Kirby-a in #67-80	7.00	21.00	50.00
79-Dr. Strange prototype story (12/60)	8.00	24.00	55.00
81-83,85-92: Ditko/Kirby-a in all. 89-1st app. Fin Fang Foom (10/61) by Kirby. 92-Last 10 cent issue	6.50	19.00	45.00
84-Magneto prototype (5/61); has powers like Magneto of X-Men over two years later; Ditko/Kirby-a	7.00	21.50	50.00
93-96,98-100-Kirby-a	5.70	17.00	40.00
97-Aunt May & Uncle Ben prototype by Ditko, 3 months before Amazing Fantasy #15. Kirby-a	10.00	30.00	70.00
101-Human Torch begins by Kirby (10/62)			
	57.00	170.00	400.00
102-1st app. Wizard	25.00	75.00	175.00
103-105: 104-1st app. Trapster	19.00	58.00	135.00
106,108,109: 106-Fantastic Four guests (3/63)			
	13.00	40.00	90.00
107-Human Torch/Sub-Mariner battle	16.00	48.00	110.00
110-(7/63)-Intro Doctor Strange, Ancient One & Wong by Ditko			
	72.00	216.00	500.00
111-2nd Dr. Strange	25.00	75.00	175.00
112,113	9.30	28.00	65.00
114-Acrobat disguised as Captain America, 1st app. since the G.A.; intro. & 1st app. Victoria Bentley; 3rd Dr. Strange app. & begin series (11/63)	22.00	65.00	150.00

Strange Tales #111, © Marvel Comics

	Good	Fine	N-Mint
115-Origin Dr. Strange; early Spider-Man x-over (12/63); 2nd app. & origin Sandman (Spidey villain)	32.00	96.00	220.00
116-Human Torch battles The Thing; 1st Thing x-over	8.50	25.50	60.00
117,118,120: 120-1st Iceman x-over (from X-Men)	5.70	17.00	40.00
119-Spider-Man x-over	8.50	25.50	60.00
121,122,124-134: Thing/Torch team-up in all. 125-Torch & Thing battle Sub-Mariner (10/64). 126-Intro Clea. 130-The Beatles cameo. 134-Last Human Torch; Wood-a(i)	4.30	13.00	30.00
123-1st Thor x-over	5.00	15.00	35.00
135-Col. (formerly Sgt.) Nick Fury becomes Nick Fury Agent of Shield (origin/1st app.) by Kirby (8/65); series begins, ends #168	7.00	21.00	50.00
136-147,149: 146-Last Ditko Dr. Strange who is in consecutive stories since #113	2.85	8.50	20.00
148-Origin Ancient One	3.60	11.00	25.00
150(11/66)-John Buscema's 1st work at Marvel	2.85	8.50	20.00
151-1st Marvel work by Steranko (w/Kirby)	3.60	11.00	25.00
152,153-Kirby/Steranko-a	2.85	8.50	20.00
154-158-Steranko-a/script	2.85	8.50	20.00
159-Origin Nick Fury retold; Intro Val; Captain America-c/story; Steranko-a	3.60	11.00	25.00
160-162-Steranko-a/scripts; Capt. America app.	2.85	8.50	20.00

	Good	Fine	N-Mint
163-166,168-Steranko-a(p). 168-Last Nick Fury			
	2.85	8.50	20.00
167-Steranko pen/script; classic flag-c	4.00	12.00	28.00

169-177: 169-1st app. Brother Voodoo(origin in 169,170) & begin series, ends #173. 174-Origin Golem. 177-Brunner-c

	.40	1.25	2.50

178-(6/74)-Warlock by Starlin begins; origin Warlock & Him retold; Starlin-c/a & scripts in 178-181 (all before Warlock #9)

	2.65	8.00	18.00

179-181-All Warlock. 179-Intro/1st app. Pip the Troll. 180-Intro Gamora. 181-Warlock story continued in Warlock #9

	1.30	4.00	9.00
182-188	.40	1.25	2.50

Annual 1(1962)-Reprints from Strange Tales #73,76,78, Tales of Suspense #7,9, Tales to Astonish #1,6,7, & Journey Into Mystery #53,55,59

	32.00	96.00	220.00

Annual 2(7/63)-r/from Strange Tales #67, Strange Worlds (Atlas) #1-3, World of Fantasy #16; new Human Torch vs. Spider-Man story by Kirby/Ditko (1st Spidey x-over); Kirby-c

	37.00	110.00	260.00

STRANGE TALES
Apr, 1987-No. 19, Oct, 1988
Marvel Comics Group

	Good	Fine	N-Mint
V2#1		.60	1.20
2-12,15-19: 5,7-Defenders app. 18-X-Factor app.		.50	1.00
13,14-Punisher app.	.35	1.00	2.00

STRANGE TALES OF THE UNUSUAL
Dec, 1955-No. 11, Aug, 1957
Atlas Comics (ACI No. 1-4/WPI No. 5-11)

	Good	Fine	N-Mint
1-Powell-a	16.00	48.00	110.00
2	8.00	24.00	55.00
3-Williamson-a, 4 pgs.	8.50	25.50	60.00
4,6,8,11	5.00	15.00	35.00
5-Crandall, Ditko-a	8.00	24.00	55.00
7,9: 7-Kirby, Orlando-a. 9-Krigstein-a	5.70	17.00	40.00
10-Torres, Morrow-a	5.30	16.00	38.00

STRANGE WORLDS
Dec, 1958-No. 5, Aug, 1959
Marvel Comics (MPI No. 1,2/Male No. 3,5)

	Good	Fine	N-Mint
1-Kirby & Ditko-a; flying saucer issue	29.00	85.00	200.00
2-Ditko-c/a	17.00	51.00	120.00
3-Kirby-a(2)	13.00	40.00	90.00
4-Williamson-a	14.00	43.00	100.00
5-Ditko-a	11.50	34.00	80.00

SUB-MARINER, THE (See The Defenders, Fantastic Four #4, The
     Invaders, Iron Man &..., Marvel Spotlight #27, Namor, The...,
     Prince Namor, The..., Saga Of The..., Tales to Astonish #70 &
     T.T.A., 2nd series)
May, 1968-No. 72, Sept, 1974 (No. 43: 52 pgs.)
Marvel Comics Group

1-Origin Sub-Mariner; story continued from Iron Man & Sub-
     Mariner #1   17.00   51.00   120.00
2-Triton app.   5.70   17.00   40.00
3-10: 5-1st Tiger Shark. 7-Photo-c. 8-Sub-Mariner vs. Thing. 9-1st
     app. Serpent Crown (origin in #10 & 12)
                                           3.15   9.50   22.00
11-13,15: 15-Last 12 cent issue   2.00   6.00   14.00
14-Sub-Mariner vs. G.A. Human Torch; death of Toro (1st modern
     app. & only app. Toro)   4.30   13.00   30.00
16-20: 19-1st Sting Ray; Stan Lee, Romita, Heck, Thomas, Everett &
     Kirby cameos. 20-Dr. Doom app.   1.50   4.50   10.00
21-40: 22-Dr. Strange x-over. 30-Capt. Marvel x-over. 34-Silver
     Surfer & Hulk x-over. 35-Ties into 1st Defenders story. 37-Death
     of Lady Dorma. 38-Origin. 40-Spider-Man x-over
                                           1.00   3.00   7.00
41-72: 42-Last 15 cent issue. 44,45-Sub-Mariner vs. H. Torch. 47,48-
     Dr. Doom app. 50-1st app. Nita, Namor's niece (later Namorita in
     New Warriors). 59-1st battle with Thor. 61-Last artwork by
     Everett; 1st 4 pgs. completed by Mortimer; pgs. 5-20 by Mooney.
     62-1st Tales of Atlantis, ends 66. 64-Hitler cameo. 67-F.F. x-over.
     69-Spider-Man x-over   .70   2.00   4.00
Special 1,2: 1(1/71)-r/Tales to Astonish #70-73. 2(1/72)-r/T.T.A. #74-
     76; Everett-a   1.00   3.00   6.00

SUB-MARINER COMICS (1st Series) (The Sub-Mariner #1,2,33-42;
     also see All-Select, Marvel Comics & Marvel Mystery) Spring,
     1941-No. 23, Sum, '47; No. 24, Wint, '47-No. 31, 4/49; No. 32,
     7/49; No. 33, 4/54-No. 42, 10/55
Timely/Marvel Comics (TCI 1-7/SePI 8/MPI 9-32/Atlas Comics
(CCC 33-42)

	Good	Fine	VF-NM
1-The Sub-Mariner by Everett & The Angel begin			
	570.00	1420.00	3400.00

	Good	Fine	N-Mint
2-Everett-a	258.00	645.00	1550.00
3-Churchill assassination-c; 40 pg. Sub-Mariner story			
	200.00	500.00	1200.00
4-Everett-a, 40 pgs.; 1 pg. Wolverton-a	167.00	415.00	1000.00
5	125.00	315.00	750.00
6-10: 9-Wolverton-a, 3 pgs.; flag-c	92.00	230.00	550.00
11-15	64.00	160.00	385.00
16-20	58.00	145.00	350.00
21-Last Angel; Everett-a	50.00	125.00	300.00
22-Young Allies app.	50.00	125.00	300.00
23-The Human Torch, Namora x-over	50.00	125.00	300.00
24-Namora x-over	50.00	125.00	300.00
25-The Blonde Phantom begins, ends No. 31; Kurtzman-a; Namora			
x-over	60.00	150.00	360.00
26-28: 28-Namora cover; Everett-a	50.00	125.00	300.00
29-31 (4/49): 29-The Human Torch app. 31-Capt. America app.			
	50.00	125.00	300.00
32 (7/49, Scarce)-Origin Sub-Mariner	92.00	230.00	550.00
33 (4/54)-Origin Sub-Mariner; The Human Torch app.; Namora			
x-over in Sub-Mariner #33-42	50.00	125.00	300.00
34,35-Human Torch in each	40.00	100.00	240.00
36,37,39-41: 36,39-41-Namora app.	40.00	100.00	240.00
38-Origin Sub-Mariner's wings; Namora app. Last pre-code (2/55)			
	50.00	125.00	300.00
42-Last issue	50.00	125.00	300.00

SUGAR & SPIKE
Apr-May, 1956-No. 98, Oct-Nov, 1971
National Periodical Publications

1 (Scarce)	86.00	260.00	600.00
2	39.00	118.00	275.00
3-5	36.00	107.00	250.00
6-10	22.00	65.00	150.00
11-20	19.00	58.00	135.00
21-29,31-40: 26-XMas-c	10.00	30.00	70.00
30-Scribbly x-over	11.50	34.00	80.00
41-60	5.70	17.00	40.00
61-80: 72-Origin & 1st app. Bernie the Brain			
	3.60	11.00	25.00

	Good	Fine	N-Mint
81-98: 85-(68 pgs.); r-#72. #96-(68 pgs.). #97,98-(52 pgs.)			
	2.65	8.00	18.00

SUPERBOY (... & the Legion of Super-Heroes with #231; becomes
The Legion of Super-Heroes #259 on; also see Adventure, 80 Page
Giant #10 & Superman Family #191)
Mar-Apr, 1949-No. 258, Dec, 1979 (#1-16: 52 pgs.)
National Periodical Publications/DC Comics

	Good	Fine	VF-NM
1-Superman cover	335.00	835.00	2000.00
	Good	**Fine**	**N-Mint**
2-Used in **SOTI**, pg. 35-36,226	115.00	345.00	800.00
3	82.00	245.00	575.00
4,5: 5-Pre-Supergirl tryout	68.00	205.00	475.00
6-10: 8-1st Superbaby. 10-1st app. Lana Lang			
	50.00	150.00	350.00
11-15	36.00	107.00	250.00
16-20	27.00	80.00	185.00
21-26,28-30	20.00	60.00	140.00
27-Low distribution	22.00	65.00	150.00
31-38: 38-Last pre-code issue	14.00	43.00	100.00
39-48,50 (7/56)	11.50	34.00	80.00
49 (6/56)-1st app. Metallo (Jor-El's robot)			
	13.50	41.00	95.00
51-60: 55-Spanking-c	8.50	25.50	60.00
61-67	7.00	21.00	50.00
68-Origin/1st app. original Bizarro (10-11/58)			
	36.00	108.00	250.00
69-77,79: 75-Spanking-c. 76-1st Supermonkey. 77-Pre-Pete Ross tryout	5.70	17.00	40.00
78-Origin Mr. Mxyzptlk & Superboy's costume			
	10.00	30.00	70.00
80-1st meeting Superboy/Supergirl (4/60)	8.50	25.50	60.00
81,83-85,87,88: 83-Origin & 1st app. Kryptonite Kid			
	4.30	13.00	30.00
82-1st Bizarro Krypto	5.00	15.00	35.00
86(1/61)-4th Legion app; Intro Pete Ross	11.00	32.00	75.00
89(6/61)-Mon-el 1st app.	19.00	57.00	130.00
90-93: 90-Pete Ross learns Superboy's I.D. 92-Last 10 cent issue. 93-(12/61)-10th Legion app; Chameleon Boy app.			
	4.30	13.00	30.00
94-97,99	2.65	8.00	18.00

	Good	Fine	N-Mint

98(7/62)-18th Legion app; origin & 1st app. Ultra Boy; Pete Ross joins Legion

4.00 12.00 28.00

100(10/62)-Ultra Boy app; 1st app. Phantom Zone villains, Dr. Xadu & Erndine. 2 pg. map of Krypton; origin Superboy retold; r-cover of Superman #1; Pete Ross joins Legion

14.00 43.00 100.00

101-120: 104-Origin Phantom Zone. 115-Atomic bomb-c. 117-Legion app.

1.50 4.50 10.00

121-128: 124(10/65)-1st app. Insect Queen (Lana Lang). 125-Legion cameo. 126-Origin Krypto the Super Dog retold with new facts

1.00 3.00 6.00

129 (80- pg. Giant G-22)-Reprints origin Mon-el

1.15 3.50 8.00

130-137,139,140: 131-Legion statues cameo in Dog Legionnaires story. 132-1st app. Supremo

.70 2.00 4.00

138 (80- pg. Giant G-35)

1.15 3.50 8.00

141-146,148-155,157-164,166-173,175,176: 145-Superboy's parents regain their youth. 172,173,176-Legion app.; 172-Origin Yango (Super Ape)

.50 1.50 3.00

147(6/68)-Giant G-47; origin Saturn Girl, Lightning Lad, Cosmic Boy; origin Legion of Super-Pets-r/Adv. #293?

1.15 3.50 8.00

156,165,174 (Giants G-59,71,83)

1.00 3.00 6.00

177-184,186,187 (All 52 pgs.): 184-Origin Dial H for Hero-r

.35 1.00 2.00

185-DC 100 pg. Super Spectacular #12; Legion-c/story; Teen Titans, Kid Eternity, Star Spangled Kid-r

.40 1.25 2.50

188-196: 188-Origin Karkan. 191-Origin Sunboy retold; Legion app. 193-Chameleon Boy & Shrinking Violet get new costumes. 195-1st app. Erg/Wildfire; Phantom Girl gets new costume. 196-Last Superboy solo story

.25 .75 1.50

197-Legion series begins; Lightning Lad's new costume

.85 2.50 5.00

198,199: 198-Element Lad & Princess Projectra get new costumes

.35 1.00 2.00

200-Bouncing Boy & Duo Damsel marry; Jonn' Jonzz' cameo

.75 2.25 4.50

201,204,206,207,209: 201-Re-intro Erg as Wildfire. 204-Supergirl resigns from Legion. 206-Ferro Lad & Invisible Kid app. 209-Karate Kid new costume

.35 1.00 2.00

202,205-(100 pgs.): 202-Light Lass gets new costume

.45 1.25 2.50

	Good	Fine	N-Mint
203-Invisible Kid dies	.50	1.50	3.00

208,210: 208-(68 pgs.). 210-Origin Karate Kid

	.45	1.25	2.50

211-220: 212-Matter-Eater Lad resigns. 216-1st app. Tyroc who joins Legion in #218

	.30	.90	1.80

221-249: 226-Intro. Dawnstar. 228-Death of Chemical King. 240-Origin Dawnstar. 242-(52 pgs.). 243-Legion of Substitute Heroes app. 243-245-(44 pgs.)

	.60	1.20

250-258: 253-Intro Blok. 257-Return of Bouncing Boy & Duo Damsel by Ditko

	.50	1.00

| Annual 1(Sum/64, 84 pgs.)-Origin Krypto-r | 9.50 | 28.50 | 66.00 |

...Spectacular 1(1980, Giant)-Distr. through comic stores; mostly-r

	.50	1.00

SUPERBOY (TV) (The Adventures of... #19 on)
Feb, 1990-No. 22, Dec, 1991 ($1.00-$1.25, color)
DC Comics

1-15: Mooney-a(p) in 1-8,18-20; 1-Photo-c from TV show. 8-Bizarro-c/story; Arthur Adams-a(i). 9-12,14-17,20-Swan-p

	.50	1.00
16-22: 16-Begin $1.25-c	.65	1.30

SUPERCAR (TV)
Nov, 1962-No. 4, Aug, 1963 (All painted covers)
Gold Key

	Good	Fine	N-Mint
1	17.00	51.00	120.00
2,3	8.50	25.50	60.00
4	13.00	40.00	90.00

SUPER COMICS
May, 1938-No. 121, Feb-Mar, 1949
Dell Publishing Co.

1-Terry & The Pirates, The Gumps, Dick Tracy, Little Orphan Annie, Gasoline Alley, Little Joe, Smilin' Jack, Smokey Stover, Smitty, Tiny Tim, Moon Mullins, Harold Teen, Winnie Winkle begin

	Good	Fine	N-Mint
begin	117.00	291.00	700.00
2	50.00	150.00	350.00
3	44.00	132.00	310.00
4,5	36.00	107.00	250.00
6-10	29.00	85.00	200.00
11-20	23.00	70.00	160.00

	Good	Fine	N-Mint
21-29: 21-Magic Morro begins (Origin, 2/40). 22-Ken Ernst-c			
	19.00	58.00	135.00
30-"Sea Hawk" movie adaptation-c/story with Errol Flynn			
	19.00	58.00	135.00
31-40	16.00	48.00	110.00
41-50: 43-Terry & The Pirates ends	13.00	40.00	90.00
51-60	9.30	28.00	65.00
61-70: 65-Brenda Starr-r begin? 67-X-mas-c			
	8.00	24.00	55.00
71-80	7.00	21.00	50.00
81-99	5.30	16.00	38.00
100	7.00	21.00	50.00
101-115-Last Dick Tracy (moves to own title)			
	4.30	13.00	30.00
116,118-All Smokey Stover	3.60	11.00	25.00
117-All Gasoline Alley	3.60	11.00	25.00
119-121-Terry & The Pirates app. in all	3.60	11.00	25.00

SUPER DC GIANT (25-50 cents, all 68-52 pg. Giants)
No. 13, 9-10/70-No. 26, 7-8/71; V3#27, Summer, 1976 (No #1-12)
National Periodical Publications

S-13-Binky	.50	1.50	3.00
S-14-Top Guns of the West; Kubert-c; Trigger Twins, Johnny Thunder, Wyoming Kid-r; Moreira-r (9-10/70)			
	.50	1.50	3.00
S-15-Western Comics; Kubert-c; Pow Wow Smith, Vigilante, Buffalo Bill-r; new Gil Kane-a (9-10/70)	.70	2.00	4.00
S-16-Best of the Brave & the Bold; Batman-r & Metamorpho origin-r from Brave & the Bold	.70	2.00	4.00
S-17-Love 1970	.40	1.25	2.50
S-18-Three Mouseketeers; Dizzy Dog, Doodles Duck, Bo Bunny-r; Sheldon Mayer-a	.50	1.50	3.00
S-19-Jerry Lewis; no Neal Adams-a	.50	1.50	3.00
S-20-House of Mystery; N. Adams-c; Kirby-r(3)			
	.50	1.50	3.00
S-21-Love 1971	.35	1.00	2.00
S-22-Top Guns of the West	.40	1.25	2.50
S-23-The Unexpected	.35	1.00	2.00
S-24-Supergirl	.35	1.00	2.00
S-25-Challengers of the Unknown; all Kirby/Wood-r			
	.50	1.50	3.00

	Good	Fine	N-Mint
S-26-Aquaman (1971)	.50	1.50	3.00
27-Strange Flying Saucers Advs. (Sum, '76)			
	.35	1.00	2.00

SUPER FRIENDS (TV)
Nov, 1976-No. 47, Aug, 1981 (#14 is 44 pgs.)
National Periodical Publications/DC Comics

	Good	Fine	N-Mint
1-Superman, Batman, Robin, Wonder Woman, Aquaman, Atom, Wendy, Marvin & Wonder Dog begin	.25	.75	1.50

2-47: 7-1st app. Wonder Twins, & The Seraph. 8-1st app. Jack
   O'Lantern. 9-1st app. Icemaiden. 13-1st app. Dr. Mist. 14-Origin
   Wonder Twins. 25-1st app. Fire & Green Fury. 31-Black Orchid
   app. 36,43-Plastic Man app. 47-Origin Fire & Green Fury

		.50	1.00

...Special 1 (1981, giveaway, no ads, no code or price)-r/Super Friends
   #19 & 36

		.50	1.00

SUPERGIRL (See Action, Adventure #281, Crisis on Infinite Earths
     Super DC Giant, Superman Family, & Super-Team Family)
Nov, 1972-No. 9, Dec-Jan, 1973-74; No. 10, Sept-Oct, 1974
National Periodical Publications

	Good	Fine	N-Mint
1-1st solo title; Zatanna begins, ends #5	.35	1.00	2.00
2-10: 5-Zatanna origin-r. 8-JLA x-over; Batman cameo			
		.50	1.00

SUPER GOOF (Walt Disney)
Oct, 1965-No. 74, 1982
Gold Key No. 1-57/Whitman No. 58 on

	Good	Fine	N-Mint
1	1.70	5.00	12.00
2-10	1.00	3.00	6.00
11-20	.70	2.00	4.00
21-30	.50	1.50	3.00
31-50	.25	.75	1.50
51-74		.50	1.00

SUPER HEROES
Jan, 1967-No. 4, June, 1967
Dell Publishing Co.

	Good	Fine	N-Mint
1-Origin & 1st app. Fab 4	2.15	6.50	15.00
2-4	1.15	3.50	8.00

SUPERMAN (Becomes Adventures of... #424 on; also see Action
   Comics, Brave & the Bold, Cosmic Odyssey, DC Comics Presents
   & World's Finest)
Summer, 1939-No. 423, Sept, 1986 (#1-5 are quarterly)
National Periodical Publications/DC Comics

	Good	Fine	VF-NM
1(nn)-1st four Action stories reprinted; origin Superman by Siegel & huster; has a new 2 pg. origin plus 4 pgs. omitted in Action story			
	5,500.00	16,500.00	40,000.00

(Prices vary widely on this book)

	Good	Fine	N-Mint
2-All daily strip-r	667.00	1670.00	4000.00
3-2nd story-r from Action #5; 3rd story-r from Action #6			
	485.00	1210.00	2900.00
4-2nd mention of Daily Planet (Spr/40); also see Action #23; 2nd app. Luthor (1st Luthor-c & 1st bald Luthor; also see Action #23)			
	367.00	915.00	2200.00
5	267.00	665.00	1600.00
6,7: 7-1st Perry White?	208.00	520.00	1250.00
8-10: 10-Luthor app.	167.00	415.00	1000.00
11-13,15: 13-Jimmy Olsen app.	125.00	315.00	750.00
14-Patriotic Shield-c by Fred Ray	183.00	455.00	1100.00
16-20: 17-Hitler, Hirohito-c	108.00	270.00	650.00
21-23,25	87.00	220.00	525.00
24-Flag-c	100.00	250.00	600.00
26-29: 28-Lois Lane Girl Reporter series begins, ends #40,42			
	79.00	200.00	475.00
28-Overseas edition for Armed Forces; same as reg. #28			
	79.00	200.00	475.00
30-Origin & 1st app. Mr. Mxyztplk (pronounced "Mix-it-plk") in comic books; name later became Mxyzptlk ("Mix-yez-pit-l-ick")			
	107.00	321.00	750.00
31-40: 33-(3-4/45)-3rd app. Mxyzptlk	59.00	178.00	415.00
41-50: 45-Lois Lane as Superwoman (see Action #60 for 1st app.)			
	44.00	132.00	310.00
51,52	36.00	107.00	250.00
53-Origin Superman retold; 10th anniversary			
	100.00	300.00	700.00
54,56-60	38.00	115.00	265.00
55-Used in **SOTI**, pg. 33	39.00	118.00	275.00
61-Origin Superman retold; origin Green Kryptonite (1st Kryptonite story)			
	64.00	192.00	450.00

	Good	**Fine**	**N-Mint**
62-65,67-70: 62-Orson Welles app. 65-1st Krypton Foes: Mala, K120, & U-Ban	36.00	107.00	250.00
66-2nd Superbaby story	36.00	107.00	250.00
71-75: 75-Some have #74 on-c	33.00	100.00	230.00
72-Giveaway(9-10/51)-(Rare)-Price blackened out; came with banner wrapped around book	41.00	125.00	290.00
76-Batman x-over; Superman & Batman learn each other's I.D.	86.00	257.00	600.00
77-81: 78-Last 52 pg. issue. 81-Used in **POP**, pg. 88	30.00	90.00	210.00
82-90	27.00	80.00	185.00
91-95: 95-Last precode issue	25.00	75.00	175.00
96-99	23.00	70.00	160.00
100 (9-10/55)	93.00	280.00	650.00
101-110	22.00	65.00	150.00
111-120	17.00	51.00	120.00
121-130: 123-Pre-Supergirl tryout. 127-Origin/1st app. Titano. 128-Red Kryptonite used (4/59). 129-Intro/origin Lori Lemaris, The Mermaid	14.00	43.00	100.00
131-139: 139-Lori Lemaris app.; "Untold Story of Red Kryptonite" back-up story	10.00	30.00	70.00
140-1st Blue Kryptonite & Bizarro Supergirl; origin Bizarro Jr. #1	11.50	34.00	80.00
141-145,148: 142-2nd Batman x-over	7.00	21.00	50.00
146-Superman's life story	10.00	30.00	70.00

147(8/61)-7th Legion app; 1st app. Legion of Super-Villains; 1st app.

Superman #156, © DC Comics

	Good	Fine	N-Mint
Adult Legion	10.00	30.00	70.00

149(11/61)-9th Legion app. (cameo); last 10 cent issue

	9.30	28.00	65.00

150-162: 152(4/62)-15th Legion app. 155(8/62)-19th Legion app; Lightning Man & Cosmic Man, & Adult Legion app. 156,162-Legion app. 157-Gold Kryptonite used (see Adv. 299); Mon-el app.; Lightning Lad cameo (11/62). 158-1st app. Flamebird & Nightwing & Nor-Kan of Kandor. 161-1st told death of Ma and Pa Kent
    4.30   13.00   30.00

161-2nd printing (1987, $1.25-c)-New DC logo; sold thru So Much Fun Toy Stores (cover title: Superman Classic)
    .25   .75   1.50

163-166,168-180: 166-XMas-c. 168-All Luthor issue. 169-Last Sally Selwyn. 170-Pres. Kennedy story is finally published after delay from #168 due to assassination. 172,173-Legion cameos. 174-Super-Mxyzptlk; Bizarro app.
    3.15   9.50   22.00

167-New origin Brainiac & Brainiac 5; intro Tixarla (later Luthor's wife)
    6.50   19.00   45.00

181,182,184-186,188-192,194-196,198,200: 181-1st 2965 story/series. 189-Origin/destruction of Krypton II
    2.00   6.00   14.00

183,187,193,197 (Giants G-18,G-23,G-31,G-36)
    2.30   7.00   16.00

199-1st Superman/Flash race (8/67)   12.00   36.00   85.00

201,203-206,208-211,213-216,218-221,223-226,228-231,234-238: 213-Brainiac-5 app.   1.30   4.00   9.00

202 (80- pg. Giant G-42)-All Bizarro issue   1.70   5.00   12.00

207,212,217,222,239 (Giants G-48,G-54,G-60,G-66,G-84): 207-Legion app.; 30th anniversary Superman (6/68)
    1.70   5.00   12.00

227,232(Giants, G-78,G-72)-All Krypton issues
    1.70   5.00   12.00

233-2nd app. Morgan Edge, Clark Kent switch from newspaper reporter to TV newscaster   1.30   4.00   9.00

240-Kaluta-a   .85   2.50   5.00

241-244 (All 52 pgs.): 243-G.A.-r/#38   .70   2.00   4.00

245-DC 100 pg. Super Spectacular #7; Air Wave, Kid Eternity, Hawkman-r; Atom-r/Atom #3   .85   2.50   5.00

246-248,250,251,253 (All 52 pgs.): 246-G.A.-r/#40. 248-World of Krypton story. 251-G.A.-r/#45. 253-G.A.-r/#13
    .50   1.50   3.00

249,254-Neal Adams-a. 249-(52 pgs.); origin & 1st app. Terra-Man by Neal Adams (inks)   1.15   3.50   7.00

	Good	Fine	N-Mint
252-DC 100 pg. Super Spectacular #13; Ray, Black Condor, Hawkman-r; Starman-r/Adv. #67; Dr. Fate & Spectre-r/More Fun #57; N. Adams-c	1.00	3.00	6.00
255-271,273-277,279-283: 263-Photo-c. 264-1st app. Steve Lombard. 276-Intro Capt. Thunder	.35	1.00	2.00
272,278,284-All 100 pgs. G.A.-r in all	.50	1.50	3.00
285-299: 292-Origin Lex Luthor retold	.25	.75	1.50
300-Retells origin	.85	2.50	5.00
301-399: 301,320-Solomon Grundy app. 323-Intro. Atomic Skull. 327-329-(44 pgs.). 330-More facts revealed about I. D. 338-The bottled city of Kandor enlarged. 344-Frankenstein & Dracula app. 353-Brief origin. 354,355,357-Superman 2020 stories (354-Debut of Superman III). 356-World of Krypton story (also #360, 367,375). 372-Superman 2021 story. 376-Free 16 pg. preview Daring New Advs. of Supergirl. 377-Free 16 pg. preview Masters of the Universe	.25	.75	1.50
400 (10/84, $1.50, 68 pgs.)-Many top artists featured; Chaykin painted cover, Miller back-c	.50	1.50	3.00
401-410,412-422: 405-Super-Batman story. 408-Nuclear Holocaust-c/story. 414,415-Crisis x-over. 422-Horror-c	.25	.75	1.50
411-Special Julius Schwartz tribute issue	.25	.75	1.50
423-Alan Moore scripts; Perez-a(i)	1.00	3.00	7.00
Annual 1(10/60, 84 pgs.)-Reprints 1st Supergirl story/Action #252; r/Lois Lane #1 (1st Silver Age DC annual)	43.00	130.00	300.00
Annual 2(1960)-Brainiac, Titano, Metallo, Bizarro origin-r	25.00	75.00	175.00
Annual 3(1961)	18.00	54.00	125.00
Annual 4(1961)-11th Legion app; 1st Legion origins-text & pictures	14.00	43.00	100.00
Annual 5(Sum, '62)-All Krypton issue	10.00	30.00	70.00
Annual 6(Wint, '62-'63)-Legion-r/Adv. #247	8.50	25.50	60.00
Annual 7(Sum/'63)-Origin-r/Superman-Batman team/Adv. 275; r-1955 Superman dailies	6.50	19.00	45.00
Annual 8(Wint, '63-'64)-All origins issue	5.00	15.00	35.00
Annual 9(1983)-Toth/Austin-a	.70	2.00	4.00
Annuals 10-12: 10(1984, $1.25)-M. Anderson inks. 11(1985)-Moore scripts.12(1986)	.50	1.50	3.00
...IV Movie Special (1987, $2.00, one-shot)-Movie adaptation; Heck-a	.35	1.00	2.00

	Good	Fine	N-Mint
Special 1(1983)-G. Kane-c/a; contains German-r	.50	1.50	3.00
Special 2,3(1984, 1985, $1.25, 52 pgs.)	.50	1.50	3.00

...Movie Special-(9/83)-Adaptation of Superman III; other versions exist with store logos on bottom A2> of-c   .50   1.00

SUPERMAN (2nd series)
Jan, 1987-Present (.75-$1.00)
DC Comics

1-Byrne-c/a begins; intro new Metallo	.35	1.00	2.00
2-8,10: 3-Legends x-over; Darkseid app. 7-Origin/1st app. Rampage. 8-Legion app.		.60	1.20
9-Joker-c	.50	1.50	3.00

11-49,51,52,54-56,58-67: 11-1st new Mr. Mxyzptlk. 12-Lori Lemaris revived. 13-1st app. Toyman. 13,14-Millennium x-over. 20-Doom Patrol app.; Supergirl revived in cameo. 21-Supergirl-c/story. 31-Mr. Mxyzptlk app. 37-Newsboy Legion app. 41-Lobo app. 44-Batman storyline, part 1. 45-Free extra 8 pgs. 63-Aquaman x-over. 65,66-Deathstroke app.   .50   1.00

50-($1.50, 52 pgs.)-Clark Kent proposes to Lois	.85	2.50	5.00
50-2nd printing		.50	1.00
53-Clark reveals i.d. to Lois cont'd from Action #662	.40	1.25	2.50
53-2nd printing		.50	1.00
57-($1.75, 52 pgs.)	.30	.90	1.80
68-72: 68-Deathstroke-c/story; begin $1.25-c	.65		1.30
Annual 1 (1987)-No Byrne-a	.25	.75	1.50
Annual 2 (1988)-Byrne-a; Newsboy Legion; return of the Guardian	.25	.75	1.50
Annual 3 ('91, $2.00, 68 pgs.)-Armageddon 2001 x-over; Batman app.; Austin-c(i) & part inks	.70	2.00	4.00
Annual 3-2nd & 3rd printings; 3rd has silver ink	.70	2.00	4.00
Annual 4 (1992, $2.50, 68 pgs.)-Eclipso app.	.40	1.25	2.50

SUPERMAN FAMILY, THE (Formerly Superman's Pal
    Jimmy Olsen)
No. 164, Apr-May, 1974-No. 222, Sept, 1982
National Periodical Publications/DC Comics

164-Jimmy Olsen, Supergirl, Lois Lane begin	.25	.75	1.50

	Good	Fine	N-Mint
165-176 (100-68 pgs.)		.60	1.20
177-181 (52 pgs.)		.50	1.00
182,194: Marshall Rogers-a in each. 182-$1.00 issues begin; Krypto begins, ends #192	.35	1.00	2.00
183-193,195-222: 183-Nightwing-Flamebird begins, ends #194. 189-Brainiac 5, Mon-el app. 191-Superboy begins, ends #198. 200-Book length story. 211-Earth II Batman & Catwoman marry		.50	1.00

SUPERMAN'S GIRLFRIEND LOIS LANE (See Action Comics #1, 80 Page Giant #3,14, Showcase #9,10, Superman #28 & Superman Family)

Mar-Apr, 1958-No. 136, Jan-Feb, 1974; No. 137, Sept-Oct, 1974
National Periodical Publications

	Good	Fine	N-Mint
Showcase #9 (7-8/57)-Lois Lane (pre #1); 1st Showcase character to win own series	122.00	365.00	850.00
Showcase #10 (9-10/57)-Jor-el cameo	103.00	310.00	725.00
1-(3-4/58)	98.00	294.00	685.00
2	40.00	120.00	280.00
3-Spanking panel	30.00	90.00	210.00
4,5	23.00	70.00	160.00
6-10: 9-Pat Boone app.	14.00	43.00	100.00
11-20: 14-Supergirl x-over; Batman app?	8.50	25.50	60.00
21-29: 23-1st app. Lena Thorul, Lex Luthor's sister. 27-Bizarro-c/story. 29-Aquaman, Batman, Green Arrow cameo; last 10 cent issue	5.30	16.00	38.00
30-32,34-49: 47-Legion app.	2.85	8.50	20.00
33(5/62)-Mon-el app.	3.50	10.50	24.00
50(7/64)-Triplicate Girl, Phantom Girl & Shrinking Violet app.	2.30	7.00	16.00
51-55,57-67,69: 59-Jor-el app.; Batman back-up story	1.60	4.80	11.00
56-Saturn Girl app.	1.85	5.50	13.00
68-(Giant G-26)	2.30	7.00	16.00
70-Penguin & Catwoman app. (1st S.A. Catwoman, 11/66); Batman & Robin cameo	13.50	41.00	95.00
71-Catwoman story cont'd from #70 (2nd app.)	9.30	28.00	65.00
72,73,75,76,78	1.15	3.50	8.00
74-1st Bizarro Flash; JLA cameo	2.15	6.50	15.00
77-(Giant G-39)	1.30	4.00	9.00
79-Neal Adams-c begin, end #95,108	.85	2.50	5.00

	Good	Fine	N-Mint
80-85,87-94: 89-Batman x-over; all N. Adams-c			
	.70	2.00	4.00
86,95: (Giants G-51,G-63)-Both have Neal Adams-c. 95-Wonder Woman x-over	1.00	3.00	6.00
96-103,105-111: 105-Origin/1st app. The Rose & the Thorn. 108-Neal Adams-c. 111-Morrow-a	.60	1.75	3.50
104,113-(Giants G-75,87)	1.00	3.00	6.00
112,114-123 (52 pgs.): 122-G.A.-r/Superman #30. 123-G.A. Batman-r	.50	1.50	3.00
124-137: 130-Last Rose & the Thorn. 132-New Zatanna story. 136-Wonder Woman x-over	.35	1.00	2.00
Annual 1(Sum,'62)	8.50	25.50	60.00
Annual 2(Sum,'63)	5.70	17.00	40.00

SUPERMAN'S PAL JIMMY OLSEN (Superman Family #164 on)
  (See Action Comics #6 for 1st app. & 80 Page Giant)
Sept-Oct, 1954-No. 163, Feb-Mar, 1974
National Periodical Publications

	Good	Fine	N-Mint
1	135.00	405.00	945.00
2	67.00	200.00	460.00
3-Last pre-code issue	45.00	135.00	315.00
4,5	30.00	90.00	210.00
6-10	22.00	65.00	150.00
11-20	14.00	43.00	100.0t
21-30: 29-1st app. Krypto in Jimmy Olsen	8.30	25.00	58.00
31-40: 31-Origin Elastic Lad. 33-One pg. biography of Jack Larson (TV Jimmy Olsen). 36-Intro Lucy Lane. 37-2nd app. Elastic Lad; 1st cover app.	5.70	17.00	40.00
41-50: 41-1st J.O. Robot. 48-Intro/origin Superman Emergency Squad	4.00	12.00	28.00
51-56: 56-Last 10 cent issue	2.65	8.00	18.00
57-62,64-70: 57-Olsen marries Supergirl. 62-Mon-el & Elastic Lad app. but not as Legionnaires. 70-Element Lad app.	1.50	4.50	10.00
63(9/62)-Legion of Super-Villains app.	1.60	4.80	11.00
71,74,75,78,80-84,86,89,90: 86-J.O. Robot becomes Congorilla	1.00	3.00	7.00
72(10/63)-Legion app; Elastic Lad (Olsen) joins	1.30	4.00	9.00
73-Ultra Boy app.	1.30	4.00	9.00
76,85-Legion app.	1.30	4.00	9.00
77,79: 77-Olsen with Colossal Boy's powers & costume; origin			

	Good	Fine	N-Mint
Titano retold. 79(9/64)-Titled The Red-headed Beatle of 1000 B.C.	1.00	3.00	7.00
87-Legion of Super-Villains app.	1.30	4.00	9.00
88-Star Boy app.	1.00	3.00	7.00
91-94,96-99: 99-Olsen w/powers & costumes of Lightning Lad, Sun Boy & Star Boy	.75	2.25	4.50
95,104 (Giants G-25,G-38)	1.60	4.80	11.00
100-Legion cameo	1.00	3.00	7.00
101-103,105-112,114-121,123-130,132: 106-Legion app. 110-Infinity-c	.60	1.75	3.50
113,122,131 (Giants G-50,G-62,G-74)	.60	1.75	3.50
133-Re-intro Newsboy Legion & begins by Kirby	.75	2.25	4.50
134-(12/70)-1st app. Darkseid (1 panel) & Morgan Edge	.85	2.50	5.00
135-163: 135-(1/71)-2nd app. Darkseid (1 pg. cameo; see Forever People & New Gods); G.A. Guardian app. 136-Origin new Guardian. 139-Last 15 cent issue. 140-(Giant G-86). 141-Newsboy Legion reprints by S&K begin (52 pg. issues begin). 149,150-G.A. Plastic Man reprint in both; last 52 pg. issue. 150-Newsboy Legion app.	.50	1.50	3.00

SUPERMAN: THE EARTH STEALERS
1988 (one-shot, $2.95, 52 pgs, prestige format)
DC Comics

1-Byrne scripts; painted-c	.60	1.75	3.50
1-2nd printing	.50	1.50	2.95

SUPERMAN: THE MAN OF STEEL (Also see The Man of Steel)
July, 1991-Present ($1.00-$1.25, color)
DC Comics

1-($1.75, 52 pgs.)	.30	.90	1.80
2-10: 3-War of the Gods x-over. 5-Reads sideways		.50	1.00
11-16: 11-Begin $1.25-c. 14-Robin app.		.65	1.30
Annual 1 (1992, $2.50, 68 pgs.)-Eclipso app.	.40	1.25	2.50

SUPERMAN: THE SECRET YEARS
Feb, 1985-No. 4, May, 1985 (Mini-series)
DC Comics

1-Miller-c on all	.25	.75	1.50
2-4		.50	1.00

SUPER-TEAM FAMILY
10-11/75-No. 15, 3-4/78 (#1-4: 68 pgs.; #5 on: 52 pgs.)
National Periodical Publications/DC Comics

	Good	Fine	N-Mint
1-Reprints by Neal Adams & Kane/Wood	.35	1.00	2.00
2,3-New stories	.25	.75	1.50
4-7-Reprints. 4-G.A. JSA-r & Superman/Batman/Robin-r from World's Finest		.50	1.00
8-10-New Challengers of the Unknown stories	.35	1.00	2.00
11-15-New stories		.60	1.20

SUPER-VILLAIN TEAM-UP (See Fantastic Four #6)
8/75-No. 14, 10/77; No. 15, 11/78; No. 16, 5/79; No. 17, 6/80
Marvel Comics Group

	Good	Fine	N-Mint
1-Sub-Mariner & Dr. Doom begin, end #10	.70	2.00	4.00
2-17: 5-1st Shroud. 6-F.F., Shroud app. 7-Origin Shroud. 9-Avengers app. 11-15-Dr. Doom & Red Skull app.	.35	1.00	2.00

SWAMP THING (See Challengers of the Unknown #82, House of Secrets #92, Roots of the..., & The Saga of...)
Oct-Nov, 1972-No. 24, Aug-Sept, 1976
National Periodical Publications/DC Comics

	Good	Fine	N-Mint
1-Wrightson-c/a begins	5.70	17.00	40.00
2	2.85	8.50	20.00
3-Intro. Patchworkman	1.70	5.00	12.00
4-6,8-10: 10-Last Wrightson issue	1.50	4.50	10.00
7-Batman-c/story	1.60	4.80	11.00
11-24-Redondo-a; 23-Swamp Thing reverts back to Dr. Holland. 23,24-New logo	.40	1.25	2.50

SWING WITH SCOOTER
June-July, 1966-No. 35, Aug-Sept, 1971; No. 36, Oct-Nov, 1972
National Periodical Publications

	Good	Fine	N-Mint
1	1.70	5.00	12.00
2-10: 9-Alfred E. Newman swipe in last panel	1.00	3.00	7.00
11-20	.85	2.50	5.00
21-36: 33-Interview with David Cassidy. 34-Interview with Ron Ely (Doc Savage)	.70	2.00	4.00

SWORD OF SORCERY
Feb-Mar, 1973-No. 5, Nov-Dec, 1973
National Periodical Publications

	Good	Fine	N-Mint
1-Leiber Fafhrd & The Grey Mouser; Chaykin/Neal Adams (Crusty Bunkers) art; Kaluta-c	.35	1.00	2.00
2-Wrightson-c(i); Neal Adams-a(i)	.25	.75	1.50
3-5: 3-Wrightson-i(5 pg.). 5-Starlin-a(p); Conan cameo		.60	1.20

T

TALES CALCULATED TO DRIVE YOU BATS
Nov, 1961-No. 7, Nov, 1962; 1966 (Satire)
Archie Publications

	Good	Fine	N-Mint
1-Only 10 cent issue; has cut-out Werewolf mask (price includes			
mask)	5.00	15.00	35.00
2-Begin 12 cent issues	2.65	8.00	18.00
3-6	2.15	6.50	15.00
7-Storyline change	1.70	5.00	12.00
1('66)-25 cents	2.15	6.50	15.00

TALES FROM THE CRYPT
No. 20, Oct-Nov, 1950-No. 46, Feb-Mar, 1955
E.C. Comics

20	82.00	245.00	575.00
21-Kurtzman-r/Haunt of Fear #15(#1)	68.00	205.00	475.00
22-Moon Girl costume at costume party, one panel			
	54.00	162.00	380.00
23-25: 24-E. A. Poe adaptation	41.00	122.00	285.00

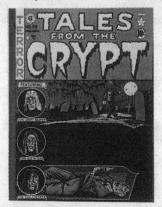

Tales From the Crypt #28, © William M. Gaines

26-30	33.00	100.00	230.00

31-Williamson-a(1st at E.C.); B&W and color illos. in **POP**; Kamen

	Good	Fine	N-Mint
draws himself, Gaines & Feldstein; Ingels, Craig & Davis draw themselves in his story	37.00	110.00	260.00
32,35-39	26.00	77.00	180.00
33-Origin The Crypt Keeper	46.00	137.00	320.00
34-Used in **POP**, pg. 83; lingerie panels	26.00	77.00	180.00
40-Used in Senate hearings & in Hartford Courant anti-comics editorials in 1954	26.00	77.00	180.00
41-45: 45-2 pgs. showing E.C. staff	24.00	73.00	170.00
46-Low distribution; pre-advertised cover for unpublished 4th horror title "Crypt of Terror" used on this book			
	30.00	90.00	210.00

TALES FROM THE CRYPT
July, 1990-No. 6, May, 1991 ($1.95, color, 68 pgs.)(#4 on: $2.00)
Gladstone Publishing

1-r/TFTC #33 & Crime S.S. #17; Davis-c(r)			
	.70	2.00	4.00
2-Davis-c(r)	.50	1.50	3.00
3-6: 3,5,6-Davis-c(r). 4-Craig-c(r)	.40	1.25	2.50

TALES OF ASGARD
Oct, 1968 (25 cents, 68 pages); Feb, 1984 ($1.25, 52 pgs.)
Marvel Comics Group

1-Reprints Tales of Asgard (Thor) back-up stories from Journey into Mystery #97-106; new Kirby-c	3.60	11.00	25.00
V2#1 (2/84)-Thor-r; Simonson-c		.50	1.00

TALES OF SUSPENSE (Becomes Captain America #100 on)
Jan, 1959-No. 99, March, 1968
Atlas (WPI No. 1,2/Male No. 3-12/VPI No. 13-18)/Marvel No. 19 on

1-Williamson-a, 5 pgs.	68.00	204.00	475.00
2,3: 3-Flying saucer-c/story	30.00	90.00	210.00
4-Williamson-a, 4 pgs; Kirby/Everett c/a			
	32.00	96.00	220.00
5-10	21.00	63.00	140.00
11-15,17-20: 12-Crandall-a. 14-Intro. Colossus			
	15.00	45.00	105.00
16-1st Metallo (7/61, Iron Man prototype)			
	18.00	54.00	125.00
21-25: 25-Last 10 cent issue	11.00	32.00	75.00
26-38: 32-Sazzik The Sorcerer app. "The Man and the Beehive;" story came out same time as "The Man in the Ant Hill" in TTA			

	Good	Fine	N-Mint
#27 (1st Ant-man)-characters were tested to see which got best fan response	9.00	27.00	63.00
39 (3/63)-Origin/1st app. Iron Man & begin series; 1st Iron Man story has Kirby layouts	170.00	680.00	1700.00
40-2nd app. Iron Man (in new armor)	93.00	280.00	650.00
41-3rd app. Iron Man	57.00	170.00	400.00
42-45: 45-Intro. & 1st app. Happy & Pepper	25.00	75.00	175.00
46,47: 46-1st app. Crimson Dynamo	16.00	48.00	110.00
48-New Iron Man armor	19.30	58.00	135.00
49-1st X-Men x-over (same date as X-Men #3, 1/64); 1st Tales of the Watcher back-up story	11.00	32.00	75.00
50-1st app. Mandarin	9.30	28.00	65.00
51-1st Scarecrow	8.00	24.00	55.00
52-1st app. The Black Widow (4/64)	11.00	32.00	75.00
53-Origin & 2nd app. The Watcher (5/64); 2nd Black Widow app.	9.30	28.00	65.00
54-56: 56-1st app. Unicorn	5.70	17.00	40.00
57-Origin/1st app. Hawkeye (9/64)	12.00	36.00	85.00
58-Captain America battles Iron Man (10/64)-Classic-c; 2nd Kraven app. (Cap's 1st app. in this title)	22.00	65.00	150.00
59-Iron Man plus Captain America double feature begins (11/64); 1st S.A. Captain America solo story; intro Jarvis, Avenger's butler; classic-c	22.00	65.00	150.00
60	9.50	28.50	66.00
61,62,64: 62-Origin Mandarin (2/65)	5.70	17.00	40.00
63-1st Silver Age origin Captain America (3/65)	14.00	43.00	100.00
65-1st Silver-Age Red Skull (6/65)	9.30	28.00	65.00
66-Origin Red Skull	9.30	28.00	65.00
67-78,81-98: 69-1st app. Titanium Man. 75-1st app. Agent 13 later named Sharon Carter. 76-Intro Batroc & Sharon Carter, Agent 13 of Shield. 92-1st Nick Fury x-over (as Agent of Shield, 8/67). 94-Intro Modok. 95-Capt. America's i.d. revealed	4.30	13.00	30.00
79-Begin 3 part Iron Man/Sub-Mariner battle; Sub-Mariner-c & cameo; 1st app. Cosmic Cube	5.00	15.00	35.00
80-Iron Man battles Sub-Mariner story continued in Tales to Astonish #82	5.70	17.00	40.00
99-Captain America story continued in Captain America #100; Iron Man story continued in Iron Man and Sub-Mariner #1	6.50	19.00	45.00

TALES OF THE GREEN HORNET
Sept, 1990-No. 2, Oct?, 1990 ($1.75, color, mini-series)
V2#1, Jan, 1992-Present ($1.95, color)
Now Comics

	Good	Fine	N-Mint
1-Painted-c/a; 1960s Green Hornet & Kato			
	.40	1.25	2.50
2-Painted-c/a	.35	1.00	2.00
V2#1-8: 1-N. Adams-c. 1,2-Origin Green Hornet			
	.35	1.00	2.00

TALES OF THE LEGION (... of Super-Heroes #332 on; formerly
    The Legion of Super-Heroes)
No. 314, Aug, 1984-No. 354, Dec, 1987 (75 cents; 353,354: $1.00-c)
DC Comics

314-320: 314-Origin The White Witch		.50	1.00
321-354-r/Legion of S.H. (Baxter series)		.50	1.00
Annual 4 (1986), 5 (1987)		.60	1.20

TALES OF THE NEW TEEN TITANS
June, 1982-No. 4, Sept, 1982 (Mini-series)
DC Comics

1-Origin Cyborg-book length story; Perez-c/a			
	.35	1.00	2.00
2-4: 2-Origin Raven. 3-Origin Changeling. 4-Origin Starfire; all issues contain Perez-c/a(p)	.25	.75	1.50

TALES OF THE TEENAGE MUTANT NINJA TURTLES
May, 1987-No. 7, Apr, 1989 (B&W, $1.50)(See Teenage Mutant...)
Mirage Studios

1	1.10	3.25	6.50
2-7: Title merges w/Teenage Mutant Ninja...			
	.60	1.75	3.50

TALES OF THE TEEN TITANS (Formerly The New Teen Titans)
    No. 41, April, 1984-No. 91, July, 1988 (75 cents)
DC Comics

41,45-59: 46-Aqualad & Aquagirl join. 50-Double size. 53-Intro Azreal. 56-Intro Jinx. 59-r/DC Comics Presents #26			
		.50	1.00

42-44: The Judas Contract part 1-3 with Deathstroke the Terminator
    in all; concludes in Annual #3. 44-Dick Grayson becomes Night-
    wing (3rd to be Nightwing) & joins Titans; Jericho (Deathstroke's

	Good	Fine	N-Mint
son) joins; origin Deathstroke	1.35	4.00	8.00

60-91-r/New Teen Titans Baxter series. 68-B. Smith-c. 70-Origin
Kole. #83-91 are $1.00 cover

		.50	1.00

Annual 3(1984, $1.25)-Part 4 of The Judas Contract; Deathstroke-
c/story; Death of Terra

	.50	1.50	3.00

Annual 4,5: 4-(1986, $1.25)-Reprints. 5(1987)

		.60	1.20

TALES OF THE UNEXPECTED (The Unexpected #105 on)
Feb-Mar, 1956-No. 104, Dec-Jan, 1967-68
National Periodical Publications

	Good	Fine	N-Mint
1	60.00	180.00	425.00
2	29.00	85.00	200.00
3-5	20.00	60.00	140.00
6-10	16.00	48.00	110.00
11,14,19,20	8.50	25.50	60.00

12,13,15-18,21-24: All have Kirby-a. 16-Character named "Thor"
with a magic hammer (not like later Thor)

	10.00	30.00	70.00
25-30	7.00	21.00	50.00
31-39	5.70	17.00	40.00

40-Space Ranger begins (8/59), ends #82 (1st app. in Showcase #15)

	43.00	130.00	300.00
41,42-Space Ranger stories	14.00	43.00	100.00

43-1st Space Ranger-c this title, plus story

	32.00	96.00	220.00
44-46	13.50	41.00	95.00
47-50	9.30	28.00	65.00
51-60: 54-Dinosaur-c/story	8.00	24.00	55.00
61-67: 67-Last 10 cent issue	6.30	19.00	44.00
68-82: 82-Last Space Ranger	3.15	9.50	22.00
83-100: 91-1st Automan (also in #94,97)	1.70	5.00	12.00
101-104	1.50	4.50	10.00

TALES TO ASTONISH (Becomes The Incredible Hulk #102 on)
Jan, 1959-No. 101, March, 1968
Atlas (MAP No. 1/ZPC No. 2-14/VPI No. 15-21/Marvel No. 22 on

	Good	Fine	N-Mint
1-Jack Davis-a	65.00	195.00	450.00
2-Ditko-c	29.00	85.00	200.00
3-5: 5-Williamson-a (4 pgs.)	23.00	70.00	160.00
6-10	19.00	58.00	135.00
11-20	14.00	43.00	100.00

	Good	Fine	N-Mint
21-26,28-34	10.00	30.00	70.00
27-1st Antman app. (1/62); last 10 cent issue			
	157.00	470.00	1100.00
35-(9/62)-2nd app. Antman, 1st in costume; begin series			
	100.00	300.00	700.00
36-3rd app. Antman	47.00	140.00	325.00
37-40	23.00	70.00	160.00
41-43	14.00	43.00	100.00
44-Origin & 1st app. The Wasp (6/63)	17.00	51.00	120.00
45-48	10.00	30.00	70.00
49-Antman becomes Giant Man	14.00	43.00	100.00

50-56,58: 50-Origin/1st app. Human Top; 1st app. Whirlwind. 52-Origin/1st app. Black Knight (2/64)   7.00   21.00   50.00

57-Early Spider-Man app. (7/64)	9.30	28.00	65.00
59-Giant Man vs. Hulk feature story	11.50	34.00	80.00
60-Giant Man plus Hulk double feature begins			
	14.00	43.00	100.00

61-69: 62-1st app./origin The Leader; new Wasp costume. 65-New Giant Man costume. 68-New Human Top costume. 69-Last Giant Man   5.70   17.00   40.00

| 70-Sub-Mariner & Incredible Hulk begins | 8.50 | 25.50 | 60.00 |

71-81,83-91,94-99: 81-1st app. Boomerang. 90-1st app. The Abomination. 97-X-Men cameo (brief)   4.00   12.00   28.00

82-Iron Man battles Sub-Mariner (1st Iron Man x-over outside The Avengers); story continued from Tales of Suspense #80   5.70   17.00   40.00

92,93-1st Silver Surfer x-over (outside of F.F., 7/67 & 8/67). 93-Hulk battles Silver Surfer   5.00   15.00   35.00

100-Hulk battles Sub-Mariner full-length story   5.00   15.00   35.00

101-Hulk story continued in Incredible Hulk #102; Sub-Mariner story continued in Iron Man and Sub-Mariner #1   6.50   19.00   45.00

TALES TO ASTONISH (2nd Series)
Dec, 1979-No. 14, Jan, 1981
Marvel Comics Group

| V1#1-Reprints Sub-Mariner #1 by Buscema | .60 | 1.20 |
| 2-14: Reprints Sub-Mariner #2-14 | .50 | 1.00 |

TARZAN (...of the Apes #138 on)
1-2/48-No. 131, 7-8/62; No. 132, 11/62-No. 206, 2/72
Dell Publishing Co./Gold Key No. 132 on

	Good	Fine	N-Mint
1-Jesse Marsh-a begins	79.00	235.00	550.00
2	47.00	140.00	325.00
3-5	34.00	103.00	240.00
6-10: 6-1st Tantor the Elephant. 7-1st Valley of the Monsters			
	27.00	81.00	190.00
11-15: 11-Two Against the Jungle begins, ends #24. 13-Lex Barker			
photo-c begin	23.00	70.00	160.00
16-20	17.00	51.00	120.00
21-24,26-30	13.00	40.00	90.00
25-1st "Brothers of the Spear" episode; series ends #156,160,161,			
196-206	16.00	48.00	110.00
31-40	8.00	24.00	55.00
41-54: Last Barker photo-c	6.50	19.00	45.00
55-60: 56-Eight pg. Boy story	5.00	15.00	35.00
61,62,64-70	4.00	12.00	28.00
63-Two Tarzan stories, 1 by Manning	4.30	13.00	30.00
71-79	3.15	9.50	22.00
80-99: 80-Gordon Scott photo-c begin	3.50	10.50	24.00
100	4.30	13.00	30.00
101-109	2.85	8.50	20.00
110 (Scarce)-Last photo-c	3.15	9.50	22.00
111-120	2.30	7.00	16.00
121-131: Last Dell issue	1.70	5.00	12.00
132-154: 132-1st Gold Key issue	1.50	4.50	10.00
155-Origin Tarzan	1.70	5.00	12.00
156-161: 157-Banlu, Dog of the Arande begins, ends #159, 195. 169-			
Leopard Girl app.	1.00	3.00	7.00
162,165,168,171 (TV)-Ron Ely photo covers			
	1.30	4.00	9.00
163,164,166-167,169-170: 169-Leopard Girl app.			
	.85	2.60	6.00
172-199,201-206: 178-Tarzan origin r-/#155; Leopard Girl app, also in			
#179, 190-193	.70	2.00	5.00
200 (Scarce)	.85	2.60	6.00
Story Digest 1(6/70)-G.K.	.85	2.60	6.00

TARZAN (Continuation of Gold Key series)
No. 207, April, 1972-No. 258, Feb, 1977
National Periodical Publications

	Good	Fine	N-Mint
207-Origin Tarzan by Joe Kubert, part 1; John Carter begins (origin); 52 pg. issues thru #209	.85	2.50	5.00
208,209: 208-210-Parts 2-4 of origin. 209-Last John Carter	.50	1.50	3.00
210,211: 210-Kubert-a. 211-Hogarth, Kubert-a	.35	1.00	2.00
212-214: Adaptations from "Jungle Tales of Tarzan." 213-Beyond the Farthest Star begins, ends #218	.35	1.00	2.00
215-218,224,225-All by Kubert. 215-part Foster-r	.35	1.00	2.00
219-223: Adapts "The Return of Tarzan" by Kubert	.35	1.00	2.00
226-229: 226-Manning-a	.35	1.00	2.00
230-100 pgs.; Kubert, Kaluta-a(p); Korak begins, ends #234; Carson of Venus app.	.40	1.25	2.50
231-234: Adapts "Tarzan and the Lion Man;" all 100 pgs.; Rex, the Wonder Dog r-#232, 233	.35	1.00	2.00
235-Last Kubert issue; 100 pgs.	.35	1.00	2.00
236-258: 238-(68 pgs.). 240-243 adapts "Tarzan & the Castaways." 250-256 adapts "Tarzan the Untamed." 252,253-r/#213	.35	1.00	2.00
Comic Digest 1(Fall,'72)(DC)-50 cents; 160 pgs.; digest size; Kubert-c, Manning-a	.50	1.50	3.00

TARZAN
June, 1977-No. 29, Oct, 1979
Marvel Comics Group

1	.25	.75	1.50
2-29: 2-Origin by John Buscema		.50	1.00
Annual 1-3: 1-(1977). 2-(1978). 3-(1979)		.50	1.00

TARZAN, LORD OF THE JUNGLE
Sept, 1965 (Giant)(soft paper cover)(25 cents)
Gold Key

1-Marsh-r	4.00	12.00	28.00

TEAM AMERICA (See Captain America #269)
June, 1982-No. 12, May, 1983
Marvel Comics Group

1-Origin; Ideal Toy motorcycle characters		.60	1.20
2-10: 9-Iron man app.		.50	1.00
11-Ghost Rider app.	.85	2.50	5.00

	Good	Fine	N-Mint
12-Double size	.35	1.00	2.00

TEENAGE MUTANT NINJA TURTLES (Also see Tales Of The...)
1984-Present ($1.50-$1.75, B&W; all 44-52 pgs.)
Mirage Studios

	Good	Fine	N-Mint
1-1st printing (3000 copies)-Only printing to have ad for Gobbledygook #1 & 2; Shredder app.	52.00	155.00	309.00
1-2nd printing (6/84)(15,000 copies)	11.00	34.00	67.00
1-3rd printing (2/85)(36,000 copies)	5.30	16.00	33.00
1-4th printing, new-c (50,000 copies)	3.15	9.50	19.00
1-5th printing, new-c (8/88-c, 11/88 inside)	.65	1.90	3.80
1-Counterfeit. Note: Most counterfeit copies have a inch wide white streak or scratch marks across the center of back cover. Black part of cover is a bluish black instead of a deep black. Inside paper is very white & inside cover is bright white. These counterfeit the 1st printings.			
2-1st printing (15,000 copies)	17.00	50.00	100.00
2-2nd printing	2.30	7.00	14.00
2-3rd printing; new Corben-c/a (2/85)	.85	2.50	5.00
2-Counterfeit with glossy cover stock.			
3-1st printing	6.70	20.00	40.00
3-Variant, 500 copies, given away in NYC. Has "Laird's Photo" in white rather than light blue	12.50	37.50	75.00
3-2nd printing; contains new back-up story	.90	2.75	5.50
4-1st printing	3.70	11.00	22.00
4-2nd printing (5/87)	.60	1.80	3.60
5-1st printing; Fugitoid begins, ends #7	2.70	8.00	16.00
5-2nd printing (11/87)	.60	1.80	3.60
6-1st printing (4/87-c, 5/87 inside)	2.30	7.00	14.00
6-2nd printing	.40	1.25	2.50
7-4 pg. Corben color insert; 1st color TMNT	2.30	7.00	14.00
7-2nd printing (1/89)	.40	1.25	2.50
8-Cerebus guest stars	1.50	4.50	9.00
9,10: 9 (9/86)-Rip In Time by Corben	1.10	3.25	6.50
11-15	.75	2.25	4.50
16-18: 18-Mark Bode'-a	.60	1.75	3.50
18-2nd printing ($2.25, color, 44 pgs.)-New-c	.35	1.00	2.00
19-49: 19-Begin $1.75-c. 24-26-Veitch-c/a. 35-Begin $2.00-c	.35	1.00	2.00

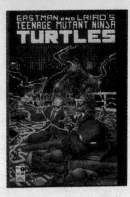

Teenage Mutant Ninja Turtles #9, © Mirage Studios

	Good	Fine	N-Mint
32-2nd printing ($2.75, color, 52 pgs.)	.45	1.40	2.80
Book 1,2($1.50, B&W): 2-Corben-c	.25	.75	1.50
...Christmas Special 1 (12/90, $1.75, B&W, 52 pgs.)-Cover title: Michaelangelo Christ. Spec.; r/Michaelangelo one-shot plus new Raphael story	.30	.90	1.80

TEENAGE MUTANT NINJA TURTLES ADVENTURES (TV)
8/88-No. 3, 12/88; 3/89-Present ($1.00, color)
Archie Comics

	Good	Fine	N-Mint
1-Adapts TV cartoon; not by Eastman/Laird	.85	2.50	5.00
2,3 (Mini-series)	.50	1.50	3.00
1 (2nd on going series)	.50	1.50	3.00
2-5: 5-Begins original stories not based on TV	.35	1.00	2.00
6-38: 14-Simpson-a(p). 19-1st Mighty Mutanimals (also in #20). 20-Begin $1.25-c. 22-Gene Colan-c/a		.65	1.30
1-11: 2nd printings w/B&W inside covers		.50	1.00
nn (Spring, 1991, $2.50, 68 pgs.)-(Meet Archie)	.40	1.25	2.50
nn (Sum, 1991, $2.50, 68 pgs.)-(Movie II)-Adapts movie sequel	.40	1.25	2.50
Special 1 (Sum, 1992, $2.50, 68 pgs.)	.40	1.25	2.50

TEEN BEAM (Formerly Teen Beat #1)
No. 2, Jan-Feb, 1968
National Periodical Publications

	Good	Fine	N-Mint

2-Orlando, Drucker-a(r); Monkees photo-c

| | 1.70 | 5.00 | 12.00 |

TEEN BEAT (Becomes Teen Beam #2)
Nov-Dec, 1967
National Periodical Publications

1-Photos & text only; Monkees photo-c   2.15   6.50   15.00

TEEN TITANS (See Brave & the Bold, DC Super-Stars #1, Marvel &
    DC Present, New Teen Titans and Showcase)
1-2/66-No. 43, 1-2/73; No. 44, 11/76-No. 53, 2/78
National Periodical Publications/DC Comics

Brave and the Bold #54 (6-7/64)-Origin & 1st app. Teen Titans; Kid
    Flash, Robin & Aqualad begin   22.00   65.00   150.00
Brave and the Bold #60 (6-7/65)-2nd app. Teen Titans; 1st app. new
    Wonder Girl (Donna Troy), who joins Titans
        8.00   24.00   55.00
Showcase #59 (11-12/65)-3rd app. Teen Titans
        8.00   24.00   55.00
1-(1-2/66)-Titans join Peace Corps; Batman, Flash, Aquaman,
    Wonder Woman cameos   18.00   54.00   125.00
2   8.50   25.50   60.00
3-5: 4-Speedy app. 6-Beast Boy x-over; readers polled on him join-
    ing Titans   4.50   14.00   32.00
6-10: 6-Doom Patrol app.   3.50   10.50   24.00
11-19: 11-Speedy app. 13-X-Mas-c. 18-1st app. Starfire (11-12/68).
    19-Wood-i; Speedy begins as regular   2.30   7.00   16.00
20-22: All Neal Adams-a. 21-Hawk & Dove app.; last 12 cent issue.
    22-Origin Wonder Girl   2.85   8.50   20.00
23-30: 23-Wonder Girl dons new costume. 25-Flash, Aquaman, Bat-
    man, Green Arrow, Green Lantern, Superman, & Hawk & Dove
    guests; 1st app. Lilith who joins T.T. West in #50. 29-Hawk &
    Dove & Ocean Master app. 30-Aquagirl app.
        1.50   4.50   10.00
31-43: 31-Hawk & Dove app. 36,37-Superboy-r. 38-Green Arrow/
    Speedy-r; Aquaman/Aqualad story. 39-Hawk & Dove-r. (36-39:
    52 pgs.)   1.00   3.00   7.00
44,45,47,49,51,52: 44-Mal becomes the Guardian
        .70   2.00   4.00
46-Joker's daughter begins (see Batman Family)
        1.35   4.00   9.00

	Good	Fine	N-Mint
48-Intro Bumblebee; Joker's daughter becomes Harlequin			
	1.35	4.00	9.00
50-1st revival original Bat-Girl; intro. Teen Titans West			
	1.15	3.50	8.00
53-Origin retold	.85	2.50	5.00

TEEN TITANS SPOTLIGHT
Aug, 1986-No. 21, Apr, 1988 (75 cents, color)(#21: $1.00-c)
DC Comics

1	.25	.75	1.50
2-21: 7-Guice's 1st work at DC. 14-Nightwing; Batman app. 18,19-			
Millennium x-over. 21-Original Teen Titans		.50	1.00

TERMINATOR, THE
Sept, 1988-No. 17, 1989 ($1.75, color, Baxter paper)
Now Comics

1-Based on movie	3.60	11.00	25.00
2	2.00	6.00	12.00
3-5	1.15	3.50	7.00
6-10	.85	2.50	5.00
11,13-17	.40	1.25	2.50
12 ($2.95, 52 pgs.)-Intro. John Connor	.50	1.50	3.00

TERMINATOR, THE
Aug, 1990-No. 4, Nov, 1990 ($2.50, color, mini-series)
Dark Horse Comics

1-Set 39 years later than the movie	1.00	3.00	6.00
2-4	.50	1.50	3.00

TERMINATOR: ALL MY FUTURES PAST, THE
V3#1, Aug, 1990-V3#2, Sept, 1990 ($1.75, color, mini-series)
Now Comics

V3#1,2	.40	1.25	2.50

TERMINATOR: ONE SHOT, THE
July, 1991 ($5.95, color, 56 pgs.)
Dark Horse Comics

nn-Matt Wagner-a; contains stiff pop-up inside

	1.00	3.00	6.00

TERMINATOR: SECONDARY OBJECTIVES, THE
July, 1991-No. 4, Oct, 1991 ($2.50, color, mini-series)
Dark Horse Comics

	Good	Fine	N-Mint
1-Gulacy-c/a(p) in all	.50	1.50	3.00
2-4	.40	1.25	2.50

TERMINATOR: THE BURNING EARTH, THE
V2#1, Mar, 1990-V2#5, July, 1990 ($1.75, color, mini-series)
Now Comics

V2#1	1.00	3.00	6.00
2	.70	2.00	4.00
3-5	.40	1.25	2.50

TERMINATOR: THE ENEMY WITHIN, THE
Nov, 1991-No. 4, Feb, 1992 ($2.50, color, mini-series)
Dark Horse Comics

1-4: All have Simon Bisley painted-c	.40	1.25	2.50

TERMINATOR 2: JUDGEMENT DAY
Early Sept, 1991-No. 3, Early Oct, 1991 ($1.00, color, mini-series)
Marvel Comics

1-Based on movie sequel; 1-3-Same as nn issues		.60	1.20
2,3		.50	1.00
nn (1991, $4.95, squarebound, 68 pgs.)-Photo-c			
	.85	2.50	5.00
nn (1991, $2.25, B&W, magazine, 68 pgs.)	.40	1.15	2.30

TEX MORGAN
Aug, 1948-No. 9, Feb, 1950
Marvel Comics (CCC)

1-Tex Morgan, his horse Lightning & sidekick Lobo begin			
	12.00	36.00	85.00
2	9.30	28.00	65.00
3-6: 3,4-Arizona Annie app.	6.00	18.00	42.00

7-9: All photo-c. 7-Captain Tootsie by Beck. 8-18 pg. story "The
Terror of Rimrock Valley;" Diablo app.

	9.30	28.00	65.00

TEX RITTER WESTERN (Movie star; singing cowboy)
Oct, 1950-No. 46, May, 1959 (Photo-c: 1-21)
Fawcett No. 1-20 (1/54)/Charlton No. 21 on

	Good	Fine	N-Mint
1-Tex Ritter, his stallion White Flash & dog Fury begin; photo front/ back-c begin	39.00	118.00	275.00
2	19.00	58.00	135.00
3-5: 5-Last photo back-c	16.00	48.00	110.00
6-10	13.00	40.00	90.00
11-19	8.50	25.50	60.00
20-Last Fawcett issue (1/54)	10.00	30.00	70.00
21-1st Charlton issue; photo-c (3/54)	10.00	30.00	70.00
22-B&W photo back-c begin, end #32	5.30	16.00	38.00
23-30: 23-25-Young Falcon app.	4.30	13.00	30.00
31-38,40-45	3.60	11.00	25.00
39-Williamson-a; Whitman-c (1/58)	5.00	15.00	35.00
46-Last issue	4.30	13.00	30.00

TEX TAYLOR
Sept, 1948-No. 9, March, 1950
Marvel Comics (HPC)

	Good	Fine	N-Mint
1-Tex Taylor & his horse Fury begin	13.00	40.00	90.00
2	8.50	25.50	60.00
3	8.00	24.00	55.00
4-6: All photo-c. 4-Anti-Wertham editorial. 5,6-Blaze Carson app.			
	8.50	25.50	60.00
7-Photo-c; 18 pg. Movie-Length Thriller "Trapped in Time's Lost Land!" with sabre toothed tigers, dinosaurs; Diablo app.			
	10.00	30.00	70.00
8-Photo-c; 18 pg. Movie-Length Thriller "The Mystery of Devil-Tree Plateau!" with dwarf horses, dwarf people & a lost miniature Inca type village; Diablo app.	10.00	30.00	70.00
9-Photo-c; 18 pg. Movie-Length Thriller "Guns Along the Border!" Captain Tootsie by Schreiber; Nimo The Mountain Lion app.			
	10.00	30.00	70.00

THANOS QUEST, THE (See Capt. Marvel #25, Infinity Gauntlet, Iron Man #55, Logan's Run, Marvel Feature #12, Silver Surfer #34 & Warlock #9) 1990-No. 2, 1990 ($4.95, color, squarebound, 52 pgs.)
Marvel Comics

	Good	Fine	N-Mint
1-Both have Starlin scripts & covers	2.30	7.00	14.00
2	1.70	5.00	10.00
1,2-2nd printings ($4.95)	.85	2.50	5.00

THING, THE (See Fantastic Four, Marvel Fanfare, Marvel Feature
  #11, 12 and Marvel Two-In-One)
July, 1983-No. 36, June, 1986
Marvel Comics Group

	Good	Fine	N-Mint
1-Life story of Ben Grimm; Byrne scripts begin			
	.35	1.00	2.00
2-36: 5-Spider-Man, She-Hulk app.	.60	1.20	

THOR (Formerly Journey Into Mystery)(The Mighty Thor #413 on;
  also see Avengers #1, Marvel Spectacular, Special Marvel Edition
  & Tales of Asgard)
March, 1966-Present
Marvel Comics Group

	Good	Fine	N-Mint
126-Thor continues	11.50	34.00	80.00
127-133,135-140	5.00	15.00	35.00
134-Intro High Evolutionary	6.50	19.00	45.00
141-157,159,160: 146-Inhumans begin, end #151. 146,147-Origin Inhumans. 148,149-Origin Black Bolt in each; 149-Origin Medusa, Crystal, Maximus, Gorgon, Kornak			
	3.60	11.00	25.00
158-Origin-r/#83; 158,159-Origin Dr. Blake			
	8.00	24.00	55.00
161,163,164,167,170-179-Last Kirby issue. 164-Brief cameo Him (5/69)	2.30	7.00	16.00
162,168,169-Origin Galactus	4.00	12.00	28.00
165-(6/69)-1st full app. Warlock (Him)(2nd since Fantastic Four #66,67)	5.70	17.00	40.00
166-(7/69)-2nd full app. Warlock (Him); Thor battles Him			
	5.00	15.00	35.00
180,181-Neal Adams-a	1.50	4.50	10.00
182-192,194-200	.85	2.50	5.00
193-(52 pgs.); Silver Surfer x-over	3.85	11.50	27.00
201-250: 225-Intro. Firelord	.60	1.75	3.50
251-280: 271-Iron Man x-over. 274-Death of Balder the Brave			
	.40	1.25	2.50
281-299: 294-Origin Asgard & Odin	.35	1.00	2.00
300-(12/80)-End of Asgard; origin of Odin & The Destroyer			
	.85	2.50	5.00
301-336: 316-Iron Man x-over	.25	.75	1.50
337-Simonson-c/a begins, ends #382; Beta Ray Bill becomes new Thor			
	1.15	3.50	7.00
338-Two variants exist, 60 & 75 cents	.50	1.50	3.00

	Good	Fine	N-Mint
339,340: 340-Donald Blake returns as Thor	.25	.75	1.50
341-373,375-381,383: 373-X-Factor tie-in		.50	1.00
374-Mutant Massacre; X-Factor app.	1.35	4.00	8.00
382-($1.25)-Anniversary issue; last Simonson-a			
	.35	1.00	2.00
384-Intro. new Thor	.35	1.00	2.00

385-399,401-410,413-428: 385-Hulk x-over. 391-Spider-Man x-over. 395-Intro Earth Force. 408-Eric Masterson becomes Thor. 427,428-Excalibur x-over

		.50	1.00
400-($1.75, 68 pgs.)-Origin Loki	.40	1.25	2.50
411-Intro New Warriors (apps. in costume in last panel)			
	.50	1.50	3.00

412-1st full app. New Warriors (Marvel Boy, Kid Nova, Namorita, Night Thrasher, Firestar & Speedball)   3.00   9.00   18.00

429,430-Ghost Rider x-over	.50	1.50	3.00

431,434-449,451,452: 434-Capt. America x-over. 437-Thor vs. Quasar; Hercules app.; Tales of Asgard back-up stories begin. 443-Dr. Strange & Silver Surfer x-over. 444-Begin $1.25-c

		.65	1.30
432-($1.50, 52 pgs.)-Thor's 300th app. (vs. Loki); reprints origin & 1st app. from Journey into Mystery #83	.50	1.50	3.00
433-Intro new Thor	.50	1.50	3.00
450-($2.50, 68 pgs.)-Double gatefold-c	.40	1.25	2.50
Special 2(9/66)-See Journey Into Mystery for 1st annual			
	5.70	17.00	40.00
King Size Special 3(1/71)	1.15	3.50	8.00
Special 4(12/71)	1.15	3.50	8.00
Annual 5,7,8: 5(11/76). 7(1978). 8(1979)	1.00	3.00	6.00
Annual 6 (10/77)-Guardians of the Galaxy app.			
	1.00	3.00	6.00
Annual 9-12: 9(1981). 10(1982). 11(1983). 12(1984)			
	.50	1.50	3.00

Annual 13-16: 13(1985). 14('89, $2.00, 68 pgs.)-Atlantis Attacks. 15('90, $2.00, 68 pgs.). 16('91, $2.00, 68 pgs.)-3 pg. origin; Guardians of the Galaxy x-over   .35   1.00   2.00

Annual 17 (1992, $2.25, 68 pgs.)	.40	1.15	2.30

3-D BATMAN (Also see Batman 3-D)
1953, Reprinted in 1966
National Periodical Publications

1953-Reprints Batman #42 & 48; Tommy Tomorrow app. (25 cents)

	Good	Fine	N-Mint
	86.00	257.00	600.00

	Good	Fine	N-Mint
1966-Tommy Tomorrow app.	29.00	85.00	200.00

THREE MOUSEKETEERS, THE (1st Series)
3-4/56-No. 24, 9-10/59; No. 25, 8-9/60-No. 26, 10-12/60
National Periodical Publications

1	11.50	34.00	80.00
2	5.70	17.00	40.00
3-10	4.30	13.00	30.00
11-26	3.60	11.00	25.00

THREE MOUSEKETEERS, THE (2nd Series) (See Super DC Giant)
May-June, 1970-No. 7, May-June, 1971 (#5-7: 68 pgs.)
National Periodical Publications

1-Mayer-a	.85	2.50	5.00
2-7-Mayer-a	.50	1.50	3.00

THREE STOOGES
No. 1043, Oct-Dec, 1959-No. 55, June, 1972
Dell Publishing Co./Gold Key No. 10 (10/62) on

4-Color 1043 (#1)	11.50	34.00	80.00
4-Color 1078,1127,1170,1187	6.50	19.00	45.00
6(9-11/61)-10: 6-Professor Putter begins; ends #16	5.00	15.00	35.00
11-14,16-20: 17-The Little Monsters begin (5/64)(1st app.?)	4.30	13.00	30.00
15-Go Around the World in a Daze (movie scenes)	5.00	15.00	35.00
21,23-30	3.60	11.00	25.00
22-Movie scenes/"The Outlaws Is Coming"	4.50	14.00	32.00
31-55	3.00	9.00	21.00

THRILLING COMICS
Feb, 1940-No. 80, April, 1951
Better Publ./Nedor/Standard Comics

1-Origin Doc Strange (37 pgs.); Nickie Norton of the Secret Service begins	72.00	215.00	500.00
2-The Rio Kid, The Woman in Red, Pinocchio begins	34.00	100.00	235.00
3-The Ghost & Lone Eagle begin	29.00	85.00	200.00
4-10	20.00	60.00	140.00

Thrilling Comics #24, © Standard Comics

	Good	Fine	N-Mint
11-18,20	15.00	45.00	105.00
19-Origin The American Crusader (1st app?), ends #39,41			
	22.00	65.00	150.00
21-30: 24-Intro. Mike, Doc Strange's sidekick. 29-Last Rio Kid			
	14.00	43.00	100.00
31-40: 36-Commando Cubs begin	11.50	34.00	80.00
41,44-Hitler-c	11.50	34.00	80.00
42,43,45-52: 52-The Ghost ends	9.30	28.00	65.00
53-The Phantom Detective begins; The Cavalier app.; no Commando Cubs	9.30	28.00	65.00
54-The Cavalier app.; no Commando Cubs			
	9.30	28.00	65.00
55-Lone Eagle ends	9.30	28.00	65.00
56-Princess Pantha begins	17.00	51.00	120.00
57-60	14.00	43.00	100.00
61-66: 61-Ingels-a; The Lone Eagle app. 65-Last Phantom Detective & Commando Cubs. 66-Frazetta text illo			
	14.00	43.00	100.00
67,70-73: Frazetta-a(5-7 pgs.) in each. 72-Sea Eagle app.			
	19.00	58.00	135.00
68,69-Frazetta-a(2), 8 & 6 pgs.; 9 & 7 pgs.			
	20.00	60.00	140.00
74-Last Princess Pantha; Tara app. Buck Ranger, Cowboy Detective begins	8.50	25.50	60.00
75-78: 75-Western format begins	4.30	13.00	30.00
79-Krigstein-a	6.00	18.00	42.00
80-Severin & Elder, Celardo, Moreira-a	5.70	17.00	40.00

THUNDER AGENTS (See Dynamo and Noman)
11/65-No. 17, 12/67; No. 18, 9/68, No. 19, 11/68, No. 20, 11/69 (No. 1-
    16: 68 pgs.; No. 17 on: 52 pgs.)(All are 25 cents)
Tower Comics

	Good	Fine	N-Mint
1-Origin & 1st app. Dynamo, Noman, Menthor, & The Thunder Squad; 1st app. The Iron Maiden	8.00	24.00	55.00
2-Death of Egghead	4.30	13.00	30.00
3-5: 4-Guy Gilbert becomes Lightning who joins Thunder Squad; Iron Maiden app.	3.15	9.50	22.00
6-10: 7-Death of Menthor. 8-Origin & 1st app. The Raven	2.00	6.00	14.00
11-15: 13-Undersea Agent app.; no Raven story	1.30	4.00	9.00
16-19	1.00	3.00	7.00
20-Special Collectors Edition; all reprints	.70	2.00	4.00

THUNDERBOLT (Peter Cannon...; see Crisis on Infinite Earths)
Jan, 1966; No. 51, Mar-Apr, 1966-No. 60, Nov, 1967
Charlton Comics

1-Origin	1.50	4.50	10.00
51-(Formerly Son of Vulcan #50)	.85	2.50	5.00
52-59: 54-Sentinels begin. 59-Last Thunderbolt & Sentinels (back-up story)	.70	2.00	4.00
60-Prankster app.	.85	2.50	5.00

TIME TUNNEL, THE (TV)
Feb, 1967-No. 2, July, 1967
Gold Key

1,2-Photo back-c	3.50	10.50	24.00

TOMAHAWK (Son of... on-c of #131-140; see Star Spangled Comics
    #69 & World's Finest Comics #65)
Sept-Oct, 1950-No. 140, May-June, 1972
National Periodical Publications

1-Tomahawk begins by F. Ray	68.00	205.00	475.00
2-Frazetta/Williamson-a (4 pgs.)	34.00	103.00	240.00
3-5	22.00	65.00	150.00
6-10: 7-Last 52 pg. issue	15.00	45.00	105.00
11-20	9.30	28.00	65.00
21-27,30: Last precode (2/55)	7.00	21.00	50.00
28-1st app. Lord Shilling (arch-foe)	9.30	28.00	65.00
29-Frazetta-r/Jimmy Wakely #3 (3 pgs.)	13.50	41.00	95.00

	Good	Fine	N-Mint
31-40	7.00	21.00	50.00
41-50	5.00	15.00	35.00
51-56,58-60	3.60	11.00	25.00
57-Frazetta-r/Jimmy Wakely #6 (3 pgs.)	8.00	24.00	55.00
61-77: 77-Last 10 cent issue	2.65	8.00	18.00
78-85: 81-1st app. Miss Liberty. 83-Origin Tomahawk's Rangers			
	1.70	5.00	12.00
86-100: 96-Origin/1st app. The Hood, alias Lady Shilling			
	1.00	3.00	6.00
101-110: 107-Origin/1st app. Thunder-Man	.85	2.50	5.00
111-130,132-138,140	.50	1.50	3.00
131-Frazetta-r/Jimmy Wakely #7 (3 pgs.); origin Firehair retold			
	.70	2.00	4.00
139-Frazetta-r/Star Spangled #113	.60	1.75	3.50

TOMB OF DRACULA
April, 1972-No. 70, Aug, 1979
Marvel Comics Group

	Good	Fine	N-Mint
1-1st app. Dracula; Colan-p in all	5.70	17.00	40.00
2	3.50	10.50	24.00
3-5: 3-Intro. Dr. Rachel Van Helsing & Inspector Chelm			
	2.00	6.00	14.00
6-10: 10-1st app. Blade the Vampire Slayer			
	1.70	5.00	12.00
11-20: 12-Brunner-c(p). 13-Origin Blade	1.30	4.00	9.00
21-40	1.00	3.00	7.00
41-60: 50-Silver Surfer app.	.75	2.25	4.50
61-70: 70-Double size	.60	1.75	3.50

TOMB OF DRACULA
1991-No. 4, 1992 ($4.95, color, mini-series, squarebound, 52 pgs.)
Epic Comics (Marvel)

	Good	Fine	N-Mint
Book 1-4: Colan/Williamson-a; Colan painted-c			
	.85	2.50	5.00

TOWER OF SHADOWS (Creatures on the Loose #10 on)
Sept, 1969-No. 9, Jan, 1971
Marvel Comics Group

	Good	Fine	N-Mint
1-Steranko, Craig-a	2.15	6.50	15.00
2-Neal Adams-a	.85	2.60	6.00
3-Barry Smith, Tuska-a	1.00	3.00	7.00

	Good	Fine	N-Mint
4-Kirby/Everett-c	.85	2.50	5.00
5,7-B. Smith(p), Wood-a (Wood draws himself-1st pg., 1st panel-#5)			
	.85	2.60	6.00
6,8: Wood-a; 8-Wrightson-c	.85	2.50	5.00
9-Wrightson-c; Roy Thomas app.	.70	2.00	4.00
Special 1(12/71)-Neal Adams-a	.85	2.50	5.00

TRANSFORMERS, THE (TV)(Also see G.I. Joe and...)
Sept, 1984-No. 80, July, 1991 (.75-$1.00)
Marvel Comics Group

	Good	Fine	N-Mint
1-Based on Hasbro toys	.40	1.25	2.50
2,3	.30	.90	1.80
4-10,75: 75-($1.50, 52 pgs.)	.25	.75	1.50
11-74,76-80: 21-Intro Aerialbots. 54-Intro Micromasters			
		.50	1.00

NOTE: *Second and third printings of all issues exist and are worth less than originals. Was originally planned as a four issue mini-series.*

TUROK, SON OF STONE
No. 596, 12/54-No. 29, 9/62; No. 30, 12/62-No. 91, 7/74; No. 92, 9/74-
No. 125, 1/80; No. 126, 3/81-No. 130, 4/82
Dell Publ. Co. No. 1-29/Gold Key No. 30-91/Gold Key or Whitman No.
92-125/Whitman No. 126 on

	Good	Fine	N-Mint
4-Color 596 (12/54)(#1)-1st app./origin Turok & Andar			
	32.00	95.00	225.00
4-Color 656 (10/55)(#2)-1st mention of Lanok			
	24.00	70.00	165.00
3(3-5/56)-5	17.00	51.00	120.00
6-10	11.50	34.00	80.00
11-20: 17-Prehistoric pygmies	7.00	21.00	50.00
21-30: 30-Back-c pin-ups begin. 30-33-Painted back-c pin-ups			
	4.00	12.00	28.00
31-40	2.85	8.50	20.00
41-50	2.00	6.00	14.00
51-60: 58-Flying Saucer c/story	1.15	3.50	8.00
61-70: 62-12 & 15 cent-c. 63-Only line drawn-c			
	.85	2.50	5.00
71-84: 84-Origin & 1st app. Hutec	.70	2.00	4.00
85-130: 114,115-(52 pgs.)	.35	1.00	2.00
Giant 1(30031-611) (11/66)	7.00	21.00	50.00

TV STARS (TV)(Hanna-Barbera)
Aug, 1978-No. 4, Feb, 1979
Marvel Comics Group

	Good	Fine	N-Mint
1-Great Grape Ape app.	.60	1.75	3.50
2,4: 4-Top Cat app.		.60	1.20
3-Toth-c/a; Dave Stevens inks	.60	1.75	3.50

12 O'CLOCK HIGH (TV)
Jan-Mar, 1965-No. 2, Apr-June, 1965 (Photo-c)
Dell Publishing Co.

1,2	3.00	9.00	21.00

TWILIGHT ZONE, THE (TV)
No. 1173, 3-5/61-No. 91, 4/79; No. 92, 5/82
Dell Publishing Co./Gold Key/Whitman No. 92

	Good	Fine	N-Mint
4-Color 1173 (#1)-Crandall/Evans-c/a	11.50	34.00	80.00
4-Color 1288-Crandall/Evans-c/a	7.70	23.00	53.00
01-860-207 (5-7/62-Dell, 15 cents)	6.00	18.00	42.00
12-860-210 on-c; 01-860-210 on inside(8-10/62-Dell)-Evans-c/a; Crandall/Frazetta-a(2)	6.00	18.00	42.00
1(11/62-Gold Key)-Crandall/Frazetta-a(10 & 11 pgs.); Evans-a	6.70	20.00	47.00
2	3.70	11.00	26.00
3-11: 3,4,9-Toth-a, 11,10 & 15 pgs.	2.70	8.00	19.00
12,13,15: 12-Williamson-a. 13-Williamson/Crandall-a. 15-Crandall-a	2.40	7.25	17.00
14-Williamson/Orlando/Crandall/Torres-a	2.40	7.25	17.00
16-20	1.70	5.00	12.00
21-27: 21-Crandall-a(r). 25-Evans/Crandall-a(r); Toth-r/#4. 26-Crandall, Evans-a(r). 27-Evans-r(2)	1.15	3.50	8.00
28-32: 32-Evans-a(r)	.70	2.00	4.00
33-51: 43-Crandall-a. 51-Williamson-a	.50	1.50	3.00
52-70	.25	.75	1.50
71-92: 71-Reprint. 83,84-(52 pgs.)		.50	1.00

TWILIGHT ZONE, THE (TV)
Nov, 1990 ($2.95, color)
V2#1, Nov, 1991-Present ($1.95, color)
Now Comics

	Good	Fine	N-Mint
1-($2.95, 52 pgs.)-Direct sale edition; Neal Adams-a, Sienkiewicz-c; Harlan Ellison scripts	1.35	4.00	8.00
1-(11/90, $1.75)-Newsstand ed. w/N. Adams-c	.30	.90	1.80
1-Prestige Format (10/91, $4.95)-Reprints above with extra Harlan Ellison short story	1.35	4.00	8.00
1-Collector's Edition (10/91, $2.50)-None-code approved and polybagged; reprints 11/90 issue; gold logo	1.70	5.00	10.00
1-Reprint ($2.50)-Reprints direct sale ed. from 11/90	.40	1.25	2.50
1-Reprint ($2.50)-Reprints newsstand ed. from 11/90	.40	1.25	2.50
V2#1-(Direct sale, non-code-c)-B. Jones scripts	.35	1.00	2.00
V2#1-(Newsstand, code approved-c)	.35	1.00	2.00
V2#2-8,10-12	.35	1.00	2.00
V2#9-($2.95)-3-D Special with hologram on-c (both versions are polybagged)	.50	1.50	3.00
V2#9-($4.95)-Prestige 3-D Special w/different hologram and extra stories	.85	2.50	5.00

2001, A SPACE ODYSSEY
Dec, 1976-No. 10, Sept, 1977 (Regular size, all 30 cent issues)
Marvel Comics Group

	Good	Fine	N-Mint
1-Based on movie; Kirby-c/a in all	.35	1.00	2.00
2-10: 8-Origin/1st app. Machine Man (called Mr. Machine)		.50	1.00

UNCANNY X-MEN, THE (See X-Men)

UNCANNY X-MEN AND THE NEW TEEN TITANS (See Marvel and DC Present...)

UNCANNY X-MEN AT THE STATE FAIR OF TEXAS, THE
1983 (36 pgs.)(One-Shot)
Marvel Comics Group

	Good	Fine	N-Mint
nn	2.50	7.50	15.00

UNCANNY X-MEN IN DAYS OF FUTURE PAST, THE
1989 ($3.95, color, squarebound, 52 pgs.)
Marvel Comics

nn-Byrne/Austin-r (2 stories); Guice-c(p)	.70	2.00	4.00

UNCLE SAM QUARTERLY (Blackhawk #9 on) (Also see National Comics)
Autumn, 1941-No. 8, Fall, 1943
Quality Comics Group

1-Origin Uncle Sam; Fine/Eisner-c, chapter headings, 2 pgs. by Eisner. (2 versions: dark cover, no price; light cover with price sticker); Jack Cole-a	130.00	385.00	900.00
2-Cameos by The Ray, Black Condor, Quicksilver, The Red Bee, Alias the Spider, Hercules & Neon the Unknown; Eisner, Fine-c/a	63.00	190.00	440.00
3-Tuska-c/a	47.00	140.00	330.00
4	39.00	120.00	275.00
5-8	34.00	100.00	235.00

UNCLE SCROOGE ADVENTURES (Walt Disney's...#4 on)
Nov, 1987-No. 21, May, 1990
Gladstone Publishing

1-Barks-r begin	.70	2.00	4.00
2-5: 5-Rosa-c/a	.25	.75	1.50
6-19: 9,14-Rosa-a. 10-r/U.S. #18 (all Barks)		.50	1.00
20,21 ($1.95, 68 pgs.) 20-Rosa-c/a. 21-Rosa-a			
	.35	1.00	2.00

UNCLE SCROOGE & DONALD DUCK
June, 1965 (25 cents) (Paper cover)
Gold Key

	Good	Fine	N-Mint
1-Reprint of 4-Color #386(#1) & lead story/F.C. #29			
	8.35	25.00	50.00

UNDERDOG (TV)
July, 1970-No. 10, Jan, 1972; Mar, 1975-No. 23, Feb, 1979
Charlton Comics/Gold Key

	Good	Fine	N-Mint
1 (1st series, Charlton)	4.30	13.00	30.00
2-10	1.70	5.00	12.00
1 (2nd series, Gold Key)	2.65	8.00	18.00
2-10	1.15	3.50	8.00
11-23: 13-1st app. Shack of Solitude	1.00	3.00	6.00

UNDERSEA AGENT
Jan, 1966-No. 6, Mar, 1967 (25 cents, 68 pages)
Tower Comics

	Good	Fine	N-Mint
1-Davy Jones, Undersea Agent begins	3.15	9.50	22.00
2-6: 2-Jones gains magnetic powers. 5-Origin & 1st app. of Merman. 6-Kane?/Wood-c(r)	2.15	6.50	15.00

UNEARTHLY SPECTACULARS
Oct, 1965-No. 3, Mar, 1967 (#1: 12 cents; #2,3: 25 cent giants)
Harvey Publications

	Good	Fine	N-Mint
1-Tiger Boy; Simon-c	1.00	3.00	6.00
2-Jack Q. Frost, Tiger Boy & Three Rocketeers app.; Williamson, Wood, Kane-a; r-1 story/Thrill-O-Rama #2	2.00	6.00	14.00
3-Jack Q. Frost app.; Williamson/Crandall-a; r-from Alarming Advs. #1, 1962	2.00	6.00	14.00

UNEXPECTED, THE (Formerly Tales of the...)
No. 105, Feb-Mar, 1968-No. 222, May, 1982
National Periodical Publications/DC Comics

105-Begin 12 cent cover price, ends ?	1.15	3.50	8.00
106-115,117,118,120,122-127	.75	2.25	4.50
116,119,121,128-Wrightson-a	1.10	3.25	6.50
129-162: 132-136-(52 pgs.). 157-162-(100 pgs.)	.40	1.25	2.50
163-188: 187,188-(44 pgs.)		.60	1.20

	Good	Fine	N-Mint
189,190,192-195 ($1.00, 68 pgs.): 189 on are combined with House of Secrets & The Witching Hour		.70	1.40
191-Rogers-a(p) ($1.00, 68 pgs.)	.40	1.25	2.50
196-221: 200-Return of Johnny Peril by Tuska. 205-213-Johnny Peril app. 210-Time Warp story		.50	1.00

UNKNOWN SOLDIER (Formerly Star-Spangled War Stories)
No. 205, Apr-May, 1977-No. 268, Oct, 1982
National Periodical Publications/DC Comics

	Good	Fine	N-Mint
205-268: 219-221-(44 pgs.). 248,249-Origin. 251-Enemy Ace begins. 268-Death of Unknown Soldier	.25	.75	1.50

UNKNOWN WORLDS
Aug, 1960-No. 57, Aug, 1967
American Comics Group/Best Synd. Features

	Good	Fine	N-Mint
1	8.50	25.50	60.00
2-5: 2-Dinosaur-c/story	4.30	13.00	30.00
6-11: 9-Dinosaur-c/story. 11-Last 10 cent issue	3.00	9.00	21.00
12-19: 12-Begin 12 cent issues?; ends #57	2.30	7.00	16.00
20-Herbie cameo (12-1/62-63)	2.65	8.00	18.00
21-35	1.70	5.00	12.00
36-"The People vs. Hendricks" by Craig; most popular ACG story ever	2.15	6.50	15.00
37-46	1.30	4.00	9.00
47-Williamson-a r-from Adventures Into the Unknown #96, 3 pgs.; Craig-a	1.50	4.50	10.00
48-57: 53-Frankenstein app.	1.00	3.00	7.00

UNTOLD LEGEND OF THE BATMAN, THE
July, 1980-No. 3, Sept, 1980 (Mini-series)
DC Comics

	Good	Fine	N-Mint
1-Origin; Joker-c; Byrne's 1st work at DC	.70	2.00	4.00
2,3	.50	1.50	3.00
1-3: Batman cereal premiums (28 pgs., 6X9''); 1st & 2nd printings known		.50	1.00

UNUSUAL TALES (Blue Beetle #50 on)
Nov, 1955-No. 49, Mar-Apr, 1965
Charlton Comics

	Good	Fine	N-Mint
1	11.00	32.00	75.00
2	4.50	14.00	32.00

	Good	Fine	N-Mint
3-5	3.15	9.50	22.00
6-8-Ditko-c/a	11.00	32.00	75.00
9-Ditko-c/a, 20 pgs.	11.50	34.00	80.00
10-Ditko-c/a(4)	13.00	40.00	90.00
11-(3/58, 68 pgs.)-Ditko-a(4)	13.00	40.00	90.00
12,14-Ditko-a	8.00	24.00	55.00
13,16-20	2.65	8.00	18.00
15-Ditko-c/a	8.00	24.00	55.00
21,24,28	1.70	5.00	12.00
22,25-27,29-Ditko-a	5.00	15.00	35.00
23-Ditko-c	2.15	6.50	15.00
30-49	1.50	4.50	10.00

USA COMICS
Aug, 1941-No. 17, Fall, 1945
Timely Comics (USA)

	Good	Fine	VF-NM
1-Origin Major Liberty (called Mr. Liberty #1), Rockman by Wolverton, & The Whizzer by Avison; The Defender with sidekick Rusty & Jack Frost begin; The Young Avenger only app.; S&K-c plus 1 pg. art	415.00	1040.00	2500.00

	Good	Fine	N-Mint
2-Origin Captain Terror & The Vagabond; last Wolverton Rockman	215.00	540.00	1300.00
3-No Whizzer	167.00	415.00	1000.00
4-Last Rockman, Major Liberty, Defender, Jack Frost, & Capt. Terror;Corporal Dix app.	132.00	335.00	800.00
5-Origin American Avenger & Roko the Amazing; The Blue Blade, The Black Widow & Victory Boys, Gypo the Gypsy Giant & Hills of Horror only app.; Sergeant Dix begins; no Whizzer. Hitler-c	112.00	280.00	675.00
6-Captain America, The Destroyer, Jap Buster Johnson, Jeep Jones begin; Terror Squad only app.	132.00	335.00	800.00
7-Captain Daring, Disk-Eyes the Detective by Wolverton app.; origin & only app. Marvel Boy; Secret Stamp begins; no Whizzer, Sergeant Dix	117.00	290.00	700.00
8-10: 9-Last Secret Stamp. 10-The Thunderbird only app.	83.00	210.00	500.00
11,12: 11-No Jeep Jones	67.00	167.00	400.00
13-17: 13-No Whizzer; Jeep Jones ends. 15-No Destroyer; Jap Buster Johnson ends	50.00	125.00	300.00

"V" (TV)
Feb, 1985-No. 18, July, 1986
DC Comics

	Good	Fine	N-Mint
1-Based on TV movie & series (Sci/Fi)	.25	.75	1.50
2-18: 17,18-Denys Cowan-c/a		.50	1.00

VAULT OF HORROR
No. 12, Apr-May, 1950-No. 40, Dec-Jan, 1954-55
E. C. Comics

12 (Scarce)	285.00	860.00	2000.00
13-Morphine story	74.00	220.00	515.00
14	64.00	193.00	450.00
15	54.00	163.00	380.00
16	41.00	125.00	290.00
17-19	32.00	95.00	220.00
20-25: 22-Frankenstein adaptation. 23-Used in **POP**, pg. 84. 24-Craig biography	24.00	73.00	170.00
26-B&W & color illos in **POP**	24.00	73.00	170.00
27-35: 31-Ray Bradbury biog. 35-X-Mas-c	18.00	54.00	125.00
36-"Pipe Dream"-classic opium addict story by Krigstein; "Twin Bill" cited in articles by T.E. Murphy, Wertham	18.00	54.00	125.00
37-1st app. Drusilla, a Vampirella look alike; Williamson-a	18.00	54.00	125.00
38-39: 39-Bondage-c	15.00	45.00	105.00
40-Low distribution	18.00	54.00	125.00

VAULT OF HORROR, THE
Aug, 1990-No. 6, June, 1991 ($1.95, color, 68 pgs.)(#4 on: $2.00)
Gladstone Publishing

1-Craig-c(r); all contain EC reprints	.70	2.00	4.00
2-Craig-c(r)	.50	1.50	3.00
3-6: 4-6-Craig-c(r). 3-Ingels-c(r)	.40	1.25	2.50

V FOR VENDETTA
Sept, 1988-No. 10, May, 1989 ($2.00, maxi-series, mature readers)
DC Comics

	Good	Fine	N-Mint
1-Alan Moore scripts in all	.70	2.00	4.00
2-10	.35	1.00	2.00

VIGILANTE, THE (Also see Action Comics #42, Justice League of
   America, New Teen Titans & World's Finest #244)
Oct, 1983-No. 50, Feb, 1988 ($1.25; Baxter paper)
DC Comics

1-Origin	.85	2.50	5.00
2	.50	1.50	3.00
3-10: 3-Cyborg app. 4-1st app. The Exterminator. 6,7-Origin			
	.35	1.00	2.00
11-49: 17,18-Alan Moore scripts. 20,21-Vs. Nightwing. 35-Origin			
Mad Bomber. 47-Batman-c/story	.30	.90	1.80
50-Death of Vigilante (suicide; shoots himself)			
	.40	1.25	2.50
Annual 1 (1985, $2.00, 52 pgs.)	.40	1.25	2.50
Annual 2 (1986. $2.00, 52 pgs.)-Bolland-c	.35	1.10	2.25

VISION AND THE SCARLET WITCH, THE (See Marvel Fanfare)
Nov, 1982-No. 4, Feb, 1983 (Mini-series)
Marvel Comics Group

1	.25	.75	1.50
2-4: 2-Nuklo & Future Man app.		.50	1.00

VISION AND THE SCARLET WITCH, THE
Oct, 1985-No. 12, Sept, 1986 (Maxi-series)
Marvel Comics Group

V2#1-Origin; 1st app. in Avengers #57	.30	.90	1.80
2-5: 2-West Coast Avengers x-over	.25	.75	1.50
6-12		.60	1.30

W

WALT DISNEY'S COMICS AND STORIES (#1-30 contain Donald
Duck newspaper reprints) (Titled "Comics And Stories" #264 on)
10/40-#263, 8/62; #264, 10/62-#510, 1984;
#511, 10/86-Present
Dell Publishing Co./Gold Key #264-473/Whitman #474-510/
Gladstone #511-547(4/90)/Disney Comics #548(5/90) on

NOTE: *The whole number can always be found at the bottom of the title
page in the lower left-hand or right-hand panel.*

	Good	Fine	VF-NM
1(V1#1-c; V2#1-indicia)-Donald Duck strip-r by Al Taliaferro & Gottfredson's Mickey Mouse begin	450.00	2000.00	3900.00

(Prices vary widely on this book)

	Good	Fine	N-Mint
2	360.00	1070.00	2500.00
3	115.00	345.00	800.00
4-X-mas-c	86.00	257.00	600.00

4-Special promotional, complimentary issue; cover same except one
corner was blanked out & boxed in to identify the giveaway (not a
paste-over). This special pressing was probably sent out to former
subscribers to Mickey Mouse Mag. whose subscriptions had
expired. *(Very rare-5 known copies)*

	Good	Fine	N-Mint
	129.00	385.00	900.00
5	71.00	215.00	500.00
6-10	57.00	170.00	400.00
11-14	50.00	150.00	350.00

15-17: 15-The 3 Little Kittens (17 pgs.). 16-The 3 Little Pigs (29
pgs.); X-mas-c. 17-The Ugly Duckling (4 pgs.)

	Good	Fine	N-Mint
	45.00	135.00	315.00
18-21	38.00	115.00	265.00
22-30: 22-Flag-c	32.00	95.00	225.00
31-Donald Duck by Carl Barks begins	215.00	645.00	1500.00
32-Barks-a	100.00	300.00	700.00
33-Barks-a (infinity-c)	71.00	215.00	500.00

34-Gremlins by Walt Kelly begin, end #41; Barks-a

	Good	Fine	N-Mint
	59.00	178.00	415.00
35,36-Barks-a	52.00	155.00	365.00
37-Donald Duck by Jack Hannah	26.00	77.00	180.00

38-40-Barks-a. 39-Christmas-c. 40-Gremlins by Kelly

	36.00	107.00	250.00

Walt Disney's Comics and Stories #16, © The Disney Company

	Good	Fine	N-Mint
41-50-Barks-a; 41-Gremlins by Kelly	29.00	85.00	200.00
51-60-Barks-a; 51-Christmas-c. 52-Li'l Bad Wolf begins, ends #203 (not in #55). 58-Kelly flag-c	22.00	65.00	150.00
61-70: Barks-a. 61-Dumbo story. 63,64-Pinocchio stories. 63-c-swipe from New Funnies #94. 64-X-mas-c. 65-Pluto story. 66-Infinity-c. 67,68-Mickey Mouse Sunday-r by Bill Wright	16.00	48.00	125.00
71-80: Barks-a. 75-77-Brer Rabbit stories, no Mickey Mouse. 76-X-Mas-c	11.50	34.00	90.00
81-87,89,90: Barks-a. 82-84-Bongo stories. 86-90-Goofy & Agnes app. 89-Chip 'n' Dale story	9.50	28.50	75.00
88-1st app. Gladstone Gander by Barks	11.50	34.00	90.00
91-97,99: Barks-a. 95-1st WDC&S Barks-c. 96-No Mickey Mouse; Little Toot begins, ends #97. 99-X-Mas-c	7.50	22.50	58.00
98-1st Uncle Scrooge app. in WDC&S	16.00	48.00	125.00
100-Barks-a	8.50	25.50	65.00
101-110-Barks-a. 107-Taliaferro-c. Donald acquires super powers	6.50	19.50	50.00
111,114,117-All Barks	5.00	15.00	40.00
112-Drug (ether) issue (Donald Duck)	5.00	15.00	40.00
113,115,116,118-123: Not by Barks. 116-Dumbo x-over. 121-Grandma Duck begins, ends #168; not in #135,142,146,155	2.25	6.75	18.00
124,126-130-All Barks. 124-X-Mas-c	4.35	13.00	35.00

	Good	Fine	N-Mint
125-1st app. Junior Woodchucks; Barks-a	7.00	21.00	55.00
131,133,135-139-All Barks	4.35	13.00	35.00
132-Barks-a(2) (D. Duck & Grandma Duck)			
	5.15	15.50	40.00
134-Intro. & 1st app. The Beagle Boys	8.50	25.50	65.00
140-1st app. Gyro Gearloose by Barks	8.50	25.50	65.00
141-150-All Barks. 143-Little Hiawatha begins, ends #151,159			
	2.65	8.00	21.00
151-170-All Barks	2.25	6.75	18.00
171-200-All Barks	2.00	6.00	16.00
201-240: All Barks. 204-Chip 'n' Dale & Scamp begin			
	1.70	5.00	14.00
241-283: Barks-a. 241-Dumbo x-over. 247-Gyro Gearloose begins, ends #274. 256-Ludwig Von Drake begins, ends #274			
	1.50	4.50	10.00
284,285,287,290,295,296,309-311-Not by Barks			
	.85	2.50	6.00
286,288,289,291-294,297,298,308-All Barks stories; 293-Grandma Duck's Farm Friends. 297-Gyro Gearloose. 298-Daisy Duck's Diary-r	1.35	4.00	9.00
299-307-All contain early Barks-r (#43-117). 305-Gyro Gearloose			
	1.50	4.50	10.00
312-Last Barks issue with original story	1.35	4.00	9.00
313-315,317-327,329-334,336-341	.85	2.50	5.00
316-Last issue published during life of Walt Disney			
	.85	2.50	5.00
328,335,342-350-Barks-r	1.00	3.00	6.00
351-360-w/posters inside; Barks reprints (2 versions of each with & without posters)-without posters...	.85	2.50	5.00
351-360-With posters	1.15	3.50	9.00
361-400-Barks-r	.85	2.50	5.00
401-429-Barks-r	.70	2.00	4.00
430,433,437,438,441,444,445,466,506-No Barks			
	.35	1.00	2.00
431,432,434-436,439,440,442,443-Barks-r	.35	1.00	2.00
446-465,467-505,507-510: All Barks-r. 494-r/WDC&S #98 (1st Uncle Scrooge)	.25	.75	1.50
511-Wuzzles by Disney studio (1st by Gladstone)			
	.85	2.50	5.00
512	.50	1.50	3.00
513-520: 518-Infinity-c	.30	.90	1.80
521-545: 522-r/1st app. Huey, Dewey & Louie from D. Duck Sunday			

	Good	Fine	N-Mint
page. 535-546-Barks-r. 541-545-(All $1.50, 52 pgs.)	.25	.75	1.50
546,547-($1.95, 68 pgs.): 546-Kelly-r. 547-Rosa-a	.35	1.00	2.00
548,549,551-570,572,573, ($1.50): 548-New-a. 549-Barks-r begin. 556-r/Mickey Mouse Cheerios Premium by Dick Moores	.25	.75	1.50
550 ($2.25, 52 pgs.)-Donald Duck by Barks; previously only printed in The Netherlands (1st time in U.S.); also reprints 1st app. Chip 'n' Dale & 1st app. Scamp. 570-Valentine's Day issue	.40	1.15	2.30
571-($2.95, 68 pgs.)-r/D.D.'s Atom Bomb by Carl Barks	.50	1.50	3.00
574-576-($2.95, 68 pgs.)-Barks-r; D. Duck & M. Mouse	.50	1.50	3.00

WANTED, THE WORLD'S MOST DANGEROUS VILLAINS
July-Aug, 1972-No. 9, Aug-Sept, 1973 (All reprints)
National Periodical Publications (See DC Special)

	Good	Fine	N-Mint
1-Batman, Green Lantern (story r-from G.L. #1), & Green Arrow	.70	2.00	4.00
2-Batman/Joker/Penguin-c/story r-from Batman #25; plus Flash story (r-from Flash #121)	1.00	3.00	6.00
3-9: 3-Dr. Fate, Hawkman(r/Flash #100), & Vigilante. 4-Gr. Lantern & Kid Eternity. 5-Dollman/Green Lantern. 6-Burnley Starman; Wildcat/Sargon. 7-Johnny Quick/Hawkman/Hourman by Baily. 8-Dr. Fate/Flash(r/Flash #114). 9-S&K Sandman/ Superman	.35	1.00	2.00

WARLOCK (The Power of...)(Also see Fantastic Four #66, 67, Incredible Hulk #178, Marvel Premiere #1, Strange Tales #178-181 & Thor #165)
Aug, 1972-No. 8, Oct, 1973; No. 9, Oct, 1975-No. 15, Nov, 1976
Marvel Comics Group

	Good	Fine	N-Mint
1-Origin by Kane	5.00	15.00	35.00
2,3	2.15	6.50	15.00
4-8: 4-Death of Eddie Roberts	1.50	4.50	10.00
9-Starlin's 2nd Thanos saga begins, ends #15; new costume for Warlock; Thanos cameo only; story cont'd from Strange Tales #178-181; Starlin-c/a in #9-15	1.75	5.25	12.50
10-Origin Thanos & Gamora; recaps events from Capt. Marvel #25-34. Thanos-c/story	4.50	14.00	32.00

	Good	Fine	N-Mint
11-Thanos app.; death of Warlock	3.60	11.00	25.00
12-14: 14-Origin Star Thief	1.75	5.25	12.50
15-Thanos-c/story	4.50	14.00	32.00

WARLOCK (...Special Edition on-c)
Dec, 1982-No. 6, May, 1983 ($2.00, 52 pgs.) (slick paper)
Marvel Comics Group

1-6: 1-Warlock-r/Strange Tales #178-180. 2-Warlock-r/Str. Tales #180,181 & Warlock #9. 3-r/Warlock #10-12(Thanos origin recap). 4-r/Warlock #12-15. 5-r/Warlock #15 & Avengers Annual #7 (Starlin-r in all w/new Starlin-c)	1.15	3.50	7.00
Special Edition #1(12/83)	1.35	4.00	8.00

WARLOCK
V2#1, May, 1992-No. 6, Oct, 1992 ($2.50, color, mini-series)
    Marvel Comics

1-Reprints Warlock reprint series above from 1982			
	.50	1.50	3.00
2-6	.40	1.25	2.50

WARLOCK AND THE INFINITY WATCH
Feb, 1992-Present ($1.75, color)(Sequel to Infinity Gauntlet)
Marvel Comics

1-Starlin scripts begin; 1,2-Austin-c/a(i)	.60	1.75	3.50
2,3	.35	1.10	2.20
4-8: 8-Infinity War x-over	.30	.90	1.80

WARLORD
1-2/76; No.2, 3-4/76; No.3, 10-11/76-No. 133, Wint, 1988-89
National Periodical Publications/DC Comics #123 on

1-Story cont'd. from First Issue Special #8			
	2.50	7.50	15.00
2-Intro. Machiste	1.35	4.00	8.00
3-5	.85	2.50	5.00
6-10: 6-Intro Mariah. 7-Origin Machiste. 9-Dons new costume			
	.70	2.00	4.00
11-20: 11-Origin-r. 12-Intro Aton. 15-Tara returns; Warlord has son			
	.50	1.50	3.00
21-40: 27-New facts about origin. 28-1st Wizard World. 32-Intro Shakira. 37, 38-Origin Omac by Starlin. 38-Intro Jennifer Morgan, Warlord's daughter. 39-Omac ends. 40-Warlord gets new costume	.35	1.00	2.00

	Good	Fine	N-Mint
41-47,49-52: 42-47-Omac back-up series. 49-Claw The Unconquered app. 50-Death of Aton. 51-Reprints #1		.50	1.00
48-(52 pgs.)-1st app. Arak; contains free 14 pg. Arak Son of Thunder; Claw The Unconquered app.	.35	1.00	2.00
53-130,132: 55-Arion Lord of Atlantis begins, ends #62. 63-The Barren Earth begins; free 16 pg. Masters of the Universe preview. 91-Origin w/new facts. 100-Double size ($1.25). 114,115-Legends x-over. 125-Death of Tara		.50	1.00
131-1st DC work by Rob Liefeld (9/88)	.35	1.00	2.00
133-($1.50, 52 pgs.)	.25	.75	1.50
Annual 1(1982)-Grell-c, a(p)	.35	1.00	2.00
Annual 2-6: 2('83). 3('84). 4('85). 5('86). 6('87)		.50	1.00

WARLORD
Jan, 1992-No. 6, June, 1992 ($1.75, color, mini-series)
DC Comics

	Good	Fine	N-Mint
1-6: Grell-c & scripts	.30	.90	1.80

WATCHMEN
Sept, 1986-No. 12, Oct, 1987 (12 issue maxi-series)
DC Comics

	Good	Fine	N-Mint
1-Alan Moore scripts in all	1.00	3.00	6.00
2,3	.70	2.00	4.00
4-10	.60	1.75	3.50
11,12	.50	1.50	3.00

WEB OF SPIDER-MAN, THE
Apr, 1985-Present
Marvel Comics Group

	Good	Fine	N-Mint
1-Painted-c (4th app. black costume?)	2.65	8.00	16.00
2,3	.90	2.75	5.50
4-8: 7-Hulk x-over; Wolverine splash	.75	2.20	4.40
9-13: 10-Dominic Fortune guest stars; painted-c	.70	2.00	4.00
14-28: 19-Intro Humbug & Solo	.55	1.65	3.30
29-Wolverine, new Hobgoblin (Macendale) app.	2.15	6.50	13.00
30-Origin recap The Rose & Hobgoblin I (entire book is flashback story); Punisher & Wolverine cameo	2.00	6.00	12.00
31,32-Six part Kraven storyline begins	1.35	4.00	8.00
33,34	.25	.75	1.50
35-37,39-47,49: 35-1st app. Tombstone		.60	1.20

Web of Spider-Man #2, © Marvel Comics

	Good	Fine	N-Mint
38-Hobgoblin app.; begin $1.00-c	1.00	3.00	6.00
48-Origin of Hobgoblin II (Demo Goblin); Kingpin app.			
	2.00	6.00	12.00
50-($1.50, 52 pgs.)	.35	1.00	2.00
51-58		.55	1.10
59-Cosmic Spidey cont./Spect. Spider-Man			
	1.35	4.00	8.00

60-65,68-89,91-94: 69,70-Hulk x-over. 74-76-Austin-c(i). 76-Fantastic Four x-over. 78-Cloak & Dagger app. 84-Begin 6 part Rose & Hobgoblin II storyline. 85-Begin $1.25-c   .65   1.30

66,67-Green Goblin (Norman Osborn) app. as a super-hero
                                                    .35   1.00   2.00

90-($2.95, 52 pgs.)-30th Anniversary issue with hologram on-c; origin retold; contains 3 page gatefold poster
                                                    .60   1.75   3.50

Annual 1 (1985)   .45   1.30   2.60

Annual 2 (1986)-New Mutants; Art Adams-a
                                                    1.15   3.50   7.00

Annual 3 (1987)   .40   1.25   2.50

Annual 4 (1988, $1.75)-Evolutionary War x-over
                                                    .50   1.50   3.00

Annual 5 (1989, $2.00, 68 pgs.)-Atlantis Attacks; Captain Universe by Ditko (p) & Silver Sable stories; F.F. app.
                                                    .40   1.25   2.50

	Good	Fine	N-Mint

Annual 6 ('90, $2.00, 68 pgs.)-Punisher back-up plus Capt. Universe
    by Ditko; G. Kane-a   .40   1.25   2.50
Annual 7 (1991, $2.00, 68 pgs.)-Origins of Hobgoblin I, Hobgoblin II,
    Green Goblin I & II & Venom; Austin-c(i)
                        .40   1.25   2.50
Annual 8 (1992, $2.25, 68 pgs.)-New Warriors x-over; part 3 of
    Venom story   .40   1.15   2.30

WEIRD, THE
Apr, 1988-No. 4, July, 1988 ($1.50, color, mini-series)
DC Comics

	Good	Fine	N-Mint
1-Wrightson-c/a in all	.40	1.25	2.50
2-4	.35	1.00	2.00

WEIRD FANTASY (Becomes Weird Science-Fantasy #23 on)
No. 13, May-June, 1950-No. 22, Nov-Dec, 1953
E. C. Comics

	Good	Fine	N-Mint
13(#1) (1950)	100.00	300.00	700.00

14-Necronomicon story; atomic explosion-c
                        55.00   165.00   385.00

	Good	Fine	N-Mint
15,16: 16-Used in **SOTI**, pg. 144	46.00	140.00	325.00
17 (1951)	39.00	118.00	275.00
6-10	29.00	86.00	200.00

11-13 (1952): 12-E.C. artists cameo. 13-Anti-Wertham "Cosmic
    Correspondence"   22.00   65.00   150.00
14-Frazetta/Williamson(1st team-up at E.C.)/Krenkel-a, 7 pgs.;
    Orlando draws E.C. staff; "Cosmic Ray Bomb Explosion" by
    Feldstein stars Gaines & Feldstein   36.00   107.00   250.00
15-Williamson/Evans-a(3), 4,3,&7 pgs.   24.00   71.00   165.00
16-19-Williamson/Krenkel-a in all. 18-Williamson/Feldstein-c
                        22.00   65.00   150.00
20-Frazetta/Williamson-a, 7 pgs.   24.00   71.00   165.00
21-Frazetta/Williamson-c & Williamson/Krenkel-a
                        36.00   107.00   250.00
22-Bradbury adaptation   16.00   48.00   110.00

WEIRD MYSTERY TALES
Jul-Aug, 1972-No. 24, Nov, 1975
National Periodical Publications

	Good	Fine	N-Mint
1-Kirby-a; Wrightson splash pg.	.35	1.00	2.00
2-24		.50	1.00

WEIRD SCIENCE (Becomes Weird Science-Fantasy #23 on)
No. 12, May-June, 1950-No. 22, Nov-Dec, 1953
E. C. Comics

	Good	Fine	N-Mint
12(#1) (1950)	105.00	310.00	725.00
13	59.00	175.00	410.00
14,15 (1950)	52.00	154.00	360.00
5-10: 5-Atomic explosion-c	33.00	100.00	230.00
11-14 (1952): 12-"Dream of Doom" star Gaines & E.C. artists			
	22.00	65.00	150.00
15-18-Williamson/Krenkel-a in each; 15-Williamson-a. 17-Used in **POP**, pgs. 81,82	24.00	73.00	170.00
19,20-Williamson/Frazetta-a, 7 pgs each. 19-Used in **SOTI**, illo-"A young girl on her wedding night stabs her sleeping husband to death with a hatpin..."	33.00	100.00	230.00
21-Williamson/Frazetta-a, 6 pgs.; Wood draws E.C. staff; Gaines & Feldstein app. in story	33.00	100.00	230.00
22-Williamson/Frazetta/Krenkel/Krigstein-a, 8 pgs.; Wood draws himself in his story (last pg. & panel)	33.00	100.00	230.00

WEIRD SCIENCE
Sept, 1990-No. 4, Mar, 1991 ($1.95, color, 68 pgs.)(#3 on: $2.00)
Gladstone Publishing

1-Wood-c(r); all reprints in each	.50	1.50	3.00
2-4: 2-4-Wood-c(r)	.40	1.25	2.50

WEIRD SCIENCE-FANTASY (Formerly Weird Science & Weird Fantasy)
No. 23 Mar, 1954-No. 29, May-June, 1955
E. C. Comics

23-Williamson, Wood-a; Bradbury adaptation			
	24.00	71.00	165.00
24-Williamson & Wood-a; Harlan Ellison's 1st professional story, "Upheaval!," later adapted into a short story as "Mealtime," and then into a TV episode of Voyage to the Bottom of the Sea as "The Price of Doom"	24.00	71.00	165.00
25-Williamson-c; Williamson/Torres/Krenkel-a plus Wood-a; Bradbury adaptation	27.00	81.00	190.00
26-Flying Saucer Report; Wood, Crandall, Orlando-a			
	22.00	65.00	155.00
27	24.00	71.00	165.00

	Good	Fine	N-Mint
28-Williamson/Krenkel/Torres-a; Wood-a			
	26.00	77.00	180.00
29-Frazetta-c; Williamson/Krenkel & Wood-a			
	45.00	135.00	315.00

WEIRD WAR TALES
Sept-Oct, 1971-No. 124, June, 1983
National Periodical Publications/DC Comics

1	.50	1.50	3.00
2-7,9,10: 7-Krigstein-a. 10-Simonson's 1st-a?			
	.25	.75	1.50
8-Neal Adams-c/a(i)	.50	1.50	3.00
11-50: 36-Crandall, Kubert-r/#2		.50	1.00

51-63,65-67,69-124: 67-69-(44 pgs.). 69-Sci-Fic issue. 93-Intro/
origin Creature Commandos. 101-Intro/origin G.I. Robot. 111-
Creature Commandos & G.I. Robot team-ups begin

		.50	1.00
64,68-Miller-a		.50	1.00

WEIRD WESTERN TALES (Formerly All-Star Western)
No. 12, June-July, 1972-No. 70, Aug, 1980 (No. 12: 52 pgs.)
National Periodical Publications/DC Comics

12-Bat Lash, Pow Wow Smith reprints; El Diablo by Neal Adams/			
Wrightson	.70	2.00	4.00
13,15-Neal Adams-a. 15-N. Adams-c	.70	2.00	4.00
14,29: 14-Toth-a. 29-Origin Jonah Hex	.35	1.00	2.00
16-28,30-70: 39-Origin/1st app. Scalphunter		.50	1.00

WEIRD WORLDS
Aug-Sept, 1972-No. 9, Jan-Feb, 1974; No. 10, Oct-Nov, 1974
National Periodical Publications

1-Edgar Rice Burrough's John Carter Warlord of Mars & David			
Innes begin (1st DC app.); Kubert-c	.50	1.50	3.00
2-7: 7-Last John Carter	.25	.75	1.50
8-10: 8-Iron Wolf begins by Chaykin (1st app.)		.50	1.00

WEREWOLF BY NIGHT (See Marvel Spotlight #2-4)
Sept, 1972-No. 43, Mar, 1977
Marvel Comics Group

1-Ploog-a-cont'd. from Marvel Spotlight #4			
	3.15	9.50	22.00
2	1.50	4.50	10.00

	Good	**Fine**	**N-Mint**
3-5	1.15	3.50	8.00
6-10	.85	2.60	6.00
11-20: 15-New origin Werewolf; Dracula app.			
	.70	2.00	5.00
21-31	.70	2.00	4.00
32-Origin & 1st app. Moon Knight (4/75?)			
	5.00	15.00	35.00
33-2nd app. Moon Knight	2.85	8.50	20.00
34-36,38-43: 35-Starlin/Wrightson-c	.40	1.25	2.50
37-Moon Knight app; part Wrightson-c	.85	2.60	6.00

WEST COAST AVENGERS
Sept, 1984-No. 4, Dec, 1984 (Mini-series; Mando paper)
Marvel Comics Group

	Good	**Fine**	**N-Mint**
1-Origin & 1st app. W.C. Avengers; Hawkeye, Iron Man, Mocking-bird & Tigra	1.15	3.50	7.00
2-4	.75	2.25	4.50

WEST COAST AVENGERS (Becomes Avengers West Coast #48 on)
Oct, 1985-No. 47, Aug, 1989 (On-going series)
Marvel Comics Group

	Good	**Fine**	**N-Mint**
V2#1	1.00	3.00	6.00
2,3	.70	2.00	4.00
4-6	.50	1.50	3.00
7-10	.40	1.25	2.50
11-20	.35	1.10	2.20
21-30	.25	.75	1.50
31-41		.60	1.20
42-Byrne-a(p)/scripts begin	.35	1.10	2.20
43-47: 46,46-Byrne-c. 46-1st Great Lakes Avengers			
		.55	1.10
Annual 1 (1986)	.35	1.10	2.20
Annual 2 (1987)	.35	1.00	2.00
Annual 3 (1988, $1.75)-Evolutionary War app.			
	.45	1.40	2.80
Annual V2#4 (1989, $2.00, 68 pgs.)-Atlantis Attacks; Byrne/Austin-a			
	.35	1.10	2.20
Annual V2#5 (1990, $2.00, 68 pgs.)	.35	1.00	2.00
Annual V2#6 (1991, $2.00, 68 pgs.)	.35	1.00	2.00
Annual V2#7 (1992, $2.25, 68 pgs.)	.40	1.15	2.30

WESTERN GUNFIGHTERS

Aug, 1970-No. 33, Nov, 1975 (#1-6: 25 cents, 68 pgs.; #7: 52 pgs.)

Marvel Comics Group

	Good	Fine	N-Mint
1-Ghost Rider begins; Fort Rango, Renegades & Gunhawk app.			
	.70	2.00	4.00
2-33: 2-Origin Nightwind (Apache Kid's horse). 7-Origin Ghost Rider retold. 10-Origin Black Rider. 12-Origin Matt Slade			
	.35	1.00	2.00

WESTERN KID, THE

Dec, 1971-No. 5, Aug, 1972 (All 20 cent issues)

Marvel Comics Group

1-Reprints; Romita-c/a(3)	.50	1.50	3.00
2,4,5: 2-Romita-a; Severin-c. 4-Everett-r	.35	1.00	2.00
3-Williamson-r	.35	1.00	2.00

WHAT IF? (What If? Featuring... #13 & #?-33)(1st series)

Feb, 1977-No. 47, Oct, 1985; June, 1988 (All 52 pgs.)

Marvel Comics Group

	Good	Fine	N-Mint
1-Brief origin Spider-Man, Fantastic Four			
	2.15	6.50	15.00
2-Origin The Hulk retold	1.30	4.00	9.00
3-5: 3-Avengers. 4-Invaders. 5-Capt. America			
	1.00	3.00	6.00
6-10: 8-Daredevil. 9-Origins Venus, Marvel Boy, Human Robot, 3-D Man. 11-Marvel Bullpen as Fantastic Four			
	.85	2.50	5.00
11,12	.70	2.00	4.00
13-Conan app.; John Buscema-c/a(p)	1.00	3.00	6.00
14-16,18-26,29,30: 18-Dr. Strange. 19,30-Spider-Man. 22-Origin Dr. Doom retold	.70	2.00	4.00
17-Ghost Rider & Son of Satan app.	1.15	3.50	7.00
27-X-Men app.; Miller-c	1.70	5.00	10.00
28-Daredevil by Miller; Ghost Rider app.	1.70	5.00	10.00
31-Featuring Wolverine & the Hulk; X-Men app.; death of Hulk, Wolverine & Magneto	2.30	7.00	14.00
32-47: 32,36-Byrne-a. 34-Marvel crew each draw themselves. 35-What if Elektra had lived?; Miller/Austin-a. 37-Old X-Men & Silver Surfer app. 39-Thor battles Conan			
	.35	1.00	2.00
Special 1 ($1.50, 6088)-Iron Man, F.F., Thor app.			
	.35	1.00	2.00

WHAT IF...? (2nd series)
V2#1, July, 1989-Present ($1.25 color)
Marvel Comics

	Good	Fine	N-Mint
V2#1-...The Avengers Had Lost the Evolutionary War			
	.85	2.50	5.00
2-5: 2-Daredevil, Punisher app.	.50	1.50	3.00
6-X-Men app.	.70	2.00	4.00
7-Wolverine app.; Liefeld-c/a(1st on Wolvie?)			
	1.00	3.00	6.00
8,11: 11-Fantastic Four app.; McFarlane-c(i)			
	.35	1.00	2.00
9,12-X-Men	.50	1.50	3.00
10-Punisher	.60	1.75	3.50

13-15,17-21,23,27-29: 13-Prof. X; Jim Lee-c. 14-Capt. Marvel;
Austin-c. 15-F.F. 17-Spider-Man/Kraven. 18-F.F. 19-Vision. 20,
21-Spider-Man. 23-X-Men. 27-Namor/F.F. 28,29-Capt. America

	.25	.75	1.50
16-Conan battles Wolverine; Red Sonja app.; X-Men cameo			
	.75	2.25	4.50
22-Silver Surfer by Lim/Austin-c/a.	.50	1.50	3.00
24-Wolverine; Punisher app.	.50	1.50	3.00
25-($1.50, 52 pgs.)-Wolverine app.	.50	1.50	3.00
26-Punisher app.	.35	1.00	2.00
30-($1.75, 52 pgs.)-Sue Richards/F.F.	.30	.90	1.80

31-40: 31-Cosmic Spider-Man & Venom app.; Hobgoblin cameo.
32, 33-Phoenix; X-Men app. 35-Fantastic Five (w/Spidey). 36-
Avengers vs. Guardians of the Galaxy. 37-Wolverine

	.25	.75	1.50
41-($1.75, 52 pgs.)-Avengers vs. Galactus			
	.30	.90	1.80
42-44		.65	1.30

WHAT THE-?!
Aug, 1988-Present ($1.25-$1.50, semi-annually #5 on)
Marvel Comics

1-All contain parodies	.40	1.25	2.50
2,4,5: 5-Punisher/Wolverine parody; Jim Lee-a			
	.25	.75	1.50
3-X-Men parody; Todd McFarlane-a	.50	1.50	3.00

6-22: 6-($1.00)-Acts of Vengeance (Punisher, Wolverine, Alpha
Flight)-Byrne/Austin-a. 7-($1.25)-Avengers vs. Justice League
parody; Patsy Walker story. 9-Wolverine. 10-Byrne-c/a. 11,13-

	Good	Fine	N-Mint

Byrne-c. 13-Silver Surfer, Batman 2 movie parody. 16-Flip comic
w/EC back-c parody. 17-Wolverine/Punisher parody. 20-Infinity

War parody		.65	1.30

WHERE CREATURES ROAM
July, 1970-No. 8, Sept, 1971
Marvel Comics Group

	Good	Fine	N-Mint
1-Kirby/Ayers-r	.50	1.50	3.00
2-8-Kirby-r	.25	.75	1.50

WHERE MONSTERS DWELL
Jan, 1970-No. 38, Oct, 1975
Marvel Comics Group

	Good	Fine	N-Mint
1-Kirby/Ditko-r; all contain pre super-hero-r			
	.50	1.50	3.00
2-10,12: 4-Crandall-a(r). 12-Giant issue	.25	.75	1.50
11,13-37: 18,20-Starlin-c		.50	1.00
38-Williamson-r/World of Suspense #3	.25	.75	1.50

Whiz Comics #1, © Fawcett Publications

WHIZ COMICS
No. 2, Feb, 1940-No. 155, June, 1953
Fawcett Publications

	Good	Fine	VF-NM

1-(nn on cover, #2 inside)-Origin & 1st newsstand app. Captain
Marvel by C. C. Beck (created by Bill Parker), Spy Smasher,
Golden Arrow, Ibis the Invincible, Dan Dare, Scoop Smith,

	Good	Fine	VF-NM
Sivana, & Lance O'Casey begin	4,080.00	11,400.00	24,500.00

	Good	Fine	N-Mint
2-(3/40, nn on cover, #3 inside)-Spy Smasher reveals I.D. to Eve			
	329.00	985.00	2300.00
3-(4/40, #3 on-c, #4 inside)-1st app. Beautia			
	207.00	621.00	1450.00
4-(5/40, #4 on cover, #5 inside)-Brief origin Capt. Marvel retold			
	171.00	515.00	1200.00
5-Captain Marvel wears button-down flap on splash page only			
	129.00	385.00	900.00
6-10: 7-Dr. Voodoo begins (by Raboy-#9-22)			
	100.00	300.00	700.00
11-14	72.00	215.00	500.00
15-Origin Sivana; Dr. Voodoo by Raboy	86.00	257.00	600.00
16-18-Spy Smasher battles Captain Marvel			
	86.00	257.00	600.00
19,20	50.00	150.00	350.00
21-Origin & 1st app. Lt. Marvels	54.00	161.00	375.00
22-24: 23-Only Dr. Voodoo by Tuska	40.00	120.00	280.00
25-(12/41)-Captain Nazi jumps from Master Comics #21 to take on Capt. Marvel solo after being beaten by Capt. Marvel/Bulletman team, causing the creation of Capt. Marvel Jr.; 1st app./origin of Capt. Marvel Jr. (part II of trilogy origin); Captain Marvel sends Jr. back to Master #22 to aid Bulletman against Capt. Nazi; origin Old Shazam in text	121.00	365.00	850.00
26-30	34.00	103.00	240.00
31,32: 32-1st app. The Trolls	29.00	86.00	200.00
33-Spy Smasher, Captain Marvel x-over on cover and inside			
	32.00	95.00	225.00
34,36-40: 37-The Trolls app. by Swayze	23.00	70.00	160.00
35-Captain Marvel & Spy Smasher-c	26.00	77.00	180.00
41-50: 43-Spy Smasher, Ibis, Golden Arrow x-over in Capt. Marvel. 44-Flag-c. 47-Origin recap (1 pg.)	16.00	48.00	110.00
51-60: 52-Capt. Marvel x-over in Ibis. 57-Spy Smasher, Golden Arrow, Ibis cameo	13.00	40.00	90.00
61-70	11.50	34.00	80.00
71,77-80	8.50	25.50	60.00
72-76-Two Captain Marvel stories in each; 76-Spy Smasher becomes Crime Smasher	9.30	28.00	65.00
81-99: 86-Captain Marvel battles Sivana Family. 91-Infinity-c	9.30	28.00	65.00
100	11.50	34.00	80.00

	Good	Fine	N-Mint
101-106: 102-Commando Yank app. 106-Bulletman app.			
	7.00	21.00	50.00
107-152: 107-White House photo-c. 108-Brooklyn Bridge photo-c.			
112-Photo-c. 139-Infinity-c. 142-Used in **POP**, pg. 89			
	7.00	21.00	50.00
153-155-(Scarce)	11.00	32.00	75.00

WHO'S WHO IN STAR TREK
March, 1987-No. 2, April, 1987
DC Comics

1,2-Chaykin-c; 1-3 pgs.-a by most DC artists			
	.85	2.50	5.00

WHO'S WHO: THE DEFINITIVE DIRECTORY OF THE DC UNIVERSE
Mar, 1985-No. 26, Apr, 1987 (26 issue maxi-series, no ads)
DC Comics

1-DC heroes from A-Z	.35	1.00	2.00
2-26: All have 1-2 pgs.-a by most DC artists		.60	1.20

WHO'S WHO UPDATE '87
Aug, 1987-No. 5, Dec, 1987 ($1.25, color)
DC Comics

1-5: contains art by most DC artists		.65	1.30

WHO'S WHO UPDATE '88
Aug, 1988-No. 4, Nov, 1988 ($1.25)
DC Comics

1-4: Contains art by most DC artists		.65	1.30

WITCHING HOUR (The ... later issues)
Feb-Mar, 1969-No. 85, Oct, 1978
National Periodical Publications/DC Comics

1-Toth-a, plus Neal Adams-a (2 pgs.)	1.85	5.50	13.00
2,6: 2-Toth-a	1.00	3.00	7.00
3,5-Wrightson-a; Toth-p. 3-Last 12 cent issue			
	.85	2.50	5.00
4,7,9-12: Toth-a in all	.70	2.00	4.00
8-Toth, Neal Adams-a	.85	2.50	5.00
13-Neal Adams-c/a, 2 pgs.	.70	2.00	4.00
14-Williamson/Garzon, Jones-a; N. Adams-c			
	.70	2.00	4.00

	Good	Fine	N-Mint
15-20	.35	1.00	2.00
21-85: 38-(100 pgs.). 84-(44 pgs.)		.50	1.00

WOLVERINE (See Alpha Flight, Daredevil #196, 249, Incredible
Hulk #180, Incredible Hulk &..., Kitty Pryde And..., Marvel Comics
Presents, Power Pack, Punisher and..., Spider-Man vs... &
X-Men #94)
Sept, 1982-No. 4, Dec, 1982 (Mini-series)
Marvel Comics Group

	Good	Fine	N-Mint
1-Frank Miller-c/a(p) in all	4.50	13.50	27.00
2,3	3.00	9.00	18.00
4	3.35	10.00	20.00
Trade Paperback #1 (7/87, $4.95)-Reprints #1-4 with new Miller-c			
	1.35	4.00	8.00

Wolverine #41 (1st printing), © Marvel Comics

WOLVERINE
Nov, 1988-Present ($1.50-$1.75, color, Baxter paper)
Marvel Comics

	Good	Fine	N-Mint
1-Buscema a-1-16, c-1-10; Williamson i-1,4-8			
	4.15	12.50	25.00
2	1.85	5.50	11.00
3-5	1.35	4.00	8.00
6-9: 6-McFarlane back-c. 7,8-Hulk app.	1.15	3.50	7.00
10-1st battle with Sabretooth (before Wolverine had his claws)			
	4.00	12.00	24.00
11-16: 11-New costume	.85	2.50	5.00
17-20: 17-Byrne-c/a(p) begins, ends #23	.60	1.75	3.50

	Good	Fine	N-Mint
21-30	.50	1.50	3.00
31-40,44,47: 26-Begin $1.75-c. 48-Sequel to Weapon X begins			
	.35	1.00	2.00
41-Sabretooth claims to be Wolverine's father; Cable cameo			
	1.70	5.00	10.00
41-Gold 2nd printing	.35	1.00	2.00
42-Sabretooth, Cable & Nick Fury app.; Sabretooth proven not to be			
Wolverine's father	.85	2.50	5.00
42-Gold ink 2nd printing ($1.75)	.30	.90	1.80
43-Sabretooth cameo (2 panels)	.70	2.00	4.00
45,46-Sabretooth-c/stories	.60	1.75	3.50
48,49-Sabretooth app.; Weapon-X sequel	.40	1.25	2.50
50-($2.50, 64 pgs.)-Die-cut-c; Nick Fury app.; Wolverine back to old			
yellow costume; Weapon-X concludes	.85	2.50	5.00
51-64: 51-Sabretooth-c & app.; Andy Kubert-c/a(p). 54-Shatterstar			
(from X-Force) app.	.30	.90	1.80
Annual nn (1990, $4.50, squarebound, 52 pgs.)-The Jungle Adventure;			
Simonson scripts; Mignola-c/a	.75	2.25	4.50
Annual 2 (12/90, $4.95, squarebound, 52 pgs.)-Bloodlust			
	.85	2.50	5.00
Annual nn (#3, 1991, $5.95, 68 pgs.)-Rahne of Terror; Cable & The			
New Mutants app.; Andy Kubert-c/a (2nd print exists)			
	1.00	3.00	6.00
...Battles the Incredible Hulk nn (1989, $4.95, squarebound, 52 pg.)-			
r/Incredible Hulk #180,181	1.35	4.00	8.00

WOLVERINE SAGA
Mid-Sept, 1989-No. 4, Dec, 1989 ($3.95, color, mini-series, 52 pgs.)
Marvel Comics

	Good	Fine	N-Mint
1-Gives history; Austin-c(i)	.85	2.50	5.00
2-4: 4-Kaluta-c	.70	2.00	4.00

WONDER WOMAN (See Adventure Comics #459, Justice League of
America and World's Finest Comics #244)
Summer, 1942-No. 329, Feb, 1986
National Periodical Publications/All-American Publ./DC Comics

	Good	Fine	VF-NM
1-Origin Wonder Woman retold; H. G. Peter-a begins			
	470.00	1170.00	2800.00

	Good	Fine	N-Mint
2-Origin & 1st app. Mars; Duke of Deception app.			
	129.00	385.00	900.00

	Good	Fine	N-Mint
3	93.00	280.00	650.00
4,5: 5-1st Dr. Psycho app.	68.00	205.00	475.00
6-10: 6-1st Cheetah app.	52.00	156.00	365.00
11-20	41.00	122.00	285.00
21-30	32.00	95.00	225.00
31-40	24.00	71.00	165.00
41-44,46-49: 49-Used in **SOTI**, pgs. 234,236; Last 52 pg. issue			
	18.00	54.00	125.00
45-Origin retold	32.00	95.00	225.00
50-(44 pgs.)-Used in **POP**, pg. 97	16.50	50.00	115.00
51-60	12.00	36.00	85.00
61-72: 62-Origin of W.W. i.d. 64-Story about 3-D movies. 70-1st Angle Man app. 72-Last pre-code	11.00	32.00	75.00
73-90: 80-Origin The Invisible Plane. 89-Flying saucer-c/story			
	8.50	25.50	60.00
91-94,96-99: 97-Last H. G. Peter-a. 98-Origin W.W. i.d. with new facts	6.00	18.00	42.00
95-A-Bomb-c	6.50	19.00	45.00
100	7.00	21.00	50.00
101-104,106-110: 107-1st advs. of Wonder Girl; 1st Merboy; tells how Wonder Woman won her costume	5.00	15.00	35.00
105-(Scarce)-Wonder Woman's secret origin; W. Woman appears as a girl (not Wonder Girl)	14.00	43.00	100.00
111-120	3.60	11.00	25.00
121-126: 122-1st app. Wonder Tot. 124-1st app. Wonder Woman Family. 126-Last 10 cent issue	2.15	6.50	15.00
127-130: 128-Origin The Invisible Plane retold			
	1.50	4.50	10.00
131-150: 132-Flying saucer-c	1.00	3.00	7.00
151-155,157,158,160-170 (1967)	.85	2.60	6.00
156-(8/65)Early mention of a comic book shop & comic collecting; mentions DCs selling for $100 a copy	.85	2.60	6.00
159-Origin retold (1/66); 1st S.A. origin?	1.00	3.00	7.00
171-178	.70	2.00	4.00
179-195: 179-Wears no costume to issue #203. 180-Death of Steve Trevor. 195-Wood inks?	.50	1.50	3.00
196-198 (52 pgs.): 196-Origin-r/All-Star #8. 197,198-Reprints			
	.60	1.75	3.50
199,200 (5-6/72)-Jeff Jones-c; 52 pgs.	.85	2.50	5.00
201-210: 204-Return to old costume; death of I Ching. 202-Fafhrd & The Grey Mouser debut	.25	.75	1.50
211-240: 211,214-(100 pgs.), 217-(68 pgs.). 220-N. Adams assist.			

	Good	Fine	N-Mint

223-Steve Trevor revived as Steve Howard & learns W.W.'s I.D.
228-Both Wonder Women team up & new World War II stories
begin, end #243. 237-Origin retold .50 1.00

241-266,269-280,284-286: 241-Intro Bouncer. 247-249-(44 pgs.).
248-Steve Trevor Howard dies. 249-Hawkgirl app. 250-Origin/
1st app. Orana, the new W. Woman. 251-Orana dies. 269-Last
Wood a(i) for DC? (7/80). 271-Huntress & 3rd Life of Steve
Trevor begin .50 1.00

267,268-Re-intro Animal Man (5/80 & 6/80)

	2.15	6.50	15.00
281-283: Joker covers & stories	.50	1.50	3.00
287-New Teen Titans x-over	.25	.75	1.50

288-299,301-328: 288-New costume & logo. 291-293-Three part epic
with Super-Heroines .50 1.00

300-($1.50, 76 pgs.)-Anniversary issue; Giffen-a; New Teen Titans,
JLA & G.A. Wonder Woman app. .25 .75 1.50

329-Double size	.25	.75	1.50

WONDER WOMAN
Feb, 1987-Present
DC Comics

1-New origin; Perez-c/a begins	.50	1.50	3.00

2-20: 8-Origin Cheetah. 12,13-Millennium x-over. 18,26-Free 16
pg. story .65 1.30

21-49,51-62: 24-Last Perez-a; scripts continue thru #62. 60-Vs.
Lobo; Last Perez-c .50 1.00

50-($1.50, 52 pgs.)-New Titans, Justice League

	.25	.75	1.50

63,64: 63-Bolland-c, new direction & $1.25-c begins; Deathstroke
x-over cont'd from W.W. Special #1 .25 .75 1.50

65-68		.65	1.30
Annual 1 ('88, $1.50)-Art Adams-a(p&i)	.35	1.00	2.00

Annual 2 ('89, $2.00, 68 pgs.)-All women artists issue; Perez-c(i)

	.35	1.00	2.00
Annual 3 (1992, $2.50, 68 pgs.)	.40	1.25	2.50

Special 1 (1991, $1.75, 52 pgs.)-Deathstroke-c/story

	.35	1.00	2.00

WORLD'S BEST COMICS (World's Finest Comics #2 on)
Spring, 1941 (Cardboard-c)(DC's 6th annual format comic)
National Periodical Publications (100 pgs.)

	Good	Fine	VF-NM
1-The Batman, Superman, Crimson Avenger, Johnny Thunder, The King, Young Dr. Davis, Zatara, Lando, Man of Magic, & Red, White & Blue begin; Superman, Batman & Robin covers begin (inside-c is blank)	550.00	1375.00	3300.00

WORLD'S FINEST
1990-No. 3, 1990 ($3.95, squarebound, mini-series, 52 pgs.)
DC Comics

	Good	Fine	N-Mint
1-3: Batman & Superman team-up against The Joker and Lex Luthor. 2,3-Joker/Luthor painted-c by Steve Rude	.70	2.00	4.00

WORLD'S FINEST COMICS (Formerly World's Best Comics #1)
No. 2, Sum, 1941-No. 323, Jan, 1986 (early issues have 100 pgs.)
National Periodical Publ./DC Comics (#1-17 have cardboard covers)

	Good	Fine	N-Mint
2 (100 pgs.)-Superman, Batman & Robin covers continue	250.00	625.00	1500.00
3-The Sandman begins; last Johnny Thunder; origin & 1st app. The Scarecrow	215.00	540.00	1300.00
4-Hop Harrigan app.; last Young Dr. Davis	150.00	375.00	900.00
5-Intro. TNT & Dan the Dyna-Mite; last King & Crimson Avenger	150.00	375.00	900.00
6-Star Spangled Kid begins; Aquaman app.; S&K Sandman with Sandy in new costume begins, ends #7	117.00	290.00	700.00
7-Green Arrow begins; last Lando, King, & Red, White & Blue; S&K art	117.00	290.00	700.00
8-Boy Commandos begin	105.00	265.00	635.00
9: S&K-a; Batman cameo in Star Spangled Kid; S&K-a; last 100 pg. issue; Hitler, Mussolini, Tojo-c	108.00	270.00	650.00
10-S&K-a	96.00	240.00	575.00
11-17-Last cardboard cover issue	87.00	220.00	525.00
18-20: 18-Paper-c begin; last Star Spangled Kid	76.00	190.00	455.00
21-30: 30-Johnny Peril app.	54.00	135.00	325.00
31-40: 33-35-Tomahawk app.	46.00	115.00	275.00
41-50: 41-Boy Commandos end. 42-Wyoming Kid begins, ends #63. 43-Full Steam Foley begins, ends #48. 48-Last square binding. 49-Tom Sparks, Boy Inventor begins	35.00	88.00	210.00

	Good	Fine	N-Mint
51-60: 51-Zatara ends. 59-Manhunters Around the World begins, ends #62	35.00	88.00	210.00
61-64: 61-Joker story. 63-Capt. Compass app.	31.00	77.00	185.00
65-Origin Superman; Tomahawk begins, ends #101	40.00	100.00	240.00
66-70-(15 cent issues)(Scarce)-Last 68 pg. issue	33.00	83.00	200.00
71-(10 cent issue)(Scarce)-Superman & Batman begin as team	50.00	125.00	300.00
72,73-(10 cent issues) (Scarce)	34.00	85.00	200.00
74-80: 74-Last pre-code issue	22.00	65.00	150.00
81-90: 88-1st Joker/Luthor team-up. 90-Batwoman's 1st app. in World's Finest (3rd app. anywhere)	14.00	43.00	100.00
91-93,95-99: 96-99-Kirby Green Arrow	9.50	29.00	66.00
94-Origin Superman/Batman team retold	36.00	108.00	250.00
100 (3/59)	20.00	60.00	140.00
101-110: 102-Tommy Tomorrow begins, ends #124	7.00	21.00	50.00
111-121: 111-1st app. The Clock King. 113-Intro. Miss Arrowette in Green Arrow; 1st Bat-Mite/Mr. Mxyzptlk team-up. 121-Last 10 cent issue	5.70	17.00	40.00
122-128,130-142: 123-2nd Bat-Mite/Mr. Mxyzptlk team-up. 125-Aquaman begins, ends #139. 135-Last Dick Sprang story. 140-Last Green Arrow. 142-Origin The Composite Superman (villain); Legion app.	2.85	8.50	20.00
129-Joker/Luthor team-up-c/story	4.30	13.00	30.00
143-150: 143-1st Mailbag	1.70	5.00	12.00
151-155,157-160	1.50	4.50	10.00
156-1st Bizarro Batman; Joker-c/story	7.00	21.00	50.00
161,170 (80-pg. Giants G-28,G-40)	1.70	5.00	12.00
162-165,167-169,171-174: 168,172-Adult Legion app.	1.00	3.00	7.00
166-Joker-c/story	1.70	5.00	12.00
175,176-Neal Adams-a; both r-J'onn J'onzz origin/Detective #225, 226	1.50	4.50	10.00
177-Joker/Luthor team-up-c/story	1.50	4.50	10.00
178,180-187: 182-Silent Knight-r/Brave & Bold #6. 186-Johnny Quick-r. 187-Green Arrow origin-r/Adv. #256	.65	2.00	4.00
179,188 (80-pg. Giants G-52,G-64): 179-r/#94	.85	2.50	5.00

	Good	Fine	N-Mint
189-196: 190-193-Robin-r	.50	1.50	3.00
197-80 pg. Giant G-76	.65	2.00	4.00
198,199-3rd Surperman/Flash race	3.60	11.00	25.00
200-204	.40	1.25	2.50

205-6 pgs. Shining Knight by Frazetta/Adv. #153; 52 pgs.; Teen Titans
x-over   .40   1.25   2.50

206 (80-pg. Giant G-88)   .40   1.25   2.50

207-248: 207-212-(52 pgs.). 208-Origin Robotman-r/Det. #138. 215-
Intro Batman Jr. & Superman Jr. 217-Metamorpho begins, ends
#220; Batman/Superman team-ups begin. 223-228-(100 pgs.).
223-Neal Adams-r. 223-Deadman origin. 226-N. Adams S&K,
Toth-r; Manhunter part origin-r/Det. #225,226. 229-r/origin
Superman-Batman team. 244-Green Arrow, Black Canary, Won-
der Woman, Vigilante begin; $1.00, 84 pg. issues begin. 246-
Death of Stuff in Vigilante; origin Vigilante retold. 248-Last
Vigilante   .35   1.00   2.00

249-The Creeper begins by Ditko, ends #255 .70   2.00   4.00

250-270,272-299: 250-The Creeper origin retold by Ditko. 252-Last
84 pg. issue. 253-Capt. Marvel begins; 68 pgs. begin, end #265.
255-Last Creeper. 256-Hawkman begins. 257-Black Lightning
begins. 266-282-(52 pgs.). 267-Challengers of the Unknown app.
268-Capt. Marvel Jr. origin retold. 274-Zatanna begins. 279,280-
Capt. Marvel Jr. & Kid Eternity learn they are brothers. 284-
Legion app. 298-Begin 75 cent-c   .25   .75   1.50

271-Origin Superman/Batman team retold   .35   1.00   2.00

300-($1.25, 52 pgs.)-Justice League of America, New Teen Titans &
The Outsiders app.; Perez-a(3 pgs.)   .35   1.00   2.00

301-323: 304-Origin Null and Void. 309,319-Free 16 pg. story in each
(309-Flash Force 2000, 319-Mask preview)
                                          .25   .75   1.50

WOW COMICS
Winter, 1940-41; No. 2, Summer, 1941-No. 69, Fall, 1948
Fawcett Publications

	Good	Fine	VF-NM
nn(#1)-Origin Mr. Scarlet by S&K; Atom Blake, Boy Wizard, Jim Dolan, & Rick O'Shay begin; Diamond Jack, The White Rajah, & Shipwreck Roberts, only app.; 1st mention of Gotham City in comics; the cover was printed on unstable paper stock and is rarely found in fine or mint condition; blank inside-c; bondage-c by Beck	770.00	2000.00	5400.00

	Good	Fine	N-Mint
2 (Scarce)-The Hunchback begins	85.00	260.00	600.00

	Good	Fine	N-Mint
3 (Fall, 1941)	54.00	160.00	375.00
4-Origin Pinky	57.00	171.00	400.00
5	39.00	120.00	275.00
6-Origin The Phantom Eagle; Commando Yank begins			
	34.00	100.00	235.00
7,8,10: 10-Swayze-c/a on Mary Marvel	30.00	90.00	210.00
9 (1/6/43)-Capt. Marvel, Capt. Marvel Jr., Shazam app.; Scarlet & Pinky x-over; Mary Marvel c/stories begin (cameo #9)			
	57.00	170.00	400.00
11-17,19,20: 15-Flag-c	19.00	58.00	135.00
18-1st app. Uncle Marvel (10/43); infinity-c			
	24.00	70.00	165.00
21-30: 28-Pinky x-over in Mary Marvel	11.50	34.00	80.00
31-40: 32-68-Phantom Eagle by Swayze	8.00	24.00	55.00
41-50	6.50	19.00	45.00
51-58: Last Mary Marvel	5.70	17.00	40.00
59-69: 59-Ozzie begins. 62-Flying Saucer gag-c (1/48). 65-69-Tom Mix stories			
	5.00	15.00	35.00

X

X-FACTOR (Also see The Avengers #263 & Fantastic Four #286)
Feb, 1986-Present
Marvel Comics Group

	Good	Fine	N-Mint
1-($1.25, 52 pgs)-Story recaps 1st app. from Avengers #263; story continued from F.F. #286; return of original X-Men (X-Factor); Layton/ Guice-a	1.35	4.00	8.00
2,3	.85	2.50	5.00
4,5: 5-1st app. Apocalypse	.75	2.25	4.50
6-10	.60	1.75	3.50
11-20: 15-Intro wingless Angel	.50	1.50	3.00
21-23: 23-1st app. Archangel (cameo)	.40	1.25	2.50
24-Fall Of The Mutants begins; 1st full app. Archangel (now in Uncanny X-Men); origin Apocalypse	2.00	6.00	12.00
25,26-Fall of the Mutants storyline. 26-New outfits	.70	2.00	4.00
27-30	.35	1.00	2.00
31-37,39,41-49: 35-Origin Cyclops	.25	.75	1.50
38,50-($1.50, 52 pgs.): 50-Liefeld/McFarlane-c	.35	1.00	2.00
40-Rob Liefield-c/a (4/88, 1st at Marvel?)	1.00	3.00	6.00
51-53-Sabretooth app. 52-Liefeld-c(p)	.85	2.50	5.00
54-59: 54-Intro Crimson		.50	1.00
60-X-Tinction Agenda x-over; New Mutants (Cable) x-over in #60-62	1.35	4.00	8.00
60-Gold 2nd printing	.40	1.25	2.50
61,62-X-Tinction Agenda. 62-J. Lee-c; Wolverine app.	1.00	3.00	6.00
63-Whilce Portacio-c/a(p) begins, ends #69	1.00	3.00	6.00
64-67,69,70: 65-68-Lee co-plots. 67-Inhumans app. 69,70-X-Men x-over	.35	1.00	2.00
68-Baby Nathan (Cable?) apps. & is sent into the future.	.85	2.50	5.50
71-New team begins (Havok, Polaris, Wolfsbane & Madrox); Stroman-c/a begins	1.00	3.00	6.00
71-2nd printing ($1.25)		.65	1.30
72-74	.25	.75	1.50
75-($1.75, 52 pgs.)	.30	.90	1.80

X-Factor #71, © Marvel Comics

	Good	Fine	N-Mint
76-84: 76-Begin $1.25-c; Stroman-c(p) only		.65	1.30
Annual 1 (10/86), 2 (10/87)	.40	1.25	2.50
Annual 3 ('88, $1.75)-Evolutionary War app.	.40	1.25	2.50
Annual 4 ('89, $2.00, 68 pgs.)-Atlantis Attacks; Byrne/Simonson-a;			
Byrne-c	.40	1.25	2.50
Annual 5 ('90, $2.00, 68 pgs.)-F.F., New Mutants x-over			
	.40	1.25	2.50
Annual 6 ('91, $2.00, 68 pgs.)-New Warriors & X-Force app.			
	.40	1.25	2.50
Annual 7 ('92, $2.25, 68 pgs.)-No Stroman-c/a			
	.40	1.15	2.30
...Prisoner of Love nn (1990, $4.95, 52 pgs.)-Starlin scripts; Guice-a			
	.85	2.50	5.00

X-FORCE (Also see The New Mutants #100)
Aug, 1991-Present ($1.00-$1.25, color)
Marvel Comics

1-($1.50, 52 pgs.)-Sealed in plastic bag with 5 different Marvel Universe trading cards inside (1 each); Liefeld-c/a begins			
	.70	2.00	4.00
1-1st printing with Cable trading card inside			
	1.00	3.00	6.00
1-2nd printing; metallic ink-c (no bag or card)			
	.25	.75	1.50
2,3: 2-Deadpool-c/story. 3-New Brotherhood of Evil Mutants app.			
	.35	1.00	2.00
4-Spider-Man x-over; cont'd from Spider-Man #16; reads sideways.			

	Good	Fine	N-Mint
8,9,11-Liefeld-c only. 8-11-Liefeld plots only			
	.50	1.50	3.00
5-10	.25	.75	1.50
11-16		.65	1.30
Annual 1 (1992, $2.25, 68 pgs.)-No Liefeld-c/a			
	.40	1.15	2.30

X-MEN, THE (X-Men #94-141; The Uncanny X-Men #142 on; see
Amazing Adventures, Capt. America #172, Classic X-Men, Heroes
For Hope..., Kitty Pryde &..., Marvel & DC Present, Marvel
Fanfare, Marvel Super Heroes, Marvel Team-up, Marvel Triple
Action, Nightcrawler, Special Edition..., The Uncanny..., X-Factor
& X-Terminators)
Sept, 1963-Present
Marvel Comics Group

	Good	Fine	N-Mint
1-Origin/1st app. X-Men; 1st app. Magneto & Professor X			
	180.00	720.00	1600.00
2-1st app. The Vanisher	68.00	205.00	475.00
3-1st app. The Blob	36.00	107.00	250.00
4-1st Quick Silver & Scarlet Witch & Brotherhood of the Evil Mutants; 1st app. Toad; Magneto app.	30.00	90.00	210.00
5	23.00	70.00	160.00
6-10: 6-Sub-Mariner app. 8-1st Unus the Untouchable. 9-Early Avengers app. 10-1st S.A. app. Ka-Zar			
	17.00	51.00	120.00
11,13-15: 11-1st app. The Stranger. 14-1st app. Sentinels. 15-Origin Beast	11.50	34.00	80.00
12-Origin Prof. X; Origin/1st app. Juggernaut			
	18.00	54.00	125.00
16-20: 19-1st app. The Mimic	8.00	24.00	55.00
21-27,29,30: 27-Re-enter The Mimic (r-in #75)			
	6.50	19.00	45.00
28-1st app. The Banshee (r-in #76)	8.50	25.50	60.00
31-34,36,37,39,40: 39-New costumes	4.50	14.00	32.00
35-Spider-Man x-over (8/67)(r-in #83); 1st app. Changeling			
	7.00	21.00	50.00
38-Origins of the X-Men series begins, ends #57			
	7.00	21.00	50.00
41-49: 42-Death of Prof. X (Changeling disguised as). 44-1st S.A. app. G.A. Red Raven. 49-Steranko-c; 1st Polaris			
	3.60	11.00	25.00
50,51-Steranko-c/a	4.50	14.00	32.00

	Good	Fine	N-Mint
52	2.85	8.50	20.00
53-Barry Smith-c/a (1st comic book work)	4.30	13.00	30.00

54,55-B. Smith-c. 54-1st app. Alex Summers who later becomes
Havok. 55-Alex Summers discovers he has mutant powers

	4.00	12.00	28.00

56-Intro Havoc without costume; Neal Adams-a(p)

	4.50	14.00	32.00

57,59-63,65-N. Adams-a(p). 65-Return of Professor X

	4.50	14.00	32.00
58-1st app. Havok (in costume)	6.50	19.00	45.00
64-1st app. Sunfire	5.00	15.00	35.00

66-Last new story w/original X-Men (3/70); X-Men battle Hulk

	2.65	8.00	18.00

67-70,72: (52 pgs.). 67-Reprints begin, end #93

	2.15	6.50	15.00

71,73-93: 73-86-r/#25-38 w/new-c. 87-93-r/#39-45 with-c

	1.85	5.50	13.00

94(8/75)-New X-Men begin (See Giant-Size X-Men for 1st app.);
Colossus, Nightcrawler, Thunderbird, Storm, Wolverine, &
Banshee join; Angel, Marvel Girl, & Iceman resign

	23.00	70.00	160.00
95-Death of Thunderbird	6.50	19.00	45.00
96-99: 98,99-25 cent & 30 cent-c exist	5.00	15.00	35.00

100-Old vs. New X-Men; part origin Phoenix; last 25 cent issue (8/76)

	5.30	16.00	38.00
101-Phoenix origin concludes	4.30	13.00	30.00

X-Men #100, © Marvel Comics

	Good	Fine	N-Mint
102-107: 102-Origin Storm. 104-1st app. Starjammers (brief cameo). 106-Old vs. New X-Men; 30 & 35 cent issues exist. 107-1st full app. Starjammers; last 30 cent issue	2.15	6.50	15.00
108-Byrne-a begins (see Marvel Team-Up #53)	4.35	13.00	30.00
109-1st Vindicator	3.70	11.00	25.00
110,111: 110-Phoenix joins	2.15	6.50	15.00
112-119: 117-Origin Professor X	1.70	5.00	12.00
120-1st app. Alpha Flight (cameo), story line begins; last 35 cent issue	4.00	12.00	28.00
121-1st full Alpha Flight story	4.35	13.00	30.00
122-128: 123-Spider-Man x-over. 124-Colossus becomes Proletarian	1.85	5.50	11.00
129-Intro Kitty Pryde; last Banshee	2.15	6.50	13.00
130-1st app. The Dazzler by Byrne	2.35	7.00	14.00
131-135: 131-Dazzler app. 132-1st White Queen. 133-Wolverine app. 134-Phoenix becomes Dark Phoenix	1.70	5.00	10.00
136,138: 138-Dazzler app.; Cyclops leaves	1.45	4.25	8.50
137-Giant; death of Phoenix	1.85	5.50	11.00
139-Alpha Flight app.; Kitty Pryde joins; new costume for Wolverine	3.35	10.00	20.00
140-Alpha Flight app.	3.00	9.00	18.00
141-Intro Future X-Men & The New Brotherhood of Evil Mutants; death of Frank Richards; 1st app. Rachel (Phoenix)	3.35	10.00	20.00
142-Deaths of Wolverine, Storm & Colossus; Rachel app.	2.50	7.50	15.00
143-Last Byrne issue	1.15	3.50	7.00
144-150: 144-Man-Thing app. 145-Old X-Men app. 148-Spider-Woman & Dazzler app. 150-Double size	1.00	3.00	6.00
151-157,159-161,163,164: 161-Origin Magneto. 163-Origin Binary. 164-1st app. Binary as Carol Danvers	.70	2.00	4.00
158-1st app. Rogue in X-Men (see Avengers Annual #10)	.85	2.50	5.00
162-Wolverine solo story	1.35	4.00	8.00
165-Paul Smith-a begins	1.00	3.00	6.00
166-Double size; Paul Smith-a	.85	2.50	5.00
167-170: 167-New Mutants app. (3/83); same date as New Mutants #1; 1st meeting w/X-Men; ties into N.M. #3,4. 168-1st app. Madelyne Pryor in X-Men (see Avengers Annual #10)	.65	2.00	4.00

	Good	Fine	N-Mint
171-Rogue joins X-Men; Simonson-c/a	1.15	3.50	7.00
172-174: 172,173-Two part Wolverine solo story. 173-Two cover variations, blue & black. 174-Phoenix cameo	.70	2.00	4.00
175-Double size; anniversary issue; Phoenix returns. Last Paul Smith-c/a	.85	2.50	5.00
176-185: 181-Sunfire app. 182-Rogue solo story. 184-1st app. Forge	.50	1.50	3.00
186-Double-size; Barry Smith/Austin-a	.70	2.00	4.00
187-192,194-199: 190,191-Spider-Man & Avengers x-over. 195-Power Pack x-over	.50	1.50	3.00
193-Double size; 100th app. New X-Men	.85	2.50	5.00
200-(12/85, $1.25, 52 pgs.)	1.35	4.00	8.00
201-(1/86)-1st app. Cable? (as baby Nathan); 1st Whilce Portacio-c/a(i) on X-Men (guest artist)	2.15	6.50	15.00
202-204,206-209: 204-Nightcrawler solo story. 207-Wolverine/Phoenix story	.85	2.50	5.00
205-Wolverine solo story by Barry Smith	1.50	4.50	9.00
210,211-Mutant Massacre begins	2.65	8.00	18.00
212,213-Wolverine vs. Sabretooth (Mutant Ma.)	4.50	14.00	32.00
214-221,223,224: 219-Havok joins	.65	2.00	4.00
222-Wolverine battles Sabretooth	2.50	7.00	15.00
225-227: Fall Of The Mutants. 226-Double size	1.35	4.00	8.00
228-239,241: 229-$1.00 begin	.70	2.00	4.00
240-Sabretooth app.	.85	2.50	5.00
242-Double size, X-Factor app., Inferno tie-in	.70	2.00	4.00
243-247: 244-1st Jubilee. 245-Rob Liefeld-a(p)	.50	1.50	3.00
248-1st Jim Lee art on X-Men (1989)	4.00	12.00	28.00
248-2nd printing (1992, $1.25)	.25	.75	1.50
249-252: 252-Lee-c	.35	1.00	2.00
253-255: 253-All new X-men begin	.65	2.00	4.00
256,257-Jim Lee-c/a begins	1.70	5.00	10.00
258-Wolverine solo story; Lee-c/a	2.00	6.00	12.00
259-Sylvestri-a; no Lee-a	.85	2.50	5.00
260-265-No Lee-a	.35	1.00	2.00
266-1st full app. Gambit; no Lee-a	3.35	10.00	20.00
267-Jim Lee-c/a resumes	1.70	5.00	12.00

	Good	Fine	N-Mint
268-Capt. America, Black Widow & Wolverine team-up; Lee-a			
	3.35	10.00	20.00
269-Lee-a	1.00	3.00	6.00
270-X-Tinction Agenda begins	1.70	5.00	10.00
270-Gold 2nd printing	.50	1.50	3.00
271,272-X-Tinction Agenda	1.15	3.50	7.00
273-New Mutants (Cable) & X-Factor x-over; Golden, Byrne & Lee			
part pencils	1.00	3.00	6.00
274	.85	2.50	5.00
275-($1.50, 52 pgs.)-Tri-fold-c by Jim Lee (p)			
	1.00	3.00	6.00
275-Gold 2nd printing	.35	1.00	2.00
276-280: 277-Last Lee-c/a. 280-X-Factor x-over			
	.25	.75	1.50
281-New team begins (Archangel, Colossus, Iceman, Marvel Girl &			
Storm); Whilce Portacio-c/a begins; Byrne scripts begin			
	1.00	3.00	6.00
281-Red metallic ink 2nd printing w/o UPC box ($1.00)			
		.50	1.00
282-1st app. Bishop (cover plus 1 pg. cameo)	.70	2.00	4.00
282-Gold 2nd printing ($1.00)		.50	1.00
283-1st full app. Bishop	1.15	3.50	7.00
284-294: 285-Begin $1.25-c. 286-Lee-c & plots. 287-Bishop joins			
team		.65	1.30
Special 1(12/70)-Kirby-c/a; origin The Stranger			
	4.30	13.00	30.00
Special 2(11/71)	4.30	13.00	30.00
Annual 3('79, 52 pgs.)-New story; Miller/Austin-c; Wolverine still in			
old yellow costume	2.00	6.00	12.00
Annual 4(1980, 52 pgs.)-Dr. Strange guest stars			
	1.15	3.50	7.00
Annual 5(1981, 52 pgs.)	.85	2.50	5.00
Annual 6(1982, 52 pgs.)	.70	2.00	4.00
Annual 7,8: 7-(1983, 52 pgs.). 8-(1984, 52 pgs.)			
	.70	2.00	4.00
Annual 9(1985)-New Mutants; Art Adams-a			
	2.00	6.00	12.00
Annual 10(1986)-Art Adams-a	2.00	6.00	12.00
Annual 11(1987)	.50	1.50	3.00
Annual 12(1988, $1.75)-Evolutionary War app.			
	.70	2.00	4.00

	Good	Fine	N-Mint
Annual 13(1989, $2.00, 68 pgs.)-Atlantis Attacks	.50	1.50	3.00

Annual 14(1990, $2.00, 68 pgs.)Fantastic Four, New Mutants (Cable) & X-Factor x-over; Arthur Adams-c/a(p); 1st app. Gambit (minor app.) 1.00 3.00 6.00

Annual 15 (1991, $2.00, 68 pgs.)-4 pg. origin; X-Force & New Mutants x-over; 4 pg. Wolverine solo back-up story .70 2.00 4.00

Annual 16(1992, $2.25, 68 pgs.)-No Lee or Portacio-a .40 1.15 2.30

Giant-Size X-Men 1 (Summer, 1975, 50 cents, 68 pgs.)-1st app. New X-Men; intro Nightcrawler, Storm, Colossus & Thunderbird; 2nd full app. Wolverine after Incredible Hulk #181 25.00 75.00 175.00

Giant-Size X-Men 2 (11/75)-Neal Adams-r (51 pgs.) 3.60 11.00 25.00

X-MEN (2nd series)
Oct, 1991-Present ($1.00-$1.25, color)
Marvel Comics

1-($1.50, 52 pgs.)-Four different-c by Jim Lee; new team begins (Beast, Cyclops, Gambit, Psylocke, Rogue & Wolverine) .35 1.00 2.00

1-($3.95)-Double gate-fold-c consisting of all four regular covers by Jim Lee; contains fold-out poster; Lee-c/a begins .70 2.00 4.00

| 2 | .35 | 1.00 | 2.00 |
| 3,4 | .25 | .75 | 1.50 |

5-14: 5-Begin $1.25-c. 6-Sabretooth-c/story. 8-Ghost Rider cameo cont'd in G.R. #26. 9-Ghost Rider x-over cont'd from G.R. #26 .65 1.30

Annual 1 (1992, $2.25, 68 pgs.) Jim Lee-c and layouts

X-MEN/ALPHA FLIGHT
Jan, 1986-No. 2, Jan, 1986 ($1.50, mini-series)
Marvel Comics Group

1,2: 1-Intro The Berserkers; Paul Smith-a .60 1.75 3.50

X-MEN AND THE MICRONAUTS, THE
Jan, 1984-No. 4, April, 1984 (Mini-series)
Marvel Comics Group

1-4: Guice-c/a(p) in all .25 .75 1.50

X-MEN CLASSIC (Formerly Classic X-Men)
No. 46, Apr, 1990-Present ($1.25, color)
Marvel Comics

	Good	Fine	N-Mint
46-69,71-78: Reprints from X-Men. 54-($1.25, 52 pgs.). 57,60-63,65-Russell-c (i); 62-r/X-Men #158(Rogue). 66-r/#162 (Wolvie)		.65	1.30
70-($1.75, 52 pgs.)	.30	.90	1.80

X-MEN CLASSICS
Dec, 1983-No. 3, Feb, 1984 ($2.00; Baxter paper)
Marvel Comics Group

1-3: X-Men-r by Neal Adams	.50	1.50	3.00

X-MEN SPOTLIGHT ON... STARJAMMERS (See X-Men #104)
1990-No. 2, 1990 ($4.50, squarebound, 52 pgs.)
Marvel Comics

1,2-Cockrum/Albrecht-a	.75	2.25	4.50

X-MEN VS. THE AVENGERS
Apr, 1987-No. 4, July, 1987 ($1.50, mini-series, Baxter paper)
Marvel Comics Group

1	.60	1.75	3.50
2-4	.40	1.25	2.50

X-O MANOWAR
Feb, 1992-Present ($1.95, color, high quality)
Valiant

1-Barry Windsor-Smith/Layton-a; Layton-c			
	2.30	7.00	14.00
2-Smith-c(p)	1.35	4.00	8.00
3	.85	2.50	5.00
4,5	.50	1.50	3.00
6-10: 6-Begin $2.25-c	.40	1.15	2.30

X-TERMINATORS
Oct, 1988-No. 4, Jan, 1989 ($1.00, color, mini-series)
Marvel Comics

1-1st app.; X-Men/X-Factor tie-in; Williamson-i			
	.50	1.50	3.00
2	.30	.90	1.80
3,4		.65	1.30

YOUNG ALL-STARS
June, 1987-No. 31, Nov, 1989 ($1.00, deluxe format, color)
DC Comics

	Good	Fine	N-Mint
1-1st app. Iron Munro & The Flying Fox		.50	1.00
2-31: 7-18-$1.25. 8,9-Millennium tie-ins. 19-23-$1.50. 24-Begin			
$1.75-c		.50	1.00
Annual 1 (1988, $2.00)	.35	1.00	2.00

YOUNGBLOOD
Apr, 1992-No. 4, 1992 ($2.50, color, mini-series)
Image Comics (Malibu)

1-Rob Liefeld-c/a in all; flip book format; trading cards			
	.50	1.50	3.00
1-2nd printing	.40	1.25	2.50
2,3: Contains trading cards	.40	1.25	2.50
4-Glow-in-the-Dark-c	.40	1.25	2.50
0-(8/92)-Includes 2 trading cards	.35	1.00	2.00

YOUNG MEN (...on the Battlefield #12-20(4/53); ...In Action #21)
No. 4, 6/50-No. 11, 10/51; No. 12, 12/51-No. 28, 6/54
Marvel/Atlas Comics (IPC)

4-(52 pgs.)	8.00	24.00	55.00
5-11	4.30	13.00	30.00
12-23: 15-Colan, Pakula-a	3.60	11.00	25.00
24-Origin Captain America, Human Torch, & Sub-Mariner which are			
revived thru #28. Red Skull app.	43.00	130.00	300.00
25-28: 25-Romita-c/a	36.00	107.00	250.00

ZIP COMICS
Feb, 1940-No. 47, Summer, 1944
MLJ Magazines

	Good	Fine	N-Mint
1-Origin Kalathar the Giant Man, The Scarlet Avenger, & Steel Sterling; Mr. Satan, Nevada Jones & Zambini, the Miracle Man, War Eagle, Captain Valor begins	150.00	375.00	900.00
2	64.00	193.00	450.00
3	50.00	150.00	350.00
4,5	43.00	130.00	300.00
6-9: 9-Last Kalathar & Mr. Satan	34.00	103.00	240.00
10-Inferno, the Flame Breather begins, ends #13	37.00	110.00	260.00
11,12: 11-Inferno without costume	34.00	103.00	240.00
13-17,19: 17-Last Scarlet Avenger	34.00	103.00	240.00
18-Wilbur begins (1st app.)	37.00	110.00	260.00
20-Origin Black Jack (1st app.)	46.00	140.00	325.00
21-26: 25-Last Nevada Jones. 26-Black Witch begins; last Captain Valor	32.00	95.00	225.00
27-Intro. Web	46.00	140.00	325.00
28-Origin Web	46.00	140.00	325.00
29,30	25.00	75.00	175.00
31-38: 34-1st Applejack app. 35-Last Zambini, Black Jack. 38-Last Web issue	19.00	58.00	135.00
39-Red Rube begins (origin, 8/43)	19.00	58.00	135.00
40-47: 45-Wilbur ends	14.00	43.00	100.00

ZORRO (Walt Disney with #882)(TV)
May, 1949-No. 15, Sept-Nov, 1961 (Photo-c #882 on)
Dell Publishing Co.

4-Color 228	19.00	57.00	135.00
4-Color 425,497,617,732	11.50	34.00	80.00
4-Color 538,574-Kinstler-a	12.00	36.00	85.00
4-Color 882-Photo-c begin; Toth-a	10.00	30.00	70.00
4-Color 920,933,960,976-Toth-a in all	10.00	30.00	70.00
4-Color 1003('59)-Toth-a	8.50	25.50	60.00
4-Color 1037-Annette Funicello photo-c	11.00	32.00	75.00
8(12-2/59-60)	5.70	17.00	40.00

	Good	Fine	N-Mint
9,12-Toth-a. 12-Last 10 cent issue	6.50	19.00	45.00
10,11,13-15-Last photo-c	4.30	13.00	30.00

ZORRO (Walt Disney)(TV)
Jan, 1966-No. 9, March, 1968 (All photo-c)
Gold Key

	Good	Fine	N-Mint
1-Toth-a	4.50	14.00	32.00
2,4,5,7-9-Toth-a. 5-r/F.C. #1003 by Toth			
	3.15	9.50	22.00
3,6-Tufts-a	2.65	8.00	18.00

ZORRO (TV)
Dec, 1990-No. 12, Nov, 1991 ($1.00, color)
Marvel Comics

	Good	Fine	N-Mint
1-12: Based on new TV show. 12-Toth-c		.50	1.00

Introduction

Big Little Books first appeared in 1933 in the heart of the depression, the same year that the first comic books were being tested. The idea for Big Little Books came about through a series of circumstances set in motion by a young Samuel Lowe, who headed the creative marketing and sales staff at Whitman. Sam frequently went into the shop to get a first-hand view of what the equipment could do. On one such trip through the bindery, he saw strips or blocks of paper falling from lifts of printed sheets on the cutter. It seemed to him that this paper was being wasted, and he picked up a handful. Holding it between thumb and middle finger, he walked around the office for several days asking people, "Don't you think this would make a nice book? It just fits a small hand. But what should go into it?"

The rest is history. They decided upon *Dick Tracy, Orphan Annie,* and *Mickey Mouse* for the first books. The first shipments went into nearby Milwaukee stores late in the year and before Christmas the phones were ringing like mad. Of course, the paper at the end of the sheets was not used except for the initial dummies — it was simply the source of the idea which created Big Little Books. Over the next three decades, after a title change to Better Little Books in 1938, hundreds of Big Little Books were produced.

Big Little Books all sold for 10 cents and were generally available at 10 cent stores such as Woolworths, Kresgge, W.T. Grant, etc. They were displayed on shelves in a glass case with the spines facing front.

In the beginning, famous newspaper strips were adapted to the Big Little Book format, followed by popular movies, classic novels and some original material. The colorful covers and spines of these fat little books were eye-catching and caught on instantly. Other companies followed Whitman's lead and began their series of similarly formatted books. The largest of these was the Saalfield Publishing Co. who latched onto exclusive rights to publishing *Shirley Temple* books. Saalfield also published several collectible movie books as well as a few popular strip characters such as *Brick Bradford, Just Kids* and *Popeye.* However, most of their books were original western, crime and sport oriented themes. No other publisher ever came close to competing with the avalanche of Whitman titles satisfying consumer demand. Whitman had all the best syndicated stars wrapped up early-on, including *Tarzan, Dick Tracy, Buck Rogers, Flash Gordon, Disney,* and a host of others, and never lost their hold on the market.

The public recognized from the beginning the uniqueness of these colorful children's books, and many collectors began saving them. Although the paper drives of the '40s consumed untold thousands, many survived and show up at flea markets, antique shows and comic book conventions for sale.

The name Big Little Book has now become a generic term in describing books of this type. It is believed that the name Big Little Book was changed to Better Little Book because the term had previously been used by another publisher. It is known that Little Big Book had been used in the late 1920s.

Today the collector's market for Big Little Books is very healthy and growing. These books are rare in mint condition and sell rapidly whenever they turn up in this grade.

Big Little Books are collected in many ways. Some collectors only want Whitman books. Others collect special characters or genres such as *Dick Tracy, Tarzan, Popeye,* westerns or *Disney.* Still others want them all. The most popular titles, of course, correspond with the most popular characters. *Flash Gordon, Buck Rogers, Donald Duck, Mickey Mouse, Dick Tracy, Popeye, Tarzan, The Shadow, Captain Midnight, The Green Hornet,* etc. are high on everyone's list. Whatever your collecting interest, most Big Little Books are under $50.00, except for the highest grades, and are affordable to most budgets.

As supplies dry up with an ever-increasing demand, the future growth should continue to be good. No time is better than now to begin your collection. The following listing was completely compiled from several large private collections. It is not complete, but is nearly so, and will be expanded and improved with each new future edition.

Other variants of the Big Little Book are also listed, such as Big Big Books, Dime Action Books, Fast-Action Books, Nickel Books, Penny Books, Pop-Up books, Top-Line Comics and Wee Little Books. The author would be grateful to know of any omissions or errors in the listings.

Big Little Book Giveaways

Many popular titles were republished as giveaways or premiums and are listed alphabetically under the original version listing in most cases. Otherwise they will appear after the regular listings under each character.

The best known and most commonly found are the premiums issued by the Cocomalt Company (Cocomalt is a chocolate additive to milk). It was long known among collectors that the rarest and most sought after Cocomalt BLB was the Buck Rogers "City of Floating Globes." Most Cocomalt BLBs were condensed versions of the same Whitman BLB of the same title. With the exception of one, all featured the same cover as their Whitman counterpart. All covers were soft. Cocomalt was the first company to give away BLBs as premiums.

All Whitman BLBs as well as the giveaway spin-offs were produced by Western Publishing Co. in Racine, Wis. Western also produced more Whitman condensed version premiums for American Gas Co., Kolynos Dental Cream and Phillips Tooth Paste.

A few special BLBs were prepared by Western to be given away by Santas in the toy department of large department stores such as Macy's, Stewart's, Mandel's (Chicago), Sears and others. Some of these premiums are very rare and difficult to obtain.

Soon after the Cocomalt BLBs appeared, several dairy companies contracted Western to produce premiums for them. The best known of this type were produced by dairies of Tarzan Ice Cream and Buddy Ice Cream. Tarzan Ice Cream was purchased in cups and a BLB premium could be ordered through the mail only by sending in 12 cup lids. Buddy Ice Cream gave out coupons for each cone of ice cream purchased. A premium book of your choice would be sent for 12 coupons. More premiums were offered in the books by sending in 12 back covers. Consequently, many books turn up missing the back cover. Since these books were not distributed to the stands and were so difficult to obtain, they are today among the rarest of the BLB premiums.

There were many other companies that used BLB type premiums to promote their products. A few are: Poll Parrot shoes, Karmetz and Perkins.

In the late 1930s more premiums were offered to the public by gas companies such as Pan-Am and Gilmore. These were also produced by Western.

Many of these books are scarce and very popular with BLB collectors who are lucky enough to find copies for their collections.

How to Use the Listings

All titles are listed alphabetically, regardless of publisher, with the following exception. When more than one book was published of a given character, they are listed numerically within that grouping. For instance, to look up a *Dick Tracy* book, you would go to the *Dick Tracy* listing first and then find the book listed numerically. If it is a giveaway with no number, you will usually find it listed under the original book and title it reprints. Generally, the earlier the date, the closer to the beginning of the listing the book will appear. The information is listed in this order: Issue number, title, date, publisher, page count (which includes covers and end sheets), special information, artists, etc.

Grading

Before a Big Little Book's value can be assessed, its condition or state of preservation must be determined. A book in **Mint** condition will bring many times the price of the same book in **Poor** condition. Many variables influence the grading of a Big Little Book and all must be considered in the final evaluation. Due to the way they are constructed, damage occurs with very little use — usually to the spine, book edges and binding. Consequently, books in near mint to mint condition are scarce. More important defects that affect grading are: Split spines, pages missing, page browning or brittleness, writing, crayoning, loose pages, color fading, chunks missing, and rolling or out of square. The following grading guide is given to aid the novice:

Mint: Absolutely perfect in every way, regardless of age; white pages, original printing luster retained on covers and spine; no color fading; no wear on edges or corners of book; virtually an unread copy with binding still square and tight.

Near Mint: Almost perfect; full cover gloss and white pages with only very slight wear on book corners and edges; binding still square and tight with no pages missing.

Very Fine: Most of cover gloss retained with minor wear appearing at corners and around edges; paper quality still fresh from white to off-white; spine tight with no pages missing.

Fine: Slight wear beginning to show; cover gloss reduced but still clean; pages still relatively fresh and white; very minor splits and wear at spine and book edges. Relatively flat and square with no pages missing.

Very Good: Obviously a read copy with original printing luster almost gone; some fading and discoloration, but not soiled; some signs of wear such as minor corner splits, rolling and page yellowing with possibly one of the blank inside pages missing; no chunks missing.

Good: An average used copy complete with only minor pieces missing from spine which may be partially split; slightly soiled or marked with rolling, color flaking and wear around edges, but perfectly sound and legible; could have minor tape repairs or one or more of blank inside pages missing, but otherwise complete.

Fair: Very heavily read and soiled with small chunks missing from cover; most or all of spine could be missing; multiple splits in spine and loose pages, but still sound and legible, bringing 50 to 70 percent of good price.

Poor: Damaged, heavily weathered, soiled or otherwise unsuited for collecting purposes.

IMPORTANT

Most BLBs on the market today will fall in the very good to fine grade category. **Rarely** will very fine to near mint BLBs be offered for sale. When they are, they usually bring premium prices.

A Word on Pricing

The prices are given for good, fine and near-mint condition. A book in fair would be 50–70% of the good price. Very good would be halfway between the good and fine price, and very fine would be halfway between the fine and near mint price. The prices listed were averaged from convention sales, dealers' lists, adzines, auctions, and by special contact with dealers and collectors from coast to coast. The prices and the spreads were determined from sales of copies in available condition or the highest grade known. Since most available copies are in the good to fine range, neither dealers nor collectors should let the mint column influence the prices they are willing to charge or pay for books in less than perfect condition.

In the past, the BLB market has lacked a point of focus due to the absence of an annual price guide that accurately reports sales and growth in the market. Due to this, current prices for BLBs still vary considerably from region to region. It is our hope that this book will contribute to the stability of the BLB market. The prices listed reflect a six times spread from good to near mint (1 - 3 - 6). We feel this spread accurately reflects the current market, especially when you consider the scarcity of books in NM-Mint condition. When one or both end sheets are missing, the book's value would drop about a half grade.

Books with movie scenes are of double importance due to the high cross over demand by movie collectors.

Abbreviations: *a*-art; *c*-cover; *nn*-no number; *p*-pages; *r*-reprint.

Publisher Codes: *BRP*-Blue Ribbon Press; *ERB*-Edgar Rice Burroughs; *EVW*-Engel van Wiseman; *FAW*-Fawcett Publishing Co.; *Gold*-Goldsmith Publishing Co.; *Lynn*-Lynn Publishing Co.; *McKay*-David McKay Co.; *Whit*-Whitman Publishing Co.; *World*-World Syndicate Publishing Co.

Terminology: *All Pictures Comics*-no text, all drawings; *Fast Action*-A special series of Dell books highly collected; *Flip Pictures*-upper right corner of interior pages contain drawings that are put into motion when rifled; *Movie Scenes-*book illustrated with scenes from the movie. *Soft Cover-*A thin single sheet of cardboard used in binding most of the giveaway versions.

"Big Little Book" is a registered trademark of Whitman Publishing Co.
"Pop-Up" is a registered trademark of Blue Ribbon Press.
"Little Big Book" is a registered trademark of the Saalfield Co.

*Top 20 Big Little Books**

Issue#	Rank	Title	Price
W-707	1	Dick Tracy The Detective	$1,000
717	2	Mickey Mouse	770
725	3	Big Little Mother Goose	700
721	4	Big Little Paint Book	630
710	5	Dick Tracy & Dick Tracy Jr.	350
1056	6	Krazy Kat, Advs. of	335
1126	7	Laughing Dragon of Oz	315
708	8	Little Orphan Annie	280
1119	9	Betty Boop in Snow White	265
1158	10	Betty Boop in Miss Gullivers Travels	245
1402	11	John Carter of Mars	245
770	12	Tarzan Twins, 1934	250
742	13	Buck Rogers in 25th Century A.D.	245
1430	14	The Shadow & the Living Death	230
1443	15	The Shadow and the Master of Evil	230
1495	16	The Shadow & the Ghost Makers	230
1453	17	Green Hornet Strikes!	190
1051	18	Popeye, The Advs. of	190
1480	19	Green Hornet Cracks Down	160
1496	20	Green Hornet Returns	160

* Includes only standard format BLBs; no premiums, giveaways or other divergent forms are included.

Big Little Book Listings

	Good	Fine	N-Mint
1175-0-Abbie an' Slats, 1940, Sal, 400p	7.00	25.00	50.00
1182-Abbie an' Slats-and Becky, 1940, Sal, 400p	7.00	25.00	50.00
1177-Ace Drummond, 1935, Whit, 432p	6.00	21.00	42.00
Admiral Byrd (See Paramount Newsreel...)			
nn-Adventures of Charlie McCarthy and Edgar Bergen, The, 1938, Dell, 194p, Fast-Action Story, soft-c	18.00	62.00	125.00
1422-Adventures of Huckleberry Finn, The, 1939, Whit, 432p, Henry E. Vallely-a	6.00	21.00	42.00
1648-Adventures of Jim Bowie (TV Series), 1958, Whit, 280p	3.00	9.00	18.00
1056-Adventures of Krazy Kat and Ignatz Mouse in Koko Land, 1934, Sal, 160p, oblong size, hard-c, Herriman c/a	48.00	170.00	335.00
1306-Adventures of Krazy Kat and Ignatz Mouse in Koko Land, 1934, Sal, 164p, oblong size, soft-c, Herriman c/a	48.00	170.00	335.00
1082-Adventures of Pete the Tramp, The, 1935, Sal, hard-c, by C. D. Russell	9.00	31.00	62.00
1312-Adventures of Pete the Tramp, The, 1935, Sal, soft-c, by C. D. Russell	9.00	31.00	62.00
1053-Adventures of Tim Tyler, 1934, Sal, hard-c, oblong size, by Lyman Young	16.00	55.00	110.00
1303-Adventures of Tim Tyler, 1934, Sal, soft-c, oblong size, by Lyman Young	16.00	55.00	110.00
1058-Adventures of Tom Sawyer, The, 1934, Sal, 160p, hard-c, Park Sumner-a	6.00	21.00	42.00
1308-Adventures of Tom Sawyer, The, 1934, Sal, 160p, soft-c, Park Sumner-a	6.00	21.00	42.00
1448-Air Fighters of America, 1941, Whit, 432p, flip pictures	5.50	19.00	38.00

	Good	Fine	N-Mint

Alexander Smart, ESQ. (See Top-Line Comics)

759-Alice in Wonderland, 1933, Whit, 160p, hard photo-c, movie
scenes   17.00   60.00   120.00

Alice in Wonderland #759, © Paramount Productions, 1933

1481-Allen Pike of the Parachute Squad U.S.A., 1941, Whit, 432p
                                       5.50   19.00   38.00
763-Alley Oop and Dinny, 1935, Whit, 384p, V. T. Hamlin-a
                                       11.00   37.50   75.00
1473-Alley Oop and Dinny in the Jungles of Moo, 1938, Whit,
432p, V. T. Hamlin-a   10.00   35.00   70.00
nn-Alley Oop and the Missing King of Moo, 1938, Whit, 36p,
2½×3½", Penny Book   5.00   17.50   35.00
nn-Alley Oop in the Kingdom of Foo, 1938, Whit, 68p, 3¼×3½",
Pan-Am premium   11.00   37.50   75.00
nn-"Alley Oop the Invasion of Moo," 1935, Whit, 260p, Cocomalt premium, soft-c; V. T. Hamlin-a
                                       12.50   42.50   85.00

Andy Burnette (See Walt Disney's...)
Andy Panda (See Walter Lantz...)
531-Andy Panda, 1943, Whit, 3¾×8¾", Tall Comic Book, All
Pictures Comics   18.00   62.50   125.00
1425-Andy Panda and Tiny Tom, 1944, Whit, All Pictures Comics
                                       8.00   27.50   55.00
1431-Andy Panda and the Mad Dog Mystery, 1947, Whit, 288p,
by Walter Lantz   6.00   21.00   42.00
1441-Andy Panda in the City of Ice, 1948, Whit, All Pictures
Comics, by Walter Lantz   7.50   26.00   52.00
1459-Andy Panda and the Pirate Ghosts, 1949, Whit, 288p, by
Walter Lantz   6.00   21.00   42.00
1485-Andy Panda's Vacation, 1946, Whit, All Pictures Comics, by
Walter Lantz   7.50   26.00   52.00

	Good	**Fine**	**N-Mint**
15-Andy Panda (The Adventures of), 1942, Dell, Fast-Action Story	18.00	62.50	125.00
707-10-Andy Panda and Presto the Pup, 1949, Whit	5.00	17.50	35.00
1130-Apple Mary and Dennie Foil the Swindlers, 1936, Whit, 432p (Forerunner to Mary Worth)	7.00	25.00	50.00
1403-Apple Mary and Dennie's Lucky Apples, 1939, Whit, 432p	5.50	19.00	38.00
2017-(#17)-Aquaman-Scourge of the Sea, 1968, Whit, 260p, 39 cents, hard-c, color illos	2.50	7.50	15.00
1192-Arizona Kid on the Bandit Trail, The, 1936, Whit, 432p	5.00	17.50	35.00
1469-Bambi (Walt Disney's), 1942, Whit, 432p	16.00	55.00	110.00
1497-Bambi's Children (Disney), 1943, Whit, 432p, Disney Studio-a	16.00	55.00	110.00
1138-Bandits at Bay, 1938, Sal, 400p	5.00	17.50	35.00
1459-Barney Baxter in the Air with the Eagle Squadron, 1938, Whit, 432p	7.00	25.00	50.00
1083-Barney Google, 1935, Sal, hard-c	12.50	42.50	85.00
1313-Barney Google, 1935, Sal, soft-c	12.50	42.50	85.00
2031-Batman and Robin in the Cheetah Caper, 1969, Whit, 258p	2.50	7.50	15.00
5771-2-Batman and Robin in the Cheetah Caper, 1975?, Whit, 258p	.50	1.50	3.00
nn-Beauty and the Beast, nd (1930s), np (Whit), 36p, 3×3½" Penny Book	1.50	4.50	9.00
760-Believe It or Not!, 1933, Whit, 160p, by Ripley (c. 1931)	7.50	22.50	45.00

Betty Bear's Lesson (See Wee Little Books)

Betty Boop in Snow White #1119, © Whitman Publishing, 1934

	Good	Fine	N-Mint

1119-Betty Boop in Snow White, 1934, Whit, 240p, hard-c; adapted from Max Fleischer Paramount Talkartoon

    38.00   132.50   265.00

1158-Betty Boop in "Miss Gullivers Travels," 1935, Whit, 288p, hard-c   35.00   122.50   245.00

1432-Big Chief Wahoo and the Lost Pioneers, 1942, Whit, 432p, Elmer Woggon-a   6.00   21.00   42.00

1443-Big Chief Wahoo and the Great Gusto, 1938, Whit, 432p, Elmer Woggon-a   6.00   21.00   42.00

1483-Big Chief Wahoo and the Magic Lamp, 1940, Whit, 432p, flip pictures, Woggon-c/a   6.00   21.00   42.00

725-Big Little Mother Goose, The, 1934, Whit, 580p (Rare)

    100.00   350.00   700.00

1006-Big Little Nickel Book, 1935, Whit, 144p, Blackie Bear stories, folk tales in primer style   5.00   17.50   35.00

1007-Big Little Nickel Book, 1935, Whit, 144p, Wee Wee Woman, etc.   5.00   17.50   35.00

1008-Big Little Nickel Book, 1935, Whit, 144p, Peter Rabbit, etc.

    5.00   17.50   35.00

721-Big Little Paint Book, The, 1933, Whit, 336p, $3\frac{3}{4} \times 8\frac{1}{2}$", for crayoning (Rare)   90.00   315.00   630.00

1178-Billy of Bar-Zero, 1940, Sal, 400p   5.00   17.50   35.00

773-Billy the Kid, 1935, Whit, 432p, Hal Arbo-a

    7.00   25.00   50.00

1159-Billy the Kid on Tall Butte, 1939, Sal, 400p

    5.00   17.50   35.00

1174-Billy the Kid's Pledge, 1940, Sal, 400p

    5.00   17.50   35.00

nn-Billy the Kid, Western Outlaw, 1935, Whit, 260p, Cocomalt premium, Hal Arbo-a, soft-c   8.00   27.50   55.00

1057-Black Beauty, 1934, Sal, hard-c   5.00   17.50   35.00

1307-Black Beauty, 1934, Sal, soft-c   5.00   17.50   35.00

1414-Black Silver and His Pirate Crew, 1937, Whit, 300p

    5.50   19.00   38.00

1447-Blaze Brandon with the Foreign Legion, 1938, Whit, 432p

    5.50   19.00   38.00

1410-Blondie and Dagwood in Hot Water, 1946, Whit, 352p, by Chic Young   6.00   21.00   42.00

1415-Blondie and Baby Dumpling, 1937, Whit, 432p, by Chic Young   7.50   26.00   52.00

1419-Oh, Blondie the Bumsteads Carry On, 1941, Whit, 432p, flip pictures, by Chic Young   7.50   26.00   52.00

1423-Blondie Who's Boss?, 1942, Whit, 432p, flip pictures, by Chic Young   7.50   26.00   52.00

	Good	**Fine**	**N-Mint**

1429-Blondie with Baby Dumpling and Daisy, 1939, Whit, 432p,
by Chic Young   7.50   26.00   52.00

1430-Blondie Count Cookie in Too!, 1947, Whit, 288p, by Chic
Young   6.00   21.00   42.00

1438-Blondie and Dagwood Everybody's Happy, 1948, Whit,
288p, by Chic Young   6.00   21.00   42.00

1450-Blondie No Dull Moments, 1948, Whit, 288p, by Chic Young
6.00   21.00   42.00

Blondie Fun for All #1463, © King Features Syndicate, 1949

1463-Blondie Fun For All!, 1949, Whit, 288p, by Chic Young
6.00   21.00   42.00

1466-Blondie or Life Among the Bumsteads, 1944, Whit, 352p, by
Chic Young   7.50   26.00   52.00

1476-Blondie and Bouncing Baby Dumpling, 1940, Whit, 432p,
by Chic Young   7.50   26.00   52.00

1487-Blondie Baby Dumpling and All!, 1941, Whit, 432p, flip
pictures, by Chic Young   7.50   26.00   52.00

1490-Blondie Papa Knows Best, 1945, Whit, 352p, by Chic Young
6.00   21.00   42.00

1491-Blondie-Cookie and Daisy's Pups, 1943, Whit, 432p
7.50   26.00   52.00

703-10-Blondie and Dagwood Some Fun!, 1949, Whit, by Chic
Young   5.00   17.50   35.00

21-Blondie and Dagwood, 194?, Lynn, by Chic Young
12.00   42.00   85.00

1108-Bobby Benson on the H-Bar-O Ranch, 1934, Whit, 300p,
based on radio serial   7.00   25.00   50.00

Bobby Thatcher and the Samarang Emerald (See Top-Line
Comics)

1432-Bob Stone the Young Detective, 1937, Whit, 240p, movie
scenes   8.00   27.50   55.00

	Good	Fine	N-Mint
2002-(#2)-Bonanza-The Bubble Gum Kid, 1967, Whit, 260p,			
39 cents, hard-c, color illos	3.00	9.00	18.00
1139-Border Eagle, The, 1938, Sal, 400p			
	5.00	17.50	35.00
1153-Boss of the Chisholm Trail, 1939, Sal, 400p			
	5.00	17.50	35.00
1425-Brad Turner in Transatlantic Flight, 1939, Whit, 432p			
	5.50	19.00	38.00
1058-Brave Little Tailor, The (Disney), 1939, Whit, 5×5½", 68p,			
hard-c (Mickey Mouse)	9.00	31.00	62.00
1427-Brenda Starr and the Masked Impostor, 1943, Whit, 352p,			
Dale Messick-a	8.50	30.00	60.00
1426-Brer Rabbit (Walt Disney's...), 1947, Whit, All Pict, Comics,			
from *Song Of The South* Movie	13.00	45.00	90.00
704-10-Brer Rabbit, 1949?, Whit	12.00	42.00	85.00
1059-Brick Bradford in the City Beneath the Sea, 1934, Sal,			
hard-c, by William Ritt & Clarence Gray			
	12.00	42.00	85.00
1309-Brick Bradford in the City Beneath the Sea, 1934, Sal,			
soft-c, by Ritt & Gray	12.00	42.00	85.00
1468-Brick Bradford with Brocco the Modern Buccaneer, 1938,			
Whit, 432p, by Wm. Ritt & Clarence Gray			
	7.00	25.00	50.00
1133-Bringing Up Father, 1936, Whit, 432p, by George McManus			
	11.00	37.50	75.00
1100-Broadway Bill, 1935, Sal, photo-c, 4½×5¼", movie scenes			
(Columbia Pictures, horse racing)	9.00	31.00	62.00
1580-Broadway Bill, 1935, Sal, soft-c, photo-c, movie scenes			
	9.00	31.00	62.00
1181-Broncho Bill, 1940, Sal, 400p	5.00	17.50	35.00
nn-Broncho Bill in Suicide Canyon (See Top-Line Comics)			
1417-Bronc Peeler the Lone Cowboy, 1937, Whit, 432p, by Fred			
Harman, forerunner of Red Ryder	7.00	25.00	50.00
1470-Buccaneer, The, 1938, Whit, 240p, photo-c, movie scenes			
	8.50	30.00	60.00
1646-Buccaneers, The (TV Series), 1958, Whit, 4½×5¾", 280p,			
Russ Manning-a	2.50	7.50	15.00
1104-Buck Jones in the Fighting Code, 1934, Whit, 160p, hard-c,			
movie scenes	11.00	37.50	75.00
1116-Buck Jones in Ride 'Em Cowboy (Universal Presents), 1935,			
Whit, 240p, photo-c, movie scenes			
	11.00	37.50	75.00
1174-Buck Jones in the Roaring West (Universal Presents),			
1935, Whit, 240p, movie scenes	11.00	37.50	75.00

	Good	Fine	N-Mint
1188-Buck Jones in the Fighting Rangers (Universal Presents), 1936, Whit, 240p, photo-c, movie scenes	11.00	37.50	75.00
1404- Buck Jones and the Two-Gun Kid, 1937, Whit, 432p	6.00	21.00	42.00
1451-Buck Jones and the Killers of Crooked Butte, 1940, Whit, 432p	6.00	21.00	42.00
1461-Buck Jones and the Rock Creek Cattle War, 1938, Whit, 432p	6.00	21.00	42.00
1486-Buck Jones and the Rough Riders in Forbidden Trails, 1943, Whit, flip pictures, based on movie; Tim McCoy app.	8.00	27.50	55.00
3-Buck Jones in the Red Ryder, 1934, EVW, 160p, movie scenes	15.00	52.50	105.00
15-Buck Jones in Rocky Rhodes, 1935, EVW, 160p, photo-c, movie scenes	15.00	52.50	105.00
4069-Buck Jones and the Night Riders, 1937, Whit, 7×9½", 320p, Big Big Book	32.00	112.50	225.00
nn-Buck Jones on the Six-Gun Trail, 1939, Whit, 36p, 2½×3½", Penny Book	6.00	21.00	42.00
nn-Buck Jones Big Thrill Chewing Gum, 1934, Whit, 8p, 2½×3½" (6 diff.) ea...	8.50	30.00	60.00

Buck Rogers in the 25th Century A.D. #742, © John F. Dille Co., 1938

742-Buck Rogers in the 25th Century A.D., 1933, Whit, 320p, Dick Calkins-a	35.00	122.50	245.00
nn-Buck Rogers in the 25th Century A.D., 1933, Whit, 204p, Cocomalt premium, Calkins-a	20.00	70.00	140.00
765-Buck Rogers in the City Below the Sea, 1934, Whit, 320p, Dick Calkins-a	18.00	62.50	125.00
765-Buck Rogers in the City Below the Sea, 1934, Whit, 324p, soft-c, Dick Calkins c/a	35.00	122.50	245.00
1143-Buck Rogers on the Moons of Saturn, 1934, Whit, 320p,			

	Good	Fine	N-Mint
Dick Calkins-a	18.00	62.50	125.00

nn-Buck Rogers on the Moons of Saturn, 1934, Whit, 324p, premium w/no ads, soft 3-color-c, Dick Calkins-a

	35.00	122.50	245.00

1169-Buck Rogers and the Depth Men of Jupiter, 1935, Whit, 432p, Calkins-a

	18.00	62.50	125.00

1178-Buck Rogers and the Doom Comet, 1935, Whit, 432p, Calkins-a

	17.00	60.00	120.00

1197- Buck Rogers and the Planetoid Plot, 1936, Whit, 432p, Calkins-a

	17.00	60.00	120.00

1409-Buck Rogers Vs. the Fiend of Space, 1940, Whit, 432p, Calkins-a

	17.00	60.00	120.00

1437-Buck Rogers in the War with the Planet Venus, 1938, Whit, 432p, Calkins-a

	17.00	60.00	120.00

1474-Buck Rogers and the Overturned World, 1941, Whit, 432p, flip pictures, Calkins-a

	17.00	60.00	120.00

1490-Buck Rogers and the Super-Dwarf of Space, 1943, Whit, ll Pictures Comics, Calkins-a

	17.00	60.00	120.00

4057-Buck Rogers, The Adventures of, 1934, Whit, 7×9½", 320p, Big Big Book, "The Story of Buck Rogers on the Planet Eros," Calkins-c/a

	63.00	220.00	440.00

nn-Buck Rogers, 1935, Whit, 4×3½", Tarzan Ice Cream cup premium (Rare)

	65.00	225.00	450.00

nn-Buck Rogers in the City of Floating Globes, 1935, Whit, 258p, Cocomalt premium, soft-c, Dick Calkins-a

	45.00	157.50	315.00

nn-Buck Rogers Big Thrill Chewing Gum, 1934, Whit, 8p, 2½×3" (6 diff.) ea...

	12.00	42.00	85.00

1135-Buckskin and Bullets, 1938, Sal, 400p

	5.00	17.50	35.00

Buffalo Bill (See Wild West Adventures of...)

nn-Buffalo Bill, 1934, World, All pictures, by J. Carroll Mansfield

	5.50	19.00	38.00

713-Buffalo Bill and the Pony Express, 1934, Whit, 384p, Hal Arbo-a

	7.00	25.00	50.00

1194-Buffalo Bill Plays a Lone Hand, 1936, Whit, 432p, Hal Arbo-a

	5.50	19.00	38.00

530-Bugs Bunny, 1943, Whit, All Pictures Comics, Tall Comic Book, 3¾×8¾", reprints/Looney Tunes 1 & 5

	18.00	62.50	125.00

1403-Bugs Bunny and the Pirate Loot, 1947, Whit, All Pictures Comics

	7.00	25.00	50.00

1435-Bugs Bunny, 1944, Whit, All Pictures Comics

	8.00	27.50	55.00

Bugs Bunny in Risky Business #1440, © Warner Bros., 1948

	Good	Fine	N-Mint
1440-Bugs Bunny in Risky Business, 1948, Whit, All Pictures & Comics	7.00	25.00	50.00
1455-Bugs Bunny and Klondike Gold, 1948, Whit, 288p	7.00	25.00	50.00
1465-Bugs Bunny The Masked Marvel, 1949, Whit, 288p	7.00	25.00	50.00
1496-Bugs Bunny and His Pals, 1945, Whit, All Pictures Comics; r/4-Color 33	8.00	27.50	55.00
706-10-Bugs Bunny and the Giant Brothers, 1949, Whit	4.50	16.00	32.00
2007-(#7)-Bugs Bunny-Double Trouble on Diamond Fountain, 1967, Whit, 260p, 39 cents, hard-c, color illos	2.00	6.00	12.00
2952-Bugs Bunny's Mistake, 1949, Whit, 3¼×4", 24p, Tiny Tales, full color (5 cents)	5.00	17.50	35.00
5757-2-Bugs Bunny in Double Trouble on Diamond Island, 1967, (1980-reprints #2007), Whit, 260p, soft-c, 79 cents, B&W	.50	1.50	3.00
5772-2-Bugs Bunny the Last Crusader, 1975, Whit, 79 cents, flip-it book	.50	1.50	3.00
13-Bugs Bunny and the Secret of Storm Island, 1942, Dell, 194p, Fast-Action Story	18.00	62.50	125.00
1169-Bullet Benton, 1939, Sal, 400p	5.00	17.50	35.00
nn-Bulletman and the Return of Mr. Murder, 1941, Faw, 196p, Dime Action Book	27.00	95.00	190.00
1142-Bullets Across the Border (A Billy The Kid story), 1938, Sal, 400p	5.00	17.50	35.00
Bunky (See Top-Line Comics)			
837-Bunty (Punch and Judy), 1935, Whit, 28p, Magic-Action with 3 pop-ups	10.00	30.00	60.00
1091-Burn 'Em Up Barnes, 1935, Sal, hard-c, movie scenes	8.50	30.00	60.00

	Good	Fine	N-Mint

1321-Burn 'Em Up Barnes, 1935, Sal, soft-c, movie scenes
                                          8.50   30.00   60.00
1415-Buz Sawyer and Bomber 13, 1946, Whit, 352p, Roy Crane-a
                                          8.50   30.00   60.00
1412-Calling W-I-X-Y-Z, Jimmy Kean and the Radio Spies,
1939, Whit, 300p   7.00   25.00   50.00
Call of the Wild (See Jack London's...)
1107-Camels are Coming, 1935, Sal, movie scenes
                                          7.00   25.00   50.00
1587-Camels are Coming, 1935, Sal, movie scenes
                                          7.00   25.00   50.00
nn-Captain and the Kids, Boys Will Be Boys, The, 1938, 68p,
Pan-Am Oil premium, soft-c   8.50   30.00   60.00
1128-Captain Easy Soldier of Fortune, 1934, Whit, 432p, Roy
Crane-a   10.00   35.00   70.00
nn-Captain Easy Soldier of Fortune, 1934, Whit, 436p,
Premium-no ads, soft 3-color-c, Roy Crane-a
                                         17.00   60.00   120.00
1474-Captain Easy Behind Enemy Lines, 1943, Whit, 352p, Roy
Crane-a   9.00   31.00   62.00
nn-Captain Easy and Wash Tubbs, 1935, 260p, Cocomalt
premium, Roy Crane-a   9.00   31.00   62.00
1444-Captain Frank Hawks Air Ace and the League of Twelve,
1938, Whit, 432p   6.00   21.00   42.00
nn-Captain Marvel, 1941, Faw, 196p, Dime Action Book
                                         30.00   105.00   210.00
1402-Captain Midnight and Sheik Jomak Khan, 1946, Whit,
352p   15.00   52.00   105.00
1452-Captain Midnight and the Moon Woman, 1943, Whit, 352p
                                         15.00   52.00   105.00
1458-Captain Midnight Vs. The Terror of the Orient, 1942, Whit,
432p, flip pictures, Hess-a   15.00   52.00   105.00
1488-Captain Midnight and the Secret Squadron, 1941, Whit,
432p   15.00   52.00   105.00
Captain Robb of... (See Dirigible ZR90...)
L20-Ceiling Zero, 1936, Lynn, 128p, 7½×5", hard-c, James
Cagney, Pat O'Brien photos on-c, movie scenes, Warner Bros.
Pictures   7.50   26.00   52.00
1093-Chandu the Magician, 1935, Sal, 5×5¼", 160p, hard-c, Bela
Lugosi photo-c, movie scenes   11.00   37.50   75.00
1323-Chandu the Magician, 1935, Sal, 5×5¼", 160p, soft-c, Bela
Lugosi photo-c   11.00   37.50   75.00
Charlie Chan (See Inspector...)
1459-Charlie Chan Solves a New Mystery (See Inspector...), 1940,

Charlie Chan Solves a New Mystery #1459,
© McNaught Syndicate, 1940

	Good	Fine	N-Mint
Whit, 432p, Alfred Andriola-a	10.00	35.00	70.00

1478-Charlie Chan of the Honolulu Police, Inspector, 1939,
Whit, 432p, Andriola-a   10.00   35.00   70.00

Charlie McCarthy (See Story Of...)

734-Chester Gump at Silver Creek Ranch, 1933, Whit, 320p,
Sidney Smith-a   10.00   35.00   70.00

nn-Chester Gump at Silver Creek Ranch, 1933, Whit, 204p,
Cocomalt premium, soft-c, Sidney Smith-a
   12.00   42.00   85.00

nn-Chester Gump at Silver Creek Ranch, 1933, Whit, 52p,
4×5½", premium-no ads, soft-c, Sidney Smith-a
   17.00   60.00   120.00

766-Chester Gump Finds the Hidden Treasure, 1934, Whit,
320p, Sidney Smith-a   10.00   35.00   70.00

nn-Chester Gump Finds the Hidden Treasure, 1934, Whit,
52p, 3½×5¾", premium-no ads, soft-c, Sidney Smith-a
   17.00   60.00   120.00

nn-Chester Gump Finds the Hidden Treasure, 1934, Whit,
52p, 4×5½", premium-no ads, Sidney Smith-a
   17.00   60.00   120.00

1146-Chester Gump in the City Of Gold, 1935, Whit, 432p,
Sidney Smith-a   10.00   35.00   70.00

nn-Chester Gump in the City Of Gold, 1935, Whit, 436p,
premium-no ads, 3-color, soft-c, Sidney Smith-a
   20.00   70.00   140.00

1402-Chester Gump in the Pole to Pole Flight, 1937, Whit, 432p
   8.50   30.00   60.00

5-Chester Gump and His Friends, 1934, Whit, 132p, 3½×3½",
soft-c, Tarzan Ice Cream cup lid premium
   22.00   75.00   155.00

	Good	Fine	N-Mint

nn-Chester Gump at the North Pole, 1938, Whit, 68p, soft-c, 3¾×3½", Pan-Am giveaway   12.00   42.00   85.00

nn-Chicken Greedy, nd(1930s), np(Whit), 36p, 3×2½", Penny Book   1.50   4.50   9.00

nn-Chicken Licken, nd (1930s), np (Whit), 36p, 3×2½", Penny Book   1.50   4.50   9.00

1101-Chief of the Rangers, 1935, Sal, hard-c, Tom Mix photo-c, movie scenes from "The Miracle Rider"
   12.50   45.00   90.00

1581-Chief of the Rangers, 1935, Sal, soft-c, Tom Mix photo-c, movie scenes   12.50   45.00   90.00

Child's Garden of Verses (See Wee Little Books)

L14-Chip Collins' Adventures on Bat Island, 1935, Lynn, 192p
   8.50   30.00   60.00

2025- Chitty Chitty Bang Bang, 1968, Whit, movie photos
   2.50   7.50   15.00

Chubby Little Books, 1935, Whit, 3×2½", 200p

W803-Golden Hours Story Book, The   4.00   12.00   24.00

W803-Story Hours Story Book, The   4.00   12.00   24.00

W804-Gay Book of Little Stories, The   4.00   12.00   24.00

W804-Glad Book of Little Stories, The   4.00   12.00   24.00

W804-Joy Book of Little Stories, The   4.00   12.00   24.00

W804-Sunny Book of Little Stories, The 4.00   12.00   24.00

1453-Chuck Malloy Railroad Detective on the Streamliner, 1938, Whit, 300p   5.50   19.00   38.00

Cinderella (See Walt Disney's...)

Clyde Beatty (See The Steel Arena)

1410-Clyde Beatty Daredevil Lion and Tiger Tamer, 1939, Whit, 300p   8.50   30.00   60.00

1480-Coach Bernie Bierman's Brick Barton and the Winning Eleven, 1938, 300p   5.50   19.00   38.00

1446-Convoy Patrol (A Thrilling U.S. Navy Story), 1942, Whit, 432p, flip pictures   5.50   19.00   38.00

1127-Corley of the Wilderness Trail, 1937, Sal, hard-c
   6.00   21.00   42.00

1607-Corley of the Wilderness Trail, 1937, Sal, soft-c
   6.00   21.00   42.00

1-Count of Monte Cristo, 1934, EVW, 160p, (Five Star Library), movie scenes, hard-c   12.00   42.00   85.00

1457-Cowboy Lingo Boys' Book of Western Facts, 1938, Whit, 300p, Fred Harman-a   6.00   21.00   42.00

1171-Cowboy Malloy, 1940, Sal, 400p   5.00   17.50   35.00

1106-Cowboy Millionaire, 1935, Sal, movie scenes with George O'Brien, photo-c, hard-c   10.00   35.00   70.00

	Good	**Fine**	**N-Mint**
1586-Cowboy Millionaire, 1935, Sal, movie scenes with George O'Brien, photo-c, soft-c	10.00	35.00	70.00
724-Cowboy Stories, 1933, Whit, 300p, Hal Arbo-a	9.00	31.00	62.00
nn-Cowboy Stories, 1933, Whit, 52p, soft-c, premium-no ads, 4×5½", Hal Arbo-a	10.00	35.00	70.00
1161-Crimson Cloak, The, 1939, Sal, 400p	5.00	17.50	35.00
L19-Curley Harper at Lakespur, 1935, Lynn, 192p	6.00	21.00	42.00
5785-2-Daffy Duck in Twice the Trouble, 1980, Whit, 260p, 79 cents, soft-c	.50	1.50	3.00
2018-(#18)-Daktari-Night of Terror, 1968, Whit, 260p, 39 cents, hard-c, color illos	2.50	7.50	15.00
1010-Dan Dunn And The Gangsters' Frame-Up, 1937, Whit, 7¼×5½", 64p, Nickle Book	9.00	31.00	62.00
1116-Dan Dunn "Crime Never Pays," 1934, Whit, 320p, by Norman Marsh	8.50	30.00	60.00
1125-Dan Dunn on the Trail of the Counterfeiters, 1936, Whit, 432p, by Norman Marsh	8.50	30.00	60.00
1171-Dan Dunn and the Crime Master, 1937, Whit, 432p, by Norman Marsh	8.50	30.00	60.00
1417-Dan Dunn and the Underworld Gorillas, 1941, Whit, All Pictures Comics, flip pictures, by Norman Marsh	8.50	30.00	60.00
1454-Dan Dunn on the Trail of Wu Fang, 1938, Whit, 432p, by Norman Marsh	10.00	35.00	70.00
1481-Dan Dunn and the Border Smugglers, 1938, Whit, 432p, by Norman Marsh	8.50	30.00	60.00
1492-Dan Dunn and the Dope Ring, 1940, Whit, 432p, by Norman Marsh	8.50	30.00	60.00

Dan Dunn and the Border Smugglers #1481,
© Publishers Syndicate, Inc., 1938

	Good	Fine	N-Mint

nn-Dan Dunn and the Bank Hold-Up, 1938, Whit, 36p,
2½×3½", Penny Book　　　　6.00　　21.00　　42.00

nn-Dan Dunn and the Zeppelin Of Doom, 1938, Dell, 196p,
Fast-Action Story, soft-c　　18.00　　62.50　　125.00

nn-Dan Dunn Meets Chang Loo, 1938, Whit, 66p, Pan-Am
premium, by Norman Marsh　10.00　　35.00　　70.00

nn-Dan Dunn Plays a Lone Hand, 1938, Whit, 36p, 2½×3½",
Penny Book　　　　　　　　6.00　　21.00　　42.00

6-Dan Dunn and the Counterfeiter Ring, 1938, Whit, 132p,
3¾×3½", Buddy book　　　　22.00　　77.00　　155.00

9-Dan Dunn's Mysterious Ruse, 1936, Whit, 132p, soft-c,
3½×3½", Tarzan Ice Cream cup lid premium
　　　　　　　　　　　　　22.00　　77.00　　155.00

1177-Danger Trail North, 1940, Sal, 400p
　　　　　　　　　　　　　　5.00　　17.50　　35.00

1151-Danger Trails in Africa, 1935, Whit, 432p
　　　　　　　　　　　　　　6.00　　21.00　　42.00

nn-Daniel Boone, 1934, World, High Lights of History Series,
hard-c, All in Pictures　　　5.50　　19.00　　38.00

1160-Dan of the Lazy L, 1939, Sal, 400p
　　　　　　　　　　　　　　5.00　　17.50　　35.00

1148-David Copperfield, 1934, Whit, hard-c, 160p, photo-c, movie
scenes (W. C. Fields)　　　12.00　　42.00　　85.00

nn-David Copperfield, 1934, Whit, soft-c, 164p, movie scenes
　　　　　　　　　　　　　12.00　　42.00　　85.00

1151-Death by Short Wave, 1938, Sal　8.00　　27.50　　55.00

1156-Denny the Ace Detective, 1938, Sal, 400p
　　　　　　　　　　　　　　5.00　　17.50　　35.00

1431-Desert Eagle and the Hidden Fortress, The, 1941, Whit,
432p, flip pictures　　　　　6.00　　21.00　　42.00

1458-Desert Eagle Rides Again, The, 1939, Whit, 300p
　　　　　　　　　　　　　　6.00　　21.00　　42.00

1136-Desert Justice, 1938, Sal, 400p　5.00　　17.50　　35.00

1484-Detective Higgins of the Racket Squad, 1938, Whit, 432p
　　　　　　　　　　　　　　6.00　　21.00　　42.00

1124-Dickie Moore in the Little Red School House, 1936, Whit,
240p, photo-c, movie scenes (Chesterfield Motion Picts. Corp)
　　　　　　　　　　　　　　8.50　　30.00　　60.00

W-707-Dick Tracy the Detective, the Adventures of, 1933, Whit,
320p (The 1st Big Little Book), by Chester Gould (Scarce)
　　　　　　　　　　　　150.00　　525.00　　1050.00

nn-Dick Tracy Detective, The Adventures of, 1933, Whit, 52p,
4×5½", premium-no ads, soft-c, by Chester Gould
　　　　　　　　　　　　　50.00　　175.00　　350.00

The Adventures of Dick Tracy the Detective #W-707,
© Chester Gould, 1933

	Good	Fine	N-Mint

710-Dick Tracy and Dick Tracy, Jr. (The Advs. of...), 1933,
 Whit, 320p, by Chester Gould   45.00   157.00   315.00

nn-Dick Tracy and Dick Tracy, Jr. (The Advs. of...), 1933,
 Whit, 52p, premium-no ads, soft-c, 4×5½", by Chester Gould
  45.00   157.00   315.00

nn-Dick Tracy the Detective and Dick Tracy, Jr., 1933, Whit,
 52p, premium-no ads, 3½×5¾", soft-c, by Chester Gould
  45.00   157.00   315.00

723-Dick Tracy Out West, 1933, Whit, 300p, by Chester Gould
  30.00   105.00   210.00

749-Dick Tracy from Colorado to Nova Scotia, 1933, Whit,
 320p, by Chester Gould   25.00   75.00   175.00

nn-Dick Tracy from Colorado to Nova Scotia, 1933, Whit,
 204p, premium-no ads, soft-c, by Chester Gould
  30.00   105.00   210.00

1105-Dick Tracy and the Stolen Bonds, 1934, Whit, 320p, by
 Chester Gould   17.00   57.00   115.00

1112-Dick Tracy and the Racketeer Gang, 1936, Whit, 432p, by
 Chester Gould   13.00   45.00   90.00

1137-Dick Tracy Solves the Penfield Mystery, 1934, Whit, 320p,
 by Chester Gould   17.00   60.00   120.00

nn-Dick Tracy Solves the Penfield Mystery, 1934, Whit, 324p,
 premium-no ads, 3-color, soft-c, by Chester Gould
  30.00   105.00   210.00

1163-Dick Tracy and the Boris Arson Gang, 1935, Whit, 432p, by
 Chester Gould   12.50   45.00   90.00

1170-Dick Tracy on the Trail of Larceny Lu, 1935, Whit, 432p,
 by Chester Gould   12.50   45.00   90.00

1185-Dick Tracy in Chains of Crime, 1936, Whit, 432p,
 by Chester Gould   12.50   45.00   90.00

1412- Dick Tracy and Yogee Yamma, 1946, Whit, 352p, by
 Chester Gould   11.00   37.50   75.00

	Good	Fine	N-Mint

1420-Dick Tracy and the Hotel Murders, 1937, Whit, 432p, by
 Chester Gould   12.50   45.00   90.00

1434-Dick Tracy and the Phantom Ship, 1940, Whit, 432p, by
 Chester Gould   12.50   45.00   90.00

1436-Dick Tracy and the Mad Killer, 1947, Whit, 288p, by
 Chester Gould   11.00   37.50   75.00

1439-Dick Tracy and His G-Men, 1941, Whit, 432p, Flip pictures,
 by Chester Gould   12.50   45.00   90.00

1445-Dick Tracy and the Bicycle Gang, 1948, Whit, 288p, by
 Chester Gould   11.00   37.50   75.00

1446-Detective Dick Tracy and the Spider Gang, 1937, Whit,
 240p, movie scenes from "Adventures of Dick Tracy"
 (Republic serial)   18.00   62.50   125.00

1449-Dick Tracy Special F.B.I. Operative, 1943, Whit, 432p by
 Chester Gould   12.50   45.00   90.00

1454-Dick Tracy on the High Seas, 1939, Whit, 432p, by Chester
 Gould   12.50   45.00   90.00

1460-Dick Tracy and the Tiger Lilly Gang, 1949, Whit, 288p, by
 Chester Gould   11.00   37.50   75.00

1478-Dick Tracy on Voodoo Island, 1944, Whit, 352p, by Chester
 Gould   11.00   37.50   75.00

1479-Detective Dick Tracy Vs. Crooks in Disguise, 1939, Whit,
 432p, flip pictures, by Chester Gould
     12.50   45.00   90.00

1482-Dick Tracy and the Wreath Kidnapping Case, 1945, Whit,
 352p   11.00   37.50   75.00

1488-Dick Tracy the Super-Detective, 1939, Whit, 432p, by
 Chester Gould   12.50   45.00   90.00

1491-Dick Tracy the Man with No Face, 1938, Whit, 432p
     12.50   45.00   90.00

1495-Dick Tracy Returns, 1939, Whit, 432p, based on Republic
 Motion Picture serial, Chester Gould-a
     12.50   45.00   90.00

2001-(#1)-Dick Tracy-Encounters Facey, 1967, Whit, 260p,
 39 cents, hard-c, color illos   2.50   7.50   15.00

4055-Dick Tracy, The Adventures of, 1934, Whit, 7×9½", 320p,
 Big Big Book, by Chester Gould   53.00   185.00   370.00

4071-Dick Tracy and the Mystery of the Purple Cross, 1938,
 7×9½", 320p, Big Big Book, by Chester Gould (Scarce)
     83.00   290.00   580.00

nn-Dick Tracy and the Invisible Man, 1939, Whit, 3¾×3¾",
 132p, stapled, soft-c, Quaker Oats premium; NBC radio play
 script, Chester Gould-a   25.00   87.50   175.00

Vol. 2-Dick Tracy's Ghost Ship, 1939, Whit, 3½×3½", 132p, soft-c,

	Good	Fine	N-Mint

stapled, Quaker Oats premium; NBC radio play script episode
from actual radio show; Gould-a   25.00   87.50   175.00

3-Dick Tracy Meets a New Gang, 1934, Whit, 3×3½", 132p,
soft-c, Tarzan Ice Cream cup lid premium
40.00   140.00   280.00

11-Dick Tracy in Smashing the Famon Racket, 1938, Whit,
3¾×3½", Buddy Book-ice cream premium, by Chester Gould
40.00   140.00   280.00

nn-Dick Tracy Gets His Man, 1938, Whit, 36p, 2½×3½", Penny
Book   8.00   27.50   55.00

nn-Dick Tracy the Detective, 1938, Whit, 36p, 2½×3½", Penny
Book   8.00   27.50   55.00

9-Dick Tracy and the Frozen Bullet Murders, 1941, Dell,
196p, Fast-Action Story, soft-c, by Gould
27.00   95.00   190.00

6833-Dick Tracy Detective and Federal Agent, 1936, Dell, 244p,
Cartoon Story Books, hard-c, by Chester Gould
30.00   105.00   210.00

nn-Dick Tracy Detective and Federal Agent, 1936, Dell, 244p,
Fast-Action Story, soft-c, by Gould
27.00   95.00   190.00

nn-Dick Tracy and the Blackmailers, 1939, Dell, 196p, Fast-
Action Story, soft-c, by Gould   27.00   95.00   190.00

nn-Dick Tracy and the Chain of Evidence, Detective, 1938,
Whit, 196p, Fast-Action Story, soft-c, by Chester Gould
27.00   95.00   190.00

nn-Dick Tracy and the Crook Without a Face, 1938, Whit, 68p,
3¾×3½", Pan-Am giveaway, Gould c/a
16.00   55.00   110.00

nn-Dick Tracy and the Maroon Mask Gang, 1938, Dell, 196p,
Fast-Action Story, soft-c, by Gould
27.00   95.00   190.00

nn-Dick Tracy Cross-Country Race, 1934, Whit, 8p, 2½×3",
Big Thrill chewing gum premium (6 diff.)
10.00   35.00   70.00

nn-Dick Whittington and his Cat, nd(1930s), np(Whit), 36p,
Penny Book   1.50   4.50   9.00

Dinglehoofer und His Dog Adolph (See Top-Line Comics)

Dinky (See Jackie Cooper in...)

1464-Dirigible ZR90 and the Disappearing Zeppelin (Captain
Robb of...), 1941, Whit, 300p, Al Lewin-a
13.00   45.00   90.00

1167-Dixie Dugan Among the Cowboys, 1939, Sal, 400p
6.00   21.00   42.00

	Good	Fine	N-Mint

1188-Dixie Dugan and Cuddles, 1940, Sal, 400p, by Striebel &
McEvoy   6.00   21.00   42.00
    Doctor Doom (See Foreign Spies... & International Spy...)
    Dog of Flanders, A (See Frankie Thomas in...)
1114-Dog Stars of Hollywood, 1936, Sal, photo-c, photo-illos
                                    10.00   35.00   70.00
1594-Dog Stars of Hollywood, 1936, Sal, photo-c, soft-c, photo-
illos   10.00   35.00   70.00
    Donald Duck (See Silly Symphony... & Walt Disney's...)

Donald Duck (Says Such a Life) #1404,
© Walt Disney Productions, 1939

1404-Donald Duck (Says Such a Life) (Disney), 1939, Whit, 432p,
Taliaferro-a   13.00   45.00   90.00
1411-Donald Duck and Ghost Morgan's Treasure (Disney),
1946, Whit, All Pictures Comics, Barks-a; R/4-Color 9
                                    15.00   52.50   105.00
1422-Donald Duck Sees Stars (Disney), 1941, Whit, 432p, flip
pictures, Taliaferro-a   13.00   45.00   90.00
1424-Donald Duck Says Such Luck (Disney), 1941, Whit, 432p
flip pictures, Taliaferro-a   13.00   45.00   90.00
1430-Donald Duck Headed For Trouble (Disney), 1942, Whit,
432p, flip pictures, Taliaferro-a   13.00   45.00   90.00
1432-Donald Duck and the Green Serpent (Disney), 1947, Whit,
All Pictures Comics, Barks-a; R/4-Color 108
                                    15.00   52.50   105.00
1434-Donald Duck Forgets To Duck (Disney), 1939, Whit, 432p,
Taliaferro-a   13.00   40.00   90.00
1438-Donald Duck Off the Beam (Disney), 1943, Whit, 352p, flip
pictures, Taliaferro-a   13.00   40.00   90.00
1438-Donald Duck Off the Beam (Disney), 1943, Whit, 432p, flip
pictures, Taliaferro-a   13.00   40.00   90.00
1449-Donald Duck Lays Down the Law, 1948, Whit, 288p,

	Good	Fine	N-Mint
Barks-a	15.00	52.50	105.00

1457-Donald Duck in Volcano Valley (Disney), 1949, Whit, 288p,
Barks-a 15.00 52.50 105.00

1462-Donald Duck Gets Fed Up (Disney), 1940, Whit, 432p,
Taliaferro-a 13.00 45.00 90.00

1478- Donald Duck-Hunting For Trouble (Disney), 1938, Whit,
432p, Taliaferro-a 13.00 45.00 90.00

1484-Donald Duck is Here Again!, 1944, Whit, All Pictures
Comics, Taliaferro-a 13.00 45.00 90.00

1486-Donald Duck Up in the Air (Disney), 1945, Whit, 352p,
Barks-a 15.00 52.50 105.00

705-10-Donald Duck and the Mystery of the Double X (Disney),
1949, Whit, Barks-a 8.00 27.50 55.00

2009-(#9)-Donald Duck-The Fabulous Diamond Fountain (Walt
Disney), 1967, Whit, 260p, 39 cents, hard-c, color illos
1.70 5.00 10.00

nn-Donald Duck and the Ducklings, 1938, Whit, 194p, Fast-
Action Story, soft-c, Taliaferro-a 25.00 87.50 175.00

nn-Donald Duck Out of Luck (Disney), 1940, Dell, 196p, Fast-
Action Story, has 4-Color No. 4 on back-c, Taliaferro-a
25.00 87.50 175.00

8-Donald Duck Takes It on the Chin (Disney), 1941, Dell,
196p, Fast-Action Story, soft-c, Taliaferro-a
25.00 87.50 175.00

5760-2-Donald Duck in Volcano Valley (Disney), 1973, Whit,
79 cents, flip-it book .50 1.50 3.00

L13-Donnie and the Pirates, 1935, Lynn, 192p
8.00 27.50 55.00

1438-Don O'Dare Finds War, 1940, Whit, 432p
5.50 19.00 38.00

1107-Don Winslow, U.S.N., 1935, Whit, 432p
10.00 35.00 70.00

nn-Don Winslow, U.S.N., 1935, Whit, 436p, premium-no ads,
3-color, soft-c 17.00 60.00 120.00

1408-Don Winslow and the Giant Girl Spy, 1946, Whit, 352p
7.50 26.00 52.00

1418-Don Winslow Navy Intelligence Ace, 1942, Whit, 432p, flip
pictures 10.00 35.00 70.00

1419-Don Winslow of the Navy Vs. the Scorpion Gang, 1938,
Whit, 432p 10.00 35.00 70.00

1453-Don Winslow of the Navy and the Secret Enemy Base,
1943, Whit, 352p 10.00 35.00 70.00

1489-Don Winslow of the Navy and the Great War Plot, 1940,
Whit, 432p 10.00 35.00 70.00

Don Winslow of the Navy Vs. the Scorpion Gang #1419,
© Frank V. Martinek, 1938

	Good	Fine	N-Mint
nn-Don Winslow U.S. Navy and the Missing Admiral, 1938, Whit, 36p, 2½×3½", Penny Book			
	6.00	21.00	42.00
1137-Doomed To Die, 1938, Sal, 400p	5.00	17.50	35.00
1140- Down Cartridge Creek, 1938, Sal, 400p			
	5.00	17.50	35.00
1416-Draftie of the U.S. Army, 1943, Whit, All Pictures Comics			
	6.00	21.00	42.00
1100B-Dreams (Your dreams & what they mean), 1938, Whit, 36p, 2½×3½", Penny Book	2.00	6.00	12.00
L24-Dumb Dora and Bing Brown, 1936, Lynn			
	10.00	35.00	70.00
1400-Dumbo of the Circus-Only His Ears Grew! (Disney), 1941, Whit, 432p, based on Disney movie			
	14.00	50.00	100.00
10-Dumbo the Flying Elephant (Disney), 1944, Dell, 194p, Fast-Action Story, soft-c	20.00	70.00	140.00
nn-East O' the Sun and West O' the Moon, nd (1930s), np (Whit), 36p, 3×2½", Penny Book	1.50	4.50	9.00
774-Eddie Cantor in an Hour with You, 1934, Whit, 154p, 4¾×5¼", photo-c, movie scenes	11.00	37.50	75.00
nn-Eddie Cantor in Laughland, 1934, Gold, 132p, soft, photo-c, Vallely-a	10.00	35.00	70.00
1106-Ella Cinders and the Mysterious House, 1934, Whit, 432p			
	9.00	31.00	62.00
nn-Ella Cinders and the Mysterious House, 1934, Whit, 52p, premium-no ads, soft-c, 3½×5¾"	13.00	45.00	90.00
nn-Ella Cinders, 1935, Whit, 148p, 3¾×4", Tarzan Ice Cream cup lid premium	22.00	77.00	155.00
nn-Ella Cinders Plays Duchess, 1938, Whit, 68p, 3¾×3½", Pan-Am Oil premium	10.00	35.00	70.00

	Good	Fine	N-Mint
nn-**Ella Cinders Solves a Mystery,** 1938, Whit, 68p, Pan-Am Oil premium, soft-c	10.00	35.00	70.00
11-**Ella Cinders' Exciting Experience,** 1934, Whit, 3½×3½", 132p, Tarzan Ice Cream cup lid giveaway	22.00	77.00	155.00
1406-**Ellery Queen the Adventure of the Last Man Club,** 1940, Whit, 432p	8.50	30.00	60.00
1472-**Ellery Queen the Master Detective,** 1942, Whit, 432p, flip pictures	8.50	30.00	60.00
1081-**Elmer and his Dog Spot,** 1935, Sal, hard-c	6.00	21.00	42.00
1311-**Elmer and his Dog Spot,** 1935, Sal, soft-c	6.00	21.00	42.00
722-**Erik Noble and the Forty-Niners,** 1934, Whit, 384p	7.00	21.00	42.00
nn-**Erik Noble and the Forty-Niners,** 1934, Whit, 386p, 3-color, soft-c	10.00	30.00	70.00
1058-**Farmyard Symphony, The** (Disney), 1939, 5×5½", 68p, hard-c	9.00	31.00	62.00
1129-**Felix the Cat,** 1936, Whit, 432p, Messmer-a	20.00	70.00	140.00
1439-**Felix the Cat,** 1943, Whit, All Pictures Comics, Messmer-a	18.00	62.50	125.00

Felix the Cat #1465, © King Features Syndicate, 1945

	Good	Fine	N-Mint
1465-**Felix the Cat,** 1945, Whit, All Pictures Comics, Messmer-a	16.00	55.00	110.00
nn-**Felix** (Flip book), 1967, World Retrospective of Animation Cinema, 188p, 2½×4", by Otto Messmer	2.50	7.50	15.00
nn-**Fighting Cowboy of Nugget Gulch, The,** 1939, Whit, 36p,			

	Good	Fine	N-Mint
2½×3½", Penny Book	5.00	17.50	35.00

1401-Fighting Heroes Battle for Freedom, 1943, Whit, All Pictures Comics, from "Heroes of Democracy" strip, by Stookie Allen 5.50 19.00 38.00

6-Fighting President, The, 1934, EVW (Five Star Library), 160p, photo-c, photo ill., F. D. Roosevelt
8.00 27.50 55.00

nn-Fire Chief Ed Wynn and "His Old Fire Horse," 1934, Gold, 132p, H. Vallely-a, photo, soft-c 8.00 27.50 55.00

1464-Flame Boy and the Indians' Secret, 1938, Whit, 300p, Sekakuku-a (Hopi Indian) 5.50 19.00 38.00

22-Flaming Guns 1935, EVW, with Tom Mix, movie scenes
12.00 42.00 85.00

1110-Flash Gordon on the Planet Mongo, 1934, Whit, 320p, by Alex Raymond 21.00 72.50 145.00

1166-Flash Gordon and the Monsters of Mongo, 1935, Whit, 432p, by Alex Raymond 17.00 60.00 120.00

nn-Flash Gordon and the Monsters of Mongo, 1935, Whit, 436p, premium-no ads, 3-color, soft-c, by Alex Raymond
28.00 95.00 195.00

1171-Flash Gordon and the Tournaments of Mongo, 1935, Whit, 432p, by Alex Raymond 17.00 60.00 120.00

1190-Flash Gordon and the Witch Queen of Mongo, 1936, Whit, 432p, by Alex Raymond 15.00 52.50 105.00

1407-Flash Gordon in the Water World of Mongo, 1937, Whit, 432p, by Alex Raymond 15.00 52.50 105.00

1423-Flash Gordon and the Perils of Mongo, 1940, Whit, 432p, by Alex Raymond 14.00 47.50 95.00

1424-Flash Gordon in the Jungles of Mongo, 1947, Whit, 352p, by Alex Raymond 12.50 42.50 85.00

1443-Flash Gordon in the Ice World of Mongo, 1942, Whit, 432p, flip pictures, by Alex Raymond 14.00 47.50 95.00

1447-Flash Gordon and the Fiery Desert of Mongo, 1948, Whit, 288p, Raymond-a 12.50 42.50 85.00

1469-Flash Gordon and the Power Men of Mongo, 1943, Whit, 352p, by Alex Raymond 14.00 47.50 95.00

1479-Flash Gordon and the Red Sword Invaders, 1945, Whit, 352p, by Alex Raymond 12.50 42.50 85.00

1484-Flash Gordon and the Tyrant of Mongo, 1941, Whit, 432p, flip pictures, by Alex Raymond 14.00 47.50 95.00

1492-Flash Gordon in the Forest Kingdom of Mongo, 1938, Whit, 432p, by Alex Raymond 15.00 52.50 105.00

12-Flash Gordon and the Ape Men of Mor, 1942, Dell, 196p, Fast-Action Story, by Raymond 30.00 105.00 210.00

Flash Gordon and the Power Men of Mongo #1469,
© King Features Syndicate, 1943

	Good	Fine	N-Mint
6833-Flash Gordon Vs. the Emperor of Mongo, 1936, Dell, 244p, Cartoon Story Books, hard-c, Alex Raymond c/a	35.00	122.50	245.00
nn-Flash Gordon Vs. the Emperor of Mongo, 1936, Dell, 244p, Fast-Action Story, soft-c, Alex Raymond c/a	30.00	105.00	210.00
1467-Flint Roper and the Six-Gun Showdown, 1941, Whit, 300p	5.50	19.00	38.00
2014-(#14)-Flintstones-The Case of the Many Missing Things, 1968, Whit, 260p, 39 cents, hard-c, color illos	2.00	6.00	12.00
2003-(#3)-Flipper-Killer Whale Trouble, 1967, Whit, 260p, hard-c, 39 cents, color illos	1.70	5.00	10.00
1108-Flying the Sky Clipper with Winsie Atkins, 1936, Whit, 432p	5.50	19.00	38.00
1460-Foreign Spies Doctor Doom and the Ghost Submarine, 1939, Whit, 432p, Al McWilliams-a	7.50	26.00	52.00
1100B-Fortune Teller, 1938, Whit, 36p, 2½×3½" Penny Book	2.00	6.00	12.00
1175-Frank Buck Presents Ted Towers Animal Master, 1935, Whit, 432p	6.00	21.00	42.00
2015-(#15)-Frankenstein, Jr.-The Menace of the Heartless Monster, 1968, Whit, 260p, 39 cents, hard-c, color illos	2.00	6.00	12.00
16-Frankie Thomas in A Dog of Flanders, 1935, EVW, movie scenes	10.00	35.00	70.00
1121-Frank Merriwell at Yale, 1935, 432p	6.00	21.00	42.00

Freckles and His Friends in the North Woods (See Top-

	Good	Fine	N-Mint
Line Comics)			
nn-Freckles and his Friends Stage a Play, 1938, Whit, 36p, 2½×3½", Penny Book	6.00	21.00	42.00
1164-Freckles and the Lost Diamond Mine, 1937, Whit, 432p, Merrill Blosser-a	7.50	26.00	52.00
nn-Freckles and the Mystery Ship, 1935, Whit, 66p, Pan-Am premium	10.00	35.00	70.00
1100B-Fun, Puzzles, Riddles, 1938, Whit, 36p, 2½×3½", Penny Book	2.00	6.00	12.00
1433-Gang Busters Step In, 1939, Whit, 432p, Henry E. Vallely-a	7.00	25.00	50.00
1437-Gang Busters Smash Through, 1942, Whit, 432p	7.00	25.00	50.00
1451-Gang Busters in Action!, 1938, Whit, 432p	7.00	25.00	50.00
nn-Gangbusters and Guns of the Law, 1940, Dell, 4×5", 194p, Fast-Action Story, soft-c	17.00	62.00	125.00
nn-Gang Busters and the Radio Clues, 1938, Whit, 36p, 2½×3½", Penny Book	6.00	21.00	42.00
1409-Gene Autry and Raiders of the Range, 1946, Whit, 352p	8.00	27.50	55.00
1425-Gene Autry and the Mystery of Paint Rock Canyon, 1947, Whit, 288p	8.00	27.50	55.00
1428-Gene Autry Special Ranger, 1941, Whit, 432p, Erwin Hess-a	9.00	31.00	62.00
1430-Gene Autry and the Land Grab Mystery, 1948, Whit, 288p	7.00	25.00	50.00
1433-Gene Autry in Public Cowboy No. 1, 1938, Whit, 240p, photo-c, movie scenes (1st Autry BLB)	17.00	60.00	120.00
1434-Gene Autry and the Gun-Smoke Reckoning, 1943, Whit, 352p	9.00	31.00	62.00
1456-Gene Autry in Special Ranger Rule, 1945, Whit, 352p, Henry E. Vallely-a	9.00	31.00	62.00
1461-Gene Autry and the Red Bandit's Ghost, 1949, Whit, 288p	7.00	25.00	50.00
1483-Gene Autry in Law of the Range, 1939, Whit, 432p	9.00	31.00	62.00
1493-Gene Autry and the Hawk of the Hills, 1942, Whit, 428p, flip pictures, Vallely-a	9.00	31.00	62.00
1494-Gene Autry Cowboy Detective, 1940, Whit, 432p, Erwin Hess-a	9.00	31.00	62.00
700-10-Gene Autry and the Bandits of Silver Tip, 1949, Whit	5.00	17.50	35.00

	Good	Fine	N-Mint
714-10-Gene Autry and the Range War, 1950, Whit			
	5.00	17.50	35.00
nn-Gene Autry in Gun Smoke, 1938, Whit, 196p, Fast-Action Story, soft-c	20.00	70.00	140.00
1176-Gentleman Joe Palooka, 1940, Sal, 400p			
	10.00	35.00	70.00
George O'Brien (See The Cowboy Millionaire)			
1101-George O'Brien and the Arizona Badman, 1936?, Whit			
	10.00	35.00	70.00
1418-George O'Brien in Gun Law, 1938, Whit, 240p, photo-c, movie scenes, RKO Radio Pictures			
	10.00	35.00	70.00
1457-George O'Brien and the Hooded Riders, 1940, Whit, 432p, Erwin Hess-a	6.00	21.00	42.00
nn-George O'Brien and the Arizona Bad Man, 1939, Whit, 36p, 2½×3½", Penny Book	6.00	21.00	42.00
1462-Ghost Avenger, 1943, Whit, 432p, flip pictures, Henry Vallely-a	6.00	21.00	42.00
nn-Ghost Gun Gang meet Their Match, The, 1939, Whit, 36p, 2½×3½", Penny Book	6.00	21.00	42.00
nn-Gingerbread Boy, The, nd(1930s), np(Whit), 36p, Penny Book	1.50	4.50	9.00
1173-G-Man in Action, A, 1940, Sal, 400p, J.R. White-a			
	5.00	17.50	35.00
1118-G-Man on the Crime Trail, 1936, Whit, 432p			
	7.00	25.00	50.00
1147-G-Man Vs. the Red X, 1936, Whit, 432p			
	7.00	25.00	50.00
1162-G-Man Allen, 1939, Sal, 400p	5.00	17.50	35.00
1173-G-Man in Action, A, 1940, Sal, 400p			
	5.00	17.50	35.00

G-Man Vs. the Fifth Column #1470, © Stephen Slesinger, 1941

	Good	Fine	N-Mint

1434-G-Man and the Radio Bank Robberies, 1937, Whit, 432p
                              7.00   25.00   50.00

1469-G-Man and the Gun Runners, The, 1940, Whit, 432p
                              7.00   25.00   50.00

1470-G-Man Vs. the Fifth Column, 1941, Whit, 432p, flip pictures
                              7.00   25.00   50.00

1493-G-Man Breaking the Gambling Ring, 1938, Whit, 432p,
        James Gary-a   7.00   25.00   50.00

4-G-Men Foil the Kidnappers, 1936, Whit, 132p, 3½×3½",
        soft-c, Tarzan Ice Cream cup lid premium
                             20.00   70.00   140.00

nn-G-Man on Lightning Island, 1936, Dell, 244p, Fast-Action
        Story, soft-c, Henry E. Vallely-a   15.00   52.50   105.00

6833-G-Man on Lightning Island, 1936, Dell, 244p, Cartoon Story
        Book, hard-c, Henry E. Vallely-a   15.00   52.50   105.00

1157-G-Men on the Trail, 1938, Sal, 400p
                              5.00   17.50   35.00

1168-G Men on the Job, 1935, Whit, 432p
                              7.00   25.00   50.00

nn-G-Men on the Job Again, 1938, Whit, 36p, 2½×3½", Penny
        Book   6.00   21.00   42.00

nn-G-Men and Kidnap Justice, 1938, Whit, 68p, Pan-Am
        premium, soft-c   8.00   27.50   55.00

nn-GMen and the Missing Clues, 1938, Whit, 36p, 2½×3½",
        Penny Book   6.00   21.00   42.00

1097-Go Into Your Dance, 1935, Sal, 160p, photo-c, movie scenes
        with Al Jolson & Ruby Keeler   10.00   35.00   70.00

1577-Go Into Your Dance, 1935, Sal, 160p, photo-c, movie scenes,
        soft-c   10.00   35.00   70.00

5751-Goofy in Giant Trouble (Walt Disney's...), 1968, Whit, 260p,
        39 cents, soft-c, color illos   1.70   5.00   10.00

5751-2-Goofy in Giant Trouble, 1968 (1980-reprint of '67 version),
        Whit, 260p, 79 cents, soft-c, B&W   .50   1.50   3.00

8-Great Expectations, 1934, EVW, (Five Star Library), 160p,
        photo-c, movie scenes   12.00   42.00   85.00

1453-Green Hornet Strikes!, The, 1940, Whit, 432p, Robert
        Weisman-a   27.00   95.00   190.00

1480-Green Hornet Cracks Down, The, 1942, Whit, 432p, flip
        pictures, Henry Vallely-a   23.00   80.00   160.00

1496-Green Hornet Returns, The, 1941, Whit, 432p, flip pictures
                             23.00   80.00   160.00

1172-Gullivers' Travels, 1939, Sal, 320p, adapted from Paramount
        Pict. Cartoons   12.00   42.00   85.00

nn-Gumps in Radio Land, The (Andy Gump and the Chest of

	Good	Fine	N-Mint

Gold), 1937, Lehn & Fink Prod. Corp., 100p, 3¼×5½", Pebeco Tooth Paste giveaway, by Gus Edson

    14.00   50.00   100.00

nn-Gunmen of Rustlers' Gulch, The, 1939, Whit, 36p, 2½×3½", Penny Book   6.00   21.00   42.00

1426-Guns in the Roaring West, 1937, Whit, 300p

    5.50   19.00   38.00

1647-Gunsmoke (TV Series), 1958, Whit, 280p, 4½×5¾"

    4.50   13.50   27.00

1101-Hairbreath Harry in Department QT, 1935, Whit, 384p, by J. M. Alexander   7.50   26.00   52.00

1413-Hal Hardy in the Lost Land of Giants, 1938, Whit, 300p, "The World 1,000,000 Years ago" 6.00   21.00   42.00

1159-Hall of Fame of the Air, 1936, Whit, 432p, by Capt. Eddie Rickenbacker   5.50   19.00   38.00

nn-Hansel and Grethel, The Story of, nd (1930s), no publ.,36p, Penny Book   1.50   4.50   9.00

1145-Hap Lee's Selection of Movie Gags, 1935, Whit, 160p, photos of stars   8.50   30.00   60.00

Happy Prince, The (See Wee Little Books)

1111- Hard Rock Harrigan-A Story of Boulder Dam, 1935, Sal, photo-c, photo illos.   5.50   19.00   38.00

1591-Hard Rock Harrigan-A Story of Boulder Dam, 1935, Sal, photo-c, photo illos.   5.50   19.00   38.00

1418-Harold Teen Swinging at the Sugar Bowl, 1939, Whit, 432p, by Carl Ed   7.00   25.00   50.00

1100B-Hobbies, 1938, Whit, 36p, 2½×3½", Penny Book

    2.00   6.00   12.00

1125-Hockey Spare, The, 1937, Sal, sports book

    4.50   13.50   27.00

1605-Hockey Spare, The, 1937, Sal, soft-c

    4.50   13.50   27.00

728-Homeless Homer, 1934, Whit, by Dee Dobbin, for young kids 2.00   6.00   12.00

17-Hoosier Schoolmaster, The, 1935, EVW, movie scenes

    10.00   35.00   70.00

715-Houdini's Big Little Book of Magic, 1927 (1933), Whit, 300p   9.50   32.50   65.00

nn-Houdini's Big Little Book of Magic, 1927 (1933), Whit, 196p, American Oil Co. premium, soft-c

    8.50   30.00   60.00

nn- Houdini's Big Little Book of Magic, 1927 (1933), Whit, 204p, Cocomalt premium, soft-c   8.50   30.00   60.00

Huckleberry Finn (See The Adventures of ...)

	Good	Fine	N-Mint
1644-Hugh O'Brian TV's Wyatt Earp (TV Series), 1958, Whit, 280p	4.00	12.00	24.00
1424-Inspector Charlie Chan Villainy on the High Seas, 1942, Whit, 432p, flip pictures	10.00	35.00	70.00
1186-Inspector Wade of Scotland Yard, 1940, Sal, 400p	6.00	21.00	42.00
1448-Inspector Wade Solves the Mystery of the Red Aces, 1937, Whit, 432p	6.00	21.00	42.00
1148-International Spy Doctor Doom Faces Death at Dawn, 1937, Whit, 432p, Arbo-a	7.50	26.00	52.00

In the Name of the Law #1155, © Stephen Slesinger, 1937

	Good	Fine	N-Mint
1155-In the Name of the Law, 1937, Whit, 432p, Henry E. Vallely-a	7.00	21.00	42.00
2012-(#12)-Invaders, The-Alien Missile Threat (TV Series), 1967, Whit, 260p, hard-c, 39 cents, color illos	2.35	7.00	14.00
1403-Invisible Scarlet O'Neil, 1942, Whit, All Pictures Comics, flip pictures	7.00	25.00	50.00
1406-Invisible Scarlet O'Neil Versus the King of the Slums, 1946, Whit, 352p	6.00	21.00	42.00
1098-It Happened One Night, 1935, Sal, 160p, Little Big Book, Clark Gable, Claudette Colbert photo-c, movie scenes from Academy Award winner	13.00	45.00	90.00
1578-It Happened One Night, 1935, Sal, 160p, soft-c	13.00	45.00	90.00
Jack and Jill (See Wee Little Books)			
1432-Jack Armstrong and the Mystery of the Iron Key, 1939, Whit, 432p, Henry E. Vallely-a	7.50	26.00	52.00
1435-Jack Armstrong and the Ivory Treasure, 1937, Whit, 432p, Henry Vallely-a	7.50	26.00	52.00
Jackie Cooper (See Story Of...)			

Jack Armstrong and the Mystery of the Iron Key #1432,
© General Mills, Inc., 1939

	Good	**Fine**	**N-Mint**

1084-Jackie Cooper in Peck's Bad Boy, 1934, Sal, 160p, hard, photo-c, movie scenes 10.00 35.00 70.00

1314-Jackie Cooper in Peck's Bad Boy, 1934, Sal, 160p, soft, photo-c, movie scenes 10.00 35.00 70.00

1402-Jackie Cooper in "Gangster's Boy," 1939, Whit, 240p, photo-c, movie scenes 8.50 30.00 60.00

13-Jackie Cooper in Dinky, 1935, EVW, 160p, movie scenes 10.00 35.00 70.00

nn-Jack King of the Secret Service and the Counterfeiters, 1939, Whit, 36p, 2½×3½", Penny Book, by John G. Gray 6.00 21.00 42.00

L11-Jack London's Call of the Wild, 1935, Lynn, 20th Cent. Pic., movie scenes with Clark Gable 10.00 35.00 70.00

nn-Jack Pearl as Detective Baron Munchausen, 1934, Gold, 132p, soft-c 8.00 27.50 55.00

1102-Jack Swift and His Rocket Ship, 1934, Whit, 320p 12.00 42.00 85.00

1498-Jane Arden the Vanished Princess, Whit, 300p 7.00 25.00 50.00

1179-Jane Withers in This is the Life (20th Century-Fox resents...), 1935, Whit, 240p, photo-c, movie scenes 9.00 31.00 62.00

1463-Jane Withers in Keep Smiling, 1938, Whit, 240p, photo-c, movie scenes 9.00 31.00 62.00

Jaragu of the Jungle (See Rex Beach's...)

1447-Jerry Parker Police Reporter and the Candid Camera Clue, 1941, Whit, 300p 5.50 19.00 38.00

Jim Bowie (See Adventures of...)

nn-Jim Bryant of the Highway Patrol and the Mysterious Accident, 1939, Whit, 36p, 2½×3½", Penny Book 6.00 21.00 42.00

1466-Jim Craig State Trooper and the Kidnapped Governor,

	Good	Fine	N-Mint
1938, Whit, 432p	5.50	19.00	38.00

nn-Jim Doyle Private Detective and the Train Hold-Up, 1939, Whit, 36p, 2½×3½", Penny Book   6.00   21.00   42.00

1180-Jim Hardy Ace Reporter, 1940, Sal, 400p, Dick Moores-a
6.00   21.00   42.00

1143-Jimmy Allen in the Air Mail Robbery, 1936, Whit, 432p
5.50   19.00   38.00

L15-Jimmy and the Tiger, 1935, Lynn, 192p
6.00   21.00   42.00

Jimmy Skunk's Justice (See Wee Little Books)

1428-Jim Starr of the Border Patrol, 1937, Whit, 432p
5.50   19.00   38.00

Joan of Arc (See Wee Little Books)

1105-Joe Louis the Brown Bomber, 1936, Whit, 240p, photo-c, photo-illos.   12.00   42.00   85.00

Joe Palooka (See Gentleman...)

1123-Joe Palooka the Heavyweight Boxing Champ, 1934, Whit, 320p, Ham Fisher-a   10.00   35.00   70.00

1168-Joe Palooka's Greatest Adventure, 1939, Sal
10.00   35.00   70.00

nn-Joe Penner's Duck Farm, 1935, Gold, Henry Vallely-a
8.00   27.50   55.00

1402-John Carter of Mars, 1940, Whit, 432p, John Coleman Burroughs-a   35.00   122.50   245.00

nn-John Carter of Mars, 1940, Dell, 194p, Fast-Action Story, soft-c   40.00   140.00   280.00

1164-Johnny Forty Five, 1938, Sal, 400p
5.00   17.50   35.00

John Wayne (See Westward Ho!)

1100B-Jokes (A book of laughs galore), 1938, Whit, 36p, 2½×3½", Penny Book   2.00   6.00   12.00

1100B-Jokes (A book of side-splitting funny stories), 1938, Whit, 36p, 2½×3½", Penny Book   2.00   6.00   12.00

2026-Journey to the Center of the Earth, The fiery Foe, 1968, Whit   2.00   6.00   12.00

Jungle Jim #1138, © King Features Syndicate, 1936

	Good	Fine	N-Mint

Jungle Jim (See Top-Line Comics)

1138-Jungle Jim, 1936, Whit, 432p, Alex Raymond-a
| | 12.00 | 42.00 | 85.00 |

1139-Jungle Jim and the Vampire Woman, 1937, Whit, 432p,
Alex Raymond-a　　　　13.00　　45.00　　90.00

1442-Junior G-Men, 1937, Whit, 432p, Henry E. Vallely-a
| | 6.00 | 21.00 | 42.00 |

nn-Junior G-Men Solve a Crime, 1939, Whit, 36p, 2½×3½",
Penny Book　　　　　6.00　　21.00　　42.00

	Good	Fine	N-Mint

1422-Junior Nebb on the Diamond Bar Ranch, 1938, Whit, 300p,
by Sol Hess　　　　　6.00　　21.00　　42.00

1470-Junior Nebb Joins the Circus, 1939, Whit, 300p, by Sol Hess
| | 6.00 | 21.00 | 42.00 |

nn-Junior Nebb Elephant Trainer, 1939, Whit, 68p, Pan-Am
Oil premium, soft-c　　　8.00　　27.50　　55.00

1052-"Just Kids" (Adventures of...), 1934, Sal, oblong size, by Ad
Carter　　　　　　　15.00　　52.50　　105.00

1094-Just Kids and the Mysterious Stranger, 1935, Sal, 160p,
by Ad Carter　　　　　9.00　　31.00　　62.00

1184-Just Kids and Deep-Sea Dan, 1940, Sal, 400p, by Ad Carter
| | 7.00 | 25.00 | 50.00 |

1302-Just Kids, The Adventures of, 1934, Sal, oblong size, soft-c,
by Ad Carter　　　　　15.00　　52.50　　105.00

1324-Just Kids and the Mysterious Stranger, 1935, Sal, 160p,
soft-c, by Ad Carter　　9.00　　31.00　　62.00

1401-Just Kids, 1937, Whit, 432p, by Ad Carter
| | 8.00 | 27.50 | 55.00 |

1055-Katzenjammer Kids in the Mountains, 1934, Sal, Oblong,
H. H. Knerr-a　　　　14.00　　50.00　　100.00

14-Katzenjammer Kids, The, 1942, Dell, 194p, Fast-Action
Story, H. H. Knerr-a　　15.00　　52.50　　105.00

1411-Kay Darcy and the Mystery Hideout, 1937, Whit, 300p,
Charles Mueller-a　　　7.00　　25.00　　50.00

1180-Kayo in the Land of Sunshine (With Moon Mullins), 1937,
Whit, 432p, by Willard　8.00　　27.50　　55.00

1415-Kayo and Moon Mullins and the One Man Gang, 1939,
Whit, 432p, by Frank Willard　8.00　　27.50　　55.00

7-Kayo and Moon Mullins 'Way Down South, 1938, Whit,
132p, 3½×3½", Buddy Book　22.00　　77.00　　155.00

1105-Kazan in Revenge of the North (James Oliver Curwood's...),
1937, Whit, 432p, Henry E. Vallely-a
| | 5.50 | 19.00 | 38.00 |

1471-Kazan, King of the Pack (James Oliver Curwood's...), 1940,
Whit, 432p　　　　　5.00　　17.50　　35.00

	Good	Fine	N-Mint

1420-Keep 'Em Flying! U.S.A. for America's Defense, 1943, Whit, 432p, Henry E. Vallely-a, flip pictures
| | 5.50 | 19.00 | 38.00 |

1133-Kelly King at Yale Hall, 1937, Sal 5.00 17.50 35.00

Ken Maynard (See Strawberry Roan, Western Frontier & Wheels of Destiny)

776-Ken Maynard in "Gun Justice," 1934, Whit, 160p, movie scenes (Universal Pic.)   12.00 42.00 85.00

1430-Ken Maynard in Western Justice, 1938, Whit, 432p, Irwin Myers-a   7.00 25.00 50.00

Ken Maynard and the Gun Wolves of Gila #1442,
© Ken Maynard, 1939

1442-Ken Maynard and the Gun Wolves of the Gila, 1939, Whit, 432p   7.00 25.00 50.00

nn-Ken Maynard in Six-Gun Law, 1938, Whit, 36p, 2½×3½", Penny Book   6.00 21.00 42.00

1134-King of Crime, 1938, Sal, 400p 5.00 17.50 35.00

King of the Royal Mounted (See Zane Grey)

1010-King of the Royal Mounted in Arctic Law, 1937, Whit, 7¼×5½", 64p, Nickel Book   9.00 31.00 62.00

nn-Kit Carson, 1933, World, by J. Carroll Mansfield, High Lights Of History Series, hard-c 5.50 19.00 38.00

nn-Kit Carson, 1933, World, same as hard-c above but with a black cloth-c   5.50 19.00 38.00

1105-Kit Carson and the Mystery Riders, 1935, Sal, hard-c, Johnny Mack Brown photo-c, movie scenes
| | 12.00 | 42.00 | 85.00 |

1585-Kit Carson and the Mystery Riders, 1935, Sal, soft-c, Johnny Mack Brown photo-c, movie scenes
| | 12.00 | 42.00 | 85.00 |

Krazy Kat (See Advs. of...)

	Good	**Fine**	**N-Mint**

2004-(#4)-Lassie-Adventure in Alaska (TV Series), 1967, Whit, 260p, 39 cents, hard-c, color illos   2.00   6.00   12.00

2027-Lassie and the Shabby Sheik (TV Series), 1968, Whit
2.00   6.00   12.00

1132-Last Days of Pompeii, The, 1935, Whit, 5¼×6¼", 260p, photo-c, movie scenes   10.00   35.00   70.00

1128-Last Man Out (Baseball), 1937, Sal, hard-c
4.50   16.00   32.00

L30-Last of the Mohicans, The, 1936, Lynn, 192p, movie scenes with Randolph Scott, United Artists Pictures
10.00   35.00   70.00

1126-Laughing Dragon of Oz, The, 1934, Whit, 432p, by Frank Baum   45.00   157.50   315.00

1086-Laurel and Hardy, 1934, Sal, 160p, hard-c, photo-c, movie scenes   12.00   42.00   85.00

1316-Laurel and Hardy, 1934, Sal, 160p, soft-c, photo-c, movie scenes   12.00   42.00   85.00

1092-Law of the Wild, The, 1935, Sal, 160p, photo-c, movie scenes of Rex, The Wild Horse & Rin-Tin-Tin Jr.
5.50   19.00   38.00

1322-Law of the Wild, The, 1935, Sal, 160p, photo-c, movie scenes, soft-c   5.50   19.00   38.00

1100B-Learn to be a Ventriloquist, 1938, Whit, 36p, 2½×3½", Penny Book   2.00   6.00   12.00

1149-Lee Brady Range Detective, 1938, Sal, 400p
5.00   17.50   35.00

L10-Les Miserables (Victor Hugo's...), 1935, Lynn, 192p, movie scenes   9.00   31.00   62.00

1441-Lightning Jim U.S. Marshal brings Law to the West, 1940, Whit, 432p, based on radio program
5.50   19.00   38.00

nn-Lightning Jim Whipple U.S. Marshal in Indian Territory, 1939, Whit, 36p, 2½×3½", Penny Book
6.00   21.00   42.00

653-Lions and Tigers (With Clyde Beatty), 1934, Whit, 160p, photo-c, movie scenes   10.00   35.00   70.00

1187-Li'l Abner and the Ratfields, 1940, Sal, 400p, by Al Capp
12.00   42.00   85.00

1193-Li'l Abner and Sadie Hawkins Day, 1940, Sal, 400p, by Al Capp   12.00   42.00   85.00

1198-Li'l Abner in New York, 1936, Whit, 432p, by Al Capp
12.00   42.00   85.00

1401-Li'l Abner among the Millionaires, 1939, Whit, 432p, by Al Capp   12.00   42.00   85.00

	Good	Fine	N-Mint

1054-Little Annie Rooney, 1934, Sal, Oblong-4×8", All Pictures
Comics, hard-c   13.00   45.00   90.00

1304-Little Annie Rooney, 1934, Sal, Oblong-4×8", All Pictures,
soft-c   13.00   45.00   90.00

1117-Little Annie Rooney and the Orphan House, 1936, Whit,
432p   7.00   25.00   50.00

1406-Little Annie Rooney on the Highway to Adventure, 1938,
Whit, 432p   7.00   25.00   50.00

1149-Little Big Shot (With Sybil Jason), 1935, Whit, 240p, photo-c,
movie scenes   7.00   25.00   50.00

nn-Little Black Sambo, nd (1930s), np (Whit), 36p, 3×2½",
Penny Book   7.00   20.00   40.00

Little Bo-Peep (See Wee Little Books)

Little Colonel, The (See Shirley Temple)

1148-Little Green Door, The, 1938, Sal, 400p
                                         5.00   17.50   35.00

1112-Little Hollywood Stars, 1935, Sal, movie scenes (Little
Rascals, etc.), hard-c   8.50   30.00   60.00

1592-Little Hollywood Stars, 1935, Sal, movie scenes, soft-c
                                         8.50   30.00   60.00

1087-Little Jimmy's Gold Hunt, 1935, Sal, 160p, hard-c, Little Big
Book, by Swinnerton   7.50   26.00   52.00

1317-Little Jimmy's Gold Hunt, 1935,Sal, 160p, 4¼×5¾", soft-c,
by Swinnerton   7.50   26.00   52.00

Little Joe and the City Gangsters (See Top-Line Comics)

Little Joe Otter's Slide (See Wee Little Books)

1118-Little Lord Fauntleroy, 1936, Sal, movie scenes, photo-c,
4½×5¼", starring Mickey Rooney & Freddie Bartholomew,
hard-c   7.50   26.00   52.00

1598-Little Lord Fauntleroy, 1936, Sal, photo-c, movie scenes,
soft-c   7.50   26.00   52.00

1192-Little Mary Mixup and the Grocery Robberies, 1940, Sal
                                         6.00   21.00   42.00

8-Little Mary Mixup Wins A Prize, 1936, Whit, 132p,
3½×3½", soft-c, Tarzan Ice Cream cup lid premium
                                        22.00   77.00   155.00

1150-Little Men, 1934, Whit, 4¾×5¼", movie scenes (Mascot
Prod.), photo-c, hard-c   7.50   26.00   52.00

9-Little Minister, The-Katharine Hepburn, 1935, 160p,
4¼×5½", EVW (Five Star Library), movie scenes (RKO)
                                        10.00   35.00   70.00

1120-Little Miss Muffet, 1936, Whit, 432p, by Fanny Y. Cory
                                         7.00   25.00   50.00

708-Little Orphan Annie, 1933, Whit, 320p, by Harold Gray, the

	Good	Fine	N-Mint
2nd Big Little Book	40.00	140.00	280.00

nn-Little Orphan Annie, 1928 ('33), Whit, 52p, 4×5½", premium-no ads, soft-c, by Harold Gray
| | 22.00 | 77.00 | 155.00 |

716-Little Orphan Annie and Sandy, 1933, Whit, 320p, by Harold Gray
| | 17.00 | 60.00 | 120.00 |

716-Little Orphan Annie and Sandy, 1933, Whit, 300p, by Harold Gray
| | 17.00 | 60.00 | 120.00 |

nn-Little Orphan Annie and Sandy, 1933, Whit, 52p, premium-no ads, 4×5½", soft-c, by Harold Gray
| | 20.00 | 77.00 | 155.00 |

748-Little Orphan Annie and Chizzler, 1933, Whit, 320p, by Harold Gray
| | 14.00 | 50.00 | 100.00 |

1010-Little Orphan Annie and the Big Town Gunmen, 1937, 7¼×5½", 64p, Nickel Book
| | 9.00 | 31.00 | 62.00 |

1103-Little Orphan Annie with the Circus, 1934, Whit, 320p, by Harold Gray
| | 12.00 | 42.00 | 85.00 |

1140-Little Orphan Annie and the Big Train Robbery, 1934, Whit, 300p, by Gray
| | 12.00 | 42.00 | 85.00 |

1140-Little Orphan Annie and the Big Train Robbery, 1934, Whit, 300p, premium-no ads, soft-c, by Harold Gray
| | 18.00 | 62.50 | 125.00 |

1154-Little Orphan Annie and the Ghost Gang, 1935, Whit, 432p, by Harold Gray
| | 12.00 | 42.00 | 85.00 |

nn-Little Orphan Annie and the Ghost Gang, 1935, Whit, 436p, premium-no ads, 3-color, soft-c, by Harold Gray
| | 18.00 | 62.50 | 125.00 |

1162-Little Orphan Annie and Punjab the Wizard, 1935, Whit, 432p, by Harold Gray
| | 12.00 | 42.00 | 85.00 |

1186-Little Orphan Annie and the $1,000,000 Formula, 1936, Whit, 432p, by Gray
| | 10.00 | 35.00 | 70.00 |

Little Orphan Annie in the Thieves' Den #1446,
© Chicago Tribune-N.Y. News Syndicate, 1948

	Good	Fine	N-Mint
1414-Little Orphan Annie and the Ancient Treasure of Am, 1939, Whit, 432p, by Gray	8.50	30.00	60.00
1416-Little Orphan Annie in the Movies, 1937, Whit, 432p, by Harold Gray	8.50	30.00	60.00
1417-Little Orphan Annie and the Secret of the Well, 1947, Whit, 352p, by Gray	7.50	26.00	52.00
1435-Little Orphan Annie and the Gooneyville Mystery, 1947, Whit, 288p, by Gray	7.50	26.00	52.00
1446-Little Orphan Annie in the Thieves' Den, 1948, Whit, 288p, by Harold Gray	7.50	26.00	52.00
1449-Little Orphan Annie and the Mysterious Shoemaker, 1938, Whit, 432p, by Harold Gray	8.50	30.00	60.00
1457-Little Orphan Annie and Her Junior Commandos, 1943, Whit, 352p, by H. Gray	7.50	26.00	52.00
1461-Little Orphan Annie and the Underground Hide-Out, 1945, Whit, 352p, by Gray	7.50	26.00	52.00
1468-Little Orphan Annie and the Ancient Treasure of Am, 1949 (Misdated 1939), 288p, by Gray	8.00	27.50	55.00
1482-Little Orphan Annie and the Haunted Mansion, 1941, Whit, 432p, flip pictures, by Harold Gray	8.50	30.00	60.00
4054-Little Orphan Annie, The Story of, 1934, 7×9½", 320p, Big Big Book, Harold Gray c/a	43.00	150.00	300.00
nn-Little Orphan Annie gets into Trouble, 1938, Whit, 36p, 2½×3½", Penny Book	6.00	21.00	42.00
nn-Little Orphan Annie in Hollywood, 1937, Whit, 3½×3¼", Pan-Am premium, soft-c	11.00	37.50	75.00
nn-Little Orphan Annie in Rags to Riches, 1938, Dell, 194p, Fast-Action Story, soft-c	20.00	70.00	140.00
nn-Little Orphan Annie Saves Sandy, 1938, Whit, 36p, 2½×3½", Penny Book	6.00	21.00	42.00
nn-Little Orphan Annie Under the Big Top, 1938, Dell, 194p, Fast-Action Story, soft-c	20.00	70.00	140.00
nn-Little Orphan Annie Wee Little Books (In open box) nn, 1934, Whit, 44p, by H. Gray			
L.O.A. And Daddy Warbucks	6.00	21.00	42.00
L.O.A. And Her Dog Sandy	6.00	21.00	42.00
L.O.A. And The Lucky Knife	6.00	21.00	42.00
L.O.A. And The Pinch-Pennys	6.00	21.00	42.00
L.O.A. At Happy Home	6.00	21.00	42.00
L.O.A. Finds Mickey	6.00	21.00	42.00
Complete set with box	43.00	150.00	300.00
nn-Little Polly Flinders, The Story of, nd (1930s), no publ., 36p, 2½×3", Penny Book	1.50	4.50	9.00

	Good	Fine	N-Mint

nn-Little Red Hen, The, nd(1930s), np(Whit), 36p, Penny Book

　　　　　　　　　　　　　1.50　　4.50　　9.00

nn-Little Red Riding Hood, nd (1930s), np (Whit), 36p, 3×2½",
Penny Book　　　　　　1.50　　4.50　　9.00

nn-Little Red Riding Hood and the Big Bad Wolf (Disney),
1934, McKay, 36p, stiff-c, Disney Studio-a

　　　　　　　　　　　18.00　　62.50　　125.00

757-Little Women, 1934, Whit, 4¾×5¼", 160p, photo-c, movie
scenes, starring Katharine Hepburn

　　　　　　　　　　　11.00　　37.50　　75.00

Littlest Rebel, The (See Shirley Temple)

1181-Lone Ranger and his Horse Silver, 1935, Whit, 432p,
Hal Arbo-a　　　　　　15.00　　50.00　　100.00

The Lone Ranger and the Vanishing Herd #1196,
© The Lone Ranger, Inc., 1936

1196-Lone Ranger and the Vanishing Herd, 1936, Whit, 432p

　　　　　　　　　　　12.00　　42.00　　85.00

1407-Lone Ranger and Dead Men's Mine, The, 1939, Whit, 432p

　　　　　　　　　　　11.00　　37.50　　75.00

1421-Lone Ranger on the Barbary Coast, The, 1944, Whit, 352p,
Henry Vallely-a　　　　9.00　　31.00　　62.00

1428-Lone Ranger and the Secret Weapon, The, 1943, Whit,
352p　　　　　　　　　9.00　　31.00　　62.00

1431-Lone Ranger and the Secret Killer, The, 1937, Whit, 432p,
H. Anderson-a　　　　12.00　　42.00　　85.00

1450-Lone Ranger and the Black Shirt Highwayman, The, 1939,
Whit, 432p　　　　　　11.00　　37.50　　75.00

1465-Lone Ranger and the Menace of Murder Valley, The, 1938,
Whit, 432p, Robert Wiseman-a　11.00　　37.50　　75.00

1468-Lone Ranger Follows Through, The, 1941, Whit, 432p,
H. E. Vallely-a　　　　11.00　　37.50　　75.00

1477-Lone Ranger and the Great Western Span, The, 1942,

	Good	Fine	N-Mint
Whit, 424p, H.E. Vallely-a	9.00	31.00	62.00

1489-Lone Ranger and the Red Renegades, The, 1939, Whit,
432p   11.00   37.50   75.00

1498-Lone Ranger and the Silver Bullets, 1946, Whit, 352p,
Henry E. Vallely-a   9.00   31.00   62.00

712-10-Lone Ranger and the Secret of Somber Cavern, The, 1950,
Whit   5.00   17.50   35.00

2013-(#13)-Lone Ranger Outwits Crazy Cougar, The, 1968,
Whit, 260p, 39 cents, hard-c, color illos
                                               2.00   6.00   12.00

nn-Lone Ranger and the Lost Valley, The, 1938, Dell, 196p,
Fast-Action Story, soft-c   20.00   70.00   140.00

1405-Lone Star Martin of the Texas Rangers, 1939, Whit, 432p
                                               5.00   17.50   35.00

19-Lost City, The, 1935, EVW, movie scenes
                                              10.00   35.00   70.00

1103-Lost Jungle, The (With Clyde Beatty), 1936, Sal, movie
scenes, hard-c   10.00   35.00   70.00

1583-Lost Jungle, The (With Clyde Beatty), 1936, Sal, movie
scenes, soft-c   9.00   31.00   62.00

753-Lost Patrol, The, 1934, Whit, 160p, photo-c, movie scenes
with Boris Karloff   9.00   31.00   62.00

1189-Mac of the Marines in Africa, 1936, Whit, 432p
                                               7.00   25.00   50.00

1400-Mac of the Marines in China, 1938, Whit, 432p
                                               7.00   25.00   50.00

1100B-Magic Tricks (With explanations), 1938, Whit, 36p, 2½×3½",
Penny Book   2.00   6.00   12.00

1100B-Magic Tricks (How to do them), 1938, Whit, 36p, 2½×3½",
Penny Book   2.00   6.00   12.00

Major Hoople (See Our Boarding House)

Mandrake the Magician and the Flame Pearls #1418,
© King Features Syndicate, 1946

	Good	Fine	N-Mint

1167-Mandrake the Magician, 1935, Whit, 432p, by Lee Falk &
　　Phil Davis　　　　　　　　　12.00　　42.00　　85.00

1418-Mandrake the Magician and the Flame Pearls, 1946,
　　Whit, 352p, by Lee Falk & Phil Davis
　　　　　　　　　　　　　　　8.00　　27.50　　55.00

1431-Mandrake the Magician and the Midnight Monster, 1939,
　　Whit, 432p, by Lee Falk & Phil Davis
　　　　　　　　　　　　　　　9.00　　31.00　　62.00

1454-Mandrake the Magician Mighty Solver of Mysteries, 1941,
　　Whit, 432p, by Lee Falk & Phil Davis, flip pictures
　　　　　　　　　　　　　　　9.00　　31.00　　62.00

2011-(#11)-Man From U.N.C.L.E., The-The Calcutta Affair (TV
　　Series), 1967, Whit, 260p, 39 cents, hard-c, color illos
　　　　　　　　　　　　　　　2.50　　8.00　　16.00

1429-Marge's Little Lulu Alvin and Tubby, 1947, Whit, All
　　Pictures Comics, Stanley-a　　15.00　　52.50　　105.00

1438-Mary Lee and the Mystery of the Indian Beads, 1937, Whit,
　　300p　　　　　　　　　　　　5.50　　19.00　　38.00

1165-Masked Man of the Mesa, The, 1939, Sal, 400p
　　　　　　　　　　　　　　　5.00　　17.50　　35.00

1436-Maximo the Amazing Superman, 1940, Whit, 432p,
　　Henry E. Vallely-a　　　　　8.50　　30.00　　60.00

**1444-Maximo the Amazing Superman and the Crystals of
　　Doom,** 1941, Whit, 432p, Henry E. Vallely-a
　　　　　　　　　　　　　　　8.50　　30.00　　60.00

1445-Maximo the Amazing Superman and the Supermachine,
　　1941, Whit, 432p　　　　　　8.50　　30.00　　60.00

755-Men of the Mounted, 1934, Whit, 320p
　　　　　　　　　　　　　　　8.50　　30.00　　60.00

nn-Men of the Mounted, 1933, Whit, 52p, 3½×5¾", premium-no
　　ads; another versions with Poll Parrot & Perkins ad; soft-c
　　　　　　　　　　　　　　　13.00　　45.00　　90.00

nn-Men of the Mounted, 1934, Whit, Cocomalt premium, soft-c,
　　by Ted McCall　　　　　　　7.50　　26.00　　52.00

1475-Men With Wings, 1938, Whit, 240p, photo-c, movie scenes
　　(Paramount Pics.)　　　　　7.00　　25.00　　50.00

1170-Mickey Finn, 1940, Sal, 400p, by Frank Leonard
　　　　　　　　　　　　　　　7.00　　25.00　　50.00

717-Mickey Mouse (Disney), 1933, Whit, 320p, Gottfredson-a
　　(Two diff. covers printed)　　110.00　　385.00　　770.00

726-Mickey Mouse in Blaggard Castle (Disney), 1934, Whit,
　　320p, Gottfredson-a　　　　20.00　　70.00　　140.00

731-Mickey Mouse the Mail Pilot (Disney), 1933, Whit, 300p,
　　Gottfredson-a　　　　　　　20.00　　70.00　　140.00

	Good	Fine	N-Mint

nn-Mickey Mouse the Mail Pilot (Disney), 1933, Whit, 292p,
American Oil Co. premium, soft-c, Gottfredson-a; another
version 3½×4¾"   20.00   70.00   140.00

750-Mickey Mouse sails for Treasure Island (Disney), 1933,
Whit, 320p, Gottfredson-a   20.00   70.00   140.00

*Mickey Mouse Sails for Treasure Island (Kolynos Dental Cream
premium), © Walt Disney Enterprises, 1935*

nn-Mickey Mouse sails for Treasure Island (Disney), 1935,
Whit, 196p, premium-no ads, soft-c, Gottfredson-a (Scarce)
                                  22.00   77.00   155.00

nn-Mickey Mouse Sails for Treasure Island (Disney), 1935,
Whit, 196p, Kolynos Dental Cream premium (Scarce)
                                  22.00   77.00   155.00

756-Mickey Mouse Presents a Walt Disney Silly Symphony
(Disney), 1934, Whit, 240p, Bucky Bug app.
                                  17.00   60.00   120.00

**1111-Mickey Mouse Presents Walt Disney's Silly Symphonies
Stories,** 1936, Whit, 432p, Donald Duck, Bucky Bug app.
                                  17.00   60.00   120.00

1128-Mickey Mouse and Pluto the Racer (Disney), 1936, Whit,
432p, Gottfredson-a   15.00   52.50   105.00

1139-Mickey Mouse the Detective (Disney), 1934, Whit, 300p,
Gottfredson-a   17.00   60.00   120.00

1139-Mickey Mouse the Detective (Disney), 1934, Whit, 304p,
premium-no ads, soft-c, Gottfredson-a (Scarce)
                                  25.00   87.50   175.00

1153-Mickey Mouse and the Bat Bandit (Disney), 1935, Whit,
432p, Gottfredson-a   16.00   55.00   110.00

nn-Mickey Mouse and the Bat Bandit (Disney), 1935, Whit,
436p, premium-no ads, 3-color, soft-c, Gottfredson-a (Scarce)
                                  25.00   87.50   175.00

	Good	Fine	N-Mint
1160-Mickey Mouse and Bobo the Elephant (Disney), 1935, Whit, 432p, Gottfredson-a	16.00	55.00	110.00
1187-Mickey Mouse and the Sacred Jewel (Disney), 1936, Whit, 432p, Gottfredson-a	14.00	50.00	100.00
1401-Mickey Mouse in the Treasure Hunt (Disney), 1941, Whit, 430p, flip pictures with Pluto, Gottfredson-a	13.00	45.00	90.00
1409-Mickey Mouse Runs His Own Newspaper (Disney), 1937, Whit, 432p, Gottfredson-a	13.00	45.00	90.00
1413-Mickey Mouse and the "Lectro Box" (Disney), 1946, Whit, 352p, Gottfredson-a	11.00	37.50	75.00
1417-Mickey Mouse on Sky Island (Disney), 1941, Whit, 432p, flip pictures, Gottfredson-a; considered by Gottfredson to be his best Mickey story	13.00	45.00	90.00
1428-Mickey Mouse in the Foreign Legion (Disney), 1940, Whit, 432p, Gottfredson-a	13.00	45.00	90.00
1429-Mickey Mouse and the Magic Lamp (Disney), 1942, Whit, 432p, flip pictures	13.00	45.00	90.00
1433-Mickey Mouse in the Lazy Daisy Mystery (Disney), 1947, Whit, 288p	11.00	37.50	75.00
1444-Mickey Mouse in the World of Tomorrow (Disney), 1948, Whit, 288p, Gottfredson-a	14.00	50.00	100.00
1451-Mickey Mouse and the Desert Palace (Disney), 1948, Whit, 288p	11.00	37.50	75.00
1463-Mickey Mouse and the Pirate Submarine (Disney), 1939, Whit, 432p, Gottfredson-a	13.00	45.00	90.00
1464-Mickey Mouse and the Stolen Jewels (Disney), 1949, Whit, 288p	12.00	42.00	85.00
1471-Mickey Mouse and the Dude Ranch Bandit (Disney), 1943, Whit, 432p, flip pictures	13.00	45.00	90.00
1475-Mickey Mouse and the 7 Ghosts (Disney), 1940, Whit, 432p, Gottfredson-a	13.00	45.00	90.00
1476-Mickey Mouse in the Race for Riches (Disney), 1938, Whit, 432p, Gottfredson-a	13.00	45.00	90.00
1483-Mickey Mouse Bell Boy Detective (Disney), 1945, Whit, 352p	12.00	42.00	85.00
1499-Mickey Mouse on the Cave-Man Island (Disney), 1944, Whit, 352p	12.00	42.00	85.00
4062-Mickey Mouse, The Story Of, 1935, Whit, 7×9½", 320p, Big Big Book, Gottfredson-a	60.00	210.00	420.00
4062-Mickey Mouse and the Smugglers, The Story Of, (Scarce), 1935, Whit, 7×9½", 320p, Big Big Book, same contents as above version; Gottfredson-a	80.00	280.00	560.00
708-10-Mickey Mouse on the Haunted Island (Disney), 1950, Whit,			

	Good	Fine	N-Mint
Gottfredson-a	7.00	25.00	50.00

nn-Mickey Mouse and Minnie at Macy's, 1934, Whit, 148p, 3¼×3½", soft-c, R. H. Macy & Co. Xmas giveaway

	75.00	262.00	525.00

nn-Mickey Mouse and Minnie March to Macy's, 1935, Whit, 148p, 3½×3½", soft-c, R. H. Macy & Co. Xmas giveaway

	75.00	262.00	525.00

nn-Mickey Mouse and the Magic Carpet, 1935, Whit, 148p, 3½×4", soft-c, giveaway, Gottfredson-a, Donald Duck app.

	55.00	192.00	385.00

nn-Mickey Mouse Silly Symphonies, 1934, Dean & Son, Ltd (England), 48p, with 4 pop-ups, Babes In The Woods, King Neptune, with dust jacket

	60.00	210.00	420.00
Without dust jacket	43.00	150.00	300.00

3061-Mickey Mouse to Draw and Color (The Big Little Set), nd (early 1930s), Whit, with crayons; box contains 320 loose pages to color, reprinted from early Mickey Mouse BLBs

	60.00	210.00	420.00

16-Mickey Mouse and Pluto (Disney), Dell, 196p, Fast-Action Story

	27.00	95.00	190.00

nn-Mickey Mouse the Sheriff of Nugget Gulch (Disney), 1938, Dell, 196p, Fast-Action Story, soft-c, Gottfredson-a

	27.00	95.00	190.00

Mickey Mouse with Goofy and Mickey's Nephews,
© Walt Disney Productions, 1938

nn-Mickey Mouse with Goofy and Mickey's Nephews, 1938, Dell, 196p, Fast-Action Story, Gottfredson-a

	27.00	95.00	190.00

Series A-Mickey Mouse (In actual Motion Pictures), nd (1932?), Moviescope Corp., 50p, stapled, 1¾×2½" flip book. Earliest known M. Mouse flip book

	7.00	25.00	50.00

	Good	Fine	N-Mint

512-Mickey Mouse Wee Little Books (In open box), nn, 1934, 44p, small size, soft-c

	Good	Fine	N-Mint
M. Mouse and Tanglefoot	7.00	25.00	50.00
M. Mouse at the Carnival	7.00	25.00	50.00
M. Mouse Will Not Quit!	7.00	25.00	50.00
M. Mouse Wins the Race!	7.00	25.00	50.00
M. Mouse's Misfortune	7.00	25.00	50.00
M. Mouse's Uphill Fight	7.00	25.00	50.00
Complete set with box	50.00	175.00	350.00

1493-Mickey Rooney and Judy Garland and How They Got into the Movies, 1941, Whit, 432p, photo-c

	8.50	30.00	60.00

1427-Mickey Rooney Himself, 1939, Whit, 240p, photo-c, movie scenes, life story

	8.50	30.00	60.00

532-Mickey's Dog Pluto (Disney), 1943, Whit, All Picture Comics, A Tall Comic Book, 3¾×8¾"

	18.00	62.50	125.00

2113-Midget Jumbo Coloring Book, 1935, Sal

	22.00	77.00	155.00

21-Midsummer Night's Dream, 1935, EVW, movie scenes

	10.00	35.00	70.00

nn-Minute-Man (Mystery of the Spy Ring), 1941, Faw, Dime Action Book

	27.00	95.00	190.00

710-Moby Dick the Great White Whale, The Story of, 1934, Whit, 160p, photo-c, movie scenes from "The Sea Beast"

	8.50	30.00	60.00

746-Moon Mullins and Kayo (Kayo and Moon Mullins-inside), 1933, Whit, 320p, Frank Willard c/a

	11.00	37.50	75.00

nn-Moon Mullins and Kayo, 1933, Whit, Cocomalt premium, soft-c, by Willard

	11.00	37.50	75.00

Moon Mullins and Kayo #746, © Frank Willard, 1933

	Good	Fine	N-Mint

1134-Moon Mullins and the Plushbottom Twins, 1935, Whit, 432p, Willard c/a   10.00   35.00   70.00

nn-Moon Mullins and the Plushbottom Twins, 1935, Whit, 436p, premium-no ads, 3-color, soft-c, by Frank Willard
19.00   66.00   132.00

1058-Mother Pluto (Disney), 1939, Whit, 68p, hard-c
9.00   31.00   62.00

1100B-Movie Jokes (From the talkies), 1938, Whit, 36p, 2½×3½", Penny Book   2.00   6.00   12.00

1408-Mr. District Attorney on the Job, 1941, Whit, 432p, flip pictures   5.50   19.00   38.00

nn-Musicians of Bremen, The, nd (1930s), np (Whit), 36p, 3×2½", Penny Book   1.50   4.50   9.00

1113-Mutt and Jeff, 1936, Whit, 300p, by Bud Fisher
15.00   52.50   105.00

1116-My Life and Times (By Shirley Temple), 1936, Sal, Little Big Book, hard-c, photo-c/illos   10.00   35.00   70.00

1596-My Life and Times (By Shirley Temple), 1936, Sal, Little Big Book, soft-c, photo-c/illos   10.00   35.00   70.00

1497-Myra North Special Nurse and Foreign Spies, 1938, Whit, 432p   7.00   25.00   50.00

1400-Nancy and Sluggo, 1946, Whit, All Pictures Comics, Ernie Bushmiller-a   7.00   25.00   50.00

1487-Nancy has Fun, 1944, Whit, All Pictures Comics
7.00   25.00   50.00

1150-Napoleon and Uncle Elby, 1938, Sal, 400p, by Clifford McBride   7.00   25.00   50.00

1166-Napoleon Uncle Elby And Little Mary, 1939, Sal, 400p, by Clifford McBride   7.00   25.00   50.00

1179-Ned Brant Adventure Bound, 1940, Sal, 400p
6.00   21.00   42.00

1146-Nevada Rides The Danger Trail, 1938, Sal, 400p, J. R. White-a   5.00   17.50   35.00

1147-Nevada Whalen, Avenger, 1938, Sal, 400p
5.00   17.50   35.00

Nicodemus O'Malley (See Top-Line Comics)

1115-Og Son of Fire, 1936, Whit, 432p   5.00   17.50   35.00

1419-Oh, Blondie the Bumsteads (See Blondie)

11-Oliver Twist, 1935, EVW (Five Star Library), movie scenes, starring Dickie Moore (Monogram Pictures)
10.00   35.00   70.00

718-"Once Upon a Time....," 1933, Whit, 364p, soft-c
10.00   35.00   70.00

712-100 Fairy Tales for Children, The, 1933, Whit, 288p,

	Good	Fine	N-Mint
Circle Library	5.00	17.50	35.00

1099-One Night of Love, 1935, Sal, 160p, hard-c, photo-c, movie scenes, Columbia Pictures, starring Grace Moore

	8.50	30.00	60.00

1579-One Night of Love, 1935, Sal, 160p, soft-c, photo-c, movie scenes, Columbia Pictures, starring Grace Moore

	8.50	30.00	60.00

1155-$1000 Reward, 1938, Sal, 400p   5.00   17.50   35.00

Orphan Annie (See Little Orphan ...)

L17-O'Shaughnessy's Boy, 1935, Lynn, 192p, movie scenes, w/Wallace Beery & Jackie Cooper (Metro-Goldwyn-Mayer)

	7.50	26.00	52.00

Oswald the Lucky Rabbit #1109, © Whitman Publishing Co., 1934

1109-Oswald the Lucky Rabbit, 1934, Whit, 288p

	11.00	37.50	75.00

1403-Oswald Rabbit Plays G Man, 1937, Whit, 240p, movie scenes by Walter Lantz   12.00   42.00   85.00

1190-Our Boarding House, Major Hoople and his Horse, 1940, Sal, 400p   8.00   27.50   55.00

1085-Our Gang, 1934, Sal, 160p, photo-c movie scenes, hard-c

	8.50	30.00	60.00

1315-Our Gang, 1934, Sal, 160p, photo-c movie scenes, soft-c

	8.50	30.00	60.00

1451-"Our Gang" on the March, 1942, Whit, 432p, flip pictures, Vallely-a   8.50   30.00   60.00

1456-Our Gang Adventures, 1948, Whit, 288p

	7.00	25.00	50.00

nn-Paramount Newsreel Men with Admiral Byrd in Little America, 1934, Whit, 96p, 6¼×6¾", photo-c, photo ill.

	7.00	25.00	50.00

	Good	Fine	N-Mint

nn-Patch, nd (1930s), np (Whit), 36p, 3×2½", Penny Book
| | 1.50 | 4.50 | 9.00 |

1445-Pat Nelson Ace of Test Pilots, 1937, Whit, 432p
| | 5.00 | 17.50 | 35.00 |

1411-Peggy Brown and the Mystery Basket, 1941, Whit, 432p, flip pictures, Henry E. Vallely-a
| | 6.00 | 21.00 | 42.00 |

1423-Peggy Brown and the Secet Treasure, 1947, Whit, 288p, Henry E. Vallely-a
| | 6.00 | 21.00 | 42.00 |

1427-Peggy Brown and the Runaway Auto Trailer, 1937, Whit, 300p, Henry E. Vallely-a
| | 6.00 | 21.00 | 42.00 |

1463-Peggy Brown and the Jewel of Fire, 1943, Whit, 352p, Henry E. Vallely-a
| | 6.00 | 21.00 | 42.00 |

1491-Peggy Brown in the Big Haunted House, 1940, Whit, 432p, Vallely-a
| | 6.00 | 21.00 | 42.00 |

1143-Peril Afloat, 1938, Sal, 400p
| | 5.00 | 17.50 | 35.00 |

1199-Perry Winkle and the Rinkeydinks, 1937, Whit, 432p, by Martin Branner
| | 8.50 | 30.00 | 60.00 |

1487-Perry Winkle and the Rinkeydinks get a Horse, 1938, Whit, 432p, by Martin Branner
| | 8.50 | 30.00 | 60.00 |

Peter Pan (See Wee Little Books)

nn-Peter Rabbit, nd(1930s), np(Whit), 36p, Penny Book, 3×2½"
| | 2.00 | 6.00 | 12.00 |

Peter Rabbit's Carrots (See Wee Little Books)

The Phantom #1100, © King Features Syndicate, 1936

1100-Phantom, The, 1936, Whit, 432p, by Lee Falk & Ray Moore
| | 20.00 | 70.00 | 140.00 |

1416-Phantom and the Girl of Mystery, The, 1947, Whit, 352p, by Falk & Moore
| | 10.00 | 35.00 | 70.00 |

1421-Phantom and Desert Justice, The, 1941, Whit, 432p, flip pictures, by Falk & Moore
| | 12.50 | 42.50 | 85.00 |

1468-Phantom and the Sky Pirates, The, 1945, Whit, 352p, by

	Good	Fine	N-Mint
Falk & Moore	10.00	35.00	70.00

1474-Phantom and the Sign of the Skull, The, 1939, Whit, 432p, by Falk & Moore
| | 14.00 | 50.00 | 100.00 |

1489-Phantom, Return of the..., 1942, Whit, 432p, flip pictures, by Falk & Moore
| | 12.50 | 42.50 | 85.00 |

1130-Phil Barton, Sleuth (Scout Book), 1937, Sal, hard-c
| | 4.50 | 16.00 | 32.00 |

Pied Piper of Hamlin (See Wee Little Books)

1466-Pilot Pete Dive Bomber, 1941, Whit, 432p, flip pictures
| | 5.50 | 19.00 | 38.00 |

5783-2-Pink Panther at Castle Kreep, The, 1980, Whit, 260p, soft-c, 79 cents, B&W
| | .50 | 1.50 | 3.00 |

Pinocchio and Jiminy Cricket (See Walt Disney's...)

nn-Pioneers of the Wild West (Blue-c), 1933, World, High Lights of History Series
| | 5.50 | 19.00 | 38.00 |

nn-Pioneers of the Wild West (Red-c), 1933, World, High Lights of History Series
| | 5.50 | 19.00 | 38.00 |

1123-Plainsman, The, 1936, Whit, 240p, photo-c, movie scenes (Paramount Pics.)
| | 7.00 | 25.00 | 50.00 |

Pluto (See Mickey's Dog . . . & Walt Disney's . . .)

2114-Pocket Coloring Book, 1935, Sal
| | 20.00 | 70.00 | 140.00 |

1060-Polly and Her Pals on the Farm, 1934, Sal, 164p, hard-c, by Cliff Sterrett
| | 10.00 | 35.00 | 70.00 |

1310-Polly and Her Pals on the Farm, 1934, Sal, soft-c
| | 10.00 | 35.00 | 70.00 |

1051-Popeye, Adventures of..., 1934, Sal, oblong-size, E. C. Segar-a, hard-c
| | 27.00 | 95.00 | 190.00 |

1088-Popeye in Puddleburg, 1934, Sal, 160p, hard-c, E. C. Segar-a
| | 12.00 | 42.00 | 85.00 |

1113-Popeye Starring in Choose Your Weppins, 1936, Sal, 160p, hard-c, Segar-a
| | 12.00 | 42.00 | 85.00 |

1117-Popeye's Ark, 1936, Sal, 4½×5½", hard-c, Segar-a
| | 12.00 | 42.00 | 85.00 |

1163-Popeye sees the Sea, 1936, Whit, 432p, Segar-a
| | 13.00 | 45.00 | 90.00 |

1301-Popeye, Adventures of..., 1934, Sal, oblong-size, Segar-a
| | 27.00 | 95.00 | 190.00 |

1318-Popeye in Puddleburg, 1934, Sal, 160p, soft-c, Segar-a
| | 12.00 | 42.00 | 85.00 |

1405-Popeye and the Jeep, 1937, Whit, 432p, Segar-a
| | 13.00 | 45.00 | 90.00 |

1406-Popeye the Super-Fighter, 1939, Whit, All Pictures Comics, flip pictures, Segar-a
| | 12.50 | 42.00 | 85.00 |

	Good	Fine	N-Mint
1422-Popeye the Sailor Man, 1947, Whit, All Pictures Comics			
	9.00	31.00	62.00
1450-Popeye in Quest of His Poopdeck Pappy, 1937, Whit, 432p,			
Segar c/a	13.00	45.00	90.00
1458-Popeye and Queen Olive Oyl, 1949, Whit, 288p, Sagendorf-a			
	8.50	30.00	60.00

Popeye and the Quest for the Rainbird #1459,
© King Features Syndicate, 1943

	Good	Fine	N-Mint
1459-Popeye and the Quest for the Rainbird, 1943, Whit, Winner			
& Zaboly-a	10.00	35.00	70.00
1480-Popeye the Spinach Eater, 1945, Whit, All Pictures Comics			
	9.00	31.00	62.00
1485-Popeye in a Sock for Susan's Sake, 1940, Whit, 432p,			
flip pictures	10.00	35.00	70.00
1497-Popeye and Caster Oyl the Detective, 1941, Whit, 432p, flip			
pictures, Segar-a	12.00	42.00	85.00
1499-Popeye and the Deep Sea Mystery, 1939, Whit, 432p,			
Segar-c/a	12.00	42.00	85.00
1593-Popeye Starring in Choose Your Weppins, 1936, Sal, 160p,			
soft-c, Segar-a	12.00	42.00	85.00
1597-Popeye's Ark, 1936, Sal, 4½×5½", soft-c, Segar-a			
	12.00	42.00	85.00
2008-(#8)-Popeye-Ghost Ship to Treasure Island, 1967, Whit,			
260p, 39 cents, hard-c, color illos	2.00	6.00	12.00
4063-Popeye, Thimble Theatre Starring, 1935, Whit, 7×9½",			
320p, Big Big Book, Segar c/a; (Cactus cover w/yellow logo)			
	43.00	150.00	300.00
4063-Popeye, Thimble Theatre Starring, 1935, Whit, 7×9½",			
320p, Big Big Book, Segar c/a; (Big Balloon-c w/red logo),			
(2nd printing w/same contents as above)			
	45.00	157.00	315.00

	Good	Fine	N-Mint

5761-2-Popeye and Queen Olive Oyl, 1973 (1980-reprint of 1973 version), 260p, 79 cents, B&W, soft-c

	.50	1.50	3.00

The "Pop-Up" Buck Rogers in the Dangerous Mission #103,
© John F. Dille Co., 1934

103-"Pop-Up" Buck Rogers in the Dangerous Mission (with Pop-Up picture), 1934, BRP, 62p, The Midget Pop-Up Book w/Pop-Up in center of book, Calkins-a

	47.00	165.00	330.00

206-"Pop-Up" Buck Rogers-Strange Adventures in the Spider-Ship, The, 1935, BRP, 24p, 8×9", 3 Pop-Ups, hard-c, by Dick Calkins

	68.00	237.50	475.00

nn-"Pop-Up" Cinderella, 1933, BRP, 7½×9¾", 4 Pop-Ups, hard-c w/dust jacket ($2.00)

	57.00	200.00	400.00
Without dust jacket	43.00	150.00	300.00

207-"Pop-Up" Dick Tracy-Capture of Boris Arson, 1935, BRP, 24p, 8×9", 3 Pop-Ups, hard-c, by Gould

	57.00	200.00	400.00

210-"Pop-Up" Flash Gordon Tournament of Death, The, 1935, BRP, 24p, 8 9", 3 Pop-Ups, hard-c, by Alex Raymond

	57.00	200.00	400.00

202-"Pop-Up" Goldilocks and the Three Bears, The, 1934, BRP, 24p, 8×9", 3 Pop-Ups, hard-c

	18.00	62.50	125.00

nn-"Pop-Up" Jack and the Beanstalk, 1933, BRP, hard-c (50 cents), 1 Pop-Up

	12.50	42.00	85.00

nn-"Pop-Up" Jack the Giant Killer, 1933, BRP, hard-c (50 cents), 1 Pop-Up

	12.50	42.00	85.00

nn-"Pop-Up" Jack the Giant Killer, 1933, BRP, 4 Pop-Ups, hard-c w/dust jacket ($2.00)

	57.00	200.00	400.00

	Good	Fine	N-Mint
Without dust jacket	43.00	150.00	300.00

nn-"Pop-Up" Little Black Sambo (with Pop-Up picture), 1934, BRP, 62p, The Midget Pop-Up Book, one Pop-Up in center of book

	40.00	140.00	280.00

208-"Pop-Up" Little Orphan Annie and Jumbo the Circus Elephant, 1935, BRP, 24p, 8×9", 3 Pop-Ups, hard-c, by H. Gray

	43.00	150.00	300.00

nn-"Pop-Up" Little Red Ridinghood, 1933, BRP, hard-c (50 cents), 1 Pop-Up

	12.50	42.00	85.00

nn-"Pop-Up" Mickey Mouse, The, 1933, BRP, 34p, 6½×9", 3 Pop-Ups, hard-c, Gottfredson-a (75 cents)

	68.00	237.50	475.00

nn-"Pop-Up" Mickey Mouse in King Arthur's Court, The, 1933, BRP, 56p, 7½×9¾", 4 Pop-Ups, hard-c w/dust jacket, Gottfredson-a ($2.00)

	88.00	307.00	615.00
Without dust jacket	70.00	245.00	490.00

101-"Pop-Up" Mickey Mouse in "Ye Olden Days" (with Pop-Up picture), 1934, 62p, BRP, The Midget Pop-Up Book, one Pop-Up in center of book, Gottfredson-a

	47.00	165.00	330.00

nn-"Pop-Up" Minnie Mouse, The, 1933, BRP, 36p, 6½×9", 3 Pop-Ups, hard-c (75 cents), Gottfredson-a

	68.00	237.50	475.00

203-"Pop-Up" Mother Goose, The, 1934, BRP, 24p, 8×9¼", 3 Pop-Ups, hard-c

	33.00	115.00	230.00

nn-"Pop-Up" Mother Goose Rhymes, The, 1933, BRP, 96p, 7½×9¾", 4 Pop-Ups, hard-c w/dust jacket ($2.00)

	57.00	200.00	400.00
Without dust jacket	47.00	165.00	330.00

209-"Pop-Up" New Adventures of Tarzan, 1935, BRP, 24p, 8×9", 3 Pop-Ups, hard-c

	57.00	200.00	400.00

104-"Pop-Up" Peter Rabbit, The (with Pop-Up picture), 1934, BRP, 62p, The Midget Pop-Up Book, one Pop-Up in center of book

	27.00	95.00	190.00

nn-"Pop-Up" Pinocchio, 1933, BRP, 7½×9¾", 4 Pop-Ups, hard-c w/dust jacket ($2.00)

	73.00	255.00	510.00
Without dust jacket	62.00	215.00	430.00

102-"Pop-Up" Popeye among the White Savages (with Pop-Up picture), 1934, BRP, 62p, The Midget Pop-Up Book, one Pop-Up in center of book, E. C. Segar-a

	43.00	150.00	300.00

205-"Pop-Up" Popeye with the Hag of the Seven Seas, The, 1935, BRP, 24p, 8×9", 3 Pop-Ups, hard-c, Segar-a

	43.00	150.00	300.00

	Good	Fine	N-Mint

201-"Pop-Up" Puss In Boots, The, 1934, BRP, 24p, 3 Pop-Ups, hard-c
| | 18.00 | 62.50 | 125.00 |

nn-"Pop-Up" Silly Symphonies, The (Mickey Mouse Presents His...), 1933, BRP, 56p, 9¾×7½", 4 Pop-Ups, hard-c w/dust jacket ($2.00)
| | 83.00 | 290.00 | 580.00 |
Without dust jacket
| | 70.00 | 245.00 | 490.00 |

nn-"Pop-Up" Sleeping Beauty, 1933, BRP, hard-c (50 cents), 1 Pop-Up
| | 26.00 | 90.00 | 180.00 |

212-"Pop-Up" Terry and the Pirates in Shipwrecked, The, 1935, BRP, 24p, 8×9", 3 Pop-Ups, hard-c
| | 43.00 | 150.00 | 300.00 |

211-"Pop-Up" Tim Tyler in the Jungle, The, 1935, BRP, 24p, 8×9", 3 Pop-Ups, hard-c
| | 26.00 | 90.00 | 180.00 |

1404-Porky Pig and His Gang, 1946, Whit, All Pictures Comics, Barks-a r/4-Color 48
| | 13.00 | 45.00 | 90.00 |

1408-Porky Pig and Petunia, 1942, Whit, All Pictures Comics, flip pictures, r/4-Color 16 & Famous Gang Book of Comics
| | 8.50 | 30.00 | 60.00 |

1176-Powder Smoke Range, 1935, Whit, 240p, photo-c, movie scenes, Hoot Gibson, Harey Carey app. (RKO Radio Pict.)
| | 8.50 | 30.00 | 60.00 |

1058-Practical Pig!, The (Disney), 1939, Whit, 68p, 5×5½", hard-c
| | 7.50 | 26.00 | 52.00 |

758-Prairie Bill and the Covered Wagon, 1934, Whit, 384p, Hal Arbo-a
| | 7.00 | 25.00 | 50.00 |

nn-Prairie Bill and the Covered Wagon, 1934, Whit, 390p, premium-no ads, 3-color, soft-c, Hal Arbo-a
| | 12.00 | 42.00 | 85.00 |

1440-Punch Davis of the U.S. Aircraft Carrier, 1945, Whit, 352p
| | 5.00 | 17.50 | 35.00 |

nn-Puss in Boots, nd(1930s), np(Whit), 36p, Penny Book
| | 1.50 | 4.50 | 9.00 |

1100B-Puzzle Book, 1938, Whit, 36p, 2½×3½", Penny Book
| | 2.00 | 6.00 | 12.00 |

1100B-Puzzles, 1938, Whit, 36p, 2½×3½", Penny Book
| | 2.00 | 6.00 | 12.00 |

1100B-Quiz Book, The, 1938, Whit, 36p, 2½×3½", Penny Book
| | 2.00 | 6.00 | 12.00 |

1142-Radio Patrol, 1935, Whit, 432p, by Eddie Sullivan & Charlie Schmidt (#1)
| | 7.50 | 26.00 | 52.00 |

1173-Radio Patrol Trailing the Safeblowers, 1937, Whit, 432p
| | 6.00 | 21.00 | 42.00 |

1496-Radio Patrol Outwitting the Gang Chief, 1939, Whit, 432p
| | 6.00 | 21.00 | 42.00 |

	Good	Fine	N-Mint

1498-Radio Patrol and Big Dan's Mobsters, 1937, Whit, 432p
| | 6.00 | 21.00 | 42.00 |

1441-Range Busters, The, 1942, Whit, 432p, Henry E. Vallely-a
| | 6.00 | 21.00 | 42.00 |

1163-Ranger and the Cowboy, The, 1939, Sal, 400p
| | 5.00 | 17.50 | 35.00 |

1154-Rangers on the Rio Grande, 1938, Sal, 400p
| | 5.00 | 17.50 | 35.00 |

1447-Ray Land of the Tank Corps, U.S.A., 1942, Whit, 432p, flip pictures, Hess-a
| | 5.00 | 17.50 | 35.00 |

1157-Red Barry Ace-Detective, 1935, Whit, 432p, by Will Gould
| | 7.00 | 25.00 | 50.00 |

1426-Red Barry Undercover Man, 1939, Whit, 432p, by Will Gould
| | 6.00 | 21.00 | 42.00 |

20-Red Davis, 1935, EVW, 160p
| | 8.00 | 27.50 | 55.00 |

1449-Red Death on the Range, The, 1940, Whit, 432p, Fred Harman-a (Bronc Peeler)
| | 7.00 | 25.00 | 50.00 |

nn-Red Hen and the Fox, The, nd(1930s), np(Whit), 36p, 3×2½", Penny Book
| | 1.50 | 4.50 | 9.00 |

1145-Red Hot Holsters, 1938, Sal, 400p
| | 5.00 | 17.50 | 35.00 |

1400-Red Ryder and Little Beaver on Hoofs of Thunder, 1939, Whit, 432p, Harman c/a
| | 10.00 | 35.00 | 70.00 |

1414-Red Ryder and the Squaw-Tooth Rustlers, 1946, Whit, 352p, Fred Harman-a
| | 7.00 | 25.00 | 50.00 |

1427-Red Ryder and the Code of the West, 1941, Whit, 432p, flip pictures, by Harman
| | 9.00 | 31.00 | 62.00 |

Red Ryder the Fighting Westerner #1440, © NEA Service, 1940

1440-Red Ryder the Fighting Westerner, 1940, Whit, Harman-a
| | 9.00 | 31.00 | 62.00 |

	Good	Fine	N-Mint

1443-Red Ryder and the Rimrock Killer, 1948, Whit, 288p,
Harman-a 6.00 21.00 42.00

1450-Red Ryder and Western Border Guns, 1942, Whit, 432p,
flip pictures, by Harman 9.00 31.00 62.00

1454-Red Ryder and the Secret Canyon, 1948, Whit, 288p,
Harman-a 6.00 21.00 42.00

1466-Red Ryder and Circus Luck, 1947, Whit, 288p, by Fred
Harman 6.00 21.00 42.00

1473-Red Ryder in War on the Range, 1945, Whit, 352p, by Fred
Harman 7.00 25.00 50.00

1475-Red Ryder and the Outlaws of Painted Valley, 1943, Whit,
352p, by Harman 7.50 26.00 52.00

702-10-Red Ryder acting Sheriff, 1949, Whit, by Fred Harman
5.00 17.50 35.00

nn-Red Ryder Brings Law to Devil's Hole, 1939, Dell, 196p,
Fast-Action Story, Harman c/a 20.00 70.00 140.00

nn-Red Ryder and the Highway Robbers, 1938, Whit, 36p,
2½x3½", Penny Book 6.00 21.00 42.00

754-Reg'lar Fellers, 1933, Whit, 320p, by Gene Byrnes
9.00 31.00 62.00

nn-Reg'lar Fellers, 1933, Whit, 202p, Cocomalt premium, by
Gene Byrnes 10.00 35.00 70.00

1424-Rex Beach's Jaragu of the Jungle, 1937, Whit, 432p
5.50 19.00 38.00

12-Rex, King of Wild Horses in "Stampede," 1935, EVW,
160p, movie scenes, Columbia Pictures
7.00 25.00 50.00

1100B-Riddles for Fun, 1938, Whit, 36p, 2½x3½", Penny Book
2.00 6.00 12.00

1100B-Riddles to Guess, 1938, Whit, 36p, 2½x3½", Penny Book
2.00 6.00 12.00

1425-Riders of Lone Trails, 1937, Whit, 300p
5.00 17.50 35.00

1141-Rio Raiders (A Billy The Kid Story), 1938, Sal, 400p
5.00 17.50 35.00

5767-2-Road Runner, The Lost Road Runner Mine, The, 1974
(1980), 260p, 79 cents, B&W, soft-c
.50 1.50 3.00

Robin Hood (See Wee Little Books)

10-Robin Hood, 1935, EVW, 160p, movie scenes w/Douglas
Fairbanks (United Artists), hard-c 12.00 42.00 85.00

719-Robinson Crusoe (The Story of...), nd (1933), Whit, 364p,
soft-c 9.00 31.00 62.00

1421-Roy Rogers and the Dwarf-Cattle Ranch, 1947, Whit, 352p,

	Good	Fine	N-Mint
Henry E. Vallely-a	8.00	27.50	55.00
1437-Roy Rogers and the Deadly Treasure, 1947, Whit, 288p			
	7.00	25.00	50.00
1448-Roy Rogers and the Mystery of the Howling Mesa, 1948, Whit, 288p			
	7.00	25.00	50.00
1452-Roy Rogers in Robbers' Roost, 1948, Whit, 288p			
	7.00	25.00	50.00

Roy Rogers Robinhood of the Range #1460, © Roy Rogers, 1942

	Good	Fine	N-Mint
1460-Roy Rogers Robinhood of the Range, 1942, Whit, 432p, Hess-a (1st)	8.00	27.50	55.00
1462-Roy Rogers and the Mystery of the Lazy M, 1949, Whit	6.00	21.00	42.00
1476-Roy Rogers King of the Cowboys, 1943, Whit, 352p, Irwin Myers-a, based on movie	9.00	31.00	62.00
1494-Roy Rogers at Crossed Feathers Ranch, 1945, Whit, 320p, Erwin Hess-a	7.00	25.00	50.00
701-10-Roy Rogers and the Snowbound Outlaws, 1949, 3¼x5½"	4.50	16.00	32.00
715-10-Roy Rogers Range Detective, 1950, Whit, 2½x5"	4.50	16.00	32.00
nn-Sandy Gregg Federal Agent on Special Assignment, 1939, Whit, 36p, 2½x3½", Penny Book	6.00	21.00	42.00
Sappo (See Top-Line Comics)			
1122-Scrappy, 1934, Whit, 288p	12.00	42.00	85.00
L12-Scrappy (The Adventures of...), 1935, Lynn, 192p, movie scenes	12.00	42.00	85.00
1191-Secret Agent K-7, 1940, Sal, 400p, based on radio show	5.00	17.50	35.00
1144-Secret Agent X-9, 1936, Whit, 432p, Charles Flanders-a	9.00	31.00	62.00

	Good	Fine	N-Mint

1472-Secret Agent X-9 and the Mad Assassin, 1938, Whit, 432p,
   Charles Flanders-a   9.00   31.00   62.00
1161-Sequoia, 1935, Whit, 160p, photo-c, movie scenes
                                   8.50   30.00   60.00
1430-Shadow and the Living Death, The, 1940, Whit, 432p, Erwin
   Hess-a   33.00   115.00   230.00
1443-Shadow and the Master of Evil, The, 1941, Whit, 432p, flip
   pictures, Hess-a   33.00   115.00   230.00
1495-Shadow and the Ghost Makers, The, 1942, Whit, 432p, John
   Coleman Burroughs-c   33.00   115.00   230.00
2024-Shazzan, The Glass Princess, 1968, Whit
                                   2.00   6.00   12.00
Shirley Temple (See My Life and Times & Story of...)
1095-Shirley Temple and Lionel Barrymore Starring in
   "The Little Colonel," 1935, Sal, photo-c, movie scenes
                                  10.00   35.00   70.00
1115-Shirley Temple in the Littlest Rebel, 1935, Sal, photo-c,
   movie scenes, hard-c   10.00   35.00   70.00
1595-Shirley Temple in the Littlest Rebel, 1935, Sal, photo-c,
   movie scenes, soft-c   10.00   35.00   70.00
1195-Shooting Sheriffs of the Wild West, 1936, Whit, 432p
                                   5.50   19.00   38.00

Silly Symphony Featuring Donald Duck #1441,
© *Walt Disney Productions, 1937*

1169-Silly Symphony Featuring Donald Duck (Disney), 1937,
   Whit, 432p, Taliaferro-a   14.00   50.00   100.00
1441-Silly Symphony Featuring Donald Duck and His (Mis)
   Adventures (Disney), 1937, Whit, 432p, Taliaferro-a
                                  14.00   50.00   100.00
1155-Silver Streak, The, 1935, Whit, 160p, photo-c, movie scenes
   (RKO Radio Pict.)   7.00   25.00   50.00
Simple Simon (See Wee Little Books)

	Good	Fine	N-Mint

1649-Sir Lancelot (TV Series), 1958, Whit, 280p
                                         3.00   9.00   18.00

1112-Skeezix in Africa, 1934, Whit, 300p, Frank King-a
    7.50   26.00   52.00

1408-Skeezix at the Military Academy, 1938, Whit, 432p, Frank King-a
    6.00   21.00   42.00

1414-Skeezix goes to War, 1944, Whit, 352p, Frank King-a
    6.00   21.00   42.00

1419-Skeezix on His Own in the Big City, 1941, Whit, All Pictures Comics, flip pictures, Frank King-a
    7.00   25.00   50.00

761-Skippy, 1934, Whit. 320p, by Percy Crosby
   10.00   35.00   70.00

4056-Skippy, The Story of, 1934, Whit, 320p, 7×9½", Big Big Book, Percy Crosby-a   33.00 115.00 230.00

nn-Skippy, The Story of, 1934, Whit, Phillips Dental Magnesia premium, soft-c, by Percy Crosby 8.50   30.00   60.00

1439-Skyroads with Clipper Williams of the Flying Legion, 1938, Whit, 432p, by Lt. Dick Calkins, Russell Keaton-a
    6.00   21.00   42.00

1127-Skyroads with Hurricane Hawk, 1936, Whit, 432p, by Lt. Dick Calkins, Russell Keaton-a 6.00   21.00   42.00
    Smilin' Jack and his Flivver Plane (See Top-Line Comics)

1152-Smilin' Jack and the Stratosphere Ascent, 1937, Whit, 432p, Zack Mosley-a 10.00   35.00   70.00

Smilin' Jack in Wings Over the Pacific #1416, © Zack Mosley, 1939

1412-Smilin' Jack Flying High with "Downwind," 1942, Whit, 432p, Zack Mosley-a 9.00   31.00   62.00

1416-Smilin' Jack in Wings over the Pacific, 1939, Whit, 432p, Zack Mosley-a 9.00   31.00   62.00

	Good	Fine	N-Mint

1419-Smilin' Jack and the Jungle Pipe Line, 1947, Whit, 352p, Zack Mosley-a   8.00   27.50   55.00

1445-Smilin' Jack and the Escape from Death Rock, 1943, Whit, 352p, Mosley-a   8.00   27.50   55.00

1464-Smilin' Jack and the Coral Princess, 1945, Whit, 352p, Zack Mosley-a   8.00   27.50   55.00

1473-Smilin' Jack Speed Pilot, 1941, Whit, 432p, Zack Mosley-a   9.00   31.00   62.00

2-Smilin' Jack and his Stratosphere Plane, 1938, Whit, 132p, Buddy Book, soft-c, Zack Mosley-a

22.00   77.00   154.00

nn-Smilin' Jack Grounded on a Tropical Shore, 1938, Whit, 36p, 2½×3½", Penny Book   6.00   21.00   42.00

11-Smilin' Jack and the Border Bandits, 1941, Dell, 196p, Fast-Action Story, soft-c, Zack Mosley-a

20.00   70.00   140.00

745-Smitty Golden Gloves Tournament, 1934, Whit, 320p, Walter Berndt-a   9.00   31.00   62.00

nn-Smitty Golden Gloves Tournament, 1934, Whit, 204p, Cocomalt premium, soft-c, Walter Berndt-a

11.00   37.50   75.00

1404-Smitty and Herbie Lost Among the Indians, 1941, Whit, All Pictures Comics   6.00   21.00   42.00

1477-Smitty in Going Native, 1938, Whit, 300p, Walter Berndt-a

6.00   21.00   42.00

2-Smitty and Herby, 1936, Whit, 132p, 3½×3½", soft-c, Tarzan Ice Cream cup lid premium   22.00   77.00   154.00

9-Smitty's Brother Herby and the Police Horse, 1938, Whit, 132p, 3¾×3½", Buddy Book-ice cream premium, by Walter Berndt   22.00   77.00   154.00

1010-Smokey Stover Firefighter of Foo, 1937, Whit, 7¼×5½", 64p, Nickel Book, Bill Holman-a   8.50   30.00   60.00

1413-Smokey Stover, 1942, Whit, All Pictures Comics, flip pictures, Bill Holman-a   7.00   25.00   50.00

1421-Smokey Stover the Foo Fighter, 1938, Whit, 432p, Bill Holman-a   7.00   25.00   50.00

1481-Smokey Stover the Foolish Foo Fighter, 1942, Whit, All Pictures Comics   7.00   25.00   50.00

1-Smokey Stover the Fireman of Foo, 1938, Whit, 3¾×3½", 132p, Buddy Book-ice cream premium, by Bill Holman

22.00   77.00   155.00

1100A-Smokey Stover, 1938, Whit, 36p, 2½×3½", Penny Book

6.00   21.00   42.00

nn-Smokey Stover and the Fire Chief of Foo, 1938, Whit, 36p,

	Good	Fine	N-Mint
2½×3½", Penny Book, yellow shirt on-c			
	6.00	21.00	42.00

nn-Smokey Stover and the Fire Chief of Foo, 1938, Whit, 36p,
Penny Book, Green shirt on-c   7.00   25.00   50.00

Snow White and the Seven Dwarfs #1460,
© Walt Disney Productions, 1938

1460-Snow White and the Seven Dwarfs (The Story of Walt
Disney's...), 1938, Whit, 288p   15.00   52.50   105.00
1136-Sombrero Pete, 1936, Whit, 432p   5.50   19.00   38.00
1152-Son of Mystery, 1939, Sal, 400p   5.00   17.50   35.00
1191-SOS Coast Guard, 1936, Whit, 432p, Henry E. Vallely-a
    5.00   17.50   35.00
2016-(#16)-Space Ghost-The Sorceress of Cyba-3 (TV Cartoon),
1968, Whit, 260p, 39 cents, hard-c, color illos
    4.50   14.00   28.00
**1455-Speed Douglas and the Mole Gang-The Great Sabotage
Plot,** 1941, Whit, 432p, flip pictures
    5.00   17.50   35.00
5779-2-Spider-Man Zaps Mr. Zodiac, 1976 (1980), 260p, 79 cents,
soft-c, B&W   .50   1.50   3.00
1467-Spike Kelly of the Commandos, 1943, Whit, 352p
    5.00   17.50   35.00
1144-Spook Riders on the Overland, 1938, Sal, 400p
    5.00   17.50   35.00
768-Spy, The, 1936, Whit, 300p   7.00   25.00   50.00
nn-Spy Smasher and the Red Death, 1941, Faw, 4×5½", Dime
Action Book   27.00   95.00   190.00
1120-Stan Kent Freshman Fullback, 1936, Sal, 148p, hard-c
    4.50   13.50   27.00
1132-Stan Kent, Captain, 1937, Sal   4.50   13.50   27.00

	Good	Fine	N-Mint

1600-Stan Kent Freshman Fullback, 1936, Sal, 148p, soft-c

4.50   13.50   27.00

1123-Stan Kent Varsity Man, 1936, Sal, 160p, hard-c

4.50   13.50   27.00

1603-Stan Kent Varsity Man, 1936, Sal, 160p, soft-c

4.50   13.50   27.00

1104-Steel Arena, The (With Clyde Beatty), 1936, Sal, hard-c,
movie scenes adapted from *The Lost Jungle*

8.00   27.50   55.00

1584-Steel Arena, The (With Clyde Beatty), 1936, Sal, soft-c,
movie scenes

8.00   27.50   55.00

**1426-Steve Hunter of the U.S. Coast Guard Under Secret
Orders,** 1942, Whit, 432p

5.00   17.50   35.00

1456-Story of Charlie McCarthy and Edgar Bergen, The, 1938,
Whit, 288p

7.00   25.00   50.00

Story of Daniel, The (See Wee Little Books)

Story of David, The (See Wee Little Books)

1110-Story of Freddie Bartholomew, The, 1935, Sal, 4½×5¼",
hard-c, movie scenes (MGM)

7.00   25.00   50.00

1590-Story of Freddie Bartholomew, The, 1935, Sal, 4½×5¼",
soft-c, movie scenes (MGM)

7.00   25.00   50.00

Story of Gideon, The (See Wee Little Books)

W714-Story of Jackie Cooper, The, 1933, Whit, 240p, photo-c,
movie scenes, "Skippy" & "Sooky" movie

9.00   31.00   62.00

Story of Joseph, The (See Wee Little Books)

Story of Moses, The (See Wee Little Books)

Story of Ruth and Naomi (See Wee Little Books)

1089-Story of Shirley Temple, The, 1934, Sal, 160p, hard photo-c,
movie scenes

10.00   35.00   70.00

1319-Story of Shirley Temple, The, 1934, Sal, 160p, soft photo-c,
movie scenes

10.00   35.00   70.00

1090-Strawberry-Roan, 1934, Sal, 160p, hard-c, Ken Maynard
photo-c, movie scenes

10.00   35.00   70.00

1320-Strawberry-Roan, 1934, Sal, 160p, soft-c, Ken Maynard
photo-c, movie scenes

10.00   35.00   70.00

Streaky and the Football Signals (See Top-Line Comics)

5780-2-Superman in the Phantom Zone Connection, 1980, 260p,
79 cents, soft-c, B&W

.50   1.50   3.00

747-Tailspin Tommy in the Famous Pay-Roll Mystery, 1933,
Whit, 320p, Hal Forrest-a (#1)

10.00   35.00   70.00

nn-Tailspin Tommy the Pay-Roll Mystery, 1934, Whit, 52p,
3½×5¼", premium-no ads, soft-c; another version with Perkins
ad, Hal Forrest-a

15.00   52.50   105.00

	Good	Fine	N-Mint
1110-Tailspin Tommy and the Island in the Sky, 1936, Whit, 432p, Hal Forrest-a	8.00	27.50	55.00
1124-Tailspin Tommy the Dirigible Flight to the North Pole, 1934, Whit, 432p, H. Forrest-a	9.00	31.00	62.00
nn-Tailspin Tommy the Dirigible Flight to the North Pole, 1934, Whit, 436p, 3-color, soft-c, premium-no ads, Hal Forrest-a	19.00	66.00	132.00
1172-Tailspin Tommy Hunting for Pirate Gold, 1935, Whit, 432p, Hal Forrest-a	8.00	27.50	55.00
1183-Tailspin Tommy Air Racer, 1940, Sal, 400p, hard-c	8.00	27.50	55.00
1184-Tailspin Tommy in the Great Air Mystery, 1936, Whit, 240p, photo-c, movie scenes	10.00	35.00	70.00
1410-Tailspin Tommy the Weasel and His "Skywaymen," 1941, Whit, All Pictures Comics, flip pictures	7.00	25.00	50.00
1413-Tailspin Tommy and the Lost Transport, 1940, Whit, 432p, Hal Forrest-a	7.00	25.00	50.00
1423-Tailspin Tommy and the Hooded Flyer, 1937, Whit, 432p, Hal Forrest-a	8.00	27.50	55.00
1494-Tailspin Tommy and the Sky Bandits, 1938, Whit, 432p, Hal Forrest-a	8.00	27.50	55.00
nn-Tailspin Tommy and the Airliner Mystery, 1938, Whit, 196p, Fast-Action Story, soft-c, Hal Forrest-a	20.00	70.00	140.00
nn-Tailspin Tommy in Flying Aces, 1938, Dell, 196p, Fast-Action Story, soft-c, Hal Forrest-a	20.00	70.00	140.00
nn-Tailspin Tommy in Wings Over the Arctic, 1934, Whit, Cocomalt premium, Forrest-a	11.00	37.50	75.00
nn-Tailspin Tommy Big Thrill Chewing Gum, 1934, Whit, 8p, 2½×3" (6 diff.) ea...	8.50	30.00	60.00
3-Tailspin Tommy on the Mountain of Human Sacrifice, 1938, Whit, soft-c, Buddy Book	22.00	77.00	155.00
7-Tailspin Tommy's Perilous Adventure, 1934, Whit, 132p, 3½×3½", soft-c, Tarzan Ice Cream cup premium	22.00	77.00	155.00
L16-Tale of Two Cities, A, 1935, Lynn, movie scenes	10.00	35.00	70.00
744-Tarzan of the Apes, 1933, Whit, 320p, by Edgar Rice Burroughs (1st)	20.00	70.00	140.00
nn-Tarzan of the Apes, 1935, Whit, 52p, 3½×5¾", soft-c, stapled, premium, no ad; another version with a Perkins ad	27.00	95.00	190.00
769-Tarzan the Fearless, 1934, Whit, 240p, Buster Crabbe			

The Tarzan Twins #770, © Edgar Rice Burroughs, 1935

	Good	Fine	N-Mint
photo-c, movie scenes, ERB	18.00	62.50	125.00

770-Tarzan Twins, The, 1934, Whit, 432p, ERB

	42.00	125.00	250.00

770-Tarzan Twins, The, 1935, Whit, 432p, ERB

	27.00	80.00	160.00

nn-Tarzan Twins, The, 1935, Whit, 52p, 3½×5¾", premium-no ads, soft-c, ERB · 30.00 · 105.00 · 210.00

nn-Tarzan Twins, The, 1935, Whit, 436p, 3-color, soft-c, premium-no ads, ERB · 32.00 · 112.00 · 225.00

778-Tarzan of the Screen (The Story of Johnny Weissmuller), 1934, Whit, 240p, photo-c, movie scenes, ERB · 18.00 · 62.50 · 125.00

1102-Tarzan, The Return of, 1936, Whit, 432p, Edgar Rice Burroughs · 13.00 · 45.00 · 90.00

1180-Tarzan, The New Adventures of, 1935, Whit, 160p, Herman Brix photo-c, movie scenes, ERB · 15.00 · 52.00 · 105.00

1182-Tarzan Escapes, 1936, Whit, 240p, Johnny Weissmuller photo-c, movie scenes, ERB · 18.00 · 62.00 · 125.00

1407-Tarzan Lord of the Jungle, 1946, Whit, 352p, ERB · 10.00 · 35.00 · 70.00

1410-Tarzan, The Beasts of, 1937, Whit, 432p, Edgar Rice Burroughs · 12.00 · 42.00 · 85.00

1442-Tarzan and the Lost Empire, 1948, Whit, 288p, ERB · 11.00 · 37.50 · 75.00

1444-Tarzan and the Ant Men, 1945, Whit, 352p, ERB · 11.00 · 37.50 · 75.00

1448-Tarzan and the Golden Lion, 1943, Whit, 432p, ERB · 12.00 · 42.00 · 85.00

1452-Tarzan the Untamed, 1941, Whit, 432p, flip pictures, ERB · 12.00 · 42.00 · 85.00

	Good	Fine	N-Mint

1453-Tarzan the Terrible, 1942, Whit, 432p, flip pictures, ERB
                      12.00   42.00   85.00

1467-Tarzan in the Land of the Giant Apes, 1949, Whit, ERB
                      11.00   37.50   75.00

1477-Tarzan, The Son of, 1939, Whit, 432p, ERB
                      12.00   42.00   85.00

1488-Tarzan's Revenge, 1938, Whit, 432p, ERB
                      12.00   42.00   85.00

1495-Tarzan and the Jewels of Opar, 1940, Whit, 432p
                      12.00   42.00   85.00

4056-Tarzan and the Tarzan Twins with Jad-Bal-Ja the Golden Lion, 1936, Whit, 7×9½", 320p, Big Big Book
                      70.00   245.00   490.00

709-10-Tarzan and the Journey of Terror, 1950, Whit, 2½×5", ERB, Marsh-a   6.00   21.00   42.00

2005-(#5)-Tarzan: The Mark of the Red Hyena, 1967, Whit, 260p, 39 cents, hard-c, color illos   2.50   7.50   15.00

nn-Tarzan, 1935, Whit, 148p, soft-c, 3½×4", Tarzan Ice Cream cup premium, ERB (Scarce)   65.00   225.00   450.00

nn-Tarzan and a Daring Rescue, 1938, Whit, 68p, Pan-Am premium, soft-c, ERB   17.00   60.00   120.00

nn-Tarzan and his Jungle Friends, 1936, Whit, 132p, soft-c, 3½×3½", Tarzan Ice Cream cup premium, ERB (Scarce)   65.00   225.00   450.00

nn-Tarzan in the Golden City, 1938, Whit, 68p, Pan-Am premium, soft-c, ERB   18.00   62.00   125.00

nn-Tarzan The Avenger, 1939, Dell, 194p, Fast-Action Story, ERB, soft-c   27.00   95.00   190.00

nn-Tarzan with the Tarzan Twins in the Jungle, 1938, Dell, 194p, Fast-Action Story, ERB   27.00   95.00   190.00

1100B-Tell Your Fortune, 1938, Whit, 36p, 2½×3½", Penny Book
                        2.30   7.00   14.00

1156-Terry and the Pirates, 1935, Whit, 432p, Milton Caniff-a (#1)   12.00   42.00   85.00

nn-Terry and the Pirates, 1935, Whit, 52p, 3½×5¾", soft-c, premium, Milton Caniff-a; 3 versions: No ad, Sears ad & Perkins ad   17.00   60.00   120.00

1412-Terry and the Pirates Shipwrecked on a Desert Island, 1938, Whit, 432p, Milton Caniff-a   9.00   31.00   62.00

1420-Terry and War in the Jungle, 1946, Whit, 352p, Milton Caniff-a   8.00   27.50   55.00

1436-Terry and the Pirates the Plantation Mystery, 1942, Whit, 432p, flip pictures, Milton Caniff-a
                      9.00   31.00   62.00

	Good	Fine	N-Mint

1446-Terry and the Pirates and the Giant's Vengeance, 1939, Whit, 432p, Caniff-a   9.00   31.00   62.00

1499-Terry and the Pirates in the Mountain Stronghold, 1941, Whit, 432p, Caniff-a   9.00   31.00   62.00

4073-Terry and the Pirates, The Adventures of, 1938, Whit, 7×9½", 320p, Big Big Book, Milton Caniff-a
                                    53.00   185.00   370.00

10-Terry and the Pirates Meet Again, 1936, Whit, 132p, 3½×3½", soft-c, Tarzan Ice Cream cup lid premium
                                    27.00   95.00   190.00

nn-Terry and the Pirates, Adventures of, 1938, 36p, 2½×3½", Penny Book, Caniff-a   7.00   25.00   50.00

nn-Terry and the Pirates and the Island Rescue, 1938, Whit, 68p, 3¾×3½", Pan-Am premium   12.00   42.00   85.00

nn-Terry and the Pirates on Their Travels, 1938, 36p, 2½×3½", Penny Book, Caniff-a   7.00   25.00   50.00

nn-Terry and the Pirates and the Mystery Ship, 1938, Dell, 194p, Fast-Action Story, soft-c   25.00   87.50   175.00

1492-Terry Lee Flight Officer U.S.A., 1944, Whit, 352p, Milton Caniff-a   8.00   27.50   55.00

7-Texas Bad Man, The (Tom Mix), 1934, EVW, 160p, (Five Star Library), movie scenes   14.00   50.00   100.00

1429-Texas Kid, The, 1937, Whit, 432p   5.50   19.00   38.00

1135-Texas Ranger, The, 1936, Whit, 432p, Hal Arbo-a
                                    5.50   19.00   38.00

nn-Texas Ranger, The, 1935, Whit, 260p, Cocomalt premium, soft-c, Hal Arbo-a   7.00   25.00   50.00

nn-Texas Ranger in the West, The, 1938, Whit, 36p, 2½×3½", Penny Book   6.00   21.00   42.00

nn-Texas Ranger to the Rescue, The, 1938, Whit, 36p, 2½×3½", Penny Book   6.00   21.00   42.00

12-Texas Rangers in Rustler Strategy, The, 1936, Whit, 132p, 3½×3½", soft-c, Tarzan Ice Cream cup lid premium
                                    20.00   70.00   140.00

Tex Thorne (See Zane Grey)

Thimble Theatre (See Popeye)

L26-13 Hours By Air, 1936, Lynn, 128p, 5×7½", photo-c, movie scenes (Paramount Pictures)   10.00   35.00   70.00

nn-Three Bears, The, nd (1930s), np (Whit), 36p, 3×2½", Penny Book   1.50   4.50   9.00

1129-Three Finger Joe (Baseball), 1937, Sal, Robert A. Graef-a
                                    5.00   17.50   35.00

nn-Three Little Pigs, The, nd(1930s), np(Whit), 36p, 3×2½", Penny Book   1.50   4.50   9.00

	Good	Fine	N-Mint

1131-Three Musketeers, 1935, Whit, 182p, 5¼×6¼", photo-c, movie scenes   10.00   35.00   70.00

1409-Thumper and the Seven Dwarfs (Disney), 1944, Whit, All Pictures Comics   11.00   37.50   75.00

1108-Tiger Lady, The (The life of Mabel Stark, animal trainer), 1935, Sal, photo-c, movie scenes, hard-c
          7.00   25.00   50.00

1588-Tiger Lady, The, 1935, Sal, photo-c, movie scenes, soft-c
          7.00   25.00   50.00

1442-Tillie the Toiler and the Wild Man of Desert Island, 1941, Whit, 432p, Russ Westover-a   8.00   27.50   55.00

1058-"Timid Elmer" (Disney), 1939, Whit, 5×5½", 68p, hard-c
          7.50   26.00   52.00

1152-Tim McCoy in the Prescott Kid, 1935, Whit, 160p, hard photo-c, movie scenes   13.00   45.00   90.00

1193-Tim McCoy in the Westerner, 1936, Whit, 240p, photo-c, movie scenes   12.50   42.00   85.00

1436-Tim McCoy on the Tomahawk Trail, 1937, Whit, 432p, Robert Weisman-a   7.00   25.00   50.00

1490-Tim McCoy and the Sandy Gulch Stampede, 1939, Whit, 424p   7.00   25.00   50.00

2-Tim McCoy in Beyond the Law, 1934, EVW, Five Star Library, photo-c, movie scenes (Columbia Pictures)
          14.00   50.00   100.00

10-Tim McCoy in Fighting the Redskins, 1938, Whit, 130p, Buddy Book, soft-c   22.00   77.00   155.00

14-Tim McCoy in Speedwings, 1935, EVW, Five Star Library, 160p, photo-c, movie scenes (Columbia Pictures)
          14.00   50.00   100.00

nn-Tim the Builder, nd (1930s), np (Whit), 36p, 3×2½", Penny Book   1.50   4.50   9.00

Tim Tyler (See Adventures of...)

1140-Tim Tyler's Luck Adventures in the Ivory Patrol, 1937, Whit, 432p, by Lyman Young   7.00   25.00   50.00

1479-Tim Tyler's Luck and the Plot of the Exiled King, 1939, Whit, 432p, by Lyman Young   6.00   21.00   42.00

767-Tiny Tim, The Adventures of, 1935, Whit, 384p, by Stanley Link   9.00   31.00   62.00

1172-Tiny Tim and the Mechanical Men, 1937, Whit, 432p, by Stanley Link   8.00   27.50   55.00

1472-Tiny Tim in the Big, Big World, 1945, Whit, 352p, by Stanley Link   7.00   25.00   50.00

2006-(#6)-Tom and Jerry Meet Mr. Fingers, 1967, Whit, 39 cents, 260p, hard-c, color illos   2.00   6.00   12.00

	Good	Fine	N-Mint

5787-2-Tom and Jerry Under the Big Top, 1980, Whit, 79 cents, 260p, soft-c, B&W

.50   1.50   3.00

723-Tom Beatty Ace of the Service, 1934, Whit, 256p, George Taylor-a

8.00   27.50   55.00

nn-Tom Beatty Ace of the Service, 1934, Whit, 260p, soft-c

8.00   27.50   55.00

1165-Tom Beatty Ace of the Service Scores Again, 1937, Whit, 432p, Weisman-a

7.00   25.00   50.00

1420-Tom Beatty Ace of the Service and the Big Brain Gang, 1939, Whit, 432p

7.00   25.00   50.00

nn-Tom Beatty Ace Detective and the Gorgon Gang, 1938?, Whit, 36p, 2½×3½", Penny Book   6.00   21.00   42.00

nn-Tom Beatty Ace of the Service and the Kidnapers, 1938? Whit, 36p, 2½×3½", Penny Book   6.00   21.00   42.00

1102-Tom Mason on Top, 1935, Sal, 160p, Tom Mix photo-c, from Mascot serial "The Miracle Rider," movie scenes, hard-c

12.00   42.00   85.00

1582-Tom Mason on Top, 1935, Sal, 160p, Tom Mix photo-c, movie scenes, soft-c   12.00   42.00   85.00

Tom Mix (See Chief of the Rangers, Flaming Guns & Texas Bad Man)

762-Tom Mix and Tony Jr. in "Terror Trail," 1934, Whit, 160p, movie scenes   12.00   42.00   85.00

1144-Tom Mix in the Fighting Cowboy, 1935, Whit, 432p, Hal Arbo-a   8.50   30.00   60.00

nn-Tom Mix in the Fighting Cowboy, 1935, Whit, 436p, premium-no ads, 3 color, soft-c, Hal Arbo-a

17.00   60.00   120.00

1166-Tom Mix in the Range War, 1937, Whit, 432p, Hal Arbo-a

8.00   27.50   55.00

1173-Tom Mix Plays a Lone Hand, 1935, Whit, 288p, hard-c, Hal

Tom Mix and His Circus on the Barbary Coast #1482,
© Stephen Slesinger, 1940

	Good	Fine	N-Mint
Arbo-a	8.00	27.50	55.00
1183-Tom Mix and the Stranger from the South, 1936, Whit, 432p	8.00	27.50	55.00
1462-Tom Mix and the Hoard of Montezuma, 1937, Whit, 432p, H. E. Vallely-a	8.00	27.50	55.00
1482-Tom Mix and His Circus on the Barbary Coast, 1940, Whit, 432p, James Gary-a	8.00	27.50	55.00
4068-Tom Mix and the Scourge of Paradise Valley, 1937, Whit, 7×9½", 320p, Big Big Book, Vallely-a	32.00	112.50	225.00
nn-Tom Mix Riders to the Rescue, 1939, 36p, 2½×3", Penny Book	6.00	21.00	42.00
6833-Tom Mix in the Riding Avenger, 1936, Dell, 244p, Cartoon Story Book, hard-c	20.00	70.00	140.00
nn-Tom Mix Avenges the Dry Gulched Range King, 1939, Dell, 196p, Fast-Action Story, soft-c	20.00	70.00	140.00
nn-Tom Mix in the Riding Avenger, 1936, Dell, 244p, Fast-Action Story	20.00	70.00	140.00
4-Tom Mix and Tony in the Rider of Death Valley, 1934, EVW, Five Star Library, 160p, movie scenes (Universal Pictures), hard-c	14.00	50.00	100.00
7-Tom Mix in the Texas Bad Man, 1934, EVW, Five Star Library, 160p, movie scenes	14.00	50.00	100.00
10-Tom Mix in the Tepee Ranch Mystery, 1938, Whit, 132p, Buddy Book, soft-c	22.00	77.00	155.00
nn-Tom Mix the Trail of the Terrible 6, 1935, Ralston Purina Co., 84p, 3×3½", premium	12.50	42.00	85.00
1126-Tommy of Troop Six (Scout Book), 1937, Sal, hard-c	4.50	13.50	27.00
1606-Tommy of Troop Six (Scout Book), 1937, Sal, soft-c	4.50	13.50	27.00
Tom Sawyer (See Adventures of...)			
1437-Tom Swift and His Magnetic Silencer, 1941, Whit, 432p, flip pictures	10.00	35.00	70.00
1485-Tom Swift and His Giant Telescope, 1939, Whit, 432p, James Gary-a	10.00	35.00	70.00
540-Top-Line Comics (In Open Box), 1935, Whit, 164p, 3½×3½", 3 books in set, all soft-c:			
Bobby Thatcher and the Samarang Emerald	12.00	40.00	80.00
Broncho Bill in Suicide Canyon	12.00	40.00	80.00
Freckles and His Friends in the North Woods	12.00	40.00	80.00

	Good	Fine	N-Mint
Complete set with box	44.00	150.00	300.00

541-Top-Line Comics (In Open Box), 1935, Whit, 164p, 3½×3½", 3 books in set; all soft-c:

Little Joe and the City Gangsters	12.00	40.00	80.00
Smilin' Jack and His Flivver Plane			
	12.00	40.00	80.00
Streaky and the Football Signals	12.00	40.00	80.00
Complete set with box	44.00	150.00	300.00

542-Top-Line Comics (In Open Box), 1935, Whit, 164p, 3½×3½", 3 books in set; all soft-c:

Dinglehoofer Und His Dog Adolph by Knerr			
	12.00	40.00	80.00
Jungle Jim by Alex Raymond	17.00	55.00	110.00
Sappo by Segar	17.00	55.00	110.00
Complete set with box	53.00	187.50	375.00

543-Top-Line Comics (In Open Box), 1935, Whit, 164p, 3½×3½", 3 books in set; all soft-c:

Alexander Smart, ESQ by Winner	12.00	40.00	80.00
Bunky by Billy de Beck	12.00	40.00	80.00
Nicodemus O'Malley by Carter	12.00	40.00	80.00
Complete set with box	44.00	150.00	300.00

1158-Tracked by a G-Man, 1939, Sal, 400p

	5.00	17.50	35.00

L25-Trail of the Lonesome Pine, The, 1936, Lynn, movie scenes

	10.00	35.00	70.00

nn-Trail of the Terrible 6 (See Tom Mix...)

1185-Trail to Squaw Gulch, The, 1940, Sal, 400p

	5.00	17.50	35.00

720-Treasure Island, 1933, Whit. 362p

	10.00	35.00	70.00

1141-Treasure Island, 1934, Whit, 160p, 4¾×5¼", Jackie Cooper photo-c, movie scenes

	8.00	27.50	55.00

1100B-Tricks Easy to Do (Slight of hand & magic), 1938, Whit, 36p, 2½×3½", Penny Book

	2.00	6.00	12.00

1100B-Tricks You can Do, 1938, Whit, 36p, 2½×3½", Penny Book

	2.00	6.00	12.00

1104-Two-Gun Montana, 1936, Whit, 432p, Henry E. Vallely-a

	5.50	19.00	38.00

nn-Two-Gun Montana Shoots it Out, 1939, Whit, 36p, 2½×3½", Penny Book

	6.00	21.00	42.00

1058-Ugly Duckling, The (Disney), 1939, Whit, 68p, 5×5½", hard-c

	9.00	31.00	62.00

nn-Ugly Duckling, The, nd(1930s), np(Whit), 36p, 3×2½", Penny Book

	1.50	4.50	9.00

	Good	Fine	N-Mint

Unc' Billy Gets Even (See Wee Little Books)

1114-Uncle Don's Strange Adventures, 1935, Whit, 300p, radio
star-Uncle Don Carney   6.00   21.00   42.00

 722-Uncle Ray's Story of the United States, 1934, Whit, 300p
                                         7.00   25.00   50.00

1461-Uncle Sam's Sky Defenders, 1941, Whit, 432p, flip pictures
5.50   19.00   38.00

1405-Uncle Wiggily's Adventures, 1946, Whit, All Pictures
Comics   8.00   27.50   55.00

Union Pacific #1411, © Whitman Publishing Co., 1939

1411-Union Pacific, 1939, Whit, 240p, photo-c, movie scenes
                                         8.00   27.50   55.00

1189-Up Dead Horse Canyon, 1940, Sal, 400p
                                         5.00   17.50   35.00

1455-Vic Sands of the U.S. Flying Fortress Bomber Squadron,
1944, Whit, 352p   5.00   17.50   35.00

1645-Walt Disney's Andy Burnett on the Trail (TV Series), 1958,
Whit, 280p   3.00   9.00   18.00

711-10-Walt Disney's Cinderella and the Magic Wand, 1950, Whit,
2½×5", based on Disney movie   6.00   21.00   42.00

 845-Walt Disney's Donald Duck and his Cat Troubles (Disney),
1948, Whit, 100p, 5×5½", hard-c   7.00   25.00   50.00

 845-Walt Disney's Donald Duck and the Boys, 1948, Whit,
100p, 5×5½", hard-c, Barks-a   20.00   60.00   120.00

2952-Walt Disney's Donald Duck in the Great Kite Maker, 1949,
Whit, 24p, 3¼×4", Tiny Tales, full color (5 cents)
                                         5.00   17.50   35.00

 804-Walt Disney's Mickey and the Beanstalk, 1948, Whit,
hard-c   7.00   25.00   50.00

Walt Disney's Donald Duck and His Cat Troubles #845,
© Walt Disney Productions, 1948

	Good	Fine	N-Mint
2952-Walt Disney's Mickey Mouse and the Night Prowlers, Whit, 1949, 24p, 3¼×4", Tiny Tales, full color (5 cents)			
	5.00	17.50	35.00
845-Walt Disney's Mickey Mouse and the Boy Thursday, 1948, Whit, 5×5½", 100p	7.00	25.00	50.00
845-Walt Disney's Mickey Mouse the Miracle Maker, 1948, Whit, 5×5½", 100p	7.00	25.00	50.00
845-Walt Disney's Minnie Mouse and the Antique Chair, 1948, Whit, 5×5½", 100p	7.00	25.00	50.00
1435-Walt Disney's Pinocchio and Jiminy Cricket, 1940, Whit, 432p	11.50	40.00	80.00
845-Walt Disney's Poor Pluto, 1948, Whit, 5×5½", 100p, hard-c	7.00	25.00	50.00
1467-Walt Disney's Pluto the Pup (Disney), 1938, Whit, 432p, Gottfredson-a	12.50	42.00	85.00
1066-Walt Disney's Story of Clarabelle Cow (Disney), 1938, Whit, 100p	7.00	25.00	50.00
1066-Walt Disney's Story of Dippy the Goof (Disney), 1938, Whit, 100p	7.00	25.00	50.00
1066-Walt Disney's Story of Donald Duck (Disney), 1938, Whit, 100p, hard-c, Taliaferro-a	7.00	25.00	50.00
1066-Walt Disney's Story of Mickey Mouse (Disney), 1938, Whit, 100p, hard-c, Gottfredson-a, Donald Duck app.			
	7.00	25.00	50.00
1066-Walt Disney's Story of Minnie Mouse (Disney), 1938, Whit, 100p, hard-c	7.00	25.00	50.00
1066-Walt Disney's Story of Pluto the Pup, (Disney), 1938, Whit, 100p, hard-c	7.00	25.00	50.00
2952-Walter Lantz Presents Andy Panda's Rescue, 1949, Whit, Tiny Tales, full color (5 cents)	5.00	17.50	35.00

	Good	Fine	N-Mint
751-Wash Tubbs in Pandemonia, 1934, Whit, 320p, Roy Crane-a			
	8.00	27.50	55.00
1455-Wash Tubbs and Captain Easy Hunting For Whales, 1938,			
Whit, 432p, Roy Crane-a	7.00	25.00	50.00
6-Wash Tubbs in Foreign Travel, 1934, Whit, soft-c, 3½×3½",			
Tarzan Ice Cream cup premium	22.00	77.00	155.00
nn-Wash Tubbs, 1934, Whit, 52p, 4×5½", premium-no ads,			
soft-c, Roy Crane-a	12.00	42.00	85.00

Walt Disney's Story of Dippy the Goof #1066,
© Walt Disney Productions, 1938

513-Wee Little Books (In Open Box), 1934, Whit, 44p, small size,			
6 books in set			
Child's Garden of Verses	2.00	7.00	14.00
The Happy Prince (The Story of)	2.00	7.00	14.00
Joan of Arc (The Story of)	2.00	7.00	14.00
Peter Pan (The Story of)	2.50	9.00	18.00
Pied Piper Of Hamlin	2.00	7.00	14.00
Robin Hood (A Story of...)	2.00	7.00	14.00
Complete set with box	17.00	55.00	110.00
514-Wee Little Books (In Open Box), 1934, Whit, 44p, small size,			
6 books in set			
Jack And Jill	2.00	7.00	14.00
Little Bo-Peep	2.00	7.00	14.00
Little Tommy Tucker	2.00	7.00	14.00
Mother Goose	2.00	7.00	14.00
Simple Simon	2.00	7.00	14.00
Complete set with box	17.00	55.00	110.00
518-Wee Little Books (In Open Box), 1933, Whit, 44p, small size,			
6 books in set, written by Thornton Burgess			
Betty Bear's Lesson-1930	3.00	10.00	20.00

	Good	**Fine**	**N-Mint**
Jimmy Skunk's Justice-1933	3.00	10.00	20.00
Little Joe Otter's Slide-1929	3.00	10.00	20.00
Peter Rabbit's Carrots-1933	3.50	11.00	22.00
Unc' Billy Gets Even-1930	3.00	10.00	20.00
Whitefoot's Secret-1933	3.00	10.00	20.00
Complete set with box	23.00	75.00	150.00

519- Wee Little Books (In Open Box) (Bible Stories), 1934, Whit, 44p, small size, 6 books in set, Helen Janes-a

The Story of David	1.35	6.00	12.00
The Story of Gideon	1.35	6.00	12.00
The Story of Daniel	1.35	6.00	12.00
The Story of Joseph	1.35	6.00	12.00
The Story of Ruth and Naomi	1.35	6.00	12.00
The Story of Moses	1.35	6.00	12.00
Complete set with box	13.00	45.00	90.00

1471- Wells Fargo, 1938, Whit, 240p, photo-c, movie scenes
        8.50   30.00   60.00

L18- Western Frontier, 1935, Lynn, 192p, starring Ken Maynard, movie scenes   14.00   50.00   100.00

1121- West Pointers on the Gridiron, 1936, Sal, 148p, hard-c, sports book   4.50   16.00   32.00

1601- West Pointers on the Gridiron, 1936, Sal, 148p, soft-c, sports book   4.50   16.00   32.00

1124- West Point Five, The, 1937, Sal, 4¾×5¼", sports book, hard-c
        4.50   16.00   32.00

1604- West Point Five, The, 1937, Sal, 4¾×5¼", sports book, soft-c
        4.50   16.00   32.00

1164- West Point of the Air, 1935, Whit, 160p, photo-c, movie scenes   7.00   25.00   50.00

18- Westward Ho!, 1935, EVW, 160p, movie scenes, starring John Wayne (Scarce)   30.00   105.00   210.00

1109- We Three, 1935, Sal, 160p, photo-c, movie scenes, by John Barrymore, hard-c   6.00   21.00   42.00

1589- We Three, 1935, Sal, 160p, photo-c, movie scenes, by John Barrymore, soft-c   6.00   21.00   42.00

5- Wheels of Destiny, 1934, EVW, 160p, movie scenes, starring Ken Maynard   14.00   50.00   100.00

Whitefoot's Secret (See Wee Little Books)

nn- Who's Afraid of the Big Bad Wolf, "Three Little Pigs" (Disney), 1933, McKay, 36p, 6×8½", stiff-c, Disney studio-a
        22.00   77.00   155.00

nn- Wild West Adventures of Buffalo Bill, 1935, Whit. 260p, Cocomalt premium, soft-c, Hal Arbo-a
        8.50   30.00   60.00

	Good	Fine	N-Mint
1096-Will Rogers, The Story of, 1935, Sal, photo-hard-c	7.00	25.00	50.00
1576-Will Rogers, The Story of, 1935, Sal, photo-soft-c	7.00	25.00	50.00
1458-Wimpy the Hamburger Eater, 1938, Whit, 432p, E.C. Segar-a	12.00	42.00	85.00
1433-Windy Wayne and His Flying Wing, 1942, Whit, 432p, flip pictures	5.00	17.50	35.00
1131-Winged Four, The, 1937, Sal, sports book, hard-c	5.00	17.50	35.00
1407-Wings of the U.S.A., 1940, Whit, 432p, Thomas Hickey-a	5.00	17.50	35.00
nn-Winning of the Old Northwest, The, 1934, World, High Lights of History Series	5.50	19.00	38.00
1122-Winning Point, The, 1936, Sal, (Football), hard-c	4.50	13.50	27.00
1602-Winning Point, The, 1936, Sal, soft-c	4.50	13.50	27.00
710-10-Woody Woodpecker Big Game Hunter, 1950, Whit, by Walter Lantz	4.50	16.00	32.00
2010-(#10)-Woody Woodpecker-The Meteor Menace, 1967, Whit, 260p, 39 cents, hard-c, color illos	2.00	6.00	12.00
2028-Woody Woodpecker-The Sinister Signal, 1969, Whit	2.00	6.00	12.00
23-World of Monsters, The, 1935, EVW, Five Star Library, movie scenes	10.00	35.00	70.00
779-World War in Photographs, The, 1934, photo-c, photo illus.	5.50	19.00	38.00
Wyatt Earp (See Hugh O'Brian...)			
nn-Zane Grey's Cowboys of the West, 1935, Whit, 148p, 3¾x4", Tarzan Ice Cream Cup premium, soft-c, Arbo-a	22.00	77.00	155.00
Zane Grey's King of the Royal Mounted (See Men of the Mounted)			
1103-Zane Grey's King of the Royal Mounted, 1936, Whit, 432p	9.00	31.00	62.00
nn-Zane Grey's King of the Royal Mounted, 1935, Whit, 260p, Cocomalt premium, soft-c	12.00	42.00	85.00
1179-Zane Grey's King of the Royal Mounted and the Northern Treasure, 1937, Whit, 432p	8.50	30.00	60.00
1405-Zane Grey's King of the Royal Mounted the Long Arm of the Law, 1942, Whit, All Pictures Comics	8.50	30.00	60.00

	Good	Fine	N-Mint

1452-Zane Grey's King of the Royal Mounted gets His Man,
1938, Whit, 432p   8.50   30.00   60.00

**1486-Zane Grey's King of the Royal Mounted and the Great
Jewel Mystery,** 1939, Whit, 432p 8.50   30.00   60.00

5-Zane Grey's King of the Royal Mounted in the Far North,

*Zane Grey's Tex Thorne Comes Out of the West #1440,
© Stephen Slesinger, 1937*

1938, Whit, 132p, Buddy Book, soft-c
                            22.00   77.00   155.00

**nn-Zane Grey's King of the Royal Mounted in Law of the
North,** 1939, Whit, 36p, 2½×3½", Penny Book
                            6.00   21.00   42.00

**nn-Zane Grey's King of the Royal Mounted Policing the
Frozen North,** 1938, Dell, 196p, Fast-Action Story, soft-c
                            18.00   62.50   125.00

1440-Zane Grey's Tex Thorne Comes Out of the West, 1937,
Whit, 432p   5.00   17.50   35.00

1465-Zip Saunders King of the Speedway, 1939, 432p, Weisman-a
                            5.00   17.50   35.00

Character &
Premium
Rings

Foreword
By Bob Hritz

"The tolling of the tower bell" and "drone of a plane"; the magic word "Shazam," a clap of thunder and bolt of lightning; "who knows what evil lurks in the hearts of men?": These opening phrases of yesteryear's heroes left an indelible mark on the minds of countless children.

Every character from radio programs, pulps, comic books, movies and serials became a part of the lives of thousands of Americans. Needless to say, the producers and sponsors also were aware of America's love affair with these imaginary heroes. Their connection was making sure we remained loyal to the character and the product—and, what better way than to provide a simple device to guarantee this—The Ring! A small item that was worn was certainly the most astonishingly clever marketing devise ever created. The ring provided the sponsor with the demographics it needed to find its place in the market as well as targeting a group for future product sales. Today, it costs companies millions to find out the same information. Being the first kid on the block to display this new treasure was undoubtedly this week's claim to fame. "How do I get one?" was repeated over and over and the marketing hook was taken. An advertising genius never had the power of persuasion that any child possesses. We raced to the corner to get a copy of that special comic, urged mom and dad to use only "clean buring Blue Coal" in the furnace, nagged for more boxes of instant Ralston, and argued the health value of "nutritious, delicious, Ovaltine." How else could a sponsor place a sales representative in every home? Not only were boys & girls sales reps, but they also learned the value of work. It took all day to mow a lawn with the push mower to earn 50 cents to send for a Blue Coal Shadow glow in the dark ring and a Green Hornet secret compartment seal ring.

We can look back on these rings with more than fondness. If you doubt this, how can you explain their survival? These treasures of childhood were placed carefully in our special boxes and bags to avoid the ultimate demise of premiums—mom throwing them away. They survived teen years, dating, and even raising our own families. Today, the collector awaits the mail anxiously for his newest rings purchased from fellow collectors. The thrill rivals that of his childhood. Going through a portfolio of investments never brought forth the flashes of excitement and wonderful memories that handling one of these rings can. Today's ring collector pursues his hobby with no less zeal than when he first wanted one way back then. And he's not alone.

Special Advisors
John Snyder, Bob Hritz, Ed Pragler, Steve Geppi, Bruce Rosen, Robert Hall, Art Thomas, Steve Ison, Harry Matetsky

Introduction

Listed on the following pages is the most comprehensive list of rings ever assembled. As you will note, every major radio, T.V., movie and comic character star was honored with his own personalized rings. The premium and store bought items created a desire for the child to listen to and watch many programs and cartoons offered by sponsors of various products. Even today this marketing approach still works. Many rings are offered each year to attract new collectors in this market. For instance, DC recently produced the Superman magnet and Green Lantern squirt rings. Matchbox developed a beautiful set of 68 rings called the ''Ring Raiders'' and Mattel produced a popular series called ''Polly Pockets'' with its own styled ring box. Many cereal boxes are adorned with offers for rings. Teenage Mutant Ninja Turtles cereal offered 8 different rings. Lucky Charms displayed the Lucky Horseshoe ring and King Vitamin also got into the act with the offering of the Hologram ring. Kelloggs Sugar Corn Pops offered a set of 28 football insignia rings—a classic set of metal beauties. Disney offered a set of 5 different stamp rings featuring Minnie Mouse in 1991. Thousands of collectors are eagerly waiting each year for new offerings to add to their collections.

This prompted Overstreet Publications to develop the following reference and price report. We hope it will provide up-to-date information in this new and exciting part of collecting comic related memorabilia. A special thanks to all who helped in the compilation of this unique listing of these wonderful little toys—the rings!

A WORD ABOUT GRADE AND ITS RELATION TO VALUE:
The rare rings usually sell for high prices, regardless of condition, as long as they are complete with all parts. Perfect examples would sell for more if the collector had a choice of condition, but in most cases, these rings are rarely offered for sale. The collector is lucky just to find an example in any condition. The top ten rings are very rare with only 2 to 10 copies of each known to exist.

On the other hand, condition plays a larger role in terms of the price spread on the more common rings. Complete rings in lower grades can be worth as much as 2 to 3 times less than in Mint condition. The two retail values listed in this section are for rings in good and near mint condition.

TOP 10 MOST VALUABLE

VALUE	RANK	& RING TYPE
$100,000	1	Supermen Of America (prize)(comic books)
$70,000	2	Superman Secret Compartment (candy)
$70,000	2	Superman Secret Compartment (gum)
$15,000	4	Radio Orphan Annie Altascope
$15,000	4	Superman Tim
$14,000	6	Operator Five
$9,000	7	Spider
$6,000	8	Cisco Kid Secret Compartment
$5,500	9	Valric The Viking
$5,000	10	Howdy Doody Jack in Box

2ND TOP TEN

VALUE	RANK	AND RING TYPE
$5,000	10	Tom Mix Deputy
$4,500	12	Lone Ranger Meteorite
$4,000	13	Radio Orphan Annie Magnifying
$4,000	13	Radio Orphan Annie Initial
$3,500	15	Frank Buck Black Leopard (W. Fair)
$3,000	16	Lone Ranger (ice cream)
$2,500	17	Frank Buck Black Leopard (bronze)
$2,400	18	Buck Rogers Sylvania Bulb
$2,000	19	Captain Marvel
$2,000	19	Captain Midnight Mystic Sun God

3RD TOP TEN

VALUE	RANK	& RING TYPE
$2,000	19	Tonto (ice cream)
$2,000	19	Buck Rogers Repeller Ray
$1,800	23	Knights of Columbus
$1,600	24	Green Hornet (plastic)
$1,500	25	Quisp Figural
$1,500	25	Dick Tracy Monogram
$1,500	25	Lone Ranger Photo (test)
$1,500	25	Frank Buck Black Leopard (silver)
$1,500	25	Joe Louis Face
$1,500	25	Quisp Figural

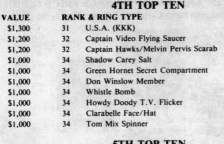

4TH TOP TEN

VALUE	RANK & RING TYPE	
$1,300	31	U.S.A. (KKK)
$1,200	32	Captain Video Flying Saucer
$1,200	32	Captain Hawks/Melvin Pervis Scarab
$1,000	34	Shadow Carey Salt
$1,000	34	Green Hornet Secret Compartment
$1,000	34	Don Winslow Member
$1,000	34	Whistle Bomb
$1,000	34	Howdy Doody T.V. Flicker
$1,000	34	Clarabelle Face/Hat
$1,000	34	Tom Mix Spinner

5TH TOP TEN

VALUE	RANK & RING TYPE	
$1,000	34	Radio Orphan Annie Triple Mystery
$1,000	34	Barnabas Collins (Dark Shadows)
$850	43	Captain Video Pendant
$850	43	Buck Rogers Ring of Saturn
$800	45	Sky King Aztec
$800	45	Captain Midnight Signet
$800	45	Space Patrol Cosmic Glow
$800	45	Ted Williams Baseball
$800	45	Jack Armstrong Crocodile
$800	45	Roy Rogers Hat

NOTE: Prices vary widely on the top 20 rings due to rarity. Rings complete in original box with instructions can be worth up to double the list value.

If you have additional rings not listed, please send information to:

Overstreet Publications, Inc.
780 Hunt Cliff Dr. NW, Cleveland, TN 37311

CHARACTER AND PREMIUM RINGS PRICE GUIDE
(Prices listed represent Good and Near Mint condition)

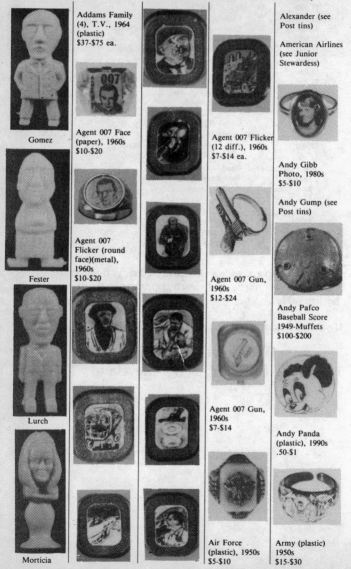

Addams Family (4), T.V., 1964 (plastic) $37-$75 ea.

Gomez

Agent 007 Face (paper), 1960s $10-$20

Agent 007 Flicker (round face)(metal), 1960s $10-$20

Fester

Lurch

Morticia

Agent 007 Flicker (12 diff.), 1960s $7-$14 ea.

Agent 007 Gun, 1960s $12-$24

Agent 007 Gun, 1960s $7-$14

Air Force (plastic), 1950s $5-$10

Alexander (see Post tins)

American Airlines (see Junior Stewardess)

Andy Gibb Photo, 1980s $5-$10

Andy Gump (see Post tins)

Andy Pafco Baseball Score 1949-Muffets $100-$200

Andy Panda (plastic), 1990s .50-$1

Army (plastic) 1950s $15-$30

Arthur Godfrey
Photo, 1950s
$10-$20

Atlanta Crackers
1954
$25-$50

Babe Ruth
(plastic),
Kellogg's, 1949
$25-$50

Babe Ruth (gold),
Muffets, 1934
$150-$300

Barnabas Collins
(Dark Shadows,
T.V.), Gum, 1969
$500-$1000

Baseball Centen-
nial (see Jack
Armstrong)

Baseball-
Cincinatti Reds
1970s
$10-$20

Baseball logos
1960-plastic, 15
red, 15 blue, 15
white, Post, '60s
$20-$40 ea.

Baseball Game
(pin ball),
Kellogg's, 1949
$150-$300

Basketball, metal
base, 1960s
$50-$100

Bat Signal (Dia-
mond Comics
Distr.), 14k gold
w/diamond chips
(25 made), 1992
$375-$750

Bat Signal (Dia-
mond Comics
Distr.), silver
(550 made)
1992
$100-$200

Batman
(flicker)(set of
12), 1966
(silver base)
$10-$20 ea.

Batman (flicker)
1966 (blue base)
$10-$20 ea.

Batman (metal) (3-diff.), 1960s
$10-$20 ea.

Batman Paper Disc, 1960s
$25-$50

Batman (rubber bat, glow-in-dark) (blue, red, black), '70s
$25-$50

Batman Logo Nestle's (blue) 1980s
$25-$50 ea.

Batman Logo Nestle's (red) 1980s
$25-$50

Batman Party (plastic), 1982
$1-$2

Batman (plastic bat), 1970s
$10-$20

Bazooka Joe Baseball, 1950s
$30-$60

Bazooka Joe Printing Stamp, 1940s
$60-$120

George

John

Paul

Ringo

Beatles Flicker (set of 4), 1966
$5-$10

Betty Boop (12 on card, generic) 1990s, $10-$20 (set)

Betty Grable Photo, 1950
$15-$30

Billy The Kid Saddle, 1940
$60-$120

Billy West Club, 1940 (see Tom Mix Circus)
$50-$100

Bing Crosby Photo, 1950s
$20-$40

Black Flame (Hi Speed Gas), 1930s
$125-$250

Bob Hope Photo, 1950
$20-$40

Boy Scout (silver), 1940a
$25-$50

Bozo's Circus 1960s
$50-$100

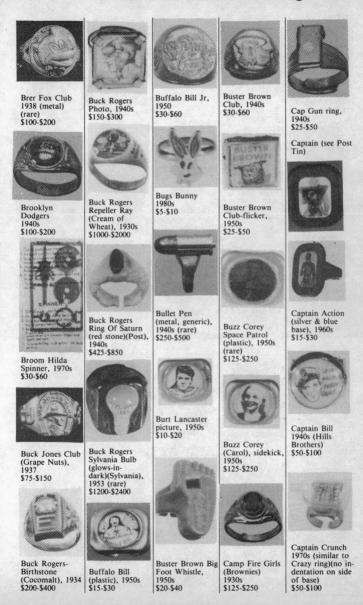

Brer Fox Club 1938 (metal) (rare) $100-$200

Buck Rogers Photo, 1940s $150-$300

Buffalo Bill Jr, 1950 $30-$60

Buster Brown Club, 1940s $30-$60

Cap Gun ring, 1940s $25-$50

Captain (see Post Tin)

Brooklyn Dodgers 1940s $100-$200

Buck Rogers Repeller Ray (Cream of Wheat), 1930s $1000-$2000

Bugs Bunny 1980s $5-$10

Buster Brown Club-flicker, 1950s $25-$50

Broom Hilda Spinner, 1970s $30-$60

Buck Rogers Ring Of Saturn (red stone)(Post), 1940s $425-$850

Bullet Pen (metal, generic), 1940s (rare) $250-$500

Buzz Corey Space Patrol (plastic), 1950s (rare) $125-$250

Captain Action (silver & blue base), 1960s $15-$30

Buck Jones Club (Grape Nuts), 1937 $75-$150

Buck Rogers Sylvania Bulb (glows-in-dark)(Sylvania), 1953 (rare) $1200-$2400

Burt Lancaster picture, 1950s $10-$20

Buzz Corey (Carol), sidekick, 1950s $125-$250

Captain Bill 1940s (Hills Brothers) $50-$100

Buck Rogers-Birthstone (Cocomalt), 1934 $200-$400

Buffalo Bill (plastic), 1950s $15-$30

Buster Brown Big Foot Whistle, 1950s $20-$40

Camp Fire Girls (Brownies) 1930s $125-$250

Captain Crunch 1970s (similar to Crazy ring)(no indentation on side of base) $50-$100

Captain Hawks Air Hawks, 1930s $75-$150

Captain Midnight Flight Commander, Ovaltine, 1941 $200-$400

Captain Midnight Marine Corps (Ovaltine), 1942 $200-$400

Captain Planet (6 diff.), 1990s $5-$10 ea.

Captain Video Pendant, 1950s (rare) $425-$850

Captain Hawks Secret Scarab, 1937 (rare, Post Bran Flakes), same as Melvin Purvis Secret Scarab (green top) $600-$1200

Captain Midnight Flight Commander Signet (Ovaltine), 1957 $400-$800

Captain Midnight Mystic Sun God (Ovaltine) 1947 $1000-$2000

Captain Planet Sound Ring 1991 $12-$25

Captain Video photo, 1940s $175-$350

Captain Midnight Game?, 1940s $50-$100

Captain Midnight Secret Compartment (Ovaltine), 1942 $75-$150

Captain Hawks Sky Patrol, 1930s $75-$150

Captain Midnight Initial Printing (Ovaltine), 1948 $250-$500

Captain Video Flying Saucer (gold & silver base versions), 2 saucers, one glows in dark, 1940s (rare) $600-$1200

Captain Marvel, 1940s (rare) $1000-$2000

Captain Midnight Whirlwind Whistle (Ovaltine), 1941 $250-$500

Captain Midnight (red V), Skelly Oil, 1940s $100-$200

Captain Midnight Look Around (Ovaltine), 1942 (same as L. Ranger & ROA Mystic Eye) $75-$150

Captain Video Flying Saucer (view of base) $100-$200

Captain Video Secret Seal (copper top), 1940s $300-$600

Captain Video Secret Seal (gold top), 1940s
$250-$500

Charles Starrett photo, 1950s (square)(cereal)
$20-$40

Chicago White Sox (aluminum), 1960s
$10-$20

Cisco Kid Hat, 1950s (rare)
$300-$600

Cleveland Indians, 1950s
$30-$60

Carrot Ring (3), 1960s
$5-$10

Casper (see Post Tin)

Charles Starrett Photo, 1950s (round)(store)
$10-$20

Chief Wahoo (Goudy Gum), 1941
$100-$200

Cisco Kid Saddle, 1950 (rare)
$250-$500

Clyde Beatty Lions Head (Quaker Crackles), 1930s (rare)
$200-$400

Charlie Chaplin, 1940s (rare)
$100-$200

China Clipper (Quaker), 1936
$50-$100

Cisco Kid Secret Compartment, 1950s (rare)
$3000-$6000

Cocomalt Compass, 1936
$25-$50

Compass (see Black Flame, Cocomalt, Davy Crockett, Nabisco & Wheaties)

Casper-Flasher (2 diff.), 1960s
$10-$20

Charlie McCarthy 1940s (metal)
$200-$400

Circus-Lucky Horseshoe, 1940s
$30-$60

Clarabelle Face/Hat, 1950s (rare)
$500-$1000

Compass ring, 1950s
$30-$60

Casper (plastic), 1950s
$25-$50

Charlie McCarthy Photo, 1950s
$10-$20

Cisco Kid Club 1950 (gold & silver versions)
$150-$300

Clarabelle Horn, 1950s
$200-$400

Cousin Eerie, Warren, 1960s (gold metal)
$40-$80

Cowboy Boot
(see Goudy--)

Cowboy Hat (see
Goudy--)

Cowboy Riding
Horse, 1950s
(silver & gold versions) (gumball)
$10-$20

Cowboy Riding
Horse, 1950s
(silver)
$5-$10

Crazy Rings (See
Quaker--)

Daffy Duck
(Arby's, 10 diff.)
1987
$10-$20

Dagwood (See
Post Tin)

Daniel Boone
(plastic),1960s
$10-$20

Dark Shadows
(see Barnabas
Collins)

Davey Adams
(Lava)(siren),
1940
$200-$400

Davy Crockett
(blue enamel),
1950s
$50-$100

Davy Crockett
(green enamel),
1950s
$50-$100

Davy Crockett
Compass, elastic
band, 1950s
$150-$300

Davy Crockett
Face (raised)
(plastic, yellow,
red), 1950s
$30-$60

Davy Crockett
Face (raised)
1950s
$30-$60

Davy Crockett
Face (raised)
(silver), 1960s
$20-$40

Davy Crockett
Face (square)
(brass), 1950s
$30-$60

Davy Crockett
Face (metal),
1950s
$40-$80

Davy Crockett
Face (metal)
1950s
$40-$60

Davy Crockett
Fess Parker
figure photo
1960s
$30-$60

Davy Crockett
Fess Parker head
photo
1960s
$30-$60

Davy Crockett
Figure, 1960s
$15-$30

Davy Crockett
Figure, 1960s
$15-$30

Davy Crockett
Figure (silver)
1950s
$30-$60

Davy Crockett
Figure (silver)
(oval), 1950s
$30-$60

Davy Crockett
Flasher, T.V.
Screen (rare),
1950s
$250-$500

Davy Crockett
Head (bronze)
(plastic), 1950s
$30-$60

Davy Crockett
Head (silver)
(plastic), 1950s
$30-$60

Davy Crockett
Head (gold)
(plastic), 1950s
$30-$60

Davy Crockett Rifle (silver or bronze), 1950s
$30-$60

Dennis O'Keefe Photo, 1950s
$10-$20

Devil Dog (movie), Quaker, 1938
$75-$150

Dick Tracy Crimestoppers, 1991
$25-$50

Dick Tracy Hat 1930s (var. exists w/enamel hat)
$150-$300

Dick Tracy Monogram, 1930s (rare)
$750-$1500

Dick Tracy Secret Compartment, 1940s
$250-$500

Dinosaurs (5 diff.), 1970s
$2-$4 ea.

Disney (Sugarjets) (9 diff.), 1950s
$40-$80 ea.

Dixie (Hanna-Barbara), aluminum, 1960s
$15-$30

Dizzy Dean Winners (Post Grapenuts), 1936
$75-$150

Dizzy Dean (Win With) (Post Grapenuts), 1930s
$80-$160

Doctor Doolittle Flasher, 1970s
$10-$20

Don Winslow Member (Kelloggs), 1938
$500-$1000

Donald Duck (with Pep box), 1949
$200-$400

Donald Duck (sterling, color & plain, round & square top, glow-in-dark), 1950s
$50-$100

Donald Duck (square top, glow-in-dark), (color & plain) 1950s
$50-$100

Donald Duck Big Face, 1980s
$2-$4

Donald Duck Good Luck Portrait, 1950s
$50-$100

Donald Duck Small Face (2 diff.), 1990s
$5-$10

Dukes of Hazzard (Hazzard County Police) (plastic), 1983
$50-$100

Elsie The Cow (plastic), 1950s
$15-$30

Donald Duck, sterling, square, no color, 1950s
$50-$100

Baby Donald, 1980s
$3-$6

Ed Sullivan Photo, 1950s
$10-$20

Elvis Flicker, 1960s
$60-$120

Finger Fighters (3 diff.) 1989
$5-$10

Donald Duck Figure, 1990s
$5-$10

Dorothy Hart, 1940s
$150-$300

Eddie Fisher Photo, 1950s
$10-$20

E.T. Face (movie, 1980s)
$50-$100

Felix (see Post Tin)

Donald Duck Full Figure, with color, 1940s
$125-$250

Douglas DC-6 (cereal), 1950s
$30-$60

Fireball Twigg 1948, Post's Grape Nuts (see Sundial Shoes)
$30-$60

Fish (see Sword In The Stone)

Flash Gordon (see Post Tin)

Donald Duck (gold & silver face versions), 1980s
$3-$6

Douglas F-3D Sky Knight, (cereal), 1950s
$30-$60

Elizabeth Taylor Photo, 1940s
$25-$50

Felix Face, 1970s
$10-$20

Flight Commander (generic), 1940s
$50-$100

Douglas MacArthur Photo, 1950s
$15-$30

Elmer Fudd Flasher, 1950s
$2-$5

Felix Flicker (3 diff.), 1960s
$5-$10 ea.

Flying Saucer (see Capt. Video & Wheaties)

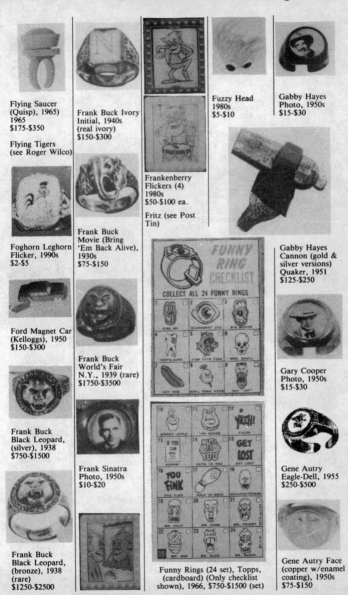

Flying Saucer
(Quisp), 1965)
1965
$175-$350

Flying Tigers
(see Roger Wilco)

Foghorn Leghorn
Flicker, 1990s
$2-$5

Ford Magnet Car
(Kelloggs), 1950
$150-$300

Frank Buck
Black Leopard,
(silver), 1938
$750-$1500

Frank Buck
Black Leopard,
(bronze), 1938
(rare)
$1250-$2500

Frank Buck Ivory
Initial, 1940s
(real ivory)
$150-$300

Frank Buck
Movie (Bring
'Em Back Alive),
1930s
$75-$150

Frank Buck
World's Fair
N.Y., 1939 (rare)
$1750-$3500

Frank Sinatra
Photo, 1950s
$10-$20

Frankenberry
Flickers (4)
1980s
$50-$100 ea.

Fritz (see Post
Tin)

FUNNY
RING
CHECKLIST

COLLECT ALL 24 FUNNY RINGS

Funny Rings (24 set), Topps,
(cardboard) (Only checklist
shown), 1966, $750-$1500 (set)

Fuzzy Head
1980s
$5-$10

Gabby Hayes
Photo, 1950s
$15-$30

Gabby Hayes
Cannon (gold &
silver versions)
Quaker, 1951
$125-$250

Gary Cooper
Photo, 1950s
$15-$30

Gene Autry
Eagle-Dell, 1955
$250-$500

Gene Autry Face
(copper w/enamel
coating), 1950s
$75-$150

Gene Autry Face
(copper), 1950s
$75-$150

Gene Autry
Photo, 1950s
$15-$30

G-Man Club,
1930s
$20-$40

Goudy Gum
Cowboy Hat,
1940s
$30-$60

Green Hornet
Rubber, 1966
$10-$20

Gene Autry Face
(Aluminum w/
gold face, 1950s
$75-$150

Gene Kelly
Photo, 1940s
$$20-$40

G-Men (name in
G), 1930s
$25-$50

Goudy Gum In-
dian, 1940s
$75-$150

Green Hornet
Seal, 1966
$20-$40

Gene Autry Face
(silver), 1950s
$75-$150

Gene Tunney
(plastic), 1950s
$20-$40

G-Men (name
below G), 1930s
$30-$60

Green Beret
(movie), 1970s
$10-$20

Green Hornet
Secret Compart-
ment, General
Mills, 1947
$500-$1000

Gene Autry Flag-
Dell, 1950s, gold
& silver versions
$75-$150

Genie Squirt
Ring, 1990s
$2-$4

Golden Nugget
Cave (casino),
1950s (rare)
(see Straight
Arrow Nugget)
$200-$400

Green Hornet
Flicker (12 diff.),
1960s
$10-$20 ea.

Green Lantern
Glow-in-dark,
1992 comic
giveaway
$2-$4

Gene Autry Nail
on Card, 1950
$100-$200

G.I. Joe, 1982
$50-$100

Goudy Gum
Cowboy Boot,
1940s
$30-$60

Green Hornet
Plastic, 1930s
(rare)
$800-$1600

Green Lantern
Squirt, 1980s
$12-$24

Have Gun Will Travel (Paladin), (white & black top versions) T.V., 1960s $30-$60

Henry (see Post Tin)

Henry The Chicken Hawk 1990s $2-$5

Hills Brothers (see Captain Bill)

Hopalong Cassidy Bar 20 (brass), 1950s $30-$60

Horseshoe (see Tiger Eye)

Hopalong Cassidy Bar 20 (silver), 1950s $30-$60

Gumby, 1980s (7 diff.) $5-$10 ea.

Hans (see Post Tin)

Harold Teen (see Post Tin)

Hopalong Cassidy Compass/Hat, 1950s $100-$200

Hopalong Cassidy Photo, 1950s $30-$60

Hopalong Cassidy Steer Head, ring/slide, 1950s (rare) $250-$500

Howdy Doody Flashlight, 1950s $100-$200

Howdy Doody Poll Parrot Flicker, 1950s $15-$30

Buffalo Bee

Buffalo Bob

Chief Thunderthud

Clarabelle

Flubadub

Howdy Doody

Mr. Bluster

Princess

Howdy Doody Flicker (8), 1950s $15-$30 ea.

Howdy Doody Glow Photo, 1950s $75-$150

Howdy Doody Insert (red base), 1950s $75-$150

Howdy Doody Jack In Box, 1950s (rare) $2500-$5000

Howdy Doody
Raised Face
(white & silver
base versions)
1950s
$75-$150

Howdy Doody
T.V., 1950s (rare)
$500-$1000

H.R. Puff 'n
Stuff (7 diff.),
1970s
$30-$60 ea.

Huckleberry
Hound Club,
1960s
$50-$100

Huckleberry
Hound-
aluminum, 1960s
$15-$30

Huskies Club,
cereal, 1936
(rare)
$200-$400

Ice Maiden
Magnet, 1990s
$3-$6

Ingred Bergman
Photo, 1950s
$10-$20

Inspector (see
Post Tin)

Jack Armstrong
Crocodile (green
stone), 1940s
$400-$800

Jack Armstrong
Egyptian Whistle,
1940s
$50-$100

Jack Armstrong
100 Anniversary
Baseball, 1930s
(rare)
$290-$580

Jack Benny
Photo, 1950s
$10-$20

Jack Kramer
(plastic, orange
top, brown base)
& (blue top,
green base),
1950s
$20-$40

Jackie Gleason
Photo, 1950s
$20-$40

Jackie Kennedy
Photo, 1960s
$5-$10

James Bond (see
Agent 007)

Jiggs (see Post
Tin)

Jimmy Allen Fly-
ing Club, 1930s
$50-$100

Jimmy Durante
Photo, 1950s
$10-$20

Jinx (Hanna-
Barbera),
aluminum, 1960s
$15-$30

Joanne Dru,
1950s
$10-$20

Joe Dimaggio
Club, 1940s
$150-$300

Joe E. Brown,
1940s
$50-$100

Joe Louis Face,
1940s (rare)
$750-$1500

Joe Louis Photo,
1940s
$40-$80

Joe Penner Face
Puzzle, 1940s
(rare)
$225-$450

Joel McCrae
Photo, 1950s
$10-$20

John Kennedy Photo, 1960s $5-$10

Junior Pilot, 1955 $10-$20

Henry

Kit Carson T.V. 1950s (rare) $100-$200

John Wayne Photo, 1940s $25-$50

Junior Stewardess, (American Airlines), 1955 (metal) $10-$20

Inspector

Knights of Columbus, radio, 1940s (rare) $900-$1800

John Wayne Photo, 1950s $25-$50

Captain

Jiggs

John Wayne Rectangle, 1950s $50-$100

Felix

Maggie

Kolonel Keds (see U.S. Keds) 1950s $30-$60

June Allyson Photo, 1950s $10-$20

Fritz

Mama

King Comics (set 20), 1953 $20-$40 ea.

Kool Aid Treasure, 1930s $55-$110

Junior Fire Marshal, 1950s $25-$50

Hans

King Vitamin Hologram, 1970s $120-$240

Lassie Face, 1950s $80-$160

Laughin Flicker (7 diff.), 1970s $10-$20 ea.

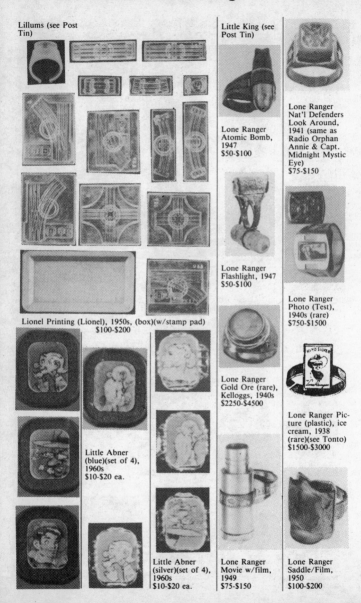

Lillums (see Post Tin)

Lionel Printing (Lionel), 1950s, (box)(w/stamp pad) $100-$200

Little Abner (blue)(set of 4), 1960s $10-$20 ea.

Little Abner (silver)(set of 4), 1960s $10-$20 ea.

Little King (see Post Tin)

Lone Ranger Atomic Bomb, 1947 $50-$100

Lone Ranger Flashlight, 1947 $50-$100

Lone Ranger Gold Ore (rare), Kelloggs, 1940s $2250-$4500

Lone Ranger Movie w/film, 1949 $75-$150

Lone Ranger Nat'l Defenders Look Around, 1941 (same as Radio Orphan Annie & Capt. Midnight Mystic Eye) $75-$150

Lone Ranger Photo (Test), 1940s (rare) $750-$1500

Lone Ranger Picture (plastic), ice cream, 1938 (rare)(see Tonto) $1500-$3000

Lone Ranger Saddle/Film, 1950 $100-$200

Lone Ranger Seal
Print Face, 1940s
$150-$300

*Lone Ranger
Secret Com-
partment-Air
Force, 1942
$375-$750

*Lone Ranger
Secret
Compartment-
Army, 1940s
$375-$750

*Lone Ranger
Secret
Compartment-
Marines, 1940s
$375-$750

*Lone Ranger
Secret
Compartment-
Navy, 1940s
$375-$750

Lone Ranger Six
Shooter, 1947
$75-$150

*(Includes photos of Silver & Lone
Ranger. Beware of repro photos.

Lone Ranger
Weather, 1947
$50-$100

Lone Wolf (see
Thunderbird)

Lone Wolf
Tribal, Wrigley,
silver, 1932
$100-$200

Lucky Buddha
1940s
$25-$50

Lucky Charms
Horseshoe
(boys), 1985
$60-$120

Lucky Charms
Initial (girls),
1985
$75-$150

Lucky Horseshoe
(see Circus--)

Lucky Skull
(see Montrose--)

McDonalds Big
Mac, 1970s
$5-$10

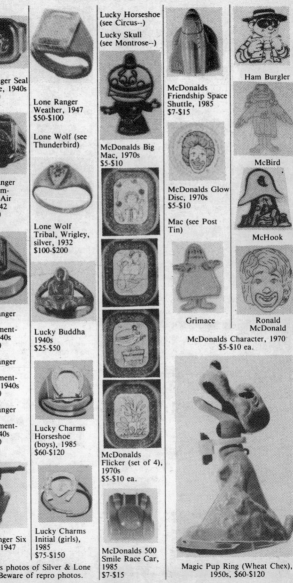

McDonalds
Flicker (set of 4),
1970s
$5-$10 ea.

McDonalds 500
Smile Race Car,
1985
$7-$15

McDonalds
Friendship Space
Shuttle, 1985
$7-$15

McDonalds Glow
Disc, 1970s
$5-$10

Mac (see Post
Tin)

Grimace

Ham Burger

McBird

McHook

Ronald
McDonald

McDonalds Character, 1970
$5-$10 ea.

Magic Pup Ring (Wheat Chex),
1950s, $60-$120

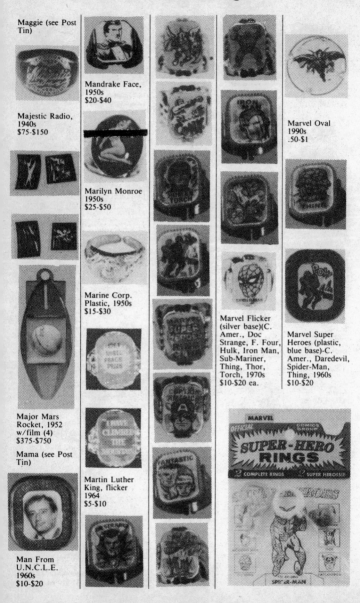

Maggie (see Post Tin)

Majestic Radio, 1940s
$75-$150

Mandrake Face, 1950s
$20-$40

Marilyn Monroe 1950s
$25-$50

Marine Corp. Plastic, 1950s
$15-$30

Major Mars Rocket, 1952 w/film (4)
$375-$750

Mama (see Post Tin)

Martin Luther King, flicker 1964
$5-$10

Man From U.N.C.L.E. 1960s
$10-$20

Marvel Flicker (silver base)(C. Amer., Doc Strange, F. Four, Hulk, Iron Man, Sub-Mariner, Thing, Thor, Torch, 1970s
$10-$20 ea.

Marvel Oval 1990s
.50-$1

Marvel Super Heroes (plastic, blue base)-C. Amer., Daredevil, Spider-Man, Thing, 1960s
$10-$20

Melvin Purvis
Secret Operator
(Post), 1936
$75-$150

Mickey Mouse
Figure (color)
1980s
$5-$10

Mickey Mouse
15th Anniversary,
1980s
$50-$100

Mets Baseball
1970s (metal)
$30-$60

Mickey Mouse
Figure Mounted
1950s
$10-$20

Mickey with
stone, 1990s
$5-$10

Mickey Mouse
Club Flicker,
1950s
$25-$50

Mickey Mouse
Gold Face, 1980s
(in box)
$30-$60

Milton Berle
Photo, 1950s
$15-$30

Marvel Super-
Hero (on card)
(3 card sets with
2 rings per card)
1980s
$30-$60

Variant with 4
rings per card
$50-$100

Melvin Purvis G-
Man, Post, 1937
$25-$50

Mickey Mouse
Face (color)
1960s
$5-$10

Mickey Mouse
Silver Face,
1980s
$20-$40

Minnie Mouse
Face (Oval),
1950s
$10-$20

Melvin Purvis
Birthstone, 1930s
$75-$150

Melvin Purvis
Secret Scarab,
Post, 1937
(same as Capt.
Hawks Secret
Scarab)(rare)
$600-$1200

Mickey Mouse
Face Ornament
1990s
$5-$10

Mickey Mouse
Small Black
Figure, 1980s
(silver & gold
versions)
$5-$10

Minnie Mouse
Stamp (5 diff.),
1990s
$5-$10 ea.

Mister Softee Face, 1950s $25-$50

Model Airplane Club, 1940s $50-$100

David

Mike

Peter

Monkees Flicker (3), 1960s $20-$40

Monkees Flicker (4 heads), 1960s $20-$40

Monster Flicker (Set 3), 1950s $15-$30 ea.

Montrose Lucky Skull, 1940s $50-$100

Mr. Magoo, 1960s $20-$40

Mr. Peanut, 1950s $40-$80

Munster Flickers (Set 4), 1960s $20-$40 ea.

Mutant Ninja Turtles (see Teenage--)

Nabisco Compass, 1950s (gold w/red dial) $25-$50

National Baseball, 1950s $50-$100

Atlanta Falcons

Buffalo Bills

Chicago Bears

Cin. Bengals

Clev. Browns

Dallas Cowboys

Denver Broncos

Detroit Lions

Gr.Bay Packers

Houston Oilers

Ind. Colts

Kan.City Chiefs

L.A. Rams

Miami Dolphins

Phoenix Card.

NY Yankee
(aluminum),
1970s
$10-$20

Olive Oyl (see
Post Tin)

Ovaltine Signet,
1937
$25-$50

Paladin (see Have
Gun Will Travel)

Peter Paul
Weather, 1950s
$25-$50

Minn. Vikings

Pitts. Steelers

Olympic Ring
1950s
$30-$60

Pan American
Clipper
(cereal), 1950s
$30-$60

PF Flyer Decoder
1949
$20-$40

Phantom (see
Post Tin)

N. Eng. Patriots

S.F. 49'ers

Operator 5, Pulp,
1934 (rare)
$7,000-$14,000

Orphan Annie
(see Post Tin &
Radio--)

Paul Winchell &
Jerry Mahoney
Photo, 1950s
$15-$30

Perry Winkle (see
Post Tin)

Phantom
(plastic), 1950s
$20-$40

N. Or. Saints

Seat. Seahawks

N.Y. Giants

Tampa Bay
Buccaneers

Oscar Meyer
Weiner (plastic,
red & yellow)
$10-$20

Peter Paul Face,
1950s
$10-$20

Pharoah, 1950s
$25-$50

N.Y. Jets

Wash. Redskins

NFL Football
Logo (28 diff.),
Kelloggs
$20-$40 ea.

Ovaltine Bir-
thstone, 1930s
(same as ROA
Birthstone)
$100-$200

Peter Paul Glow-
In-Dark Secret
Compartment,
1940s
$175-$350

Pinocchio Nose,
1940s
$200-$400

Oak. Raiders

Pirate Glow Skull, 1940s
$25-$50

Pirate Skull, Carribean (Disney), 1980s
$10-$20

Pluto (colored & plain), International, silver, 1950s
$50-$100

Pocahontas, 1960s
$10-$20

Poll Parrot Face (gold & silver versions), 1950s
$20-$40

Polly Pocket (10 diff.), 1990s
$2-$4 ea.

Polly Pocket Throne, 1990s
$10-$20

Popeye (see Post Tin)

Popeye, 1960s
$10-$20

Popeye Flicker (4 diff.), 1960s
$10-$20 ea.

Popsicle Boot with paper code, 1951
$50-$100

Popsicle Skull, red eyes (silver), 1940s
$50-$100

Porky Pig (hand painted) (metal), 1970
$7-$14

Porky Pig Flasher, 1950s
$2-$5

Post Tin Rings- (rare unbent with no rust). 1948, 1949 (priced below)

Alexander
$5-$25

Andy Gump
$5-$25

Captain, $5-$25

Casper, $5-$25

Casper, $5-$25

Dagwood, $10-$50

Dick Tracy, $20-$100

Felix The Cat, $20-$100

Flash Gordon, $20-$100

Fritz, $5-$25

Hans, $5-$25

Mama, $5-$25

Harold Teen, $5-$25

Olive Oyl, $10-$50

Henry, $5-$25

Orphan Annie, $10-$50

Herby

Perry Winkle, $5-$25

Inspector, $5-$25

Phantom, $20-$100

Jiggs, $5-$25

Popeye, $20-$100

Lillums, $5-$25

Little King, $10-$50

Mac, $5-$25

Maggie, $5-$25

Roy Rogers, $8-$40

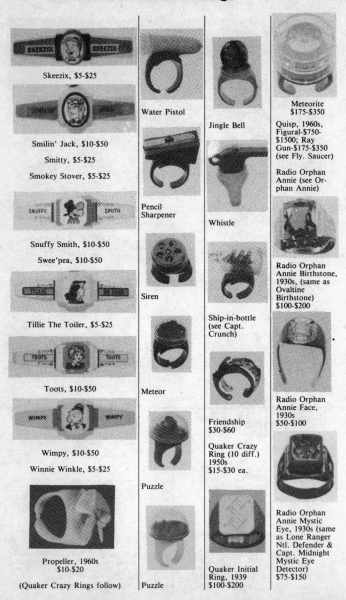

Skeezix, $5-$25

Water Pistol

Jingle Bell

Meteorite
$175-$350

Smilin' Jack, $10-$50

Smitty, $5-$25

Smokey Stover, $5-$25

Quisp, 1960s,
Figural-$750-
$1500; Ray
Gun-$175-$350
(see Fly. Saucer)

Radio Orphan
Annie (see Or-
phan Annie)

Pencil
Sharpener

Whistle

Snuffy Smith, $10-$50

Swee'pea, $10-$50

Radio Orphan
Annie Birthstone,
1930s, (same as
Ovaltine
Birthstone)
$100-$200

Siren

Tillie The Toiler, $5-$25

Ship-in-bottle
(see Capt.
Crunch)

Toots, $10-$50

Meteor

Radio Orphan
Annie Face,
1930s
$50-$100

Wimpy, $10-$50

Winnie Winkle, $5-$25

Friendship
$30-$60

Quaker Crazy
Ring (10 diff.)
1950s
$15-$30 ea.

Puzzle

Radio Orphan
Annie Mystic
Eye, 1930s (same
as Lone Ranger
Ntl. Defender &
Capt. Midnight
Mystic Eye
Detector)
$75-$150

Propeller, 1960s
$10-$20

(Quaker Crazy Rings follow)

Puzzle

Quaker Initial
Ring, 1939
$100-$200

Radio Orphan Annie Secret Guard Altascope, 1940s (rare) $7,500-$15,000

Radio Orphan Annie Triple Mystery (secret compartment), 1930s $500-$1000

Range Rider (TV), 1950s $100-$200

Red Goose Secret Compartment, 1940s $55-$110

Ring Raiders 68 diff.), 1990s $5-$10 ea.

Radio Orphan Annie Secret Guard Initial, 1940s (rare) $2000-$4000

Radio Orphan Annie Two Initial, 1930s $110-$220

Range Rider (TV), 1950s (rare) $250-$500

Red Ryder 1940s (metal) $75-$150

Radio Orphan Annie Secret Guard Magnifying, 1940s (rare) $2000-$4000

Raggedy Ann (metal) $7.50-$15

Ranger Rick (T.V.), 1950s $50-$100

Republic XF-91 Thunderceptor (cereal), 1950s $30-$60

GENUINE 10¢ RatFink RING YOU TOO CAN BE A RAT FINK

Ratfink 1950s $20-$40

Radio Orphan Annie Signet, 1930s $125-$250

Randolf Scott Photo, 1950s $10-$20

Radio Orphan Annie Silver Star, 1930s $200-$400

Randolph Scott Photo, 1950s $10-$20

Red Ball Super Space Decoder, 1950s, $15-$30

Republic F-84E Thunderjet (cereal), 1950s $30-$60

Rin Tin Tin, plastic (8 diff.), 1960s $20-$40 ea.

Rin Tin Tin Magic, with pencil, 1950s $300-$600

Rocket Whistle, 1953 $25-$50

Romper Room T.V. (silver), 1960s $40-$80

Roy Rogers Branding Iron (black cap), 1950s $100-$200

Roy Rogers Photo, 1950s $25-$50

Rita Hayworth Photo, 1950s $10-$20

Roger Wilco Flying Tiger, 1940s (w/metal whistle inside) $115-$230

Rootie Kazootie T.V., 1950s $75-$150

Roy Rogers Branding Iron (white cap), 1950s $150-$300

Roy Rogers Saddle, 1950s $250-$500

Robin Hood Shoes (silver), 1950s (rare) $175-$350

Roger Wilco Rescue, 1949 (w/metal whistle inside) $75-$150

Rootie Kazootie Lucky Spot, 1940s (rare) $200-$400

Roy Rogers (see Post Tin)

Roy Rogers Hat, 1950s (rare) $400-$800

Sears Christmas Flicker, 1950s $20-$40

Robin Logo, 1980s (Nestles) $25-$50

Robin (rubber) 1970s $25-$50

Roger Wilco Magniray, 1940s $30-$60

Roy Rogers on horse (silver) 1950s $125-$250

Roy Rogers Microscope, 1950s $50-$100

Secret Compartment Generic, 1950s $10-$20

Rocket To Moon, 1951 (w/3 glow-in-dark rockets) (gold & silver) $375-$750

Romper Room T.V. (gold), 1960s $50-$100

Roy Rogers on horse (oval) (silver), 1950s $125-$250

Roy Rogers Photo, 1950s $25-$50

Shadow Blue Coal, glows-in-dark, 1941 $225-$450

Shadow Carey Salt (black stone), glows-in-dark, 1947
$500-$1000

Shirley Temple 1930s (rare)
$200-$400

Sir Ector (see Sword In The Stone)

Shield (generic)(2 diff.), 1930s
$25-$50

Siren Ring, elephant base (gold & silver versions), 1930s
$25-$50

Sitting Bull (plastic), 1950s
$15-$30

Skeezix (see Post Tin)

Skull (gold w/red eyes), 1939
$50-$100

Skull 1950s (foreign)
$20-$40

Skull (see Montrose--, Pirate-- & Popsicle--)

Sky Bar Pilot, 1940s
$150-$300

Sky Bird, 1940s
$75-$150

Sky King Aztec, 1940s
$400-$800

Sky King Electronic T.V., (w/photos), 1940s
$100-$200

Sky King Magni-glo Writing, 1940s
$50-$100

Sky King Mystery Picture 1940s
$300-$600

Sky King Navajo, 1950s
$100-200

Sky King Radar, 1940s
$75-$150

Shmoo Luck Rings on Card 1950s, $30-$60 ea.

Sky King Teleblinker, 1950s
$75-$150

Sliding Whistle
(generic), 1940s
(rare)
$100-$200

Smilin' Jack (see
Post Tin)

Smith Brothers
Cough Drops,
Air Force, 1940s
$50-$100

Smith Brothers
Marine, 1940s
$50-$100

Smith Brothers
Navy, 1940s
$50-$100

Smith Brothers
Saddle, 1940s
$20-$40

Smitty (see Post
Tin)

Smokey Bear
1990s
.50-$1

Smokey Stover
(see Post Tin)

Smurfs
1980s
$10-$20

Snap
$250-$500
white hat

Crackle
$150-$300
red hat

Pop
$300-$600
yellow hat

Snap, Crackle &
Pop (3 ring set),
Kelloggs, 1950s
(rare)

Snuffy Smith (see
Post Tin)

Soupy Sales
Flicker, 1960s
$20-$40

Space Flicker (8
diff.), 1960s
$2-$4 ea.

Space (plastic) (10 diff.), 1960s $5-$10 ea.

Space Patrol (see Buzz Corey)

Space Patrol Compass (gold & silver versions), 1950s $75-$150

Space Patrol Cosmic Glow, 1950s $400-$800

Space Patrol Hydrogen Ray, 1950s $150-$300

Space Patrol Printing, 1950s w/stamp pad $200-$400

Speedy Gonzales (hand painted) 1970 $6-$12

Spider (pulp), 1930s (theater) (rare) $4,500-$9,000

Spiderman Face (green),1980s (see Marvel) $30-$60

Spiderman (vitamins), 1960s (rare) $150-$300

Spinner (see Broom Hilda)

Stanley Club (radio) (green stone, gold metal), 1940s $150-$300

Star Trek (McDonalds)(4 diff.), 1979 $30-$60 ea.

Star Wars (3 in box), 1977 $60-$120 (set)

MAY THE FORCE BE WITH YOU

Star Wars (8 diff.), (C3PO, Fighter, Force(lg.), Force(sm.), R2D2, Vader, Xfighter, Yoda), 1980s $7-$15 ea.

Starriors (on card, 2 diff.), 1984, came with comic book $10-$20 ea.

Steer Head (generic), 1940s $75-$150

Story Book, 1960s $50-$100

Straight Arrow Face, 1950s $25-$50

Straight Arrow Gold Arrow 1940s $25-$50

Straight Arrow Nugget, 1940s w/photo inside (see Golden Nugget Cave) $125-$250

Sunbeam Bread Flicker, 1950s $10-$20

Sundial Shoes 1940s (see Fireball Twigg) $30-$60

Superman Crusader, metal, 1940s $100-$200

Superman F87, 1940s $125-$250

Superman Flicker (8 diff.), 1960s $50-$100 ea.

Superman Prize (Membership) 1940s (rare) $30,000-100,000 (A VF sold for $125,000)

Target Comics 1940s (rare) (sterling silver) $250-$500

Tarzan Flicker (6 blue), 1960s $15-$30 ea.

Sword In The Stone (hard plastic) (Disney), 1960s $37-$75

Superman Kryptonite, 1980s $15-$30

Tarzan, 1930s (rare) $200-$400

Superman Secret Compartment (gum), 1940s, (rare) $25,000-$70,000 (A Vg-Fn sold for $80,000)

Superman Logo (blue logo) Nestle's, 1980 $25-$50

Sword In The Stone (soft plastic) (3 diff.), 1960s $25-$50

Superman Secret Compartment (candy), 1940s, (rare) $25,000-$70,000

Fish

Superman Logo, movie, 1970s $25-$50

Sir Ector

Superman Tim, 1940s (rare) $7,500-$15,000

Squirrel

Superman Pep Airplane, 1940s $125-$250

Swastika 1940s $75-$150

Sword In The Stone (8 diff.) 1960s $12-$25

Tarzan Flicker (6 silver), 1960s $15-$30 ea.

Ted Williams
Baseball, 1940s
$400-$800

Tennessee Jed
Look-around,
1940s
$200-$400

Terry & Pirates
Gold Detector,
1940s
$75-$150

Terry & Pirates
plastic, 1950s
$25-$50

Teenage Mutant
Ninja Turtles,
1990s (8 diff.)
$25-$50 ea.

Moe

Three Stooges
(3 diff.), 1960s
$20-$40 ea.

Thunderbird
1930s (rare)
(see Lone Wolf)
$200-$400

Thunderceptor
(see Republic)

Curley

Larry

Tiger Eye (4
diff.), (blue,
green, red tops)
1960s
$25-$50 ea.

Tillie The Toiler
(see Post Tin)

Tim Ring, 1930s
(rare)
$250-$500

Timothy (Disney)
oval, 1950s
$50-$100

Timothy (Disney)
square, 1950s
$50-$100

Tom Corbett
Face, 1950s
$125-$250

Tom Mix Elephant Hair Good Luck 1940s (rare) $100-$200

Tom Mix Signature, 1940s $100-$200

Tom Mix Straight Shooters, 1930s $50-$100

Tonto Picture (plastic), ice cream, 1938 (rare) $1000-$2000

Toots (see Post Tin)

Tom Corbett (plastic) (12 diff.), 1950s $20-$40 ea.

Tom Mix Initial Signet, 1930s $100-$200

Tom Mix Siren, 1940s $50-$100

Tom Mix Target, 1930s $125-$250

Tom Corbett Rocket, 1950s $225-$450

Tom Mix Look Around, 1940s $75-$150

Tom Mix Sliding Whistle, 1940s $50-$100

Tom Mix Tiger Eye, plastic, 1950s $125-$250

Troll Doll, 1960s $10-$20

Tom Mix Circus, 1930s (see Billy West) $50-$100

Tom Mix Magnet, 1940s $75-$150

Tom Mix Spinner, 1940s (rare) $500-$1000

Tonka Jewell, 1990s $5-$10

Twist Flicker, 1950s $10-$20

Tom Mix Deputy 1935 (rare) $2500-$5000

Tom Mix Nail, 1930s (same as Gene Autry Nail) $20-$40

Tom Mix Stanhope Image, 1930s $200-$400

Tonto Looking Photo, 1940s? $20-$40

Uncle Creepy, Warren, 1960s $100-$200

U.N.C.L.E. Flicker (see Man From --)

USA Ring
(100%),1930s
(flips to reveal
KKK)
(radio)(rare)
$650-$1300

U.S. Keds
(metal)(see
Kolonel Keds),
1960s
$55-$110

U.S. Marshal
1930s (rare)
$250-$500

Victor Mature
Photo, 1950s
$10-$20

USN Store Card,
1950s
$10-$20

Valentine Flicker,
1950s
$5-$10

Valric the Viking
Magnifying (All
Rye Flakes),
1940s (rare)
$2750-$5500

Walnettos Initial
(Saddle), 1940s
$30-$60

Wanda Hendrix
Photo, 1950s
$10-$20

Weather Bird
1950s
$75-$150

Wheat Chex
Decoder, 1940s
$30-$60

Wheaties Com-
pass, 1940s
$30-$60

Wheaties Flying
Saucer (plastic),
1940s
$50-$100

Whistle Bomb
(glow-in-dark),
1940s (rare)
$500-$1000

William Boyd
(see Hopalong
Cassidy)

Winnie Winkle
(see Post Tin)

Wonder Bread
(plastic), 1960s
$5-$10

Wonder Woman
Logo, 1980s
$25-$50

Woody
Woodpecker
Club, 1960s
$100-$200

Woody
Woodpecker
(plastic), 1990s
.50-$1

World's Fair,
1933 Chicago
$15-$50

World's Fair,
1933 Chicago
$15-$50

World's Fair
1933 Chicago
$15-$50

World's Fair
1933 Chicago
(silver/blue top)
$15-$50

World's Fair 1933 Chicago (Indian head) (bronze) $20-$60

World's Fair 1934 Chicago $15-$50

World's Fair 1934 Chicago (gold) $15-$50

World's Fair 1934 Chicago (Indian head) (pewter) $20-$60

World's Fair 1934 Hall Of Science (2 diff.) $15-$50

World's Fair 1939, metal (blue) $15-$50

World's Fair, 1939, metal (silver) $15-$50

World's Fair 1939 (plastic top) $15-$50

World's Fair, 1939, plastic (white, blue, green, orange tops; silver, gold metal base versions) $50-$100 ea.

World's Fair, 1939 (gold) $15-$50

Wyatt Earp Marshall, 1950s $40-$80

Yogi Bear (aluminum), 1960s $15-$30

Yosemite Sam (hand painted) 1970s $5-$10

Your Name (Kelloggs), 1950s $20-$40

Zorro Logo 1960s (silver & black base versions) $30-$60

Zorro (Z), 1960s $40-$80

About the Author

Bob Overstreet, the leading authority on comic book values in the United States, can always be found rummaging through boxes of old comic books looking for data. He attends most of the major comic book conventions and has appeared on numerous radio and television shows across the country. He maintains an extensive collection of comic books and Big Little Books as well as radio premiums, Indian relics and antiques.

He began collecting comic books in 1952 and published his first book *The Comic Book Price Guide* in 1970. This book was one of the first price guides published outside of the top hobbies of coins, stamps and antiques. The success of *The Comic Book Price Guide* and the fledgling field it represented inspired many other price guides to follow. Now known as *The Overstreet Comic Book Price Guide,* it has become the standard reference work in the field.

Bob Overstreet resides in Cleveland, Tennessee, with his wife Martha. He only collects and has no comic books for sale.

About the Cover Artist

Adam Kubert

Adam was born in Boonton, New Jersey, in 1959 and has a wife and two kids, a boy and a girl. Adam's father, Joe, has been drawing comic books since the early 1940s and now owns the Kubert School of Cartoon and Graphic Art.

Adam grew up with comic books always available to him. He learned lettering at his dad's school and began lettering professionally at the age of 13. His first published comic art was a back-up story in Sgt. Rock back in 1983. He also did a story published in Pacific Comics, "Edge of Chaos."

Currently he is doing the smash hit Ghost Rider comic book "Spirits of Vengeance."

Cover character: Ghost Rider, who first appeared in Marvel Comic's Marvel Spotlight #5 in August of 1972. He graduated into his own title in September of 1973 and has today become one of the most exciting costume hero characters.

The CONFIDENT COLLECTOR™

KNOWS THE FACTS

Each volume packed with valuable information that
no collector can afford to be without

**THE OVERSTREET COMIC BOOK
PRICE GUIDE, 22nd Edition**
by Robert M. Overstreet   76912-3/$15.00 US/$17.50 Can

**THE OVERSTREET COMIC BOOK
GRADING GUIDE, 1st Edition**
by Robert M. Overstreet and Gary M. Carter   76910-7/$12.00 US/$15.00 Can

**THE OVERSTREET COMIC BOOK
PRICE GUIDE COMPANION, 6th Edition**
by Robert M. Overstreet   76911-5/$6.00 US/$8.00 Can

● ● ●

FINE ART
Identification and Price Guide, 2nd Edition
by Susan Theran   76924-7/$20.00 US/$24.00 Can

QUILTS
Identification and Price Guide, 1st Edition
by Liz Greenbacker and Kathleen Barach   76930-1/$14.00 US/$17.00 Can